RESEARCH HANDBOOK ON INTELLECTUAL PROPERTY AND MORAL RIGHTS

RESEARCH HANDBOOKS IN INTELLECTUAL PROPERTY

Series Editors: Jeremy Phillips, *Intellectual Property Consultant, Olswang, Research Director, Intellectual Property Institute and co-founder, IPKat weblog*

Under the general editorship and direction of Jeremy Phillips comes this important new *Research Handbook* series of high quality, original reference works that cover the broad pillars of intellectual property law: trademark law, patent law and copyright law – as well as less developed areas, such as geographical indications, and the increasing intersection of intellectual property with other fields. Taking an international and comparative approach, these *Research Handbooks*, each edited by leading scholars in the respective field, will comprise specially commissioned contributions from a select cast of authors, bringing together renowned figures with up-and-coming younger authors. Each will offer a wide-ranging examination of current issues in intellectual property that is unrivalled in its blend of critical, innovative thinking and substantive analysis, and in its synthesis of contemporary research.

Each *Research Handbook* will stand alone as an invaluable source of reference for all scholars of intellectual property, as well as for practising lawyers who wish to engage with the discussion of ideas within the field. Whether used as an information resource on key topics, or as a platform for advanced study, these *Research Handbooks* will become definitive scholarly reference works in intellectual property law.

For a full list of Edward Elgar published titles, including the titles in this series, visit our website at www.e-elgar.com.

Research Handbook on Intellectual Property and Moral Rights

Edited by

Ysolde Gendreau

Professor of Law, Université de Montréal, Canada

RESEARCH HANDBOOKS IN INTELLECTUAL PROPERTY

Edward Elgar
PUBLISHING

Cheltenham, UK • Northampton, MA, USA

Published by
Edward Elgar Publishing Limited
The Lypiatts
15 Lansdown Road
Cheltenham
Glos GL50 2JA
UK

Edward Elgar Publishing, Inc.
William Pratt House
9 Dewey Court
Northampton
Massachusetts 01060
USA

A catalogue record for this book
is available from the British Library

Library of Congress Control Number: 2023941851

This book is available electronically in the **Elgar**online
Law subject collection
http://dx.doi.org/10.4337/9781789904871

ISBN 978 1 78990 486 4 (cased)
ISBN 978 1 78990 487 1 (eBook)

Printed and bound by CPI Group (UK) Ltd, Croydon, CR0 4YY

Contents

Contributors

Johan Axhamn, Senior Lecturer, Department of Business Law, Lund University; Research associate, IFIM and IRI, Stockholm University, Sweden.

Sérgio Branco, Professor, IBMEC University, Co-founder and Director of the Institute for Technology & Society of Rio de Janeiro (ITS Rio), Brazil.

Jhonny Antonio Pabón Cadavid, Adjunct Research Fellow, School of Accounting and Commercial Law, Victoria University of Wellington, New Zealand.

Hannah Carnegy-Arbuthnott, Lecturer, Department of Philosophy, York Centre for Political Theory, University of York.

Silmara Juny de Abreu Chinellato, Full Professor at the Faculty of Law of the University of São Paulo, Head of Department of Private Law (2016 to 2019), Brazil.

Carys Craig, Associate Dean of Research & Institutional Relations and Associate Professor, Osgoode Hall Law School, York University, Toronto, Canada.

Gillian Davies, Barrister, Hogarth Chambers, Lincoln's Inn, London, and Hon. Professor of EU and International IP Law at the Centre for Commercial Law Studies (CCLS) at Queen Mary, University of London, UK.

Anupriya Dhonchak, Faculty of Law, University of Oxford; National Law University Delhi, India.

F. Jay Dougherty, Professor (emeritus), Loyola Marymount University Law School (Los Angeles), Director Emeritus, Loyola Entertainment & New Media Law Institute, USA.

Katharina de la Durantaye, Chair for Private Law, Business Law, Competition Law and Intellectual Property at Free University Berlin, Germany.

Ezieddin Elmahjub, Associate Professor, College of Law, Qatar University, Qatar.

Susy Frankel, Professor of Law, FRSNZ, Chair in Intellectual Property and International Trade, Faculty of Law, Te Herenga Waka – Victoria University of Wellington, New Zealand.

Christophe Geiger, Professor of Law at the Luiss Guido Carli University, Rome, Italy.

Ysolde Gendreau, Professor, Faculty of Law, Université de Montréal, Canada.

Alexandra Giannopoulou, Post-doctoral researcher, Faculty of Law, University of Amsterdam, The Netherlands.

Darren Hudson Hick, Assistant Professor, Department of Philosophy, Furman University, South Carolina, USA.

Elena Izyumenko, Case-processing Lawyer at the European Court of Human Rights, Council of Europe, Strasbourg, France.

Pascal Kamina, Professeur agrégé de droit privé, Université Jean-Moulin Lyon 3, Director, Centre Paul-Roubier, France.

Nari Lee, Professor of Intellectual Property Law, Hanken School of Economics, Helsinki, Finland.

Rudolf Leška, Štaidl Leška Advokáti; Senior Assistant Professor, Copyright and Media Law, University of Finance and Administration, Czech Republic.

Brigitte Lindner, Barrister, Rechtsanwältin (Berlin Bar/Germany), Associate Member, Serle Court, Lincoln's Inn, London, UK.

Laura Moscati, Professor, Faculty of Law, Sapienza University of Rome, Italy.

Beatriz Nunes, Specialist in Intellectual Property (PUC Rio), Brazil.

John Peffer, Professor of Art History, Ramapo College, New Jersey, USA.

Giorgio Spedicato, Associate Professor of Business Law, Department of Legal Sciences, University of Bologna, Italy.

Irini A. Stamatoudi, Professor, Faculty of Law, University of Nicosia, Cyprus.

Sybilla Stanisławska-Kloc, Senior Lecturer, Faculty of Law, Chair of Intellectual Property Law, Jagiellonian University, Cracow, Poland.

Tatiana Synodinou, Professor, Law Department, University of Cyprus, Nicosia, Cyprus.

Paul L. C. Torremans, Professor of Intellectual Property Law, School of Law Faculty of Social Sciences, University of Nottingham, UK.

Tatsuhiro Ueno, Professor of Law, Waseda University, Deputy Director, Research Center for the Legal System of Intellectual Property (RCLIP), Tokyo, Japan.

Yong Wan, Professor, School of Law, Renmin University of China, Beijing, China.

Genevieve Wilkinson, Senior Lecturer, University of Technology Sydney, Sydney, Australia.

Richard Watt, Professor of Economics, University of Canterbury, Christchurch, New Zealand.

Acknowledgments

The inclusion of an excerpt from Milan Kundera's essay *Testaments Betrayed: An Essay in Nine Parts* has been made possible thanks to Mr Milan Kundera, Mrs Věra Kunderová, the Wylie Agency, and the publisher Faber and Faber. Many thanks also to the law firm ŠTAIDL LEŠKA ADVOKÁTI that has generously supported this endeavour.

Very sincere thanks are owed to the artist who has spontaneously and generously accepted to allow the reproduction of his painting for the cover of the book. Even if this authorization was conditional upon a pseudonymous publication, it is only fitting in a book on moral rights that the artist should eventually see a public acknowledgment.

Epigraph: Excerpt from 'You're Not in Your Own House Here, My Dear Fellow', *Testaments Betrayed: An Essay in Nine Parts*

Milan Kundera

Toward the end of his life, Stravinsky decided to bring his whole oeuvre together in a great recorded edition of his own performances, as pianist or conductor, so as to establish an authorized sonic version of all his music. This wish to take on the role of performer himself often provoked an irritated response: how fiercely Ernest Ansermet mocked him in his 1961 book: when Stravinsky conducts an orchestra, he is seized 'by such panic that, for fear of falling, he pushes his music stand up against the podium rail, cannot take his eyes off a score he knows by heart, and counts time!'; he interprets his own music 'literally and slavishly'; 'when he performs all joy deserts him'.

Why such sarcasm?

I open the Stravinsky letters: the correspondence with Ansermet starts in 1914; 146 letters by Stravinsky: My dear Ansermet, My dear fellow, My dear friend, Very dear, My dear Ernest; not a hint of tension; then, like a thunderclap:

Paris, October 14, 1937:

'In great haste, my dear fellow.

'There is absolutely no reason to make cuts in *Jeu de cartes* in concert performances. ... Compositions of this type are dance suites whose form is rigorously symphonic and require no audience explanation, because there are no descriptive elements illustrating theatrical action, which would interfere with the symphonic evolution of the pieces as they are played in sequence.

'If this strange idea occurred to you, of asking me to make cuts, it must be that you personally find the sequence of movements in *Jeu de cartes* a little boring. I cannot do anything about that. But what amazes me most is that you try to convince *me* to make cuts in it – me, who just conducted it in Venice and who reported to you the enthusiastic response of the audience. Either you forgot what I told you, or else you do not attach much importance to my observations or to my critical sense. Furthermore, I really do not believe that your audience would be less intelligent than the one in Venice.

'And to think that it is you who proposed to cut my composition, with every likelihood of distorting it, in order that it might be better understood by the public – you, who were not afraid to play a work as risky from the standpoint of success and listener comprehension as the *Symphonies of Wind Instruments*!

'So I cannot let you make cuts in *Jeu de cartes*; I think it is better not to play it at all than to do so with reservations.

'I have nothing to add, period.'

You're Not in Your Own House Here, My Dear Fellow

On October 15, Ansermet's reply:

'I ask only if you would forgive me the small cut in the March from the second measure after 45 to the second measure after 58.'

Stravinsky reacted on October 19:

> '... I am sorry, but I cannot allow you *any* cuts in *Jeu de cartes*.
> 'The absurd one that you propose *cripples* my little March, which has its form and its structural meaning in the totality of the composition (a *structural meaning* that you claim to be protecting). You cut my March only because you like the middle section and the development less than the rest. In my view, this is not sufficient reason, and I would like to say: 'But you're not in your own house, my dear fellow'; I never told you: 'Here, take my score and do whatever you please with it.'
> 'I repeat: either you play *Jeu de cartes* as it is or you do not play it at all.
> 'You do not seem to have understood that my letter of October 14 was quite categorical on this point.'

Thereafter they exchanged only a few letters, chilly, laconic. In 1961 Ansermet published in Switzerland a voluminous book of musicology, including a lengthy chapter that is an attack on the insensitivity of Stravinsky's music (and his incompetence as a conductor). Only in 1966 (twenty-nine years after their dispute) was there this brief response from Stravinsky to a conciliatory letter from Ansermet:

> 'My dear Ansermet,
> 'Your letter touched me. We are both too old not to think about the end of our days; and I would not want to end these days with the painful burden of an enmity.'

An archetypal phrase for an archetypal situation: often toward the end of their lives, friends who have failed one another will call off their hostility this way, coldly, without quite becoming friends again.

It's clear what was at stake in the dispute that wrecked the friendship: Stravinsky's author's rights, his *moral* rights; the anger of an author who will not stand for anyone tampering with his work; and, on the other side, the annoyance of a performer who cannot tolerate the author's proud behavior and tries to limit his power.

Introduction: a contemporary take on moral rights in intellectual property

Ysolde Gendreau

When Edward Elgar reached out to me to edit a *Research Handbook on Intellectual Property and Moral Rights*, the mandate seemed clear: I was encouraged to examine moral rights from any angle possible, including from the unusual perspective of industrial property. Those who are already familiar with the subject know about its continental European origins and the clichés that are associated with it. While it always remains topical to revisit one's classics, in whatever field one works, the contemporary relevancy of a concept requires that it be repeatedly studied through different frames of references. Some of these points of view may not seem so new: the seeds of reflection had already been planted here and there as doctrine has patiently sought to bring new light to moral rights. In particular, one must acknowledge the pioneering work in English that has been accomplished in this century by Elizabeth Adeney,[1] Gillian Davies and Kevin Garnett,[2] and Mira T. Sundara Rajan.[3] In a similar vein, the two congresses on moral rights that the Association littéraire et artistique internationale (ALAI), an association that gave the impetus for the creation of the Berne Convention, has held in Belgium 21 years apart have shown how the copyright community is willing to revisit one of the fundamental components of copyright law.[4] More recently, the International Association for the Protection of Intellectual Property (AIPPI), an eminent association of intellectual property practitioners since 1897, has adopted a resolution on moral rights that represents the summation of 37 national reports.[5] Something about moral rights is definitely afoot.

International guidance as to the standards of moral rights is not very constraining. Since the Rome Act of the Berne Convention in 1928, only two prerogatives – the right of attribution and the right of integrity – have been identified as the minimum requirements of protection. Indications as to their regime are also fairly minimal; there seems to have been concern mostly about their duration, although the identity of the persons who may exercise them deserved some mention too. What has really dealt a blow to their legitimacy, however, has been their

---

[1]   E. Adeney, *The Moral Rights of Authors and Performers – An International and Comparative Analysis* (Oxford, Oxford University Press 2006).
[2]   G. Davies and K. Garnett, *Moral Rights* (London, 1st edn, 2nd edn, Sweet and Maxwell 2010, 2016).
[3]   M.T. Sundara Rajan, *Moral Rights – Principles, Practice and New Technology* (Oxford, Oxford University Press 2011).
[4]   ALAI (ed.), *The Moral Rights of the Author* (Paris, ALAI, 1994); F. Brison, S. Dusollier, M.-C. Janssens, and H. Vanhees (eds), *Moral Rights in the 21st Century – The Changing Role of the Moral Rights in an Era of Information Overload* (Brussels, Larcier 2015).
[5]   2022 AIPPI World Congress, *Resolution 2022 – Study Question – Copyright Moral Rights*, 13 September 2022, available at https://aippi.soutron.net/Portal/DownloadImageFile.ashx?fieldValueId= 5418.

express exclusion from the TRIPs Agreement.[6] Moral rights are thus free to develop nationally according to the specificities they have acquired over time.

The lack of elaborate international constraints does not mean that there is no general framework within which to delineate their contours. Indeed, much of the debate takes place, either consciously or unconsciously, in reference to the cliché assumptions about moral rights. Therefore, the first part of this book deals with philosophical issues that can infuse moral rights with particular meanings. Some of the chapters deal with traditional referents. Such is the case with Hannah Carnegy-Arbuthnott's philosophical take on moral rights. To a certain extent, Laura Moscati's chapter on civil codes and authors' rights also brings the reader to the fundamentals of copyright protection since the decision to situate authors' rights within or outside the basic legal regulation that civil codes represent can lead to different positionings with respect to the contents of that protection. Some other ideological approaches reflect more recent preoccupations. There is greater curiosity today about Islamic perspectives, which Ezieddin Elmahjub brings forth, just as feminist studies, which Carys Craig and Anupriya Dhonchak here represent, have become standard interrogations for any field of law. Time elapsed since the fall of the Berlin Wall also means that reflections on the Communist past of the Central and Eastern European countries, as evidenced in the chapter written by Sybilla Stanisławska-Kloc, can shed a light on the impact of general political orientations on moral rights.

Why not, then, measure up these fundamental backgrounds against industrial property rights that are definitely not the usual references in moral rights literature? This was the task entrusted to Nari Lee, Giorgio Spedicato, and Genevieve Wilkinson with patents, industrial designs, and trademarks respectively, whose analyses make up the second part of the book. This exploration is in contrast with the third part where traditional moral rights debates are updated. Readers who are unfamiliar with the German monist author's rights tradition will discover, thanks to Katharina de la Durantaye's chapter, how the dualist/monist dichotomy can create distinctions within the European Union. F. Jay Dougherty's chapter, on the other hand, takes the reader to the well-known US stance on moral rights through the example of one of its iconic copyright industries, the film sector.

The longest part of the book is the fourth one, which deals with challenges that moral rights face today. There is resistance in some quarters to the recognition that moral rights have economic connotations. It is a myth that Richard Watt debunks in his chapter on the economic dimensions of moral rights. The issue of collective creation permeates to varying degrees the chapters on corporate entities (Pascal Kamina), multiple ownership (Tatiana Synodinou), Creative Commons (Alexandra Giannopoulou), and even artificial intelligence (Sérgio Branco and Beatriz Nunes). Just as in the area of economic rights, concerns about limitations to moral rights also exist. They can be examined generally (Johan Axhamn) or through one particular country, to wit Greece (Irini A. Stamatoudi); they can inform the debate on the relationship between copyright law and freedom of expression (Christophe Geiger and Elena Izyumenko). Their enforcement has often proved to be contentious, whether it be because of conflicts of laws issues when there is a foreign element at stake (Paul L.C. Torremans) or because they are not intuitively associated with the alternative dispute resolution schemes that are much touted today (Brigitte Lindner).

---

[6]   TRIPs Agreement, Art. 9(1).

Another myth about moral rights that must be tackled is the impression that they are essentially a continental European development. Though it is where they started, Europe is not the only place where moral rights exist. It must be acknowledged that the Berne Convention has accomplished its mission of imposing a minimal standard in most countries of the world. Perhaps because they are freer from doctrinal traditions, other countries or continents can allow for more daring propositions. Authors in Japan (Tatsuhiro Ueno), China (Yong Wan), Brazil (Silmara Juny de Abreu Chinellato), or Spanish-speaking Latin America (Jhonny Antonio Pabón Cadavid) can describe matter-of-factly situations that are less common or less accepted on the Old Continent. In their own ways, Commonwealth (copyright) countries bring new perspectives on moral rights (Gillian Davies) which can even become an analytical tool to study traditional knowledge issues (Susy Frankel).

The last part of the book deals with practical issues that authors have experienced while they were grappling with moral rights dilemma, often without actual knowledge that their situation had something to do with moral rights. John Peffer brings to light a case where the status of a work changes over time so that what may have initially seemed a banal work free from copyright considerations may become one that raises real moral rights interrogations later. Darren Hudson Hick describes a practice in the US film industry that was infused with moral rights issues without naming it as such. Lastly, Rudolf Leška adds the moral rights perspective to the real dilemmas with which authors' heirs have been confronted when authors wish to control the fate of their works beyond their death. The book concludes with my own take on moral rights that has been enriched by all these contributions.

The contributors to this book have all enthusiastically met the challenge they were requested to take up. Thanks to them, I hope the readers will find multiple reasons to continue to think about the role of moral rights in copyright law, of course, but also in patent law, designs law, and trademarks law. I am very conscious of the gaps in the issues that could have been treated on this occasion and can only wish that the existence of this book will spur other commentators to tackle them.

My most sincere thanks go to all those who have been so patient during the making of this book. This project started before the Covid-19 pandemic and has been plagued by the delays that have accompanied perhaps every major task that had to be undertaken during that time. The total absence of pressure from Edward Elgar has been a blessing. The contributors' patience cannot be underestimated either! I am very grateful for their unwavering collaboration and kind understanding. It is also impossible not to mention the two assistants who have worked in the shadows of such a project. The help provided by Eva Gallo and Sabrina Roy has been invaluable.

Lastly, special thanks must be expressed to Rudolf Leška, one of the contributors, and his law firm, Štaidl Leška Advokáti, who have enabled me to include as an epigraph an excerpt from Milan Kundera's essay, *Testaments Betrayed*. From the start, I had wanted to include contributions that would deal with the way authors themselves experience moral rights. They make up the last part of the book. However, the opportunity to include the very words that an author of such literary stature has penned down to show how authors/composers and performers intuitively experience moral rights has been the icing on the cake.

Ysolde Gendreau, Montreal
September 2022

PART I

PHILOSOPHICAL ISSUES

1. In defence of honour? A case for moral rights from relational autonomy

Hannah Carnegy-Arbuthnott

1.   INTRODUCTION

One of the most philosophically interesting aspects of moral rights is the way in which they constrain the economic element of property rights in works of art by attributing to authors certain inalienable rights of control over their creations.[1] Alienability is typically considered a hallmark of property rights. To have full ownership of something is taken to include the ability to dispose of it, sell it, give it away, or lend it to someone else under conditions of your own choosing.[2] Limits to the alienability of property rights therefore require special justification. With respect to moral rights, the Berne Convention stipulates: "Independently of the author's economic rights, and even after the transfer of the said rights, the author shall have the right to claim authorship of the work and to object to any distortion, mutilation or other modification of, or other derogatory action in relation to, the said work, which would be prejudicial to his honour or reputation."[3] As such, it would be apt to question whether the concept of honour could play a part in the justification of moral rights, and if so, what concept of honour might be up to the job. This chapter will focus specifically on the justification of inalienable rights of attribution and integrity.

The restrictions that moral rights impose on property rights in creative works have historically been justified by appeal to the idea that there is a special relation between an author and their work, such that moral rights are required in order to protect the personality of the author.[4] This approach poses a distinct philosophical challenge to justifying alienability constraints on a person's rights over their own creative output. The crux of the puzzle is how to justify

---

[1]   A note on terminology: I will use the word "author" throughout to refer to creators of works, in line with the terminology of the Berne Convention, though I do not mean to restrict this to literary works only. The argument I put forward will apply, I take it, to any creative works protected under systems of intellectual property that assign property rights to authors on the basis that their work constitutes original expression.

[2]   For a detailed explication of the incidents of ownership see Anthony M. Honoré, "Ownership" in *Readings in the Philosophy of Law* (Routledge 2013) 563–4.

[3]   (1967). Berne Convention for the Protection of Literary and Artistic Works, of 9 September 1886, completed at Paris on 4 May 1896, revised at Berlin on 13 November 1908, completed at Berne on 20 March 1914, revised at Rome on 2 June 1928, revised at Brussels on 26 June 1948, and revised at Stockholm on 14 July 1967. Geneva, United International Bureaux for the Protection of Intellectual Property.

[4]   Cf. Gillian Davies and Kevin M. Garnett, *Moral Rights* (Sweet & Maxwell 2010). "The concept and justification for moral rights is the notion that the personality of the author is bound up in and expressed by his work. Thus, the term moral rights refers collectively to a number of rights which are concerned with protecting the expression of the author's personality and his personal and continuing relationship to his work."

constraints on an author's ability to alienate their moral rights by their own free choice. What is it about an author's relation to their work that requires their control over it to be protected, even if the author would prefer to transfer those rights to someone else?[5] It is unsurprising, then, that the question of whether an author can contractually bind themselves not to exercise their moral right of attribution has been referred to as "one of the most difficult in the entire realm of moral rights".[6]

This chapter interrogates the philosophical justifications for the alienability restrictions that moral rights impose. I will argue that personality-based approaches provide a more limited justification for moral rights than they have typically been taken to yield. In particular, I will argue that a Kantian personality-based approach fails to establish that the relation between an author and their work is such that moral rights are required as a matter of moral necessity. In light of these shortcomings, I argue that the best explanation for such alienability restrictions are not that they are deeply "moral rights" in the sense that any system would, as a matter of moral necessity, have to protect such rights. Instead, in the context of an economic system that allows private property rights in creative works, that system gives rise to reasons that stand in favour of including some alienability restrictions. In particular, I will suggest a possible case in favour of protecting rights of attribution and integrity by drawing on insights from theories which emphasize the relational dimensions of autonomy.

Examining the reasons that stand in favour of moral rights from the perspective of relational autonomy offers a different perspective on the concept of honour such rights might serve to protect. This involves moving away from the traditional notion of honour as a mark of esteem judged by reference to existing social norms. Instead, I will suggest that we can think of the sphere of art as a domain in which individuals contribute to the very shaping of social norms. In a free market system where works of art are up for sale to the highest bidder, concerns arise about people's contributions to that process being undermined or distorted by economic forces. In that context, moral rights can be seen as protecting individuals' equal standing in the process of norm-creation. If the ability to participate in the shaping of social norms is an important aspect of functioning as an autonomous individual embedded in a web of social relations with others, then there is a relational autonomy-based case for protecting the expressive contributions of artists from manipulation by others.

2.   THE PERSONALITY-BASED APPROACH

The most robust philosophical case for protecting inalienable rights of attribution and integrity comes from conceptions of creative expression which view authorial works as constitutive elements of an author's personality. Chief among these are Kantian approaches which assume

---

[5]   The form of this problem is the same as the famous problem in political philosophy of what to make of voluntary slavery contracts. While writers such as J.S. Mill and Rousseau sought to argue that there is an inherent contradiction in the idea of allowing an autonomous person to voluntarily sell themselves into slavery, others such as Robert Nozick have been open to accepting that having full ownership of oneself would include full powers of alienation, including the ability to voluntarily bind oneself under a slavery contract. John Stuart Mill, "On Liberty", in *A Selection of His Works* (Springer 1966) 1–147, ch 5; Robert Nozick, *Anarchy, State, and Utopia*, vol 5038 (Basic Books 1974).

[6]   Martin A. Roeder, "Doctrine of Moral Right: A Study in the Law of Artists, Authors and Creators", *Harv. L. Rev.* 53 (1939): 554. p. 564

a moral connection between an author and their work as a form of expression. For Kant, literary works constitute an act of communication between an author and the public.[7] As acts of communication, literary works count as an aspect of the person, rather than as external objects of property.[8] Unconsented uses of an author's communicative works are therefore protected by the author's innate and inalienable right in their own person. From a Kantian perspective, unauthorized publication of or modifications to an author's work can be considered a form of compelled speech.[9]

The basics of the Kantian approach, however, do not yet provide a full response to the alienability puzzle. We can push the puzzle as follows against the Kantian account: Even if one accepts that each person has an inalienable right to engage in acts of communication, one might question why the relation between an author and an individual instance of communication, as expressed in a particular work, may not be alienated. That is, accepting the inalienability of the general right to engage in communicative act-types does not explain why each token of communication must also be inalienable. Why should a general and inalienable right to engage in communicative acts by publishing my thoughts in writing prevent me on occasion from contracting to allow someone else to permanently use my words in their name (waiving my right of attribution), or indeed to allow them to modify or alter my text as they please, without requiring my consent (waiving the right to integrity)? To allow such individual instances of alienation would not necessarily undercut my general right to engage in authorial acts.[10]

From this perspective, we can notice that the Kantian approach supports a connection between the right of attribution and the right of integrity, rather than establishing each as severally necessary. If authorial works constitute acts of communication, whenever a piece of work is presented with attribution to its author, it must be presented in its original form. Otherwise, it constitutes a distortion of the author's communication in their own name, amounting to compelled speech. This leaves open, however, the possibility that altering an author's work and presenting the altered form without attribution is not wrongful.[11] In other words, on a view

---

[7]   Immanuel Kant, "On the Wrongfulness of Unauthorized Publication of Books", *Practical Philosophy (Cambridge Edition of the Works of Immanuel Kant)*, 1996, 23–36. For arguments as to the implications of this view for copyright more widely, see Abraham Drassinower, "Authorship as Public Address: On the Specificity of Copyright Vis-à-Vis Patent and Trade-Mark", *Mich. St. L. Rev.* (2008): 199.

[8]   On literary works, emphasizing their status as actions of an author, Kant writes, "Hence these latter belong exclusively to the person of the author*, and the author has in them an inalienable right (*ius personalissimum*) always *himself* to speak through anyone else, the right, that is, that no one may deliver the same speech to the public other than in his (the author's) name." Kant (n 7) 35.

[9]   Abraham Drassinower, "Copyright Infringement as Compelled Speech," in Annabelle Lever (ed.), *New Frontiers in the Philosophy of Intellectual Property* (Cambridge University Press 2011).

[10]   John Christman makes a similar argument, though not directly against a Kantian account of IP. Christman takes the view that selves are socially constituted in the sense that relations to other persons, traditions and social institutions are part of the defining conditions of constituting the self. Even so, Christman argues, autonomy-based defences of intellectual property rights would need to show that the denial of rights of intellectual property would erode cultural practices to such a devastating effect as to undermine the defining conditions of selfhood. Simply allowing some alienability of moral rights would not erode the conditions of autonomy to that extent. John Christman, "1 Autonomy, Social Selves and Intellectual Property Claims," in Annabelle Lever (ed.), *New Frontiers in the Philosophy of Intellectual Property* (Cambridge University Press 2012).

[11]   This would appear to be consistent with Kant's view of the permissibility of editors making changes to an author's text, as long as the editor's role is clearly publicized: "But if someone so alters

of authorial works as acts of communication, the justification of an inalienable integrity right hangs on the question of author attribution. If there is no right of attribution, there may yet be a right of integrity, but only in cases where a distorted work has been attributed to you as the author. If there is an inalienable right to attribution, then the integrity right follows in its wake.

The most robust way to justify inalienable rights of attribution and integrity, then, would be to show that there is an innate personal right to be identified as the author of one's works whenever they are published or presented to an audience. But as Anne Barron points out, "at no point does [Kant] argue that individual rights to freedom of expression, much less authors' rights, are directly deducible from the idea of moral autonomy".[12] That is, such rights are not required as a matter of necessity due to the moral nature of persons. The most promising path to establishing authors' rights from a Kantian perspective comes instead from accounts which contextualize the role of authorial speech in establishing the necessary social conditions for the right to freedom of thought.[13] Barron explains that for Kant, freedom of thought requires more than mere liberty of expression. Freedom of thought involves attaining enlightenment or maturity of thought, which requires the ability to think for oneself, to think from the perspective of others, and to think consistently. This can only be attained with the right social and institutional conditions that make that kind of self-reflection towards enlightenment possible. What is required is a system of communicative freedom that supports equal access to free, critical debate.[14]

3.   THE CASE FROM THE PUBLIC USE OF REASON

Taking as its starting point a moral imperative for intellectual autonomy, the Kantian account establishes the necessity of having social and institutional structures of the right kind to support communicative freedom. But the precise form those structures must take is not determined – there could be any number of different institutional structures which could fulfil the conditions of communicative freedom. Several scholars have explored the implications of this argument for assessing the limits of copyright as balanced against the interests of the public in having access to works in order to engage in the system of public reason.[15] Our question for current purposes is what to make of authors' rights of attribution on this Kantian picture. According to Barron, Kantian communicative freedom requires "the freedom to articulate one's thoughts in public, subject to principles entailed by the internal logic of communication itself as a mode

---

another's book … that it would even be a wrong to pass it off any longer in the name of the author of the original, then the revision in the editor's own name is not unauthorized publication and therefore impermissible." Kant (n 7) 35. The point I am making here is that in the absence of author attribution, the case that presenting the author's ideas to the public in the abstract would amount to compelled speech becomes less compelling.

[12]   Anne Barron, "Kant, Copyright and Communicative Freedom", *Law and Philosophy* 31, no. 1 (2012): 1–48, p. 29.

[13]   See Anne Barron and Laura Biron, "Public Reason, Communication and Intellectual Property", *New Frontiers in the Philosophy of Intellectual Property* 18, no. 2 (2012): 225.

[14]   Barron (n 12).

[15]   Barron and Biron (n 13); Drassinower, "Copyright Infringement as Compelled Speech" (n 9); Drassinower, "Authorship as Public Address" (n 7).

of interaction between a plurality of (at least potentially) rational persons".[16] The point I wish to press here is to what extent this requires each individual to be able to publish their thoughts *as their own*.

Imagine, for example, a system in which individuals were able to publish their thoughts through various means, though no works were ever published with author attribution, and authors had no right to be identified as the originators of specific works. Relative to the Kantian aim of establishing a culture of maturity of thought, such a public forum of ideas unattached from the identities of specific persons might have some distinct advantages – for example, by minimizing forms of cognitive bias which can impede the ability to think consistently, such as authority bias or the halo effect.

If the kind of institutional system described above for regulating the exchange of ideas could be justified on the basis of Kantian principles without ascribing a right of attribution, then the Kantian approach would seem to leave us with a more limited defence of the moral rights of authors. Specifically, rather than defending rights of attribution and integrity as morally necessary, it would leave a more limited formulation of the integrity right. That is, an author would have a claim to object to distortions of their work only in cases where they were publicly identified as the author of that work.[17] Under a system where all authorial communications were required to be published anonymously, the question of authors having a personal right to object to false attribution would not arise, as those actions would be precluded by the rules of the system. That is, the justification of a rule requiring author anonymity is available at the level of providing a good communicative system for the public use of reason towards enlightenment. Moreover, in light of the absence of a Kantian argument to demonstrate that the moral connection between an author and their work requires rights of attribution, such a proposed system would not obviously violate the rights of individuals within it.

On the question of whether there is a special personal relation between an author and their work that necessitates rights of attribution and integrity, this suggests that even a Kantian approach may have to concede that these rights are contingent on the shape of the existing institutional conditions under which authorial works are made public. Under systems which do protect authors' rights to publish in their own name, there may nevertheless be a robust Kantian case for protecting rights of integrity and attribution on the basis that publishing content under a person's name that distorts their originally intended communication amounts to compelled speech. In summary, it seems that rights of attribution and integrity are not necessary, on a Kantian view. They may, however, be justifiable within some forms of institutional arrangements aimed at establishing adequate conditions for the public use of reason. If rights of attribution are protected, then rights of integrity which give authors claims against distorted work being presented in their name will be necessary too.[18]

The point of engaging with Kantian arguments for authorial rights is not merely to downplay the extent to which rights of attribution and integrity are necessary as a matter of

---

[16]   Barron (n 12).

[17]   One might think other questions arise with respect to claims typically protected under the right to attribution, namely the right to object to false attribution of authorship, and the right to remain anonymous as the author of a piece. However, the question of the necessity of these rights only arises within a system where author attribution is assumed as the norm.

[18]   Though as Drassinower points out, drawing on Kant's remarks on edited works cited above, if the work is sufficiently modified and presented as edited by a transformative author, this will not amount to compelled speech. Drassinower, "Copyright Infringement as Compelled Speech" (n 9).

protecting an innate right of personality. Rather, we can draw some insights from the Kantian approach which indicate a different, and perhaps surprising, justificatory basis for moral rights even from the perspective of systems of intellectual property rights premised on Lockean or utilitarian justifications. The insight is this: once you have an institutional system that attributes to authors certain rights over their works by virtue of being the originators of those works, that system might function to instantiate the kind of authorial relations which require moral rights-type protections. In other words, if we happen to have a system that protects private intellectual property rights in creative works, there may be reasons that arise from the existence of that system in favour of protecting inalienable rights of attribution and integrity.

In the next sections, I will make the case that systems of intellectual property that privilege original expression as a property-right creating act may create the conditions under which the protection of moral rights of attribution and integrity becomes important, even if those systems are initially justified on Lockean or utilitarian grounds. That is, even in contexts where the justification for having a system of intellectual property rights is neither taken to be rooted in the importance of providing the right kind of communicative forum for achieving enlightenment of thought, nor in the importance of protecting any special moral relation between an author and their work.

4.   DEPARTING FROM PERSONALITY

Legal systems which have historically taken Lockean or utilitarian arguments as the justificatory basis of intellectual property (IP) have tended to provide weaker protections for moral rights than their continental counterparts. From a philosophical perspective, this coheres with the fact that both Lockean and utilitarian approaches to property rights presuppose alienability.[19] This is perhaps most obvious on the utilitarian picture: if the main justification for having a system of intellectual property rights is to maximize the availability of new inventions and cultural goods to the public, granting authors intellectual property rights over their work is justified to the extent that it incentivizes the production of such goods. The basic premises of the utilitarian justification for IP do not place any inherent value in the relation between an author and their work. Instead, they prioritize the instrumental value to the community of the work being produced. Alienability restrictions might be justifiable on such a view, but they would hang on empirical evidence about the extent to which providing authors with inalienable rights of integrity would maximize incentives for production, resulting in more or better access to cultural goods for the public.

In contrast to utilitarian views, Lockean approaches see property rights as justified on the basis that each individual has a property in their own person, which gives them exclusive ownership of their labour and the products thereof. One might think, then, that a Lockean approach to intellectual property would be more amenable to protecting a special relation between authors and their work. However, Lockean approaches tend to see the products of one's labour as straightforwardly alienable. While the Lockean approach differs from utilitarian approaches

---

[19]   See Neil Netanel, "Alienability Restrictions and the Enhancement of Author Autonomy in United States and Continental Copyright Law", *Cardozo Arts & Ent. LJ* 12 (1994): 1. And Neil Netanel, "Copyright Alienability Restrictions and the Enhancement of Author Autonomy: A Normative Evaluation", *Rutgers LJ* 24 (1992): 347.

by starting from the premise of authors having natural rights over the products of their intellectual labour, unlike the Kantian approach, it sees no contradiction in the possibility of alienating those products.

As we saw, Kantian theory provides principles to underpin the inalienability of moral rights as part of its rationale for the general structure of rights governing the dissemination of intellectual works. To the extent that authorial expression constitutes an extension of the self within a given institutional structure, it must be protected as an inalienable aspect of personality. Utilitarian and Lockean approaches to intellectual property, however, do not provide any such alienability constraints as a necessary requirement of the principles that underpin such property rights. However, one might still seek to justify moral rights on the basis of a specific conception of the values or interests which systems of intellectual property are supposed to protect. For example, while rejecting as obscure the notion that an "intimate bond" between an author and their work makes the work a constitutive element of their personality, Charles Beitz proposes an analysis of the interests of creators, audiences, and society at large which he argues may justify some protection for moral rights, but not their inalienability.[20] Taking the perspective of the social value of art, Burton Ong has provided a defence of moral rights based on the idea that moral rights function as a mark of respect for the artistic contribution of authors, thus expressing norms about the value of art and artists within the community, as prioritized above the pecuniary interests of owners and traders of the objects of art.[21]

These kinds of arguments need not rely on premises about creative expression requiring protection as a constitutive element or extension of personality. Rather, they assert the importance of constraining the commodification of art as a purely economic good by emphasizing the value of art as art. In doing so, that approach assumes that the value of art depends on it being preserved in the original state in which it was created. The idea that the best way to protect the value of art is by reference to the original intentions of the artist is open to the criticism that this simply misconstrues the value of art. By holding the artist's original intentions to be the prime source of value in art, it ignores the fact that art exists in a dynamic social context in which it may be exposed to interpretation, modification, and a process of change over time in a way that enriches, rather than diminishes, its artistic value.[22]

So far, then, we have seen that personality-based views that seek to establish a necessary moral connection between an author and their work as an aspect of the self end up making only a contingent case for the protection of moral rights. The necessity of protecting a right of integrity appears to hang on the question of whether authors are granted rights of attribution, and the Kantian account does not appear to require rights of attribution as a necessary condition of autonomous expression. Alternatively, making the case for moral rights as constraints to a system of intellectual property rights justified on utilitarian or Lockean principles by reference to the value of art comes with its own challenges and involves relying on contested claims about the primacy of the original author's intentions to the value of art.

In what follows, I will suggest an alternative approach to establishing moral rights which relies neither on a strong personality view of authorial works as an extension of the self, nor

---

[20]   Charles R. Beitz, "The Moral Rights of Creators of Artistic and Literary Works", *Journal of Political Philosophy* 13, no. 3 (2005): 330–58.

[21]   Burton Ong, "Why Moral Rights Matter: Recognizing the Intrinsic Value of Integrity Rights", *Colum. JL & Arts* 26 (2002): 297.

[22]   See e.g., Amy M. Adler, "Against Moral Rights", *Calif. L. Rev.* 97 (2009): 263.

on claims about the value of art requiring preservation in its original form. Instead of seeing moral rights as standing in tension with the principles of intellectual property, we can see the way in which assumptions embedded in even utilitarian or Lockean justifications of IP can fit with justifications for moral rights in a mutually reinforcing manner. This happens when we consider the way in which systems of IP function within a wider system of the rights of individuals.

5. THE CASE FROM RELATIONAL AUTONOMY

I started the chapter by indicating that it would be worth interrogating the place of the concept of honour or reputation in the justification for moral rights. In this section, I will suggest that we can draw on insights from theories that emphasize the relational dimensions of autonomy to make a case for the role of moral rights in protecting the standing of authors and artists as contributors in the process of shaping of social norms. While this represents a departure from the traditional concept of honour, the notion of standing I discuss can be thought of as a reimagining of a concept analogous to honour which the law may have reason to protect.

First, however, it will be instructive to compare an approach to justifying a more limited conception of moral rights by direct reference to the notion of reputational damage, namely, as a way of protecting against defamation. Rights against defamation are one of the mechanisms that have been used in common law countries to provide authors with some limited claims of integrity.[23] However, rather than protecting the integrity of the work itself as a matter of principle, rights against defamation only allow an artist to object to their work being used or modified in a way that is detrimental to their reputation. This would not preclude modifications to a work which detract from its artistic integrity (by the lights of the artist's original intentions) while leaving the artist's reputation intact relative to the normative standards of the community. From that perspective, while rights against defamation might provide recourse to protect the integrity of a work in some limited cases, they typically fall short of protecting a full moral right of integrity. To seek to justify moral rights by appeal to the right against defamation will thus fall short of justifying inalienable rights of attribution or integrity. In order to develop a conception of honour that could underpin such inalienable moral rights, it will therefore be necessary to go beyond the limited conception of honour or reputation that rights against defamation protect. In this section, I will interrogate the reasons why we might value rights against defamation in the first place, and see how those could be harnessed to underpin an alternative justification for inalienable rights of attribution and integrity.

The case I will put forward here is that some assumptions behind the reasons that support rights against defamation also stand in support of protecting more extensive moral rights under certain institutional structures of intellectual property. This becomes most evident when we examine the way in which systems of IP privilege acts of individual expression as meriting property-type protections.

I argued above that the Kantian approach to intellectual property fails to establish that rights of attribution and integrity are required as a matter of moral necessity. I also argued that Kantian arguments about the importance of providing the right conditions for the public use

---

[23] Netanel, "Alienability Restrictions and the Enhancement of Author Autonomy in United States and Continental Copyright Law" (n 19).

of reason do not establish the necessity of a system of private rights in intellectual property. However, we can still draw some insights from the general structure of the Kantian approach to thinking about the role of institutions in regulating our social practices and the standing of individuals within them. When it comes to assessing systems of intellectual property, we can think of legal institutions for regulating the public sharing of private expression as shaping the conditions in which we exchange ideas and contribute to public discourse.

In addition to providing a sphere in which ideas can be robustly challenged by reference to standards of rationality and reason, the public exchange of ideas also serves as a mechanism for contributing to and contesting the shared norms of a community. From that perspective, systems of IP which attach significance to authorial creation as a property-right creating act support a culture in which we expect objects of art to function as acts of expression of identifiable individuals. In that context, to manipulate the object plausibly can have the effect of distorting the original expression it represents.

That does not yet provide an answer to the question of how to justify attributing to authors an inalienable right to the integrity of their expression. The clearest path to identifying reasons to support moral rights, I suggest, comes from understanding authorial expression as an institutionally constructed way for individuals to participate in the process of shaping the norms of the community. By that, I mean that the way in which the law defines the conditions for attributing intellectual property shapes the conditions in which authorial expression becomes socially significant in various ways. That social significance, in turn, gives rise to reasons that speak in favour of protecting the connection between authors and their work in various ways. One justifiable way to do that may be by attributing inalienable rights of attribution and integrity.

The right against defamation protects individuals from other people making false claims about them which damage their reputation. The standard of whether a false claim is defamatory is whether it lowers the standing of the defamed person in the eyes of the community – that is, judged by reference to existing community norms. This reference to community norms makes sense in the context of defamation construed as a right that protects each person's entitlement that no other person determines one's standing in the eyes of others.[24] One can see how a standard of defamation could apply to cases where works of art are distorted or manipulated in such a way to make them seem like the artist's intended message was one that is deemed wrong or offensive by the community. But as I pointed out above, this would fall far short of supporting inalienable rights to attribution and integrity.

Taking a view of authorial expression as a way of participating in the very shaping of community norms reveals further limitations of applying rights against defamation straightforwardly to the manipulation of authorial works. That is because within the context of an institutional structure which functions as one of the forums for shaping, testing, and contesting community norms, it does not make sense to apply a test of interference with a person's reputation by the standards of existing community norms. Rather, there is a case to be made in favour of protecting the integrity of authorial expression by reference to the author's own expressive intentions in creating the work. That case emerges once we start to interrogate the importance of the way in which individuals stand to systems of honour or reputation to which the right against defamation makes reference.

---

[24]   For a detailed account interpreting the right against defamation in this way, see Arthur Ripstein, *Private Wrongs* (Harvard University Press 2016).

Arthur Ripstein argues that the interest in reputation protected by the right against defamation is "fundamentally juridical" in nature, as it arises not from a contingent interest that individuals have in being thought well of by others, but rather from the basic structuring ideas presupposed by private law: "Like other rights that figure in tort law, it is not an interest that the law has contingently taken up and given relational form. Your right to your own good name is relational in a sense that goes beyond the mode of its protection. It is already present in the very possibility of a system of relational rights."[25] When we hold people accountable for wrongs they do to others, we assume as a basic ordering principle that each person should be made to answer only for things that are properly attributable to them, not on the basis of false allegations made by others.

One might ask why the norms of any given community should matter so much in a system of relational rights. That is, why should the standard of defamation be that the false allegations against me count as wrongful in the eyes of the community, rather than by the standards of conduct to which I hold myself? Why should my right to my own reputation not extend to being able to shape it the way I want – whether that be as a rebel or a conformist – as long as I am judged on my actions rather than what other people say about me (or even lies I might tell about myself)? Ripstein's explanation is that the right against defamation is not a right to a certain state of affairs that everyone only believe true things about you. Rather, it is a constraint on the conduct of others, that they not put you in a position to answer for wrongs that you have not done.

This juridical view of the right to one's own good name contains no value judgement on the content of the existing norms of the community. In applying the standard of which false claims count as defamatory, it takes no account of the moral status of the community's norms. Consider, for example, the fact that false allegations that a person had leprosy or a sexually transmitted disease have historically been considered defamatory, on the basis that a person who had such a disease was considered to have brought it upon themselves through sinful behaviour, and was therefore fit to be shunned by polite society.[26]

If the right against defamation is based on the principle that an individual not have their social standing damaged by dishonest interference by others, this assumes a view of the individual as embedded within a social structure in which reputation matters. More precisely, it matters that each person stand on an equal footing with respect to their own reputation, answerable to society on the basis of their own deeds. One way to interpret the function of such a right is to see it as securing a condition for individuals to stand as independent responsible agents, even as they are embedded within a social structure which imposes certain expectations and norms of conduct on all members of the community.

Putting things this way, however, invites questions about the position of the individual in relation to the very shaping of the community norms to which they are held accountable. This is where we can instructively draw on insights from theories that emphasize the relational dimensions of autonomy. If it is important not to be held answerable to the community for things that one did not do, once we push the question back to a slightly higher level of abstraction, one might also think it important that individuals not be held accountable to social norms imposed on them in unilateral or arbitrary ways. One way to think of the relation between these two levels is that the value to any given individual of the right against defamation will at

[25] Ibid 189.
[26] For discussion of these, see ibid 189.

least partially depend on the extent to which they take the system of social norms that govern one's reputation in the first place not to be overly constrictive or oppressive. To explain this by example, it would be cold comfort to have a right against being defamed as promiscuous in a puritanical society if what one really wanted was to be able to have sexual relationships outside of marriage without facing social sanctions or stigma.[27]

The idea that the concept of individual autonomy itself can only be fully understood by taking into account the way in which individuals are embedded in a complex social environment has been a key focus of feminist approaches to relational autonomy.[28] Accounts that conceptually define individual autonomy in terms of the individual's wider social relationships have been criticized as being overly perfectionist in their criteria for determining which relationships and social values are constitutive of autonomy.[29] In rejoinder to the charge of perfectionism, some proponents of relational autonomy have sought to focus on the importance of the standing of individuals in relation to their community not by reference to the content of the social norms in question, but in the formal sense of individuals having a part in the creation and maintaining of social norms.[30]

Taking on board this insight from theories of relational autonomy of the importance of having a contributing role in the creation of social norms offers a perspective on a possible defence of moral rights of integrity which need not rely on a view of artistic expression constituting part of an author's personality. To be clear, I do not mean to argue that moral rights to the integrity of one's artistic expression are a necessary condition of relational autonomy. Rather, once there exists an institutional system which attributes property rights in expression, that creates a forum in which individuals contribute to creating, contesting, and recreating social norms. Systems of intellectual property which attribute exclusive property rights to individuals as the originators of expressive acts ensure that this forum of expression is not just one in which ideas and expressions are shared and tested in abstraction, but one in which expressions stand explicitly as the expressions of particular identifiable individuals. Moreover, by privileging original acts of expression as those which merit property-type protection, such systems explicitly designate objects of art as physical instantiations of individual expression.

In his discussion of the various interests which provide reasons in support of moral rights (though not, in the author's opinion, their inalienability), Charles Beitz draws an interesting parallel to an argument for voting rights on the basis that they "constitute a form of communal affirmation of equal individual worth".[31] Beitz suggests the relevant analogy to moral rights

---

[27]   That is not to say that the right against defamation would be worthless under such circumstances. No doubt someone would still wrong you by defaming you in a puritanical society by levelling false allegations of promiscuity against you, even if you didn't believe that acting promiscuously should result in social disapprobation.

[28]   For a collection of essays exploring the social and relational dimensions of autonomy, see Catriona Mackenzie and Natalie Stoljar, *Relational Autonomy: Feminist Perspectives on Autonomy, Agency, and the Social Self* (Oxford University Press 2000).

[29]   See John Christman, "Relational Autonomy, Liberal Individualism, and the Social Constitution of Selves", *Philosophical Studies: An International Journal for Philosophy in the Analytic Tradition* 117, no. 1/2 (2004): 143–64.

[30]   See Andrea C. Westlund, "Rethinking Relational Autonomy", *Hypatia* 24, no. 4 (2009): 26–49; Ann E. Cudd, "Connected Self-Ownership and Our Obligations to Others", *Social Philosophy and Policy* 36, no. 2 (ed 2019): 154–73, https://doi.org/10.1017/S0265052519000402.

[31]   Beitz (n 20) 343.

is that they "give public recognition to the social value of creative activity".[32] The case I am making here suggests a different take on the analogy to voting rights, which is the case for the procedural importance of individual voters having an equal voice in shaping the political landscape. The analogy is not direct, at least not if voting rights are considered necessary to the legitimacy of the democratic process. It may be possible to secure the conditions in which individuals can participate in the creation of social norms without giving property protection to acts of expression. However, once such a system of IP is in place, the way in which it functions as a forum for contributing to norm-creation gives rise to reasons that support protecting the integrity of the expressive works of individuals produced within that framework.

On this view, the case for protecting the integrity of expressive works can be linked to the importance of individuals having standing as contributors to the shaping of social norms. If systems of intellectual property provide a forum for individuals to make public authorial expressions as a way of contributing to and contesting social norms, the full commodification of the objects in which those expressions are reified raises a distinct set of concerns. We can tease out a few of these by taking the right of attribution and the right of integrity in turn.

The case in favour of the right to be attributed as the author of a work derives from the importance of protecting an individual's ability to claim standing as an independent contributor to the process of shaping social norms. The right to remain anonymous can be defended on the basis of the same principle. This is most clear if we consider the dangers of expressing disagreement with deeply entrenched social norms. A right to remain anonymous protects each individual's ability to publish controversial or dissenting views without exposing the author to social stigma or shunning. To allow these rights to be alienated along with the economic rights to the work in question would threaten to undermine the standing of individuals as equal participants in the system of norm shaping. It would allow those with more purchasing power to exert greater influence by accumulating authorial objects and presenting them as their own contributions.

Similar reasons can be marshalled in defence of the right to integrity. Full commodification of creative works with no integrity protections would raise concerns about those with less commercial power having their contributions co-opted or manipulated by those with more purchasing power. This concern would perhaps be most evident in cases where a piece of work was distorted but still presented to the public or to the market as the work of its originator. This would amount to a manipulation of the author's contribution to the shaping of social norms, while still ostensibly presenting the contribution as her own. But one might equally raise concerns about the contributions of anonymous authors being distorted beyond their original meaning, insofar as this would erase their contribution entirely. Considering some of the reasons that stand in favour of the right to remain anonymous, there may be particularly strong reasons to protect the right to integrity for anonymous authors whose work may be most vulnerable to being manipulated into a more socially palatable form.

It should be evident from the above that a right against defamation would not provide adequate protection from the perspective of protecting authors' standing as contributors to the shaping of social norms. If systems of intellectual property provide the institutional conditions under which authorial expression functions as a way of contributing to the very shaping of social norms, the importance of integrity protections cannot be established by reference only

---

[32]   Ibid. For a similar case in favour of the expressive value of moral rights, see Ong (n 21).

to existing normative standards of reputation. Such defamation-based integrity rights would only stand in protection of the status-quo, and risk stifling the ability of individuals to stand not only as subjects of, but contributors to the construction of those social norms.

6.   CONCLUSION

This chapter sought to interrogate what concept of honour, if any, might play a part in the justification for attributing to authors inalienable rights of attribution and integrity with regard to their creative output. I argued that the Kantian personality-based approach falls short of justifying such rights as morally necessary. Appeals to the importance of securing the right conditions for the public use of reason also fail to establish the moral necessity of a system of copyright in which rights of attribution and integrity would require protection. As such, we have reason to be sceptical that there is anything intrinsically special about the connection between an author and their work which requires special protection.

The case for moral rights from relational autonomy from the perspective I have offered avoids the pitfalls of the personality-based approach. It need not commit to the idea that any instance of interference with the integrity of an authorial expression constitutes an interference with an aspect of that person, and therefore an affront to their autonomy. Instead, it offers reasons from the perspective of the existing legal context in favour of preserving the conditions to support relational autonomy. The form of the argument is as follows: when you have an existing system of copyright which protects artistic contributions as the property of creators, and in which art functions as a way of contributing to shaping the norms of the community, then we can think of the domain of art and copyright as part of the conditions for relational autonomy.

If we think it important that individuals have equal standing in the process of norm shaping, this gives rise to reasons in favour of attributing to authors inalienable rights of attribution and integrity with respect to their artistic creations. Even if it would not necessarily threaten a particular individual's autonomy to allow her to alienate her moral rights with respect to a certain piece of work, the general implications of allowing widespread market alienability of authorial expression without protecting rights of attribution or integrity would undermine an important aspect of the conditions of autonomous participation. In that sense, the case from relational autonomy provides a system-level, rather than personality-based justification for limiting the alienability of moral rights. This idea that moral rights could serve to protect the standing of artists to contribute to the process of shaping social norms could, I suggest, be seen as a re-interpretation of the concept of honour referenced in the Berne Convention.

That said, there may well be a balance to be struck in favour of allowing some ways for authors to waive rights of attribution or integrity in limited or specific ways, in order to allow for dynamics of creative collaboration, evolution and interpretation such as those performed by transformative authors. The case I have put forward from the value of relational autonomy does not mandate moral rights as absolutely inalienable or non-waivable, but it provides a robust way of defending moral rights protections that goes beyond rights against defamation, without relying on a strong view of the significance of authorial output as a constitutive element of personality.

2. The moral rights of the author – "All Quiet on the Eastern Front"? (a Polish perspective)

Sybilla Stanisławska-Kloc[1]

1. INTRODUCTION

In three years' time, we will be celebrating the 100th anniversary of the protection of the author's moral (personal) rights in Poland. Adopted in 1926, the Copyright Act (CA 1926)[2] contained detailed regulations on the author's moral (personal) rights. It was the first Polish Copyright Act, adopted a few years after Poland regained its independence (which took place in 1918, after 123 years of Partition), and two years before the Rome (1928) revision of the Berne Convention, during which authors' moral rights were "born" for the whole world.

The aim of this chapter is to present almost 100 years of authors' moral rights from the perspective of three legal systems; rights which, interestingly enough, almost perfectly coincide with significant socio-political and economic changes. In the interwar period and for several years immediately after the war (between WWI and WWII, and during early post-WWII years), the aforementioned Act of 1926 was in force. From 1952 to 1994, a second law functioned (Copyright Act – CA 1952[3]) and three years ago marked a quarter of a century since the current Act of Copyright and Related Rights of 1994 was passed (CA 1994[4]). The delay of several years for these legal acts in relation to various ground-breaking events (1945 to the end of WWII, 1989 to the fall of the Berlin Wall) was due to the fact that copyright issues were not as politically "sensitive" as other more pressing issues.

Comparing the content of these regulations, the case law and doctrine will allow us to assess the condition of authors' moral rights. The title of this chapter is inspired by the title of E.M. Remarque's book, *All Quiet on the Western Front*, which was recently invoked at the beginning of the Advocate General A. Szpunar's opinion (Case C-469/17 *Funke Medien*, which concerned the copyright protection of military reports). I hope I will be justified in referring to the title of this novel, as I will try to present a "report" on the historical development and current state of authors' moral rights in Central and Eastern Europe, using the example of Poland[5] and a few references to other countries in this region of the world.[6]

---

[1]   English version prepared by DvM and SSK, further edited by EG.
[2]   Law from 29 March 1926, binding from 14 June 1926, Dziennik Ustaw (Official Journal) – Dz.U. from 1926, nr 48, item 286, consolidated text Dz.U. from 1935, nr 36, item. 260.
[3]   Law from 10 July, 1952, binding from 31 July 1952, Dz.U. from 1952, nr 234, item 286, changed twice in 1975 and 1989, provisions regarding the author's moral rights were not amended.
[4]   Law from 4 February 1994, binding from 23 May 1994, consolidated text Dz.U. 2021, item 1062; provisions regarding the author's moral rights were not amended.
[5]   During WWI, the eastern front ran across the south-east territory of present-day Poland.
[6]   For details see: Mihály Ficsor, The Past, Present and Future of Copyright in the European Socialist Countries, 118 RIDA 33, 61 (1983); Adolf Dietz, Intellectual Property and Desocialization in Eastern Europe, 26 IIC 851 (1995), 865; Péter Gyertyanfy, On the Evolution of Copyright Legislation in Central

First, it is important to underline that Central and Eastern Europe have a long (dating from the 1920s[7]), rich and strong tradition of protecting authors' moral rights.[8] As pointed out by S. von Lewinski: "A clear indication of the adherence of Central and Eastern European countries to the continental European system is their recognition of far-reaching moral rights, which extend beyond the minimum rights contained in article 6bis of the Berne Convention."[9] A. Dietz states that a common feature of those copyright systems are their roots: the influence of the French *droit d'auteur* in the field of moral rights[10] and the perpetuity of the author's moral rights.[11] As will be shown below, Poland is a noticeable element of the European legal landscape defined by strong moral rights for the author.

2.   GENERAL REMARKS – MORAL RIGHTS IN POLISH LAW

Regulation regarding moral (personal) rights in the Polish legal system is dichotomic: in the Civil Code and in intellectual property laws, but with additional interesting "legal chimera" features (see Section 2.2 below).

2.1   The Civil Code – Act from 1964

Personal rights (general) protecting personal interests are regulated in the Civil Code of 1964 (CC 1964)[12] where Art. 23 contains an open catalogue[13] (exemplary) of those interests including: name and image, scientific, artistic, inventive and rationalizing creativity (in addition to the protection provided by other regulations such as the Copyright Act).[14] Pertaining to moral

---

and Eastern Europe up to January 1999, 182 RIDA 5 (1999) 23–5; Péter Mezei, A Development of Hungarian Copyright Law until the Creation of the First Copyright Act (1793–1884). Available at SSRN: https://ssrn.com/abstract=2890496 or http://dx.doi.org/ 10.2139/ssrn.2890496.

[7]   In Bulgaria, Romania, Hungary, Czechoslovakia, and Poland in the 1920s, and Yugoslavia in the 1930s. See Péter Gyertyanfy, On the Evolution of Copyright Legislation in Central and Eastern Europe up to January 1999, 182 RIDA 5 (1999); and in 1922 Swiss Copyright Act, 1920 Austrian Copyright Reform, Italian law (1925).

[8]   M.T. Sundara Rajan writes: "post-socialist copyright represents an expansion of moral rights into new areas", M.T. Sundara Rajan, *Moral Rights – Principles, Practice and New Technology* (Oxford, Oxford University Press 2011) pp. 187–8.

[9]   S. von Lewinski, Copyright in Central and Eastern Europe: An Intellectual Property Metamorphosis, 8 Fordham Intell. Prop. Media & Ent. L.J. 39 (1997). Available at: https://ir.lawnet.fordham.edu/iplj/vol8/iss1/4, p. 53.

[10]   See Adolf Dietz, Intellectual Property and Desocialization in Eastern Europe, 26 IIC 868 (1995).

[11]   S. von Lewinski, Copyright in Central and Eastern Europe: An Intellectual Property Metamorphosis, 8 Fordham Intell. Prop. Media & Ent. L.J. 39 (1997). Available at: https://ir.lawnet.fordham.edu/iplj/vol8/iss1/4, p. 53.

[12]   Law from 23 April 1964, consolidated text Dz.U. 2022, item 1360. Outside the scope of this article are the protection of moral (personal) right (attribution right) under law of industrial property (the act from 30 June 2000, consolidated text Dz.U. 2021, item 324).

[13]   The most important, but only exemplary listed in Art. 23 CC, are: health, freedom, dignity, freedom of conscience, name, pseudonym, image, privacy (secrecy) of correspondence, inviolability of home.

[14]   Author's moral rights are a specific type of general personal rights, see J. Barta, R. Markiewicz (in:) *International Copyright Law and Practice*, ed. E. Geller, 2020, 32-12/2020, p. POL-39.

rights, there are four main features of this protection. Firstly, personal interests from the CC 1964 are protected for a natural person's lifetime and extinguish upon their death.[15] Secondly, this statutory exemplary catalogue of protected personal interests (a total of ten) from the CC 1964 is constantly expanded by the judiciary, which, among other things, has also extended personal interest protections to the relatives[16] of a deceased person in the form of "worship". It enables them, to some extent, to seek the protection of the personal rights of deceased authors, as part of the preservation of their memory and achievements (scientific, artistic, etc.).[17] Thirdly, as part of the personal interests under Art. 23 CC 1964, the authorship of a scientific finding or discovery is protected, which at present, remains outside the scope of copyright protection in Poland.[18]

Finally, this last feature, together with the first one, is relevant to the main topic of this paper: protection under the CC 1964 for authors of copyrightable works and artists of artistic performances is "independent" of copyright protection found in the CA 1994, and the entitled person (during their lifetime) may decide to use either, or both regimes of protection. The entitled person benefits from the choice of which legal instruments they will use to fully implement the protection of their personal interests. However, this does not mean opening the way to multiple civil sanctions under CC 1964 and CA 1994.[19]

Even in this cursorily outlined background, we can see how important it was to regulate the moral rights of authors in Copyright Acts as perpetual rights (i.e., unlimited in time). Whether this also applies to the moral rights of performers will be the subject of further analysis.

2.2 "Legal Chimera" – A Special Act of Protection of the Heritage of Fryderyk Chopin

The only Polish artist whose heritage (including works and posthumous personal interests) has been regulated in a special legal act is Fryderyk Chopin. Article 1 of the Act of 3 February 2001 on the protection of the heritage of Fryderyk Chopin (hereinafter referred to as PHFCh) states that the composer's works and related items constitute a national good and are subject to special protection exercised by the Minister of Culture and National Heritage. Moreover, the name of Fryderyk Chopin and his image are *similarly protected* on the basis of personal interests.[20] However, the PHFCh displays significant differences from the general principles

---

[15] Exceptionally, only protection of their image was provided for 20 years after the death of a person (see: Arts 81 and 83 CA 1994) as well as the privacy (secrecy) of correspondence (see: Arts 82 and 83 CA 1994).
[16] Not only limited to relatives interpreted as next of kin, but also close friends, see: judgment of the Supreme Court of 6 April 2004, I CK 484/03, OSNC 2005, nr 4 item 69.
[17] It must be emphasized, that this refers to their "own" protected personal interests (not the personal interests of this dead person), which will be executed by relatives.
[18] See Art. 1 p. 1 p. 2¹ CA 1994 and also Art. 9 p. 2 TRIPS Agreement.
[19] According to Art. 479⁸⁹ § 2 p. 3 Code of civil procedure (law from 17 November 1964 – *kodeks postępowania cywilnego*, consolidated text Dz.U. 2021, item. 1805 with amd.) infringement of personal rights done in connection with scientific and inventive activities are considered as intellectual property cases and decided in special procedure by intellectual property courts.
[20] J. Barta, R. Markiewicz even pointed out that in fact it is not protection based on the rules from Art. 23 and 24 CC 1964; J. Barta, R. Markiewicz (in:) J. Barta, M. Czajkowska-Dąbrowska, Z. Ćwiąkalski, R. Markiewicz, E. Traple, *Prawo autorskie i prawa pokrewne. Komentarz* [Copyright and related rights. Commentary.] (Warsaw 2005) p. 592. Additional English-language versions of titles of books, commen-

of the protection of name and image in the CC 1964 and form a specific system of *sui generis* protection.[21] Firstly, the protection was introduced *post mortem*, more precisely 150 years after the composer's death. Secondly, the protection is eternal, unlimited in time, and will last as long as this Act is in force. Finally, the scope of protection appears to be specific. The PHFCh does not affect the provisions of the CA 1994 (there is no need to obtain permission to use the name of Fryderyk Chopin as the author of the copyrightable work). The Minister is an entity authorized to claim the protection of Fryderyk Chopin's moral rights (pursuant to Art. 78 CA 1994) and also is entitled to seek the protection of personal interests (his surname and image) if they are used in a dishonourable manner.

What is worth emphasizing is that the phrase "in a dishonourable manner" from Art. 1 PHFCh does not appear in other regulations concerning the protection of personal rights. Hence, views have been reasonably expressed that this protection should only be granted in cases of pejorative (i.e., dishonourable to Fryderyk Chopin) uses of his name and image.[22] In my opinion, a specific prohibition on the use of the name or image of Fryderyk Chopin could only be imposed by a court if it was established that the specific use of his name or image is truly demeaning.

Characterizing this issue, attention is drawn to another important issue: "the Chopin Act provides neither the obligation to seek the protection of Chopin's honour nor the right to seek its protection", and the special title granted to The Fryderyk Chopin Institute (F.Ch.I.)[23] is primarily intended "to exercise general custody over this heritage, and it is not a system of specific rights and corresponding claims".[24]

PHFCh does not result in the revival of the protection of the author's economic rights to Chopin's works. Nevertheless, it "confirms" the protection of the deceased author's moral rights, and clearly indicates that the Minister is the person entitled to claim infringement on the composer's moral rights. However, there have yet to be any court disputes related to the application of PHFCh.

---

taries and articles published in Polish are given in square brackets for the convenience of readers not familiar with the Polish language.

[21]   See G. Tylec, *Dobra osobiste a inne dobra o charakterze osobistym chronione post mortem* (in:) *Non omnis moriar: osobiste i majątkowe aspekty prawne śmierci człowieka. Zagadnienia wybrane* [Personal rights and other rights of a personal nature protected postmortem (in:) Non omnis moriar: personal and property legal aspects of human death] ed. J. Gołaczyński, J. Mazurkiewicz, J. Turłukowski, D. Karkut (Wrocław 2015) p. 834.

[22]   See M. Kruk, *W 200. rocznicę urodzin Wielkiego Polskiego Kompozytora o ochronie jego dóbr osobistych* [On the 200th birth anniversary of the Great Polish Composer – about the protection of his personal rights] (Palestra 2010), nr 11-12, p. 91; J. Mazurkiewicz, Non omnis moriar: ochrona dóbr osobistych zmarłego w prawie polskim [Non omnis moriar: Protection of personal rights of deseased in Polish law], p. 728, 2011, on-line version, https://www.bibliotekacyfrowa.pl/dlibra/publication/28023/edition/34548?language=pl; D. Flisak (in:) M. Bukowski, D. Flisak (ed.), Z. Okoń, P. Podrecki, J. Raglewski, S. Stanisławska-Kloc, T. Targosz, *Prawo autorskie i prawa pokrewne* [Copyright and related rights. Commentary]; 2015, point 20 in the commentary to Art. 81 CA 1994.

[23]   The Fryderyk Chopin Institute, https://nifc.pl/en//.

[24]   M. Poźniak-Niedzielska, *Osobiste prawa autorskie po upływie czasu ochrony* [Author's moral rights after the expiration of the term of protection] (in:) M. Poźniak-Niedzielska, A. Niewęgłowski, A. Przyborowska-Klimczak, *Ochrona niematerialnego dziedzictwa kulturalnego* [Protection of intangible cultural heritage], A. Niewęgłowski, A. Przyborowska-Klimczak, p. 1.2.2 (Warsaw 2015), on-line version.

With regard to the score of an unknown work by Fryderyk Chopin that was recently found[25] and might be published or otherwise distributed for the first time, it would be legally possible to create a related right to the first editions (the so-called *editio princeps* – cf. Art. 99¹ CA 1994) and the publisher's related right to a critical and scientific edition (cf. Art. 99² CA 1994; both related rights are only economic character[26]). In practice, this means that a posthumously discovered score, and more precisely the work contained therein, would be protected for a period of 25 years in all fields of exploitation (Art. 99¹ CA 1994). Any derivative work of such a score would, of course, be protected by the CA 1994 as a derivative work.

The PHFCh is a national Act, thus, is valid only in Poland. It is also not the subject of any international agreements (including bilateral ones).[27]

2.3 A Special Protection of the Author's Right to Attribution – An Act of Higher Education and Science ("University Act")

The special protection of authors' moral rights (their right to attribution) is established in the Act of Higher Education and Science of 2018 (AHES).[28] Such a new, detailed regulation has existed since the beginning of the twenty-first century.

In order to prevent plagiarism (the misappropriation of authorship of copyright works) in the academic and scientific environment, certain solutions were introduced. Firstly, the AHES makes it possible to deprive a person who has infringed on the right of authorship[29] of their Master title, PhD title, habilitation title (in case of the misappropriation of the authorship of a substantial part or element of a copyrightable work, but also including substantial scientific findings in a Master's thesis, PhD thesis, and postdoctoral/habilitation thesis).[30] Such a solution did not exist under the Copyright Act. The CA 1994 is focused on the protection of authors and offers no opportunity for a civil or criminal court to deprive a third person of their Master's degree or science degrees and titles; this is possible only under the AHES with an administrative procedure.

Secondly, the AHES provides detailed rules of disciplinary liability.[31] According to Art. 275 p. 1: "an academic teacher shall be subject to disciplinary liability for any disciplinary

---

[25]   Copies of which had not previously been publicly accessible.

[26]   See Art. 4 (protection of previously unpublished works) and Art. 5 (critical and scientific publications) EC Directive 2006/116 of 12 December 2006 on the protection of copyright and certain related rights.

[27]   Some trademarks with Fryderyk Chopin's name are registered in the EU IPO, without any prior permission of the Ministry.

[28]   Consolidated text Dz.U. 2022, item. 574 with amendments. Previous acts: (a) Act on academic degrees and academic title and degrees and title in art (valid till 2018); and (b) the Act on Higher Education from 2005 also provided such regulation. English version of AHES (not legally binding) available here: https://konstytucjadlanauki.gov.pl/content/uploads/2020/06/act-of-20-july-2018-the-law -on-higher-education-and-science.pdf. It should be explained that "higher education" (as in the title of law regulation-English version) in Poland means education at the university level.

[29]   But also the misappropriation of the authorship of the substantial part or elements of scientific discoveries (scientific findings, which per se are not copyrightable works).

[30]   Declare the invalidity of the diploma, see Art. 77 p. 5, 194–5, 225 AHES.

[31]   Previous Acts also provided disciplinary liability, but did not regulate in such detail as regards copyright matters. AHES also provides the possibility of disciplinary liability in case of the falsification of scientific research or its results or other scientific fraud.

misconduct which constitutes an act which defaults on the duties of an academic teacher, or which offends the dignity of the academic profession". The AHES states that some copyright infringements also entail disciplinary liability. The disciplinary investigation process is initi-ated *ex officio* in the case of an act consisting of copyright infringements such as (1) misap-propriating the authorship or misleading as to the authorship of the whole or part of another person's work or artistic performance; and (2) dissemination, without providing the name or pseudonym of the author, of another person's work in its original version or in the form of a derivative work.[32]

The AHES creates an additional instrument of protection for authors' and performers' moral rights (mostly rights of attribution) in the interest of the public, universities and scientific community. The AHES obliges universities to use anti-plagiarism software in order to check the diploma theses of all students[33] (including PhD students' theses).

3.   COPYRIGHT HORIZON – AUTHOR'S MORAL RIGHTS CENTENNIAL PERSPECTIVE

3.1   The Act of 1926 – A Solid "Foundation" of Polish Authors' Moral Rights

In 1918, Poland regained its independence (after 123 years of Partition), which was confirmed by the Treaty of Versailles. One of the first tasks facing its leaders was to rebuild the legal system to replace the regulations introduced by the partitioning powers. Art. 19 of the Little Treaty of Versailles of 1919[34] imposed an obligation on Poland to join, inter alia, the Berne Convention. On 28 January 1920, before the first Polish copyright law was passed, Poland acceded to the Berne Convention.[35] Whether due to the first prime Minister Ignacy Jan Paderewski's friendship with US President Woodrow Wilson, his status as an outstanding pianist (his concerts in the US were a great success) and a publisher of Chopin's works,[36] or because the works of Polish authors (poets, writers, artists) during Partition played a signifi-cant role in uniting the nation, actions were promptly taken to enact appropriate regulation in the field of copyright. It is difficult to say why this was unequivocally the case. For certain, these circumstances, as well as the importance of economic development and awareness as to the importance of intellectual property rights in the system of international law played a significant role.

---

[32]   And also in case of: (3) the dissemination, without providing the name or pseudonym of the author, of another person's artistic performance or the public distortion of such work, artistic performance, phonogram, videogram or broadcast; (4) infringement of someone else's copyright or related rights in a manner other than specified in points 1–3. Above points 1–4 are almost verbal copies of Art. 115 CA 1994, which provides criminal liability of infringement of authors and performers moral rights. That disciplinary liability is independent from civil (Arts 78–9 CA 1994) and criminal (Art. 115 CA 1994) liability.

[33]   A national repository of diploma theses was established.

[34]   Treaty was signed on 28 June 1919; published in Dz.U. 1920, nr 110, item 728.

[35]   Government statement dated 12 May 1921, published in Dz.U. 1922, nr 3, item 150. In 1920 The Codification Commission appointed reporter (F. Zoll) and co-reporter (J. Litauer) of the bill of copyright.

[36]   *Chopin. Complete works.* Editor Paderewski, Fryderyk Chopin Institute and PWM Edition Kraków.

In the period from 1795 to 1918, Poland was divided into Partitions under the control of the Russian Empire (part: the Kingdom of Poland, including Warsaw), the Kingdom of Prussia (part: Wielkopolska, including Poznań) and the Habsburg Monarchy of Austria (part: Małopolska – Galicja, including Krakow, Lviv and Cieszyn Silesia). The law of the partitioning powers was in force in Poland. Hence, the Polish regulation of 1926 was not the first Act of Copyright that would be known and applied by Polish authors.[37] This was especially true in Krakow, where it was possible to enjoy the benefits of the relatively large autonomy of Galicia, and where the scientific community was well developed (including the first Polish university founded in 1364, the Jagiellonian University) and artistic life flourished (theatres, and the Academy of Fine Arts founded in 1818, were continuously being developed). Admittedly, in a study on Austrian private law at Jagiellonian University, F. Zoll explained his concept of copyright as "rights similar to in rem", that is, rights that were proprietary and transferable. Nevertheless, he pointed to one right connected to copyright, which could not be transferred either *inter vivos* or *mortis causa*, namely the right to declare to the public that you are the author of a work.[38] In connection with authors' moral rights, two issues were present. First, some artists working in Partitions used pseudonyms. This was partly due to the nineteenth-century fashion for pseudonyms, which were considered part of the artistic dimension of a work (they created a certain mystery). Second, for political reasons, these pseudonyms made it possible to conceal an author's identity and thus avoid repression due to the content of the work, especially if the author decided to publish a work with patriotic and political content. In all Partitions (and particularly in Russia and Prussia), the content of published works was extensively supervised and censored. Partitions imposed changes and ordered the removal of inappropriate fragments or works.

Cicero famously wrote "*inter arma silent Musae*" ("in times of war, the Muses fall silent"), but art was a very important weapon in the fight to preserve the Polish identity against invaders, especially after several unsuccessful uprisings. Following the suppression of the November Uprising in 1831, Fryderyk Chopin composed an étude in C minor (Op. 10 No. 12, also known as Revolutionary) in Paris. According to some sources, it was banned in Warsaw and in the entire Russian Partition at the request of Tsar Nicholas I, who not only suppressed the uprising, but also sent thousands of Poles to Siberia (a distant part of Russia). The tsar was afraid of the composer's work; he is quoted as having said that Fryderyk Chopin's music "is cannons buried in flowers".[39] After this uprising, many Poles (the political and artistic elite) emigrated to France (the so-called Great Emigration[40]), and more groups came in the wake of

---

[37]   See E. Ferenc-Szydełko, Prawo autorskie na ziemiach polskich do 1926 Roku [Copyright on the Polish territory until 1926], ZN UJ PzWiOWI [Zeszyty Naukowe Uniwersytetu Jagiellońskiego, Prace z Wynalazczości i Ochrony Własności Intelektualnej], z. 75 (Cracow 2000); Leonard Górnicki, *Rozwój idei praw autorskich: od starożytności do II wojny światowej* [The development of the idea of copyright: from antiquity to World War II] (Wrocław 2013), access: http://www.bibliotekacyfrowa.pl/Content/42471/Rozwoj_idei_praw_autorskich.pdf.
[38]   F. Zoll, *Austriackie prawo prywatne. Część ogólna* [Austrian Private Law. General part] (Kraków 1909) pp. 165–8.
[39]   This was quoted by a friend of F. Chopin – Robert Schumann, see A. Walker, *Fryderyk Chopin. A Life and Times* (Faber and Faber 2018) p. 305.
[40]   See A. Zamoyski, *Poland a History* (London 2009); Prince Adam Jerzy Czartoryski was the leader of Polish emigration in France, he founded a conservative-liberal camp, which was called the "Lambert hotel", after the prince's palace located on the island of St. Louis in Paris.

the Krakow Uprising (1846) and January Uprising (1863–1864). The works of many Polish authors were banned, including national poets such as A. Mickiewicz, J. Słowacki and C.K. Norwid.[41] Emigration to French also played an important role in the period after WWII (cf. Section 3.2).

The Berne Convention, Art. 6*bis*, which concerned the moral (personal) rights of authors, was added in 1928 during a revision congress in Rome.[42] Polish lawyers also contributed to the adoption of this regulation.[43] Prof. F. Zoll was even invited to the most important authority body of the congress: the Drafting Commission, which, at the time, only had five members: Piola Caselli (Italy), G. Maillard (France), Beckett (Great Britain), Coloman de Alker (Hungary) and F. Zoll (Poland).[44]

With Art. 6*bis*, the Berne Convention introduced the protection of the right of attribution and the right of integrity[45] independent of an author's economic rights. The conditions for the exercise of authors' moral rights, including the choice of specific protection measures, are left to national-level legislation. To this day, Art. 6*bis* has yet to be amended.[46]

In Poland, since 29 March 1926, that is, since the adoption of the first Act on Copyright, a strong protection of the moral (personal) rights of authors has been in force.[47] The system

---

[41]   After the failure of the January Uprising, he wrote a patriotic poem "Chopin's Piano", referring to an authentic event, i.e., the removal of the piano on which F. Chopin played from the Zamoyski palace by the Russians. A bomb had been dropped from this palace earlier during an unsuccessful attempt on the tsarist governor.

[42]   See S. Ricketson, J. Ginsburg, *International Copyright and Neighbouring Rights: The Berne Convention and Beyond*, 2d ed., vol. 1 (Oxford, Oxford University Press 2005) pp. 589–90; E. Adeney, *The Moral Rights of Authors and Performers. An International and Comparative Analysis* (Oxford, Oxford University Press 2006) pp. 103–34; E. Adeney, Of Moral Rights and Legal Transplants Connecting Laws, Connecting Cultures (in:) *Across Intellectual Property. Essays in Honour of Sam Ricketson*, ed. by G.W. Austin, A.F. Christie, A.T. Kenyon, M. Richardson (Cambridge, Cambridge University Press 2020) pp. 67–8.

[43]   "Moral rights were promoted at Rome by the delegations of Italy, France, Poland, Romania and Czechoslovakia", E. Adeney, *The Moral Rights of Authors and Performers. An International and Comparative Analysis* (Oxford, Oxford University Press 2006) pp. 105, 108 (footnote 20).

[44]   *Wspomnienia Fryderyka Zolla* [Memoirs of Fryderyk Zoll], ed. I. Homala-Skąpska, Zakamycze 2000, ss. 320–1.

[45]   See S. Ricketson, J. Ginsburg, *International Copyright and Neighbouring Rights: The Berne Convention and Beyond*, 2d ed., vol. 1 (Oxford, Oxford University Press 2005) pp. 585–6.

[46]   Only a small editorial amendment of Art. 6*bis* was made in a Brussels revision in 1948. For details see S. Ricketson, J. Ginsburg, *International Copyright and Neighbouring Rights: The Berne Convention and Beyond*, 2d ed., vol. 1 (Oxford, Oxford University Press 2005) pp. 594–9.

[47]   But the first version of bill of copyright act (with provision relating to the authors moral rights) was prepared by F. Zoll in 1920, the final bill was accepted by Codification Committee in 1923, see S. Gołąb, Ustawa o prawie autorskim z dnia 29 marca 1926 r. z materiałami [Copyright Act of March 29, 1926 with materials] (Warsaw 1928) p. 245; *Wspomnienia Fryderyka Zolla* [Memoirs of Fryderyk Zoll], ed. I. Homala-Skąpska (Zakamycze 2000) ss. 316, 319–21; see also J. Słyszewska, Ochrona praw twórców w świetle ustawy o prawie autorskim z 29 Marca 1926 roku [Protection of authors under the Copyright Act from 29 March 1926], Civitas et Lex, 2020, 2 (26) pp. 43–5, http://www.uwm.edu.pl/elk/publikacje/wp-content/uploads/2020/05/03_Slyszewska-J.pdf.\; S. Stanisławska-Kloc, "Ab origine": The Ninetieth Anniversary of Enacting the First Polish Copyright Act, ZNUJ. PPWI (Zeszyty Naukowe UJ, Prace z Prawa Własności Intelektualnej), 2016, nr 2, pp. 157–75.

of copyright dualism (moral and economic rights) that is still in force today belongs to the tradition of Polish legislation.[48]

The first Polish regulation on authors' moral rights was very extensive: Art. 6 CA 1926 indicated that copyright belonged to the author and introduced the presumption of authorship. Due to the lack of a system of author registration in Poland (and lack of the official certification of the authorship of a work), this presumption still plays an important role to this day when it comes to making it easier for an author to assert their rights, both moral (personal) and economic.[49] Art. 12 CA 1926 clearly stated: "the protection of moral rights serves every author regardless of the existence or non-existence of copyright" (even if economic rights did not exist).[50] Such a synthetic and "short" approach to authors' moral rights was intentional, since, as aptly pointed out in the justification of the CA 1926: "these rights cannot be strictly defined according to the present state of science and therefore one must be satisfied with their exemplary enumeration, leaving the disclosure of their characteristic features and complete identification in hold of the future".[51] It was already considered at that time that moral (personal) rights protected the author's attitude to the work ("the emotional knot that connects the author with the work" – *vinculum spirituale*[52]), and not the author's personality (according to J. Kohler[53]).

Another provision, Art. 58 CA 1926 entitled "Complaints for Copyright Infringement" contained a detailed catalogue of claims that could be filed by authors whose moral (personal) rights had been violated.[54] Those claims and their penalties included omission (injunction), removal of consequences (including through a public statement, an announcement of a judgment in the press), and in the case of culpable violation, an appropriate amount of money

---

[48] See T. Targosz, *Dziewięćdziesięciolecie pierwszej polskiej ustawy prawnoautorskiej – czyli kilka uwag o żyjącej przeszłości* [Ninety years of the first Polish copyright law – a few notes on the living past]; Kwartalnik Prawa Prywatnego, year XXV, 2016, nr 4, p. 797.

[49] Or maybe especially the author's moral rights, because this original authorship designation is "petrified" (actually fixed in the face of the impossibility of transfer of moral rights), in relation to the changing of rightholders of authors' economic rights.

[50] This is also pointed out by E. Adeney, *The Moral Rights of Authors and Performers. An International and Comparative Analysis* (Oxford, Oxford University Press 2006) p. 91.

[51] See S. Gołąb, *Ustawa o prawie autorskim z dnia 29 marca 1926 r. z materiałami* [Copyright Act of March 29, 1926 with materials] (Warsaw 1928) s. 62 i 281. Especially notes it T. Targosz, *Dziewięćdziesięciolecie pierwszej polskiej ustawy prawnoautorskiej – czyli kilka uwag o żyjącej przeszłości* [Ninety years of the first Polish copyright law – a few notes on the living past]; Kwartalnik Prawa Prywatnego, year XXV, 2016, nr 4, p. 798.

[52] F. Zoll, *Polska ustawa o prawie autorskiem i Konwencja Berneńska z objaśnieniami* [Polish Copyright Act and Berne Convention] (Warsaw-Kraków-Lwów-Poznań 1926) p. 54; S. Ritterman, *Komentarz do ustawy o prawie autorskim* [Commentary to copyright law] (Kraków 1937) p. 77.

[53] This is pointed out in more recent literature by T. Targosz, *Dziewięćdziesięciolecie pierwszej polskiej ustawy prawnoautorskiej – czyli kilka uwag o żyjącej przeszłości.* [Ninety years of the first Polish copyright law – a few notes on the living past] Kwartalnik Prawa Prywatnego, year XXV, 2016, nr 4, ss. 798–9 and B. Giesen, E. Wojnicka (in:) *System prawa prywatnego*, tom 13, *Prawo autorskie* [System of Private Law, Volume 13. Copyright Law] ed. J. Barta, p. 279.

[54] F. Zoll, *Polska ustawa o prawie autorskiem i konwencja berneńska* [Polish Copyright Act and Berne Convention] (Warsaw Kraków-Lwów-Poznań 1926) p. 8.

(*solatium*/penitence[55]). However, what should be emphasized is that the infringement of the author's economic rights was regulated separately.

F. Zoll pointed out that this civil protection should be based on principles analogous to the Roman *actio iniuriarum aestimatoria* (action for delict). Additionally, the provision of Art. 58 CA 1926 listed the exemplary but most important[56] types of violations of moral rights; this catalogue started with the misappropriation of authorship, but misrepresentation of authorship was separately indicated. Furthermore, it provided protection for the decision over the first publication, integrity and improper use of works. While at that time, the sphere of authors' moral rights also included criticism devaluing the copyrightable work, today this protection exists only as part of the personal rights of the author in the CC 1964 (their good name, in the case of unfair criticism of their work).

This method of regulation resulted from the difficulty in precisely defining the full breadth of moral rights.[57] Delineating which actions violated moral rights had an even greater social impact and introduced an instructive dimension to the law, making it easier to recognize unlawful activities that encroach on the personal rights of authors and caution against them.

The biggest novelty in the CA 1926, even on an international scale, was the inclusion of authors' moral rights (not only in terms of authorship) as perpetual rights, not limited in time.[58] They served the author regardless of the existence of an author's economic rights.

Granting the perpetual protection of authors' moral rights meant that it covered the period after an author's death. Although the assumption was that these rights could not be inherited,[59] they were to be protected after the author's death. This required identifying the circle of

---

[55]   That is, awarding an amount for the incurred "unpleasantness and other personal detriment", but only in the case of a culpable violation of the author's moral rights. After 1935, this right was granted only to the author, and not to persons who exercised moral rights after their death, including the Prosecutor's Office; see the judgment of the Supreme Court of 19 February 1937, file ref. I K 1117/36, in which it was assumed that penitential (*solatium*) is not a punishment imposed by a criminal court, but "a lump-sum cash remuneration claimed in a general procedure of civil proceedings, or by way of a civil claim". Publ. in OSN (K) 1937/7/203. At the same time, the court could refuse to carry out *solatium* when "the moral harm suffered by the author was made up in a different way", judgment of the Supreme Court of 1 September 1936, II C 822/36.

[56]   Art. 62 CA 1926: "Such personal harm is: when someone appropriates the authorship, the name of the author or a pseudonym; when he does not provide the author or the source from which he took the content or excerpts in his work, resulting in an incorrect opinion as to authorship, or gives a false author or source; when he publishes a work, not intended for publication by the author; when introducing changes, additions or shortenings to the publication that distort the content or offend the dignity and value of the work; when he publishes a work in a grossly inappropriate manner; when he makes changes to the original work, when the original work marked with the name of the author against his will, or otherwise against his will, reveals the authorship; when in criticism he lowers the value of the work by deliberately misrepresenting the facts, etc."

[57]   F. Zoll, *Polska ustawa o prawie autorskiem i konwencja berneńska* [Polish Copyright Act and Berne Convention] (Warsaw-Kraków-Lwów-Poznań 1926) p. 54.

[58]   "Such a provision is an expression of deep concern for the inviolability of cultural heritage, constituting an undeniable value for the entire nation" – wrote A. Kopff, Fryderyka Zolla koncepcja praw do rzeczowych podobnych (in:) *Fryderyk Zoll (1865–1948). Prawnik-uczony-kodyfikator* [A. Kopff, Fryderyk Zoll's concept of rights to property similar (in:) Fryderyk Zoll (1865–1948). Lawyer-scholar-codifier] (Kraków 1994) p. 49.

[59]   This raised no doubts from the very beginning, see J.L. Litauer, *Ustawodawstwo autorskie obowiązujące w Królestwie Polskiem* [Legislation of copyright in force in the Kingdom of Poland] (Warsaw 1916) p. 12, with reference to the view of F. Zoll (who wrote that there is one right that cannot

persons entitled to their enforcement. Legislators immediately provided three solutions. Either the author could indicate a person who could seek this protection, and if he did not do so, the persons entitled under the Act were: the spouse, parents, descendants, and the siblings of the deceased. The indicated persons were considered representatives of the "spiritual interests" of the deceased author, appointed as valid "substitutes" in the exercise of these rights. Two factors determined the selection: a close relationship with the author and the capacity to properly supervise the author's legacy.[60] To better implement the protection of these rights, the CA 1926 indicated that once one of the entitled persons had filed a complaint, the others could not file a new one, but had to join the already pending dispute. The third solution regarded works published under a pseudonym or anonymously; the publisher was the authorized "substitute" who could act to protect an author's moral (personal) rights. In 1935, an amendment to the CA 1926 added the Prosecutor's Office (acting per the instructions of the Ministry of Religions and Public Enlightenment, Art. 63 CA 1926) to the list of persons authorized to enforce the moral rights of deceased authors.

Authors' moral (personal) rights were also protected by other detailed provisions. In the case of the transfer of an author's economic rights to another person, the author retained his moral (personal) rights (Art. 28 CA 1926) and authors were guaranteed the right to correct and amend the work prepared for publication (Art. 38 CA 1926). Another provision required the identification of the author (and not only the source) in the case of fair use (exception/ limitation) of their work (Art. 16 CA 1926).

From the beginning, the inherent nature of the moral (personal) rights of co-authors were recognized, stressing that the primacy of majority granted by civil law (in case of ownership) could not be allowed in the sphere of authors' moral (personal) rights.[61] In practice, this meant that any disagreement between co-authors as to the exercise of their moral rights was decided by the courts (taking into consideration the interests of all co-authors, including minority ones).

As early as 1926, the protection of moral rights could also apply to foreign authors from countries that did not afford such protections.[62] This solution was of particular importance as Polish regulations were one of the first in the world, as emphasized in September 1926 during

---

pass through succession, "because the grandson of the deceased author cannot publish under his own name" – F. Zoll, *Polskie prawo autorskie i konwencja berneńska* [Polish Copyright Act and the Berne Convention] (Warsaw-Kraków-Lwów-Poznań 1926) p. 55).

[60]   "*Personae, quae sustinet personam defuncti*", see F. Zoll, *Polska ustawa o prawie autorskiem i konwencja berneńska* [Polish Copyright Act and Berne Convention] (Warsaw-Kraków-Lwów-Poznań 1926) p. 56.

[61]   See F. Zoll, *Polska ustawa o prawie autorskiem i konwencja berneńska* [Polish Copyright Act and the Berne Convention] (Warsaw-Kraków-Lwów-Poznań 1926) r., p. 45.

[62]   J.L. Litauer, *Ustawodawstwo autorskie obowiązujące w Królestwie Polskiem* [Legislation of copyright in force in the Kingdom of Poland] (Warsaw 1916) p. 36; see E. Adeney, *The Moral Rights of Authors and Performer. An International and Comparative Analysis* (Oxford, Oxford University Press 2006) p. 92.

the ALAI congress,[63] the first one held in Poland. During that event, F. Zoll dedicated the first of his commentary to the CA 1926, which was likewise issued in September 1926.[64]

Since the beginning of CA 1926, the confluence of authors' interests and societal interests was also observed in the sphere of the author's moral rights.[65] It was pointed out that criminal protection should be even more important than economic protection in the case of authors' moral rights, as "acts against the author's spiritual interests are connected with the need for repression from the standpoint of public interest" (e.g., misleading an audience as to the origin of a work, its author).[66] Therefore, intentional misappropriation (plagiarism) of someone else's work was a punishable offence.[67]

A few judgments issued at that time were insightful in identifying and resolving problems related to the sphere of authors' moral rights. For instance, the presumption of a "positive" performance in terms of marking work with a surname or a pseudonym (when sending a work for printing with the designation of the authorship of a surname;[68] but the use of a pseudonym required a clear statement). Additionally, the moral (personal) rights of translators were recognized.[69]

The newly adopted CA 1926 was accompanied by numerous studies, authored by outstanding lawyers and characterized by the transparency and elegance of their legal arguments (with vast references to foreign literature). It was pointed out in memoires that when Zoll "advocated the protection of *droit moral* after the author's death, he was looking for a structural basis in Horace: *Non omnis moriar, multaque pars mei – vitabit Libitinam*, and in Sully Prudhomme: *c'est peut-etre expirer mais ce n'est pas pourir* as well as in Kohler's *residuum*, constantly avoiding any so-called fiction in law".[70]

Such a solid foundation of protection was available to artists who, starting in 1918, were able to operate within the Union of Authors and Stage Composers (ZAiKS), Poland's largest collective copyright management organization, which still persists to this day.

The outbreak of WWII prevented the publication (made it impossible to publish) of another commentary on copyright law, which had been prepared by Jan Wiktor Lesman (publishing

---

[63]   In the resolution of the XXV ALAI Congress, held in September 1926 in Warsaw, Polish achievements in the field of the protection of moral (personal) rights were emphasized, see L. Górnicki, *Rozwój idei praw autorskich: od starożytności do II wojny światowej* [The development of the idea of copyright: from antiquity to World War II], 2013, p. 257, access: http://www.bibliotekacyfrowa.pl/Content/42471/Rozwoj_idei_praw_autorskich.pdf.

[64]   Dedication print/published on a separate cover sheet, see F. Zoll, *Polska ustawa o prawie autorskiem i konwencja berneńska* [Polish Copyright Act and the Berne Convention] (Warsaw-Kraków-Lwów-Poznań 1926).

[65]   F. Zoll, *Polska ustawa o prawie autorskiem i konwencja berneńska* [Polish Copyright Act and the Berne Convention] (Warsaw-Kraków-Lwów-Poznań 1926) pp. 8, 54, 58.

[66]   F. Zoll, *Polska ustawa o prawie autorskiem i konwencja berneńska* [Polish Copyright Act and the Berne Convention] (Warsaw-Kraków-Lwów-Poznań 1926) p. 8.

[67]   This offense was prosecuted on a private basis but until 1935 the Public Prosecutor General could also appear in court on the basis of this charge.

[68]   Supreme Court, 6 June 1928, K 715/28.

[69]   Supreme Court, 22 March 1938, I K 1985/37, the use of a fictitious name instead of the real name of the translator or his pseudonym was found to be a violation of the translator's rights and a crime. Published in OSN (K) 1938/11/257.

[70]   S. Grzybowski, Fryderyk Zoll – człowiek i jego dzieło (in:) *Fryderyk Zoll 1865–1948. Prawnik-uczony-kodyfikator* [Fryderyk Zoll – the men and his work (in:) Fryderyk Zoll (1865–1948). Lawyer-scholar-codifier] ed. A. Mączyński (Kraków 1994) p. 8.

under the pseudonym Jan Brzechwa). Lesman was a lawyer and legal advisor of ZAiKS (and its co-founder), although he is best known as a writer, an author of fairy tales for children and satirical stories, as well as a translator.[71]

The period of WWII (1939–1945)[72] and the years immediately following were not favourable to the further development of many branches of law, including this one. More exactly, they limited this development, leaving only speculation as to whether this pre-war accumulation of talents and works was providential for Polish copyright law.

3.2   The Copyright Act of 1952 – "Resistance to the Wind of Change"?

The circumstances surrounding the adoption of the CA 1952[73] (under a socialist regime), did not have a significant negative impact on the scope of protection of authors' moral (personal) rights; although one difference, discussed further, did occur due to the political change.

In the legal literature (which was not as rich after 1939), studies carried out before WWII were used.[74] Moreover, one of the main representatives of copyright doctrine, S. Grzybowski[75] (1902–2003), had published in the 1930s, 1950s, 1970s, and 1990s, making it possible to ensure the continuity of thought and the survival of the original solutions in the doctrine, as well as in judicial practice. After the adoption of the Civil Code of 1964, one of the most significant theoretical issues was the relationship between authors' moral rights under the CA 1952 and general moral (personal) rights under the CC 1964 (see Section 2.1).

CA 1952 stated *expressis verbis* that copyright covered the right to the protection of moral rights (Art. 15). There was no doubt in the doctrine that this Act was also based on the dualistic

---

[71]   See P. Polański (ed.), *Brzechwa. Poeta w adwokackiej todze* [Brzechwa. Poets in a lawyer's toga] (Warsaw 2022).

[72]   However, even in these wartime conditions, there was an awareness of the need to protect the sphere of authors' interests (including the author's moral rights). Cf. The decree of the President of the Republic of Poland of 13 April 1940 (Dz.U. 1940, No. 10, item 25) on the protection of the copyrights of Polish citizens outside the territory of the State. It was issued by the president-in-exile (Władysław Raczkiewicz) in Angers, France, pursuant to Art. 79 sec. (2) of the constitutional law. The decree allowed the curator (upon delivery of a letter of nomination) to exercise all the rights for the persons for whom copyright had been established, within the scope covered by the Copyright Act, with the exception of transfers of economic rights. The curator, as provided for in Art. 2 was obliged to keep a list of disseminated works, collect receivables due to the persons for whom it had been established, to ensure that the rights of these persons were not violated, and to protect the moral (personal) rights of the authors.

[73]   See A. Kopff (in:) S. Grzybowski, A. Kopff, J. Serda, *Zagadnienia prawa autorskiego* [Issues in Copyright Law], 1973, p. 31; M. Czajkowska – Dąbrowska, *Sytuacja prawna autorów obcych w Polsce* [Legal situation of foreign authors in Poland], 1991, postprint 2019, access: Reprinty *Pro Scientia Iuridica*: http://snpsi.umcs.pl/wp-content/uploads/2019/03/dabrowska_sytuacja_prawna_internet.pdf.

[74]   While the pre-war Polish doctrine drew on German and French studies, the post-war doctrine, taking into account political correctness and the changing conditions, referred to the literature of the socialist bloc countries, while in no way ceasing to draw on the achievements of the West. For instance, in the most important monograph on personal rights from the Civil Code, the comparative analysis included Germanic, Roman, Anglo-American, and Socialist legislation, with reference to numerous first-hand sources. See A. Szpunar, *Ochrona dóbr osobistych* [Protection of personal rights], 1979, pp. 17–77.

[75]   Who was also the Rector of the Jagiellonian University. Before the war, he prepared a monograph on the issue of moral (personal) rights after the death of a person. See S. Grzybowski, *Ochrona osobista stosunku do dzieła po śmierci twórcy: zagadnienia ogólne* [Personal protection of the relation to a work after the death of the author: general issues] (Kraków 1933).

concept of copyright.[76] As in the previous Act, a separate chapter was provided for the protection of the authors' moral rights (Arts 52–54). Art. 52 of the CA 1952 listed seven exemplary categories of infringements of moral (personal) rights: (1) misappropriation of authorship; (2) omitting the author's name when publishing or reproducing a work; (3) placing a name of author on a work or otherwise disclosing the authorship against the author's will; (4) failure to mention an author or source from which the content or an exception was taken in a work, or providing a false author or source; (5) publishing a work not intended for publication by the author; (6) introducing changes, additions or abbreviations in a work that distort the content or form or reduce the value of a work; and (7) acting in some other way detrimental to the author's personal rights (this constituted the widest category).

Any action from the above-described categories was considered a prima facie premise for being found in violation of a moral (personal) interest. However, as was pointed out, this did not rule out the admissibility of proof that "the personal relationship of the author to the work was not infringed"[77] (a fact which would result in the dismissal of the claim). On the other hand, this approach did not mean that the protection of moral (personal) rights was relativized, but rather, it offered the possibility of weighing (or balancing) protection while taking into account social interests and the interests of third parties (e.g., criticism that could be classified under category 7, or when making certain changes in a work by a successor). Moreover, particularly in the case of the right to authorship, it was pointed out that this should correspond to accepted customs (with the proviso that the adopted practice might not always be considered completely authoritative[78] or completely meaningful).

The CA 1952 provided for the protection of authors' moral (personal) rights after the death of the author, despite the debatable theoretical foundation of this protection indicated by the doctrine;[79] this debatable status has not changed until now. In the 1970s, S. Grzybowski wrote that it was not possible to create a "correct" constructive approach and, in this context, he referred to the accuracy of the French saying: *rien n'est plus pratique qu'une bonne théorie.*[80]

The CA 1952 granted authors typical remedies for the infringement of moral (personal) rights (omission (injunction), removal of consequences, public statement and/or publication of

---

[76]   See S. Grzybowski (in:) S. Grzybowski, A. Kopff, J. Serda, *Zagadnienia prawa autorskiego* [Issues in Copyright Law], 1973, pp. 243–4.

[77]   See S. Grzybowski (in:) S. Grzybowski, A. Kopff, J. Serda, *Zagadnienia prawa autorskiego* [Issues in Copyright Law], 1973, p. 249.

[78]   See J. Błeszyński, M. Staszkow, *Prawo autorskie i wynalazcze* [Copyright and patent law] (Warsaw 1983) pp. 131–2.

[79]   See J. Błeszyński, *Konwencja berneńska a polskie prawo autorskie* [Berne Convention and Polish Copyright Law] (Warsaw 1979) p. 328. See also W. Serda, Droit de moral po śmierci twórcy [Droit de moral after the death of the author], ZN UJ PzWiOWI [Zeszyty Naukowe Uniwersytetu Jagiellońskiego, Prace z Wynalazczości i Ochrony Własności Intelektualnej] (Kraków 1979), z. nr 17, pp. 71–133; the author discussed constructions in capitalist and socialist countries. For example, he stated that in the USSR, pursuant to Art. 481 of the Civil Code of 1964, after the author's death, the protection of the right to the integrity of a work was enforced/performed by a person designated by the author; and in the absence of such designation, their heirs and the organization entrusted with the protection of rights. The author gave examples of Hungarian, Czechoslovak, and Romanian solutions and wrote that the belief prevailed that a competent organization would properly ensure the authenticity of the work and its proper use. However, the was no court practice (judgments) which would confirm this.

[80]   See S. Grzybowski (in:) S. Grzybowski, A. Kopff, J. Serda, *Zagadnienia prawa autorskiego* [Issues in Copyright Law], 1973, p. 257.

the judgment in a journal/press). Importantly, these were not dependent on culpability, as liability was objective in nature. Conversely, the CA 1952 no longer provided for the possibility of pecuniary redress of moral harm (as the CA 1926 had), i.e., awarding an author a certain amount of money for the infringement of their moral (personal) rights.[81] This was the result of a general change in the legislator's approach to the possibility of awarding compensation for infringement of personal rights ("which was undoubtedly closely related to the legislator's negative attitude to pecuniary compensation for moral harm in general";[82] it was even specifically written that "the legislative climate was particularly unfavourable to the upholding of the concept of such redress"[83]).

Furthermore, in the Civil Code of 1964 adopted a bit later, pecuniary compensation (in Polish: *zadośćuczynienie*) was significantly limited (a fact which was conditioned by systemic and political considerations).[84] Thus, in the case of a culpable violation of personal rights, a certain amount (referred to as the so-called "interest" – "*nawiązka*" in Polish) could be awarded for societal interests, but only to one institution, namely the Polish Red Cross (Polski Czerwony Krzyż – PCK).[85] Thus "*nawiązka*" was a form of indirect compensation and not directly given to the person whose personal rights had been violated. Since authors' moral rights had also already been recognized as special personal rights under the CC 1964 (i.e., they had a double legal status), under the Civil Code, an author could demand this specific type of compensation for the intentional infringement moral rights and it was (though not often) awarded.[86]

---

[81] See S. Grzybowski (in:) S. Grzybowski, A. Kopff, J. Serda, *Zagadnienia prawa autorskiego* [Issues in Copyright Law], 1973, p. 255.

[82] See J. Błeszyński, *Konwencja berneńska a polskie prawo autorskie* [Berne Convention and Polish Copyright Law] (Warsaw 1979) p. 330.

[83] See S. Grzybowski, *Ochrona dóbr osobistych według przepisów ogólnych prawa cywilnego* [Protection of personal rights under the general provisions of civil law] (Warsaw 1957) p. 63.

[84] In a monograph on personal rights, the following reservations were pointed out regarding the position of Soviet law towards financial compensation for non-pecuniary damage (moral damage): (1) a lack of proportion between the non-pecuniary damage and the amount that would be awarded in respect of compensation; (2) the risk of arbitrariness in its determination, and probably most importantly at that time; (3) that the institution of compensation is contrary to the principles of socialist morality (even the perversion of the institution of compensation in the capitalist system, where everything is converted into money, was pointed out: it was considered immoral to obtain income without work). See A. Szpunar, *Ochrona dóbr osobistych* [Protection of personal rights], 1979, pp. 67–8. In the legislation of socialist countries analysed by the author, this was not actually present in Romania at that time. A. Szpunar, *Ochrona dóbr osobistych* [Protection of personal rights], 1979, pp. 70–6. On the other hand, he pointed out that in other socialist countries, even if indirectly, non-pecuniary damage was remunerated.

[85] See Arts 24 and 448 CC 1964, original wording.

[86] See A. Szpunar, *Ochrona dóbr osobistych* [Protection of personal rights], 1979, p. 218, and court judgments: Supreme Court, 5 March 1971, II CR 686/70 (protection of moral rights in the case of a work – a tombstone, the amount awarded to the Polish Red Cross was PLN 10,000) and the judgment of the Supreme Court of 22 October 1974, II CR 406/74, in which the Supreme Court changed the judgment of lower court and dismissed a claim for payment of PLN 2,500 to the Polish Red Cross. The Supreme Court assumed that: "one cannot ascribe a fault towards the author of a graphic work to a company that purchased for further sale products made according to this work from a person running an authorized engraving plant, after receiving a statement from that person that he is entitled to the copyright of the work. A different view is not acceptable because it would impose on the given enterprise obligations that would practically lead to the cessation of activity". However, in the judgment of 22 September 1972, II CR 697/71, the Supreme Court assumed that: "In the event of deliberate destruction of the work, the

In the CA 1952, additional attention to the scope of authors' moral rights can be seen on the part of the legislator. Firstly, under Art. 12, an employer or ordering party (being a special entity[87]) were granted economic author's rights in relation to a certain category of works: (1) an artistic model for industry – a design project; (2) a plan; (3) a technical or artistic drawing intended for, or in relation to industry or construction; or (4) a work intended for advertising or propaganda in the field of economic activity. The same provision clearly stated: "however, the author retains the exclusive right to protect the moral rights of the author".

However, as has been written, this provision was a declaration "suggesting, in addition, a slightly different legal picture than actually existed".[88] It should be noted that the subject of this regulation was authors' moral rights to special kind of works, and which of these rights could, in practice, be exercised in a limited way (plans were modified, an advertisement was often not made public with the name of author). I believe that this regulation could possibly be interpreted as an attempt to formally emphasize the importance of these rights, and not as an attempt to influence practice (since such an attempt had no chance of success anyway).

Secondly, in the case of a quasi-compulsory licence, where the Council of Ministers could authorize the use of a work,[89] it was also indicated that authors retained the right to the protection of their moral rights (Art. 16 CA 1952). Without the explicit wording of the provisions, moral rights would remain with the author, but such additional regulation, once again, "formally" emphasized the importance of authors' moral rights. With regard to derivative works, the obligation to disclose the author of the original was also expressly provided for (Art. 3 para. 3 CA 1952).

Thirdly, in the case of fair use of a work, a requirement to indicate the original source was included and the possibility of introducing changes to the work was excluded (Art. 21 CA 1952). The latter two solutions should be interpreted as a manifestation of the legislator's concern for authors' moral rights: indirectly, as the right to authorship (broadly understood as the requirement to indicate the source, including the author's name) and directly, as the right to the integrity of a work. These were modelled on the solutions that existed under the CA 1926.

Lastly, in a section concerning copyright contracts, there was a regulation which also dealt with authors' moral rights. A legal successor could not make changes to a work, except for those demanded by an obvious necessity, and where the author would have no justifiable basis to forbid them (Art. 31 CA 1952).[90] Under the CA 1952, the author had the right to withdraw from the contract if the work was displayed in a grossly inappropriate form or with changes to which he could rightfully object (Art. 47 CA 1952).[91] Again, it can be claimed that these

---

author could demand that the perpetrator be ordered to pay an appropriate amount of money, but only to the Polish Red Cross (Art. 448 of the Civil Code) in connection with Art. 23 of the Civil Code."

[87]   They were special entities of civil law, i.e., units of the socialized economy, no longer functioning today.

[88]   According to J. Barta, the most appropriate solution for a situation where the performance of creative work in employee relations (in cases where a certain restriction of the possibility of enforcement of author's moral rights by the author – employee), would be to regulate this issue in collective labor agreements; see J. Barta, *Artystyczna twórczość pracownicza a prawo autorskie* [Employee artistic creativity and copyright], 1988, p. 147. According to the information I have, this has not happened in practice.

[89]   In practice, this provision was not applied.

[90]   It was assumed that this rule should also apply to works in relation to which the author's economic rights had expired.

[91]   However, a publisher could withdraw from a contract for publishing a work, if the publication of the work would be contrary to the interests of the people's state, and in such a case the author was entitled to remuneration (Art. 38).

solutions strengthened the right of integrity, though in practice they were difficult to enforce. This formally extended system of protection and its statutory solutions confirm that legislative attention was given to authors' moral rights under the CA 1952.

Pursuant to Art. 33 of the CA 1952, the Council of Ministers of 1977 issued an additional regulation which gave authors the right to personal supervision over all forms of use of their work (annex 1 point 14), and the possibility of stipulating a contractual penalty for the infringement of moral and economic rights (for the significant damage, destruction or loss of a work) (annex point 16).[92]

In Poland, foreign authors' moral rights were protected, and domestic authors could claim this protection abroad on the basis of a rule of assimilation.[93] After an author's death, if not specified via will,[94] claims could be made by relatives mentioned in the Act (spouse, parents, children or siblings of the author). On the other hand, an association of authors competent in the author's field of creativity could also make claims during the author's lifetime.[95] It was assumed in the legal literature that this solution was applicable in the case where the author was inactive, although in practice it was not used.

The CA 1952 provided criminal liability in the case of any infringement of moral rights. Misappropriation of someone else's authorship was an *ex officio* crime punishable by imprisonment for up to two years and a fine of up to PLN 50,000.[96]

Cases related to moral rights were subject to court decisions. For instance, the Supreme Court signalled that "socialist morality" upheld the right to authorship, and as an example of a violation of authors' moral (personal) rights (apart from obvious plagiarism), taking "content or an exception from someone else's work without specifying the author or source in a work" was adopted.[97] Similarly, the unlawful attribution of a work to a person that "had borrowed someone else's work without documentation" was considered detrimental to the author's "good name and the fame of his work".[98] To this day, this judgment (including its practical dimension) is referred to, asserting that someone "who takes content or excerpts from someone else's work into their work, without clearly providing the source of the borrowings, violates the author's personal rights and plagiarizes"; it was emphasized that the requirements

---

[92]   The Ordinance of 11 November 1977 on the rules and rates of remuneration for authors of visual works and contracts for the performance or use of these works (Dz.U.1977, No. 36, item 158). In practice, penalties for violating moral rights did not function.

[93]   In a scope not greater than that resulting from Art. 6*bis* of the Berne Convention, see J. Błeszyński, *Konwencja berneńska a polskie prawo autorskie* [Berne Convention and Polish Copyright Law] (Warsaw 1979) p. 327.

[94]   Not only in a last will, but in any other declaration of a will.

[95]   On the legitimacy of exercising these rights by state institutions after the author's death, see Aural Benard, Gyorgy Boytha. Socialist Copyright Law: A Theoretical Approach, 89 RIDA 90 (1976).

[96]   This was a relatively high fine, with the average annual salary being about PLN 7,800. Other infringements of copyright, committed for the purpose of material or personal gain, were already subject to lesser penalties and were prosecuted on a private basis.

[97]   The judgment of the Supreme Court of 24 November 1978, I CR 185/78, LEX No. 8151: "Considerations of socialist morality, in the sphere of relations between people, the duty of mutual respect due to an individual in the public interest justifies pointing out in his own work to known and available statements of authors of scientific works on specific issues solved in a new, creative, original way, especially if the content of the work refers to them. On the other hand, the sphere of copyright protection is subject to all legal rigors (apart from obvious cases of plagiarism), if the content or an exception is taken from someone else's work without specifying the author or source in the work."

[98]   Judgment of Supreme Court, 15 June 1989, III CRN 139/89, LEX No. 70836.

of copyright (Art. 18, 21) "cannot be satisfied by listing, without specifying what content or fragments were taken from someone else's work, that work in the literature on the subject compiled by him".[99]

Pertaining to an author's moral rights, infringements were classified as follows: misappropriation of authorship in connection with the publication of a work without designating the second author's name,[100] violating the right to integrity through additions, abbreviations, drawings or interludes,[101] distortion of the reproduction of a copy of a medal,[102] a defective screen copy of a film which distorts the film music,[103] making changes to an architectural plan,[104] and even the production of subsequent editions of a work without the author's consent.[105]

Even then, the possibility of authorizing the exercise of an author's moral (personal) rights was allowed. In particular, an author may authorize another person to introduce certain changes or even consent to changes already made.[106] Research was provided in the field of the right to authorship: plagiary in music,[107] literature,[108] and the authorship of scientific works.[109]

However, the letter of the copyright law, the jurisprudence and even the legal literature does not reflect the specificity of the conditions that authors functioned under from 1945 to 1990,[110]

---

[99]   Judgment of Supreme Court, 15 June 1989, III CRN 139/89, LEX No. 70836.

[100]   Judgment of Supreme Court, 11 November 1960, I CR 234/60.

[101]   Judgment of Supreme Court, 14 November 1973, II CR 531/73.

[102]   By making them "technically sloppy, substantially deviating from the approved design assumptions", judgment of Supreme Court, 25 April 1989, I CR 141/898.

[103]   Judgment of Supreme Court, 28 February 1956, I CR 563/57.

[104]   Judgment of Supreme Court, 26 May 1988, IV CR 122/88, LEX nr 63616, in which it was confirmed that the protection of an author's personal rights was granted regardless of whether the work "met the conditions of suitability for the user". The dispute arose in connection with a change in an architectural plan (co-authored by the plaintiff) consisting in building a mezzanine and covering the windows with wooden curtains for the purpose of exhibition in a museum. In this ruling, the court analysed the justification in detail. The Supreme Court assumed that objective criteria should be decisive when assessing measures to remove the effects of the infringement of moral rights; and the means used should be deliberate and appropriate to each case. Therefore, it refused to award a publication claim in two magazines, *Życie Warszawy* and *Gazeta Krakowska*. According to the court, it was not necessary to inform the whole of society, so only the claim to publish the statement in the monthly publication *Architektura* was accepted (on the assumption that it would reach the people who knew about the infringement of the plaintiff's moral rights). The court did not admit the claim for a payment of the amount of PLN 50,000 by way of interest ("*nawiązka*"), finding no grounds to accept an intentional violation.

[105]   The judgment of the Supreme Court of 6 May 1976, IV CR 129/76, in which this was adopted said this: "Publishing a work without the author's consent constitutes not only a violation of his economic rights, but also of his personal rights. The moral rights include the author's right to freely decide whether or not it is to be published; this right extends to subsequent editions." The last part of the sentence is no longer valid.

[106]   See A. Bądkowski, J. Stankiewicz, *Prawo teatralne* [Theatre Law] (Warsaw 1970) pp. 49–50.

[107]   J. Barta, *Plagiat muzyczny* [Music plagiarism], ZN UJ PzWiOWI [Zeszyty Naukowe Uniwersytetu Jagiellońskiego, Prace z Wynalazczości i Ochrony Własności Intelektualnej] (Kraków 1979), z. 17, pp. 41–67.

[108]   R. Markiewicz, *Dzieło literackie i jego twórca w polskim prawie autorskim* [Literary work and its author in Polish copyright law] (Kraków 1984) p. 113 and next.

[109]   R. Markiewicz, *Ochrona prac naukowych* [Protection of scientific works] ZN UJ PzWiOWI [Zeszyty Naukowe Uniwersytetu Jagiellońskiego, Prace z Wynalazczości i Ochrony Własności Intelektualnej], 1990, nr 55, pp. 5–173.

[110]   M.T. Sundara also pays attention to this; M.T. Sundara Rajan *Moral Rights – Principles, Practice and New Technology* (Oxford, Oxford University Press 2011) p. 187.

and the manner in which authors' moral (personal) rights were exercised. While the copyright law (provision) on moral rights resisted "the wind from the east" (it was difficult to formally deprive authors of the protection of their moral (personal) rights or to really restrict them[111]), doctrinal additions were required to secure a new and proper place for author's moral rights in socialist copyright law.[112] The realm of authorship was heavily swept by this "wind", where political events (the Cold War 1947–1991,[113] which arose following the collapse of the Nazi coalition and the establishment of the USSR's sphere of influence in Eastern Europe) influenced artistic and scientific life. The new post-war political reality was dealt with in various ways.[114]

In August 1948, the First World Congress of Individuals in Defence of Peace was held in Poland (attended by, among others, P. Picasso,[115] F. Leger, Julian Huxley (UNESCO Director General at the time), and a letter was sent by A. Einstein). In 1949, the International Fryderyk Chopin Piano Competition,[116] established in 1927, was resumed. Several notable figures received awards in that contest: the Russian Vladimir Ashkenazy (II) in 1955, the Argentinian Martha Argerich (I) in 1965, the American Garrick Ohlsson (I), and Mitsuko Uchida from Japan (II) in 1970. In 1958, the International Congress of Literary Translators was held in Warsaw. Despite the ideological problem posed by rock and roll and popular music, some Western artists managed to perform in Poland. A 1967 Rolling Stones concert was held in Warsaw, one of the first concerts by a Western group behind the "Iron Curtain". Unfortunately, as a result of aforementioned ideological reasons, the Beatles did not perform; rock and roll and popular music were not an artistic problem, but an ideological one.

For security and political reasons, authors often had to use pseudonyms.[117] The attribution right must therefore have been exercised by some authors via pseudonym or their works would be made available anonymously. Authors had little choice, either they adapted to the political conditions[118] or emigrated (voluntarily or forcibly); this was the sad reality.

---

[111]   A complete deprivation of the protection of moral rights would not have been possible (due to international obligations, the affiliation of Eastern European countries to the Berne Convention) and deliberate (however, the authorities used creativity, its importance for society was emphasized).

[112]   How "skillfully" this was done bearing in mind that the individual was, after all, deprived of rights in totalitarian and authoritarian systems, and subject to control, the following excerpt shows: "The Socialist State guarantees the author exclusive rights over his work because of the extremely personal character of intellectual creativity. The exclusive character of socialist subjective copyright has its roots in the personality – in contrast to the absolute character of capitalist copyright originating in ownership of wealth … The creative work represents an individual reflection of reality and for this reason carries the author's personal hallmark and brings his personality across to broad strata of society. Questioning the authorship of work, omitting the acknowledgment of authorship, altering the work without the author's consent, publishing, reproducing, and disseminating it against his will are all acts regarded as violating his personality". See Aural Benard, Gyorgy Boytha. Socialist Copyright Law: A Theoretical Approach, 89 RIDA 77 (1976).

[113]   This period was called the period of the Soviet occupation that followed the Nazi occupation.

[114]   See T. Jude, *Postwar: A History of Europe Since 1945* (New York 2005).

[115]   Then a member of the French Communist Party.

[116]   See J. Ekiert, *The Endless Search for Chopin: The History of the International Fryderyk Chopin Piano Competition in Warsaw* (MUZA SA 2000).

[117]   Nobel Prize winner Cz. Miłosz used about 20 pseudonyms.

[118]   There were institutions that helped to use passive resistance to the authorities (e.g. Pen Club Poland, Radio Free Europe), and private contact with foreign countries played an important role. Adaptation was not only about cooperation, but required the use of intellectual potential in order to

Some authors were only allowed to publish abroad,[119] as their works were banned at home. It was possible to import forbidden works from abroad, for example, with a modified cover, as in the case of George Orwell's "1984" (which was issued with a cover depicting a reproduction of a Soviet poster[120]). In the years immediately following the war, at the onset of top-down cultural policy and a centrally planned economy (the so-called five-year plan), living conditions were difficult; artists were not immune to these hard times.[121] War losses and destruction were enormous, they affected the entire artistic community (the intelligentsia and artists were particularly devastated by the Nazis), cultural goods (which were stolen), as well as material resources.

After WWII, access to materials and a workplace (studio) was limited (with social owner-ship of the means of production and with limited private property). The distribution channels for artistic works were also nationalized,[122] it was not possible to freely publish and distribute works in the press, radio, television or cinemas. Only works approved by the appropriate office were printed; preventive censorship was in place. As early as July 1945, the Main Office for the Control of Press, Publications and Performances was established by decree,[123] and in 1949, an Ordinance of the Prime Minister on the organization of the Main Office for the Control of Press, Publications and Performances[124] was issued, establishing subordinate offices across the country.[125]

The tasks of the Office included, inter alia, granting publishing permits to magazines all over the country and depriving "communication debit" of printed matter published abroad and prohibiting their dissemination.[126] At the same time, local units of the Office supervised press

---

"circumvent" bans and smuggle ideological content. A certain fragment of this reality is reflected in the following statement by K. Filipowicz: "I think that the political involvement of many writers on the side of communism was not always so simple, it did not consist in mystification and self-deception ... , many personal, political decisions were then accompanied by ... – the feeling of loneliness, abandonment by the West." This author said that when he was prevented from printing two books, a friend advised him to write so that the censorship would like it. When he replied: "I can't write like that", a friend said: "Then don't write. We will translate books from Russian ... ." In such circumstances and in such an atmosphere, an ideological breakthrough took place. For many writers it was a complex psychological and moral process. A. Dauksza, *Jaremianka. Biografia* [Jaremianka, A Biography] (Krakow 2019) p. 429.

[119]   The publishing house of the Literary Institute (Instytut Literacki), established in Rome at the 2nd Polish Corps, played a special role, but in 1947 it was transferred to Paris, and finally to Maisons-Laffitte near Paris. In the first volume of the "Kultura" Library, works by W. Gombrowicz were published in 1953 ("Ślub" – "The Marriage" and "Transatlantyk" – "Trans-Atlantic", and in the next volume, "Zniewolony umysł" – "The Captive Mind" by Cz. Miłosz). For details see A. Franszek, *Miłosz. Biografia* [Milosz: A Biography.] Trans. by A. Parker and M. Parker (Harvard 2017).

[120]   https://kulturaparyska.com/pl/article/history.

[121]   However, financial support was planned for ideologically correct authors. Cf. Resolution No. 154 of the Council of Ministers of 2 June 1964 on the creation of an author's fund; in order to support literary works of high ideological-artistic, scientific, and popular science value.

[122]   See Aural Benard, Gyorgy Boytha, Socialist Copyright Law: A Theoretical Approach 89 RIDA 67–8 (1976).

[123]   Dz.U. 1946, nr 34, item 210.

[124]   Dz.U. 1949, nr 32, item 241.

[125]   In 1981, the last Act on the Control of Publications and Performances was passed, Journal of Laws of 1981, No. 20, item 99, which was in force until 1990.

[126]   In the years 1950–62, several dozen (52) orders of the General Director of the Press, Publications and Performance/Show Control Office were issued concerning the deprivation of a communication debut (including the German ones: *Das Heimatwerk, Osteuropa, Geopolitik, Deutsche Soldatenzeitung, Neues*

and book publications and the organization of shows and concerts; this control was exerted over the distribution of all kinds of works (print, image or living word). Censorship ordered the removal, addition or change of fragments of works,[127] and in such conditions there was no real room to exercise the right to the integrity of a work. Surveillance and wiretaps permeated the artistic community. A state-owned enterprise, established in 1956, organized all concerts. It is only due to an active underground press (called *"samizdat"* in Russian) that some literary works could reach parts of the society.

However, in 1989, communism came to an end in Poland.[128]

Close contacts with the Max Planck Institute for Foreign and International Patent, Copyright and Competition Law established in 1966, were of great importance to the development of Polish science in the field of intellectual property (especially copyright). Prof. E. Ulmer, F-K. Beier and Prof. G. Schricker had initiated scientific collaboration and invited scientists from Poland, especially from Krakow, where, in 1972, the Institute of Inventiveness and the Protection of Intellectual Property was founded (now, after some reorganization, the chair of Intellectual Property Law at the Law Faculty of Jagiellonian University). Prof. A. Dietz[129] and Prof. J. Strauss continued this tradition. Today, the ties between the aforementioned institutions are still close thanks to director Prof. R. Hilty. The exchange of intellectual property (IP) journals and books allowed Polish lawyers to keep abreast of mainstream changes in global IP law, which still proves fruitful today.

3.3 The Copyright and Related Rights Act from 1994 – A New Old One?

3.3.1 Author's moral rights

Poland's political transformation was associated with changes in the legal sphere, including to intellectual property rights, which began to play an increasingly important role in the

---

Europa, Man in der Zeit, Herz Dame; the American ones: *Life, Saturday Review*; French ones: *Preuves, Selection du Reader's Digest*, – for political but also religious reasons – *Ave Maria* (in Polish in the US), *Quarterly World Review, Pourquoi Pas?*, and some Polish diaspora material).

[127] For example, the above-mentioned author K. Filipowicz, wrote about his struggle with censorship in the 1950s: "they wanted a novel programmatically distorted ... I did not agree to any alteration, so only a part of the chapter was removed ... I agreed, reluctantly, of course, for deleting, but not adding. So I did not allow myself to be inspired or directed, and such a tendency was common in the cultural policy of those years." (in:) A. Dauksza, *Jaremianka. Biografia* [Jaremianka. A biography] (Krakow 2019) s. 429.

[128] One of the actresses, who on 28 October 1989, on Saturday, in the main issue of the only information television program, made history, when she announced in an interview with a TV presenter: "Ladies and Gentlemen, on June 4, 1989, Communism in Poland has ended".

[129] Who writes: "Whenever I think of the beautiful town of Krakow I am immediately reminded of my past visit to the Instytut Prawa Własności Intelektualnej where so many scholars and friends of the Munich Max Planck Institute of Intellectual Property work or have been working for a long time. This is particularly true for my personal friends and colleagues Professors Janusz Barta and Ryszard Markiewicz. In my view they are the human twin towers, the lighthouses of modern post-socialist copyright law in Poland". A. Dietz, Greetings and Congratulation from Munich to the Copyright Twin Towers in Krakow! (in:) *Spory o własność intelektualną. Księga jubileuszowa dedykowana Profesorom Januszowi Barcie i Ryszardowi Markiewiczowi* [in: Intellectual Property Disputes. A Jubilee Book Dedicated to Professors Janusz Barta and Ryszard Mariewicz], ed. A. Matlak, S. Stanisławska-Kloc (Warsaw 2013) pp. 13–15. A. Dietz also prepared a report: *Protection of Intellectual Property in Central and Eastern European Countries: The Legal Situation in Bulgaria, CSFR, Hungary, Poland and Romania* (OECD 1995).

economy.[130] In 1990, Poland signed a trade treaty with the US[131] and an association agreement with the European Community in the following year,[132] in which it undertook to improve the protection of intellectual property rights and achieve a level of protection similar to that of the European Community.

Chapter 3 of the new CA 1994 regulates the scope of copyright and begins with Art. 16, which concerns authors' moral (personal) rights.[133] First, the legislator defines the nature of a moral right (it protects an author's relationship (bond) with the work, which is unlimited in time and is not subject to any waiver or transfer). Subsequently, they list examples of such a right, the most important of which are: (1) the right to authorship of the work; (2) the author's right to mark the work with their name, a pseudonym or to make work available anonymously; (3) the right to integrity of the content and form of the work and its proper use; (4) the right to determine the first release of the work to the public; and (5) the right to supervision over the use of the work. The bond between an author and their work is an element of the *sine qua non* of moral rights. Thus, a necessary condition for recognizing an infringement of moral rights is proving that a given form of use has violated this bond.[134] Objective criteria are used to assess infringements; not every disruption of this bond constitutes a violation of moral rights.[135] One of the circumstances which excludes a violation is the consent of the author (consent to making changes to the work, marking authorship of the work in a special way or disseminating the work anonymously to a certain extent).

Authors are also entitled to protect their personal interests through means such as withdrawal from the contract or its termination due to essential creative interests (Art. 56), making changes to the work (Arts 60 and 73 CA 1994), controlling access to the work (Art. 52 p. 3 CA 1994), deciding what happens with the original of an artwork (Art. 32 p. 2 CA 1994). Legislators do not differentiate the scope of the protection given to moral rights for particular categories of works, with one exception, namely, for the author of a computer program (who has only two moral rights, Art. 16 p. 1–2 CA 1994). As per Art. 77 of the CA 1994, Art. 16 points 3–5 of the CA 1994 do not apply to computer programs. However, for protection of the

---

[130]   A. Dietz, *Protection of Intellectual Property in Central and Eastern European Countries, The Legal Situation in Bulgaria, CSFR, Hungary, Poland and Romania* (OECD 1995) pp. 15–20.

[131]   Treaty on Trade and Economic Relations between the Republic of Poland and the United States of America, drawn up in Washington on 21 March 1990, Dz.U. 1994, No. 97, item 467. See also J. Barta, R. Markiewicz (in:) *International Copyright Law and Practice*, ed. E. Geller, 2020, 32-12/2020, p. POL-39.

[132]   The Europe Agreement establishing an association between the Republic of Poland, on the one hand, and the European Communities and their Member States, on the other, drawn up in Brussels on 16 December 1991, publ. in Dz.U. 1994, No. 11, item 38. Cf. in detail provisions on intellectual property rights: Arts 66, 69, 75, 111.

[133]   See J. Barta, R. Markiewicz (in:) *International Copyright Law and Practice*, ed. E. Geller, 2020, 32-12/2020, p. POL-39-44.

[134]   See R. Markiewicz, *Ilustrowane prawo autorskie* [Illustrated Copyright Law] (Warsaw 2018) p. 203.

[135]   Judgment of Court of Appeal in Krakow of 29 October 1997, I ACa 477/97, in which it was assumed that: "Not every change of any element of the content or form of the work violates the right to its integrity (Art. 16 point 3 of the Copyright Law), but only such a change that 'breaks' or 'weakens' the author's bond with the work, removes or violates the bond between the work and the individualizing features of its author. The features of infringement of the right to the work's integrity marked in this way are not met by minor changes to its content or form, which do not derogate from the work's attribution."

right to the integrity of the work, the author-programmer may invoke Art. 6*bis* of the Berne Convention.[136]

Despite the wording of Art. 16 of the CA 1994, analysis of the jurisprudence and the views held in the doctrine may justify the conclusion that the nature of the work and the way it is used in practice[137] affect the intensity of protection for these rights, or even the boundaries of a particular author's moral rights.[138]

As for legal instruments that ensure the protection of authors' personal rights, Art. 78 of the CA 1994 specifies what recourses are available in the event of a violation of these rights and the detailed rules for claiming protection and exercising moral rights after the author's death.[139] While the adopted legislative technique and wording of the regulations are slightly different from those used in the CA 1926, the *ratio legis* and the general assumptions of protection are similar, hence, it can be stated that this legal act in the field of authors' moral rights is a new version of the pre-war Act. The CA 1994 no longer lists typical methods of copyright infringement but focuses on the nature of the moral rights and its positive content. Passed almost 70 years after the adoption of the first CA 1926, this new Act seems to be a rational (appropriate) solution to society's present stage of development and the new challenges it faces.

As far as recourse is concerned, in the event of a threat to an author's rights, the author may demand cessation. However, in the event of an infringement, there is the possibility of taking the necessary actions to rectify it, particularly through the dissemination of public statements with appropriate content and form. This is done through a court judgment, which defines the content and precise technical parameters of the process of disseminating this statement (the name of the press title or other media, e.g., private website, pixel size, frequency, language or languages of the statement, detailed time of announcement).

As a rule, professional attorneys ensure these parameters are enforced since there was a case where underhanded tactics were used to spite the plaintiff: a press publication was on part of a page, the statement was in the smallest font (since the court did not specify it in the judgment), it was difficult to read, and the rest of the page was left empty. Even if the defendant who lost the trial wanted to "punish" the plaintiff in this way, it was almost impossible to achieve as the publicized statement and violation of rights was widely commented on. Courts customarily adjust the manner of dissemination of the statement to the scale and nature of the

---

[136] J. Barta, R. Markiewicz, *International Copyright Law and Practice*, ed. E. Geller, 2020, 32-12/2020, p. POL-43-44. It was also pointed out that the right of integrity in the case of computer program was "transferred" to the sphere of authors' economic rights (Art. 74. p. 4.2 CA 1994); see J. Barta, R. Markiewicz, *Prawo autorskie* [Copyright Law] p. 299.

[137] For example, as regards attribution right in case of use such a work which is used as trademark.

[138] See J. Barta, R. Markiewicz, *Prawo autorskie* [Copyright Law] p. 121; P. Machnikowski, A. Górnicz-Mulcahy, J. Balcarczyk, "Poland". In *International Encyclopaedia of Laws: Intellectual Property,* ed. Hendrik Vanhees (Kluwer Law International 2020) p. 58. On the other hand, Art. 49 CA 1994 gives the purchaser of copyrights the opportunity to make changes to the work, but only if there is an obvious necessity, and which the author would have no legitimate reason to oppose. However, compared to CA 1952, it was added that "this applies, respectively, to works for which the term of protection of economic author's rights has expired". See also the judgment of the Court of Appeal in Warsaw of 20 February 1997, in which it was held that: "the replacement of the facade was dictated by the obvious poor technical condition of the facade to date ... the ongoing change, consisting in the removal of the horizontal fragments of the wall, which gave the building facade a characteristic and well-thought-out form...".

[139] Separately in Art. 79 CA 1994, claims related to the infringement of economic rights were settled.

violation of rights so as to ensure that it reaches the people who might have encountered (e.g., read, seen) the version of the work that violated the author's moral rights (e.g., plagiarism or breach of integrity).

In a case concerning the infringement of the author's right to conceal the authorship of his work (Art. 16 p. 2 CA 1994), the court reasonably assumed that the protection granted may not consist in the infringer's denial of the work's original authorship where the author's surname was placed in the work against their will.[140] The protection of the claimant's moral right cannot be based on the defendant's obligation in a court judgment to state that the attribution was not true (this would be lying). The aggrieved party might request the destruction or withdrawal from the market of the infringing copies and a retraction (which is beginning to be used and is relevant in cases of misappropriation of authorship in scientific works disseminated via electronic journals and databases), or demand that the work be disseminated in a form free from moral rights infringements.[141] A claim for compensation in the event of a violation of moral (personal) rights was introduced into Art. 24 of the Civil Code on 28 December 1996,[142] and "reverted" to the CA 1994; it may be awarded in the event of a culpable infringement of moral rights (but it is optional). For both the legitimacy of the award and determining the amount of compensation, the harm suffered by the author must be established.[143] The harm is considered as "negative psychological experiences which boil down to suffering. This suffering, which is an expression of harm, may be the result of lowered prestige in society, the inability to undertake creative activities, which must have a causal relationship with the infringement of moral rights."[144] As a rule, in the case of misappropriation of authorship, it should be assumed that

---

[140]   Court of Appeal, Krakow, 29 October 1997, I ACa 477/97, in such a circumstance as this case, removal of consequences of violation of authorship – a real "full" restitution is impossible, because everyone recognized the identity of the author.

[141]   Although the Court of Appeal, legitimately recognizing a violation of the right to authorship (through non-naming the work) and integrity (due to the omission of a profanity at the end of a line), refused to award a claim for re-publication in the version (in which the vulgar word was to be replaced with the first and last letter and middle dots) in a magazine. The court referred to the Press Law Act, which in Art. 12 requires journalists, inter alia, to avoid profanity. On the other hand, the awarded damages amounted to PLN 2,000 (about EUR 500 in 2006), Court of Appeal, Warsaw, 14 March 2006, VI ACa 1012/05.

[142]   Based on Art. 1 point 1 of the Act of 23 August 1996 (Journal of Laws 96.114.542) amending the Civil Code on 28 December 1996.

[143]   See M. Wałachowska, Wynagrodzenie szkody niemajątkowej w razie naruszenia autorskich praw osobistych – uwagi de lege lata i de lege ferenda (in:) *Experientia docet. Księga jubileuszowa ofiarowana Pani Profesor Elżbiecie Traple* [Compensation for non-pecuniary damage in case of infringement of author's moral rights – de lege ferenda and de lege lata in: Experentia docet. A Jubilee Book Offered to Professor Elżbieta Traple], ed. P. Kostański, P. Podrecki, T. Targosz (Warsaw 2017) pp. 448–62.

[144]   Court of Appeal, Krakow, 12 October 2017, I ACa 1104/16, which also reasonably assumed that "the harm must be proved by those seeking protection, it cannot be presumed". Moreover, it was rightly considered as completely unjustified to set an appropriate amount as compensation for the double amount of the plaintiff's average remuneration for granting a license to use the work (photo) of her authorship; because "it is inconsistent with the function of the compensation specified in Art. 78 sec. 1 CA 1994". This remuneration for granting a licence would be relevant to a claim for damages for infringement of the author's economic rights, pursuant to Art. 79 sec. 1 point 3 CA 1994.

harm is done to the author.[145] The amount of compensation must then be determined[146] (taking into account, inter alia, the motivation of the infringer[147]).

Admittedly, even if this thesis is not based on the analysis of all representative court decisions, there is a visible increased interest in the claim for moral redress through compensation. This, in my opinion, is due to two circumstances, one of a social nature and the other of an economic nature. The first is related to the increase in legal awareness among authors (artists[148]) and social acceptance surrounding their claim to moral rights. The second results from the repeal of a part of the provision of Art. 79 CA 1994. After a judgment of the Constitutional Tribunal in 2015,[149] authors' ability to claim damages for infringement of their economic rights calculated as three times[150] the appropriate remuneration was reduced to only twice this remuneration. I am not claiming that authors always try or will try to compensate for this unfavourable change in the legal status by filing a claim for additional compensation (moral rights infringement). However, the courts should, undoubtedly, carefully examine the nature of any infringement of moral rights, the degree of culpability and take into account the amount of damages awarded for infringement of economic copyright so as not to confuse the functions of both claims (i.e., compensation for moral rights and redress of economic rights). Moreover, when determining the amount of compensation, the court should also take into account other adjudicated claims that may impact the remedy for the harm, and which may be financially charged to the infringer (e.g., costly apologies through a professional publishing house, press, giving satisfaction to the author). A claim for compensation may be pursued by third parties who are entitled to bring an action for the protection of the moral

---

[145] I do not think, however, that harm will occur absolutely in the case of any non-marking of authorship (some works are usually disseminated without the name of author) although cf. Court of Appeal, Warsaw, 29 August I ACa 415/17; LEX 2547096, in which we read: "Failure to mark the authorship of works violates the personal right of the author to designate his authorship. The harm caused in this way does not require further evidence, it is obvious: but for an assessment of its extent, it is also important to determine how broad the scope of the infringement was, i.e., how large a group of recipients could read the work, which was not provided with the author's name and surname".

[146] See Court of Appeal, Szczecin, 14 February 2018, I ACa 724/17, in which it was assumed that "it was repeatedly indicated in the judicature that moral redress should be adequate to the breached good and the degree of guilt of the perpetrator. It cannot be described as symbolic, but it has a compensatory and preventive function."

[147] See Court of Appeal, Warsaw, 6 February 2018, V ACa 1040/17, LEX No. 2607164, which, however, also indicated that "the court is not obliged to award compensation in any case of moral harm caused by infringement of personal interests".

[148] In one of the cases, the court awarded the author of a tombstone design compensation to the amount of PLN 7,000 (about EUR 1,600 in 2018) in connection with its use without proper identification of author in a cemetery and on the defendant's website (where the photo of the tombstone was placed). See Court of Appeal, Szczecin, 14 February 2018, I ACa 724/17, However, in the event of a violation of the moral rights to software, the court awarded compensation to the amount of PLN 50,000 (approx. EUR 11,000 in 2019) – Court of Appeal, Cracow, 19 June 2019, I ACa720/18. In the case of violation of the moral rights of author of photo (in connection with it use without proper identification of author and infringement of integrity right because of changing the colors and cropping the photo) the court awarded compensation to the amount of PLN 5000 (approx. EUR 1060 in December 2021) See Court of Appeal in Poznan, 20 December 2021, I AGa 163/21.

[149] The judgment of the Constitutional Tribunal of 23 June 2015, SK 32/14, see also judgment ECJ, 25 January 2017, case C – 367/15.

[150] Adequate remuneration, which at the time of enforcement of right would be due as the consent granted by the author (entitled person) to use the work.

rights of a deceased author.[151] Compared to previous regulations, at present, if the author has not indicated a person[152] responsible for the protection of his moral rights after death, first the spouse has this exclusive legitimacy (moreover, in the CA 1994 the catalogue was extended to include children of siblings). The indicated persons are also entitled to exercise rights such as concluding contracts. In addition, claims of infringement of an author's moral rights may be filed by an association of authors (competent for the author's specific type of creativity) or an organization for the collective management of copyright (which manages the rights of an author), and have their own separate procedural standing.[153] A separate claim can be to demand the payment of a sum of money for a social cause.

In practice, parties to a contract increasingly regulate the scope of permitted interference with the work and the rules for denoting authorship to avoid the risk of violating moral (personal) rights. Authors' moral rights may not be transferred to another person,[154] but an author

---

[151]   As was mentioned based on Art. 78 sec. 2 CA 1994, the author's moral rights cannot be inherited, but are exercised by the indicated persons. Court of Appeal, Warsaw, 28 August 2009, VI ACa 159/09. The dispute concerned the infringement of the right to authorship and the integrity of the author of the poster entitled Steersman, prepared by the plaintiff's father for the 6th Congress of the Polish United Workers' Party (PZPR) in 1956. After 50 years, a chain of restaurants dealing with the preparation and sale of pizza used (without the consent of his son) this symbol of socialist realist art in its advertising campaign. Although there have been postulates in the literature regarding compensation sought after the death of the author: (a) limitation to a certain lump sum or maximum amount, or even (b) exclusion of a claim for compensation after the death of the author and leaving in this case only the claim for payment of a sum of money for a social purpose. See M. Wałachowska, Wynagrodzenie szkody niemajątkowej w razie naruszenia autorskich praw osobistych – uwagi de lege lata i de lege ferenda (in:) *Experientia docet. Księga jubileuszowa ofiarowana Pani Profesor Elżbiecie Traple* [Compensation for non-pecuniary damage in case of infringement of author's moral rights – de lege ferenda and de lege lata in: Experentia docet. A Jubilee Book Offered to Professor Elżbieta Traple], ed. P. Kostański, P. Podrecki, T. Targosz (Warsaw 2017) p. 462. I am not an advocate of any of these solutions, especially since this claim has been not abused, but is almost never pursued after the author's death and the courts have not been inclined to award high amounts.

[152]   From my own observations and contact with public notaries who prepare notarized wills, it appears that interest of some authors in "regulating" the exercise of moral rights after their death is also increasing to some extent. At the same time, separation in terms of the exercise of an author's moral rights (based on the author's declaration) and their economic rights (based on inheritance) may have weak points due to mutual blocking; seldom does this seem to outweigh the benefits of caring for each other's rights.

[153]   It would be difficult to mention cases where this takes place in practice. However, there are proposals to extend this catalog to include: (1) foundations, universities, research institutes, the Polish Academy of Sciences, Polish Academy of Arts and Sciences (see J. Mazurkiewicz, Non omnis moriar..., p. 131) and museums and local government units (those with which the author was associated – see M. Ożóg, Uwagi o instytucjonalnej ochronie pośmiertnych autorskich dóbr osobistych; (in:) *Własność intelektualna a dziedzictwo kulturowe. Księga jubileuszowa dedykowana Profesorowi Wojciechowi Kowalskiemu*, ed. M Jankowska, P. Gwoździewicz – Matan, P. Stec [A few comments on institutional protection of posthumous authors moral rights in: Intellectual property and cultural heritage. A Jubilee book dedicated to Professor Wojciech Kowalski] (Warsaw 2020) pp. 230–1). I have some doubts as to whether such a "massification" of legal persons entitled to the protection of an author's moral rights is justified. Collective copyright management organizations may appear before the court only after the author's death, not during his lifetime, see Court of Appeal, Krakow, 18 June 2003, I ACa 510/03.

[154]   See judgment of the Court of Appeal, 14 May 2007, I ACa 668/06. J. Barta and R. Markiewicz, clearly write: "there are, however, limits to such exercise: for example, an author may not conclude a valid contract to authorize a third party to misrepresent authorship of his work to the public ... , pursuant to Article 58 of Civil Code, an agreement with a ghost writer to renounce the right of authorship

may agree to interference of their moral rights or may undertake not to exercise (to some extent) their personal rights in relation to a contracting party or third parties, or authorize other persons (again, to some extent) to exercise these rights on their behalf.[155]

An important new sphere of consideration regarding the content and limits of the protection of personal rights is related to the fair use of works (as an exception/limitation of copyright). Often, fair use is related to the modification of a work (a potential encroachment on the right of integrity) or the selection of a fragment or fragments (a potential encroachment on the right to proper use), and raises problems with denoting authorship.[156]

Additionally, Art. 2 p. 5 of the CA 1994 specifies that copies of derivative works should mention the author and the title of the original work.[157] In turn, Art. 34 imposes an obligation to mention the name and surname of the author of the work used on the basis of fair use. In 2004, in connection with the implementation of Directive 2001/29, this requirement was alleviated by adding that the name of the author and the source should take into account existing possibilities. The provisions on fair use do not prejudice the protection of authors' moral rights; nevertheless, they require a certain adjustment (or correction) in the exercise of these rights.[158]

Today, authors' moral rights disputes are more frequently the subject of court decisions.[159] For example, it was found that placing a monument (sculpture) in the middle of a square (which was an architectural and urban copyrighted work) does not violate the right to integrity,[160] and the mixing of musical work was similarly assessed if it took place in a designated location (in a disco, in a music club[161]).

---

will generally be considered invalid *ex tunc*". J. Barta, R. Markiewicz, *International Copyright Law and Practice*, ed. E. Geller, 2020, p. POL-44-45.

[155] For details see: J. Barta, R. Markiewicz (in:) *International Copyright Law and Practice*, ed. E. Geller, 2020, p. POL-44-45; and M. Wyrwiński, Autorskie prawa osobiste w obrocie prawnym [Authors moral rights in legal transaction] (Warsaw 2019) p. 296.

[156] See T. Aplin, L. Bently, *Global Mandatory Fair Use: The Nature and Scope of the Right to Quote Copyright Works* (Cambridge 2020) pp. 57–60, 77–8; see also judgment ECJ, 3 September 2014, case C–201/13 and Reto M. Hilty, K. Köklü, V. Moscon, C. Correa, S. Dusollier, Ch. Geiger, J. Griffiths, H. Große Ruse-Khan, A. Kur, X. Lin, R. Markiewicz, S. Nérisson, A. Peukert, M. Senftleben, R. Xalabarder, *International Instrument on Permitted Uses in Copyright Law and Explanatory Note*; Max Planck Institute for Innovation and Competition Research Paper No. 21-06, p. 55, available at: SSRN https://ssrn.com/abstract=3771241 or http://dx.doi.org/10.2139/ssrn.3771241.

[157] As J. Barta and R. Markiewicz, pointed out: "Nonetheless, the right to obtain pseudonymous or dissemination under Article 16 has priority over the right under art. 2.5 CA 1994, so that an author could require that copies of a derivative work based on his prior work say nothing about his authoring that prior work" (in:) *International Copyright Law and Practice*, ed. E. Geller, 2020, p. POL-40.

[158] R. Markiewicz, *Ilustrowane prawo autorskie* [Illustrated Copyright Law], 2018, p. 210.

[159] From 1 July 2020, decided by special intellectual property courts (four district in: Gdansk, Lublin, Poznań, Warsawa and two appeal: in Warsaw and Poznan).

[160] See Court of Appeal, Kraków, 18 June 2003, I ACa 510/03; although it expresses the controversial thesis that "only aesthetic and not functional elements in the structure of an architectural work are protected under copyright law". Placing the monument in the middle of the square made it actually impossible to use the steel sockets prepared earlier by the architects for the assembly of a stage or exhibition pavilion. In my opinion, however, there are no grounds for such a differentiation of the scope of protection (as regards aesthetic or functional elements), it is not justified to assume a priori that changes to functional elements will not result in a violation of the right to integrity, which would only occur in the case of changes in the sphere of aesthetic elements.

[161] Supreme Court, 5 March 2002, II KKN 341/99. Supreme Court, 5 March 2002, II KKN 341/99. In my opinion protection has varied according to the way in which it is used; and how "ephemeral" the modified versions of the works seem to be.

Jurisprudence has confirmed that a negative exercise of the right to authorship (i.e., concealment of authorship) must result from an explicit declaration of will by the author (it is not presumed that a copyrightable work is marked with a pseudonym[162]). In one case, the court rightly concluded that, as a result of the failure of a co-author to place a biographical note on the back cover of a book, the case could not be treated as an infringement of her moral rights.[163] Moreover, the court found that since the plaintiff (co-author A) agreed in the contract that her name should be placed only on the inside cover, there was no basis for an infringement of the right to authorship, since only the image and name of the other co-author (co-author B) were placed on the outside cover (co-author B was a famous actress).[164]

The CA 1994 provides, in Art. 115, criminal liability for infringement of the right of attribution (misappropriation of authorship, misrepresentation of authorship, distribution of work without specifying authorship). This offence is punishable by a fine, restriction of liberty and imprisonment (the latter is generally not adjudicated in practice). Since the enactment of the Act, the procedure for prosecuting crimes under Art. 115 has changed from private prosecution (1994–2000) to prosecution at the request of the aggrieved party (2000–2005), and finally, to public prosecution (since 2005). The 2005 change in regulations was a response to an increased disclosure of cases involving misappropriation of authorship (incorrect citation of works) in diploma theses. In tandem with the introduction of the legal basis for the withdrawal of a professional title and academic title and degree in the case of attributing the authorship (plagiarism) of someone else's work (see Section 2.3), the procedure for prosecuting the offence under Art. 115 of the CA 1994 was supposed to be a clear signal of the strengthening protection of the right to authorship, but it also served a preventive function (by threatening the offender with a double penalty). Whether it has served this purpose is suspect (as criminal proceedings are often conditionally discontinued). Criminal law instrumentation is not the most appropriate in the face of potential mass, small-scale violations in works, such as student works (Master thesis), that are not widely disseminated.[165] It seems that a better solution would be to focus on the effectiveness of the procedures related to the revocation of professional (academic) titles (and dissemination of IP knowledge among students), thereby easing the burden on prosecution offices.

---

[162] Court of Appeal, Krakow, 29 October 1997, I ACa 477/97.

[163] Court of Appeal, Warsaw, 8 July 2016, I ACa 1432/15.

[164] But an agreement with the ghostwriter to renounce the right of authorship will generally be considered invalid *ex nunc* under Art. 58 Civil Code, see J. Barta, R. Markiewicz, *International Copyright Law and Practice*, ed. E. Geller, 2020, 32-12/2020, p. POL-44.

[165] University dissertation may occur the problem with the right of disclosure, see P. Sirinelli, A. Bensamoun, Case Law Overview, 226 RIDA 10 (2020) p. 137 and next.

3.3.2   Performer's moral rights

Protection of related rights was only envisaged in the CA 1994.[166] Only performers were granted moral (personal) rights.[167] Thus, the principle of dualism of performance artists' rights was adopted. Protections of a performer's moral (personal) rights have been shaped in such a way that they are applied according to the provisions of Art. 78 of the CA 1994, which concerns the protection of authors' moral rights. Performers' rights have been included in one provision (Art. 86 CA 1994), with sec. 1 point 1 referring to moral (personal) rights (this will be the subject of a further short analysis), and para. 1 point 2 and sec. 2–3 addressing economic rights.

The performer was granted the right to protect their moral (personal) rights, although the provision only mentions the two most important moral (personal) rights:

(a)   to authorship of the performance ("to indicate him as a performer, *except in cases where the omission is customarily accepted* [my emphasis] and deciding how the performer should be named, including maintaining anonymity or using a pseudonym";[168]

(b)   the integrity of a performance ("to oppose any distortions, misrepresentations, and other changes to the performance, which could harm/violate its good name").[169]

Contrary to the contents of Art. 16 of the CA 1994, where authors' moral (personal) rights are "unlimited in time and not subject to waiver or transfer of the bond / relationship", Art. 86 of the CA 1994 makes no such statement.[170] This has significant consequences in terms of the duration of performers' moral (personal) rights. Given the lack of an explicit legal norm regarding the duration of the protection of moral (personal) rights, the result is finding that these rights expire upon the death of the performer. However, Poland is party to the World Intellectual Property Organization (WIPO) Performances and Phonograms Treaty (WPPT) 1996, which, in Art. 5 sec. 1, introduced the protection of the moral (personal) rights of

---

[166]   Related rights include the rights of: performers, producers of phonograms and videograms, radio and television broadcasters, publishers of first editions and publishers of scientific and critical editions. Nowadays, the protection pursuant to Arts 23 and 24 of the Civil Code is of significance for those scientific (scientific findings contained in the scientific edition of the work) or artistic achievements that are outside the scope of CA 1994 and for the personal rights of performers – after the expiry of the protection provided for in CA 1994 (see Section 2.1).

[167]   It is indicated in the literature that the protection of the moral (personal) rights of performers under the Civil Code 1964 "has preceded the protection of their economic interests in Poland" in the related rights system. Cf. M. Czajkowska-Dąbrowska, (in:) *System prawa prywatnego*, tom 13, *Prawo autorskie* [System of Private Law, Volume 13. Copyright Law] ed. J. Barta, p. 487 and the judgment of the Supreme Court of 15 April 1965, I CR 58/65, in which it was assumed that the use of an actor's artistic mask for advertising purposes (selling postcards depicting this mask), "therefore the mere reproduction of this mask by the producer in a photographic manner or by another person to whom the manufacturer has explicitly or implicitly commissioned advertising activities, does not constitute the infringement of Art. 11. However, the manner of this advertising must not infringe the actor's other personal rights protected by this provision, in particular his personal dignity, good name and the position of the artist in the People's State." See also P. Machnikowski, A. Górnicz-Mulcahy, J. Balcarczyk, "Poland" in *International Encyclopaedia of Laws: Intellectual Property*, ed. Hendrik Vanhees (Kluwer Law International 2020) p. 77.

[168]   See letters "a-b" point 1 sec. 1 of Art. 86 CA 1994.

[169]   See letter "c" point 1 sec. 1 of Art. 86 CA 1994.

[170]   The "bond" itself is considered to be an element creating protection of the artist's personal rights, see the judgment of the Court of Appeal in Warsaw of 13 September 2012, I ACa 1283/11.

performers[171] (the right to the authorship of a performance and the right of integrity), at least until the expiry of the economic rights of artistic performances.[172] This allows us to reasonably assume that these two rights of performers are protected as long as the performers' economic rights last; due to the principle of a conventional minimum, this rule would also protects of foreign performers in Poland.

The WPPT 1996 and the Beijing 2012 WIPO Treaty[173] basically share the two personal rights of performers, with two explicit "disclaimers" as to their content. In the case of the performance's authorship: "except where omission *is dictated by the manner* [my emphasis] of the use of the performance", and in the case of the right of integrity: "*taking due account of the nature* [my emphasis] of audiovisual fixations".[174] A comparison of the Polish regulation with the WPPT 1996 and the Beijing 2012 WIPO Treaty allows us to establish differences in their literal wording, though whether they have significant practical consequences and require the legislator's intervention is another issue. As for the right to authorship of the performance, it consists of two elements: a right to decide the content of a performance (graded from "empty/poor" in rare cases of anonymous performance, to "full/rich" in the case of a pseudonymous one or where the real name of individual artists or a group of artists is known[175]). Regarding this right, there are no specific treaty regulations, there is no need to change the national provision.

The second element of the authorship of the performance is the right to be designated as a performer. Here we are dealing with a limit[176] to the scope of this right, external to the performer: "omission is a customary practice" (customarily accepted under the CA 1994) and "except where omission is dictated by the manner of the use of the performance" (both WIPO Treaties). Polish civil law has a long history of using custom to determine the effects of a legal act/action (Art. 56 CC 1964, "to establish custom") or the manner of performance of an obligation (Art. 354 CC 1964: "A debtor should perform his obligation in accordance with ... and if there is an established custom in this respect – also in a manner complying with this custom").

In my opinion, in this context, custom is the same as "customary practice". Customary practice should be interpreted in a dynamic way, dictated by the manner of use of a performance.

---

[171]   Modeled on Art. 6*bis* of the Berne Convention, Poland has been a party to the convention since 2003.

[172]   See M. Czajkowska – Dąbrowska, (in:) *System prawa prywatnego*, tom 13, *Prawo autorskie* [System of Private Law, Volume 13. Copyright Law] ed. J. Barta, p. 1236.

[173]   Poland is the party of Beijing 2012 WIPO Treaty, and the treaty has been in force from 28 April 2020.

[174]   With additional details in the agreed statement concerning Art. 5: "For the purposes of this Treaty and without prejudice to any other treaty, it is understood that considering the nature of audiovisual fixations and their production and distribution, modifications of a performance that are made in the normal course of exploitation of the performance, such as editing, compression, dubbing, or formatting, in existing or new media or formats, and that are made in the course of use authorized by the performer, would not in themselves amount to modifications within the meaning of Article 5(1)(ii). Rights under Article 5(1)(ii) are concerned only with changes that are objectively prejudicial to the performer's reputation in a substantial way. It is also understood that the mere use of new or changed technology or media, as such, does not amount to modification within the meaning of Article 5(1)(ii)."

[175]   Compared with authors' pseudonyms, which in practice are very often used to hide or cover their true identity, performers' pseudonyms (used by individuals or by the band, not to cover their identity) are usually common.

[176]   A little parallel to the exemption/limitation to economic rights with his unreasonably prejudice the legitimate interests of the rightsholder (see Art. 35 CA 1994).

Under the Beijing 2012 WIPO Treaty, we obtained strong grounds for the interpretation of "customary practice" in light of changing manners (usually in the technical aspects but also new artistic genres like remixing or sampling for rap and hip-hop music[177]) of use (or dissemination, e.g., in films, in metaverse) of performances. Customary practices should be fair, corresponding to the particular manner of use of performance. The previous customary practice was the full omission of performers who play in the background.[178]

The right to the integrity of a performance in the CA 1994 is not absolute. Legislation only protects some aspects of the integrity of an artistic performance. Only "qualified" distortions, misrepresentations, and other changes that harm the good name of the performer, are forbidden. This provision of Art. 86 of the CA 1994 should now be interpreted in line[179] with the agreed statement of the Beijing Treaty, which "are concerned only with changes that are objectively prejudicial to the performer's reputation in a substantial way".[180] Also, modifications such as the use of new or changed technology or modifications made in the normal course of the exploitation of the performance ("such as editing, compression, dubbing, or formatting, in existing or new media or formats"[181]), and also, among other things, audio description, should not be treated as harmful to the good name of the performer.

Technology increasingly allows for the modification of artistic performances (e.g., the *Star Wars* series, or *The Shape of Water* directed by G. del Toro), giving legitimacy to flexible limits on the scope of the right to the integrity of a performance. In film studios, computer technology has long been used in animated films to obtain technical special effects and artistic special effects. The next step is artificial intelligence (AI) performance which, however, will probably not raise any significant problems in the sphere of performers' personal rights if we assume that AI performances, like computer-generated performances, should not be considered performances protected by copyright.[182]

Another interesting aspect (despite which, has not been the subject of dispute in Poland), concerns the modification and removal of an artistic performance in the case of criminal charges against the performer. The essence of this problem is illustrated by the case of the film *All the Money in the World* directed by R. Scott. As a consequence of charges of sexual harassment against Kevin Spacey (who played the role of the main character, J.P. Getty), which occurred after filming ended, this actor's scenes were minimized for fear of negative audience

---

[177] See opinion AG M. Szpunar, delivered on 12 December 2018, in the case C – 476/17, Pelham, esp. points 2-3, and 68.

[178] See point 9 of the preambles of the directive of 27 September 2011, amending Directive 2006/116/EC on the term of protection of copyright and certain related rights, which states: "This is particularly the case for performers who play in the background and do not appear in the credits (non-featured performers) but sometimes also for performers who appear in the credits (featured performers)."

[179] In my opinion, there is no need to change the provision of Art. 86 CA 1994. On the contrary see M. Barczewski, Osobiste i majątkowe prawa do artystycznych wykonań audiowizualnych – standardy międzynarodowe i perspektywy zmian w prawie polskim [Personal and economic rights of audiovisual artistic performances – international standards and prospects for changes in Polish law], Transformacje Prawa Prywatnego, 2020, nr 2, pp. 14–15, TPP, access: http:// www .transformacje .pl/ wp -content/ uploads/2020/06/Barczewski_TPP-2-2020.pdf.

[180] In my opinion, also in the case of all kinds of artistic performance (made in the course of a use authorized by the performer), not only audiovisual performances; it is justified in the digital version.

[181] Agreed statement under Art. 5 Beijing 2012 WIPO Treaty.

[182] Richard Arnold takes the view that computer-generated performances are not protected; R. Arnold, *Performers' Rights*, 4th ed. (Sweet & Maxwell 2008) pp. 69–70.

perception of the film. Moreover, Kevin Spacey was digitally replaced with actor Christopher Plummer, and in some scenes, only their faces were swapped.[183] Whether some of these consequences are likely to result in co-performances[184] or quasi-derivative artistic performances is a question to ponder. It is important to answer the question about the scope of protection of the right to the integrity of the artistic performance of such an artist. The provisions of the CA 1994 do not provide grounds for limiting the content of the personal rights of an artist who has been convicted or against whom criminal charges have been brought. If the contract did not contain provisions on making changes to the scope of artistic performance, the changes made in the circumstances indicated above should be classified as non-prejudicial to the reputation of the performer (given their legal situation). In such a case, the institution of abuse of law (by the performer) may also be considered as a basis for dismissing any claims on the part of the performer (Art. 5 CC 1964).

The CA 1994 provides the artist with a presumption of authorship of performance (the same as in the case of written works),[185] and criminal sanctions in the case of misappropriation (plagiary) and misrepresentation of the authorship of the performance.[186] Though the mere imitation of somebody else's performance, or the presentation of a work in the same artistic way is allowed.

Polish jurisprudence on the moral (personal) rights of performers is not numerous. One judgment, interesting to the practice, concerns the qualification of the use of an artistic performance (a solo trumpet part) of a former band member (plaintiff) on an album and in a musical video. The album cover contains the proper information about the plaintiff's guest performance (as he was a former member of the musical group), while the video contains only the name of the band[187] (the trumpeter's name was not given). Moreover, the video featured (presented) a model who pretended to play the trumpet to the plaintiff's artistic performance. The court found that such use did not infringe the right of integrity (objectively, no changes were made to the plaintiff's performance as such). The plaintiff argued that viewers could mistakenly identify the person (model) appearing in the video as the actual performer, and thus his right to authorship of performance had been violated. However, the court accepted that with regard to a music video, it is customary to mention the name of the band itself and not the names of individual musicians. Nevertheless, for the defendant's action, the court found that the personal right to the proper use of the performance had been violated.[188]

---

[183]   https://www.telegraph.co.uk/news/2017/11/09/christopher-plummer-replace-kevin-spacey-ridley-scotts-getty/.

[184]   Perhaps the least probable would be such a qualification – due to a lack of agreement on the part of co-performers.

[185]   Arts 92 and 8 CA 1994.

[186]   Art. 115 CA 1994.

[187]   This was adopted in the judgment of Court of Appeal in Warsaw, of 13 September 2012, I ACa 1283/11.

[188]   Analogous right to the author's personal right indicated in Art. 16 p. 3 CA 1994. See judgment of the Court of Appeal in Warsaw on 13 September 2012, I ACa 1283/11; however, it awarded a relatively low amount of compensation of moral damage PLN 5,000 (which, in 2012, was approximately EUR 1,200): "In the opinion of the Court of Appeal, the compensation appropriate to the severity of the infringement of the claimant's personal rights should be limited to the amount of PLN 5,000 ... During the creation of the above-mentioned music videoclip, the band were not known to a wider audience, and the album was sold in a small number of copies. Thus, the videoclip itself did not reach a wider audi-

4.   CONCLUSION: DIAMONDS V. AI

The author's moral rights have been protected in Poland *ab ovo*, from the first CA 1926 (bill 1920) and two years before the Rome (1928) revision of the Berne Convention, when authors' moral rights were "born" for the whole world. Central and Eastern European countries have a long (dating from the 1920s), rich and strong tradition of protecting authors' moral rights. This solid Polish legal foundation (a treasure trove of valuable law from 1926) has resisted the winds of change. The circumstances surrounding the adoption of the CA 1952 under the socialist regime did not have a significantly negative impact on the scope of protection of the moral (personal) rights of authors, although authors were not provided pecuniary redress of moral harm (in the form of the CA 1926). However, the letter of the copyright law, jurisprudence and even the legal literature do not reflect the constraints under which authors functioned and exercised their moral (personal rights) from 1945 to 1990. The CA 1994, though slightly different from that of the CA 1926, maintains a similar *ratio legis* and general assumption of protection, and therefore it can be stated that this legal act in the field of the authors' moral rights is a new version of the pre-war act. Since the beginning of the twenty-first century the AHES has created an additional instrument of protection for authors' and performers' moral rights (mostly rights of attribution) in the interest of the public, universities and scientific society. The AHES obliges universities to use anti-plagiarism software in order to check the diploma theses of all students (and PhD students' theses).

Authors' moral rights in Poland are eternal like diamonds, and, like diamonds, required shaping, by judges and doctrine to fully shine.

Authors' moral rights are not subject to specific regulation in the EU, as pointed by F. Gotzen, and this is one of the most important gaps to the harmonization of copyright law.[189] A small preparatory step was taken ten years ago by a project of the European Copyright Code (Wittem Project).[190] Differences between the EU continental civil law approach and the Anglo-Saxon and American common law systems made it difficult to develop a common position in the sphere of authors' moral rights, but this situation is changing. As evidenced by WPPT 1996 and the Beijing 2012 WIPO Treaty and now, after Brexit, we can start to create a system of authors' moral rights in the EU.

Today, we should think about scope of the protection of moral rights in the field of AI (TDM – Text and Data mining, ML – Machine Learning).[191] Preparation for 100 years, a jubilee of moral rights in Berne Convention should open the discussion about the future of moral rights.

Authors need moral rights as they are a "jewel in the crown" of the copyright system. It is an open question as to whether the results of AI will also, in the future need such an appropriately artificial copyright piece of "jewellery".[192]

---

ence. Also, the manner of violating the claimant's personal rights did not justify the award of a higher compensation."

[189]   F. Gotzen, Autonomous concepts in the case law of the court of Justice of the European Union on Copyright, 263 RIDA 75 (2020): "The most important gap is undoubtedly that which relates to authors' moral rights".

[190]   https://www.ivir.nl/copyrightcode/introduction/.

[191]   See R. Matulionyte, The (Forgotten) Moral Rights in the Age of AI; http:// copyrightblog .kluweriplaw.com/2022/02/07/the-forgotten-moral-rights-in-the-age-of-ai/.

[192]   As regards "attribution" right (the indication of source) and integrity right.

3. Islamic legal philosophy and moral rights

Ezieddin Elmahjub

1. INTRODUCTION

This chapter provides an Islamic perspective to justify the protection of moral rights in copyright laws. It aims to extract normative theories from Islamic legal philosophy to show that Islamic sources of moral obligations recognize the ethical values underpinning different forms of moral rights as we know them today. The doctrine of moral rights' protection is an essential feature of the global copyright regime and copyright legislation worldwide. It has two main components: the moral right to attribution and the moral right to integrity. The attribution right is a positive legal right that enables the author to prevent a third party from claiming the paternity of her expression and defend her connection to it. It includes the right to be identified as the author by placing her real name on the work, using a pseudonym or remaining anonymous. The moral right to integrity gives the author a negative right to prevent others from subjecting her work to derogatory treatment, which includes doing anything that results in a material distortion, mutilation or material alteration to the work that is prejudicial to the author's honour or reputation.[1]

The positivist framework for the modern doctrine of moral rights emerged and developed in the West. Policymakers and academic commentators draw from the natural rights and personality theories of Western philosophers like John Locke, Immanuel Kant and Fredrick Hegel to evaluate, justify and develop the doctrinal features of moral rights. Comparative theoretical insights explaining moral rights are rarely found in the extensive literature of copyright even though these rights have been, for almost a century, part of the global copyright regime. The current dominant doctrine of moral rights is global and influences people across the ideological and ethical spectrum. If we believe in legal pluralism and the need to provide cross-cultural justifications for global legal rules, then there will be a good reason to see how different philosophical traditions interact with notions of moral rights.

I wish to be clear from the outset; this chapter is not seeking to convince jurisdictions with predominantly Islamic populations to accept and regulate moral rights. Almost all jurisdictions in the Islamic world already recognize and protect all forms of intellectual property rights (IP), including moral rights. The focus of this chapter is theoretical. More specifically, it aims to determine how Islamic legal theory justifies moral rights protection. This question has received very little attention from scholars interested in studying IP norms from an Islamic perspective. Copyright literature in the Islamic world tends to uncritically accept the comparative justifications for moral rights without tracing their theoretical and historical roots in Islamic traditions. Furthermore, influential Islamic bodies, including the leading Sunni Islam authority al-Azhar[2]

---

[1]   Sam Ricketson and Jane Ginsburg, *International Copyright and Neighbouring Rights: The Berne Convention and Beyond*, vol 2 (Oxford University Press, 2006) 585.
[2]   Al-Azhar Fatwa Committee in a number of opinions issued on 20 April 2000 and 16 August 2001 (cited in Heba Raslan, "Shari'a and the Protection of Intellectual Property, the Example of Egypt" (2007) Intellectual Property Law Review, 503.

and the Council of Islamic Fiqh (jurisprudence) Academy,[3] have issued legal opinions (*fatwas*) legitimizing all forms of IP protection under the textual sources of Islamic law.

However, we do not have principled justifications for moral rights that draw from Islamic normative theories and Islamic ethics of authorship. Islamic legal philosophy is equipped with multiple theological principles and human-made jurisprudence that Muslims use to engage in moral reasoning about good and evil, right and wrong, and fair and unfair.[4] This chapter shows that Islamic legal philosophy is not necessarily hostile to comparative justifications of moral rights. The underlying ethical norms for the moral rights of attribution and integrity could find ample support in Islamic sources and the ethics of authorship. I construct a theoretical framework showing that it is possible to ground the dominant aspects of moral rights in an Islamic version of natural rights theory. This theory accommodates the main features of comparative discourse on moral rights, particularly the propositions around moral rights being fair entitlements or personally satisfying for authors.

The chapter will proceed as follows: Section 2 puts into context the current protection available for moral rights in some Islamic jurisdictions. It shows that the Islamic world's legislative norms of moral rights find their material source in European moral rights schemes. Scholars of copyright in these jurisdictions accept the dominant comparative justifications of moral rights without critical evaluation of moral rights from an Islamic perspective. Section 3 shows that it is possible to construct normative theory for moral rights based on the dominant justifications for ownership in the mainstream Islamic jurisprudence. Islamic jurisprudence recognizes ownership rights as a fair reward for human labour and essential human need compatible with human nature. Section 4 reinforces the theoretical justifications for moral rights in the Islamic worldview by drawing additional support from the history of authorship in Islamic regions. For centuries, Muslim authors practised the ethical norms underpinning the main components of moral rights as we know them today.

2. MORAL RIGHTS IN ISLAMIC AND COMPARATIVE CONTEXT

The legislative norms of moral rights, like all other forms of IP, emerged and developed in Western Europe. Academic commentators and policymakers usually cite Western moral philosophy to explain the societal need to protect moral rights. The most common feature of modern literature on copyright in Muslim majority countries is its uncritical acceptance of the Western sources of moral rights in the Islamic world. There has been a sweeping movement to transplant moral rights provisions from French copyright laws into copyright law in the region.

The global colonial powers of the nineteenth century were the architects of the positivist legal systems of moral rights as we know them today. In 1886, the major European countries, including Belgium, France,[5] Italy, Portugal and the United Kingdom, introduced the Berne

---

[3]   International Islamic *Fiqh* Academy, Resolution No. 43 (5/5) 1988 regarding incorporeal rights, http://zulkiflihasan.files.wordpress.com/2009/12/majma-fiqh.pdf.

[4]   Ezieddin Elmahjub, "Islamic Jurisprudence as an Ethical Discourse: An Enquiry into the Nature of Moral Reasoning in Islamic Legal Theory" (2021) Oxford Journal of Law and Religion, 10(1), 16–42.

[5]   Generally, countries of Civil Law traditions are widely known as strong advocates for moral rights protections. John Henry Merryman et. al, *Law, Ethics, and the Visual Arts*, 5th ed. (Kluwer Law

Convention for the Protection of Literary and Artistic Works as the foundational legal instrument for the global copyright regime. In the Rome Revision of the Berne Convention in 1928, France, Italy and Germany successfully inserted Article 6*bis*[6] to protect the moral rights of attribution and integrity "independently of the author's economic rights".[7] The deliberations that led to the Berne Convention and its revisions reflected the Western ethical outlook that focuses on individual autonomy as the basis for legal entitlements. The Berne Convention, through its economic and moral rights regimes, sought to reward authors with mechanisms to control access and reuse of knowledge and culture in the hope that this would create strong markets. Sam Ricketson and Jane Ginsburg note that the drafters of the Convention were mainly "concerned with the private interests of authors and with raising the level of protection that is accorded to them".[8]

By and large, countries outside continental Europe, in Asia, Africa and South America, were not part of the standard-setting processes of the global copyright regime. Colonization transplanted the rules of the copyright regime, including those pertaining to moral rights, into the legal systems of many developing countries worldwide.[9] In fact, France, Germany and the United Kingdom, the principal architects of the Berne Convention, took advantage of Article 19 of the Berne Act to include their colonies into Berne membership. Article 19 permitted colonizers to accede to the Convention, at any time, on behalf of their colonies.[10] As a result, countries around the world, including those in the Islamic world, ended up having their copyright laws tailored for them.[11]

Nearly all countries with predominantly Islamic populations were subject to colonization or direct influence by the major colonial powers of the nineteenth century. For instance, France occupied Algeria in 1830, Tunisia in 1881 and Morocco in 1912. The French version of the Civil Law system shaped the metes and bounds of the legal systems in many Islamic countries. In particular, the Napoleonic Civil Code of 1804 was the material source for laws on contract

---

International, 2007). Copyright literature normally stresses the importance of French contributions to developing moral rights as a global norm. For instance, according to Ricketson, French courts developed an independent legal protection for moral rights. Sam Ricketson, *The Berne Convention for the Protection of Literary and Artistic Works: 1886–1986* (Centre for Commercial Law Studies, Queen Mary College: Kluwer, 1987), 457. Harold Streibich explains the French enthusiasm to protect moral rights with reference to the art culture of the Renaissance. Harold C. Streibich, "The Moral Right of Ownership to Intellectual Property: Part I – From the Beginning to the Age of Printing" (1975) 6 Memphis State University Law Review 1. According to Raymond Sarraute, the French traditions on protecting moral rights led to the first known legislative schemes that explicitly recognized the moral right of attribution and integrity, these are, the Revolutionary Decrees issued in 1791 and 1793. Raymond Sarraute, "Current Theory on the Moral Rights of Authors and Artists under French Law" (1968) American Journal of Comparative Law, 465–6.

[6]   Ricketson, above n 5, 459–60.

[7]   The Berne Convention for the Protection of Literary and Artistic Works, 1886, Art 6bis. Art 6bis only mandated the protection for the right to attribution and integrity. It does not include the right to publish and the right to withdrawal which are part of some copyright law in continental Europe.

[8]   Ricketson and Ginsburg, above n 1, 881.

[9]   Peter K. Yu, "International Enclosure, The Regime Complex, and Intellectual Property Schizophrenia" (2007) Michigan State Law Review, 1, 5.

[10]   Sam Ricketson, above n 5, 791.

[11]   Peter Drahos, "Developing Countries and International Intellectual Property Standard-Setting' (2002) 5 The Journal of World Intellectual Property, 765, 767.

and property in Egypt, Libya, Syria, Tunisia, Kuwait and Iraq.[12] Copyright legislation and its regulation of moral rights was no exception. The French Copyright Decree No. 2385 issued on 17 January 1924, was the material source for regulating moral rights in several Muslim countries, even after they gained their independence.[13] The French norms on moral rights were largely copied into the old Egyptian Copyright Act of 1954, which worked as some form of template for nearly all copyright laws in the Arab world between the 1960s and 1970s. The Explanatory Memorandum of this law makes an explicit reference to European normative influence on the emergence and development of moral rights in Egyptian law.[14] It is interesting to note that, from the very beginning, the lawmaking discourse on moral rights in the Islamic world did not attempt to theorize for the need for protecting moral rights from an Islamic perspective. Even scholars of copyright in the Islamic world took a positivist approach to the protection of moral rights. This is a very unusual position for studies written in Arabic discussing civil law matters. A common feature of socio-legal research in the Islamic world since, at least, the 1950s is to conduct a comparative analysis between Islamic norms of contract and property with their counterparts in secular civil law jurisdiction, particularly French laws.[15] The underlying assumption driving the scholarly rhetoric in the Islamic world is that protecting moral rights is a sound public policy objective since these rights are already protected in major European countries.[16] An Islamic philosophy to justify the need to recognize and protect moral rights does not clearly feature in the mainstream copyright discourses in the Islamic world.

3. ISLAMIC PHILOSOPHY OF MORAL RIGHTS

Is it possible to speak of Islamic normative principles for moral rights akin to those theories used to justify moral rights in the Western context? Mainstream copyright literature usually invokes two major theories to defend the authors' rights to the paternity and integrity of their expressive content, namely natural law theory and personality theory associated, respectively, with John Locke and Emanuel Kant. This section shows that the broad theoretical assumptions

---

[12] For instance, Egyptian Civil Codes of 1949 was the source of their counterparts in several countries throughout North Africa and the Middle East, including Libya, Syria, Kuwait and Iraq. Renowned Professor Abd al-Razzak al-Sanhūri (1895–1971) was behind importing French norms into the modern Civil Codes of these countries. He spent few years in France during the 1920s to study the French Civil Code. Upon his return from France, Professor al-Sanhuri led the drafting committees of the Egyptian Civil Law and toured several other Islamic countries in the 1950s to help draft their Civil Codes. For overview on the history of Egyptian Civil Code, see Abd al-Razzak al-Sanhūri, *al-Wasīt fī al-Qanūn al-Madanī*, vol 1 (Dār al-Nahda al-'Arabiyya, 1952).
[13] Ibrahim Ahmed Ibrahim, "Ḥuqūq al-Mu'alif wa watīq' tatbiquha fi al-watan al- 'arabi" in the Arab League Educational, Cultural and Scientific Organization (ALESCO), 1996) 13.
[14] The Explanatory Memorandum of the Egyptian Copyright Law, 1954.
[15] Abd al-Razzak al-Sanhūri, *al-Wasīt fī al-Qanūn al-Madanī*, vol 1 (Dār al-Nahda al-'Arabiyya, 1952).
[16] See for instance, Farag al-Sadda, *al-Mulkiyya al-Ma'nawiyya: Haq al-Mu'alif* (Arab Lawyers Union, 1967); Nawāf Ken'an, *Haq al-Mu'alif*, (Dār al-Thaqafa, 2004) 85; Nurī Hamād Khatar, *Sharḥ Qawā'id al- Mulkiyya al-Fikerīyyah: Ḥaqq al- Mu'alīf wa-al-Ḥuqquq al-Mujawīra* (UAE University Press, 2008) 203.

on which these two theories are founded overlap with some Islamic moral intuitions on protecting the moral rights of attribution and integrity.[17]

3.1   Natural Rights Justification

Natural rights precepts are among the most popular justifications for most of the doctrinal features of copyright law, including moral rights. French scholars often start from the proposition that authors' moral rights are natural rights that deserve legal protection in line with the strong natural rights sentiments that overshadowed the French Revolution.[18] Those who create expressive content in the form of literary, dramatic, musical or artistic works should be given legal entitlements to control how others handle their work. Theological inputs heavily influence the underlying propositions for natural law justifications of copyright doctrines. Dan Rosen attempted to summon the Thomistic perspective of natural law to justify moral rights protection. He argues that if a society is inclined to accept Thomas Aquinas' proposition that "there is in man a natural and initial inclination to good" such society will allow individuals to achieve that good. In the context of moral rights, this occurs by enabling artists to control the access, attribution and integrity of their work.[19]

However, most copyright scholars normally rely on the famous Lockean version of natural rights to private property rights to justify all legal entitlements under copyright law, including moral rights. John Locke establishes his theory of natural rights to property on a theological premise stating "God gave the world to men in common".[20] Since an individual "naturally" owns "the labor of his body and the work of his hands ... Whatever then he removes out of the state that nature hath provided, and left it in, he hath mixed his labor with, and joined to it something that is his own, and thereby makes it his property".[21] William Fisher, Justin Hughes and Robert Merges argue, albeit with few reservations, suggested that all IP entitlements follow the same underlying logic. Authors mix their intellectual labour with resources held in the public domain to create new intellectual expressions. The natural consequence for this activity is to guarantee legal protection for authors to control access and reuse of their creations.[22]

The theological foundation of the Lockean natural rights theory is emphasized throughout the Qur'ān "it is He (God) who created for you (humankind) all of that which is on the earth".[23] Muslim jurists use the same line of reasoning to establish the Islamic version of the natural right to property. They define the resources held in common as *mubaḥ*, which includes vacant

---

[17]   Ezieddin Elmahjub, *An Islamic Vision of Intellectual Property: Theory and Practice* (Cambridge University Press, 2019) 42–55.

[18]   Dan Rosen, "Artists' Moral Rights: A European Evolution, an American Revolution" (1983) 2 Cardozo Arts and Entertainment Law Journal 176.

[19]   Ibid.

[20]   Section 34, John Locke, *The Second Treatise of Civil Government* (1690), www.constitution.org/jl/2ndtreat.html.

[21]   Ibid, Section 27.

[22]   Justin Hughes, "The Philosophy of Intellectual Property" (1988) 77 Georgetown Law Journal 287; William Fisher, "Theories of Intellectual Property", in S. Munzer (ed.), *New Essays in the Legal and Political Theory of Property* (Cambridge University Press, 2001); Robert P. Merges, *Justifying Intellectual Property* (Harvard University Press, 2011) 32–33.

[23]   Qur'ān, 2:29 and 45:13.

land (*al-'arḍ al-jarda'*), marine life (*al- ḥayāt al-baḥriyya*), animals (*ḥayawanāt*), plants (*nabatāt*), and mines (*ma'adin*).[24] Those who mix their labour with *mubaḥ* to appropriate resources (*iḥraz al-mubaḥ*) are entitled to ownership and control rights (*mulkiyyah*) over whatever resources they removed from nature.[25] It is possible to extend the Islamic justifications of property to copyright and moral rights. We can think of the public domain of free ideas as *mubaḥ*. Authors who transform free ideas into literary and artistic expressions should be given legal protection to control how others access and reuse their expressions. Part of this legal protection can include a positive right to be identified as the author and a negative right to prevent others from violating the integrity of the protected expression.

3.2   Personality Justifications

Personality theories have a special place in justifying legal protection for moral rights. They are built on an overarching assumption that expressive content is an extension of the author's persona. Therefore, it is imperative to protect the personal connection between the creator and her content by ensuring legal rights to the paternity and integrity of the artistic or literary subject matter. In comparative Western literature on copyright, commentators typically rely on Kant's moral philosophy to establish the normative benchmark for protecting moral rights. In this section, I show that there are interesting similarities between the Kantian and Islamic perspectives on property and possession. Like Kantian views on property, Islamic sources of moral obligations also recognize the need for property and possession as fundamental human traits. The line of reasoning that follows the Kantian vision to justify moral rights is not alien to the Islamic sources and jurisprudence as I show below.

Kant justifies the need for ownership in *Metaphysics of Morals*. In this work, he imagines a state of affairs where individuals comply with the imperatives of natural reason. A fundamental part of the natural reason for each individual is an impulse to appropriate external objects. Humans, by their nature, seek to claim objects as their own and exclude others from interfering with their possession. Accordingly, it would be compatible with natural reason to satisfy this natural impulse by legal protection for rights to ownership and control over external objects that a person appropriates through her will.[26]

IP scholars extend the Kantian version of personality theory to justify legal protection for intellectual content. The crux of the argument scholars normally make is this: as is the case with tangible objects in the Kantian theory, the need to control expressive content through legal rights is "crucial to the satisfaction of some fundamental human needs"[27] or fulfils "human instinct", which is bound up with the existence of an individual's will.[28] Indeed, it is often argued that the personality theory has a closer affinity to the need to protect intellectual expressions. Expressions are stronger receptacles to an individual's personality compared to physical objects. Accordingly, the desire to control an intellectual expression should be more

---

[24]   Muṣṭafá al-Zarqa, *al-Mudkhal al-Fiqhī al-'am* (Dār al-Qalam, 1998) 336; Muhammed M. Shalabi, *al-Fiqh al-Islāmī: Tarīkhuhu wa Madārisuhu wa Nazarīyatahu: al- Mulkiyyah wa al-'aqd* (Al- Dār al-Jāmi'iyya, 1985), 381.

[25]   Muhammed Said, *al-Mal, Mulkkiyyatuhu, Isti'maruh wa Infāqihi* (Dār al-Wafa, 2002) 60. See also Shalabi, *al- al-Fiqh al-Islāmī*, above n 24, 381.

[26]   Immanuel Kant, *Groundwork for the Metaphysic of Morals* (Cambridge University Press, 2012).

[27]   Fisher, above n 22, 5.

[28]   Merges, above n 22, 72.

robust.[29] Justin Hughes suggests that personality theory could play a vital role in explaining some doctrines and practices in copyright laws. These include two areas: First, legal protection for highly expressive intellectual products such as poems, novels and paintings. Second, legal protection for a set of moral rights enabling authors to be acknowledged as the creators of their works and to have the right to control the publication and integrity of their work.[30]

Interestingly, Kant made a general reference to moral rights precepts in his essay "On the Wrongfulness of Unauthorized Publication of Books".[31] In this essay, Kant presents a powerful defence of authors' rights to control the attribution and integrity of their works.[32] According to Kant, an author has a personal right to be named as the creator of the expressive content that he makes. In the context of literary works, he suggests that publishers who associate a person's name on a work that they chose not to publish violate the author's will of expression. Moreover, Kant suggests that the personal connection between the author and his content creates a duty on others not to distort or mutilate that content.[33]

While Islamic sources of moral obligations do not share Kant's sophisticated analysis of property as an extension of the individual's will and autonomy, there is one joint fundamental proposition. As is the case in the Kantian justification of property, the Qur'ān and the Sunnah (the recorded tradition of the Prophet Muhammed) recognize the human need to control external objects as *fiṭrah insāniyya*, a fundamental natural disposition compatible with natural human reason. The Qur'ān states: "and you (humans) love wealth with immense love".[34] The recorded traditions of the Prophet confirms this meaning. "If the son of Adam were to possess two valleys of riches, he would long for the third one."[35] Medieval and Modern interpretations of the Qur'ān suggest that Islamic textual sources recognize that humans have an innate desire towards appropriation and possession of wealth. As such, the Islamic system of rules should manage this desire to mitigate the potential negative impact of greed that might come with expansive ownership rights. One way to achieve this objective is through imposing rules to promote the social function of private property.[36]

Islamic jurisprudence maintains that Islamic normative positions must always conform to *fiṭrah*. Ethical values and moral intuitions that jurists develop must not violate natural dispositions but instead respect and regulate them.[37] This means that if we proclaim that there is *fiṭrah*/natural disposition towards ownership, this must result in some normative implications. Those who desire ownership and employ legitimate means, such as labour, to appropriate external

---

[29]   Hughes, above n 22, 333 et seq.; Merges, above n 22, 68 et seq.

[30]   Hughes, above n 22, 333.

[31]   Immanuel Kant, *On the Wrongfulness of Unauthorized Publication of Books* (1785), in *The Cambridge Edition of the Works of Immanuel Kant, Practical Philosophy* (Mary J. Gregor (ed. & trans), Cambridge University Press, 1996) 29–35.

[32]   Kim Treiger-Bar-Am, "Kant on Copyright: Rights of Transformative Authorship" (2011) 25(3) Cardozo Arts and Entertainment Law Journal, 1062.

[33]   Kant, above n 31, 8:81–2.

[34]   Qur'ān, 89:20.

[35]   Translation of Sahih Muslim, Book 5, No. 2282, www.iium.edu.my/deed/hadith/muslim/005_smt.html

[36]   Al-Ḥusayn ibn Mas'ūd, *Tafsīr al-Baghawi*, vol 8 (Dār Taiyyba, n.d.) 509; Muhammed al-Shanqīṭī, *Adwa' al-Bayān fi Idaḥ al-Qur'ān bi al-Qur'ān*, vol 9 (Dār al-Fikre, 1995); Sayyid Qutb, *Fi Zilāl al-Qur'ān*, vol 6 (Dār al-Shurūq, 2003) 3957.

[37]   Muhammad al-Ṭāhir ibn 'Āshūr, *Maqāṣid Al-Sharī'ah al-Islāmiyya* (Dār al-nafā'is, 2001) 329.

objects should be entitled to legal protection under Islamic law. In this sense, the Islamic notion of *fiṭrah* recognizes and respects human need and desire for ownership.

Islamic literature justifying copyright does not entertain the possibility to think of *fiṭrah* as a possible justification for copyright, in general, let alone moral rights. However, I see no good reason not to do so. If we accept that there is a *fiṭrah* to control external objects, including artistic and literary content, we should be able to argue for different forms of legal protection for content creators. This legal protection will include the creators' right to be named as the authors of their work. It will also include imposing a duty on others to avoid unreasonable derogatory treatment of the protected work. In other words, it is compatible with the sentiments of *fiṭrah* to recognize and protect the moral right of attribution and integrity.

The broad theoretical justifications for protecting moral rights find further support in textual sources that condemn acts of misattribution and distortion of religious knowledge. Islamic legal theory tends to resort to the language of the Qur'ān and the recorded traditions of the Prophet to elicit normative positions on the morality, or otherwise, of acts and omissions in all areas of moral uncertainties. While textual sources do not explicitly condemn behaviours that lead to violating moral rights in the context of literary and artistic expressions, they contain multiple normative signals that could provide indirect support for moral rights precepts. For instance, the Qur'ān contains a powerful condemnation for all forms of behaviour that lead to denying to recognize the efforts of others and seeking claiming credits for such efforts.[38] On this issue, the Qur'ān states that "do not let those who rejoice in their misdeeds and love to take credit for what they have not done think they will escape torment. They will suffer a painful punishment."[39] The Qur'ān also declares as a grave sin all forms of manipulations of the divine texts.[40] In particular, it instructs Muslims to preserve the attribution and integrity of religious knowledge. For instance, it warns against any misattribution and distortion of the scripture:

> And indeed, there is among them a party who alter the Scripture with their tongues so you may think it is from the Scripture, but it is not from the Scripture. And they say, "This is from Allah," but it is not from Allah. And they speak untruth about Allah while they know.[41]

Furthermore, the Qur'ān imposes a general ethical duty on Muslims to act with utmost honesty and abstain from all forms of deceitful practices. On this, the Qur'ān says, "Indeed, Allah commands you to render trusts to whom they are due."[42] If we accept that content creators have legitimate rights to attribution and integrity under the Islamic version of natural law theory or Islamic notions of *fiṭrah*, we should be able to declare as dishonest and deceitful acts that violate those rights. In other words, violating moral rights through false attribution and

---

[38]   Similar condemnation is also found in the recorded traditions of the Prophet in the context of ownership of physical assets. The Prophet warns Muslims against misleading people and creating false impression about rightful ownership: "The one who creates a false impression of receiving what one has not been given is like one who wears two garments of falsehood". See Muhammed al-Bukhārī *Ṣaḥīḥ al-Bukhārī*, Book 18, Hadith 1549. The book is available online https://sunnah.com/riyadussaliheen/18/39.

[39]   Qur'ān, 3:188.

[40]   Ali Khan, "Islam as Intellectual Property: My Lord! Increase me in knowledge" (2001) 31 Cumberland Law Review 361.

[41]   Qur'ān, 3:78.

[42]   Qur'ān, 4:58.

distortion against the author's will are immoral/deceitful practices that fall within the scope of the mentioned Qur'ānic prohibitions.[43]

4.   THE PRACTICAL ETHICS OF ATTRIBUTION AND INTEGRITY IN ISLAMIC CULTURAL HISTORY

On a theoretical level, mainstream Islamic legal theory developed normative principles for different forms of legal rules in property, contract and torts. However, there was no separate treatment for IP precepts, including moral rights. On a practical level, Islamic cultural traditions on authorship demonstrated various forms of recognition for the underlying notions of moral rights, particularly the crude forms of the right to attribution and integrity.[44] In this section, I show that throughout the long history of literary developments in the Islamic world, Muslim religious leaders and intellectuals practised the underlying norms of moral rights as religious and ethical principles. This means that Islamic jurisdictions' cultural and social climate was always ripe for developing an indigenous positivist doctrine for moral rights. In this sense, the arguments made in the previous sections about justifying moral rights in Islamic legal philosophy find additional support in the social and cultural practices regarding literary production throughout Islamic history.

The first known practical recognition for ethical principles on attribution and integrity emerged in the eighth to ninth centuries CE concerning recording the traditions and legal rules that Prophet Muhammed communicated to his companions. For instance, Imams al-Bukhārī (d. 807 CE) and Imam Muslim (d. 875 CE), among several other leading Islamic scholars, made tremendous efforts to write down collections of *ḥadīth* (Prophet's teachings). One of the most visible features in recording the *ḥadīth* was the attention given to avoiding misattribution and distortion while transcribing its texts. Collectors of *ḥadīth* had a powerful religious duty to ensure the correct attribution and integrity of texts they transmit in their written records. The Prophet made a dire warning against using his name to mislead Muslims about his speech and action "he who attributed any falsehood to me ... deliberately ... he should in fact find his abode in the Hell-Fire".[45] Muslim jurists developed a separate branch of Islamic jurisprudence known as *'ilm al-Jarḥ wa al-Ta'dī l* (The rules of authenticating *ḥadīth*) to monitor attribution and integrity of the recorded speech. *'ilm al-Jarḥ* has an overarching objective, that is, ensuring the transmitted texts (*matn*) is not distorted, modified or misattributed to the Prophet. Jurists of *'ilm al-Jarḥ* developed the notion of as *isnād* (chain of narrators) to check that those who are mentioned in the chain of narrators are trustworthy and not suspected of known falsifications or forgery.[46]

---

[43]   Amir H. Khory, "Ancient and Islamic Sources of Intellectual Property Protection in the Middle East: A Focus on Trademarks" (2003) 43 Idea: The Journal of Law and Technology 173.

[44]   I reuse some of the material included in this section from earlier work published in 2014: Ezieddin Elmahjub, "Foundations of Moral Rights in Islamic Sources and History of Authorship in Islamic Civilisation" (2014) 22 IIUM Law Journal 2, 137–64.

[45]   Muslim ibn al-Hajjaj, *Ṣaḥīḥ* Muslim Vol. 1, Book 3, Hadīth 109. The book is available online https://sunnah.com/bukhari/3/51.

[46]   Ibnal-Mulaqin, *al-Mughnī fi 'ulum al-Hadīi* (Dār Fawāz li al-Nashr, 1992); Adnan Ahmed Atef, *'ilm al-Jarḥ wa al-Ta'dīl: ahamīyyatuhu, wa Tarekha'hu*, wa Qawa'idahu, 2, Majalat Markaz Buhūt al-Sunnah wa al-Sīrra, Qatar University (1987), 422.

The religious and ethical norms of attribution and integrity did not stop with authorship practices related to religious content. It also flourished in the non-religious spheres of literature. Paper production in Baghdad, the capital of the Abbasid Caliphate, started around 950 CE. This development was a historical landmark in the history of authorship in Islamic literary culture.[47] Other factories for paper productions were also set up in the other major cultural hubs of the ancient Islamic world including Cairo, Granada, Toledo and Cordoba.[48] These developments contributed to thriving paper production and directly influenced the number of books Muslim authors wrote.[49] An independent profession known as *warraqūn* (booksellers/publishers) existed in various Islamic regions to purchase books from authors and resell them to the public.[50] *Warraqūn* had a professional duty that fits perfectly within the underlying ethics of the right of attribution and integrity. They were required to ensure that books were not made available to the public before obtaining *ijāza* (approval) from the author. The purpose of *ijāza* was to ascertain that the author himself created the content of the book and that the content was not distorted. After new reproductions of manuscripts were made, the *warraqūn* asked authors to verify that the newly reproduced content still conveys their ideas. Reproduced books often start with a phrase stating that the book's content was transmitted from the author (*sama'un a'nn*) and copied by a professional amanuensis known as *nāsīkh*.[51]

The ethics of attribution and integrity had a critical role in Islamic traditions on poetry. There was a strict ethical norm preventing poets from intentionally copying the poems of others without attribution. When poems are transmitted to the public by text or recitation, the person making the transmission had a duty to include the full name of the original poet. The requirement to do that is considered a sign that the original poet has paternity rights over their poems.[52] Since poets enjoyed a prestigious social status in Islamic culture, many attempted to free ride by copying original poems and presenting them as their own. The poets who fail to add anything of value to the copied material face harsh social condemnation. Ibn Salām (d. 846 CE) in his highly acclaimed treaty *Tabakāt Fuḥūl Ashu'ara'* (Classifications of Prominent Poets) documents several disputes among Muslims poets about incidents of "poetry thefts".[53] Unoriginal poets normally risked facing social exclusion, which was one of the most severe punishments in tribal communities within Islamic regions.[54]

In the fifteenth century, Muḥammad Ibn Ḥasan al-Nawaāji (d. 1455) completed a book entitled *Kitāb al-Ḥujjah fī sariqāt Ibn Ḥijjah* (The Proof in the Infringements of Ibn Ḥijjah).[55] Al-Nawaāji starts his book by emphasizing an Islamic religious duty on composers of literary

---

[47] Taha Baqqer, *Mūjaz fī Tarikh al-'ulum wa al-Ma'arif*, 156 (al-Dār al- Dawlīyya li al-Estithmārāt al-Thaqafīyya, 2002).

[48] Hamid Diyab, *al-Kutub wa al-Maktabāt fī al-Andalus*, 31 (Dār Qiba, 1998).

[49] Ibid, 31.

[50] Hans H. Wellisch, *The First Arab Bibliography: Fihrist al-'Ulum*, 6 (Volume 175 of Occasional Papers, University of Illinois Graduate School of Library and Information Science, ISSN 0276-1769, 1986). See also 'Abd al-Ra'ūf, *Tārikh al-Fikr al-Islamī*, (Dār Al-Fikr al-'Arabi, 1997) 189; Hamid Diyab, *al-Kutub wa al-Maktabāt*, above n 48, 60–70 and 102.

[51] Hamid Diyab, *al-Kutub wa al-Maktabāt*, above n 48, 64–5.

[52] Khory, above n 43, 155.

[53] Muḥammad ibn Salam, al-Jamahī, *Tabakāt Fuḥūl Ashu'ara'* (Umm al-Qura University, n.d).

[54] Khory, above n 43, 155.

[55] A manuscript of the book is available at Harvard Library: Muḥammad ibn Ḥasan Al-Nawājī, Kitāb al-Ḥujjah fīsariqāt ibn Ḥijjah (manuscript, undated. MS Arab 285) 12 March 2014, http://pds.lib.harvard.edu/pds/ view/12139575?n=6&imagesize=1200&jp2Res=.25&printThumbna ils=no90.

works to ensure proper attribution of knowledge. This religious duty finds its source in the Qur'ān, which states that "Indeed, Allah commands you to render trusts to whom they are due".[56] Then al-Nawaāji proceeds to claim that another Muslim poet known as Ibn Ḥijjah (d. 1433) had frequently engaged in "poetry thefts" (*sariqāt*) by copying poems from other poets and attributing them to himself.[57] Al-Nawaāji builds his case against Ibn Ḥijjah by collecting the poems that Ibn Ḥijjah allegedly copied. Then he moves to identify their original composers and show the portions that Ibn Ḥijjah plagiarized.[58]

The final example of Muslims' practices of the ethical norms underlying moral rights can be seen in al-Suyūṭī's manuscript that was dedicated to dealing with authors' obligations to ensure attribution and integrity in literary works. 'Abd al-Raḥmān Jalāl al-Dīn al-Suyūṭī (d. 1505) composed a manuscript entitled *al-Fāriq bayn al-Muṣannif wa al-Sāriq* (On the distinction between the original author and the infringer).[59] Like al-Nawaāji, he starts by quoting religious scriptures to extend the religious duty to act honestly and refrain from dishonesty in the area of authorship. According to al-Suyūṭī, authors of literary content must act honestly by ensuring that all forms of knowledge are properly transmitted without distortion, and that literary content is appropriately attributed to its rightful authors.[60] He argues that throughout the development of authorship in the field of Islamic jurisprudence and literature, authors and jurists recognized honesty in attribution and integrity of the work of others as a firm religious duty. In transmitting the written opinions of other jurists and writers, the standard practice is to show the utmost respect for proper citation and attribution to the rightful original authors of the content.[61] Al-Suyūṭī then proceeded to speak of a personal experience complaining that other authors copied two of his books without proper attribution. He begins by showing that original authors are entitled to control access to their work because they invest a long time in composing their work. For his books, he claims that he spent 20 years collecting, refining and writing their content. He even claims that he uses expressions unique to his personality and writing style.[62] Then, he heavily criticizes scholars who copied his books without proper attribution and equates misattribution to property theft.[63] According to al-Suyūṭī, those who violate the authorial rights of attribution are committing a sin against Islamic law.[64]

5.   CONCLUSION

Islamic jurisdictions have copied European norms for moral rights protection. Muslim jurists and legal theorists would usually seek some form of Islamic philosophical or doctrinal evaluation for rules imported from the Western philosophical and legal environments. Moral rights do not feature in comparative Islamic discourse in this way. This chapter sought to

---

[56]   Ibid, 6.
[57]   Ibid, 21.
[58]   Ibid, 23.
[59]   'Abd al-Raḥmān Jalāl al-Dīn al-Suyūṭī, *al-Fariq Bina al-Musanif wa al-Sāriq* ('ālam al-Kutub, 1998).
[60]   Ibid, 33–4.
[61]   Ibid, 40.
[62]   Ibid, 33–4.
[63]   Ibid, 33.
[64]   Ibid, 44.

demonstrate that an Islamic theoretical justification for moral rights is possible. Theories that Muslim jurists used to argue that private ownership is justified in Islamic legal traditions could provide normative support for moral rights protection from an Islamic perspective. As is the case regarding control rights in physical objects, I argued that authors deserve moral rights protection as a reward for their efforts and recognition for human nature's inclination towards control and possession. This conclusion is consistent with the practical ethics of authorship throughout Islamic cultural history. For centuries, Muslim authors documented their belief in religious duty to respect the moral rights to attribution and integrity in both religious and non-religious literature.

4. Against integrity: a feminist theory of moral rights, creative agency and attribution

Carys Craig and Anupriya Dhonchak

1. INTRODUCTION

It is generally agreed that moral rights occupy a unique place within the realm of copyright law. Specifically, unlike the alienable economic rights central to today's copyright system, moral rights assume an intimate and ongoing personal connection between the author and their work that deserves acknowledgement and respect. And yet it is not generally recognized that feminist theory might have something significant to say about the nature of this intimate connection and the personal rights that it seemingly entails. In this chapter, we hope to persuade the reader that a feminist frame does indeed have much to offer when it comes to theorizing, rationalizing and instrumentalizing moral rights in the copyright landscape. Critical feminist scholarship has already explored certain core elements of copyright law, from originality to fair use, providing key insights into the triadic author-work-audience relationship upon which we hope to build.[1] Feminist engagement with moral rights should similarly offer a fresh viewpoint from which to interrogate this particularly controversial but consistently compelling aspect of copyright law and the assumptions on which it depends. Moreover, feminist inquiry serves the crucial purpose of situating power and the ability to exercise it within the privileged discourse of moral rights, authorship and reputation, illuminating a potential path towards its cautious redeployment in service of equality. By reimagining moral rights within a feminist frame, we mean to challenge the false neutrality of these rights within standard legal discourse and practice while embracing their instrumentality in advancing feminist political objectives.

---

[1] See e.g. Ann Bartow, "Fair Use and the Fairer Sex: Gender, Feminism, and Copyright Law" (2006) 14 American University Journal of Gender, Social Policy & the Law 551; Malla Pollack, "Toward a Feminist Theory of the Public Domain, or Rejecting the Gendered Scope of United States Copyrightable and Patentable Subject Matter" (2006) 12 William & Mary Journal of Women and the Law 603; Dan L Burk, "Copyright and Feminism in Digital Media" (2006) 14 American University Journal of Gender, Social Policy & the Law 519; Dan L Burk, "Feminism and Dualism in Intellectual Property Law" (2007) 15 American University Journal of Gender, Social Policy & the Law 183; Carys J Craig, "Reconstructing the Author-Self: Some Feminist Lessons for Copyright Law" (2007) 15 American University Journal of Gender, Social Policy & the Law 207; Carys J Craig, "Feminist Aesthetics and Copyright Law: Genius, Value, and Gendered Visions of the Creative Self" in Irene Calboli and Srividhya Ragavan (eds), *Protecting and Promoting Diversity with Intellectual Property Law* (Cambridge University Press 2015); Sonia K Katyal, "Slash/ing Gender and Intellectual Property: A View from Fan Fiction" in Calboli and Ragavan (eds), ibid; Rebecca Tushnet, "The Romantic Author and the Romance Writer: Resisting Gendered Concepts of Creativity" in Calboli and Ragavan (eds), ibid; John Tehranian, "Copyright's Male Gaze: Authorship and Inequality in a Panoptic World" (2018) 41 Harvard Journal of Law and Gender 343. See generally, Kara W Swanson, "Intellectual Property and Gender: Reflections on Accomplishments and Methodology" (2015) 24 American University Journal of Gender, Social Policy & the Law 175.

Section 2 begins with a brief overview of what is meant by "moral rights" and where these fit in the copyright scheme, both historically and in the current international system. It then lays out the common theoretical justifications offered in support of moral rights, with a view to identifying various facets of conventional moral rights theory that are ill-suited to, or indeed inconsistent with, a feminist philosophy and politics. Section 3 proposes an alternative feminist theoretical framework for interrogating moral rights. It begins by presenting a relational theory of the situated author-self, which in turn entails a conception of authorship as an exercise of expressive agency within a dialogic community. We then consider some potential implications of this theoretical shift for defining and limiting the moral rights of integrity and attribution. In particular, we suggest curtailing the right of integrity to create space for critical, transformative and counter-hegemonic speech; and cautiously consider the strategic power of the attribution right to advance equality through the acknowledgement and amplification of culturally marginalized voices. Ultimately, we conclude, it is possible to reimagine moral rights through a critical feminist lens in a way that better reflects and protects the personal, social and political value of dialogic creativity – but we doubt whether copyright law can serve such ends.

2.   UNDERSTANDING MORAL RIGHTS

2.1   What Are Moral Rights?

The term "moral rights" captures a collection of personal rights of the author, recognized to varying degrees around the world, which run parallel to the economic copyright interests that attach to works of authorship: the right of attribution (the author's right to claim authorship); the right of integrity (the right to object to modifications of the work); the right of disclosure (the right to decide when and how the work will be published); and the right of withdrawal (the right to withdraw a work after publication).[2] Such rights vest in the author and remain with the author (or, after death, with their estate), notwithstanding the transfer or alienation of the economic rights granted by copyright law (the exclusive rights of reproduction, public performance, first publication, and so forth).

By way of example, perhaps the most well-known moral rights action, at least in North America, is the Canadian case of *Snow v. The Eaton Centre*, in which the plaintiff artist, Snow, had sold a sculpture of a flock of geese to the Eaton Centre shopping mall in downtown Toronto. When red ribbons were placed around the necks of the geese as part of the mall's Christmas decorations, Snow sought and obtained an interim injunction, successfully arguing that the ribbons rendered ridiculous his naturalistic sculpture, and so would prejudice his honour and reputation as an artist.[3] The notion that the artist can continue to exercise control over how their work is treated, even after obtaining full value for the transfer of the property and/or the licensing or assignment of copyright to a third party, is precisely what animates the normative debate around moral rights, placing their protection in tension with the efficiencies of clean and unencumbered market transactions.

---

[2]   See Cyrill P Rigamonti, "Deconstructing Moral Rights" (2006) 47 Harv Intl LJ 353, 356.
[3]   *Snow v. The Eaton Centre* (1982) 70 CPR (2d) 105.

Some scattered varieties of moral rights emerged in continental Europe well before the inception of the modern copyright system,[4] but their conceptual solidification as a cohesive body of non-transferrable creators' rights (*droit moral* in France and *Persönlichkeitsrecht* in Germany) occurred only towards the end of the nineteenth century.[5] The internationalization of moral rights was later achieved by their inclusion, in 1928, in the Berne Convention for the Protection of Literary and Artistic Works (Berne), which essentially codified the rights of attribution and integrity.[6] Under the Berne mandate, an author "shall have the right to claim authorship of the work and to object to any distortion, mutilation or other modification of, or other derogatory action in relation to, the said work, which would be prejudicial to his honor or reputation".[7] Today, however, moral rights occupy an uneasy position in the global copyright context, assigned to a category separate from – and lesser to – the economic rights around which our international copyright system is built. When the Agreement on Trade-Related Aspects of Intellectual Property Rights Protection (TRIPS) was concluded, the relevant article of the Berne Convention was carved out of the compliance obligations of member states.[8] In spite of Berne and the "largely symbolic references to moral rights" built into the 1948 Universal Declaration of Human Rights and the 1966 International Covenant on Economic, Social, and Cultural Rights,[9] moral rights have remained the poor cousin of the economic rights enshrined in multilateral trade agreements.[10] Given the conceptual and practical cleavage between moral and economic rights, this hierarchy is readily understandable: the economic rights are an instrument of exploitation that fits well with the commodification of copyright

---

[4] See e.g. Cyrill P Rigamonti, "The Conceptual Transformation of Moral Rights" (2007) 55 Am J Comp L 67.

[5] See ibid 92–3; Marilyn Randall, *Pragmatic Plagiarism: Authorship, Profit and Power* (Toronto: University of Toronto Press, 2001), 80–1, 93.

[6] See Rigamonti (n 4) 356, citing eg Lionel Bently and Brad Sherman, *Intellectual Property Law* (2nd edn, Oxford University Press 2004) 232.

[7] Berne Convention for the Protection of Literary and Artistic Works, 24 July 1971, 25 UST 1341, 828 UNTS 221 (Berne Convention).

[8] Agreement on Trade Related Aspects of Intellectual Property Rights, Art. 9(1), 15 April 1994, Marrakesh Agreement Establishing the World Trade Organization, Annex 1C, Legal Instruments – Results of the Uruguay Round, 33 ILM 81 ("[m]embers shall not have rights or obligations under this Agreement in respect of the rights conferred under Article 6bis of that Convention or of the rights derived therefrom"); International Covenant on Economic, Social, and Cultural Rights, GA Res 2200A (XXI), art 15(1)(c), UN GAOR, 21st Sess, Supp No 16, at 49, UN Doc A/6316 (1966), 993 UNTS 3 (declaring the right of every individual to "benefit from the protection of the moral and material interests resulting from any scientific, literary or artistic production of which he is the author").

[9] Universal Declaration of Human Rights, GA Res 217A (III), art 27(2), UN Doc A/810 (10 December 1948) (stating "the right to the protection of the moral and material interests resulting from any scientific, literary or artistic production of which he is the author").

[10] Moral rights provisions were also notably absent from The Universal Copyright Convention, 6 September 1952, 6 UST 2731, 216 UNTS 132, *revised* 24 July 1971, 25 UST 1341, 943 UNTS 178, and the North American Free Trade Agreement US-Can.-Mex., 17 December 1992, §§ 1701(2)(b), 1701(3), annex 1701.3(2), 32 ILM 605 ("[n]otwithstanding Article 1701(2)(b), this Agreement confers no rights and imposes no obligations on the United States with respect to Article 6bis of the Berne Convention, or the rights derived from that Article"), *revised* 30 November 2018. One notable exception to the general exclusion of moral rights from international treaties post-*Berne* is the World Intellectual Property Organization (WIPO) Copyright Treaty (WCT), Art. 1(4), 20 December 1996, 36 ILM 65, and indeed the expansion of moral rights to performing artists by the WIPO Performances and Phonograms Treaty (WPPT), Art. 5, 20 December 1996, 36 ILM 76. See generally Rigamonti (n 4) 356–9.

in the international trade regime, while moral rights are effectively (and by design) a potential restraint on such economic exploitation. But it is worth interrogating further our sense of these competing conceptualizations of economic and moral rights – and asking what else, beyond the machinations of the modern marketplace, is at stake in the distinction.

2.2   Troubling Traditional Moral Rights Theories

2.2.1   The economic/moral divide

The distinction between moral and economic rights is indeed typically cast as one between the mundanity of the market and the spirituality of the authorial enterprise. Canada's Supreme Court has explained it thus, in the paradigm shifting case of *Théberge v. Galerie d'Art du Petit Champlain Inc.*:

> The economic rights are based on a conception of artistic and literary works essentially as articles of commerce. (Indeed, the initial *Copyright Act, 1709* (U.K.), 8 Ann., c. 21, was passed to assuage the concerns of printers, not authors.) Consistently with this view, such rights can be bought and sold … The owner of the copyright, thus, can be, but need not be, the author of the work … Moral rights, by contrast, descend from the civil law tradition. They adopt a more elevated and less dollars and cents view of the relationship between an artist and his or her work. They treat the artist's *œuvre* as an extension of his or her personality, possessing a dignity which is deserving of protection. They focus on the artist's right … to protect throughout the duration of the economic rights (even where these have been assigned elsewhere) both the integrity of the work and his or her authorship of it (or anonymity, as the author wishes).[11]

Almost a century prior to this ruling in *Théberge*, Chief Justice Fitzpatrick of the Supreme Court of Canada drew the distinction along similar lines in *Morang & Co. v. LeSueur* when interpreting the rights of an author to reclaim his alienated but unpublished manuscript:

> I cannot agree that the sale of the manuscript of a book is subject to the same rules as the sale of any other article of commerce, *e.g.*, paper, grain or lumber. The vendor of such things loses all dominion over them when once the contract is executed and the purchaser may deal with the thing which he has purchased as he chooses. It is his to keep, to alienate or to destroy. But … [a]fter the author has parted with his pecuniary interest in the manuscript, he retains a species of personal or moral right in the product of his brain.[12]

For our purposes, it is worth pausing here to note that this distinction between the public and the private – between the public realm of commercial exchange and the intimate realm of personal relationship – maps onto the public/private divide that "is central to almost two centuries of feminist writing and political struggle; it is, ultimately, what the feminist movement is about".[13] Recognizing the way in which the law perpetuated inequality by separating the public from the private sphere, first wave feminists mobilized under the banner "The personal is political".[14] Second wave feminists sought to show how the gendering of public and private

---

[11]   2002 SCC 34, [2002] 2 SCR 336 [12]–[14] (*Théberge*).
[12]   *Morang & Co v. LeSueur* (1911), 45 SCR 95 [97]–[98], cited in ibid [16].
[13]   Carole Pateman, "Feminist Critiques of the Public/Private Dichotomy" in SI Benn and GF Gaus (eds), *Public and Private in Social Life* (Croom Helm 1983) 281.
[14]   See Charlotte Krølokke and Anne Scott Sørenson, "Three Waves of Feminism: From Suffragettes to Grrls" in Charlotte Krølokke and Anne Scott Sørenson (eds), *Gender Communication Theories & Analyses: From Silence to Performance* (SAGE Publications 2005) 1–23.

explained the subordination of women, while subsequent waves have sought to destabilize the conceptual pairing, deconstructing the distinction.[15] A critical theoretical approach understands such binaries in law as choices about what to privilege and what to suppress. By mapping economic/moral rights onto a gendered binary of public/private, it can come as no surprise to the critical feminist scholar that the distinction between economic and moral rights would be a hierarchical one, with the feminized personal side of the binary being marginalized in law and structurally subordinated.

Similarly, feminists might note, the economic/moral divide mirrors the rational/emotional binary that is even more obviously infused with a gendered masculine/feminine hierarchy. In copyright circles, the moral rights' claim of the author is often eyed with suspicion as inherently subjective and vulnerable to the artist's emotional caprice, in contrast to the practical reason and rationality that surely steers the copyright owner and their exploitation of the economic right.

Already, then, a critical feminist insight reveals the gendered nature of the moral right and its "feminization", and offers up a way to understand – and to question – the relative subordination of moral rights within the conventional copyright scheme. But of course, this is not the end of the matter. It should also come as no surprise that the defence of moral rights and their import is typically presented in terms that implicitly resist this feminization by reframing the personal or emotional connection at the core of the moral right claim in more masculinized terms of individual proprietary right (the power to exclude others) or paternal control, measured in terms of public reputation and honour. So let us turn now to consider this conventional moral rights' orthodoxy and its feminist critique.

2.2.2   Moral rights and personhood theories

The common theoretical justification for the protection of moral rights rests upon personhood theories "derived loosely from the writings of Kant and Hegel".[16] These personhood theories emphasize the author's special connection with his work, which is, in the Hegelian formulation, regarded as an extension of the author's personality into the external world.[17] What follows as a matter of natural justice from this outward externalization of the author's free will is the appropriative power to claim ownership over the work as an externalized object, and for that property right to be recognized as such by others.[18] In the Kantian formulation,

---

[15]   See Michael Warner, "Public/Private" in Catharine R Stimpson and Gilbert Herdt (eds), *Critical Terms for the Study of Gender* (University of Chicago Press 2014).

[16]   William W Fisher, "Theories of Intellectual Property" in Stephen R Munzer (ed.), *New Essays in the Legal and Political Theory of Property* (Cambridge University Press 2001) 171. See also Neil Netanel, "Alienability Restrictions and the Enhancement of Author Autonomy in United States and Continental Copyright Law" (1994) 12 Cardozo Arts & Entertainment Law Journal 1, 7–20.

[17]   GWF Hegel, *The Philosophy of Right* (TM Knox tr, Oxford University Press 1967); Hegel, "Remarks on Intellectual Property" (Berlin 1821) in L Bently and M Kretschmer (eds), *Primary Sources on Copyright (1450–1900)* (2008) http://www.copyrighthistory.org/record/d_1821. See generally, Justin Hughes, "The Philosophy of Intellectual Property" (1988) 77 Geo L J 287.

[18]   Maurizio Borghi, "Copyright, property and personality. Note on Hegel" https:// eprints .bournemouth.ac.uk/31036/3/Copyright%20property%20and%20personality_final.pdf; Hughes (n 17); Peter Drahos, *A Philosophy of Intellectual Property* (Dartmouth 1996). But see also Jeanne L Schroeder, "Unnatural Rights: Hegel and Intellectual Property" (2006) 60 U Miami L Rev 453 (disputing the conventional Hegelian theory of copyright and moral rights, and explaining that, for Hegel, such a right is actually *unnatural*).

the work is cast not as a thing but rather as a speech act, uttered by the author in his own name (and which no one else can therefore copy without speaking on his behalf).[19] In both versions, however, the author's entitlement to control the work – *le droit d'auteur* – emanates from the investment of his personality and individuality, through which he lays a proprietorial claim to the externalized products of his free and independent mind.

The scope of this entitlement, and in particular the degree of ongoing control over use and alienability that the author enjoys – or that Kant or Hegel would have approved – over the work remain the subject of debate amongst proponents of either variety of personhood theory; but our interest here is not in debating the nuances of Kant or Hegel's philosophical contentions. What is clear is that the author's rights, presented through a personhood frame, are firmly rooted in enlightenment notions of independence, free will and private appropriation. Moreover, rightly or wrongly, these personality-based justifications are ideologically intertwined with romantic conceptions of the individualized self.[20]

Of course, such enlightenment conceptions of selfhood have also been a target of sustained feminist critique. The fiction of the atomistic self, with its dual claim to individuality and universalizability, has been attacked as disguising difference and so neutralizing a history of domination, subordination and exclusion. It also discounts the lived reality of interdependence and social situatedness. This omission, as Shelley Wright explains, is reflected in the copyright discourse:

> The existing definition of copyright as both economic and personal within a political or civil context presupposes that individuals live in isolation from one another, that the individual is an autonomous unit who creates artistic works and sells them, or permits their sale by others, while ignoring the individual's relationship with others within her community, family, ethnic group, religion … The community has only the most tenuous identity. Society itself is seen as an aggregate of anomic individuals, each separate, segregated, fragmented … , This vision … places the emphasis on the individual rights of the artist as a "creator"…[21]

A significant body of copyright scholarship has directed critical attention to the mythology of this romantic authorship – the lone original genius that inhabits copyright's normative core – arguing that it distorts our understanding of deserving authorship, neglecting the role of community, shared culture and collaboration in the creative process.[22] As one of us (Craig) has argued elsewhere, this romantic author-figure is not only profoundly ideological and

---

[19]   Abraham Drassinower, *What's Wrong with Copying?* (Harvard University Press 2015). See also Anne Barron, "Kant, Copyright and Communicative Freedom" (2012) 31 Law and Philosophy 1; Kim Treiger-Bar-Am, "Kant on Copyright: Rights of Transformative Authorship" (2008) 25:3 Cardozo Arts & Entertainment Law Journal 1059.

[20]   See Schroeder (n 18) 453–4 ("The personality theory of property that dominates American intellectual property scholarship is imbued by a romanticism that is completely antithetic to Hegel's project").

[21]   Shelley Wright, "A Feminist Exploration of the Legal Protection of Art" (1994) 7 Canadian Journal of Women and the Law 59, 73–4.

[22]   See e.g. Martha Woodmansee, "The Genius and the Copyright: Economic and Legal Conditions of the Emergence of the 'Author'" (1984) 17 Eighteenth-Century Studies 425; Peter Jaszi, "Toward a Theory of Copyright: The Metamorphoses of 'Authorship'" [1991] Duke LJ 455; Martha Woodmansee and Peter Jaszi (eds), *The Construction of Authorship: Textual Appropriation in Law and Literature* (Duke University Press 1994); James Boyle, "The Search for an Author: Shakespeare and the Framers" (1988) 37 Am U L Rev 625; James Boyle, *Shamans, Software and Spleens: Law and the Construction of the Information Society* (Harvard University Press 1996).

historically contingent, but also reflects a patriarchal ideal derived from what feminist literary theorists have identified as a strongly gendered vision of creativity and genius.[23]

But perhaps the easier route to the conclusion that Hegelian theories of selfhood and artistic expression are inherently gendered is to point to the words of Hegel himself:

> the difference in the physical characteristics of the two sexes has a rational basis and consequently acquires an intellectual and ethical significance ... man has his actual and substantive life in the state, in learning and so forth, as well as in labour and struggle with the external world ... Woman, on the other hand, has her substantive destiny in the family and to be imbued with family piety is her ethical frame of mind.[24]
>
> Women are capable of education, but they are not made for activities which demand a universal faculty such as the more advanced sciences, philosophy and certain forms of artistic production. Women may have happy ideas, taste and elegance, but they cannot attain to the ideal.[25]
>
> Women are educated – who knows how? – as it were by breathing in ideas, by living rather than by acquiring knowledge. The status of manhood, on the other hand is attained only by the stress of thought and much technical exertion.[26]

Similarly, Kant's writing on aesthetics and the sublime[27] explicitly excluded women from the ranks of genius on the basis that woman are passionate creatures, whereas genius is a matter of reason.[28] For Kant, women's overriding duty was to *be* beautiful, to pursue feminine qualities of grace, charm, domesticity, from which it followed that the pursuit of knowledge or deep understanding was defeminizing: the woman who knew Greek or mechanics "might as well even have a beard", he wrote, and the woman who succeeds in laborious learning "destroy[s] the merits that are proper to her sex".[29] Further denigrating remarks about women are scattered throughout Kant's writings,[30] earning him the "unhappy status as the modern moral philosopher feminists find most objectionable".[31]

It might reasonably be objected that these statements of Hegel and Kant simply reflect an essentialism around sexual difference that is more attributable to historical context and a failure of imagination than any inherent flaw in their theories of personhood per se.[32] Indeed, many scholars have looked to rehabilitate Hegelian and even Kantian philosophies for feminist

---

[23]   See Carys J Craig, "Reconstructing the Author-Self: Some Feminist Lessons for Copyright Law" (2007) 15 American University Journal of Gender, Social Policy & the Law 207.

[24]   GWF Hegel, *The Phenomenology of Spirit* (AV Miller tr, Oxford University Press 1977) #474, 287 (cited in Antoinette M Stafford, "The Feminist Critique of Hegel on Women and the Family" (Animus 2, 1997) https://www2.grenfell.mun.ca/animus/Articles/Volume%202/stafford1.pdf 69).

[25]   Hegel (n 24) #166 Addition (cited in Stafford (n 24) 69).

[26]   Hegel (n 24) #166 Addition (cited in Stafford (n 24) 70).

[27]   Immanuel Kant, *The Critique of Judgment* (first published 1790, Werner S Pluhar tr, Hackett 1987).

[28]   Christine Battersby, *Gender and Genius: Towards a Feminist Aesthetics* (Quartet Books 1994) 113.

[29]   Immanuel Kant, *Observations on the Feeling of the Beautiful and Sublime* (first published 1764, John T Goldthwait tr, University of California Press 1960) 78 (cited in ibid 112).

[30]   See generally Kurt Mosser, "Kant and Feminism" (1999) *Philosophy Faculty Publications* 21 https://ecommons.udayton.edu/phl_fac_pub/21.

[31]   Barbara Herman, "Could It Be Worth Thinking about Kant on Sex and Marriage?" in L Antony and C Witt, (eds), *A Mind of One's Own* (Westview Press 1993) 50.

[32]   Compare Seyla Benhabib, "On Hegel, Women and Irony" in Mary Shanley and Carol Pateman (eds), *Feminist Interpretations and Political Theory* (Pennsylvania University Press 1991) 84.

purposes.[33] We do not mean to dismiss the value or promise of such efforts, broadly speaking. More specifically, in the intellectual property context, we recognize the important work of scholars such as Margaret Jane Radin and Anne Barron who draw on Hegelian and Kantian philosophies, respectively, to advance positions on art and ownership that arguably avoid patriarchal assumptions and resonate with a feminist politics of empowerment.[34]

In our view, however, statements such as those of Hegel and Kant quoted above reveal the fundamentally gendered nature of the theoretical premises – the conceptions of selfhood, autonomy, ethics and aesthetics – upon which the conventional moral rights orthodoxy is built. These justificatory frameworks have their foundations in theories that specifically and explicitly denied the intellectual capabilities and creative capacities of women. As Deborah Halbert notes, "[t]he origins of intellectual property law, authorship, originality, and plagiarism are indebted to understanding creation as the domain of males who are the only ones authorized to speak and write".[35] From a feminist perspective, then, it is hard to imagine why these theoretical frameworks, extracted and extrapolated from the misogynistic musings of eighteenth century white men, should be endorsed today and embraced as a conceptual starting point for a normative theory of moral rights.[36] As we suggest below, from such a starting point, further silencing and systematic exclusion seem all but inevitable.

2.2.3 Paternity and patriarchy

It should also be unsurprising that what flows from masculinist theories of authorship and entitlement is, predictably, a claim right over the work with its own tinge of patriarchy. The author's moral right to have their name attached to a work they created is commonly known as the "right to *paternity*".[37] Authorial attribution is the right to be identified and so to protect the patrilineal line, as it were. The paternity metaphor supports the notion that "the work of art is an extension of the artist himself", such that the artist/father feels personal anguish when something is done to his artist/child (even if the artist/father has chosen to sell that artwork/child, as Amy Adler wryly notes).[38] Indeed, the integrity right extends to protect the artist/father against associations that might be prejudicial to his honour and reputation. The notion

---

[33] See e.g. Kimblerly Hutchings, *Hegel and Feminist Philosophy* (Wiley 2003); Kimberley Hutchings and Tuija Pulkkinen (eds.) *Hegel's Philosophy and Feminist Thought: Beyond Antigone?* (Palgrave Macmillan 2010); Carol Hay, "A Feminist Defence of Kant" in *Kantianism, Liberalism, and Feminism: Resisting Oppression* (Palgrave MacMillan 2013); Anne Barron, "Feminism, Aestheticism and the Limits of Law" (2000) 8(3) Feminist Legal Studies 275.

[34] See e.g. Margaret Jane Radin, "Property and Personhood" (1982) 34 Stanford Law Review 5; Anne Baron, "Kant, Copyright and Communicative Freedom" (2012) 31 Law and Philosophy 1.

[35] Deborah Halbert, "Poaching and Plagiarizing: Property, Plagiarism, and Feminist Futures" in Lise Buranen and Alice M Roy (eds), *Perspectives on Plagiarism and Intellectual Property in a Postmodern World* (State University of New York Press 1999).

[36] We recognize, however, the important work that has been done by feminist scholars bringing both Hegelian and Kantian theory to bear in respect of intellectual property, art and ownership. See especially, Anne Barron, "Kant, Copyright and Communicative Freedom" (2012) 31 Law and Philosophy 1.

[37] See Mark Rose, "Mothers and Authors: Johnson v. Calvert and the New Children of Our Imaginations" (1996) 22 Critical Inquiry 613, 614. See also Amy Adler, "Against Moral Rights" (2009) 97 Cal L Rev 263 at 269 (critiquing the notion that the "work of art is an extension of the artist himself", and noting her choice of the term "himself" in light of the "metaphor of paternity").

[38] Adler (n 37) 269.

that one's metaphorical offspring can, in their social or cultural interactions or adaptations, bring shame or dishonour to the paternal line is similarly a deeply patriarchal one.

Christine Battersby's blistering critique of the gendering of genius takes aim at the metaphor of authorship as "male motherhood", which became common in nineteenth century aesthetics and still persists in the portrayal of the author as conceiving, gestating, labouring and birthing the creative work.[39] As Mark Rose observes in his insightful article on "Mothers and Authors", the analogy of authorship to procreation invokes the gendered mind/body (male/female, intellect/matter) dichotomy, with the necessary implication that "authorship is a gendered category".[40]

William Patry has also criticized the "creation-as-birth" metaphor and the way it is wielded to suggest that authors should enjoy extensive control over their works.[41] In urging the passage of the first modern copyright statute, Daniel Defoe declared: "A Book is the Author's Property, 'tis the Child of his Inventions, the Brat of his Brain; ... 'tis as much his own, as his Wife and Children."[42] The oft-quoted words of Nathaniel Shaler also exemplify this link between paternity and property: "The man who brings out of the nothingness some child of his thought, has rights therein which cannot belong to any other sort of property."[43] Such statements gesture at the patriarchal link between Romantic authorship and *le droit d'auteur*: conjuring up "patriarchal domesticity; the author as master of his household".[44] The relationship between the male author-mother and his text-child is not presented as one of maternal nurturing, but rather one of paternal control. The author's work is complete – his paternal claim established – with the act of conception/creation; it requires no ongoing relationship of care.[45] The paternal author-figure seeks only recognition for the work's successes and control over its subsequent social interactions lest they diminish the esteem in which he is held. But more fundamentally, the male motherhood metaphor mischaracterizes the creative process itself. Recast through the prism of patriarchy, the collaborative conditions of creative (re)production – biological and authorial – disappear from view:

> [T]he paternity metaphor obscures the fact that literary works are the products of complex collaborations in which many individuals are involved ... , and that literary works are produced through acts of generation that involve the adaptation and transformation of materials from the literary gene pool rather than creation out of nothingness ... The paternity metaphor is patriarchal and obsolete. More significantly, the entire conception of authorship embedded in the paternity trope is obsolete. We need a better biology of authorship.[46]

The masculinist underpinnings of traditional theories of personhood, authorship and appropriative power cast a shadow over conventional conceptions of moral rights and their common

---

[39]   Battersby (n 28) 107 ("The artist conceived, was pregnant, labored (in sweat and pain), was delivered, and (in an uncontrolled ecstasy of agonized – male – control) brought forth. These were the images of 'natural' childbirth that the male creators elaborated").

[40]   Rose (n 37) 623.

[41]   William Patry, *Moral Panics and the Copyright Wars* (Oxford University Press 2009) 69–70.

[42]   Mark Rose, *Authors and Owners: The Invention of Copyright* (Harvard University Press 1993) 39.

[43]   ibid 9 (quoting Nathan Shaler, *Considerations on the Nature of Intellectual Property and Its Importance to the State* (1878) 9).

[44]   Mark Rose, "Copyright and its Metaphors" (2002) 50 U Cal LA L Rev 1, 5.

[45]   Thanks are due to Wendy Gordon for bringing this point into focus.

[46]   ibid 14–15.

justifications. Any feminist reimagining of moral rights must therefore begin by rejecting this gendered vision of the author-self and reconceptualizing creativity. Only with a better *ontology* of authorship can we conceive a different vision of the author's moral claim – and its limits.

3.   REIMAGINING MORAL RIGHTS

3.1   A Feminist Relational Theory of the Author-self

As we have seen, copyright law protects the moral rights of the artist, but "[t]he image of the 'artist' underlying the words of the *Copyright Act* is that of the solitary male genius, isolated both spatially and temporally from his community and the background of the art in which he works".[47] A feminist theory of authorship resists the romantic myth of individual origination and instead firmly locates the creativity of author-self in the context of cultural situation and social relations. In doing so, however, feminist theorists must also be wary of communitarian conceptions of selfhood that threaten to undermine agency by subsuming the self within her social situation; and of postmodernist deconstructions of the author-figure that potentially disaggregate both her selfhood and meaning-making capacity. Feminist political engagements with moral rights must, after all, begin from a place of reckoning with the invisibilization of women's artistic productions and the "scratching out of women's writing as a historical and political process".[48] The challenge is to interrogate the systematic exclusion, suppression, appropriation and mutilation of women's creative contributions without falling into the trap of reinforcing the ideologies of possessive individualism, romantic aesthetic value and patriarchal control that the feminist project seeks to upset.

One possible path to this end, as Craig has argued more fully elsewhere, begins with a feminist relational understanding of the author-self.[49] Relational theory takes as its premise that "persons are socially embedded and that their identities form within the context of social relationships".[50] Genuine autonomy is not a matter of independence but product of *inter*dependence, as legal theorist Jennifer Nedelsky explains, and the exercise of "autonomy within relations" demands that we are "always in a creative process of interaction, of mutual shaping, with all the dimensions of our existence".[51] Creativity – including artistic creativity – is a vital component of this capacity to resist and transform existing patterns and structures:

> Part of what we cherish in the *human capacity* for innovation, for *artistic creation*, for new forms of social relations … is the ability of individuals not to be determined by their history or the prevailing

---

[47]   Shelley Wright, "A Feminist Exploration of the Legal Protection of Art" (1994) 7 Canadian Journal of Women and the Law 59, 62.

[48]   Somer Brodribb, *Nothing Mat(t)ers: A Feminist Critique of Postmodernism* (Spinifex Press 1992) xxiii.

[49]   See Carys J Craig, *Copyright, Communication and Culture: Towards a Relational Theory of Copyright Law* (Edward Elgar Publishing 2011). See also, Carys Craig and Ian Kerr, "The Death of the AI Author" (2021) 52 Ottawa Law Review 31, 81–6.

[50]   Catriona Mackenzie and Natalie Stoljar, *Relational Autonomy: Feminist Perspectives on Autonomy, Agency, and the Social Self* (Oxford University Press 2000) 4 (cited in Robert Leckey, *Contextual Subjects: Family, State and Relational Theory* (University of Toronto Press 2008) 18).

[51]   ibid.

norms and practices of their communities. We observe and honour the capacity to bring forth the new, to create, to transform, to resist.[52]

The human creative capacity allows us "to envision something new, to shift ... the terms of relations – whether through an idea, an invention, art ...". Although this involves a capacity, "at least in small ways to be imaginative and innovative", she explains, "[i]t is important not to read the above as invoking a human capacity for greatness or genius".[53] A relational approach means resisting the "caricature" of the independent man and recognizing that the creative capacity for imagination comes from within the human actor "enabled by her relational web".[54]

Recast in these terms, what is at stake when we talk about the author's "honour" is not protecting the reputation and honour of the great artist as independent originator, but rather honouring the creative capacity of the author as an exercise of expressive agency and relational autonomy. What may merit or require protection, then, is not "the fundamental category of the-man-and-his-work",[55] but the "mutual, reciprocal, communicative social interactions [that] are necessary for the formation, sustenance, and repair of the self".[56] What might this mean for our vision of moral rights?

3.2   A Feminist Reflection on the Right of Integrity

3.2.1   Authorship as dialogue

A relational theory casts authorship as discursive interaction as opposed to independent origination. The author's work is not reducible, from this perspective, to a stable object of property to be owned, but is rather an act of communication – and so a site of discursive struggle. It is, in the terms of literary scholar Mikhail Bakhtin, a dialogic utterance. The idea of authorship as relational meaning-making – as *dialogue* – is a powerful one that resists the reification of the text while also refusing to deny the creative capacity of the author-as-speaker. A Bakhtinian approach portrays discourse as inherently dialogic and multivocal: every text contains within it a myriad of voices that stand in dialogic relationship with one another. From a feminist perspective, this discredits formalistic, ahistorical analyses of language and literature (those which privileged the solitary author as the monologic source of meaning) while also emancipating subordinated voices (which are recognized as interactive and interanimating).[57] Rather than a binary opposition between, say, the marginal woman's voice and the central dominant male voice, dialogism invites "exploration and activating of the unvoiced exiled world of women".[58]

---

[52]   ibid 51 (emphasis added).
[53]   Jennifer Nedelsky, *Law's Relations: A Relational Theory of Self, Autonomy, and Law* (Oxford University Press 2011) 48.
[54]   ibid 73.
[55]   Michel Foucault, "What Is an Author?" in Paul Rabinow (ed.), *The Foucault Reader* (Vintage 1984) 101.
[56]   Amy Allen, "Foucault, Feminism and the Self: The Politics of Personal Transformation" in Dianna Taylor and Karen Vintges (eds), *Feminism and the Final Foucault* (University of Illinois Press 2004) 240 (quoted by Leckey, *Contextual Subjects: Family, State and Relational Theory* (University of Toronto Press 2008) 8).
[57]   Laurie A Finke, *Feminist Theory, Women's Writing* (Cornell University Press 1992) 111.
[58]   Mary O'Connor, "Subject, Voice, and Women in Some Contemporary Black American Women's Writing" in David M Bauer and Susan J McKinstry (eds), *Feminism, Bakhtin, and the Dialogic* (State University of New York Press 1991) 214–15.

Moreover, dialogic textuality drags the power struggle over meaning out into the open: "by articulating otherness, [it] inevitably articulates the powers attempting to marginalize or eliminate otherness".[59] It also illuminates the way that texts exist within and over time (in the context of an "utterance chain") responding to what has gone before (the *already spoken*), and anticipating that which might be to come (the *not yet spoken*).[60] It is along this "chain of speech communication" that meaning-making happens.[61] The social nature of dialogue defies closure and finality and perpetually serves, instead, as a "vehicle for reformulating old elements into new patterns".[62]

The dialogic nature of authorship has much to tell us about the appropriate limits of copyright and the power of control that it can and should confer to the author of any particular text. It throws into doubt the "original" author's claim over the work, by revealing the extent to which each utterance is informed by and dependent on others for its meaning; and it underscores the need to leave space for others' dialogic responses along the utterance chain.[63] The work that copyright hails as one author's original expression is in fact "a profoundly intertextual social unit".[64] In Bakhtin's terms, "[t]he speaker is not [the biblical] Adam, and therefore the subject of his speech itself inevitably becomes the arena where his opinions ... meet others' speech ...".[65] When each work is seen as a link in the chain of communication, we can see more clearly the harm that can be done to communicative practices when we seek to sever those links through law's construction of copyright. In the arena of social discourse, there is a risk to rendering the work as a stable, free-standing entity, somehow shielded by law from the dynamics of dialogism.

It could reasonably be contended, at this point, that the dialogic nature of authorship supports the protection of the moral right of integrity. Lior Zemer argues along these lines that moral rights "foster genuine dialogue" by ensuring that "the author, in his capacity as the other, received protection for his expression and that the public receives accurate information based on the real message and meaning intended by the author".[66] The notion is that "genuine dialogue requires seeing the other *qua* other, that is, as he wishes to be seen and treated" – a principle that is protected "by moral rights that preserve the integrity of the author's creative

---

[59] See Gale M Schwab, "Irigarayan Dialogism: Play and Powerplay" in ibid. See generally Dale Bauer, *Feminist Dialogics: A Theory of Failed Community* (State University of New York Press 1988) (adding gender considerations to refashion Bakhtin's sociological stylistics into feminist dialogics).

[60] Carys J Craig, "Transforming 'Total Concept & Feel': Dialogic Creativity and Copyright's Substantial Similarity Doctrine" (2021) 38 Cardozo Arts & Entertainment Law Journal 603, 609–12. See also, Leslie Baxter, *Voicing Relationships: A Dialogic Perspective* (Sage Publications 2010) 51.

[61] ibid 51, quoting Mikhail Bakhtin, "The Problem of Speech Genres" in Caryl Emerson and Michael Holquist (eds), *Speech Genres & Other Late Essays* (Vern W McGee tr, University of Texas Press 1986) 93.

[62] Lior Zemer, "Dialogical Transactions" (2016) 95 Oregon Law Review 141.

[63] See generally Craig (n 60).

[64] Baxter (n 60) 52.

[65] Bakhtin (n 61) 94. Bakhtin continues: "[A]n utterance is a link in the chain of speech communication, and it cannot be broken off from the preceding links that determine it both from within and from without, giving rise within it to unmediated responsive reactions and dialogic reverberations."

[66] Zemer (n 62) 187–8.

text its 'meaning and message'".[67] The idea of seeing and being seen surely appeals to feminists seeking recognition of women's voices and involvement in the creation of meaning.

In our view, however, this vision of dialogue that supports the integrity right still clings to a Romantic vision of the author-work relationship (the text as bounded by the intentions of the author and therefore as a projection of his creative soul),[68] and gives insufficient regard to intertextuality and the centrality of dialogic practice. Taking dialogue seriously means abandoning the belief "that we can discern, let alone police, artistic intention, that it is necessarily relevant to the meaning of a work".[69] A multitude of meanings and a myriad of voices already reside *within* the work, which is – even if unaltered – in a constant process of being reworked and re-authored. Dialogism wholly displaces the premise that a work contains a true and intended "meaning and message", bestowed by the author and under his control; it therefore rejects the conclusion that other meanings and messages imposed upon or extracted from the work are mistaken or distortive and to be prevented.[70] The notion of an author's authority and capacity to control meaning beyond the act of communication simply suffers from a fatal "confusion about the ontological status of ideal objects and their relationship to their creators".[71]

3.2.2   The politics of protecting integrity

From a critical feminist perspective, it should be stressed, there is an important political component to what might seem like a philosophical quibble: the moral right of integrity – the power to prevent unwelcome distortions, modifications and associations – erects barriers to dialogue in ways that we believe threaten to disempower the transformative and critical voices of those who do not fit the dominant authorial mould. Of course, the idea of preventing the mutilation or distortion of works may hold appeal for those who are used to seeing their narratives twisted and their stories co-opted by dominant culture – and to the extent that moral rights can be politically harnessed to push back against such uses, we support that pragmatic stance as a matter of social justice.[72] But if, as we know, the copyright system privileges a par-

---

[67]   ibid 187, citing Roberta Rosenthall Kwall, *The Soul of Creativity: Forging A Moral Rights Law For The United States* (Stanford University Press 2010) 58.

[68]   ibid 187 (explaining that the right of integrity "gives an author the exclusive right to project his 'soul of creativity,'" and describing the relationship between work and author as resembling that of "a parent and child". Citing Kwall (n 67) 6, XIV). But see also Lior Zemer, "Moral Rights: Limited Edition" (2011) 91 B U L Rev 1519, 1561-7 (agreeing with Kwall on the need for moral rights, but departing from the neo-Romantic individualism that grounds her argument).

[69]   Adler (n 37) 277.

[70]   Compare Rebecca Tushnet, "Naming Rights: Attribution and Law" (2007) 3 Utah Law Review 781, 801–2 (rejecting the premise that works contain "a proper, intended message or set of messages" and that "unintended interpretations are misreadings to be minimizing").

[71]   Tom Palmer, "Are Patents and Copyright Morally Justified? The Philosophy of Property Rights and Ideal Objects" (2001) 13 Harv J L & Pub Policy 817, 843. See also Adler (n 37).

[72]   See e.g. Kevin J Greene, "'Copynorms,' Black Cultural Production, and the Debate over African-American Reparations" (2008) 25 Cardozo Arts & Entertainment Law Journal 1179, 1203 (noting that "African-American artists have been particularly vulnerable to moral rights violations of attribution and integrity", such that US copyright law's refusal to protect the right of paternity "further burden[s] Black cultural production"); KJ Greene, "Intellectual Property at the Intersection of Race and Gender: Lady Sings the Blues" (2008) 16 American University Journal of Gender, Social Policy & the Law 365, 372 (identifying the general absence, in the US copyright law, of moral rights protections against harms to authorial dignity as a doctrinal factor that disadvantages black cultural production). See also Anthea Kraut, *Choreographing Copyright: Race, Gender, and Intellectual Property Rights in*

ticular kind of creator – the dominant author hailed for his ostensible original genius – then the right to integrity is most likely to disproportionately disadvantage downstream creators excluded from this authorship trope. In particular, we fear, it can be wielded against culturally subordinated creators who "use the expressive tools of the dominant culture to 'talk back' to inequality".[73] When the author's right to control his intended meaning is invoked, we have to ask for whom his message was intended. This use of existing works to create new meanings, by those who were never intended to interact with the work concerned, is transgressive. It is a means to claim cultural space by those who have been ousted from it.

Sarah Ahmed describes the ability of "queer use" to disrupt existing meanings, to make audible alternative interpretations, and so to deny history (or those who would write it) a final say over what *the* meaning of anything can be.[74] Acts of recycling, reusing and reorienting works to alter one's historic relation to them powerfully reveal the temporality and fragility of meaning signified by existing cultural expressions. Consider, for example, the queering of *Swan Lake*. Choreographer Matthew Bourne's celebrated re-gendering of the ballet upsets the conventional categories of sex, gender and desire, subverting the "traditional expectations of male spectatorship and female objectification" that permeates the world of classical ballet, and the "taken-for granted heterosexuality" of the "male gaze".[75] Challenging the established meaning and value of existing works communicates a refusal by the later user-creator to venerate – or serve as a willing vessel of – dominant cultural understandings. Now consider the controversy over Samuel Beckett's classic play, *Waiting for Godot*, traditionally played by five male actors. Beckett's estate has actively sought to enjoin productions that cast women in these roles, demanding fidelity to Beckett's original intentions.[76] As Guy Rub notes, however, it is not obvious that Beckett would have held the same views were he alive today. Nor is it obvious why we should permit the diversity norms of a prior era to dictate the rules for performances today. Norms evolve, and so freezing a work's meaning to accord with the dominant standards of the artist's lifetime "seems undesirable from both artistic and broader societal perspectives".[77] As Rebecca Tushnet has argued, then, "there are good reasons to deny authors control over *interpretations* of their works, including interpretations driven by authorial identity".[78] The right of the author to guard his intended meaning, throughout his lifetime and thereafter, allows him to claim his role as "originator" by "removing traces of those who were here before",[79] and to constrain future creators by preventing those who come after from recharting his chosen path.

American Dance (Oxford University Press 2016) (exploring the racialized power of intellectual propertization in the context of dance).

[73] Elizabeth L Rosenblatt, "Copyright's One-Way Racial Appropriation Ratchet" (2019) 53 U Cal Davis L Rev 591, 594.

[74] Sara Ahmed, "Queer Use" (*feministkilljoys*, 7 November 2018) https://feministkilljoys.com/2018/11/08/queer-use/.

[75] See Kent G Drummond, "The Queering of Swan Lake" (2003) 45 Journal of Homosexuality 235, 237–8.

[76] Barbara McMahon, "Beckett Estate Fails to Stop Women Waiting for Godot" *The Guardian* (4 February 2006). See Robert Spoo, "Ezra Pound's Copyright Statute: Perpetual Rights and the Problem of Heirs" (2009) 56 UCLA L Rev 1775, 1824–5.

[77] Guy A Rub, "The Challenges of Posthumous Moral Rights" in Peter Karol and Sharon Hecker (eds), *Posthumous Art, Law and the Art Market: The Afterlife of Art* (Routledge, 2022), 26–7.

[78] Tushnet (n 70) 802 (emphasis original).

[79] Ahmed (n 74).

Elizabeth Rosenblatt has argued that copyright's hierarchies of value – informed by "a historically Eurocentric, male conception of authorship"[80] – are implicitly racialized, disadvantaging certain speakers and denying the merit in culture "outside the colonizer's frame".[81] When copyright gives control over discourse to "dominant-culture creators", it allows them "to silence challenges to copyright's value hierarchy". Moreover, by framing this control in terms of "deserving" authors, Rosenblatt cautions, it "teaches that this hierarchy is somehow necessary or correct".[82] John Tehranian has also argued that copyright empowers the person hailed as author to shape and control the representation of others – often the bodies of women and racialized minorities rendered visible as "fungible commodities"[83] – while suppressing counter-hegemonic narratives that resist these dominant representations.[84]

In our view, the moral right of integrity potentially serves in this way to sanctify and solidify the "male gaze", as it were, of the author who speaks from a position of cultural dominance, preserving his vision of the world. Through a feminist lens, in a cultural context of colonization, dominance and subordination, the demand for the integrity of the already-created is akin to a demand to revere a thing bestowed upon the masses as an imperial gift – whereas the political act of "talking back" to power or "decolonizing culture" sometimes requires, instead, "an act of vandalism, a willful destruction of our universals; knocking off the heads of statues, snapping at the thrones of the philosopher kings".[85] The recent toppling of statues and dismantling of monuments to history's "great men" should have attuned our senses to the suppression of political speech that could be served by the invocation of artists' moral rights to prevent the mutilation of their work.[86]

An illustrative controversy is the installation, on International Women's Day in 2017, of the *Fearless Girl* statue in front of the *Charging Bull* on Wall Street. Kristen Visbal, the sculptor of the statue of the young girl obstinately facing the bull, meant to address the issue of gender representation on corporate boards.[87] Arturo DiModica, the sculptor of the famous bull statue, intended to portray a positive message about the ambition of Wall Street, and objected to its prejudicial co-optation as a symbol of male dominance.[88] For the many visitors to the statue who created their own downstream works, taking photographs of their daughters replicating the girl's stance, for example, the work represented something larger about feminism and the power of resistance.[89] Most recently, following the death of US Supreme Court Justice Ruth Bader Ginsburg, photographs circulated of the *Fearless Girl* (now relocated) with the Ruth

---

[80]   Rosenblatt (n 73) 598.

[81]   ibid 605.

[82]   ibid 597.

[83]   Kraut (n 72) xviii.

[84]   Tehranian (n 1) 343.

[85]   Ahmed (n 74).

[86]   See e.g. "How Statues are Falling Around the World" (*New York Times*, 24 June 2020) https://www.nytimes.com/2020/06/24/us/confederate-statues-photos.html.

[87]   See Annemarie Bridy, "Fearless Girl Meets Charging Bull: Copyright and the Regulation of Intertextuality" (2018) 9 U Cal Irvine L Rev 293, 295–6.

[88]   Specifically, it was claimed that the alteration of *Charging Bull* by the addition of the *Fearless Girl* damaged its integrity and was prejudicial to the sculptor's honour and reputation. See Letter from Norman Siegel, Partner, Siegel Teitelbaum & Evans, LLP, and Steven Hyman, Partner, McLaughlin & Stern, LLP, to The Honorable Bill de Blasio (11 April 2017) https://www.scribd.com/document/344998311/Letter-to-Mayor-DeBlasio-on-Charging-Bull-vs-Fearless-Girl.

[89]   Bridy (n 87) 297.

Bader Ginsburg's famous "dissent collar" lace around her neck.[90] (We would be remiss not to note the parallel to the placement of ribbons around the necks of Snow's geese.) With each contribution to the chain of communication we see the transformation of meaning laced with the politics of power.

Annemarie Bridy examines the *Fearless Girl* controversy through the frame of Bakhtinian dialogism, concluding that copyright law, as an engine of free speech and an incentive to promote artistic progress, should encourage and not prohibit this discursive interplay of meaning.[91] For Bridy, the absence of broad moral rights protections and the availability of fair use in the US copyright system "encodes the principle that cultural production is inherently dialogic and intertextual".[92] But in jurisdictions with strong moral rights and minimal exceptions – and even in Canada, where a broadly framed right of fair dealing appears not to afford a defence to moral rights violations[93] – such dialogic practice could potentially be enjoined in the name of the author's integrity right. Such a result would cede dialogic creativity to the dominant author's control over meaning, silencing critical transformative speech.

The capacity to modify, mutilate and resituate others' words and works is a powerful way to challenge privileged voices and artefacts of the dominant culture, to re-tell stories from different social sites, and so to advance a counter-hegemonic narrative.[94] To endorse the right of integrity misunderstands the relationship between author, text and public in a way that casts disruptive dialogic engagement as a moral – and legal – wrong. This is not, in our view, a position that ultimately aligns with a feminist politics of confrontation, resistance and social reform.

3.3   A Feminist Reimagining of the Right of Attribution

3.3.1   Dialogic creativity and the demand for authorship credit

We have argued that a relational feminist theory of dialogic authorship resists the idea of the individual author's control over his work, meaning and message. It therefore grounds a feminist position *against integrity*. But there is a distinction to be drawn between control over meaning and the attribution of authorship that merits more attention. Once again, a feminist political critique of moral rights must begin by recognizing that such rights operate within a copyright system that systematically misunderstands and misattributes authorship, routinely denying credit to the creative contributions of woman and others from racialized and culturally

---

[90]   See e.g. Ryan Millar, "NYC's 'Fearless Girl' statue dons white, lace collar to honor Ruth Bader Ginsburg" (*USA Today*, 21 September 2020) https://www.usatoday.com/story/news/nation/2020/09/21/ruth-bader-ginsburg-fearless-girl-statue-dons-white-lace-collar/5852310002/.

[91]   Bridy (n 87) 299.

[92]   ibid 300.

[93]   Copyright Act, RSC 1985, c C-42, ss 29, 29.1, 29.2 prescribe that fair dealing "does not infringe copyright", but makes no mention of moral rights.

[94]   See e.g. "A Conversation with Alice Randall" (*HOUGHTON MIFFLIN HARCOURT*) http://www.houghtonmifflinbooks.com/readers_guides/wind_done_gone/index2.shtml. #conversation accessed 19 November 2019 [https://perma.cc/S98H-RSDF], cited by Rosenblatt (n 73) 642. See also Rebecca Tushnet, "Comments of the Organization for Transformative Works" (13 November 2013) https://www.transformativeworks.org/wp-content/uploads/old/Comments%20of%20OTW%20to%20PTO-NTIA.pdf, 29–38.

marginalized groups.[95] When the (mis)attribution of authorship is recognized as a function of power in the context of inequality, then the demand for attribution appears as a potential route towards empowerment – and so a tempting avenue of feminist activism.

But the notion that the right of attribution can aid in the furtherance of social justice and equality – that it can be opportunistically wielded as a tool against oppression and silencing rather than to discount the creative contributions of the culturally marginalized – is sustainable only if and to the extent that the copyright system corrects course on its (mis)construction of what it means to be an "author". The concept of dialogic authorship describes a work's complex multivocality, while the notion that one person should wear the Original Author badge of honour reifies a monologic ideal. In the context of a system that venerates ostensible originality, attribution rights will misallocate the title of author by denying the contributions of other voices that inhabit the text and potentially silencing those who seek to respond to it. They will also risk reinforcing the idea of the work as a stable object to be owned, rather than a dialogic, communicative act. As Berenice Carroll explains: "claims of 'originality' and associated terms ('innovation,' 'creativity,' etc.) [are used] to rationalize and justify claims to property in ideas and lines of inheritance, preserving for small groups ... both intellectual hegemony and control of a variety of rewards and privileges". Such claims of ownership and inheritance, based on traditional conceptions of individual entitlement, will only preserve "the class system of the intellect" – a system that, as one might expect, operates on "appropriation and exploitation of the ... labor of those relegated to lower classes, including predecessors erased from memory and history".[96] From a feminist political perspective, however, acknowledging those voices from the margins has the transformative potential to disrupt this class system. Recognizing the subaltern speaker-as-author in turn recognizes her expressive agency and her capacity, through creative acts, to challenge hegemonic knowledge production, rewrite narratives, influence and undermine existing spatial arrangements.[97] Naming, in itself, signifies a reclamation of power that resists epistemic erasures of personhood.[98]

Through the feminist lens, then, one can reconceive of the demand for authorial attribution as seeking recognition of a contribution to the collective conversation that is cultural discourse. When authorship is regarded as fundamentally dialogic and relational, to attribute authorship

---

[95]   See Catherine L Fisk, "Credit Where It's Due: The Law and Norms of Attribution" (2006) 95 Geo L J 49, 55–6 ("Women have long provided uncredited research, editorial, and technical assistance on creative projects undertaken by the men in their lives. Who can and should be credited with invention is thus culturally specific and wrapped up as much in norms about honor and credit as in the supposedly simple fact of who conceived a new idea").

[96]   Berenice A Carroll, "The politics of 'originality': Women and the class system of the intellect" (1990) 2(2) Journal of Women's History 136, 138 (quoted in Richa Nagar, "Storytelling and co-authorship in feminist alliance work: reflections from a journey" (2013) 20:1 Gender, Place & Culture 1, 3).

[97]   Katherine McKittrick, *Demonic grounds: Black women and the Cartographies of Struggle* (University of Minnesota Press 2006), xxiii.

[98]   See Suze G Berkhout, "Private talk: testimony, evidence and the practice of anonymization in research" (2013) 6(1) International Journal of Feminist Approaches to Bioethics 19; Carol Smart, Jenny Hockey and Allison Janes, *The Craft of Knowledge: Experiences of Living with Data* (Palgrave Macmillan 2014) 1–20. See also Anupriya Dhonchak, "Interrogating the Norm of Anonymity in Research Ethics: Visibility, Representation and the Right to Attribution" (August 2020), SpicyIP https:// spicyip.com/2020/08/interrogating-the-norm-of-anonymity-in-research-ethics-visibility-representation -and-the-right-to-attribution.html.

to another is to recognize the other's creative capacity, which is, in turn, to acknowledge their relational autonomy. The claim to attribution need not silence the *already-spokens* or the *not-yet-spokens*, but merely acknowledge the voice of the speaker as an active agent of discourse. If this sounds somewhat Kantian, the distinction is worth underscoring. Whereas a Kantian theory of the author's entitlement turns on the harm of "compelled speech" – the copier speaks for the author and not on his own behalf – from our perspective, the harm, if any, of using another's expressive work without acknowledgement, is rather that of *silencing*: it is the refusal to acknowledge the other as speaker, and in many cases, the power to deny that they spoke at all.[99] Such refusal reproduces the muted subject of the subaltern woman.[100] The role for attribution that we see is therefore not about natural right and individual entitlement but about shaping relations of communication to advance social values of equality and shared participation in cultural dialogue. It is not about hailing the author's unique personality but acknowledging her expressive agency as a situated, speaking subject. It is not, therefore, a paternal claim to authority, but an appeal to be seen and heard.

3.3.2 The politics of attribution

Actor and activist Ossie Davis notes the political power of art: "[I]t has impact, it can affect change – it can not only move us, it makes us move."[101] This power of art to make us *feel* has the potential to spur engagement, mobilization, empathy and action.[102] As Martha Nussbaum observes, art and its narratives expose us to alternate emotional perspectives, refining our moral and emotional sensitivities.[103] The creation of expressive narrative allows the articulation of lived experiences of marginalization from the perspective of those who experience it, engendering empathy, and challenging the objectivity of truth perpetuated by dominant narratives.[104] In Foucauldian terms, it supports the emergence of subjugated knowledges from below and outside the institutions of official knowledge production.[105]

---

[99]   See Bita Amani, "Disabused of Copyright's Use?: Not Quite But You Had Me at Non-use" (2016) 29 Intellectual Property Journal 141 (arguing that Drassinower's Kantian frame fails to account for copyright's discrimination between authors and exclusion of marginalized authors-in-fact from the category of author-in-law).

[100]   Gayatri Chakravorty Spivak, "Can the Subaltern Speak?" in Cary Nelson and Lawrence Grossberg (eds), *Marxism and the Interpretation of Culture* (Macmillan 1988) 271–313.

[101]   "Truth: Ossie Davis" (*Charter for Compassion*) https://charterforcompassion.org/truth-anti-war -and-human-rights-activists/truth-ossie-davis.

[102]   Olafur Eliasson, "Why Art Has the Power to Change the World" (*World Economic Forum*, 18 January 2016) https://www.weforum.org/agenda/2016/01/why-art-has-the-power-to-change-the-world/.

[103]   Martha C Nussbaum, *Love's Knowledge: Essays on Philosophy and Literature* (Oxford University Press 1990).

[104]   This also aligns with the emphasis in Critical Race Theory on narrative as a valuable research methodology for articulation of concerns around equality, involving "autobiographies, self-portraits, allegories, fables, and fictive narratives": Margaret E Montoya, "Celebrating Racialized Legal Narratives" in Francisco Valdes, Jerome McCristal Culp and Angela Harris Jerome (eds), *Crossroads, Directions, and a New Critical Race Theory* (Temple University Press 2002) 243. See also Anjali Vats and Deirdré Keller, "Critical Race IP" (2018) 36 Cardozo Arts & Entertainment Law Journal 735, 767–9 (reflecting on the power of story-telling specifically in the context of a critical race theory of intellectual property law).

[105]   Michel Foucault, *Power/Knowledge: Selected Interviews and Other Writings* (Pantheon Press, 1980) 81–2. See also Avery F Gordon, *Ghostly Matters* (University of Minnesota Press 2008) xviii.

Creative agency resides at the heart of the feminist conception of selfhood and its political project: the discursive subject that is constituted by discourse also has the capacity to revise and resist discourses from within.[106] In India, Dalit feminism advocates for social change through engagement that involves non-linear, ever-involving dialogue, intertwining education with the organization of struggles, attentive to the unknowable "possibilities and constraints on agency as it intersects with social formation".[107] For the resistive potential of that creative agency to be fully realized, however, it is important to locate and identify the speaking subject within her socio-political circumstances, allowing the work to circle back to the contexts from which resistance emerges. The power to subvert hegemonic discourses depends in part upon the nature of the dialogic engagement and the source of the disruption.[108] Moreover, as Richa Nagar powerfully reminds us:

> For each one of us who is afforded the means or tools to step in with an authority to make knowledge claims, there are millions of others whose words and knowledges we stand on, but who have been systematically erased from, or made invisible, on the pages and spaces of formal learning ...

In the context of the historical and ongoing violence of these absences and erasures, it becomes important to ask:

> [W]ho else do we bring with ourselves onto the page or stage? Whose are the voices we rely on for weaving our stories, but whose tones and accents remain unheard and unacknowledged in our scripts? Who are the people who remain forgotten in our citational practices ...?[109]

Reimagined in relational terms, a demand for attribution uses the subject's situatedness to convey information about the work *as dialogue*, building the links in the speech chain of communication, and so enabling a more meaningful dialogic response.[110] It is a small step towards "radically reworking the ways in which these unheard tones, stolen voices, and erased knowledges are rendered".[111] In this sense, a relational right of attribution recognizes voices

---

[106]   Susan Hekman, "Reconstituting the Subject: Feminism, Modernism and Postmodernism" (1991) 6 Hypatia 44; Julia Kristeva, *In the Beginning Was Love: Psychoanalysis and Faith* (Columbia University Press 1987).

[107]   Richa Nagar, "Storytelling and Co-authorship in Feminist Alliance Work: Reflections from a Journey" (2013) 20 Gender, Place & Culture 1, 3 (citing Sharmila Rege, "Education as Trutiya Ratna: Towards Phule-Ambedkarite Feminist Pedagogical Practice" (2010) 45 Economic and Political Weekly 88, 95).

[108]   Compare Tushnet (n 70) 811 (describing the problem of misrepresentation when authors write as if they belonged to historically disadvantaged minority groups, but in fact were members of the majority).

[109]   Richa Nagar, *Hungry Translations: Relearning the World through Radical Vulnerability* (University of Illinois 2019), 1.

[110]   This conclusion ultimately dovetails with arguments by other commentators that focus on the public interest in identifying the author as the source of the work. The public interest here is in knowing the source of the work, although the capacity of authorial attribution to function as an accurate identifier of source should not be assumed. For further discussion on this point, see e.g. Jane C Ginsburg, "The Right to Claim Authorship in U.S. Copyright and Trademarks Law" (2004) 41 Houston Law Review 263; Laura A Heymann, "The Birth of the Authornym: Authorship, Pseudonymity, and Trademark Law" (2005) 80 Notre Dame L Rev 1377; Greg Lastowka, "The Trademarks Function of Authorship" (2005) 85 B U L Rev 1171; Tushnet (n 70).

[111]   Nagar (n 109).

from the margins while potentially facilitating the transformative act of "talking back".[112] It also serves a broader public interest by illuminating the exchange of knowledge and our collective "drive to meaning".[113]

Importantly, however, the attribution right includes the right to be associated with a work under a pseudonym or to remain anonymous. This too finds a firm foothold in a feminist political theory of moral rights. For artists whose works challenge established hierarchies – especially those who hail from marginalized communities, are subject to restrictive gender norms, or fear retaliation and other adverse consequences to their privacy and safety – anonymity can be wielded as a shield.[114] In this context, the right to prevent attribution by name becomes a tool to enable a contribution to the cultural dialogue by a speaker who might otherwise remain silent. Indeed, anonymity can emerge as an expressive strategy in itself; part of the power to represent oneself (or not) on one's own terms – but only if the author enjoys meaningful agency to opt for or out of anonymity. After all, "for much of history, anonymity did not protect the vulnerable, but excluded women and others from authorship and ownership of their own words, erasing them from the archive, even from history and in the process creating vulnerability through rendering people nameless".[115] As Niamh Moore reminds us, "anonymity has a history – and a politics – as well as an ethics".[116] Its moral weight and political potential is necessarily contingent on place and time.

Judith Butler writes that "there is no self ... who maintains 'Integrity' prior to its conflictual cultural field. There is only a taking up of the tools where they lie, where the very 'taking up' is enabled by the tools lying there."[117] A feminist politics of moral rights, in our view, cannot permit existing works, as tools of expressive resistance, to be occupied or frozen in time and place by any particular author in the name of protecting "integrity"; but feminist politics can support the assertion that it matters who is taking up these tools and where they are situated in our social and knowledge hierarchy. Without contradiction, we suggest, a feminist reimagining of moral rights can accommodate the author's claim to attribution as a matter of theory and politics, even as it resists the normative assumptions behind the rights to integrity and paternity.

---

[112] Rosenblatt (n 73) 634.

[113] Rosemary J Coombe, "Objects of Property and Subjects of Politics: Intellectual Property Laws and Democratic Dialogue" (1991) 69 Texas Law Review 1853, 1878.

[114] During the eighteenth and nineteenth centuries, of course, many acclaimed women writers published their work under male pseudonyms because scholarly writing was considered an exclusively male bastion. See Greg Buzwell, "Women Writers, Anonymity and Pseudonyms" The British Library, https://www.britishlibrary.cn/en/articles/women-writers-anonymity-and-pseudonyms/. Virginia Woolf was surely right when she "ventur[ed] to guess that Anon ... was often a woman". Virginia Woolf, *A Room of One's Own* (Penguin Classics 1929/89) 49. But Woolf also spoke with envy of the anonymous creative artist whose authorship was profoundly *communal*, with "no sense of property" or need to "stamp one's name", in contrast to "the isolation of the individual writer who emerged in the Renaissance". Virginia Woolf (Brenda R Silver (ed.)), "'Anon' and 'The Reader': Virginia Woolf's Last Essays" (1979) Twentieth Century Literature 356. See Sharon O'Dair, "Laboring in Anonymity" (2008) 16 symplokē 7, 8–10.

[115] Niamh Moore, "The Politics and Ethics of Naming: Questioning Anonymisation in (archival) Research" (2012) 15(4) International Journal of Social Research Methodology 331, 332.

[116] ibid.

[117] Judith Butler, *Gender Trouble: Feminism and the Subversion of Identity* (Routledge 1990) 145.

And so, our feminist theory of moral rights grounds a stance against integrity but in favour of attribution. It does not follow, however, that the structures of copyright law as currently constructed are – or are likely to become – the appropriate vehicle through which to achieve the political goals of attribution described here.[118] The political potential of moral rights to upset the stability of gender, caste and class hegemonies is sobered by the unabating risk of further harms within these contexts of cultural dominance and subordination – harms of misattribution, exclusion and the chilling threat of legal sanction. There may indeed be moments when the moral right to attribution can be harnessed as a tool against oppression and silencing and a means to better realize the political power of our creative agency. But we are not blind to the bluntness of such legal tools, nor to the power needed to wield them.

What is really called for, we suggest, is a wider politics and an ethical practice of attribution – in and between creative communities, in the academy, in the media, in public discourse – that acknowledges the contributions and amplifies the voices of women and other marginalized actors as equal participants in our cultural dialogue. We can (and must) critique conventional conceptions of authorship, creativity and originality without denying the critical importance of creative agency and attribution. Indeed, the call for advancing a *feminist praxis* of attribution and acknowledgment is ultimately aimed at disrupting traditional assumptions about authority, voice and value. It builds not upon tired patriarchal norms of individual ownership and control ("it is mine"), but upon aspirations of inclusion in the dialogic process of meaning-making ("I hear you and am heard").

4.   CONCLUSION

There is so much more that could be said from a feminist perspective about particular aspects or applications of moral rights – and their appropriate limits – in law, policy and practice. Our goal here, however, has been more modest. First, we hope to have convinced our reader that feminist theory has something to say about moral rights in the copyright system, and that this, in itself, pushes toward a new way of situating, defining and debating moral rights claims and requests for reform. Beyond that, we hope to have unsettled the moral rights system from its comfortable perch atop copyright's moral high ground. Far from the pure and spiritual *Other* of copyright's much maligned commodified form, moral rights as currently theorized represent a similar kind of claim to dominance, exclusion and control. Whether moral rights can now be reimagined to advance equality and expressive agency is a question we mean to pose – but not one we purport to answer.

---

[118]   Compare Tushnet (n 70) 820 (concluding that the norms of credit are a moral matter, which is best left separate from law "when law's tools are too crude to make the fine distinctions that prevail in ethics").

5.   Civil Codes and authors' rights

Laura Moscati

1.   FRENCH CODIFICATION AND AUTHORS' RIGHTS

Since the bicentennial of the *Code Napoléon*, I have had some opportunities to further study the correlations between codification and authors' rights.[1] Although not included in the Civil Code, the French principle at the base of the protection of these rights was widespread in Europe and stands today in many codes of the civil law countries. As is generally known, the initial protection concerns the economic rights of the authors. For the development of moral rights, it is necessary to wait, as we will see, until the twentieth century, when analogous choices were able to constitute their foundation.

To develop the analysis, we must reconstruct the origins and the evolution of intellectual property in France from the Revolution until the promulgation of the Code. Moreover, the viewpoints of legal science and case law during the first period of application of the Code are to be studied thoroughly, as France heavily influenced other continental countries since the beginning.

It was only after the Revolution, with the abolition of privileges and the claim of the freedom of the press, that authors began to have some sort of protection.[2] An economic type of safeguard arose, that is to say the exclusive right of the author to exploit his work, although without having moral rights over it. In fact, for a long time thereafter, until the beginning of the twentieth century, the nature of the granted protection was linked to property rather than to personal rights.

Even though with the decree of 1793 the *droit intermédiaire* legislation had not translated all the expectations of the *ancient régime* intellectuals into a law, what it did grant was exceptional for the time. While the *Philosophes* argued that this type of property was exactly the same as tangible property, in practice, with the first law authors had to be satisfied with the recognition of their exploitation rights within the sphere of property rights by the creation of

---

[1]   L. Moscati, "Napoléon et la propriété intellectuelle" (2006) 84 *RHD* 551–67; L. Moscati, "Le Code civil et le destin de la propriété intellectuelle en Europe" (2008) 47 *Droits. Rev. Fr.* 149–71; L. Moscati, *Diritti d'autore. Storia e comparazione nei sistemi di* civil law *e di* common law (Giuffrè Francis Lefebvre, 2020) 80–93. I wish to thank my colleague Prof. Ysolde Gendreau who, by inviting me to participate in this *Handbook*, stimulated me to come back to these topics and to deepen them.

[2]   See, in particular, M. Dury, *La censure. La prédication silencieuse* (Publisud, 1995); B. Edelman *Le sacre de l'auteur* (Editions du Seuil, 2004) and especially L. Pfister, *L'auteur, propriétaire de son œuvre? La formation du droit d'auteur du XVIe siècle à la loi de 1957*, 2 vols. (Université de Strasbourg III, 1999); L. Pfister, "Particularismes nationaux et influences étrangères dans la construction du droit d'auteur français" in L. Pfister & Y. Mausen (eds), *La construction du droit d'auteur entre autarcie et dialogue*, préface par N. Binctin (Presse de la Faculté de droit et de science politique de Montpellier, 2013) 51–100. For the European context, see L. Moscati, "Intellectual Property in the European Legal Context: Tools and Perspectives" (2011) 22 *EBLR* 79–92.

a new category of property, namely, a time-limited property.[3] Consequently, the *droit inter-médiaire* created a law on literary property – that Le Chapelier argued to be "la plus sacrée"[4] – with the introduction of inheritance rights over it limited to ten years. The 1793 text was to constitute the foundation of the French legislation, and in many respects of the European ones throughout the nineteenth century and the first half of the twentieth century.

The main issue neglected by the *droit intermédiaire* was the determination of the very nature of this right and above all, as clearly perceived by the intellectuals during the same century, the possibility of identifying it for all intents and purposes within the category of tangible property. The problem needed to be dealt with in the light of the imminent drafting of the *Code civil*. The absolute fullness and exclusiveness of exploitation and use of the Napoleonic property rights, however, implied that the authors' rights could not be included in a Code that assigned importance only to concrete items, with an overwhelming dignity attributed to tangible property.[5] Even though the compilers clearly put authors' rights on the same level as property rights, they deemed it necessary that the former were to be regulated by a special legislation.

As a result, the French regulatory activity concerning the *droit intermédiaire* for authors' rights was given the status of a special legislation, and in spite of its undeniable importance, it was not included among the articles of the *Code civil*. In fact, the 1793 decree was not taken into account by the subsequent various projects of the Code. In the complex process of preparing the *Code civil*, there was not even a single reference to the opportunity to include at least one article on the principle relative to intellectual property. The Napoleonic jurists had a clear idea to place the rights regarding authors in the sphere of material property, but they had "*évidemment supposé que d'autres lois s'en occuperaient, qu'elles le suppléeraient et le compléteraient à cet égard*".[6]

The absence of a specific rule, earlier in the projects and later in the *Code civil*, seems to be recognized by the contemporaries themselves, and the exclusion of the regulation of authors' rights posed an immediate problem, that was entrusted to the preparatory works of the *Code pénal* and to a project of a decree relative to the organization of *L'imprimerie et la librairie*, both enacted in a definitive form in 1810.

In the 1801 Penal Code project set out by Target and Oudart[7] there are evident traces of civil law references to authors' rights among the crimes and delicts against properties. It is clear that something missing was noted in the projects of the *Code civil*, which were up to that time

---

[3]   *Décret relatif aux droits de propriété des auteurs d'écrit, en tout genre, compositeurs de musique, peintres et dessinateurs*, of 19–24.7.1793 in *Bulletin des lois*, IV, no. 615 (Imprimerie Royale, 1835) 307–10.

[4]   The expression is used by Le Chapelier during the Constituent Assembly: *Archives parlementaires de 1787 à 1860. Recueil complet des débats législatifs et politiques des chambres françaises... Première série (1787 à 1799)*, XVIII (Société Paul Dupont, 1884) 212.

[5]   L. Moscati, "Napoléon et la propriété intellectuelle", *supra* note 1.

[6]   J.-G. Locré, *La législation civile, commerciale et criminelle de la France, ou commentaire et complément des Codes Français*, VIII (Treuttel et Würtz Libraires, 1827) 7.

[7]   *Projet du Code criminel, correctionnel et de police, présenté par la Commission nommée par le Gouvernement* [1801]. For further details about all the questions see L. Moscati, "Napoléon et la propriété intellectuelle", *supra* note 1.

ready, that is the lack of an article that at least outlined the principle. Therefore, the choices made by the legislators in the civil field are reflected in the Penal Code.[8]

The compilers of the *Code pénal* had a clear idea that they were dealing with a property of a particular nature, "*plus chères à l'homme, qu'elles lui appartiennent plus immédiatement, et sont en quelque sorte une partie de lui-même*".[9] They reached the conclusion that they would extract from the articles the parts that were not strictly penal, according to the essence of the Code, and then move elsewhere the inclusion '*de ses dispositions sur la propriété des auteurs qui devaient trouver leur place dans les lois civiles*'.[10] Even if aware of the shortfall, they considered neither opportune nor possible to compensate for it with the *Code pénal*, which should have only referred to the related crimes.

Consequently, the Penal Code presents itself as deprived of any civil law reference, which is instead placed in the contemporary *Règlement sur L'imprimerie et la librairie*.[11] Starting from 1808, an effort was made to define a comprehensive project[12] to cope with the evident necessity to organize the collection of the legal provisions regarding the press, the relationship between authors and publishers, and the related property of works. Authors' rights, therefore, are left in a special law.

Napoleon himself, in 1808, during one of the meetings of the *Conseil d'État* in which the project of the *Règlement* was being discussed, imposed a remarkable improvement to this form of property by defining it "*propriété incorporelle*",[13] and thus excluded any reference to perpetuity. The aim was to encourage it without hindering the spread of knowledge and the development of science.

In practice, the desire to confine all the legal aspects ensuing from intellectual property within a special legislation has meant that subsequent scholarship and case law have themselves attempted to shape embryonic forms of new categories. They have done so in fascinating ways, in an effort to make up for the regulatory gaps in the revolutionary legislation, and in any case, to let them fit into the construction of the French civil law.[14]

A few years after the promulgation of the *Code civil*, the idea started to emerge among the most advanced French legal scholars that intangible property does not change the general principles of property rights, and that its exclusion is due, in fact, to the unification of property

---

[8] See S. Solimano, "L'edificazione dell'ordine giuridico napoleonico: il ruolo di Guy Jean-Baptiste Target" in S. Vinciguerra (ed.), *Codice dei delitti e delle pene pel Regno d'Italia (1811)*, anast. repr. (Cedam, 2001) 147.

[9] In the *Exposé des motifs*, the councilor Louvet de la Somme argues that: "*le but est d'assurer des propriétés d'un ordre différent; des propriétés d'autant plus chères à l'homme, qu'elles lui appartiennent plus immédiatement, et sont en quelque sorte une partie de lui-même*": J.-G. Locré, *La législation, supra* note 6, XXXI, 156; 186–7.

[10] Ibid. 70–1.

[11] *Décret impérial contenant Règlement sur l'Imprimerie et la Librairie* in *Bulletin des lois*, XII (Imprimerie Royale, 1810), no. 5155: 5 February.

[12] The first session in which the state of the question, and above all, the problems to be faced and resolved are outlined, is on 26 August 1808: J.-G. Locré, *Discussion sur la liberté de la presse, la censure, la propriété littéraire, l'imprimerie et la librairie* (Garnery, 1819) 1–15.

[13] Ibid. 18: 2 September 1808. This is one of the meetings of the Council of State devoted to projects about the decree on the press and publishing promulgated in 1810.

[14] I refer above all to some initial steps of the interpretation given by legal science. For the second half of the nineteenth century see L. Pfister, "Particularismes nationaux et influences étrangères dans la construction du droit d'auteur français", *supra* note 2.

categories and to the elimination of different forms. They attempt to supplement the limits of codification. Literary property is thus implicitly inserted among movable goods, letting the necessity for a framework appear, at least in principle.

Some jurists go even further. Pardessus and Renouard, indeed, separate the tangible category from the intangible one and start to forge the latter with alternative solutions.[15] In this way, they anticipate the more systematic constructions of German science of the end of the century and the formation of Kohler's *Immaterialgüterrecht* theory.[16]

By means of other rights such as the *usufruit* and the *réservation de jouissance*, the aforementioned scholars also modify the terminology, moving from the traditional connotation of *propriété* to *droit de copie* and to *droit d'auteur*. They dwell on the exclusive enjoyment of a productive activity remunerated in response to a service rendered to the authority that granted it to be of public interest. In this case, the discriminating factor is the time during which the exclusive right can be enjoyed. The legislators continued to analyse its limitation throughout the nineteenth century, while during the twentieth century they sought to define its specific attributes.

2.   FRENCH MODEL AND CIVIL CODES

In continental Europe where, due to the substantial uniformity of the legislation, individual rights derive from the French system, the *droit d'auteur* was adopted as a model. Although excluded from the *Code civil*, it first took root in the territories occupied by Napoleon and then in the main European countries, stemming from the importance and novelty of the legislation.[17] The differences from the original paradigm described here only refer to the early phase of development,[18] but the evolutionary impact they would have in the future is absolutely clear. Such differences concern the addition or the modification of specific aspects, namely, the different duration of inheritance rights, the requirement or not of formalities, and the greater or lesser breadth of the categories of rightholders which, on the other hand, do not undermine the substance of the model.

Belgium and Holland, at least initially, passed in 1817 their legislation on artistic and literary property, drawing on the 1793 French Act. In Holland, it followed the 1796 Act to briefly

---

[15]   Starting with the first edition of his *Cours de droit commercial* (Garnery & Fournier Jeune, 1814–1816), Pardessus introduces the analysis of intellectual property, but it is necessary to note that earlier he had already anticipated the same concept: J.-M. Pardessus, *Elémens de jurisprudence commercial* (Durand Libraire, 1811) 88–93; A.-Ch. Renouard, *Traité des droits d'auteurs dans la littérature, les sciences et les beaux-arts*, 2 vols. (Chez Jules Renouard, 1838–1839). On Pardessus and Renouard, see L. Moscati, "Origins, Evolution and Comparison of Moral Rights between Civil and Common Law Systems" (2021) 32 *EBLR* 28–34.

[16]   J. Kohler, "Zur Konstruktion des Urheberrechts" (1897) 10 *Arch. f. bürg. R.* 241–86, and more in general, J. Kohler, *Urheberrecht an Schriftwerken und Verlagsrecht* (F. Enke, 1907).

[17]   For an overview of the main sources of European copyright, see B. Dölemeyer, "Urheber- und Verlagsrecht" in H. Coing (ed.), *Handbuch der Quellen und Literatur*, III/3 (C.H. Beck Verlag, 1986) 3955–4066; see also E. Wadle (ed.), *Historische Studien zum Urheberrecht in Europa. Entwicklungslinien und Grundfragen* (Duncker & Humblot, 1993); E. Wadle, *Beiträge zur Geschichte des Urheberrechts. Etappen auf einem langen Weg* (Duncker & Humblot, 2012).

[18]   In this regard, of particular interest is the international conference on *La construction du droit d'auteur: entre autarcie et dialogue*, Montpellier 10–11 May 2007, published 2013, quoted above.

acknowledge perpetual rights of authors.[19] In Belgium, a comprehensive legislation was enacted only towards the end of the century after a long parliamentary process, which started in 1878 and aimed at issuing an act that would ensure equal rights for the various categories of intellectual products. A particularly significant aspect was the use of the expression "exclusive right".

In German-speaking countries, specifically the Prussian Code, the Baden Code and the Austrian Civil Code mainly include provisions on the relationships between authors and publishers. A unique case is the 1809 Baden Code, which is not just a simple translation of the *Code Napoléon*, and was still in force until the promulgation of the German Civil Code. The second book, concerning property, contains an article on the property of writings[20] in which the property of the work is given to the author, although limited to his lifetime, and the authorship, if granted, to the publisher.

This represents an atypical transposition of the French paradigm. The *Schrift-Eigenthum* emerges, in fact, more as a right of the person, which is far from the sphere of material property, as well as some additional variations of the French model that will have a specific development for moral rights.

The 1837 Prussian Act,[21] whose main promoter was Savigny,[22] is, however, based on the French model, the only exception being the period of protection. Moreover, in 1846 Austria adopted an advanced piece of legislation grounded also on the French regulations,[23] but important innovations were added concerning translations.[24]

This is also the case with Portugal and Spain. In Portugal the first decree on literary property, based on the 1793 French one, was enacted in 1851.[25] It recognized the exclusive, whole lifetime property right of authors as well as towards the heirs for 30 years after their decease.

In Spain, a decree of 1813,[26] following the French Act and supplemented in 1826 by another on inventions,[27] was replaced by the 1847 Act that extended the duration of inheritance rights to 50 years.[28] Moreover, the later Spanish Civil Code introduces a general principle as well as a reference to specific regulations. In all the cases that are not regulated or resolved by the

---

[19]   I refer to the Law of 8.12.1796, in B. Van den Velden *Over het Kopijregt in Nederland* ('s-Gravenhage, 1835) 33–47.

[20]   Civil Code, Baden 1809, Art. 577 da-dg.

[21]   Law of 11.6.1837 in *Gesetz zum Schutze des Eigenthums an Werken der Wissenschaft und Kunst gegen Nachdruck und Nachbildung*, in *Preußische Gesetzsammlung* (Staatsministerium, 1837) 165–71.

[22]   E. Wadle "Friedrich Carl von Savignys Beitrag zum Urheberrecht", in G. Lüke (ed.), *Grundfragen des Privatrechts*, Köln 1989, 3–59. See also E. Wadle, *Beiträge zur Geschichte des Urheberrechts*, supra note 17, 137ff; H. Akamatsu, *Savignys Beitrag zum preußischen Urhebergesetz von 1837, sein Leben als akademischer Lehrer und seine Rechtslehre* in (2014) 78 *UFITA. Archiv für Urheber- und Medienrecht* 141–64.

[23]   *Gesetz zum Schutze des literarischen und artistischen Eigenthumes gegen unbefugte Veröffentlichung, Nachdruck und Nachbildung* in L. Geller (ed.), *Oesterreichische Justizgesetze mit Erläuterung aus der oberstgerichtlicher Rechtsprechung*, II (Verlag von Moritz Perles, 1882) 232–41: 19 October 1846.

[24]   These innovations were modelled on the Austro-Sardinian Convention of 1840.

[25]   See *Dos direitos dos Autores* in Collecção official da Legislação Portugueza (Imprensa Nacional, 1852) 232–7: 8 July 1851.

[26]   T. R. Férnandez & J. A. Santamaría (eds), *Legislación administrativa española del siglo XIX* (Instituto de Estudios Administrativos, 1977), § 288, 1267.

[27]   Ibid., § 289, 1267–70.

[28]   Ibid., § 291, 1270–3.

special law, one should defer the application to the general rules on property as established by the Code itself.

The dissemination of the French model brings with it a number of unresolved issues closely connected with the fate of intellectual property in the civil law countries. The nature of the changes concerns the systematic structure, whose traces can be found, in Baden, primarily in Italy, later also in Portugal, in Spain and in some codes of Central and Latin America thereafter. In all these cases, one or more general articles on the *droit d'auteur* are contained in the Civil Code,[29] while a specific regulation is assigned to a special legislation; rarely, the whole regulation is introduced into the Code, putting the principle and its framework on the same level.[30]

In general, the Code attributes to authors the ownership of their work leaving the elaboration to special laws to keep the general principle unchanged, while the adaptation of the specific provisions to the circumstances makes it easier to modify its application. This choice derives from the aim to face more general legal issues such as the relationship between Code and special legislation, which clearly implies the idea of the Code as a code of principles[31] that are still of topical importance and will be a core issue in a hopeful European Private Code.[32]

In this context, the problematic correlation with tangible property re-emerges. According to the French equation, the reference to authors' rights comes immediately after the opening articles under the title about property.[33] This shows the will of the compilers to place authors' rights at the very heart of the law on property rights, hence confirming the enduring equivalence of this right with tangible property.

An autonomous and innovative position was adopted instead in some later codes, which placed authors' rights in the section of the acquisition of rights within the chapter on labour.[34] It is to be noted that, although literary property is not included in the book on property rights, it is regulated as all other personal properties unless otherwise established by the law, given the special nature of such rights.[35] In the same manner, the rights on intellectual works and on industrial inventions deal with the rules of economic activities and enterprises, opening new frontiers to intellectual property and to immaterial goods.

---

[29]   For the most important see: Civil Code, Baden 1809 (Art. 577, da-dg), Civil Code, Kingdom of Sardinia 1837 (Art. 440), Civil Code, Chile 1855 (Art. 584), Civil Code, Italy 1865 (Art. 437), Civil Code, Nicaragua 1867 (Art. 584), Civil code, Venezuela 1867 (Art. 353), Civil Code, Uruguay 1868 (Art. 443), Civil Code, Honduras 1880 (Art. 663), Civil Code, El Salvador 1880 (Art. 610), Civil Code, Mexico 1884 (Arts 1130–271), Civil Code, Russia 1835–1887 (suppl. Art. 420), Civil Code, Spain 1889 (Arts 428–9).

[30]   Civil Code, Portugal 1867 (Arts 570–640).

[31]   L. Moscati, "Sul diritto d'autore tra Codice e leggi speciali" in *Iuris Vincula. Studi in onore di Mario Talamanca*, VI (Jovene, 2001) 497–527.

[32]   On the perspective for private law in Europe, see D. Corapi, *Comparazione e diritto privato nella tradizione giuridica occidentale* (Editoriale scientifica, 2020).

[33]   These are all the codes listed above in note 29, except those mentioned in the following note.

[34]   I am referring to Civil Code, Portugal 1867, Civil Code, Mexico 1884, Civil Code, Nicaragua 1904, Civil Code, Italy 1942.

[35]   Civil Code, Portugal 1867, Art. 590.

3.   CODIFICATION AND MORAL RIGHTS

Following the promulgation of the Berne Convention, an increasing attention emerges towards the recognition and the protection of moral rights.[36] They were to become the most important innovation concerning intellectual property rights in the twentieth century. Since the beginning, it was characterized by the willingness to grant wider protection to authors and their rights, in light of the technological innovations and the proliferation of the new reproduction devices, especially regarding musical works.

At the time when the need for protection of authors' personal rights arose, the problem of the relation between codification and intellectual property had already been defined, thus the recognition of moral rights followed the same choices that had been made for the economic exploitation of the author's work. In the countries that included the principle of protection within their Civil Codes, such principle would either be amplified for the general and explicit safeguard of economic and personal rights or implicitly recognized in a unitary conception of authors' rights.

Many nations, on the basis of the French example, built the regulation of these new rights through special laws. After Japan in 1899,[37] followed by the five states of South America that joined the Havana Convention in 1910[38] and by the first official Chinese Copyright Law enacted in the same year,[39] as well as the first acts in Europe, namely Romania (1923),[40] Czechoslovakia (1926)[41] and, to some extent, Poland (1926)[42] and Portugal (1927),[43] a number of aspects of moral rights began to be protected at national level.

Among them, the first most comprehensive act was the Italian royal decree-law of 1925,[44] while on the international scene, with the 1928 revision in Rome of the Berne Convention, an article was introduced on the protection of the rights of attribution and integrity.

The Italian decree provided for a mature definition of moral rights and immediately gained international support.[45] It established that authors' rights do not concern only economic, but also personal rights. As a consequence, their duration – set at 50 years differently from the previous legislation – merely applies to the economic exploitation, as moral rights do not have any expiration date.[46]

---

[36]   For a more extensive analysis of moral rights see L. Moscati, "Origins, Evolution and Comparison of Moral Rights", *supra* note 15, 25–51.

[37]   See (1899) 12 *Le Droit d'Auteur* 141–4, which contains the text of all the Acts regarding authors' rights translated into French with the relative comments.

[38]   Ibid. (1911) 24 62–4.

[39]   Ibid. 54–5.

[40]   Ibid. (1924) 37 25–30.

[41]   Ibid. (1927) 40 97–100.

[42]   Ibid. (1926) 39 97–9.

[43]   Ibid. (1928) 41 85–90; 92–6.

[44]   RDL no. 1950, 7 November 1925, Art. 16, in *Gazzetta Ufficiale del Regno d'Italia*, no. 270, 20 November 1925.

[45]   See (1925) 38 *Le Droit d'Auteur* 121–2.

[46]   E. Piola Caselli, *Trattato del diritto di autore e del contratto di edizione nel Diritto interno Italiano comparato col Diritto straniero* (2nd ed, UTET & Marghieri, 1927) 23–30; 559–63.

Such a complete text was lacking in the above-mentioned European legislations, even in the French bills in progress,[47] which were to become law only in 1957[48] and in the German project which is the same law enacted in 1901.[49] A resemblance can be observed instead with the Austrian-German model, that provided for the protection of some personal rights in the Baden Code, the Austrian Code and the earliest specific considerations of a part of the legal science.[50]

The new Italian Act was well received, mostly thanks to its protection of the authors' moral rights. It incorporated and developed in a unitary theory on authors' rights the achievements of the Italian and European legal science and courts between the end of the nineteenth and the beginning of the twentieth century. The 1925 Decree will be later substituted with the more comprehensive one of 1941, which is still in force in a renewed text. Moreover, intellectual property would be protected in the new Civil Code of 1942 through a detailed regulation inserted in the book on labour law, differently from the single article of the previous Code. In this way, the new Code embeds also moral rights into the outstanding principle of protection of creator's economic rights, based on the monistic theory, as an important example of a unitary notion of authors' rights.

Even at an international level, in the same period, there was a tendency to prioritize moral rights and to propose a new regulatory system through the Berne Convention of 1886, to avoid protecting economic rights only. The process was slow and complex. The first international conventions struggled to regulate moral rights, as evidenced by the lively debate concerning the specific article of the draft submitted to the Berne Diplomatic Convention in 1884, which stated that the name of the author must always be mentioned.[51]

The importance and centrality of the techniques designed to protect these rights fall within the "new conception of the authors' rights" pointed out by the legal science of the twentieth century. It tends to decouple authors' rights from property rights, typical correlation of the previous century, and to consider such rights as autonomous, inalienable, inviolable, exercisable also beyond the author's demise, continuing to connect the author to his work even after his death, unlike economic rights. In this context, the legal science itself started to deepen the nature of the rights connected to the person of the author and laid claim to the prominence of the protection of personal rights and supported their international dimension.

---

[47]   For the projects see M. Plaisant, "Proposition de loi tendant à compléter la loi des 19/24 juillet 1793 et la loi du 14 juillet 1866 sur la propriété littéraire et artistique pour assurer la protection du droit moral de l'auteur" (1921) 34 *Le Droit d'Auteur* 58–60; A. Vaunois, "Rapport présenté au nom de la Commission chargée d'étudier 'la Protection du droit moral des Auteurs'" (1922) 18 *Bulletin de la Société d'Études législatives* 229–37; for the discussions see ibid. (1923) 19 173–219.

[48]   *Loi n. 57-298 du 11 mars 1957 sur la propriété littéraire et artistique*, in *Journal officiel de la République française du 14 Mars 1957*, no. 89, 2723–30.

[49]   *Gesetz betreffend das Urheberrecht an Werken der Literatur und der Tonkunst*, 9 June 1901 in (1901) 27 *RGBl* 227ff, Art. 9; (1901) 34 *Le Droit d'Auteur* 85–9.

[50]   L. Moscati, "Origins, Evolution and Comparison of Moral Rights", *supra* note 15, 31–2.

[51]   "It is understood that the name of the author from whom, or of the source from which, the excerpts, passages, fragments or writings referred to in the above two paragraphs have been borrowed shall always be mentioned": *Draft Convention respecting the formation of a General Union for the Protection of the Rights of Authors formulated by the 1884 Diplomatic Conference at Berne (original French text)*, Art. VIII in S. Ricketson & J. C. Ginsburg, *International Copyright and Neighbouring Rights. The Berne Convention and Beyond, App. 2* (2nd ed, Oxford University Press, 2006) 1360.

During the revision of the Berne Convention held in Rome in 1928,[52] moral rights were moved upwards on the agenda and received due consideration at an international level.[53] The Italian delegation proposed a draft of the article about moral rights that recognized a protection of the rights of attribution, divulgation, integrity and of the right to exercise them after the author's decease.

In its final version, Article 6*bis*, according to what was provided for under the Berne Convention, recognized the principle of protection and entrusted national legislations with the task of deciding how such rights should be implemented. Among the authors' personal rights proposed by the Italian delegation, only those on authorship and integrity received full approval. Moral rights after the death of the author failed to be protected, although they were mentioned in the first resolution advanced by the Italian delegation and were adopted at the end of the Rome Conference.

Moreover, the opposition of the British and of other delegations led to ruling out the protection of the right of divulgation that was believed to be detrimental to the interests of publishers. It also entrusted national legislations with the task of deciding how inheritance rights should be enforced.[54] In general, Piola Caselli, the promoter of the Italian Act and the Rome Conference, was satisfied with the result because Article 6*bis* acknowledged moral rights at an international level and defined their configuration.[55]

Almost every country joined the Berne Convention. As is well known, the United States ratified their membership only one century after its promulgation, through the Berne Convention Implementation Act of 1988.[56] It included the protection of the rights to attribution and to integrity provided by Article 6*bis* of the Convention.[57] In turn, Canada acceded to the Berne Convention at first as a British dominion and as a contracting country in 1928,[58] marking an often-occurring extensive distance between the two North American countries in this subject matter.

---

[52]   *Convention de Berne pour la protection des œuvres littéraires et artistiques révisée à Rome le 2 juin* 1928. Some reflections on the Conference and the evolution of moral rights in the United States are in E.M. Bock, "Using Public Disclosure as the Vesting Point for Moral Rights under the Visual Artists Rights Act" (2011) 1 *Mich. L. Rev.* 153–74.

[53]   *Actes de la Conférence de Rome* 7 May–2 June 1928 (Bureau de l'Union Internationale pour la Protection des Œuvres Littéraires et Artistiques, 1929). See also the English translation edited by P. Tisseyre, *Proceedings of the Conference Held at Rome from May 7, to June 2, 1928* (International Union for the Protection of Literary and Artistic Works, 1936).

[54]   *Actes de la Conférence de Rome, supra* note 53, 201–2.

[55]   "*L'œuvre intellectuelle n'est pas assimilable à un sac de pommes de terre ... L'œuvre est rattachée indissolublement à la personnalité de l'auteur et même après la simple cession du droit exclusif patrimonial l'auteur peut conserver des droits sur son œuvre dépendant de ses intérêts personnels*": E. Piola Caselli, "A propos de l'article 6 bis de la Convention de Berne révisée" (1935) 48 *Le Droit d'Auteur* 66–8.

[56]   Berne Convention Implementation Act of 1988, 17 U.S.C. 101.

[57]   See L. Moscati, "Some Considerations on Moral Rights in the USA and in the EU Today" (2020) 42 *DPCE online* 189–98.

[58]   L. Carrière, *Adherence of Canada to the Rome Revision of the Berne Convention. Some Comments on Section 71 of the Canadian Copyright Act* (1995), available at https://silo.tips/download/adherence-of-canada-to-the-rome-revisionof-the-Berne-convention; S. Bannerman "Canadian Copyright: History, Change, and Potential" (2011) 36 *Canadian Journal of Communication* 31–7. The intention to join had been clearly expressed since the 1921 Act (Art. 49), in (1921) 34 *Le Droit d'Auteur* 85–7; 98–104.

4.   NEW PERSPECTIVES ON CIVIL CODES AND INTELLECTUAL PROPERTY

In the last decades there have been various initiatives that led to a renewal of the relationship between codification, intellectual property and tangible property, which can be understood and identified in light of the past experience that strongly marked current problems. In particular, I am referring to the draft of the revision of Book II of the *Code civil français* and to the European Copyright Code.

Through an intense programme of *"codification à droit constant"* – a phenomenon defined as legislative inflation – since the end of the 1980s about 60 codes have been promulgated in France. The one on intellectual property,[59] in particular, was intended to gather all the existing legislative material instead of selecting and redirecting it towards the general principles.

Even more recently, during the bicentennial of the French *Code civil*, one can witness the reform of Book II on goods, under the direction of Hugues Périnet-Marquet,[60] along the lines of the revision of some parts of the Code undertaken in the 1970s and starting from Book I.

It should be noted that the *Conseil Constitutionnel*, with the decision of 2006[61] on some articles of the newly enacted authors' rights and neighbouring rights law (DADVSI) argued, in particular, that property was part of the human rights enshrined in the Declaration of 1789. The objectives and conditions of exercising property rights had since then undergone an extension of the field of application to new dominions, namely that of intellectual property.[62] Moreover, the French highest constitutional authority states that the *Code Napoléon* may not have considered the existence of these rights – recent studies seem to show this as not plausible, however[63] – but the exclusion later on can be seen as a voluntary choice.

This innovative and clear-cut position had an immediate effect in the *avant-projet* of the reform of Book II on goods. It was therefore possible to consider whether to include within the revised Code one or several articles on intellectual property, which lacked in the *Code Napoléon*. I am obviously referring only to the general principles and not to the specific regulation, on the basis of the first codes and more recently of the United Nations Universal Declaration of Human Rights and the Charter of Fundamental Rights of the European Union.

In the *avant-projet*, it was acknowledged that intellectual property had never been included in the Code, with a consequential request to classify it within the category of goods.[64] Thus, under Article 517, the project states that the provisions of Book II shall not be detrimental

---

[59]   M. Vivant & J.-M. Bruguière, *Code de la propriété intellectuelle – Édition 2022* (LexisNexis, 2021), text consolidated at 2 December 2021.

[60]   The Henri Capitant Association established, in July 2006, a working group for the reform of property rights, chaired by H. Périnet-Marquet, on which see "L'immeuble et le code civil" in Y. Lequette & L. Leveneur (eds), *1804–2004. Le Code civil: Un passé, un présent, un avenir* (Dalloz, 2004) 395–408. For the results obtained, see H. Périnet-Marquet, *Propositions de l'Association Henri Capitant pour une réforme du droit des biens* (LexisNexis, 2009).

[61]   Conseil constitutionnel, *Décision n. 2006-540 DC* of 27 July 2006.

[62]   This position was reiterated with similar expressions in two subsequent judgments: Conseil constitutionnel, *Décision n. 2009-580 DC* of 10 June 2009; Conseil constitutionnel, *Décision n. 2013-370 QPC* of 28 February 2014.

[63]   Cf. L. Moscati, "Napoléon et la propriété intellectuelle", *supra* note 1.

[64]   Cf. F. Pollaud-Dulian, "Le patrimoine et les biens qui le composent" in H. Périnet-Marquet, *Propositions*, *supra* note 60, 17.

to the special law governed by the *Code de la propriété intellectuelle*.[65] It is interesting to underline that in the just enacted Belgian reform of the Book II of goods, an analogous article is introduced.[66]

However, the systematic innovation introduced by the French reformers seems to exclude a renewed attention to the problems relative to the nature of these rights, considering them as solved. This is the case concerning the relationship between intellectual property and the material one. The project considers intellectual property as *droit spécial* or *domaine autonome*, which led the legal science of the nineteenth century to write some memorable pages, primarily driven by the anxiety to protect the author rather than a genuine interest in the specific study of these rights.[67] In my opinion, the connection with the material property is one of the main topics that characterize the history of the *droit d'auteur*, which plunges its roots in the historical tradition and finds today a basis for the debate in the examined *avant-project*.

Something more could have been expected,[68] even though the editors of the project think that "*ce domaine est ... très profondément communautarisé et que l'importation des règles du Code civil pourrait se trouver en porte à faux avec les nombreuses directives applicables à la matière*".[69] The fact that the *Code de la propriété intellectuelle* prevails on the *Code civil* derives from the specificity of the object, together with certain tools of protection and the communitarization of the framework. There is an echo also in the discipline of possession, whose rules are applied only to movable tangible goods,[70] whereas the immaterial ones are regulated by special laws.[71] On the contrary, the rule on usufruct refers to material as well as immaterial goods.[72]

Apart from the recognition of intellectual property, for which reference shall be made to the specific and complex body of rules it consists of, the *avant-projet* of the reform of Book

---

[65]   Ibid. Art. 517: "*Les dispositions du présent livre ne préjudicient pas à celles du code de la propriété intellectuelle ni aux autres dispositions spéciales régissant des biens particuliers*". For some comments, see namely F. Zenati-Castaing, "La proposition de refonte du livre II du code civil" (2009) 2 *RTDCiv.* 211–44; G.B. Ferri, "L'Avant-projet dell'Association Henri Capitant per una réforme du droit des biens e l'attualità del 'modello' codice civile" (2011) 109 *Riv. dir. comm.* 537–70; J. Payet, "Les définitions dans l'avant-projet de réforme du Livre II du Code civil" (2012) 14 *RJOI* 139–245; F. Mezzanotte, "'Liberté contractuelle' e 'droits réels' (a proposito di un recente dialogo tra formanti nell'ordinamento francese)" (2013) 59 *Riv. dir. civ.* 857–73. See also S. Zolea, "La difficoltosa ascesa dell'immateriale nelle codificazioni francese e italiana" (2016) *Comparazione e diritto civile* 140–54, that mentions the historical roots of the French reform of the book II without citing the specific studies.

[66]   *Loi portant le livre 3 "Les biens" du Code civil* (4 February 2020) ch. 2, Art. 3.2: "*Les dispositions du présent Livre ne préjudicient pas aux dispositions spéciales régissant des biens particuliers tels que les droits de propriété intellectuelle ou les biens culturels*".

[67]   R. Boffa & Ph. Chauvire, "Le changement en droit des biens" (2015) 10 *Le changement du droit*, *numéro spécial Revue de droit d'Assas* 67–80 and, more in general, R. Boffa (ed.), *L'avenir du droit des biens* (L.G.D.J, 2016).

[68]   For the same opinion, see A. Lucas, "Droit des biens et biens spéciaux, l'exemple de la propriété intellectuelle", in *Les modèles propriétaires au XXIe siècle. Actes du colloque international organisé par le CECOJI à la Faculté de Droit et des Sciences sociales de l'Université de Poitiers 10–11 décembre 2009. En hommage du professeur H.-J. Lucas* (Faculté de droit et des sciences sociales de Poitiers, 2012) 15–24.

[69]   F. Pollaud-Dulian, "Le patrimoine et les biens qui le composent", *supra* note 64, 20.

[70]   H. Périnet-Marquet, *Propositions*, *supra* note 60, Arts 555–6.

[71]   Ibid. Art. 558.

[72]   Ibid. Art. 575, according to which the usufruct "*peut être établi sur toute espèce de biens ou tout ensemble de biens, meubles ou immeubles, corporels ou incorporels*".

II could have been a relevant opportunity to reflect on the autonomy of the rules relative to authors' rights and on the uniqueness of their object. It was important not only to ascertain a chance of including them within the Code, but also and above all to make it desirable to reach a collocation of these rights, providing a special and independent section to regulate them and to define and specify the single hypothetical situations and cases.

The European Copyright Code (ECC) or Wittem Project of April 2010 is a specific project stemming from the collaboration among some European scholars and funded by the Dutch government; it aims to become a model for the future development of copyright law in Europe and in the single countries.[73] This Code is not a tabula rasa re-codification of the European Union copyright law. Since it must operate within the limits of the international commitments of the European Union and its Member States, the Code takes account of the substantive rules of the Berne Convention and the TRIPS Agreement. While drafted in the form of a legislative instrument and thereby exceeding the level of detail normally associated with common principles of law, this Code is not comprehensive since it focuses only on the issues deemed essential.[74]

Despite the 20 years passed since the Directive 2001/29/EC (InfoSoc) and the even more numerous years of case law, the European Union Member States continue to lack uniformity. The Wittem Group's attempt can be considered as a starting point for the evaluation of a unique plan to regulate intellectual property in Europe, which even triggers the thought of the world of *common law* in the round.[75] The project should therefore be considered in the light of the same sources used by the compilers, that is to say, the directive, the *acquis communautaire*, the Berne Convention, the Charter of Fundamental Rights and the rules of the individual Member States. The ECC could also have a specific influence on the latter, analogously to the InfoSoc Directive, as the attempt to harmonize laws in this area has contributed significantly to the development of national laws.

However, the ECC does not seem specifically designed for European countries and for the civil law system, but it seems rather to have been developed to combine the two systems, starting from the title itself (*copyright* and *code*). This conception finds its most immediate evidence in the position granted to the author within the project, compared to the two systems: a little less capable of protection than the civil law regime, a little more than that of common law. In fact, the whole project aims at inspiring harmonization.

A number of elements need to be stressed, in general. Compared to the Charter of Fundamental Rights of the European Union, where the principle of the protection of intellectual property is affirmed – without explaining how it unravels – the ECC is the result of principles belonging to different systems. And above all, the centrality taken on by the proprietary position must be remarked, in contrast to the European Private Law draft,[76] in which the right of property is marginal.

---

[73]   The ECC was prepared by a Drafting Committee composed of seven members from different European countries.

[74]   The chapters in which the Code is divided are the following: Chapter 1: Works, Chapter 2: Authorship and ownership, Chapter 3: Moral rights, Chapter 4: Economic rights, and Chapter 5: Limitations.

[75]   J.C. Ginsburg, "'European Copyright Code' – Back to First Principles (with some additional detail)" (2011) 58 *J. Copyright Soc'y* 265–99.

[76]   C. Von Bar, E. Clive & H. Schulte-Nölke (eds), *Principles, Definitions and Model Rules of European Private Law. Draft Common Frame of Reference (DCFR). Outline Edition* (Sellier, 2009).

The definition of authors' rights is built starting from the person itself that is the author identified as creator,[77] to whom, just as a two-faced Janus, the two main elements that characterize the complex of rights are attributed, namely the economic and the moral one.[78] In defining the economic rights attributed to the author,[79] although the term "property" is not used, it is evident that they are part of the world of ownership.

The regulation of moral rights[80] is reinforced compared to the Berne Convention and chiefly to the European Directives, which expressly declare no intention to harmonize them,[81] leaving this role to the national legislations. In the ECC such rights are limited in time and their inspiring model seems to be the Canadian copyright, because it establishes the same term for both economic and moral rights. At any rate, it is a clear departure from the *droit d'auteur* system, that historically has always considered moral rights as perpetual and associated with the concept of *personne morale*.

The aim of the Wittem Group is to promote transparency and consistency in the ECC and to highlight the too often unheard voice of Academia. The Group believes that this Code might serve as a model or at least as a reference tool for future harmonization or even unification of authors' rights at the European level. The hope is that it will contribute to the establishment of a consistent body of law to protect the moral and economic interests of creators, while serving the public interest by promoting the production and dissemination of works in the field of literature, art and science.

To conclude, some Civil Codes that are in force in civil law countries, from the Italian legislation,[82] to the renewed Guatemalan,[83] Portuguese,[84] Venezuelan[85] and the Spanish ones,[86] show still today the principle of intellectual property protection and refer to the special law for the detailed regulation. More recently, certain examples as the Vietnamese[87] and the Chinese[88] ones, have come to place the protection principle in the context of the safeguard of civil rights.

It is remarkable that the Portuguese Civil Code moves away from the aforementioned choices of the nineteenth century, which consisted in the abrogation of the particular law and the insertion of the entire subject matter within the Code itself. An analogous approach can still be found in the recent Russian Civil Code that incorporates the previous specific law through

---

[77] ECC, Art. 2.1: "the author of a work is the natural person or group of natural persons who created it".

[78] Ibid. Art. 2.3 (1): "the initial owner of the economic rights in a work is its author"; Art. 2.2: "the author of the work has the moral rights".

[79] Ibid. Art. 4.1: "the economic rights in a work are the exclusive rights to authorize or prohibit the reproduction, distribution, rental, communication to the public and adaptation of the work, in whole or in part".

[80] Ibid. chapter 3: *Moral Rights*.

[81] "Moral rights are not harmonised at EU level": *Commission Staff Working Document, Impact Assessment on the modernisation of EU Copyright Rules Accompanying the document Proposal for a Directive of the European Parliament and of the Council on copyright in the Digital Single Market*, 1/3, 6.

[82] Civil Code, Italy 1942, Art. 2575.

[83] Civil Code, Guatemala 1963, Art. 470.

[84] Civil Code, Portugal 1966, Art. 1303.

[85] Civil Code, Venezuela 1982, Art. 546.

[86] Civil Code, Spain 1889, Art. 428.

[87] Civil Code, Vietnam 2015, Art. 8 no. 4.

[88] Civil Code, China 2020, Art. 123.

a large number of articles.[89] What is more, some countries adopt an intermediate solution, such as the Ukrainian Code,[90] where an entire book on intellectual property is sided by a dedicated law. Ukraine,[91] together with the Russian Federation[92] and Vietnam,[93] displays the additional peculiarity of considering intellectual property among the rights explicitly protected by the Constitution, so as to emphasize the personal component of such rights.

Other countries, namely France, but also Germany[94] or Brazil,[95] protect such rights exclusively in special laws, leaving open the issue relative to the relationship between codification and intellectual property and sometimes also the matter concerning the relationship with the property of tangible goods, created by Napoleon's Civil Code.

---

[89] Civil Code, Russian Federation, Part IV 2006, Arts 1225–551.
[90] Civil Code, Ukraine 2004, Arts 418–508; law no. 3792-XII del 1993, *Про авторське право і суміжні права.*
[91] Constitution, Ukraine 1996, Arts 41, 54.
[92] Constitution, Russian Federation 1993, Art. 44 no. 1.
[93] Constitution Vietnam 1992, Arts 40, 62 no. 2.
[94] *Gesetz über Urheberrecht und verwandte Schutzrechte (Urheberrechtsgesetz)* 1965.
[95] The Brazilian Civil Code of 2002 confirms the departure from the 1916 text, which provided for a chapter dedicated to literary, scientific and artistic property, later repealed following the enactment of law no. 9.610 of 1998, which "*altera, atualiza e consolida a legislação sobre direitos autorais e dá outras providências*".

PART II

MORAL RIGHTS IN INDUSTRIAL PROPERTY RIGHTS

6. Inventor's moral right and morality of patents

Nari Lee

1. INTRODUCTION

Morality is closely connected to property. While morality and its counterpart of the natural right to property may be an unacceptable justification to a pure utilitarian or pure positivist or those who may deny any kind of morality giving rise to property,[1] nevertheless morality provides a normative justification for property with effect.[2] Over the years, philosophers have debated the nature of property, which will not be recounted here.[3] Regardless of its philosophical basis, a property right imposes 'duties of abstention on all other members of the relevant community'.[4] The moral nature of such duties of abstention requires acceptance by society. Acceptance by the community may be seen as an indication that a property right ultimately includes a 'moral right'[5] dimension, making it a fundamental right of inviolable value that the community accepts in order to guarantee its protection.[6]

Intellectual property rights are a species of property right over abstract objects. The moral dimension of property logically extends to intellectual property rights. The morality that is implicated in duties of abstention is often expressed as the property guarantee in constitutional law against undue taking of intellectual property.[7] However, the moral rights discussion has an

---

[1]   Jeremy Bentham notably observed that 'property and law are born together, and die together. Before laws were made there was no property; take away laws and property ceases.' Jeremy Bentham, *Theory of Legislation: Translated from the French of Etienne Dumont, by R. Hildreth* (2nd edn, Trübner 1871) 113.

[2]   Raz seems to distinguish rights-based morality from individual moral claims. As rights alone cannot provide a complete account of morality, there are some fundamental moral duties that do not stem from rights, See J Raz, 'Right-based Moralities,' in *The Morality of Freedom* (Oxford University Press 1988) at 193. http://www.oxfordscholarship.com/view/10.1093/0198248075.001.0001/acprof-9780198248071.

[3]   For example, Hegel observed that individual property rights allow property ownership using 'subjective will' through 'participation with others in a common will'. Georg Wilhelm Friedrich Hegel, *Hegel's Philosophy of Right* (first published 1821, Thomas Malcolm Knox tr, Clarendon Press 1942) §51 & §71–2.

[4]   For example, Henry E Smith & Thomas W Merrill, 'The Morality of Property', 48 *Wm & Mary L Rev* (2007) 1849.

[5]   Smith and Merrill, n 4.

[6]   See for example, European Convention on Human Rights (ECHR) Art 1 Protocol. Similarly, Art 17 of the EU Charter of Fundamental Rights. In the US, the Fifth Amendment to the US Constitution provides a property guarantee and the Supreme Court has reiterated the principle by declaring in *Ruckelshaus v. Monsanto Co*, 467 U.S. 986, 1003 (1984) that intangible 'products of an individual's "labour and invention"' can be 'property' subject to the protection of the Fifth Amendment to the US Constitution, including *trade secrets* (1001–4).

[7]   See for example, Tuomas Mylly, *Intellectual Property and European Economic Constitutional Law – The Trouble with Private Informational Power*, IPR University Center Publication No. 4 (2009) 150–225.

additional dimension in intellectual property, as intellectual property rights contain elements of inalienable, personal interests. These elements are seen in justificatory theories for intellectual property in that the individual personality of the creator is embodied in abstract objects[8] so that protecting those interests as an element of the property right would allow exercise of subjective freedom.[9] The universality of the rhetoric of morality has been made clearly visible in political debates surrounding international harmonization of intellectual property norms, where developed countries have engaged in a process of moral persuasion by emphasizing the equivalence or the justness of protecting intellectual output globally with the rhetoric of theft, attaching natural right-based arguments to the right to intellectual property.[10]

In positive law, moral right is clearly visible in copyright, as seen in statutory text such as Article 6*bis* of the Berne Convention, establishing a permanent and inalienable personal moral right of attribution (or paternity) and integrity to authors.[11] In contrast, debates on morality as a basis to form a 'right' in the positive law of industrial property have been rather scarce. For example, in trademarks, the moral right of a trader as part of the exclusive right of trademark is rarely raised. At a glance, trademark holders, who are often legal entities, do not seem to have moral interests to be protected, although the reputation of a trademark belonging to legal entities is protected in practice, albeit in limited cases.[12]

However, a closer examination reveals that moral right considerations do indeed exist in trademark law. Considering that the essential function of a trademark is to maintain a version of commercial morality as to the source of goods and services, a version of the right of attribution to the authentic source seems to lie at the heart of a trademark right, despite the absence of statutory expression of moral right granted to businesses. As an extension of this, the moral interests of natural persons to trade in their own names against trade secret holders are expressed as the 'own name use defence', as seen in the status of current EU trademark law.[13]

This chapter explores whether such moral rights are also provided in patent law and how morality is conceptualized in patent law. At first glance, in patent law, moral rights to inven-

---

[8]   For example, one of the most well-known quotations in literary works that emphasizes how a creative work is a manifestation of the author's personality is Gustave Flaubert, who allegedly stated that 'Mme Bovary, c'est moi', as cited in Michel Vivant, 'Le droit moral sous un regard français' 25(1) *Cahiers de propriété intellectuelle* (2013) 365 at 366. However, the attribution of the statement has been questioned. See, for example, Yvan Leclerc 'Madame Bovary c'est moi, formule apocryphe' (2014) https://flaubert.univ-rouen.fr/ressources/mb_cestmoi.php, last visited 20 September 2020.

[9]   Hegel, n 3 at §51. See also Peter Drahos, *A Philosophy of Intellectual Property* (Routledge 1996) 75.

[10]   Samuel Oddi, 'TRIPs – Natural Rights and a "Polite Form of Economic Imperialism?"' 29 *Vand J of Transnat'l L* (1996) 425.

[11]   Art 6*bis* Berne Convention for the Protection of Literary and Artistic Works, 9 September 1886, (Berne Convention) 28 UST 7645; 1160 UNTS 231; 9 ILM 978 (1970).

[12]   See Art 9.2(c) Regulation (EU) 2017/1001 of the European Parliament and of the Council of 14 June 2017 on the European Union trade mark OJ L 154, 16 June 2017, 1–99 (EUTMR), and Art 10.2(c) Directive (EU) 2015/2436 of the European Parliament and of the Council of 16 December 2015 to approximate the laws of the Member States relating to trade marks, OJ L 336, 23 December (EUTMD). See also Guido Westkamp, 'Intellectual Property and Human Rights: Reputation, Integrity and the Advent of Corporate Personality Rights', in Christophe Geiger (ed.), *Research Handbook on Intellectual Property and Human Rights* (Edward Elgar Publishing 2016) 389–409.

[13]   For example, EUTMR Art 14(1)(a) and EUTMD Art 14(1)(a). Under the previous law, such limitation applied to all kinds of names including company names, as seen in Case C-245/02, *Anheuser-Busch v. BudějovickýBudvar*, [2004] ECR I-10989.

tions do not seem to be discussed at all. The absence of academic discussion on moral rights to patented inventions begs the question whether morality means or should mean different values in patents than in other intellectual property rights and begs the further question whether indeed there are no 'moral interests' of inventors that are worth protecting. This chapter aims to answer these questions by first exploring how morality is conceptualized in patent law, and then identifying areas where morality may be expressed in patent law. Finally, the chapter explores one concrete example by way of a case study in positive patent law where the moral interest of an inventor is indeed protected under the European Patent Convention (EPC).[14] In particular, using an opposition decision on a CRIPSR invention before the European Patent Office (EPO),[15] this chapter illustrates a case of inventor's moral right under the EPC as an active right of attribution granted only to natural persons. As the case demonstrates, when used in combination with the right to claim priority in international application, the moral right of an inventor becomes a positive right to control the patenting process, which in this case was proven to be fatal for the patent application. Based on the case study, it is arguable that as a matter of positive law, patent law not only grants an instrumentalist economic right for particular policy purposes, but also provides a moral right of attribution to a natural person as inventor. As such a right is limited in scope, this chapter cautiously claims that recognizing moral right in the patent system calls for some adjustment in patent law from the standpoint of the individual inventor, and argues that introducing a fairness-based own use defence to a named inventor would be one such step.

2.   MORAL INTERESTS OF INVENTORS AND MORALITY IN PATENT LAW

Discourses on morality in intellectual property seem to follow two distinctive paths – first where morality forms the basis of a right granted to the creators, and second where morality is used as a way to place limitations on the right – to oppose the grant or to restrict uses of registered rights. Notably, in the first case, a prominent example is found in copyright law, while the second path seems to be more visible in registrable rights, such as patents and trademarks. This is because the second path would require an explicit act of morality-based screening in the formation of rights, which can be done during the process of grant and registration, based on substantive examination.

---

[14]   Arts 61, 62, 81, and 87 Convention on the Grant of European Patents of 5 October 1973 as revised by the Act revising Article 63 EPC of 17 December 1991 and the Act revising the EPC of 29 November 2000 (EPC). See also Art 4*ter* Paris Convention for the Protection of Industrial Property, as last revised at the Stockholm Revision Conference, 20 March 1883, 21 UST 1583; 828 UNTS 305 (Paris Convention).

[15]   Decision of the Opposition Division (26 March 2018), EP 2771458, Grounds for the decision (Annex), Opposition File No. 13818570.7. (CRISPR Opposition 2018) Text available on searchable EPO online register, https://register.epo.org/, last visited 1 October 2020. The appeal to an enlarged board of appeal (T0844/18) was dismissed in the oral hearing held on 16 January 2020 and the EPO thus maintained its revocation decision. A reasoned decision for dismissal has not been published at the time of this writing.

2.1   Moral Interests of Inventors as a Right

Do inventors enjoy moral rights? Discussions are scarce on whether inventors have moral interests that need protection as a right, and a patent right seems agnostic in terms of the morality of patents granted. In contrast, the presence of a positive moral right in copyright law is often used as a touchstone that identifies the genealogy of the copyright system, whether it is based on the so-called 'economic right' regime of common law tradition or based on the so-called 'author's right' regime of the continental legal tradition.[16] Notably, it is argued that the economic right regime lacks a general moral right. In countries where moral right is an embedded part of copyright, it is often characterized as the right that protects natural-person authors against alienation and misappropriation of their authorship from their works when economic rights are assigned. Authors maintain a right of attribution or of integrity against reprehensible uses of their works. These rights are cast as non-economic rights, personal and non-alienable, and are granted for non-economic and non-utilitarian purposes. As a personal right, the justification for the right is often tied to a personhood thesis that copyright should promote human flourishing by protecting the autonomy, dignity and self-determination of the creators.

Article 6*bis*(1) of the Berne Convention offers a model typology of moral rights. It provides that:

> independently of the author's economic rights, and even after the transfer of the said rights, the author shall have *the right to claim authorship* of the work and *to object to any distortion, mutilation or other modification of, or other derogatory action* in relation to, the said work, *which would be prejudicial to his honour or reputation*.[17]

In addition, some countries grant an author the right of divulgation and withdrawal, in addition to the economic right of first publication.[18]

Moral rights in copyright are seen to be clearly motivated as protection against subjectively conceptualized harm. In contrast to economic rights that provide an economic opportunity benefiting from creation (i.e. objects of rights) and redress against potential loss, moral rights are provided as protection against reputational harm done to the creator (i.e. subjects of the right). As such, enforcing moral rights requires a determination of harm, which means that courts would need to decide what may constitute harmful conduct that negatively affects the honour or reputation of the creator. Harmful 'distortion and mutilation' or derogatory action which would be prejudicial to the honour and reputation of an author require some judgement as to *the essential quality* of the work that defines the work as the work of the creator, and the honour and reputation of the author. Prejudice or reputation may be socially determined, but what would constitute honour may require subjective judgement. In other words, the redress

---

[16]   A good review can be found in such volumes as M T Sundara Rajan. *Moral Rights: Principles, Practice and New Technology* (Oxford University Press 2011); R R Kwall. *The Soul of Creativity: Forging a Moral Rights Law for the United States* (Stanford Law Books 2010). See also for comparison, Vivant, n 8.

[17]   Berne Convention Art 6*bis*(1), emphasis added.

[18]   France, L121-2 & L121-3, Intellectual Property Code (consolidated version of 17 March 2017) Code de la propriété intellectuelle – Dernière modification le 17 mars 2017. The right can be read from the Berne Convention Arts 10 and 10*bis*.

provided by moral rights leaves room for subjective criteria and whether the creator perceives the difference between the protected work and the actual use complained of as a distorting, derogatory and mutilating modification.

In contrast, patent rights are often viewed as purely economic utilitarian instruments, without any moral dimension. In patent law, the concept of morality may be used to ground ineligibility or invalidation but not as an argument for rights that should be granted to inventors against personal harm to their integrity or reputation. Moreover, in academic discussions on patent law – other than discussion on justification as an individual private property right – the perception of a patent right as a personal moral right is no longer a widely accepted position, although it is noted as being part of discussions in the nineteenth century.[19] In contemporary patent law, a patent right is strictly an economic right to exclude and, as a result, the 'moral right' of the inventor is not found as a statutory expression in positive patent law in most countries.

From a policy perspective, the absence of an explicit moral right for inventors in the context of patent law may be both rational and yet surprising. It is rational, because the nature and purpose of the rights differ. Although copyright protects a wide range of subject matter with varying utilitarian value, from fine art to computer program codes, copyrighted expressions are often expected to be preserved intact and used as they are. This is because the value of creative works is presumed to be in the expression. In contrast, as a patent protects functional objects, the embodiments of inventions are used as such, but the inventions are expected be taken apart, experimented on, so that the underlying inventive ideas teach and stimulate follow-on inventions and promote technological progress. The patent system is founded upon trade-offs between disclosure of an invention and limited monopoly, so that teaching of inventions would widely benefit society. Considering the purpose of the patent system, it may be rational to deny the right of integrity for functional and utilitarian inventions, as that right would prevent or at least restrict all partial uses of a patented invention or any improvement replicating parts of a protected invention.

On the other hand, the absence of moral rights for inventors would be surprising when one considers the fact that both inventors and creators make intellectual investments into intellectual objects. The moral interests that need protection against personal harm are not tied to a particular type of object. Harm to the person, be they creator or inventor, can be done by false attribution or objectionable use of a highly creative artistic work or of a utilitarian or functional invention. Thus, if moral rights are necessary to prevent moral harm, there is little logic in distinguishing the interests of inventors from those of creators.

Philosophically, protection against such harm may be based on the concept of Hegelian subjective will, which forms the basis of personal property rights as would be necessary for the survival and flourishing of a human being as a person.[20] If the presence of personal will and its embodiment in a protected object is reason to acknowledge claims of moral right in the resulting intangible objects, then both inventors and creators are in an equal position to claim that right. Likewise, the will of inventors and creators as embodied in protected objects may suffer

---

[19]   This discussion, formulated as a natural right-based argument for patent rights, was raised in the nineteenth century but discarded. See for example, H I Dutton, *The Patent System and Inventive Activity during the Industrial Revolution, 1750–1852* (Manchester University Press 1984) at 17–18. Nari Lee, 'Toward a Pluralistic Theory on an Efficacious Patent Institution', 6 *J. Marshall Rev Intell Prop L* (2007) 220 at 231–2.

[20]   See Hegel, n 3 above.

from harm equally. Thus, as long as utilitarian objects as well as creative objects embody the subjective will of their makers, there are moral interests to protect in both. In other words, if moral rights are justified in copyright, then for the same reasons the inventor's moral right may need to be protected as well. The differences in the types of objects of protection does little to justify why the moral interests of inventors related to inventions should be treated differently from those of creators' works of expression.

If economic rights to exclude provide a utilitarian incentive to inventors, then acknowledging a moral right to be able to claim paternity would appeal to academic inventors. The paternity of an invention is an important dimension of a moral right. Indeed in 1951, the heirs to the inventor and renowned physicist Édouard Branly notably sued Turpain for omission without citation of his name in an article describing the history of the invention of wireless telegraphy and did so in order to restore his honour.[21]

2.2   Morality as a Restriction on Patent Rights

In contrast to the absence of a statutory expression of an inventor's moral right, patent law-related moral interests are manifested more evidently as morality-based restrictions. Immorality does not itself form a bar against protection of creative works as such. Rarely in copyright, exception-based privilege may be seen as 'infringing' when particular uses of a work may constitute immoral or morally objectionable conduct.[22] In contrast, in the registration of industrial property rights – patents and trademarks – morality may be invoked as a ground for refusal or ineligibility for protection. The TRIPS Agreement, for example, in its Article 27.2, lays down that patentable subject matter excludes any inventions whose commercial exploitation is against *ordre public* or morality.[23] Similarly, public policy-violating or morally reprehensible signs cannot be registered as trademarks in Europe.[24]

Such restrictions are found prominently in discussion on the requirement for protection for patents and the role of morality. Morality is used as a way to represent societal concerns about commodification of subject matter whose commercial use may be socially objectionable. This is because a patent would inevitably frame the relationship between the object and the rightholder (subject) in terms of property, thus inevitably commodifying the object of protection. A moral objection may exist to formation of a property-based relationship on particular objects. A human being as a potential patentable object is one such example as the relationship between two human beings should not be a property relation and such objection should not depend on technical jargon concerning excluded subject matter.[25]

---

[21]   Cour de Cassation, première chambre civile, Arrêt du 27 février 1951, Branly.

[22]   Exceptions are sometimes recalibrated in consideration of other copyright holders, based on morality. See for example, on parody, Daniël Jongsma, 'Parody after Deckmyn – A Comparative Overview of the Approach to Parody Under Copyright Law in Belgium, France, Germany and the Netherlands', 48 *IIC – International Review of Intellectual Property and Competition Law* (2017) 1–31.

[23]   See for example, Art 27.2, Agreement on Trade-Related Aspects of Intellectual Property Rights, Marrakesh Agreement Establishing the World Trade Organization, Annex 1C, 1869 UNTS 299, 33 ILM.1197 (1994) (TRIPS), and Art 53 EPC.

[24]   For example, EUTMR Art 7.1(f) provides an absolute ground for refusal of registration of trademarks which are contrary to public policy or to accepted principles of morality.

[25]   Abstract conceptualization may be used as a way to treat human beings not as a human being by utilizing concepts such as elements isolated from the human being. Objections to this way of thinking

When commodification of objects is contested, and as the market presupposes alienability of objects, scholars have argued that some types of 'objects' are best regulated with inalienability rules, which prohibit even voluntary alienability and commodification.[26] The persistence of inalienability rules in law testifies to the fact that general objections exist to regulation of certain objects with property rules, due to value commensurability.[27] For example, debates framing traditional knowledge and cultural expression as intellectual property manifest the dilemma of the necessity for profit sharing and the problematic nature of framing the issue.[28] In patent law, morality is used to justify exclusion of the human body from patent-eligible subject matter, as exemplified in the EU Biotechnology Directive.[29] Article 6(2) of the Directive even specifies *ordre public* and morality as grounds for exclusion. The Court of Justice of the European Union (CJEU) has addressed the morality-based objection in the Directive in two cases, *Brüstle*[30] and *ISCC*.[31] Although these cases show a different disposition on the part of the Court to the question what is a human being and who should answer this question, the cases and the text of the Biotechnology Directive affirm a clear moral objection to the idea of framing the relationship between the human body and a person (natural or legal) as a property relation, thus making the human body an object (as the subject matter of an exclusive right) claimed by another person as its rightholder.

As property implies societal acceptance of the propriety of such an arrangement, granting property rights over contested objects or over inventions using contested objects would endorse the moral propriety of that use. Morality here restricts the rightholder from commercially exploiting an invention that could be potentially immoral and, at the same time, sets a firm duty on rightholders that once the right is granted, use of the rights (i.e. commercial exploitation of the claimed invention) should be moral.

3.   INVENTOR'S MORAL RIGHT IN THE EPC

3.1   Inventorship and Right of Attribution

Despite the absence of a moral right for an inventor as a statutory expression in contemporary patent law, a closer examination of the formality of patent law reveals that some elements of

---

may be grounded in, for example, G W F Hegel, 'Who Thinks Abstractly?' (1808) translation excerpted in Walter Kaufmann, *Hegel: Texts and Commentary* (Anchor Books 1966) 113–18.

[26]   Market inalienability or inalienability rules in law often embody moral objections. Guido Calabresi and Douglas Melamed. 'Property Rules, Liability Rules, and Inalienability: One View of the Cathedral', *Harvard Law Review* (1972) 1089–1128. See also, M J Radin, *Contested Commodities* (Harvard University Press 1996).

[27]   Joseph Raz, 'Value Incommensurability: Some Preliminaries' *Proceedings of the Aristotelian Society*. Vol. 86. Aristotelian Society, (Wiley 1985).

[28]   Gunther Teubner and Andreas Fischer-Lescano, 'Cannibalizing Epistemes: Will Modern Law Protect Traditional Cultural Expressions?', in Christoph Graber (ed.), *Intellectual Property and Traditional Cultural Expressions in a Digital Environment* (Edward Elgar 2008) at 17.

[29]   Art 6(2) of Directive 98/44/EC of the European Parliament and of the Council of 6 July 1998 on the legal protection of biotechnological inventions (Biotech Directive) OJ L 213, 30.7.1998, 13–21.

[30]   CJEU, C-34/10, *Oliver Brüstle v. Greenpeace* eV. ECLI:EU:C:2011:669 (*Brüstle*).

[31]   CJEU, C-364/13, ECLI:EU:C:2014:2451, *International Stem Cell Corporation v. Comptroller General of Patents, Designs and Trade Marks* (*ISCC*).

a moral right are indeed found in the law. Whilst the right of integrity and divulgation may be against the purpose of the patent system, which encourages improvements and requires disclosure, the right of attribution granted as a personal right to the inventor is still found in contemporary patent law. This is reflected first in the definition of an inventor, and second in regulation of inventorship as opposed to patent applicants and proprietors.

Inventorship and authorship initially seem to be vested with natural-person inventors and authors,[32] while exclusive rights may be registered, owned and exercised by corporations. Moreover, to a limited degree, moral harm – at least against false attribution – seems to be acknowledged, as inventors are to be acknowledged in patent documents and the right to be named as inventor does exist as part of positive statutes.

It is commonly understood that the initial right to file for a European patent under the EPC belongs to a natural-person inventor and, as a corollary, only a natural-person inventor has the right to be named in a patent document. This position can be read from the reference under Article 58 to natural or legal persons, read together with Article 60(1), which grants the right to file for an invention to an inventor or the inventor's successor in title. It is also implied in Rule 19(1) of the EPC Regulation, which provides that the designation required of Article 81 must include 'the family name, given names and full address of the inventor, contain the statement referred to in Article 81 and bear the signature of the applicant or his representative'.[33] As only natural persons have family and given names, it follows that only a natural person may provide that information to meet the formality requirements. The EPO reiterated this view in its refusal decisions on patent applications naming artificial intelligence (AI) as an inventor.[34] Indeed, the preparatory works for EPO imply the signatory states' intent and understanding that the term was limited to natural persons, as the documents consistently referred to the inventor as a natural person,[35] often by the pronoun 'he', as does current EPC Article 60(1). Moreover, as noted in the DABUS rejection, the preparatory works of 1961 showed that there had been discussions on granting inventorship to a legal person, but this was dropped from the

---

[32]   See Jane C Ginsburg, 'The Concept of Authorship in Comparative Copyright Law', 52 *DePaul L Rev* (2003) 1063 at 1066. Based on comparative law study, Ginsburg concludes that in the US, the United Kingdom, Canada, Australia, France, Belgium, and the Netherlands, an author is 'a human being who exercises subjective judgement in composing the work and who controls its execution'.

[33]   Rule 19(1) EPC Regulation.

[34]   See EPO (2020) EP 18 275 163 and EP 18 275 174 Refusal Decision (consolidated) of 27 January 2020 (DABUS). Consolidated decision text available online on EPO website https://register.epo.org/application?number= EP18275163, last visited 20 September 2020. The applicant has appealed and the appeal is pending at the time of this writing. Other patent offices and courts have reached the same conclusion concerning AI inventor claims. In the UK, in a similar application filed by the same applicant, the court dismissed the appeal and upheld the rejection by UKIPO, under Art 13 UK Patent Act. *Stephen L Thaler v. The Comptroller-General of Patents, Designs and Trade Marks* [2020] EWHC 2412 (Pat).

[35]   See for example, Travaux préparatoires EPC 1973 Document BRl6 e/69 at 10–11. The document compares the Preliminary Draft of the EPC to the 1965 Draft and the EFTA Draft. Comparison of Art 5 (which granted the right to file for a patent, equivalent to Art 60 of the current EPC) shows a reference to natural and legal persons, or any body, limited by nationality or domicile. See also Travaux Préparatoires EPC 1973, Minutes of the 5th Meeting of the Inter-Governmental Conference for the Setting up of a European System for the Grant of Patents, Luxembourg, 26 January to 1 February 197 Document BR/169 e/72/ley/KM/PRK, at paras 30–2. All preparatory works are archived on the EPO website. Available online https://www.epo.org/law-practice/legal-texts/epc/archive/epc-1973/traveaux/documents.html, last visited 20 September 2020.

final draft adopted, cementing the view that only natural persons are to be deemed an inventor under the EPC.[36]

Article 58 EPC states that an application may be filed by 'any natural or legal person, or any body equivalent to a legal person by virtue of the law governing it'. Thus an application may be filed by a natural or legal person. In other words, the right to file for a patent may vest in any natural or legal person. In contrast, under Article 60(1): 'the right to a European patent shall belong to the inventor or his successor in title'. When read in combination, whilst the initial right to receive a patent belongs to an inventor, the inventor may transfer that right, and those who succeed to the right including legal persons may file for a patent and who may receive a patent. The EPC does not separately define an inventor, but in Article 62 lays down that 'the inventor shall have the right, *vis-à-vis the applicant* for *or proprietor* of a European patent, to be mentioned as such before the European Patent Office' (emphasis added). Moreover, in Article 81, the EPC lays down, as a matter of procedural requirement, the duty of an applicant to designate an inventor; and in case the applicant is not the inventor or sole inventor, the designation must contain a statement indicating the origin of the right to a European patent.

Thus, the inventor's attribution right or paternity right indeed exists in patent statutes. As the origin of that right is the Paris Convention, which provides in Article 4*ter* a right to be named as such in the patent, a similar right should exist in patent statutes of the signatory states to the Paris Convention.[37] The legislative history of the Paris Convention shows that Article 4*ter* was inserted only at the revision conference of 1934 resulting in the London Act.[38] The presence in a significant international patent convention of the inventor's right to be named seems to suggest that at least there has been a legitimate concern about the harm of passing off one's invention as that of another, which has to be regulated in a harmonized manner. As for justification for its insertion into the Paris Convention, in a publication commemorating the centennial of the Paris Convention, then World Intellectual Property Organization (WIPO) director Bogsch explained that the right is both '*just* since any inventor has a natural pride in his intellectual creation and the world should know that the creation is his brainchild … and *useful* … safeguarding the material interests of the inventor since it reduces the chances of fraudulent applications'.[39]

The statement of justness and usefulness highlights that the attribution right of an inventor in patent law has two important dimensions. It not only acknowledges the inventor by allowing a paternity claim by the inventor, which has subjective value for the inventor as a person, but also it serves as a procedural device to prevent fraudulent patent filing, objectively ensuring the veracity of the patent system. Thus, the inventor's moral right is further distinguished from

---

[36]   See 4860/IV/61-F Groupe de travail Brevets de la C.E.E. Travaux Préparatoires CBE 1973 (French) at 18–19. https://www.epo.org/law-practice/legal-texts/epc/archive/epc-1973/traveaux/documents.html, last visited 20 September 2020.

[37]   Paris Convention for the Protection of Industrial Property, as last revised at the Stockholm Revision Conference, 20 March 1883, 21 UST 1583; 828 UNTS 305 (Paris Convention).

[38]   London Act for the Paris Convention for the Protection of Industrial Property, revised as the London Act, 1938. Text available online https:// wipolex .wipo .int/ en/ treaties/ textdetails/ 12991, last visited 20 September 2020.

[39]   See Arpad Bogsch, 'The First Hundred Years of the Paris Convention for the Protection of Industrial Property', in WIPO, *The Paris Convention for the Protection of Industrial Property from 1883 to 1983* (International Bureau of IP 1983), 15–117 at 32, Text available online https://www.wipo.int/edocs/pubdocs/en/intproperty/875/wipo_pub_875.pdf, last visited 20 September 2020 (emphasis added).

moral rights in copyright law. Inventors are recognized but this does not seem to grant them any further right to control the outcome of their inventions; yet it is an important formality requirement for the registration-based patent system.

As a personal right, the inventor's moral right under the EPC is a relative right that works against other patent applicants or the patent proprietor only, and thus seems to be devoid of effect. Moreover, the scope is limited to patent documents only, and it is not a right to be named as the inventor outside the patent document granted. Beyond the patent documents and registry, inventors do not have a right to claim their inventorship further, whereas a patent proprietor, for example, may claim their patent ownership in products that embody their inventions.

As it is a procedural device, failure to indicate the inventor may result in rejection of the application. As the form(ality) and substance of an invention are separate requirements, formal failure does not result in automatic invalidation, as it may be corrected. Rule 19 of the EPC regulations establishes a procedure for the office to communicate failure and Rule 21 allows for rectification only with the consent of the wronged party.[40] Failure to meet formality requirements in the EPO could result in loss of a patent right. The EPC provides in Article 90(5) that if there is any deficiency including designation of the inventor according to Article 81, the application will be rejected.[41]

However, the EPO is not required to engage in verifying an inventorship claim nor has it the competence to rule on it, because national courts have jurisdiction.[42] Thus a challenge to claims of correct inventorship or false attribution cannot be raised in the EPO. Although the EPO itself does not adjudicate on the question of inventorship, a fraudulent application (i.e. a patent application filed by a person who does not have the right to do so) may have a procedural consequence by virtue of Article 61. This provides that a genuine rightholder may assume the application as their own and continue prosecuting it, file a new application or request rejection of the fraudulent application.[43] As false attribution may be an instance of fraudulent application, some remedies are reserved against applicants who are not inventors or successors in title.

In other words, a moral right granted to the inventor under the EPC seems to be a weak form of attribution right, limited to patent documents against the patent applicant or proprietor only, with limited remedies. Taken independently, it seems to be a weak relative right that may not have much value beyond the process of patent prosecution rather than as a substantive right. However, as Section 3.2 examines below, incorrect attribution may be used in combination with the procedural right of priority – a right granted to an applicant – to become a tool to dictate how subsequent patent rights may be filed, granted to an inventor, and even affect a part of the substantive patentability requirement of novelty.

---

[40] Implementing Regulations to the Convention on the Grant of European Patents of 5 October 1973 as amended 2020 (EPC Regulations). Text available on EPO website https://www.epo.org/law-practice/legal-texts/html/epc/2016/e/ma2.html.

[41] EPC, Art 90.

[42] According to Art 1(1) Protocol on Jurisdiction and the Recognition of Decisions in respect of the Right to the Grant of a European Patent (EPC Protocol on Recognition) of 5 October 1973, national courts have jurisdiction to adjudicate on claims to the right to the grant of a European Patent.

[43] EPC Art 61(1). See also EPO G 0003/92 (Unlawful applicant), Enlarged Board of Appeal Decision of 13 June 1994, interpreting Art 61(1)(b).

3.2   Inventor's Attribution Right and Priority Claim: A Case Study of CRISPR Inventorship

The disputed invention in the case study is based on a genome editor tool called the Clustered Regularly Interspaced Short Palindromic Repeats (CRISPR) Cas9 system, which allows researchers to cut and edit the genetic sequence. Dubbed as 'genetic scissors', the CRISPR Cas9 system may indeed be one of the most important research tools, as it can be used to modify genes of various organisms, from plants to animals, and is touted as a game changer in biotechnology and bio medicine.[44]

As a platform technology, CRISPR-Cas 9 has a wide range of applications and it is not surprising that several groups involved in developing the technology have rushed to patent various aspects and elements of the technology internationally. Patents on and surrounding CRISPR-Cas 9 have generated huge interest and many patent applications. Among these the most controversial aspect of the patent applications involving this technology relates not only to claims to economic rights but also to claims of inventorship – who was the original inventor? This question falls squarely within the core of the inventor's paternity or attribution right.

The case brought before the EPO[45] relates to oppositions filed against a patent granted to one of the research teams. This was one of the many strands of disputes between two groups of inventors and their successors in title, Broad Institute and MIT with the inventor Feng Zhang[46] against the University of Vienna and UC Berkeley with inventors Jennifer Doudna, Emmanuelle Charpentier and others.[47] Typically of any scientific research, these researchers at different research facilities communicated and exchanged ideas in conferences on various occasions.[48] A seminal paper was first published in 2012, authored by Jinek and others from Doudna and Charpentier's team. It showed CRISPR-Cas9 in prokaryotic cells but did not specifically apply the technology to eukaryotic cells.[49] In 2013, Cong and others in Feng Zhang's team published their results with applications to eukaryotic cells.[50] More controversy was generated as some of the inventors were widely recognized in public as the inventors pioneering the field, collecting accolades. Doudna and Charpentier eventually won the 2020 Nobel prize in chemistry for 'development of a method in genome editing'.[51]

In parallel to the EPO proceedings, there have been interference proceedings in the US. As US patent law notably employs the first-to-file principle, interference proceedings at the patent

---

[44]   E Pennisi, 'The CRISPR Craze', 341(6148) *Science* (2013), 833–6.

[45]   EPO T0844/18, n 15.

[46]   US Patent 8697359.

[47]   For example, US Patent Application 2014/0068797, which lists the inventors as 'Jennifer A. Doudna, Martin Jinek, Emmanuelle Charpentier, Krzysztof Chylinski, James Harrison Doudna Cate, Wendell Lim, Lei Qi'.

[48]   Jon Cohen, 'How the battle lines over CRISPR were drawn', *Science Magazine* 15 February 2017. Available online https://www.sciencemag.org/news/2017/02/how-battle-lines-over-crispr-were-drawn last visited 20 September 2020.

[49]   Martin Jinek, Krzysztof Chylinski, Ines Fonfara, Michael Hauer, Jennifer A. Doudna, Emmanuelle Charpentier, 'A Programmable Dual-RNA-Guided DNA Endonuclease in Adaptive Bacterial Immunity', *Science* 17 August 2012, 816–21.

[50]   Le Cong, F Ann Ran, David Cox, Shuailiang Lin, Robert Barretto, Naomi Habib, Patrick D Hsu, Xuebing Wu, Wenyan Jiang, Luciano A Marraffini, Feng Zhang, 'Multiplex Genome Engineering Using CRISPR/Cas Systems', *Science* 15 February 2013, 819–23.

[51]   See for 2020 announcement https://www.nobelprize.org/prizes/chemistry/2020/summary/.

office determine a so-called 'genuine' invention by ruling on the interference of applications filed at different times but directed to the same inventions.[52] In an interesting procedural twist, a later-filed application with a narrower scope led to the first patent grant, naming Feng Zhang as the inventor,[53] whilst the earlier application naming Doudna and others as the inventors was still pending.[54] In the first interference decisions, the US Patent and Trademark Office (USPTO's) Patent Trial and Appeal Board (PTAB) ruled that there was no interference and that the applications were directed to different inventions. The inference ruling was confirmed by the US Federal Court of Appeals (CAFC) on appeal.[55] A second interference hearing followed a similar path, dividing the patents derived from the inventions among different groups.[56]

Whilst the question was the identity – from among these two groups of researchers in this dispute – of the genuine inventor of CRISPR-Cas9 technology, the legal issue in the US was the scope of inventions claimed by the two different groups of patent applications; it was then a case of interference of the applications. Likewise, genuine inventorship is not a question that the EPO may decide and thus the dispute before the EPO was also not about inventorship as such, but an opposition proceeding filed by UC Berkeley's group and eight other parties seeking revocation of the patent granted naming Zhang and others as the inventors and filed by the Broad Institute and others. The main point of dispute was novelty and the priority date, as the patent used the priority date based on their many provisional applications filed in the US.

The priority right, which originates from the Paris Convention, helps inventors seeking patents over one invention in different countries. The Paris Convention in Article 4*bis* aims to prevent international patent applicants from destroying novelty over the same inventions based on their own earlier patent applications in other Paris Union countries. If priority rights are not valid, an earlier application may destroy the novelty of a second application by the same applicant. The EPC provides the same right for international applications in Article 87 stating '*Any person* who has duly filed, … an application for a patent, a utility model or a utility certificate, or his successor in title, shall enjoy, for the purpose of filing a European patent application in respect of *the same invention*, a right of priority …'.[57]

The opposing parties claimed that the patent applications were not filed by the same persons for the earlier application in respect of the same invention since one of the named inventors, as his successor in title, mentioned in the priority documents that to claim priority was not included in the EPC application.[58] Against this, the patent proprietor claimed that the law applicable to the question is US law and, among others, questioned whether the EPO has the competence to decide on the ownership of a 'priority right' as this is ultimately a question con-

---

[52]   United States Patent Act 35 USC §135(a). Interference proceedings is an *inter partes* proceeding by the administrative patent board of appeal (Patent Trials and Appels Board, PTAB).

[53]   The Broad Institute's application which has led to US Patent 8697359, granted 15 April 2014 under the expedited review procedure.

[54]   US Patent Application No. 13/842859.

[55]   See *Regents of the Univ of Cal v. Broad Inst, Inc*, No. 2017-1907, 2018 US App LEXIS 25535 (Fed Cir 10 September 2018).

[56]   See for example, Decision of the Patent Trial and Appeal Board (PTAB) Patent Interference No. 106, 115 (2020) *The Regents of the University of California; the University of Vienna; and Emmanuelle Charpentier v. The Broad Institute, Inc, Massachusetts Institute of Technology, and President and Fellows of Harvard College.*

[57]   Art 87 EPC, emphasis added.

[58]   CRISPR Opposition (2018) n 15 at para 7.

cerning inventorship. As examined in Section 3.1 above, the EPO cannot rule on the question who has the right to file for patents, which in turn means that the EPO cannot rule on who is the genuine inventor. Likewise, the EPO cannot rule on the question of ownership.[59] The EPO Opposition Division, however, considered that the question was not about ownership of the right, and inventorship, but rather an issue of the validity of a priority claim, a procedural question and thus the EPO had the competence to rule on it. It thus proceeded to interpret the meaning of 'any person ... filed on the same invention' to mean not any one of the joint applicants of the first application, but *all applicants* of the first application. This was the established practice in the EPO.[60] Thus a priority right based on a provisional application listing fewer inventors could not be relied on. The EPO also rejected the claim that the question of interpretation of 'any person' has to be decided by national law.[61] The Opposition Division ruled that the priority date based on that application could be used and, as a consequence, the patent was revoked for lack of novelty. On appeal, the EPO Board of Appeal in case T844/18 dismissed the appeal and thus maintained the revocation.

The dispute here was not about the right to be named as an inventor under the EPC as such, but about the absence of the correct inventorship attribution in the application, which was used in the equivalent manner. The case shows that, in fact, the genuine inventor enjoys entitlement in patent law based on the Paris Convention as well as the EPC. Although the attribution right provided in the EPC is a weak right to be named in the patent application *vis-à-vis* a patent applicant, nevertheless when used in the context of an application filed by entities or persons who do not have explicit consent from the original inventor, then it can be used as a strong right in international applications. The EPO's 'all applicants' approach clearly requires correct attribution to all inventors, without judging on inventorship. In the CRISPR opposition, the EPO highlights that patent applicants should correctly acknowledge the inventors and correctly receive the transfer of entitlements to priority claims from all inventors. This is an interesting case where a procedural right is used as if it is an additional property right on behalf of the inventors, although the law does not provide the named inventor any right to it against third parties, nor does it provide for a priority claim as a property right. However, as the incorrect designation could be fatal in asserting a priority right granted under the Paris Convention, the inventor's priority claim may be used as an economic right, which could be used, to an extent, to control subsequent patent filings.

3.3   Inventor's Moral Right: Prior User Right as an Own Use Defence

A third trace of the inventor's moral right in patent law could be found in the prior user right. A prior user right or a prior user defence is often considered a limitation to a patent right. Limitations and exceptions to a granted patent right are not under the EPC and thus, a remedy for the inventor against an infringement claim by the patent proprietor is not within the ambit of the EPC. The post-grant aspects of a patent granted under the EPC are national; moreover, national laws on this aspect remain largely unharmonized internationally as well as in Europe. To an extent, the TRIPS Agreement (Article 30) provides some principles on how such

---

[59]   CRISPR Opposition (2018) n 15 at paras 58–63.
[60]   CRISPR Opposition (2018) n 15 at para 66 et seq.
[61]   CRISPR Opposition (2018) n 15 at para 72.

exceptions should be made, outlining the so-called three steps test, which puts restrictions on signatory states' freedom to set limitations and exceptions on patent rights.

Historically, the 1965 EPC Draft aimed to include a prior user right.[62] However, no such right is currently found in the EPC as the project for a European patent system resulted in two tracks, namely the EPC of 1973; the Luxembourg Community Patent Convention (CPC 1975) of 1975,[63] as well as the second attempt to revive the CPC through the Community Patent Agreement (CPC 1989).[64] The CPC 1975 aimed to create a unitary title[65] autonomously in parallel to the national patent system.[66] As such, the CPC 1975 contained extensive provisions concerning post-grant aspects of the title, from Articles 27 to 32, concerning the property right, infringements,[67] exceptions,[68] exhaustion,[69] as well as both voluntary licences[70] and compulsory licences.[71] The CPC 1975 was signed but never went into effect, as there were insufficient ratifications. An amended version of the CPC 1975 with a litigation protocol was proposed as the CPC 1989, but met with the same failure.

The unitary patent package[72] was feared to inherit this history, caused by the uncertainty induced by Brexit. At least, now things are moving in a positive direction with German ratification, and the Protocol to the Agreement on a Unified Patent Court (UPCA) on provisional applications took effect on 19 January 2022.[73]

The UPCA includes substantive clauses for the post-grant aspects of a patent having a unitary effect, including a prior user right. Article 28 UPCA provides for a prior user right. However, similarly to the EPC 1965 draft, instead of creating a uniform right of prior user or a uniform defence of a prior user, the UPCA makes the right based on the participating national law, thus effectively voiding any uniform protection or harmonization. Article 28 UPCA reads (emphasis added):

> Any person, who, *if a national patent had been granted* in respect of an invention, would have had, in a Contracting Member State, a right based on prior use of that invention or a right of personal possession of that invention, *shall enjoy, in that Contracting Member State,* the same rights in respect of a patent for the same invention.

---

[62]   EPO Travaux n 35, BR/6 e/69.

[63]   Convention for the European Patent for the common market signed at Luxembourg on 15 December 1975, 17 OJ L 1 (1976) (CPC 1975).

[64]   Agreement Relating to Community Patents – Done at Luxembourg on 15 December 1989, 89/695/ EEC, OJ L 401, 30/12/1989 P 0001–0027 (CPC 1989).

[65]   CPC 1975, Art 2, para (2).

[66]   CPC 1975, Art 1; Art 2, para (2).

[67]   CPC 1975, Arts 29–30.

[68]   CPC 1975, Arts 31 and 38.

[69]   CPC 1975, Art 32.

[70]   CPC 1975, Art 44.

[71]   CPC 1975, Arts 46–8.

[72]   Regulation (EU) 1257/2012 (2012) implementing enhanced cooperation in the area of the creation of unitary patent protection, published OJEU L361/1-8, (UP Regulation), UPR; Regulation (EU) 1260/2012, implementing enhanced cooperation in the area of the creation of unitary patent protection with regard to the application translation arrangement, Published OJEU L361/89-92 (UP Translation Regulation); Agreement on a Unified Patent Court, Document no 16351/12 (11 January 2013), (UPCA).

[73]   Ratification date information to the Protocol to the Agreement on a Unified Patent Court on provisional application (PPA) is found on the website of European Council. https://www.consilium.europa.eu/ en/documents-publications/treaties-agreements/agreement/?id=2015056 last visited 22 February 2022.

Thus under the UPCA a prior user right is granted only if that right exists nationally, if a patent would have been granted instead of a unitary patent. Although the substance of the right is not provided in the UPCA, the text of Article 28 shows that a limited right is granted to a person who has used the invention prior to the patent grant, or who personally possesses the invention, implying a prior inventor or a user. The reference to a prior user or to persons who enjoy personal possession implies a genuine inventor who was unaware of – or who was not part of – the patenting process. On the other hand, the reference to 'any person' suggests that the right is not to be limited to those who can be named as an inventor but also other users of the invention and thus applicable to a broader group of users. Legislative examples from other countries with a similar right show that it is not a right that one can transfer, and is limited to those users who have independently invented the claimed inventions, prior to the grant of a patent.[74]

The prior user right is often seen as an exception that rectifies the problem created by the first-to-file rule of patent law. Patent law grants a patent right only to the first person who files for a patent and consequently the patent holder may exclude an inventor who may have actually invented the same invention as well as users who have put such inventions into practice before the patent grants without knowledge of the patent applications. In short: these prior inventors and users may be excluded from using their own inventions. In most cases, such patents should not have been granted due to lack of novelty, especially if the invention was used in public before filing of patent applications. However, in the rare instance of two or more parallel and independent inventions, the prior user right is an important right for an inventor who also employs the invention in practice[75] as it would allow continuity in using the invention but without having to seek licences from the patent holder. As it is, however, limited in scope, a prior user inventor may not be able to commercialize their invention.

The prior user right under the UPCA may be compared to the own name use exception under EU trademark law.[76] Although limited in scope, the prior user right hints at the possibility to conceptualize the prior user right as an inventor's own use defence, as an extension of moral right. An own use defence would extend not only to those who are in possession of the invention or who used it before the patent, without knowledge of the patent, but also to the inventor named in the patent document, who would clearly have knowledge of the patent, to shield themselves against infringement claims over all patents resulting from own inventions.

This defence would be useful because inventorship and ownership are indeed separate in contemporary patent law, often resulting in stories where inventors are left without much reward for their inventive ideas, and even prevented from commercially benefiting from their

---

[74]   WIPO Report SCP/20/6, 'Exceptions and Limitations to Patent Rights: Prior Use', available online http://www.wipo.int/edocs/mdocs/patent_policy/en/scp_20/scp_20_6.pdf, 14 January 2015. See also AIPPI, 'Patents Study of Prior User Rights', Summary Report, Special Committee 228 (2014), available online https://www.aippi.org/download/commitees/228/SR228English.pdf.

[75]   See for a brief summary of legislative examples, WIPO Report SCP/20/6, 'Exceptions and Limitations to Patent Rights: Prior Use', available online http://www.wipo.int/edocs/mdocs/patent _policy/en/scp_20/scp_20_6.pdf, 14 January 2015. See also AIPPI, 'Patents Study of Prior User Rights', Summary Report, Special Committee (2014), available online https://www.aippi.org/download/commitees/228/SR228English.pdf. In the context of US patent law, the own use defence was proposed earlier in the context of 'patent fair use', see K J Strandburg, 'Patent Fair Use 2.0', 1 *UC Irvine L Rev* (2011) 265, and M A O'Rourke, 'Toward a Doctrine of Fair Use in Patent Law', 100 *Colum L Rev* (2000) 1177.

[76]   The EU Trademark Regulation and Directive both provide for this. See note 14.

own inventive ideas once separated from patents.[77] Even when the inventor may agree with the first patent proprietor as to their own use, an inventor would have no claims deriving from their own invention against second or other subsequent owners of the patent, unless there is a separate agreement with them. A broad interpretation of 'prior user' to include all named inventors would prevent further alienation of the inventor from their own inventions.

4.   CONCLUDING REMARKS

The above discussion shows that although the moral right of an inventor does exist in contemporary patent law, it survives as a weak form of defensive right and the morality of the right either for or against the inventor seems to have been reduced. When one compares the idea of authorship to inventorship, the contrast is highly illustrative. One of the functions of authorship is not only for us to identify and attribute text to an author so that the author can claim it as their own, but also to make authors morally responsible for what they create, and in turn make the text reliable and authentic.[78] Can one make the same observation with respect to inventors and their inventions? If inventorship functions as does authorship as a 'set of beliefs governing the production, circulation and consumption' of an invention as in copyright discourse,[79] then the very absence of a morality-based argument removes the consideration for responsibility from the formation of patent right. As a result, we have only the owners as patent holders who cannot be morally committed to or be held responsible for the purely economic rights of patents, whereas inventors cannot govern the production, circulation and consumption of their own inventions based on their moral rights.

Focusing only on the exclusive right of patent would run contrary to the understanding that the institution of law relates and may even be founded upon morality. Raz argued that there is a necessary connection between the law and morality and that law's intrinsic virtue is to have legitimate moral authority over its subjects.[80] Based on this understanding, in the institution of law there are moral or normative principles, based on which rules, standards, rights and duties are affected, and are formed.[81] Morality may give rise to moral rights for inventors, and when morality is used as a way to impose restrictions and duties on title holders as a condition for recognition of their right, morality may be manifested as a positive legal duty on the part of owners. A positive duty-based morality then prevails over notions of the will of the community that can be found in combination with the subjective will that makes property have effect upon the world.

---

[77]   John Gapper, 'A Remote Village, A World-changing Invention and the Epic Legal Fight that Followed' *Financial Times*, 27 January 2022.

[78]   Michel Foucault, 'What Is an Author', Original Publication 1969, Translated text by Josué V Harrari, Reprinted in *The Foucault Reader*, edited by Paul Rabinow (Penguin Books 1984) at 101–20.

[79]   Martin Kretschmer, Lionel Bently and Rona Deazley, *Privilege and Property – Essays on the history of Copyright* (OpenBook Publishers 2010) at 15.

[80]   Joseph Raz, 'Can Moral Principles Change?', King's College London Dickson Poon School Of Law Legal Studies Research Paper No. 2017-40; Oxford Legal Studies Research Paper No. 58/2017 (2017). Available online https://scholarship.law.columbia.edu/faculty_scholarship/2052 last visited 20 September 2020.

[81]   Raz, n 2.

Such duties may give rise to moral rights for those who are not the owners of the exclusive right, but for others who are morally connected to an invention, that is, inventors and even the public in general. As we have seen in this chapter, the right of attribution and paternity given to an inventor protects their moral interests against patent owners. Moreover, extending the own use defence extended to the original inventors would strengthen this position against infringement claims of patents on the inventions that they have created.

Patent law's romantic vision of inventorship – a lone natural-person inventor, toiling away in a laboratory working on a spark-of-genius idea – has received much criticism for not being realistic.[82] Doctrines devised to protect such inventors may be a poor fit for the more commonly used model of a collective and company-based inventing process, where average skilled workers jointly research and develop inventions. A proposal for a stronger moral right for a natural-person inventor may seem a counter-intuitive recommendation as it proposes making the romantic vision more complete, rather than bringing the current law closer to the realities of corporate inventors where most invention is done by employees working in a collective and cumulative process, for juridical persons – a corporation. However, considering how individual inventors have all but disappeared from the actual registry of patent owners of economic rights, staying the course of the romantic vision of inventorship with individual moral value may be necessary to make patent law morally proper and acceptable, so that geniuses are indeed properly protected against the owners of the economic right. A fair patent system may need to provide not only economic but also moral incentives as fuel for the fire of genius.

---

[82]   James Boyle, *Shamans, Software, and Spleens: Law and the Construction of the Information Society* (Harvard University Press 1996).

7.   Moral rights and industrial design
Giorgio Spedicato

1.   THE ROLE OF MORAL RIGHTS WITHIN THE INTELLECTUAL PROPERTY SYSTEM

In the intellectual property domain, one instinctively tends to associate the notion of "moral rights" with copyright, and especially with the (more clearly author-centric) legal framework associated with copyright in the countries of continental Europe.[1] In fact, it is specifically in the copyright context that the need to provide legal protection to creators' personality began to emerge, around the middle of the nineteenth century, mainly driven by French case law and German legal scholarship.[2]

During the following century, however, the need for protection progressively exceeded the limited scope of copyright, and currently moral rights are no longer the exclusive prerogative of authors of copyrighted works, but are granted by some (primarily continental European) legislations – albeit to a variable extent from sector to sector, and from country to country – even to certain creators of immaterial goods protected by an industrial property right.

However, in these latter cases, moral rights are markedly more circumscribed than those granted to the author of a copyrighted work, and are often limited to the right to be mentioned as the author/creator of the immaterial good in the owner's patent application or application for registration.

This is not surprising, at least prima facie. In the copyright context, moral rights primarily have the purpose of protecting the author's personality to the extent it is expressed in his or her creation: thus, their purpose is to protect the personality of the individual *as the author* of an intellectual creation. The personal connection between the author and his or her work in fact constitutes – as noted by Advocate General Szpunar in his conclusions in the *Cofemel* case – the "axiological foundation" of copyright protection.[3] And it is no accident that the requirement to grant copyright protection to a work – i.e. its originality – is interpreted in the EU law context in terms of reflection of the author's personality.[4]

---

[1]   Cf. among the many studies, Adolf Dietz, "The Moral Right of the Author: Moral Rights and the Civil Law Countries" [1994] Colum.–VLA J. L. & Arts 199. For a survey on the position of moral rights in common law jurisdictions see Gerald Dworkin, "The Moral Right of the Author: Moral Rights and the Common Law Countries" [1994] Colum.–VLA J. L. & Arts 229. For a vast and classic comparative study on moral rights see Stig Strömholm, *Le droit moral de l'auteur en droit allemand, francais et scandinave avec un aperçu de l'évolution internationale: étude de droit comparé* (Norstedt 1966–1973).

[2]   Gillian Davies and Kevin Garnett (eds), *Moral Rights* (Sweet & Maxwell 2010) 21.

[3]   Cf. the Opinion of AG Szpunar in Case C-683/17 *Cofemel* ECLI:EU:C:2019:363, [2019] para 3.

[4]   Cf. whereas (17) of the Council Directive (EEC) No. 93/98 harmonizing the term of protection of copyright and certain related rights [1993] OJ L290/9. See also Case C-145/10 *Painer* EU:C:2011:798, [2011] ECR I-12533, para 94; Case C-604/10 *Football Dataco* ECLI:EU:C:2012:115, [2012] para 38; Case C-161/17 *Renckhoff* EU:C:2018:634, [2018] para 14; Case C-683/17 *Cofemel* EU:C:2019:721, [2019] para 30.

According to a widespread theoretical approach, the subjective element of the author's personality – and, consequently, the needs to protect the author's moral rights – take on much less significance for intellectual products that are of an essentially technical or functional nature.[5] Indeed, inventions are not protected if they are original because they reflect the inventor's personality, but if they are original because the technical solution they embody is "not obvious to a person skilled in the art".[6] Similarly, trademarks are not protected if they reflect the personality of the subject who created them, but, more objectively, if they have a "distinctive character".[7] The limited role of the creator's personality thus entails, in the context of patents and trademarks, a more limited recognition of the creator's moral rights.

Whether one agrees in general terms with this theoretical approach or not, it cannot be denied that the sector of industrial design is rather unique, because it is significantly more heterogeneous than other areas of industrial property:[8] it protects creations of a markedly, although not exclusively,[9] functional nature (e.g., the design of the pistons of an engine), creations that are both functional and aesthetic (e.g., the design of some appliances), and even creations that are almost exclusively aesthetic (e.g., the design of rings or other jewellery). The considerable heterogeneity of this conceptual category makes it significantly more complex, compared to other areas of industrial property, to provide a single response to the question of what should be the most appropriate level of protection for the designer's personality.

Moreover, apart from their traditional justification, it is widely recognized among legal scholars that moral rights have a purpose, or at least an effect, that goes beyond protecting the creator's personality as it is expressed in his or her creation. Recognizing the paternity of the work – and, secondly, the guarantee of its non-alteration (integrity) – translates into a reputational advantage for the creator that also has a clear economic dimension,[10] allowing the creator to commercially exploit his or her creations at a higher price (depending on the designer's reputation[11]) or, more generally, having better opportunities in the labour market.[12] This constitutes an economic interest that certainly does not relate solely to authors of works

---

[5]   In this sense see Alberto Musso, *Ditta e insegna. Marchio. Brevetti. Disegni e modelli. Concorrenza* (Zanichelli – Il Foro italiano 2012) 743.

[6]   Cf. e.g., Article 56 of the Convention on the Grant of European Patents (hereinafter "EPC").

[7]   Cf. e.g., Article 4 of Regulation (EU) 2017/1001 of the European Parliament and of the Council of 14 June 2017 on the European Union trade mark [2017] OJ L 154/1.

[8]   Cf. Thomas Margoni, "Not for Designers: On the Inadequacies of EU Design Law and How to Fix It" [2013] J. Intell. Prop. Info. Tech. & Elec. Com. L. 225.

[9]   Article 8 of the Regulation (EC) No. 6/2002 on Community designs [2002] OJ L3/1 explicitly excludes design protection with respect to features dictated *solely* by a technical function.

[10]   In this vein see, e.g., Catherine Fisk, "Credit Where It's Due: The Law and Norms of Attribution" [2006] Geo. L. J. 49, maintaining that "[i]f professional reputation were property, it would be the most valuable property that most people own". In general terms see Jacques De Werra, "The Moral Right of Integrity", in Estelle Derclaye (ed.), *Research Handbook on the Future of EU Copyright* (Edward Elgar 2009) 268.

[11]   An interesting case study is presented in A Gandini, I Pais and A Beraldo, "Reputation and Trust on Online Labour Markets: The Reputation Economy of Elance" [2016] Work Organis. Lab. & Globalis. 27.

[12]   In this vein see H Hansmann and M Santilli, "Authors' and Artists' Moral Rights: A Comparative and Legal Economic Analysis" [1997] J. Leg. Stud. 104, pointing out that the "alteration of works that an artist has already sold can, by damaging his reputation, lower the prices he can charge for other work that he sells subsequently".

protected by copyright, but potentially also all the other creators of intangible products protected by an industrial property right.

But moral rights also take on economic significance in a respect other than that just indicated.[13] Since they are typically independent of economic rights[14] and attribute to a certain extent a power of prohibition on their owner, they confer on the author of an intellectual creation prerogatives that can be enforced even against (1) the owner of the tangible good that incorporates the intellectual creation, and/or (2) the successor in title of the creator (e.g., his or her employer), thus potentially conflicting with the economic rights of those subjects. It can therefore be said that, from a certain perspective, moral rights constitute an external limit on the exercise of the economic rights: anyone economically using an intellectual creation, for whatever reason, will be bound to do so in accordance with the moral rights that the legislature has conferred on the creator.

This potential conflict between the creator and other subjects who own the economic rights to the intellectual creation (or good incorporating it) is normally solved by limiting the creator's ability to enforce the moral rights when exercising them would conflict with the needs of industrial production, making compliance with them excessively problematic or burdensome for the owner of the economic rights. In other words, the legislature generally does not deprive the author of his or her moral rights, but determines the best way that they can be exercised in a manner compatible with the exercise of the economic rights that may be held by third parties. And one can already anticipate that, not only under a *de lege ferenda* perspective, but also under existing law, this approach, normally adopted in the copyright context, also seems to be the most reasonable in the industrial property context: thus, not an approach that leads to precluding the attribution of moral rights to the author of an intellectual creation, but determining the manner in which exercising them can be harmonized with the exercise of the economic rights. This aspect seems to be particularly important in industrial design. The latter, in fact, poses significant challenges for the interpreter. Of the various fields of industrial property, it is conceptually the closest to copyright. That is not only because its creations are on the boundary between the artistic domain and the more strictly industrial domain but also because, specifically due to that characteristic, they can be protected (as will be clarified in greater detail below) by either an ad hoc industrial property right or by copyright, posing problems of harmonization of the norms regarding moral rights of one or the other sector.

2.   MORAL RIGHTS OF THE DESIGNER IN THE EU DESIGN LEGISLATION

Outside of the normative perimeter of copyright, international treaties on the protection of industrial design do not expressly grant moral rights to the designer.[15] In fact, Article 5(2)

---

[13]   For an economic perspective see Michael Rushton, "The Moral Rights of Artists: Droit Moral ou Droit Pécuniaire?" [1998] J. Cult. Econ. 15.

[14]   See e.g., Article 6*bis* of the Berne Convention for the Protection of Literary and Artistic Works, according to which the author shall have moral rights (more specifically: the moral right to claim authorship and to object to certain modifications and other derogatory actions) "[i]ndependently of the author's economic rights, and even after the transfer of the said rights".

[15]   No reference whatsoever to any moral right granted to the designer is contained in the Paris Convention for the Protection of Industrial Property of 1883 (its Article 4*ter* only provides that the

of the Geneva Act of the Hague Agreement Concerning the International Registration of Industrial Designs (1999) merely alludes to the possibility that a contracting party can establish by law that a national application for the grant of protection to an industrial design may contain "indications concerning the identity of the creator of the industrial design that is the subject of that application". Indirectly, therefore, what can be gleaned from the Geneva Act is that, within the legal systems that expressly so provide, the designer can, within the limits that will be examined below, be granted a right of paternity to his or her own design. This is the case, among others, for EU legislation.

While, on the one hand, Directive 98/71/EC on the legal protection of designs[16] does not grant to the designer any specific moral right[17] (and thus, from this standpoint, does not harmonize the legislations of the individual Member States, which remain somewhat fragmented),[18] Article 18 of Regulation (EC) No. 6/2002 on Community designs (CDR)[19] recognizes that the designer "shall have the right, in the same way as the applicant for or the holder of a registered Community design, to be cited as such" (i.e., to be cited as the designer) in the procedures before the Office – formerly the Office for Harmonisation in the Internal Market (OHIM), now the European Union Intellectual Property Office (EUIPO) – and in the Register of Community Designs.

The likening, suggested by the wording of the provision ("in the same way as …"), of the designer to the applicant for, or the holder of, a registered design, far from lacking significance, clearly shows that, in the intention of the European Union legislature, the purpose sought by granting a right to be cited to the designer is not so much to protect his or her personality against the applicant or the owner of the model,[20] but only to equalize those different subjects from the standpoint of their mention in the application for registration.

---

author of an invention has the moral right to be mentioned as such in the patent), the Hague Agreement Concerning the International Deposit of Industrial Designs of 1925 or the TRIPS Agreement of 1994. In a broader context, however, Article 15(1)(c) of the International Covenant on Economic, Social and Cultural Rights (1966) – which is modelled after Article 27(2) of the Universal Declaration of Human Rights (1948) and recognizes the right of everyone to "benefit from the protection of the moral and material interests resulting from any scientific, literary or artistic production of which he is the author" – does not expressly limit such right to copyrighted works, but refers more generally to creations eligible for some form of intellectual property protection: in this vein see also Fisk (n 10) 67.

[16]   Directive 98/71/EC of the European Parliament and of the Council of 13 October 1998 on the legal protection of designs [1998] OJ L 289/28.

[17]   There are, however, EU countries expressly granting moral rights to the designer: see, e.g., Article 38, para 3, of the Italian Industrial Property Code which, while granting to the employer the economic rights on a registered design or model, grants to the designer the moral right to be acknowledged as the author of the design or model and to have his or her name entered in the certificate of registration. On this provision see Philipp Fabbio, *Disegni e modelli* (Cedam 2012) 138. For a similar rule in Portugal, see Article 182 of the Portuguese Industrial Property Code.

[18]   The lack of harmonization at the European level is, however, not deemed to create any problem by some scholars: see, e.g., De Werra (n 10) 270.

[19]   Council Regulation (EC) No. 6/2002 of 12 December 2001 on Community designs [2002] OJ L3/1.

[20]   And, in this sense, it is worth noting that the text of Article 18 CDR differs from the text of the corresponding Article 19 of the original Proposal – see Proposal for a European Parliament and Council Regulation on the Community Design presented by the Commission on 3 December 1993, COM(93) 342 final, COD 463 [1994] OJ C29/20 – pursuant to which the designer shall have the right "as against the applicant for or the holder of a Registered Community Design" to be cited as such before the Office or in the Register.

In this regard, the assertion in the Official Commentary of the proposal of Regulation of 1993 that "the Community Design only confers economic rights, but no moral rights"[21] seems particularly suggestive (although not entirely accurate[22]). And the fact that the right to be cited specifically set forth in Article 18 of the Regulation is not comparable to a "genuine moral right"[23] – or at least the form that such type of right assumes in the European copyright context – is also apparent from a number of other sources.

Firstly, Article 18 of the Regulation provides that "[i]f the design is the result of teamwork, the citation of the team may replace the citation of the individual designers". Apparently, the European Union legislature's choice is based on practical considerations. In that regard, the Official Commentary of the proposal of Regulation stated that, when a design is "created by design departments of an industry or by teams of designers … it may be very cumbersome, if not sometimes impossible, to indicate the names of all the participants in the development of a design" and, therefore, "[i]n such cases it is sufficient to indicate, for example, that the design has been developed by the design department of the enterprise in question".

It is evident that the problem of multiple co-creators is in no way specific to production in the industrial design sector, and can also (and normally does) manifest itself in the case of many patentable inventions – which, more and more often, are created by teams of scientists and technicians – as well as works of authorship that are particularly complex, such as computer programs and databases. Neither patent law – which design law, from this standpoint, seems generally to be modelled after[24] – nor copyright law provide in general terms that the inventor's or author's right of paternity can be limited, on the individual level, by using a collective citation.[25] This is especially so where, as set forth in Article 18 CDR, the collective citation may consist merely of an indication of the design department of an enterprise[26] – i.e. information concerning a legal person, not a natural person (or multiple natural persons) – thus essentially disregarding the needs to protect the designer's personality[27] and, on the other

---

[21]   Cf. Official Commentary of the proposal of Regulation of 1993, 16, where, however, it is further stated that "the transfer of the right from the designer to the successor in title is total, except for the right established by Article 19 to be mentioned as designer before the Office in case of a Registered Community Design".

[22]   Cf. Mario Franzosi, *European Design Protection. Commentary to Directive and Regulation Proposal* (Kluwer Law International 1996) 105.

[23]   Cf. Green Paper on the legal protection of industrial design [1991], III/F/5131/91/EN, 96. In a similar vein, Uma Suthersanen, *Design Law in Europe* (Sweet & Maxwell 1999) 64, defines the right granted to the designer pursuant to Article 18 CDR a "quasi-moral right".

[24]   Franzosi (n 22) 114 highlights the "patent approach" characterizing the EC Regulation, which is even more evident when one considers the Regulation's treatment of moral rights.

[25]   On the contrary, a number of national laws states that each co-author is entitled to exercise his or her paternity right individually.

[26]   Cf. Official Commentary of the proposal of Regulation of 1993, 19, highlighting that "[i]n a number of cases designs are created by design departments of an industry or by teams of designers and it may be very cumbersome, if not sometimes impossible, to indicate the names of all the participants in the development of a design", with the consequence that "[i]n such cases it is sufficient to indicate, for example, that the design has been developed by the design department of the enterprise in question".

[27]   It is worth mentioning that there are national laws that, while recognizing the problems arising when industrial designs are created by teams of designers, did not restrict the individual right of each designer. See e.g. Article 11(3) of the Croatian Industrial Design Act (Law No. 46/2018), pursuant to which "[i]f several designers participated in the creation of the design jointly, all designers shall be entitled to the right [to be cited as the designer in all documents and during public exhibitions of his design],

hand, that part of legal scholars, especially European,[28] that traditionally opposes granting moral rights to a legal person.[29] Furthermore, even where it is possible to actually identify the members of the team, the collective citation dilutes the actual individual contributions, thereby reducing the value – both moral and economic – of the citation.[30]

On top of that, citing the designer's name on the application for registration is a purely optional aspect of the application.[31] In this regard, both Article 36(3) CDR – according to which "the application *may contain* [emphasis added] … the citation of the designer or of the team of designers" – and Article 1(2) of Regulation No. 2245/2002 implementing Regulation (EC) No. 6/2002 are clear.[32] It is worth noting that in the proposal of Regulation of 1993 the mention of the name of the designer or the indication of the team of designers was contemplated by Article 39(4) to be a necessary element of the application, required for it to be valid. However, as has been duly pointed out in legal commentary, "[t]he citation of the designer as a necessary element of the application [was] strongly opposed in some industrial circles".[33] The pressure applied by those industrial circles on the European Union legislature was such that, in the approved final version of the Regulation, the mention of the name of the designer was changed into a purely optional element of the application. And, because it is optional, the mention of the designer's name is not even examined by the EUIPO, as made clear by the Guidelines of the Office.[34]

In addition to being optional – and contrary not only to what typically happens in the case of moral rights granted to the author of a copyrighted work (at least in continental Europe), but also to the legislation of certain countries on industrial design[35] – the right to be cited granted by European Union law to the designer can also be waived.[36] As set forth in Article 36(3), letter (e), CDR, the application may contain "a statement under the applicant's responsibility

---

notwithstanding their contribution in the creation of the design". In the same vein, see Article 14(3) of the Kosovo Law No. 05/L-058 on industrial design (2015).

[28]   But not only European: see, e.g., Ysolde Gendreau, "Moral Rights", in Gordon Henderson (ed.), *Copyright and Confidential Information Law of Canada* (Carswell 1994) 165.

[29]   See e.g. Luigi Carlo Ubertazzi, *Profili soggettivi del brevetto* (Giuffrè 1985) 233.

[30]   Cf. Fisk (n 10) 85, concluding that "[t]he expansion in who is credited … can undermine the utility of the credit list".

[31]   The opposite approach is adopted in the context of patent law: cf. Article 81 EPC and Rule 60 of the Implementing Regulations to the European Patent Convention, which expressly provides that, lacking the designation of the inventor, the European Patent Office "shall inform the applicant that the European patent application will be refused unless the designation is made within sixteen months of the date of filing of the application or, if priority is claimed, of the date of priority".

[32]   Commission Regulation (EC) No. 2245/2002 of 21 October 2002 implementing Council Regulation (EC) No. 6/2002 on Community designs [2002] OJ L341/28.

[33]   Franzosi (n 22) 210. Margoni (n 8) 225, has observed, in general terms, that "the tools created by EU intervention have been drafted paying much more attention to the industry sector rather than to designers themselves".

[34]   Cf. Rule 6.2.4 of the EUIPO Guidelines for examination of registered Community designs, pointing out that "[t]he citation, the waiver and an indication regarding the designer(s) are merely optional and are not subject to examination".

[35]   Article 30 of the Croatian Industrial Design Act, for example, expressly provides that the transfer or waiver of the moral right of the designer shall be deemed null and void.

[36]   Similarly, in the context of patent legislation, Rule 20 of the Implementing Regulations to the European Patent Convention provides that the inventor has the moral right to be mentioned in the published European patent application and the European patent specification "unless he informs the European Patent Office in writing that he has waived his right to be thus mentioned".

that the designer or the team of designers has waived the right to be cited".[37] Also in this case, the waivability of the right is a characteristic that was not contemplated by the proposal of Regulation of 1993, which leads one to assume that the legislature intended to further weaken the scope of the right of the designer to be cited.

The possibility of a collective citation, the mere possibility of the mention of the name of the designer and the fact that the right may be waived are not, however, the only aspects that make it possible to deem the protection of the designer's moral interests to be particularly weak. In this regard, it also seems relevant that the designer's name appears only in the application and in the Register of Community Designs – which, moreover, ineluctably leads to the consequence that the creator of an unregistered design does not even have a right to be cited – and not also on the products that incorporate the registered design. In this regard, the Official Commentary of the proposal of Regulation of 1993 clarified that "[i]t has not been considered feasible to require that the name of the designer (or of the team) be mentioned in other contexts, for instance on the product itself or on the packaging or in the literature accompanying the product". Apparently, therefore, the EC legislature did not seem to base the limitation in Article 18 CDR on the existence of a preclusion of principle regarding the ability to indicate the designer's name on the product, its packaging or in the literature accompanying the product. To the contrary, it is merely a practical difficulty, as it would not be advisable to require a manufacturer to perform such a burdensome activity. However, the approach taken by the EC legislature seems questionable. On the one hand, placing the name of the designer (or of the team of designers) on the product, its packaging or in the accompanying literature does not seem to be, at least in a certain number of cases, impossible or even technically or economically burdensome.[38] For example, a famous Swedish multinational that designs and sells ready-to-assemble furniture indicates the designer's name on the specific page of its website for each product and on the tags associated with the products. Another equally well-known Italian company that manufactures plastic contemporary furniture indicates the name of the designer in the technical sheets of its products, which are also available on its website. And the fact that, for the most famous designers, at times the manufacturer itself wants to indicate their name on the products they created[39] demonstrates that such mention is not only possible (at least in a certain amount of cases) but also commercially desirable.

On the other hand, when placing the name of the designer (or of the team of designers) on the product, its packaging or in the accompanying literature is technically difficult or impossible, or financially unsustainable, the problem could perhaps have been solved, as happens in some national copyright laws, by merely requiring that the mention of the name of the author

---

[37] It is not clear, however, which legal regime is applicable to the waiver by a team of designers. In particular, it is unclear, when one or more members of the team are not willing to waive their right, how a decision will be taken (if pursuant to a majority or unanimity rule). Moreover, it is not clear if the dissenting designers may retain their moral right to be cited.

[38] On the contrary, it may well be impossible in some cases, e.g. in the case of typefaces, with respect to which Section 79(2)(b) of the UK Copyright, Designs and Patents Act 1988 expressly excludes the right of the author be identified as such.

[39] This occurs more often in specific industrial sectors such as fashion and automotive. HJ Riezebos, *Brand-added Value: Theory and Empirical Research About the Value of Brands to Consumers* (Eburon 1994) 77, recalls that, for some of its models, the Italian luxury car manufacturer *Alfa Romeo* has placed the name of the designer on the car in order to evoke a sense of uniqueness and sophistication.

be made in the customary manner,[40] if any, or that in specific circumstances such mention could even be omitted, when it is unreasonable from a practical standpoint.[41]

3.   THE DESIGNER'S MORAL RIGHTS REGARDING INDUSTRIAL DESIGN WORKS (ALSO) PROTECTED BY COPYRIGHT

As indicated in the introduction, the conceptual category of industrial design is on the boundary of the artistic and the industrial domains, and the different terms used in different languages to refer to that category (*Produktgestaltung*, *esthétique industrielle*, *arte applicata*) reflect, at least on an intuitive level, the hybrid nature[42] – aesthetic and, at the same time, utilitarian – of the creations it encompasses. In obeisance to the French theory of the "unity of the art" (*unité de l'art*),[43] various legal systems have long recognized that art applied to industry does not deserve, merely because of its end use, to be discriminated against compared to other artistic creations, and that thus it can (and must) also receive protection from the specific perspective of copyright, if and when the legal requirements therefor are met. This possibility is also contemplated by the Berne Convention, Article 2(1) of which states that the notion of literary and artistic works protected by copyright shall also include works of applied art and industrial designs and models.

The principle of cumulative protection is expressly sanctioned in the European Union by Directive 98/71/EC, whose Article 17 provides that a "design protected by a design right registered in or in respect of a Member State in accordance with this Directive shall also be eligible for protection under the law of copyright of that State as from the date on which the design was created or fixed in any form".

Aware of the unusual nature of the subject of the protection and the different national sensibilities on the point, the EC legislature granted a certain margin of discretion[44] to Member States in relation to "the extent to which, and the conditions under which" the copyright protection is conferred, "including the level of originality required".[45] Some Member States have availed themselves of this discretion: Italy, for example, provides that a work of industrial

---

[40]   Cf. e.g. Article 8 of the Italian Copyright Act. For a survey of the "customary manners" in different domains see Fisk (n 10) 77 ff.

[41]   Cf. Article 14.1(1) of the Canadian Copyright Act, granting the author the right to be associated with the work by name or under a pseudonym only "where reasonable in the circumstances".

[42]   On the qualification of industrial design as a "legal hybrid" see Jerome Reichmann, "Legal Hybrids between the Patent and Copyright Paradigms", [1994] Colum. L. Rev. 2459.

[43]   On such theory and its impact on copyright legislation see Kelsey Mott, "Analysis of the 'Unity of Art' concept in European Legal Systems" [1964] Bull. Copyright Soc'y 242; Yves Gaubiac, "La théorie de l'unité de l'art", [1982] RIDA 2.

[44]   A certain margin of discretion is also left at the international level by Article 2(7) of the Berne Convention.

[45]   A similar prevision is contained in Article 96(2) RCD. However, the first paragraph of such article specifies that "[t]he provisions of this Regulation shall be without prejudice to any provisions of Community law or of the law of the Member States concerned relating to unregistered designs, trade marks or other distinctive signs, patents and utility models, typefaces, civil liability and unfair competition", thus suggesting that the possible cumulation of protection is much wider than that between the *sui generis* protection for industrial design and copyright, and may also involve other legal instruments.

design is protected by copyright only if it has, in and of itself, a creative character (*carattere creativo*[46]), as well as artistic value (*valore artistico*[47]); Portugal, on the other hand, requires that it constitute not only an intellectual creation (*criação intelectual*), but also an artistic creation (*criação artística*[48]).

The purpose of those norms is obviously to select, from among the industrial creations theoretically eligible for copyright protection, only those with a pronounced aesthetic-expressive character. The ability to subject works of industrial designs to requirements other than mere originality has, however, been scrutinized by the EU Court of Justice which, in the *Cofemel* case,[49] seemed essentially to rule out that access to copyright protection for this type of intellectual creation could be subject to further and more stringent requirements than those applied to all other types of works.[50] That decision, in confirming the principle that the fundamental criterion for entitlement to copyright protection is the work's originality,[51] seems to imply – although the Court of Justice of the European Union (CJEU) decision does not stand out for argumentative linearity[52] – that a work of industrial design can be protected by copyright on the simple condition (which is "both necessary and sufficient"[53]) that it is original,[54] or – according to the harmonized standard of originality adopted by the Court of Justice – provided that it constitutes an "author's own intellectual creation" (the so-called "AOIC standard"). The CJEU has also clarified in a number of cases that such requirement is satisfied when the author was able to express his or her creativity in the production of the work by making "free and creative choices".[55]

---

[46] "*Carattere creativo*" is the term used in the context of the Italian copyright Act to refer to the originality requirement.

[47] Cf. Article 2, No. 10, of the Italian Copyright Act. On the notion of "valore artistico" see Silvia Guizzardi, *La tutela d'autore del disegno industriale: incentivi all'innovazione e regime circolatorio* (Giuffrè 2005) 66 ff.

[48] Cf. Article 2, letter (i), of the Portuguese Copyright Code.

[49] Cf. (n 4). But cf. also, before *Cofemel*, Case C-168/09 *Flos* ECLI:EU:C:2011:29, [2011] ECR 2011 I-00181, para 34, for whose impact on the requirements for copyright protection of (unregistered) design see Lionel Bently, "The Return of Industrial Copyright?" [2012] Eur. Int. Prop. Rev. 654.

[50] In this sense cf. Annette Kur, "*Unité de l'art* Is Here to Stay – Cofemel and its Consequences" [2019] Max Planck Institute for Innovation and Competition Research Paper No. 19-16, available at SSRN: https://ssrn.com/abstract=3500845; and Estelle Derclaye, "Doceram, Cofemel and Brompton: How does the Current and Future CJEU Case Law Affect Digital Designs?" in Barbara Pasa (ed.), *Il design, l'innovazione tecnologica e digitale, Un dialogo interdisciplinare per un ripensamento delle tutele – Design, Technological and Digital Innovation. Interdisciplinary Proposals for Reshaping Legal Protections* (ESI Press 2020, forthcoming), available at SSRN: https://ssrn.com/abstract=3507802. For a critical reading of the consequences of the *Cofemel* decision both on copyright and design law see also Jens Schovsbo, "Copyright and Design Law: What Is Left after All and Cofemel? – Or: Design Law in a 'Double Whammy'" [2020] available at SSRN: https://ssrn.com/abstract=3519156.

[51] On the so-called "no other criteria"-rule see S van Gompel and E Lavik, "Quality, Merit, Aesthetics and Purpose: An Inquiry into EU Copyright Law's Eschewal of Other Criteria than Originality" [2013] RIDA 100.

[52] See Schovsbo (n 50) 6 ff.

[53] See Case C-833/18 *Brompton* ECLI:EU:C:2020:461, [2020] para 3.

[54] For an example of the same interpretative approach adopted at the national level, see BGH, 24 November 2013, I ZR 143/12 Geburtstagszug.

[55] Among the vast body of literature concerning the EU harmonized originality standard see Eleonora Rosati, *Originality in EU Copyright. Harmonizing through Case Law* (Edward Elgar 2013);

If this interpretative approach is confirmed – also considering how low the quantitative threshold of originality required for copyright protection is normally deemed to be – the consequence would be that the vast majority of (if not all) independent creations of industrial design would be eligible for copyright protection,[56] with the sole exception of those dictated solely by a technical function (and with respect to which, since the ability to exercise free creative choices is excluded from the outset, the originality requirement would not be met[57]). That type of design would also, however, be excluded from the specific protection of the design in light of Article 8(1) CDR and Article 7(1) of Directive 98/71/EC.

Many studies have addressed the problems arising from this overlapping of protection[58] and have, for the most part, criticized such kind of cumulation (inter alia, for its potential anticompetitive effects) and, in some cases, have proposed specific alternatives on the interpretative level.[59] In this chapter, however, we will primarily focus on the effects of the cumulation of protections in regard to the exercise of the designer's moral rights, at least apart from the cases where a national law dictates specific rules on moral rights applicable to works of applied art, industrial designs and works of design protected by copyright.

---

and Irini Stamatoudi, "Originality in EU Copyright Law", in Paul Torremans, *Research Handbook on Copyright Law* (Edward Elgar 2017) 57.

56   Despite the fact that the CJEU has stated that the protection of designs and the protection associated with copyright can be cumulatively granted "only in certain situations" (Cf. *Cofemel*, para 52) it seems inevitable to conclude – based on the case law of the CJEU concerning the originality requirement – that every time a designer makes free and creative choices his or her work of design is eligible for copyright protection, while paradoxically the existence of such choices does not implicate per se that the design may be protected pursuant to Regulation (EC) No. 6/2002, which grants protection only to creations showing "individual character", i.e. only "if the overall impression it produces on the informed user differs from the overall impression produced on such a user by any design which has been made available to the public" (cf. Article 4 CDR). In this sense, when one considers a creation of industrial design, it seems much easier to meet the requirements requested for copyright protection than those requested for the *sui generis* protection provided for by Regulation (EC) No. 6/2002. Some scholars have advocated against an "easy" access of industrial design to copyright protection: see, e.g., Philipp Fabbio, "Contro una tutela autoriale 'facile' del design. Considerazioni a margine di una recente pronuncia della Cassazione tedesca (Bundesgerichtshof, sent. 13 novembre 2013 – 'Geburtstagszug') e brevi note sul diritto italiano vigente" [2015] Riv. dir. ind. 45.

57   Cf. *Cofemel*, para 31. In the same vein see also the Opinion of AG Campos Sánchez-Bordona in Case C-833/18 *Brompton Bicycle* ECLI:EU:C:2020:79, [2020] para 67. On this issue see J Schovsbo and GB Dinwoodie, "Design Protection for Products That Are 'Dictated by Function'" in A Kur, M Levin and J Schovsbo (eds), *The EU Design Approach: A Global Appraisal* (Edward Elgar 2018) 142 ff.

58   See, *ex pluribus*, Estelle Derclaye, *The Copyright/Design Interface. Past, Present and Future* (Cambridge University Press 2018); JC Fromer and MP McKenna, "Claiming Design" [2018] U. Pa. L. Rev. 123.

59   See for example Gustavo Ghidini, "Cumulation of Copyright with Registration Protection of Products of Industrial Design: An Alternative Proposal" [2016] available at SSRN: https://ssrn.com/abstract=2746364 or http://dx.doi.org/10.2139/ssrn.2746364.

3.1   The Right of Paternity Granted to the Author of a Copyright-Protected Work of Industrial Design (and the Consequences of Its Overlap with the Right to Be Cited Granted by the Community Design Regulation)

The moral right of paternity granted to the author of a copyrighted work – and thus, to the extent relevant here, also to the author of a work of industrial design – has a much broader scope than the right to be cited granted to the designer pursuant to Article 18 CDR.

The right of paternity has, in most national legislations, a negative as well as a positive dimension.[60] In the negative sense, the author has the right not to reveal his or her identity and thus to publish the work in anonymous form. Similarly, the author can decide to reveal his or her identity only partially, using a pseudonym, *nom de plume*, initials or any other conventional sign. However, those choices are not unretractable: in the majority of civil law countries, the right of paternity cannot be waived,[61] with the result that the author will always be allowed to change his or her mind and take court action to obtain recognition of his or her author status.[62] Therefore, under the laws of many countries, the negative dimension of the right of paternity does not consist solely of the right to not reveal one's identity (or reveal it only partially), but also includes, from an additional standpoint, the author's right to deny paternity of a work that was falsely attributed to him or her.[63] In fact, the protection of the individual's personality consists not only of recognizing what is his or hers, but also denying what is not, and which, if falsely attributed, may alter his or her identity.

The right of paternity also has a positive dimension. It includes the right to have (by court ruling, if necessary) one's name indicated on the copies of the work in the customary manner, which can (and do) vary from one country's legislation to the other, but also, within each country's laws, based on different factors, such as the type of work, the nature and size of the copies, and the number of authors involved in the creation. In some cases, the national legislation itself indicates what the specific forms of use are in relation to specific types of works.[64] When, however, such legislation is silent in regard to the manner of indicating the author's name, the specific usages of trade must be considered (but they, too, can vary significantly). In general terms, however, national laws and the Courts tend to require that the author's name or pseudonym be placed on the copies of the work in such a way that it is reasonably clear and evident,[65] with the sole exception of cases where such an indication is not feasible or appropriate given the factors indicated above (type of work, nature and size of the copies, number of

---

[60]   Cf. Hansmann and Santilli (n 12) 130; Giorgio Spedicato, *Principi di diritto d'autore* (Il Mulino 2020) 142.

[61]   In fact, more than one scholar doubts that the possibility to waive moral rights – which is often granted in common law countries – may be compatible with Article 6*bis* of the Berne Convention: see e.g. William Cornish, "Moral Rights under the 1988 Act" [1989] Eur. Intell. Prop. Rev. 449, 452; Jane Ginsburg, "Moral Rights in a Common Law System" [1990] Entert. L. Rev. 121, 129.

[62]   And with the further consequence that the possible waiver made pursuant to Article 36(3), letter (e), CDR will be invalid from the perspective of the copyright legislation.

[63]   In the opposite sense see Ubertazzi (n 29) 383 ff.

[64]   Cf., e.g., Article 33 of the Italian Regulation No. 1369/1941, implementing the Italian Copyright Act.

[65]   Cf., e.g., Section 77(7) of the UK Copyright, Designs and Patents Act 1988 and Section 195AA of the Australian Copyright Act 1968.

authors involved, etc.[66]). In the end, although it is possible to identify national approaches that are more or less favourable to authors, the general tendency of legislatures and the Courts is to balance the two interests and rights that appear of equal rank, also on a constitutional level: on the one hand, the interest of the author to the protection of his or her personality[67] and, on the other hand, the interest of the successor in title of the author to the protection of his or her freedom to conduct a business.[68]

The particular form that the moral right of paternity takes can, however, create problems of application when it is enforced by the author of an industrial design that, in addition to being protected by copyright, is also a registered design pursuant to Regulation (EC) No. 6/2002, not so much from the standpoint of the negative dimension of that right but the positive dimension.

Under the first of the two aspects considered, Article 18 CDR does not seem to preclude the designer's ability to remain anonymous. The right to be cited set forth in that law does not impose an obligation on the applicant to mention the name of the designer in the application. At the same time, Article 18 CDR – unlike the more rigid patent system[69] – seems sufficiently flexible as not to preclude the designer's ability to be mentioned via a pseudonym: considering that, in cases where the design is the result of teamwork, the mention of the name of the designer may be replaced by the name of the team, one does not see why that name may not be replaced by a pseudonym.

Moreover, if the designer's real name is stated in the application against his or her will, there do not seem to be any restrictions on removing that indication. As noted above, the citation of the designer in the application is merely optional; however, Rule 9.3.1 of the EUIPO Guidelines expressly provides that the name of the designer is an element of the application that may be corrected at the applicant's request if it contain errors of wording or obvious mistakes and, thus, in such context, it does not seem unreasonable to assume that the mention of a designer who expressed his or her will to remain anonymous may be considered, in a certain sense, an "obvious mistake". In any event, the designer would always have the right to have the indication of his or her name corrected or even deleted pursuant to Articles 15 and 16 of Regulation (EU) 2016/679 (the General Data Protection Regulation).[70] Those latter rules also

---

[66]   Cf. *Guide to the Copyright and Related Rights Treaties Administered by WIPO and Glossary of Copyright and Related Rights Terms* (WIPO 2003) 44, available at: https://www.wipo.int/edocs/pubdocs/en/copyright/891/wipo_pub_891.pdf, which makes clear, with reference to Article 6*bis* of the Berne Convention, that the author has the right to insist that he or she be identified as such by indicating his or her name on the copies of the work "as much as it is practicable and in a way that is reasonable under the given circumstances". In this regard see also Suthersanen (n 23) 189, where it is recalled that the German Supreme Court – cf. BGH, 16 June 1994, Case No. IZR 3/92, [1995] IIC 130 – has stated that the exercise of the right of paternity can be restricted having regard to trade practices or general business usage, taking account of the type of work, whether it is difficult or impossible to affix the author's designation for technical reasons, the purpose of the work and the intensity of the moral rights.

[67]   Relevant, inter alia, pursuant to Article 27 of the Universal Declaration of Human Rights.

[68]   Relevant, inter alia, pursuant to Article 16 of the Charter of Fundamental Rights of the EU.

[69]   Cf. Rule 19 of the Implementing Regulations to the European Patent Convention providing, with respect to Article 81 EPC, that "[t]he request for grant of a European patent shall contain the designation of the inventor" which, in turn, shall "state the family name, given names and full address of the inventor", thus excluding that the inventor may be designated by a pseudonym.

[70]   Regulation (EU) 2016/679 of the European Parliament and of the Council of 27 April 2016 on the protection of natural persons with regard to the processing of personal data and on the free movement of such data, and repealing Directive 95/46/EC (General Data Protection Regulation) [2016] OJ L119/1.

appear to solve the problem of false attributions of the designer's paternity regarding any works of industrial designs for whom he or she is not the author.

Determining how the designer of a registered design which is also protected by copyright can exercise his or her moral right of paternity in the positive sense is a more complex issue. As previously noted, Article 18 CDR limits the designer's right to be cited to the mention of his or her name in the application and in the Register of Community Designs. In this case as well, it can be observed that Article 18 CDR, while granting the designer the right to be cited as such before the EUIPO and in the Register, does not per se prevent the designer's name from also being mentioned in other contexts, nor does it necessarily create a conflict with national legislations that grant a moral right of paternity to the author of a copyrighted design. In fact, those national laws merely allow the designer to seek and obtain recognition of his or her author status in other contexts in addition to those contemplated by Article 18 CDR.

Moreover, one could ask him or herself what these alternative contexts are. As noted above, laws in different jurisdictions provide that the name of the author of the work shall be made in the customary manner. One could almost be tempted to say that, since Article 18 CDR provides only that the indication of the designer's name is to be made in the application and in the Register, this is precisely the customary manner generally applicable to all works of industrial design. However, this conclusion does not seem to be correct. The reference to the customary manner in fact constitutes an open concept which the legislature uses to adapt the actual methods of exercising the right of paternity to the various types of work and to different contexts. In a certain sense, it can be said that the specific customary manner identified at the legislative, judicial or customary level constitutes the concise expression of a fundamental general principle, namely, that the author has the moral right to have his or her name indicated (1) on the copies of the work; and (2) in a reasonably clear and evident manner; but always (3) to the extent that the same appears acceptable considering a series of factors, which include the rightholder's interest in not being constrained to take actions that are impossible or excessively burdensome on a technical or financial level to satisfy the author's moral interest. In other words – adhering to the general principle laid down in Article 52 of the Charter of Fundamental Rights of the EU – the lawfulness of the restriction on the exercise of the moral right of paternity, which doubtlessly happens or can happen in the case of works of designs, must be assessed in light of the principle of proportionality, with the result that the aforesaid restriction must, firstly, occur only to the extent necessary to sufficiently satisfy the needs to safeguard the rightholder's economic interest and, secondly, not seem excessive in relation to the extent of the reasonably permissible sacrifice, which in no case can be such as to void the essential substance of the restricted moral right.

In light of the foregoing, it thus would appear possible to, at least, exclude the two extreme interpretative solutions: on the one hand, a solution that would consider it reasonable to generally preclude any possibility of mentioning the designer's name other than in the application and in the Community Design Register[71] and, on the other hand, the solution that the designer can always require the rightholder to indicate his or her name on the copies of the work of design,[72] although in some cases it is possible to imagine that such mention would be neither impossible nor excessively burdensome (technically or financially): thus, in those cases, it

---

[71]   Cf. Fabrizio Sanna, *Il messaggio estetico del prodotto* (Giuffrè 2018) 131.
[72]   In this vein see Guizzardi (n 47) 89.

makes sense that the rightholder would not be able to legitimately refuse to affix it.[73] In all other cases, which probably constitute the vast majority, the most balanced solution will be determined taking into account, inter alia, the specific usages of trade of the specific industrial sector involved, with the result that the designer will be able, from time to time, to have his or her name cited on the packaging of the product, on its labels, in the literature accompanying the product or, more generally, in the materials used for advertising or communication (such as the producer's website).[74]

3.2   Other Moral Rights Granted to the Author of a Copyright-Protected Work of Industrial Design: The Right of Integrity

The moral right of paternity is not the only moral right granted to the author of a work. Article 6*bis* of the Berne Convention also recognizes the author's right "to object to any distortion, mutilation or other modification of, or other derogatory action in relation to [a] work, which would be prejudicial to his honour or reputation" (the "right of integrity").

The right of paternity and the right of integrity thus constitute the minimum legal core under international treaty law that is intended to protect the author's personality. However, along with that minimum core, various civil law systems recognize two additional rights, namely, the right of disclosure, i.e., the right of the author to decide whether, when and in what form to publish his or her work or make it available to the public, and the right of retraction, i.e., the author's right to withdraw the work from the market.[75]

Since the specific laws on industrial design do not grant moral rights other than the right of the designer to be cited, one could ask if and how those additional rights can be exercised by the designer whose creation also received protection through copyright.

Specifically in regard to the right of integrity, it is not uncommon in different countries' copyright laws that such right appears weak – to the point, in some cases, of being non-existent – in regard to certain utilitarian works,[76] such as works of architecture,[77] computer programs[78] and – precisely – works of industrial design.[79] This is far from surprising. An infringement

---

[73]   Orit Fischman Afori, "Reconceptualizing Property in Designs" [2008] Cardozo Arts & Ent. L. J. 1105, 1152 (n 320) observes that "[i]t would be absurd for a designer's name to appear on each hairbrush handle, lamp base, etc." However, this contention seems too absolute to be accepted, as it does not consider the diversity of items which may incorporate an industrial design.

[74]   According to LC Ubertazzi and M Ammendola, *Il diritto d"autore* (UTET 1993) 56, the author has always the right to request that his or her name is indicated, if not directly on the copies of the work, at least on an element separated from the copy and easily removable from it.

[75]   The rights of disclosure and retraction are not granted by all domestic legislations. On the other hand, a few legislations grant to the author not only the four moral rights mentioned in the text, but also further moral rights, such as the right of access. This is, for instance, the case of the French and German legislation: cf. Davies and Garnett (n 2) 389, 425.

[76]   Cf. Fischman Afori, (n 73) 1153 (n 320).

[77]   Cf. e.g. Section 80(5) of the UK Copyright, Designs and Patents Act 1988.

[78]   Cf. e.g. Section 81(2) of the UK Copyright, Designs and Patents Act 1988. In France, Article 121-7 of the Intellectual Property Code provides that the right of integrity may be exercised by the author of a computer program only in case of a prejudice to the honour or reputation of the author, while, as a general rule, the modification of a work does not have to be detrimental to the author's honour or reputation in order to qualify as a violation of the right of integrity.

[79]   Cf. e.g., Article 64(2) of the Canadian Copyright Act.

of the right of integrity in fact presumes, from a teleological perspective, a prejudice to the author's honour or reputation,[80] and it is definitely less likely (although not impossible) that such prejudice can occur when an intellectual creation is the result more of practical or functional concerns than factors of an eminently artistic or expressive nature, and therefore does not obviously bear the mark of the author's personality.[81] But that is not all. Utilitarian works, like other types of works that are not strictly utilitarian but nonetheless are intended to be inputs to productive processes, require (as observed above in regard to the right to paternity) reconciling the need to protect the author's honour or reputation with the needs of the subject managing those processes.[82] The laws of the legal systems that expressly limit or preclude the exercise of the right of integrity as to certain actions taken by the author's successor in title when those actions entail modifications to the work needed to satisfy particular technical requirements seem to be particularly significant in this regard.[83]

A certain attenuation of the principle of non-negotiability of moral rights would also seem to be reflected in the laws that, in some legal systems, allow the author of a utilitarian work to authorize modifications to his or her work in advance, thereby waiving his or her moral right to the integrity of that work.[84]

In any case, outside of the scope of application of any specific national laws, it is difficult to say, in the abstract and in general terms, within which limits the designer may exercise his or her right to prevent modifications of (or other derogatory acts in relation to) his or her work which could prejudice his or her honour or reputation. Given the significant variety of intellectual creations that could fall into the category of industrial design, the most appropriate (and most generalizable) approach is probably the one taken in those legal systems where the courts seek to identify a reasonable balance between the author's moral interests and the economic interests of the author's successor in title using a case-by-case approach that takes into

---

[80]   But in some jurisdiction (e.g. in Belgium, France and Greece or, outside Europe, in China and Japan), as conveniently pointed out by Davies and Garnett (n 2) 7, the author may object to any alteration or modification of the work irrespective of their nature and their effects on the author's honor or reputation.

[81]   In this sense, for example, Italian law is paradigmatic, as it provides at Article 20(2) of the Italian Copyright Act on the one hand that "in the case of works of architecture, the author may not oppose modifications deemed necessary in the course of construction" or which may be necessary after a work of architecture has been completed. On the other hand, however, "if the work is recognized by the competent State authority as having an important artistic character, the author shall be entrusted with the study and execution of such modifications". In other terms, the greater or lesser degree of artistic quality of a work has an impact on the possibility to exercise the exclusive right of integrity.

[82]   Cf. Sanna (n 71) 133.

[83]   In the context of Italian Copyright Act, for example, see Article 20 ICA with respect to works of architecture; Article 41 ICA (similarly to Section 81 of the UK Copyright, Design and Patent Act 1988) with respect to newspaper articles; and Article 47 ICA with respect to works used in the context of a cinematographic work. Moreover, in France, CA Paris, 12 December 1988, [1990] RIDA 145, has held that the design of a logo could be modified for technical needs of the manufacturer.

[84]   Cf. e.g. Section 87(1) of the UK Copyright, Designs and Patents Act 1988, which, in general terms, provides that "[i]t is not an infringement of any of the rights conferred by this Chapter to do any act to which the person entitled to the right has consented". In the same vein, see Article 22(2) of the Italian Copyright Act and Article 59(1) of the Portuguese Copyright Code. On the opposite hand, however, Article 11(2) of the Swiss Copyright Act provides that "[e]ven where a third party is authorized by contract or law to alter the work or to use it to create a derivative work, the author may oppose any distortion of the work that is a violation of his personal rights".

account, firstly, the (more or less) utilitarian nature of the specific work and, secondly, the relevance of the technical or economic reasons that may make it necessary to modify the work.[85]

On the contrary, the approach of the legal systems that, while precluding the author from exercising his or her right of integrity in regard to certain modifications made to his or her work by certain subjects, do allow the author to have the indication of his or her name removed from the work, seem to be less generalizable.[86] It is not difficult to understand the rationale for such rules: the protection of the author's honour or reputation is logically based on the recognition of the paternity of the work,[87] with the consequence that, by removing the indication of the author's name, it can be assumed that any possible harm to his or her honour or reputation is also de facto precluded.[88] Moreover, severing the relationship between subject and object, when the continuing and manifest existence of that relationship is likely to harm the subject's personality, is the most typical remedy used, at least in the European Union, by a further area of law that is comparable (as to purpose and effects) to moral rights: i.e., data protection law.[89] However, with the elimination of the indication of his or her name from the modified work, the author would end up essentially being deprived of the ability to exercise not only his or her right of integrity, but also his or her right of paternity.[90] At this point, when modifications are made to the work by the designer's successor in title, a request for a statement in a disclaimer that the work was subsequently modified by third parties seems more reasonable.[91]

---

[85]   Which is, for instance, what typically happens in the Netherlands with the reasonableness test adopted by Dutch courts based on Article 25(1)(c) of the Dutch Copyright Act, granting the author of a work the right to oppose any other alteration to the work "unless the nature of the alteration is such that opposition would be unreasonable": cf. Davies and Garnett (n 2) 488 ff.

[86]   Cf. Section 80(5) of the UK Copyright, Designs and Patents Act 1988 with respect to architectural works.

[87]   In fact, it is difficult to imagine infringements of the right of integrity in case of anonymous works.

[88]   Cf. Section 82(2) of the UK Copyright, Designs and Patents Act 1988 where, with respect to certain categories of works, the exercise of the right of integrity is limited to the cases in which the author is identified at the time of the derogatory act.

[89]   Cf. in particular Article 17 of Regulation (EU) 2016/679 granting the data subject the "right to erasure" (or "right to be forgotten"), i.e. the right to obtain from the controller the erasure of personal data concerning him or her. On the similarities between moral rights (in the context of copyright) and the rights granted to the data subject pursuant by the EU data protection legislation see Luigi Carlo Ubertazzi, "La disciplina UE dei diritti morali d'autore" [2016] Ann. it. dir. aut. 349, 357, who expressly states that the normative sources of the European Union on moral rights include the General Data Protection Regulation. In a similar vein see also Henry Pearce, "Could the doctrine of moral rights be used as a basis for understanding the notion of control within data protection law?" [2018] Inform. Comm. Tech. L. 133.

[90]   But see De Werra (n 10) 279, suggesting that the removal of the name of the author from a work the integrity of which has been violated "could make sure that the author's name shall not be connected to a work with which the author rejects any creative connection while allowing the continued use of such work (thus preserving the financial and personal investments and efforts made in the creation of such work)".

[91]   Cf. Section 103(2) of the UK Copyright, Design and Patent Act 1988, pursuant to which in proceedings for infringement of the right of integrity "the court may, if it thinks it is an adequate remedy in the circumstances, grant an injunction on terms prohibiting the doing of any act unless a disclaimer is made, in such terms and in such manner as may be approved by the court, dissociating the author or director from the treatment of the work".

3.3   (Follows): The Right of Disclosure

As generally recognized in legal commentary, the right of disclosure is hybrid in nature, in part moral and in part economic. If we consider its positive dimension (consisting of the right to choose whether, when and in which form an intellectual creation should be published, i.e., brought to the market), the right of disclosure constitutes, in the final analysis, a reflection of the ownership of the economic rights to the protected intellectual creation. The disclosure of the intellectual creation normally coincides with the first act of economic exploitation of that creation. In this regard, then, it could be argued that, although EU legislation on industrial design – unlike many national copyright laws – does not expressly grant a right of disclosure to the designer, that ability, understood in a positive sense, reflects the fact that the designer has a right of economic exploitation of the design pursuant to Article 14 CDR.

The most genuinely moral dimension of the right of disclosure is, however, the negative aspect, which can be appreciated particularly when ownership of the economic rights to the design belongs to a subject other than the designer, as normally happens when a design is "developed by an employee in the execution of his duties or following the instructions given by his employer" (Article 14.2 CDR). The problem then arises of determining whether the designer can oppose the economic exploitation of the design by his or her successor in title by enforcing his or her own moral right of disclosure; in other words, the problem arises of determining whether the principle of the independence of the author's moral rights from the economic rights, mentioned by Article 6*bis* of the Berne Convention – and pursuant to which the author may exercise his or her moral rights even after the transfer of the economic rights – is also applicable to the right of disclosure.

If, on the one hand, one must recognize that there are legal systems (such as in France) that are extremely protective of the author's moral interests, and thus tend to interpret the moral right of disclosure broadly,[92] one cannot fail to consider that the possibility of indiscriminate recourse to that right[93] risks completely paralysing the exercise of the economic rights to the work by the author's successor in title.[94] The risk seems all the more real if one considers that recourse to the moral right of disclosure, in the legal systems that recognize it, is not normally subject to particular teleological requirements (e.g., prejudice to the author's honour or reputation), as happens in the case of the right of integrity, or the existence of serious moral reasons, required by some national laws to exercise the right of withdrawal.[95]

A further source of complexity when balancing the interests of the designer and his or her successor in title is the fact that – unlike what happens, for instance, in the case of the right of paternity – the conflict between the designer potentially desiring not to disclose the work and the desire of his or her successor in title to commercially exploit it, presents itself essentially

---

[92]   Cf. Suthersanen (n 23) 158, who observes that, if on the one hand and at a general level, in cases where the right of disclosure conflicts with an economic right, the former will normally bear priority, on the other hand such principle is particularly difficult to reconcile in the context of designs, which are industrially made and exploited.

[93]   Which, however, based on the jurisdiction, could qualify as an abuse of the moral right of the author.

[94]   Which is probably the reason why in some countries, such as in Belgium, a right of disclosure is excluded with respect to authors of certain utilitarian works (software): cf. Davies and Garnett (n 2) 354.

[95]   See e.g. Article 141 of the Italian Copyright Act.

as a zero-sum game, in which it is difficult to find compromise solutions and where, regardless of which interest wins, the other seems inevitably destined to lose.[96]

An interpretative solution that leads, in the final analysis, to recognizing the designer's right – when there are no serious moral reasons – to paralyse his or her successor in title's exploitation of the work by exercising the right of disclosure does not seem reasonably sustainable, as it would mean completely frustrating the enterprise's productive investment, while the opposite solution appears more reasonable, also considering the pronounced economic-centric approach of the industrial design legislation.[97]

Besides, at least in legal systems that allow even limited negotiability of moral rights, one could take the position that the most appropriate context to govern the potential conflict of interest from the standpoint of the disclosure of the work between author and successor in title is the contract they enter into, with the result that in cases where the contract is silent regarding the ability to prevent the disclosure of the works created pursuant to that contract, it can be said that the designer implicitly waived it (or, from a different angle, that he or she authorized disclosure in advance). To the contrary, there is nothing preventing disclosure of the work from being contractually subject to adherence to specified conditions or even the designer's mere consent.

Consistently with the purpose of moral rights being to protect the author's personality, there may be a reasonable opening for the designer to exercise the right of disclosure where the specific work of industrial design is of a more aesthetic than functional nature, and its not-expressly authorized disclosure could concretely harm the designer's honour or reputation (as could happen, for instance, if the design of the object of the industrial design has not yet been finalized). However, in that case, and unlike what has been observed in regard to the right of integrity, the interest in protecting the designer's personality could be effectively safeguarded by eliminating any reference to the designer during the economic exploitation of the work. In fact, such remedy seems reasonably adequate when the intellectual creation is not still associated with its author in the eyes of the public, contrary to what could be said when the relationship between subject (author) and object (work) has, by then, become entrenched publicly and someone interferes with it by performing derogatory acts in relation to the work.

3.4   (Follows): The Right of Withdrawal

The above remarks, which suggest significant caution in granting to the designer the ability to exercise the right of disclosure in regard to his or her protected intellectual creation when the related economic rights have been transferred to other subjects, such as to the employer, also apply a fortiori to the exercise of the right of withdrawal.

With rare exceptions, in that relatively limited number of legal systems that recognize the right of withdrawal, it is often subject to strict conditions to be applicable,[98] which are justified

---

[96]   In an attempt to reach a reasonable compromise between the conflicting interests of the parties, some legal systems grant the successor in title of the author the possibility to claim a compensation for the economic prejudice suffered in cases where the author does not allow the disclosure of the work: cf. Davies and Garnett (n 2) 354 referring the case of Belgium.

[97]   In more general terms Sanna (n 71) 130 suggests that, in the balancing between the moral interest of the designer and the economic interest of the enterprise, the latter should generally prevail.

[98]   Cf. e.g. Article 142 of the Italian Copyright Act. On this point see also Cyrill Rigamonti, "Deconstructing Moral Rights" [2006] Harvard Intern. L. J. 353, 363.

by the seriousness of the consequences to the author's successors in title if the author decides to withdraw from commerce works that were already published and which, therefore, were already invested in by those successors in title. Moreover, in some legal systems, specifically for that reason, exercise of the right of withdrawal requires the author to indemnify the subject to whom the economic rights to the protected intellectual creation were transferred.[99]

We must also point out, in this context as well, that the peculiar functional nature of works of industrial design makes it difficult to imagine that, when a protected creation has been placed in commerce with its author's consent (implied or express), circumstances can arise in which the author's moral rights can be concretely harmed if that creation remains in commerce.[100] Where the designer asserts that such circumstances exist, proof in court will have to be particularly rigorous. In this context as well, an initial determination must be made as to whether the designer's moral interest can be adequately satisfied by measures that are less likely to interfere with the economic interests of the designer's successor in title, such as the elimination of all references to the designer during the further commercial exploitation of the product.

4. LOOKING AHEAD: AI-CREATED INDUSTRIAL DESIGN AND MORAL RIGHTS OF THE ARTIFICIAL DESIGNER

In recent years, recourse to artificial intelligence systems (AIS) to produce intellectual creations that are typologically eligible for intellectual property protection has become increasingly common.[101] Industrial design is certainly no exception to that tendency, and in fact constitutes one of the contexts in which the use of AIS is appearing more and more frequently.[102]

Obviously, the use of AIS that do not completely preclude some form of human intervention should not significantly affect the discussion to this point regarding granting moral rights to the human author who used those AIS. In such cases, the AIS are merely a technical tool, albeit an exceptionally sophisticated one, available to the designer in a manner that is not too conceptually dissimilar from computer-aided design (CAD) programs, which have been used in the sector for years.[103]

However, situations where the AIS is substantially autonomous,[104] and thus can create products of industrial design without decisive human creative intervention, are quite different.

---

[99] Cf. e.g. Article 143 of the Italian Copyright Act.

[100] Cf. Sanna (n 71) 133.

[101] For a general introduction to the topic of "artificial creativity" and the possibility to protect the relative outputs by means of an intellectual or industrial property right see Giorgio Spedicato, "Creatività artificiale, mercato e proprietà intellettuale" [2019] Riv. Dir. Ind. 253.

[102] Roger Burt and Colin Davies, "Software: Intellectual property and artificial intelligence" in Abbe Brown and Charlotte Waelde (eds), *Research Handbook on Intellectual Property and Creative Industries* (Edward Elgar 2018) 247.

[103] Cf. WIPO Conversation on Intellectual Property (IP) and Artificial Intelligence (Revised Issues Paper on Intellectual Property Policy and Artificial Intelligence), 20 May 2020, at: https://www.wipo.int/edocs/mdocs/mdocs/en/wipo_ip_ai_2_ge_20/wipo_ip_ai_2_ge_20_1_rev.pdf, p. 8.

[104] On the notion of "autonomy" applied to AIS see WF Lawless, R Mittu, D Sofge and S Russell (eds), *Autonomy and Artificial Intelligence: A Threat or Savior?* (Springer 2017).

In recent years there has been a lively debate about the possibility of granting intellectual property rights to creations produced autonomously by AIS.[105] Although some legal systems seem to allow for that possibility,[106] including with specific reference to creations of industrial design,[107] a more cautious interpretative approach has been gaining ground recently, in which intellectual property protection, and especially copyright protection, would generally be subject to a "human-creation requirement".[108]

If that approach becomes prevalent internationally, or at least in Europe, the result should be that an AI-created work of industrial design would not be able to receive protection, at least under copyright provisions, and thus the topic of an artificial designer's moral rights would not even arise. It is also significant to note, in this context, that even in the most open legal systems, such as in the United Kingdom, the granting of moral rights is expressly precluded in the case of computer-created works.[109] In fact, considering that (at least currently) robots are not considered legal entities in a philosophical and legal perspective,[110] there obviously

---

[105]   Among the vast body of literature that has grown around this fundamental issue see (with no pretense of being exhaustive) Ana Ramalho, "Will Robots Rule the (Artistic) World? A Proposed Model for the Legal Status of Creations by Artificial Intelligence Systems" [2017] J. Internet L. 12; Jane Ginsburg, "People Not Machines: Authorship and What It Means in the Berne Convention" [2018] IIC 131; in the field of patent law, see Ryan Abbott, "I Think, Therefore I Invent: Creative Computers and the Future of Patent Law" [2016] BC L. Rev. 1079; in more general terms see Spedicato (n 101); RM Hilty, J Hoffman and S Scheuerer, "Intellectual Property Justification for Artificial Intelligence", in J-A Lee, K-C Liu and RM Hilty (eds), *Artificial Intelligence and Intellectual Property* (Oxford University Press 2021). The debate, however, started almost 40 years ago: see Timothy Butler, "Can a Computer Be an Author – Copyright Aspects of Artificial Intelligence" [1981] Hastings Comm. & Ent. L. J. 707; Stephen Hewitt, "Protection of Works Created by the Use of Computers" [1983] New L. J. 235; Pamela Samuelson, "Allocating Ownership Rights in Computer-Generated Works" [1985] U. Pitt. L. Rev. 1185; Sam Ricketson, "People or Machines: The Berne Convention and the Changing Concept of Authorship" [1991] Colum. – VLA J. L. & Arts 1.

[106]   Cf. Section 9(3) of the UK Copyright, Designs and Patents Act 1988, which grants to the subject "by whom the arrangements necessary for the creation of the work are undertaken" the copyright on a computer-created work (i.e. a work which is "generated by computer in circumstances such that there is no human author of the work"). In a similar vein see also Section 11 of the Hong Kong Copyright Ordinance (Cap. 528) of 1997 and Article 2 of the Copyright Act of New Zealand of 1994.

[107]   Cf. e.g. Article 2(4) of the UK Registered Design Act 1949; Article 10(5) of the Industrial Designs Act 1996 of Malaysia; Article 4(3) of the Registered Designs Act of Singapore; and Article 3(5) of the Hong Kong Registered Designs Ordinance.

[108]   As far as copyright protection is concerned, the Compendium of the US Copyright Office Practices: Chapter 300 [2017] 4 makes clear that the US Copyright Office "will register an original work of authorship, provided that the work was created by a human being" (§ 306.1) and "will not register works produced by a machine or mere mechanical process that operates randomly or automatically without any creative input or intervention from a human author" (§ 313.2). In the same vein, the Beijing Internet Court in the case *Beijing Feilin Law Firm v. Baidu Corporation*, No. 239 [2019], Civil First Instance, 25 April 2019, has stated that Chinese copyright law may only accommodate works created by humans. For a brief comment on this case see Ming Chen, "Beijing Internet Court Denies Copyright to Works Created Solely by Artificial Intelligence" [2019] J. Intell. Prop. L. & Pract. 593.

[109]   Cf. Section 79 of the UK Copyright, Designs and Patents Act 1988.

[110]   Cf. the European Parliament resolution of 16 February 2017 with recommendations to the Commission on Civil Law Rules on Robotics [2018] OJ C 252/239, p. 250, in which the Parliament calls the Commission to explore, analyse and consider the possibility of "creating a specific legal status for robots in the long run, so that at least the most sophisticated autonomous robots could be established as having the status of electronic persons responsible for making good any damage they may cause, and possibly applying electronic personality to cases where robots make autonomous decisions or otherwise

appears to be no need to protect AIS' personality, even if one believes that exclusive (economic) rights can be granted on their creative results.

However, the discussion could be different if one considers the exclusive rights guaranteed to creations of industrial design by Regulation (EC) No. 6/2002, which is much less author-centric than current copyright laws. In fact, there seem to be no rules in the Regulation that absolutely preclude the possibility of registering a design autonomously created by an artificial designer as a Community design, and it would be necessary, in that case, to determine whether, and to what extent, it is possible to grant a right to be cited under Article 18 of Regulation (EC) No. 6/2002 to the artificial designer (which right, obviously, would be exercised by the applicant for that specific registered Community design).

A similar question was recently addressed in the context of patent legislation, where the European Patent Office (EPO) clarified that the designation of an AIS as the inventor in the context of a European patent application does not meet the formal requirements under Article 81 of the Convention on the Grant of European Patents (EPC) and, more generally, that AI systems or machines have no rights to be mentioned as the inventor or to be designated as the inventor in the patent application.[111]

In spite of the substantial symmetries between patent law and industrial design law, it is still possible to imagine that, unlike what happens in the patent law context, it may be possible for the applicant to indicate the name of the AIS as the designer in an application for registration for a Community design. While the EPC is clear in requiring that the first and last name of the designer be indicated in the patent application,[112] leaving little doubt that it must be a natural person, the fact that Article 18 CDR – and, moreover, Article 14(2)(f) of Regulation No. 2245/2002 – provide that the indication of the designer's name may be replaced by the name of the team of designers, and thus, de facto, by the name of the design department of an enterprise, leads one to believe that European law on industrial design is less rigid than patent law[113] and therefore that scenario, even though it has not yet occurred, could soon become reality.

---

interact with third parties independently". For a recent comment in the legal scholarship see Eliza Mik, "AI as a Legal Person?", in J-A Lee, K-C Liu and RM Hilty (n 105).

[111] Cf. EPO decisions of 27 January 2020 on patent applications EP 18 275 163 and EP 18 275 174, available at: https://www.epo.org/news-events/news/2020/20200128.html. For a comment on the EPO decisions see Daria Kim, "'AI-Generated Inventions': Time to Get the Record Straight?" [2020] GRUR Int. 443. A few months later, the US Patent and Trademark Office joined EPO in rejecting the possible mention of an AIS as inventor: cf. USPTO decision of 17 February 2020 on patent application No. 16/524,350, available at: https://www.uspto.gov/sites/default/files/documents/16524350_22apr2020 .pdf.

[112] Cf. Rule 19(1) of the Implementing Regulation of the European Patent Convention, which expressly provides that "[t]he designation shall state the family name, given names and full address of the inventor, contain the statement referred to in Article 81 and bear the signature of the applicant or his representative".

[113] On the contrary, for example, the Japanese legislation – cf. Article 6(1) of the Japanese Design Act of 1959 – provides that the name and domicile or residence of the creator of the design shall be indicated in the application for registration of an industrial design.

8. Exploring moral interests in the intellectual creations underlying trademarks[1]

Genevieve Wilkinson

1. INTRODUCTION

Intellectual creations underlie inherently distinctive trademarks. The words and images underlying trademarks for famous brands including I love New York, Barbie and Marlboro are intellectual creations of human beings. The inalienable personal link between authors and intellectual objects was recognised in the development of two separate regimes: protection for moral rights in the Berne Convention for the Protection of Literary and Artistic Works (Berne Convention)[2] and human rights protection for moral interests in the International Covenant on Economic, Social and Cultural Rights (ICESCR).[3] The relevance of these two types of protection to trademarks has been underexplored, a reflection of the emphasis historically placed on the commercial function of trademarks. Yet, it is increasingly apparent that trademarks can have moral, cultural and personal significance beyond their commercial significance as indicators of source. This chapter explores examples where parties other than owners of trademarks may have moral rights and interests in respect of trademark subject matter.

How can moral rights and interests for creators of trademarks be justified? The second part of this chapter considers the drafting history of the two international agreements that can support this protection. These reflect an intention to protect the personal character of creations of the human mind and advance public goals of protecting the integrity of these products and advancing creativity.[4] The third part of this chapter explores the implications of this for individual and collective human rights. Human rights protection for the moral interests of authors of literary and artistic productions found in the ICESCR[5] may support authors seeking to control use of words and images underlying trademarks. Protection for moral interests underlies copyright-like rights to attribution and protection from adverse treatment, but does not depend on entitlement to copyright protection and can be used more broadly than copyright-based moral rights to control trademark use. Human rights protection could also

---

[1]   Many thanks to the anonymous reviewer, Isabella Alexander, Evana Wright and Louise Buckingham for their very helpful comments on earlier drafts of this chapter.

[2]   Berne Convention for the Protection of Literary and Artistic Works (opened for signature 9 September 1886, entered into force 2 May 1896) 828 UNTS 221 (as amended 28 September 1979) (Berne Convention) Art 6*bis*.

[3]   International Covenant on Economic, Social and Cultural Rights (opened for signature 16 December 1966, entered into force 3 January 1976) 993 UNTS 3 (ICESCR)), Art 15(1)(c); Universal Declaration of Human Rights (adopted 10 December 1948) UNGA Res 217 A(III) (UDHR), Art 27.

[4]   Committee on Economic, Social and Cultural Rights, 'The Right of Everyone to Benefit from the Protection of the Moral and Material Interests Resulting from Any Scientific, Literary or Artistic Production of which He or She is the Author (article 15, paragraph 1 (c), of the Covenant)' (2005) General Comment No 17 UN ESCOR E/C.12/GC/17; ('GC17'), para 12.

[5]   ICESCR Art 15(1)(c).

be used to control the content of registered trademarks such as trademarks derived from traditional cultural expressions that have significance for Indigenous persons. The fourth part of this chapter considers the way that the recent *Australia – Tobacco Plain Packaging* decision by the World Trade Organization (WTO) Appellate Body can support states that protect these human rights of Indigenous persons even if this encumbers the use of trademarks by their owners.[6]

In many jurisdictions, creators of trademarks that contain subject matter protectable through copyright have entitlements as authors to control some uses of trademark subject matter that are inconsistent with their moral rights to attribution and to protect their works from derogatory treatment.[7] The fifth section explores this and identifies additional moral rights found in some jurisdictions, to protect from false attribution, when the wrong author is named, and to withdraw a work in certain circumstances, where the author has assigned alienable property rights but their personal relationship with the work has changed.[8]

Moral interests and copyright-based moral rights can be used to control trademark use but this needs to be balanced against other considerations such as protection of freedom of expression. Although there may also be human rights protection available for material interests for some trademark creators, moral rights and interests should be distinguished from the alienable property interests of corporate trademark owners, particularly where owners assert broad rights such as entitlements to dilution and tarnishment protection. Dilution and tarnishment can sometimes be likened to moral rights or moral interests to protect trademarks because they are used to protect the reputation or honour of corporate trademark owners. These rights also engage questions of control over the use of material underlying trademarks. However, dilution and tarnishment protections depend on transferrable economic interests that do not preserve the inalienable personal relationship between human beings and intellectual creations.

2.   JUSTIFICATIONS FOR MORAL PROTECTION OF TRADEMARK CREATORS AND THEIR INFLUENCE IN INTERNATIONAL LAW

As authors, creators of signs that function as trademarks can be entitled to protection of moral rights based in copyright protection or moral interests based in human rights protection. International copyright and human rights law recognised moral protection for authors in 1928 and 1948, respectively. Pre-existing European recognition of moral rights strongly influenced the inclusion of moral rights in the Berne Convention.[9] Rene Cassin, who led the French delegation was influential in debates that resulted in the inclusion of moral protection in the

---

[6]   Appeal Report, *Australia – Certain Measures Concerning Trademarks, Geographical Indications and Other Plain Packaging Requirements Applicable to Tobacco Products and Packaging* (WTO Doc WT/DS435/R, WT/DS441/R (9 June 2020)) (Appeal Report).

[7]   GC17, para 13.

[8]   Graham Dutfield and Uma Suthersanen, *Dutfield and Suthersanen on Global Intellectual Property Law* (Edward Elgar 2020) 134.

[9]   Elizabeth Adeney, 'The Moral Right of Integrity: The Past and Future of "Honour"' (2005) 2 Intellectual Property Quarterly, 111, 113–18.

Universal Declaration of Human Rights (UDHR).[10] French advocacy for moral protection for authors during the drafting debates reinforces links between moral rights protection and Hegel's personality theory.[11] Hegel's arguments that products of the mind can become intellectual objects and the author has ownership in the property associated with those intellectual objects influenced French protection for authors' rights.[12] These rights protect intellectual objects as an expression of the author. The author can alienate some property rights, for example by assignment of the right to reproduce the object, but certain rights are inalienable, such as rights of attribution and integrity.[13] Article 6*bis* of the Berne Convention protects moral rights of attribution and of integrity, independent of economic rights.[14] The nature of copyright-based moral rights protection and the type of trademarks that qualify for protection will vary depending on jurisdiction.[15]

Human rights law distinguishes between alienable material rights and inalienable moral rights for authors of intellectual objects. Human rights protection available for the moral interests for authors in Article 27(2) of the UDHR is reaffirmed in Article 15(1)(c) of the ICESCR. Both provisions recognize the rights of everyone to 'protection of the moral and material interests resulting from any scientific, literary or artistic production of which he is the author'.[16] The French again advocated for the inclusion of these rights in the ICESCR.[17] Drafters intended protection for moral rights to safeguard the 'intrinsically personal character of every creation of the human mind and the ensuing durable link between creators and their creations'.[18] Green identifies recognition of public goals of 'encouragement of creativity and the protection for the public of the integrity of finished products'[19] during debates about the form of ICESCR Article 15(1)(c). Interpreting the right, the Committee for Economic Social and Cultural Rights (CESCR) links material interests to the enjoyment of the right to an adequate standard of living, stating that this right is not directly linked to the personality of the creator.[20] The CESCR explicitly distinguishes Article 15(1)(c) rights from the rights found in intellectual property agreements that can be 'revoked, licenced or assigned'.[21] Material interests of authors may be ongoing but a single instance of remuneration may also satisfy those interests,[22] whilst domestic protection permits intellectual property owners to exploit

---

[10]   Aurora Plomer, 'The Human Rights Paradox: Intellectual Property Rights and Rights of Access to Science' (2013) 35(1) Human Rights Quarterly, 143, 167–8.

[11]   Maria Green, *Implementation of the International Covenant on Economic, Social and Cultural Rights: Drafting History of Article 15 (1) (c) of the International Covenant on Economic, Social and Cultural Rights. Background Paper*, UN ESCOR, 24th sess, Agenda Item 3, UN Doc E/C.12/2000/15 (9 October 2000) [4]–[7].

[12]   Neil Netanel, 'Copyright Alienability Restrictions and the Enhancement of Author Autonomy: A Normative Evaluation' (1993) 24(2) Rutgers Law Journal, 347, 379–82.

[13]   Dutfield and Suthersanen (n 8) 48–9.

[14]   Berne Convention, Art 6*bis*.

[15]   For example, moral rights protection is very limited in the United States, applying only to single copies of visual artwork: 17 U.S. Code § s106A.

[16]   ICESCR, Art 15(1)(c); UDHR, Art 27(2).

[17]   Green (n 11) paras 22, 27, 35.

[18]   GC17, para 12.

[19]   Ibid, para 46.

[20]   Ibid, para 12.

[21]   Ibid, para 2. Higher protection standards are permissible 'provided that these standards do not unjustifiably limit the enjoyment by others of their rights under the Covenant': GC17, para 11.

[22]   GC17 also contemplates a limited duration monopoly for authors: para 16.

broad rights within a defined grant of monopoly.[23] Although there appears to be more overlap between the examples of moral interests provided by CESCR and copyright protections for moral rights in many jurisdictions,[24] there are important differences in relation to scope of protection and eligibility for protection. For example, terms of moral interest protection will vary. Although the Berne Convention only requires moral rights protection for a term no shorter than the legislative protection subsisting for economic rights,[25] General Comment 17 recognizes the moral interests conferred by ICESCR as enduring.[26]

3. HUMAN RIGHTS FOR MORAL INTERESTS AND TRADEMARKS

Human rights protection for authors' moral interests expands opportunities for control over the use of culturally significant literary and artistic productions in trademarks. Article 15(1)(c) recognizes the rights of everyone to 'protection of the moral and material interests resulting from any scientific, literary or artistic production of which he is the author'. Protected moral interests include attribution rights and rights to object to derogatory actions in relation to productions 'which would be prejudicial to their honour and reputation'.[27] Custodians of traditional knowledge may also be able to use moral interests to 'prevent the unauthorized use of scientific, literary and artistic productions of Indigenous peoples by third parties'.[28] The CESCR recognizes that the realization of Article 15(1)(c) is intrinsically linked to the right to take part in cultural life found in Article 15(1)(a).[29] The realization of Article 15(1)(c) is also dependent on the enjoyment of other rights, including the right to own property, freedom of expression, the right to full development of the human personality and 'rights of cultural participation, including cultural rights in specific groups.'[30] Because human rights are indivisible and interdependent, human rights protection for moral interests must be balanced against other considerations such as the freedom of expression interests in permitting criticism of intellectual creations. The interplay of these rights is particularly complex in Europe where fundamental rights protect the right to property for corporate owners.[31] Despite this, as Geiger recognizes, the rights protected in Article 15 need greater protection in European human rights instruments.[32] This should include explicit recognition of moral interests as fundamental rights.

Protection for 'creations of the human mind' in ICESCR Article 15 'seeks to encourage the active contribution of creators to the arts and sciences and to the progress of society as

---

[23] GC17 states that 'intellectual property regimes primarily protect business and corporate interests and investments': para 2.

[24] GC17 paras 13–14.

[25] Berne Convention, Art 6*bis*.

[26] GC17, para 12.

[27] GC17, para 13.

[28] Ibid, para 32.

[29] Ibid, para 4.

[30] Ibid.

[31] *Anheuser-Busch Inc v. Portugal* (2007) 44 EHRR 42, IHRL 3436 (ECHR).

[32] Geiger argues that fundamental protection for property should be broadened to consider Article 27/15: Christophe Geiger, 'Implementing Intellectual Property Provisions in Human Rights Instruments: Towards a New Social Contract for the Protection of Intangibles', in Christophe Geiger (ed.), *Research Handbook on Human Rights and Intellectual Property* (Edward Elgar 2015) 661.

a whole.'[33] The significant role of trademarked images and words in culture has been recognized for decades.[34] The CESCR does not exhaustively define literary productions but interprets it to include poems, novels and paintings.[35] This means that Article 15 has the potential to expand the kinds of things that could merit protection for moral interests beyond copyright works. One example could be the case of a highly distinctive word or short phrase. Attempts to use copyright to protect trademarks have failed on the basis that single word marks are too 'trivial' to meet protection thresholds;[36] only *obiter dicta* has contemplated that copyright protection may be available for distinctive titles.[37] Accordingly, protection for word marks is unlikely unless the words form part of a composite trademark.[38] However, if a highly distinctive word mark constituted a 'literary production' within the meaning of ICESCR, protection of its author may be consistent with the objectives of encouraging creators to contribute to the arts and social progress.[39]

The interpretation of moral interests by CESCR in General Comment 17 acknowledges that some protection for moral interests already exists in domestic legislation.[40] However, the CESCR also separates human rights protection for both moral and material interests from intellectual property protection for both agreements and domestic law.[41] This is important for individuals and groups that are excluded from domestic moral rights protection because it is linked to eligibility for copyright protection.[42] In Australia, moral rights protection implementing the Berne Convention is part of copyright legislation that primarily protects economic interests of copyright owner.[43] The term of protection for literary and artistic works extends until 70 years following the death of the author.[44] This contrasts to the obligation in ICESCR Article 15 for states to provide enduring protection for moral interests, to ensure a 'durable link between creators and their creations'.[45]

Recognition of group or community ownership of enduring moral interests in literary and artistic productions could support efforts to protect traditional cultural expressions by custodians of traditional knowledge. Traditional cultural expressions may include 'art, designs, names, signs and symbols'[46] but it can be difficult for traditional owners to protect them

---

[33]   GC17, para 4.

[34]   Rosemary Coombe, *The Cultural Life of Intellectual Properties: Authorship, Appropriation and the Law* (Duke University Press 1999) 86.

[35]   GC17, para 9.

[36]   See *Exxon Corporation v. Exxon Insurance Consultants International Ltd* [1982] Ch 119, 136–7 (Stephenson LJ).

[37]   *Fairfax Media Publications Pty Ltd v. Reed International Books Australia Pty Ltd* [2010] FCA 984, para 46.

[38]   *Advantage-Rent-A-Car Inc v. Advantage Car Rental Pty Ltd* (2001) 52 IPR 24.

[39]   In human rights, culture is not defined qualitatively, so there is no reason that the cultural contribution of trademarks should be excluded from protection. See Janewa Osei Tutu, 'Corporate "Human Rights" to Intellectual Property Protection?' (2015) 55 Santa Clara Law Review, 1, 47.

[40]   GC17, para 14.

[41]   Ibid, paras 2–3.

[42]   *Bulun Bulun v. R & T Textiles Pty Ltd* [1998] FCA 1082.

[43]   Francina Cantatore and Jane Johnston, 'Moral rights: Exploring the myths, meanings and misunderstandings in Australian copyright law' (2016) 21 Deakin Law Review, 71, 74–5.

[44]   Copyright Act 1968 (Cth) s 33.

[45]   GC17, para 12.

[46]   World Intellectual Property Organization, 'Traditional Cultural Expressions', http://www.wipo.int/tk/en/folklore.

effectively through intellectual property structures that only recognize fixed expressions and require clear identification of authors or owners.[47] Trademark protection can sometimes be used to control use of signs and prevent others from using them commercially. However, this often requires not only ongoing commercial use by the custodians of traditional cultural expressions but establishing first commercial use for relevant goods or services if another party has appropriated that mark. Although the US Patent and Trademark Office has a list of traditional insignia that can be used to restrict domestic registration of these signs by unauthorized parties, this does not protect many traditional cultural expressions.[48] The situation is even more complex if public authorities appropriate traditional cultural expressions. The Zia are Indigenous persons historically residing in New Mexico in the United States. They are well-known for their pottery and their distinctive sun symbol that is used in ceremonial activities.[49] The Sun symbol was depicted on the flag of Madison, the capital city of Wisconsin, from 1962.[50] Although it was removed in 2018 in response to concerns regarding the cultural appropriation of the sacred symbol,[51] the Sun symbol remains featured in the flag of New Mexico and this restricts the ability of the Zia people to obtain trademark registration.[52] Requirements of commercial use further restrict the ability of the Zia to register related symbols.[53] In other jurisdictions, traditional knowledge custodians have been able to use trademark registration defensively to restrict use of these types of symbols[54] but this type of protection is not always available or appropriate.[55]

Protection against inappropriate use of traditional cultural expressions using intellectual property is very limited in Australia: an opposition to the registration of the Yugumbeh word for koala, Borobi, for use in relation to the 2018 Commonwealth Games Corporation in Brisbane highlighted that there is no requirement in Australian trademark law for the applicant to consult with relevant parties when using a traditional cultural expression.[56] Although consultation with traditional owners had occurred so that consent could be obtained, the opposition evidenced dispute about the validity of this consent within the Yugumbeh people.[57] The Australian trademark system is not structured to adjudicate these concerns, and nor is the copyright regime – a 2003 bill to introduce communal moral rights protection for Indigenous

---

[47]   Dalindyebo Bafana Shabalala 'Intellectual Property, Traditional Knowledge, and Traditional Cultural Expressions in Native American Tribal Codes' (2017) 4(5) Akron Law Review, 1125, 1133–4.

[48]   Stephanie B Turner, 'The Case of the Zia: Looking Beyond Trademark Law to Protect Sacred Symbols' (2012) 11 Chicago-Kent Journal of Intellectual Property, 116, 130.

[49]   Ibid, 119–20.

[50]   Logan Wroge, 'Madison City Council Approves Modified Flag Design', Wisconsin State Journal (24 July 2018 https://madison.com/wsj/news/local/govt-and-politics/madison-city-council-approves -modified-flag-design/article_1d486328-1424-5693-9a50-2299097f545b.html).

[51]   Ibid.

[52]   Turner (n 48), 121–2, 124.

[53]   Ibid.

[54]   See Michael Brown *Who Owns Native Culture* (Harvard University Press 2003) 83–7.

[55]   See Susy Frankel, 'Trademarks and Traditional Knowledge and Cultural Intellectual Property Rights', in Graeme B Dinwoodie and Marc D Janis (eds), *Trademark Law and Theory: A Handbook of Contemporary Research* (Edward Elgar, 2008) 433.

[56]   *Jabree Ltd v. Gold Coast 2018 Commonwealth Games Corporation* (2017) 132 IPR 80; [2017] ATMO 156.

[57]   Ibid.

persons never became law.[58] By contrast, in New Zealand, trademark legislation recognizes that certain marks should not be registered because they are offensive; a Māori Advisory Board advises the Trademarks Commissioner on what is offensive to Māori.[59] The legislation does not explicitly recognize ICESCR obligations but the operation of the board can protect the moral interests of Indigenous peoples.

Drawing upon the concept of moral interests found in the ICESCR could offer a better solution for traditional knowledge custodians wishing to contest offensive use of traditional cultural expressions in trademarks.[60] Marketing activities of tobacco companies have highlighted the potential need to assert moral interests against corporate actors to protect traditional cultural expressions. In 2005, Philip Morris launched a cigarette brand called Māori Mix in Israel. The package displayed 'quasi-Māori' images.[61] This generated complaints from Māori representatives and ultimately the company apologized.[62] Asserting obligations to comply with ICESCR Article 15 obligations could strengthen similar complaints in the future.[63] Recognition that these types of uses of artistic productions are derogatory actions that are inconsistent with moral interests of Indigenous communities could become a powerful tool to safeguard expressions of cultural heritage and traditional knowledge from exploitative, unauthorized uses.[64] Recognizing these interests within a human rights framework means that they can be balanced against other important interests such as freedom of expression.

4.   MORAL ASPECTS OF TRADEMARKS AND *AUSTRALIA – TOBACCO PLAIN PACKAGING*

Another area in which moral interests may also be relevant is in relation to trade law disputes about intellectual property. Several aspects of the recent decision of the WTO Appellate Body in *Australia – Tobacco Plain Packaging* suggest that states could use human rights obligations

---

[58]   See criticisms of the proposal in Jane Anderson, 'The Politics of Indigenous Knowledge: Australia's Proposed Communal Moral Rights Bill' (2004) 27 University of New South Wales Law Journal, 585.

[59]   Section 17(1)(b)(ii) of the Trade Marks Act 2002 (NZ). See Susy Frankel, 'Third-Party Trade Marks as a Violation of Indigenous Cultural Property: A New Statutory Safeguard' (2005) 8 Journal of World Intellectual Property, 83, 89–91. Inconsistency with the ground for objection can also support revocation proceedings commenced by culturally aggrieved parties: Trade Marks Act 2002 (NZ), s 73(1).

[60]   Brown (n 54) 69–87; Turner (n 48) 121–2, 124.

[61]   A van der Sterren, E M Greenhalgh, D Knoche and M H Winstanley, '8.12 The Tobacco Industry and Indigenous Communities' in M M Scollo and M H Winstanley (eds), *Tobacco in Australia: Facts and Issues* (Cancer Council Victoria, 2016). Available from https://www.tobaccoinaustralia.org.au/chapter-8-aptsi/8-12-the-tobacco-industry-and-indigenous-communiti#x6.

[62]   *ABC News*, 'Philip Morris pulls Maori Mix cigarettes' (28 April 2006) https://www.abc.net.au/news/2006-04-28/philip-morris-pulls-maori-mix-cigarettes/1740882.

[63]   GC17 recognizes that states are obliged 'to ensure the effective protection of the moral and material interests of authors against infringement by third parties': para 32.

[64]   Williams-Davidson identifies the demoralizing impact of reproduction of cultural objects on Indigenous persons: Terri-Lynn Williams-Davidson, 'Sacred Objects, Art and Nature in a Global Economy', in Jerry Mander and Victoria Tauli-Corpuz (eds), *Paradigm Wars: Indigenous Peoples' Resistance to Globalization* (Sierra Club Books 2006) 98.

to justify restricting the rights of trademark owners to protect moral interests in the future.[65] This could support legislation addressing moral interests related to uses of traditional cultural expressions in trademarks.[66]

In *Australia – Tobacco Plain Packaging* the Appellate Body considered Australian plain packaging legislation that requires standardized packaging of all tobacco products that includes very visible graphic health warnings.[67] The requirements only permit the use of work marks in standardized font, where they are used to indicate the source of origin of the product; they do not permit trademark owners to use trademarks on packaging where they are images or device marks that combine images and text.[68] The complainants unsuccessfully argued that these requirements were contrary to the prohibition on special requirements on the use of trademarks found in Article 20 of TRIPS.[69] The Appellate Body confirmed the earlier Dispute Settlement Body Panel decision that Australia did not breach the provision. Although the trademark requirements imposed by Australia's plain packaging measures did constitute special requirements that encumbered the use of the relevant trademarks in the course of trade, TRIPS only prohibits such requirements where they are imposed unjustifiably.[70]

The Appellate Body recognized the Panel's assessment that the special requirements on the use of trademarks in the course of trade were 'far reaching'.[71] In making this assessment, the Panel found that the relevant interests of the trademark owner were not limited to the use of the trademark to distinguish goods from other goods but included economic interests such as communication of the 'tangible or intangible benefits' of a product.[72] The interpretation of Article 17 in *EC – Trade Marks and Geographical Indications (United States)* provided contextual guidance for this assessment.[73] In that complaint, the Panel interpreted the interests protected by Article 17 to include the trademark owner's legitimate interest 'in the economic value of its mark arising from the reputation that it enjoys and the quality that it denotes'.[74] These broader economic interests were also relevant to the weighing and balancing assessment of the nature of the encumbrances on trademark use that resulted from Australia's plain packaging measures. However, using TRIPS Article 7 and 8, the Panel recognized that societal

---

[65]   Christophe Geiger and Luc Desaunettes-Barbero, 'The Revitalisation of the Object and Purpose of the TRIPS Agreement: The Plain Packaging Reports and the Awakening of the TRIPS Flexibility Clauses', Centre for International Intellectual Property Studies (CEIPI) Research Paper No. 2020-01, available at SSRN: https://ssrn.com/abstract=3556585. Forthcoming in: J. Griffiths and T. Mylly (eds), *Constitutional Hedges of Intellectual Property* (Oxford University Press 2020) 45.

[66]   Protection of copyright-based moral rights found in the Berne Convention is expressly excluded from the *TRIPS* Agreement: *Marrakesh Agreement Establishing the World Trade Organization*, opened for signature 15 April 1994, 1867 UNTS 3 (entered into force 1 January 1995) annex 1C ('*Agreement on Trade-Related Aspects of Intellectual Property Rights*') art 15 ('*TRIPS*') art 9(1).

[67]   Tobacco Plain Packaging Act 2011 (Cth) s 21.

[68]   Ibid, s 20.

[69]   Appeal Report, para 7.13

[70]   TRIPS, Art 20.

[71]   Appeal Report, para 6.675.

[72]   Panel Report, *Australia – Certain Measures Concerning Trademarks, Geographical Indications and Other Plain Packaging Requirements Applicable to Tobacco Products and Packaging* (June 2018) WT/DS435/R, WT/DS441/R, WT/DS458/R, WT/DS467/R (Panel Report), para. 7.2562.

[73]   Panel Report, para 7.2562.

[74]   Panel Report, *European Communities – Protection of Trademarks and Geographical Indications for Agricultural Products and Foodstuffs. Complaint by Australia*, WTO Doc WT/DS290/R (15 March 2005) para 7.664.

interests are relevant to determining whether the measures were unjustifiable.[75] Australia's public health justifications for applying these encumbrances to protect health and life as part of a comprehensive tobacco control regime were sufficiently supported by societal interests so they were not unjustifiable, despite the extensive nature of the encumbrance.[76] The importance of Australia's public health objective was further supported by the fact that plain packaging measures were developed consistently with the 'emerging multilateral consensus' evident from the Framework Convention on Tobacco Control (FCTC).[77] Australia explicitly recognized its obligations as a party to the FCTC in the objectives clause of the primary legislation use to implement tobacco plain packaging measures.[78]

This decision can support protection of Indigenous moral interests, where traditional cultural expressions underlie trademarks and WTO members develop mechanisms to control use of trademarks that is offensive to Indigenous persons. Even where a sophisticated system for protecting traditional cultural expressions in registrations exists, as it does in New Zealand, there is still potential that a mark may be registered but its use in certain circumstances may be offensive.[79] Whilst such use could support a revocation proceeding, this may be unappealing as it requires lengthy and expensive litigation, or inappropriate, as there is a long history of inoffensive use.[80] A complaint mechanism for culturally aggrieved groups about such use could strengthen protection for moral interests for Indigenous persons.[81] An advisory body could assess use in these circumstances and provide rulings recommending changes to use. Requiring owners to implement such rulings could result in encumbrances on the use of trademarks. However, a mechanism that protects the moral interests of Indigenous persons can also be consistent with the protection of societal interests by WTO members and justify encumbrances on the use of trademarks. Although Articles 7 and 8 provide guidance for the content of these societal interests, societal interests are not restricted to 'measures necessary to protect public health and nutrition, and to promote the public interest in sectors of vital importance to their socio-economic and technological development'.[82] As Australia used the FCTC as further support for its public health objectives, a WTO member could explicitly recognize

---

[75]   Panel Report, para 7.2404, Appeal Report, para 6.660.

[76]   Appeal Report, para 6.699.

[77]   Ibid, para 6.706. WHO Framework Convention on Tobacco Control (opened for signature 21 May 2003, entered into force 27 February 2005) 2302 UNTS 166 (FCTC). The FCTC Guidelines recognize the relevance of tobacco packaging to tobacco control measures: WHO FCTC, Conference of the Parties, *Guidelines for Implementation of Article 11 of the WHO Framework Convention on Tobacco Control (Packaging and Labelling of Tobacco Products)*, Decision FCTC/COP3(10) (2 November 2008).

[78]   Tobacco Plain Packaging Act 2011 (Cth), s 3.

[79]   *Jabree Ltd v. Gold Coast 2018 Commonwealth Games Corporation* (2017) 132 IPR 80 indicates that even where consent for registration has been given, there may be unanticipated use that needs to be regulated, or concerns about the nature of that consent.

[80]   Waikato argues that such actions are unlikely to result in revocation of established marks: Tania Waikato, 'He Kaitiaki Matauranga: Building a Protection Regime for Maori Traditional Knowledge' (2005) 8.2 Yearbook of New Zealand Jurisprudence, 344.

[81]   Senftleben gives examples where this mechanism could also be relevant for non-Indigenous persons who can demonstrate that the cultural impact of a trademark poses significant cultural concern. See Martin Senftleben 'Vigeland and the Status of Cultural Concerns in Trade Mark Law – The EFTA Court Develops More Effective Tools for the Preservation of the Public Domain' (2017) 48(6) IIC-International Review of Intellectual Property and Competition Law, 683–720.

[82]   Panel Report, para. 7.2406. Article 7 recognizes that the 'protection and enforcement of intellectual property shall contribute to a balance of rights and obligations': TRIPS, Art 7.

that measures providing Indigenous persons with greater control over use of traditional cultural expressions in trademarks implements ICESCR Article 15 obligations.[83] Further support is available for this position from the United Nations Declaration on the Rights of Indigenous Persons (UNDRIP). UNDRIP recognizes the rights of Indigenous peoples over traditional cultural expressions (Article 31) and manifestations of their cultures (Article 11).

5.   NAVIGATING THE COMPLEXITIES OF COPYRIGHT-BASED MORAL RIGHTS PROTECTION FOR INDIVIDUAL TRADEMARK CREATORS

Individuals who author artistic or literary productions underlying trademarks may also assert moral interests in those works and may be able to rely on domestic copyright protection for moral rights. The extent to which this protection is consistent with the objective of human rights protection for moral interests of encouraging creators to contribute to the arts and social progress will vary, depending on the circumstances surrounding the creation of that trademark. This can influence the extent to which those moral interests could be protected if they conflicted with other human rights such as the right to freedom of expression. Although it is assumed that many creators of trademarks contractually assign their moral rights in associated works to those who commission their creation, there are other circumstances where an author may claim a more meaningful connection with the work underlying a trademark as an intellectual creation. In some cases, an author's work may be used as a trademark after copyright expires and that use can arguably conflict with the deceased author's moral interests.[84] In other cases, a living author may claim that their work contributes to the arts and social progress.

Milton Glaser is an exceptional example of a well-known trademark creator. He created the famous I (heart logo) NY trademark for the City of New York in the late 1970s. He did not accept payment for the underlying artwork and is not a registered owner; he created it to support New York tourism during a difficult economic period.[85] If a pro-gun lobby commissioned an artist to use Glaser's iconic logo and replaced the heart logo with a gun logo, Glaser would not have standing in trademark law to object to subsequent use of his work to promote the gun lobby. Nor would American moral rights protection for visual artists protect Glaser, as this only protects artworks that exist in single copy.[86] If his moral rights were protected, Glaser could contest this gun artwork as a distortion of his drawn logo.[87] In a different jurisdiction,[88] he might have a strong argument that the derivative artworks breaches his moral right in the integrity of his artistic work because the gun artwork undermines the purpose of his expres-

---

[83]   The protection provided for traditional knowledge in UNDRIP is also relevant: GA Res 61/295, United Nations Declaration on the Rights of Indigenous Peoples 4 (2 October 2007) at 11.

[84]   It is beyond the scope of this chapter to discuss the complex issues raised by cumulative protection of copyright and trademark rights. See Senftleben (n 81).

[85]   When Glaser later created a derivative 'I [heart symbol] New York more than ever' following 9/11 and permitted use of the derivative for fundraising he was threatened with an intellectual property infringement by the City of New York: Chip Kidd, 'An interview with Milton Glaser' (1 September 2003) https://believermag.com/an-interview-with-milton-glaser/.

[86]   17 U.S. Code § 101 – Definitions.

[87]   17 U.S. Code § 106A(a)(3)(A).

[88]   See, for example, Copyright Act 1968 (Cth), s 195AQ.

sion, celebrating New York, in a manner that is particularly offensive to him and detrimental to his honour or reputation.[89] However, although other jurisdictions permit copyright-based protection for moral rights, creators often remain unknown and their invisibility makes it difficult to respect their personality rights as authors. Glaser is an exceptional example of a well-known trademark creator.

To explore the way that domestic moral rights protection found in domestic copyright law can protect moral rights for creators of trademarks that constitute artistic works, this section focuses on the intellectual property law of Australia, a common law country with an intellectual property (IP) system that was originally influenced by English law. It investigates barriers to copyright-based protection of moral rights for trademark creators in Australia. These include the practice of not protecting copyright in words or short titles, the absence of an effective mechanism for attribution for creators of trademarks and the likelihood that where trademarks are created in a commercial environment, business efficacy will strongly influence a standard practice of waiver of moral rights for trademark creators.

The Copyright Act 1968 (Cth) provides moral rights protection for authors of literary or artistic works.[90] A trademark that constitutes an artistic work, such as a logo that includes artistic material,[91] is likely to entitle its creator to moral rights protected through copyright. The threshold for protection for relevant artistic works such as drawings and paintings does not require an assessment of artistic merit.[92] In contrast, thresholds for protection of literary works mean that word trademarks are rarely considered to constitute literary works: protection for single word marks has been rejected.[93] It is possible that a title may reach a threshold of originality that entitles it to copyright protection but protection is much more certain for trademarks containing artistic works.[94]

In Australia, moral rights were introduced to ensure consistency with the Berne Convention[95] and correspond to the term of copyright.[96] Moral rights are only conferred on individuals and cannot be assigned to other parties.[97] An author must be identified whenever an artistic work is reproduced or communicated[98] and an individual is also entitled not to have authorship of works falsely attributed to them.[99] However, it is not an infringement if the alleged infringer

---

[89]   Glaser has also created artwork that criticized federal government failures to reform gun laws. Joe Nocera, 'The Gun Report – April 19 2013' (19 April 2013) https:// web .archive .org/ web/ 20130422085919/https://nocera.blogs.nytimes.com/2013/04/19/the-gun-report-april-19-2013/.

[90]   Copyright Act 1968 (Cth), Part IX.

[91]   Device marks composed of words and images were found to constitute protectable artistic works in *Aussie Home Loans v. Phillips* (1998) 40 IPR 392 and *Advantage-Rent-A-Car Inc v. Advantage Car Rental Pty Ltd* [2001] FCA 683.

[92]   Copyright Act 1968 (Cth), s 10. However, a logo containing only stylized text was too 'trivial' to qualify for protection in *Cortis Exhaust Systems Pty Ltd v. Kitten Software Pty Ltd* (2001) ATPR 41-837 at [33] per Tamberlin J.

[93]   *Exxon Corporation v. Exxon Insurance Consultants International Ltd* [1982] Ch 119, 143 (Stephenson LJ).

[94]   In *Fairfax Media Publications Pty Ltd v. Reed International Books Australia Pty Ltd,* Bennett J recognized copyright might be possible in a title but did not find copyright in the newspaper titles under consideration: [2010] FCA 984, para 46.

[95]   Copyright Amendment (Moral Rights) Bill 1999 Revised Explanatory Memorandum.

[96]   Copyright Act 1968 (Cth), s 195AM (except for cinematographic films).

[97]   Ibid, ss 190, 195AN(3).

[98]   Ibid (Cth), s 195AO.

[99]   Ibid (Cth) s 195AP.

can establish that it was reasonable not to identify the author of an artistic work.[100] The function of trademarks as symbols that reduce search costs for consumers[101] and the industry practice of not identifying the creators of trademarks make it likely that attribution would not be considered reasonable where trademarks contained artistic works.[102]

Rights of integrity permit a holder of moral rights 'to prevent derogatory treatment of a work that is detrimental to their honour or reputation'[103] unless they give consent or the treatment is found to be reasonable in the circumstances. Derogatory treatment includes material distortion or mutilation of the work that is prejudicial to the author's honour or reputation, exhibition in a context that prejudices the author's honour or reputation and 'the doing of anything else in relation to the work that is prejudicial to the author's honour or reputation'.[104] It may be difficult to establish prejudice to the reputation of a trademark author if they are unknown. However, damage to honour extends beyond reputational harm; Adeney argues that the drafters of the Berne Convention intended it to be read broadly.[105] Prejudice is determined both subjectively, considering the author's response to the use, and objectively, considering the reasonableness of that response.[106] Defences to breach of moral rights consider the reasonableness of the alleged breach.[107] Assessments of reasonableness include considerations of the nature and purpose of the work; the manner and context in which the work is used; the industry practice relevant to the work or its use; any circumstances of employment surrounding use of the work and the views of the treatment by other authors, where there is more than one.[108]

Considerations such as the manner and context in which the work can be important if it is necessary to balance moral concerns against other interests such as freedom of expression interests: irreverently referencing well-known trademarks can be an important part of cultural dialogue.[109] If Glaser could assert a moral interest to stop the use of his logo by the pro-gun parodist, the parodist may argue that this restricts freedom of expression and it will be necessary to assess whether protection of Glaser's interests is a necessary, direct and proportionate restriction.[110] A necessary restriction to protect the rights of Glaser needs to be for a legitimate purpose.[111] If protection of Glaser's interest could be achieved in other ways, it may be unnecessary. Any restriction must also be proportionate and there must be a 'direct

---

[100]   Ibid, s 195AR.

[101]   William M Landes and Richard A Posner, *The Economic Structure of Intellectual Property Law* (Harvard University Press 2003) 172, 166–8.

[102]   Copyright Act 1968 (Cth), s 195AR. Industry practice is reflected in registration harmonization treaties such as the Trademark Law Treaty that only recognize owners, not authors: *Trademark Law Treaty*, opened for signature 27 October 1994, 2037 UNTS 35 (entered into force 1 August 1996).

[103]   Copyright Act 1968 (Cth), s 195AQ (2).

[104]   Ibid, s 195AK.

[105]   Adeney (n 9) 123.

[106]   This approach was taken in *Perez v. Fernandez* [2012] FMCA 2, paras 60–65. See Dennis Lim 'Prejudice to Honour or Reputation in Copyright Law' (2007) 33(2) Monash University Law Review, 290.

[107]   Copyright Act 1968 (Cth), s 195AS.

[108]   Ibid, s 195AS.

[109]   See Genevieve Wilkinson 'Mitey Marks and Expressive Uses of Culturally Significant Trade Marks in Australia' (2019) 30(1) Australian Intellectual Property Journal, 46.

[110]   UN Human Rights Committee, *General Comment No 34 – Article 19: Freedoms of Opinion and Expression*, 102nd sess, UN Doc CCPR/C/GC/34 (12 September 2011) (GC34), para 22.

[111]   Ibid, para 33.

and immediate connection between the expression and the threat'.[112] This assessment requires an understanding of the precise nature of the threat. Multiple considerations are likely to be relevant. If the creator of a trademark is hired to create a commercial work for a specific brief, it is less likely that they will view their work as an intellectual creation and any moral interest may be weak. Glaser's purpose is more difficult to categorize as it was both commercial and altruistic. If the moral interest is strong, restricting parodies of the logo may be proportionate because there are alternative ways to express an opinion about gun control that do not impact the integrity of the work.

The fact that there are barriers to effective protection of attribution rights for the creators of trademarks does not mean that copyright-based moral rights protection is not justified. The Milton Glaser example suggests that there will be situations where there is an enduring personal connection between an author and their work as an expression of themselves, even though the work is used to signify origin in trade. In these cases, the protection of moral rights for creators of trademarks that constitute artistic works fit with personhood-based justifications for preserving the integrity of a work. The recognition that industry practice is relevant in defences to breaches does not mean that industry practice necessarily results in adequate protection of the moral rights of authors.[113] It may be reasonable to change the operation of the law so that authors of trademarks can be more easily identified.

One way of doing this could be through the trademarks register. Copyright does not require registration in Australia but this should not mean that creators of trademarks who are entitled to moral rights protection should not be able to register their authorship through the trademark register, in much the same way that an inventor of a patentable invention is recorded on the Australian patent register.[114] It seems probable that trademark owners would generally wish to obtain a moral rights waiver from the creator of the trademark at the same time that they obtain an assignment or licence of the economic rights in any copyright work subsisting in the trademark.[115] This information could be recorded on the register. This might also encourage both parties to turn their mind to the need for a waiver or the consequences of that waiver.[116] The current practice of not systematically identifying these authors may present problems both for authors and for derivative users. Derivative users like parodists may use trademarks for social commentary but may not intend to offend the honour of the trademark author, nor be involved in lengthy court proceedings disputing moral right entitlements. However, it is difficult to understand the connection that creators of trademarks feel to their work when industry practice means that they remain largely invisible.

---

[112]   Ibid, paras 34–5.
[113]   See criticism of Australian industry practice for moral rights protection for authors of literary works: Cantatore and Johnston (n 43) 71.
[114]   Patent Act 1990 (Cth) s15. This is consistent with the right of recognition granted in the Paris Convention: Paris Convention for the Protection of Industrial Property, opened for signature 20 March 1883, 828 UNTS 305 (entered into force 6 July 1884, revised at Stockholm 14 July 1967, amended 28 September 1979) art 4*ter*. No analogous right exists for creators of trademarks.
[115]   Copyright Act 1968 (Cth), s 195AWA.
[116]   This could have further commercial benefits of prompting trademark owners to ensure that copyright materials contained in trademarks are properly assigned. For example, of problems with failing to assign copyright in a trademark see *Re State Government Insurance Corporation and State Government Insurance Commission v. Government Insurance Office of New South Wales; Gio Holdings Ltd and Gio Life Ltd* [1991] FCA 121 (9 April 1991) French J, para 120.

6.   DO CORPORATE TRADEMARK OWNERS POSSESS MORAL RIGHTS?

The broad economic interests of trademark owners in many jurisdictions should remain clearly distinguished from claims of moral rights or moral interests for trademark creators. For well-known marks, owners' trademark rights have expanded beyond the traditional protection available to exclude third parties from using similar marks on similar goods.[117] In Australia, protection against confusing use remains the focus of trademark legislation,[118] but in other jurisdictions, including Europe and the United States, trademark owners have broader rights to restrict non-confusing uses of their marks and some authors have characterized these as moral rights for trademark owners.[119] Protection exists for owners to restrict dilution of a mark (also known as dilution by blurring) when a well-known mark is used on unrelated goods or services in a manner that negatively impacts on the reputation and distinctiveness of the mark.[120] Tarnishment (also known as dilution by tarnishment) is alleged to occur when a mark is associated with another, usually unrelated, good or service in a manner that may not be confusing but arguably invites negative associations with the original brand and negatively impacts on the reputation of the mark.[121] These actions protect the material interests of trademark owners who are often corporations.[122] Hegel's theories have been used to argue that, as symbols of a corporation's personality, trademark rights should be broadly protected.[123] Friedmann proposes expansion of rights protecting mark integrity to grant owners a 'moral right' to integrity for their trademarked logos that would prevent any unauthorized uses of those marks in social media, even if those marks were used for expressive rather than commercial purposes and even if they did not result in confusion.[124] Such attempts to use personhood theories to support broad trademark rights for corporate trademark owners fail to recognize the emphasis on the individual author in both the Berne Convention and the ICESCR. Even if claims that the limited grant of personhood for corporations mean that personhood theory can also justify rights for corporate trademark owners,[125] this is relevant only to material interests and should not be extended to justify moral rights or moral interests for corporate owners.[126]

---

[117]   Andrew Griffiths, 'A Law-and-Economics Perspective on Trade Marks' in Lionel Bently, Jennifer Davis and Jane C Ginsburg (eds), *Trade Marks and Brands: An Interdisciplinary Critique* (Cambridge University Press 2008) 241, 265.

[118]   Handler argues this is consistent with TRIPS: Michael Handler, 'Trade Mark Dilution in Australia?' (2007) 70 Intellectual Property Forum, 36, 37–8.

[119]   Danny Friedmann, *Trademarks and Social Media: Towards Algorithmic Justice* (Edward Elgar Publishing, 2015).

[120]   Michael Handler, 'What Can Harm the Reputation of a Trademark? A Critical Re-evaluation of Dilution by Tarnishment' (2016) 106(3) Trade Mark Reporter, 639.

[121]   Ibid, 640.

[122]   Sandra Rierson, 'The Myth and Reality of Dilution' (2012) 11(2) Duke Law & Technology Review 212, 279–81.

[123]   Richard Spinello, 'Online Brands and Trademark Conflicts' (2006) 16(3) Business Ethics Quarterly, 343, 351–4. See Justin Hughes, 'The Philosophy of Intellectual Property' (1988) 77(2) Georgetown Law Journal, 287, 353–4.

[124]   Friedmann (n 119).

[125]   Spinello (n 123), 352–3.

[126]   Rierson argues that the introduction of laws protecting dilution in the United States relates directly to the economic-based power of owners of well-known trademarks: (n 122) 281.

The grant of inalienable moral rights or protection for moral interests to authors recognizes an enduring personal link between the author and the work itself.[127] Trademark rights may be enduring for a corporate owner, but that is dependent on use.[128] Unlike an author with inalienable moral rights or the custodian of those rights, an owner of a trademark can assign their rights in many jurisdictions without assigning goodwill attached to the mark.[129] The 'personal' connection between a company and a trademark largely depends on whether or not it is economically beneficial to use the mark and the connection to be maintained. The attitude of Mattel to Aqua's references to the Barbie trademark in their song 'Barbie Girl' highlights this economic interest. In *MCA Records*, Mattel unsuccessfully alleged dilution and tarnishment of their trademark by Aqua and its record company, arguing that the song depicted the iconic doll as a vacuous bimbo.[130] Over a decade later, Mattel licenced the song that they had impugned in extensive litigation and used a modified version in advertising and promotion.[131]

MCA Records illustrates that the human rights implications of trademark protection are not limited to protection for moral and material interests of authors. Protection for trademark owners to restrict non-confusing uses of their marks in dilution or tarnishment actions raises complex freedom of expression concerns.[132] In 'Barbie Girl', Aqua made expressive use of the well-known Barbie mark to comment on gender stereotypes promoted by the popular toy.[133] Expressive use of a mark occurs when someone uses or references the mark for a purpose other than distinguishing the goods or services from those of others.[134] Spence argues that there is a speech based justification for permitting a trademark owner to maintain the distinctive character of the mark by restricting some types of allusions (although others must still be able to comment on the mark).[135] If the meaning of the mark becomes unstable, the commentary may be less effective.[136] However, protecting a stable meaning of a famous trademark so that it can be used effectively in cultural dialogue may restrict the freedom of expression rights of expressive users. Even if trademark rights can support speech, these rights must still be con-

---

[127]   GC17, para 2.
[128]   See for example, non-use provisions for removal of unused marks in Trade Marks Act 1995 (Cth) Part 9.
[129]   TRIPS Art 21 explicitly permits this but some jurisdictions, including the United States, do not: Robert Burrell and Michael Handler, *Australian Trade Mark Law* (2nd edition, Oxford University Press 2016) 521.
[130]   Mattel Inc v. MCA Records Inc 296 F.3d 894 (9th Cir. 2002).
[131]   Robert Burrell and Dev Gangjee, 'Trade Marks and Freedom of Expression: A Call for Caution' (2010) 41(5) International Review of Industrial & Copyright Law, 544, 551.
[132]   See Megan Richardson, 'Trade Marks and Language' (2004) 26(2) Sydney Law Review, 193, 195, 217–20; Jason Bosland, 'The Culture of Trade Marks: An Alternative Cultural Theory Perspective' (2005) 10 Media & Arts Law Review, 99.
[133]   *Mattel, Inc. v. MCA Records, Inc.* 28 F. Supp. 2d 1120 (1998) 1138.
[134]   William McGeveran, 'Rethinking Trademark Fair Use' (2008) 94 Iowa Law Review, 49, 54; Rochelle Dreyfuss, 'Expressive Genericity: Trademarks as Language in the Pepsi Generation' (1990) 65 Notre Dame Law Review, 397, 401.
[135]   Spence recognizes that both speech and property rights operate: 'The Mark as Expression/The Mark as Property' (2005) 58(1) Current Legal Problems, 491, 510.
[136]   Robert Goldman and Stephen Papson, *Sign Wars: The Cluttered Landscape of Advertising* (Guilford Press 1996) 255. Compare Aoki's arguments against freezing a sign's meaning in different social and cultural contexts: Keith Aoki, 'Authors, Inventors and Trademark Owners: Private Intellectual Property and the Public Domain-Part II' (1993) 18 Colum.-VLA JL & Arts, 191, 266.

sistent with permissible restrictions on commercial speech.[137] A trademark monopoly restricts the ability for others to use that mark and that restriction must be necessary and proportionate, consistent with the permissible limitations found in Article 19 of the International Covenant on Civil and Political Rights (ICCPR).[138] Restricting unauthorized use by third parties may be permissible as protection for the 'rights of others' because it prevents confusing uses of speech in the marketplace but that restriction must be necessary and proportionate.[139] Although *MCA Records* demonstrates that freedom of expression interests may be recognized eventually, the nature of lengthy dilution and tarnishment actions place strong emphasis on the protection of owner interests.[140]

Protection for non-confusing uses where there are significant resources disparities between trademark owners and expressive users may operate to enable trademark owners to assert rights that are not necessary, direct and proportionate restrictions on freedom of expression.[141] Expressive use was made of the Marlboro trademark on a T-shirt available for sale in the United States that depicted an image of a tobacco packet with design elements distinctive to Marlboro trademarked cigarettes but replaced the word Marlboro with death, using the same font.[142] The relevant trademarks were the vector logos that were modified to resemble dripping blood. Although significant visual differences between the registered mark and the parodic image clearly distinguished the source, Philip Morris sent a letter of demand to the artist alleging breach of dilution protections available for its famous trademark.[143] In cases like this, artists may not have access to legal advice or the resources to contest assertions of owner rights and so they might agree to the owner's demands and cease making expressive use of the mark.[144] Such assertions of trademark rights can accordingly chill freedom of expression without court supervision. Even if there is legislative protection against unjustified threats, these activities can go unreported.[145]

The size of damages claims in litigation commenced by Philip Morris to protect its rights to use trademarks in packaging suggests that economic interests strongly motivate the corporation to threaten or commence action.[146] The artist who created the Marlboro logo may also assert moral rights or interests to protection and argue that the parody of his or her artwork

---

[137] GC34, para 11.

[138] Ibid, para 22. International Covenant on Civil and Political Rights (opened for signature 16 December 1966, entered into force 23 March 1976) 999 UNTS 171 (ICCPR), Art 19.

[139] Wilkinson (n 109) 50.

[140] Considering the links between corporate personality rights and dilution and tarnishment protection in Europe, Westkamp notes that fundamental rights in reputation and honour are usually balanced against other rights including freedom of expression but this balancing is less likely to occur where trademark tarnishment is alleged: Guido Westkamp, 'Intellectual Property and Human Rights: Reputation, Integrity and the Advent of Corporate Personality Rights' in Geiger (n 32) 392.

[141] Wilkinson (n 109) 62–3.

[142] Joe Mullin, 'Philip Morris Attacks Marlboro Parody, Runs into "Web Bully's Worst Enemy"', ARSTECHNICA (17 June 2014), https://arstechnica.com/tech-policy/2014/06/philip-morris-attacks-marlboro-parody-runs-into-web-bullys-worst-enemy/.

[143] Ibid.

[144] William T Gallagher, 'Trademark and Copyright Enforcement in the Shadow of IP Law' (2012) 28(3) Santa Clara High Technology Law Journal, 453, 492–6.

[145] McGeveran (n 134) 740.

[146] See estimate of claim of billions of dollars in *Philip Morris Asia Ltd v. Australia* (2012) UNCITRAL PCA 2012-12, para 11.

is detrimental to their honour or reputation. Should this claim restrict the parodists' right to freedom of expression? Restrictions based on protection of the author's moral rights would need to be necessary and proportionate.[147] Reasonableness defences to moral rights actions may be consistent with these requirements but the potential impact of moral rights claims on freedom of expression rights remains an area for further consideration.[148]

It may be that, once the serious negative health impacts of tobacco consumption and the role of trademarks in inducing tobacco consumption become known, the author of the Marlboro artwork would prefer to withdraw it from circulation. A moral right of withdrawal exists in some jurisdictions for authors who have transferred economic rights so they can withdraw their work from circulation if it no longer represents the personality of the author. However, this requires the author to 'indemnify the transferee for prejudice caused'.[149] The significant value of the Marlboro brand to Philip Morris makes any withdrawal action inconceivable. Authors of material underlying other valuable trademarks are likely to face similar deterrents to exercising rights of withdrawal. This reflects the complex interplay between material and moral interests in trademarks, but does not mean alienable economic rights should be conflated with inalienable moral rights and interests.

7.   CONCLUSION

This chapter has drawn out several ways in which trademarks engage questions of moral rights for authors of trademarks and moral interests for authors of the literary and artistic productions and traditional cultural expressions that may underlie or be used in trademarks. These rights permit control over the use of trademarks for individuals and groups of individuals that is consistent with recognition that there is an enduring link between authors and their intellectual creations. The inalienable interests they protect should not be conflated with rights for trademark owners to expand protection for trademarks beyond non-confusing uses. This chapter has suggested that human rights protection for moral interests may provide valuable support where trademarks are used inconsistently with the values of custodians of traditional knowledge. The WTO Appellate Body decision in *Australia – Tobacco Plain Packaging* suggests that WTO members who legislate to protect these interests may be able to use their human rights obligations as support for justifiable restrictions on trademark owners. A human rights approach reveals that interests underlying trademarks are not just economic, they are moral, cultural and expressive. Protecting these interests in a human rights framework enables us to recognize that these rights are not absolute but need to be balanced against other important human rights such as freedom of expression.

---

[147]   GC 34, para 48.
[148]   See Eugene C. Lim, 'On the Uneasy Interface between Economic Rights, Moral Rights and Users' Rights in Copyright Law: Can Canada Learn from the UK Experience' (2018) 15 SCRIPTed 70.
[149]   Dutfield and Suthersanen (n8) 134.

PART III

TRADITIONAL MORAL RIGHTS DIVISIONS

9. Dualist vs. monist approaches to copyright within the European Union – an obstacle to the harmonization of moral rights?

Katharina de la Durantaye

1. INTRODUCTION

Over the past 30 years, the EU has enacted 13 directives[1] and two regulations[2] on copyright law. The author's rights to reproduce the work,[3] to distribute it,[4] to communicate it to the public,[5] and to rent or lend it[6] have all long been harmonized – including exceptions and limitations to these rights.[7] It is no exaggeration to state that today, almost every major copyright case which is put in front of one of the Member States' highest courts involves questions of community law and gets sent to Luxemburg for a preliminary ruling by the Court of Justice of the European Union (CJEU). The CJEU has interpreted its powers broadly. It has, for

---

[1]   Directive on the legal protection of computer programs (91/250/EEC; 2009/24/EC); Directive on rental right and lending right, and on certain rights related to copyright in the field of intellectual property (92/100/EEC; 2006/115/EC); Directive on the coordination of certain rules concerning copyright and rights related to copyright applicable to satellite broadcasting and cable retransmission (93/83/EEC); Directive harmonizing the term of protection of copyright and certain related rights (93/98/EEC; 2006/116/EC; 2011/77/EU); Directive on the legal protection of databases (96/9/EC); Directive on the harmonization of certain aspects of copyright and related rights in the information society (2001/29/EC); Directive on the resale right for the benefit of the author of an original work of art (2001/84/EC); Directive on the enforcement of intellectual property rights (2004/48/EC); Directive on certain permitted uses of orphan works (2012/28/EU); Directive on collective management of copyright and related rights and multi-territorial licensing of rights in musical works for online use in the internal market (2014/26/EU); Directive on certain permitted uses of certain works and other subject matter protected by copyright and related rights for the benefit of persons who are blind, visually impaired or otherwise print-disabled (2017/1564/EU); Directive on copyright and related rights applicable to certain online transmissions of broadcasting organizations and retransmissions of television and radio programs (2019/789/EU); Directive on copyright in the digital single market (2019/790/EU). Cf. also Articles 12–15 Directive on certain legal aspects of information society services, in particular electronic commerce, in the Internal Market (2000/31/EC).
[2]   Regulation (EU) 2017/1128 on cross-border portability of online content services in the internal market; Regulation (EU) 2017/1563 on the cross-border exchange between the Union and third countries of accessible format copies of certain works and other subject matter protected by copyright and related rights for the benefit of persons who are blind, visually impaired or otherwise print-disabled.
[3]   Art. 2 Directive 2001/29/EC; Art. 4(1)(a) Directive 2009/24/EC.
[4]   Art. 4 Directive 2001/29/EC; Art. 4(1)(c) Directive 2009/24/EC.
[5]   Art. 3 Directive 2001/29/EC.
[6]   Art. 2 Directive 92/100/EEC (cf. also the Directive's Art. 4 which grants authors (and performers) an unwaivable right to equitable remuneration); Art. 4(1)(c) Directive 2009/24/EC.
[7]   Art. 5 Directive 2001/29/EC; Arts 5–6 Directive 2009/24/EC; Art. 3–6, 17(7) subpara. 2 Directive 2019/790/EU.

example, created an autonomous definition of the object of protection, the "work",[8] even though the European Commission had deemed a harmonization of the originality requirement unnecessary.[9]

One notable exception to this tendency to harmonization are moral rights. So far, these rights have not explicitly been regulated by the European Union. In the same working paper (from 2004) in which it had opted against harmonizing the requirements for copyright protection, the European Commission concluded that acts of harmonization in the area of moral rights were not warranted either: While linking and framing did often touch on the author's rights of attribution and of integrity, and while existing differences between the Member States could, in theory, create obstacles to trade within the European Community/Union, they did not do so in practice.[10] Up until today, the Commission's public stance has not changed.

In this chapter, I will first look at the existing differences between the various Member States (Section 2) and will explain the two basic approaches to moral rights within the European Union – the dualist approach (2.1) and the monist approach (2.2).[11] Then, I will examine whether the European Commission's findings that these differences do not impair the internal market are convincing, and whether the European Union is, in fact, upholding its decision not to touch upon national moral rights (Section 3). I will show that there is a growing body of European Union legislation and CJEU rulings that implicitly regulates or at least concerns moral rights (3.1). I will argue that in the long run, the European Union will have to openly tackle the issue, and will conclude by delineating possible avenues for doing so and which the European Commission might want to consider (3.2).

---

[8]   Cf. only CJEU Case C-5/08 (16 July 2009) – *Infopaq International*; CJEU Cases C-403/08 and C-429/08 (4 October 2011) – *Football Association Premier League*; CJEU Case C-406/10 (2 May 2012) – *SAS Institute*; CJEU Case 201/13 (3 September 2014) – *Deckmyn and Vrijheidsfonds*; CJEU Case C-310/17 (13 November 2018) – *Levola Hengelo and Smilde Foods*; CJEU Case C-469/17 (27 July 2019) – *Funke Medien*; CJEU Case C-683/17 (12 September 2019) – *Cofemel*; CJEU Case C-833/18 (11 June 2020) – *Brompton*.

[9]   Commission Staff Working Paper on the review of the EC legal framework in the field of copyright and related rights (19 July 2004), SEC 2004 (995), 13–14. The Commission concluded that while differences in the level of originality required within the several Member States could theoretically inhibit the functioning of the Internal Market, they did not do so in practice. Paul Hughes, "Painting on a Broader Canvas: The Need for a Wider Consideration of Moral Rights under EU law" (2018) 40 EIPR 95, 96 criticizes that the Court focuses on intellectual creativity when determining whether a work meets the originality threshold but does not recognize that the same creativity is dependent "on the authorial autonomy that moral rights promote".

[10]   Commission Staff Working Paper on the review of the EC legal framework in the field of copyright and related rights (19 July 2004), SEC 2004 (995), 16. Cf. also European Commission, Green Paper on copyright and the challenge of technology (7 June 1988), COM(88) 172 final, 197; European Commission, Follow-Up to the Green Paper. Working Programme of the Commission in the field of copyright and neighbouring rights (17 January 1991), COM(90) 584 final, 34–5; European Commission, Green Paper on copyright and related rights in the information society (19 July 1995), COM(95) 382 final, 37, 65–8; European Commission, Follow-Up to the Green Paper on copyright and related rights in the information society (20 November 1996), COM(96) 568 final, 28.

[11]   This text follows the dominant understanding of the terms dualism and monism. For a different understanding cf. Cyrill P. Rigamonti, *Urheberpersönlichkeitsrechte: Globalisierung und Dogmatik einer Rechtsfigur zwischen Urheber- und Persönlichkeitsrecht* (Stampfli Verlag AG 2013) 126–216.

2.   APPROACHES TO MORAL RIGHTS WITHIN THE MEMBER STATES

Someone who examines the two dominant approaches to moral rights[12] within the Continental European Member States might at first notice similarities:[13] Both under the (Continental European) dualist and the monist approach to copyright, moral rights are thought of as rights of the author, i.e., of the human being who created the work,[14] and of that person alone.[15] Others, such as the author's employer, or the person who commissioned the work, do not qualify. By necessity then, corporations cannot be original owners of moral rights. Since moral rights are granted because of the special relationship which an author has with their work, they provide authors with rights in their works,[16] just like the rights to reproduce, to distribute, and to make a work available to the public. As such, moral rights are, first and foremost, part of copyright law. At the same time, they form a subgroup of the right to privacy:[17] Moral rights are inalienable.[18] In theory, the author cannot transfer (and/or relinquish) their moral rights *intra vivos*.[19]

Despite these similarities, harmonization of moral rights would probably be thorny. While practical differences are not that great,[20] the decision for either the dualist or the monist approach lies at the heart of the Member States' (dominant) national copyright theory.[21] Things become even more complicated if one takes into account that even after Great Britain has left the European Union, not all EU Member States are part of the Continental European tradition.

---

[12]   As to the history of the concept of moral rights, cf. only Mira T. Sundara Rajan, *Moral Rights* (Oxford University Press 2011) 31–114.

[13]   Cf. Cyrill P. Rigamonti, "Deconstructing Moral Rights" (2006) 47 Harv. Int'l L. J. 353, 359–62.

[14]   This anthropocentric approach to copyright law is often cited as one, if not the main, reason why AI output cannot be copyrighted. Cf. only P Bernt Hugenholtz and João Pedro Quintais, "Copyright and Artificial Creation: Does EU Copyright Law Protect AI-Assisted Output?" (2021) IIC 1190, 1195; Alina Škiljić, "When Art Meets Technology or Vice Versa: Key Challenges at the Crossroads of AI-Generated Artworks and Copyright Law" (2021) IIC 1228, 1350. Cf. also Jane C Ginsburg, "People Not Machines: Authorship and What It Means in the Berne Convention" (2018) IIC 131; Florian De Rouck, "Moral Rights & AI Environments: The Unique Bond Between Intelligent Agents and Their Creations" (2019) GRUR Int. 432.

[15]   As to the psychological dimension of moral rights cf. Alexander Peukert, "Die psychologische Dimension des droit moral" in Manfred Rehbinder (ed.), *Die psychologische Dimension des Urheberrechts* (Nomos 2003) 125–48.

[16]   Cf. German Federal Court of Justice, I ZR 135/87 (8 June 1989), NJW 1986, 1987 (1990) – *Emil Nolde*.

[17]   As to the (hybrid) nature of moral rights, and its relationship to the right to privacy, cf. only Hughes, *supra* n 9, 98–9; Agnès Lucas-Schloetter, "Die Rechtsnatur des Droit Moral" (2002) GRUR Int. 809–15; Alexander Peukert, "Vor §§ 12 ff mn. 29–32", in Ulrich Loewenheim, Matthias Leistner & Ansgar Ohly (eds), *Urheberrecht* (6th ed, CH Beck 2020); Jochen Schlingloff, "Das Urheberpersönlichkeitsrecht im Spannungsverhältnis zwischen Kunstfreiheit und politischer Betätigung" (2017) GRUR 572, 576–7.

[18]   Cf. only Art. 29(1) German Copyright Act; Art. L. 121-1 French Intellectual Property Code.

[19]   As to the scope of that rule in practice, cf. French Cour de Cassastion, Cass. Civ. I (28 May 1991), Rec. D. 197 (1993); Axel Metzger, *Rechtsgeschäfte über das Droit moral im deutschen und französischen Urheberrecht* (Beck Juristischer Verlag 2002) 20–7, 140–9; Rigamonti, *supra* n 13, 372–80.

[20]   Cf. only Rigamonti, *supra* n 13, 353–412.

[21]   Carine Doutrelepont, "Das droit moral in der Europäischen Union" (1997) GRUR Int. 293, 293–5. Cf. also Irma Sirvinskaite, "Towards Copyright Europeanification: European Union Moral Rights" (2010) 3 J. Int'l Media & Ent. L. 263, 265, 278–9.

Ireland's moral rights regime is very similar to the British one and substantially different from the one in France – even though both follow the dualist approach.[22]

2.1   The Dualist Approach

The idea that the *droit moral* forms a basis for legal claims developed in nineteenth century France.[23] The term *droit moral*[24] underlines that what is at stake are the author's "intellectual" interests in their creation. The word signifies something similar as in *personne morale*, the technical term for a legal entity.[25] Such an entity is intellectual in that it does not consist of flesh and blood. Its English translation as "moral rights" is thus a bit confusing; it suggests that there is a moral/ethical dimension to these rights (or that they are the opposite of legal rights).[26]

According to the dualist approach, copyright's intellectual and moral attributes, as the French call them, i.e., moral rights, exist independently from its property attributes (exploitation rights).[27] Up until today, France follows the dualist approach to copyright.[28] The same is true not only for other Romanic countries like Italy, Portugal and Spain,[29] but also for other Continental European Member States such as Belgium, the Czech Republic, Denmark, Greece, and Poland.[30]

Common Law countries such as the United Kingdom, Ireland and the United States also follow the dualist approach to copyright. However, the Common Law variety differs from the Continental European one.[31] Common law countries protect moral rights to a much lesser extent than Continental European countries.[32]

---

[22]   Even those differences are not and never have been insurmountable, though. Cf. only Jane C Ginsburg, "A Tale of Two Copyrights: Literary Property in Revolutionary France and America" (1989–1990) 64 Tul. L. Rev. 991, 994.

[23]   Stig Strömholm, *Le droit moral de l'auteur (en droit allemand, français et scandinave)*, vol 1 (Norstedt 1967) 117–50.

[24]   The French usually use the singular and not the plural (as do Germans) in order to signal that there is one overarching interest which the author has towards their work, and that the individual morals rights (right of integrity, of attribution, of disclosure, of withdrawal) are but different manifestations of this special bond between author and work. Interestingly, however, the first chapter of the part of the French Intellectual Property Code which is dedicated to copyright (L. 121-1-121-9) is entitled "droit moraux"; here, the legislature uses the plural.

[25]   Cf. Manfred Rehbinder and Alexander Peukert, *Urheberrecht* (18th ed, CH Beck 2018) 431; Haimo Schack, *Urheber- und Urhebervertragsrecht* (10th ed, Mohr Siebeck 2021) 368.

[26]   According to Rigamonti, *supra* n 13, 355, moral rights are non-economic rights.

[27]   Art. L. 111-1 French Intellectual Property Code. Cf. also Art. 2 Spanish Copyright Act 1996.

[28]   Cf. Art. L. 121-1, L. 122-1 French Intellectual Property Code.

[29]   Cf. Art. 20(1) Italian Copyright Act; Art. 9(1) Portuguese Code of Copyright and Related Rights; Art. 2 Spanish Copyright Act 1996.

[30]   Art. XI.165(2) Belgian Code of Economic Law; Art. 11 Czech Copyright Act; Art. 3 Danish Copyright Act; Art. 1(1) Greek Copyright Law 2121/1993; Art. 16 Polish Copyright Act 1994.

[31]   As to the differences among the various copyright jurisdictions cf. Jonathan Griffiths, "Moral Rights from a Copyright Perspective", in Fabienne Brison and Séverine Dusollier (eds), *Moral Rights in the 21st Century* (Larcier 2015) 83, 83–6.

[32]   Cf. only Gerald Dworkin, "The Moral Right of the Author: Moral Rights and the Common Law Countries" (1995) 19 Col. J. L. & Arts 229–67; Jane C. Ginsburg, "Urheberpersönlichkeitsrechte im Rechtssystem des Common Law" (1991) GRUR Int 593, 595–604.

2.1.1   The Continental European variety

Many Continental European countries do not only grant authors the rights of attribution and integrity, as provided for by Article 6*bis* of the Berne Convention. In addition, they grant them the right of divulgation, i.e., the right to determine when and if a work should be released to the public, and the right to withdraw a work from the public (right of withdrawal).[33]

Structurally, there are significant differences between exploitation rights and moral rights. Exploitation rights may be assigned, while moral rights inalienably rest with the author.[34] Exploitation rights usually end 70 years after the author's death.[35] In most dualist countries, moral rights exist – at least on paper[36] – in perpetuity.[37] Once the author has died, exploitation rights are bequeathed upon the author's heirs.[38] As to ownership of moral rights, rules vary: In Italy and Poland, all moral rights are exercised by the author's closest relatives.[39] In France, this is true only for the right to divulgation (if the author has not stipulated otherwise);[40] other aspects of the *droit moral* are exercised by the author's heirs.[41] In Spain, the rights of attribution and of integrity are exercised by the person whom the author entrusted to do so, or, if no such person was chosen, they are exercised by the author's heirs.[42] In Belgium, this is true

---

[33]   Cf. only Art. L. 121-2 and Art. L. 121-4 French Intellectual Property Code; Art. 4(1)(a) and (e) Greek Copyright Law 2121/1993; Art. 12 and Art. 142 Italian Copyright Act 1941; Art. 16 no. 4 Polish Copyright Act 1994; Art. 14(1) and (6) Spanish Copyright Act 1996, Art. 11(1) Czech Copyright Act.

[34]   Cf. only Art. L. 111-1 French Intellectual Property Code; Art. 4(3) Greek Copyright Law 2121/1993; Art. 56(2) Portuguese Code of Copyright and Related Rights; Art. 14 Spanish Copyright Act 1996; Art. 11(4) Czech Copyright Act; Art. XI.165(2) Belgian Code of Economic Law.

[35]   Art. 1(1) Directive 2006/116/EC.

[36]   As to the factual limitations of such a perpetual moral right cf. Bernard Edelman, "L'œuvre ne meurt jamais" (2011) Rec. D. 1708–12; Sylvie Nérisson, "Le droit moral de l'auteur décédé on France et Allemagne" (2003) 4 Cahiers IRPI 25–40.

[37]   Cf. only Art. L. 121-1 French Intellectual Property Code; Art. 23 Italian Copyright Act 1941; Art. 56(2) Portuguese Code of Copyright and Related Rights. Cf. also Art. 75 Danish Copyright Act 1995; Art. 16 Polish Copyright Act 1994. In Spain, this is only true with respect to works that have been divulged to the public (Art. 15(1) Spanish Copyright Act 1996); rights in works which have not been divulged end 70 years after the author's death (Art. 15(2)). In the Czech Republic, moral rights expire with the death of the author (Art. 11(4) Czech Copyright Act); however, a certain level of protection remains (Art. 11(5)). In Belgium, moral rights end 70 years after the author's death (Art. XI.166(1) Belgian Code of Economic Law). For a comparative study of post-mortem moral rights in Israel, France and the US, cf. Galia Aharoni, "You Can't Take It with You When you Die ... Or Can You?" (2009) 17 U. Balt. Intell. Prop. L. J. 103.

[38]   Art. L. 123-1 French Intellectual Property Code; Art. 115 Italian Copyright Act.

[39]   Art. 23 Italian Copyright Act 1941; Art. 78(2) Polish Copyright Act 1994.

[40]   According to Art. L. 121-2 French Intellectual Property Code, the author's executor exercises the right to divulgation. If no such person exists or if that person dies, the right is – unless the author has determined otherwise – exercised by the author's descendants; if they don't exist or die, by the author's spouse (unless there is a judgement of legal separation or the spouse has entered a new marriage), and only then by the author's heirs (cf. also Art. L. 121-3 French Intellectual Property Code). Traditionally, this article was applied to other aspects of the *droit moral* as well, even though Art. L. 121-1 French Intellectual Property Code states that upon the author's death, their moral rights are transferable upon the author's heirs.

[41]   French Court of Cassation Cass. Civ. I (11 Jan 1989), D. 1989 Jur. 308. For an analysis of the relevant rules from a copyright perspective cf. John Henry Merryman, "The Moral Right of Maurice Utrillo" (1995) 43 Am. J. Comp. L. 445–54.

[42]   Art. 15(1) Spanish Copyright Act 1996.

for all moral rights.[43] In Greece and Portugal, the exercise of the author's moral rights is up to the author's heirs until the work falls into the public domain; afterwards, it is exercised by the respective Ministry of Culture as the representative of the State.[44]

2.1.2   The common law variety

Since Great Britain left the European Union, Ireland is the Union's only remaining Common Law country. In Ireland, just like in the UK, authors are granted the right of attribution ("paternity right") and the right of integrity ("integrity right").[45] The scope of these rights is broader in Ireland than it is in the UK.[46] Under Irish law, unlike under those in force on the Continent, both the right of attribution and the right of integrity may be waived – for specific works, groups of works, or all works, for existing and/or future ones, conditionally or unconditionally.[47] In addition, both rights are subject to fairly broad exceptions and limitations.[48] The right of attribution does not apply to works made for the purpose of reporting current events, or for the purpose of a newspaper, a periodical, an encyclopaedia, dictionary, yearbook, or other collective work for reference,[49] to works in which Government copyright subsists, and to works in which the copyright originally vested in a prescribed international organization.[50] If the work was made for hire, the right of attribution does not apply to anything done by or with the licence of the employer as the original copyright owner.[51]

Similarly, the right of integrity does not apply to works made for the purpose of reporting current events, or works made for the purpose of a newspaper, a periodical, an encyclopaedia, dictionary, yearbook, or other collective work for reference.[52] Authors of works made for hire, of works in which Government copyright subsists, and of works in which the copyright originally vested in a prescribed international organization cannot claim violations of their integrity right against uses by or with the licence of the copyright owner unless the author is identified at the time of the act concerned or had previously been identified.[53]

The right of attribution and the right of integrity end at the same time as the exploitation rights.[54] The right against false attribution[55] subsists for 20 years after the death of the person on whom the right is conferred.[56]

---

[43]   Art. XI.171 Belgian Code of Economic Law.
[44]   Art. 29(2) Greek Copyright Law 2121/1993; Art. 57(1), (2) Portuguese Code of Copyright and Related Rights.
[45]   Sect. 107, 109 Irish Copyright and Related Rights Act 2000. Chapter 7 of that Act is dedicated to moral rights. It is debatable whether moral rights provisions in the UK and in Ireland meet the requirements as set out by the Berne Convention. Cf. only Hughes, *supra* n 9, 101–2; Luigi Carlo Ubertazzi, "Das EU-Reglement über die Persönlichkeitsrechte" (2018) GRUR Int. 110, 119–20.
[46]   For a broader comparison of moral rights in Ireland and in the UK cf. Maureen O'Sullivan, "Irish Artistic Copyright Law: A Menagerie of Holy Cows and Turtle Doves?" (2015) 1 IPQ 31, 54–8.
[47]   Sect. 116 Irish Copyright and Related Rights Act 2000.
[48]   Sections 108, 110, 111 Irish Copyright and Related Rights Act 2000.
[49]   Sect. 108(4) Irish Copyright and Related Rights Act 2000.
[50]   Sect. 108(5) Irish Copyright and Related Rights Act 2000.
[51]   Sect. 108(2) Irish Copyright and Related Rights Act 2000.
[52]   Sect. 110(1) (a)–(b) Irish Copyright and Related Rights Act 2000.
[53]   Sect. 111(2) Irish Copyright and Related Rights Act 2000.
[54]   Sect. 115(1) Irish Copyright and Related Rights Act 2000.
[55]   Sect. 113 Irish Copyright and Related Rights Act 2000.
[56]   Sect. 115(2) Irish Copyright and Related Rights Act 2000.

2.2   The Monist Approach

Unlike the dualist approach, the monist approach does not consider moral and exploitation rights as different groups of rights which, for reasons of efficiency, are merged under the same heading. Instead, copyright is conceptualized as one unified right with two functions. The monist approach was devised by academics[57] and was first codified in 1936 in Austria's Copyright Statute. In 1965, Germany's Copyright Act followed suit.[58]

Today, almost every German copyright casebook explains the monist approach with the help of Eugen Ulmer's "tree theory".[59] In his casebook from 1980, Ulmer likened copyright to a tree trunk with two roots: the author's economic interests and the author's intellectual/ personality interests. The author's rights formed the tree's branches. Some of them drew their strength equally from both roots, others more from one or the other root.[60] Ulmer uses this metaphor to underline that exploitation rights have a moral rights component, and that moral rights are economic rights in that their violation can lead to claims for damages,[61] and in that they can be used in order to preserve a work's economic success.[62] Because of that, both groups of rights are commonly understood as rights to immaterial goods (*Immaterialgüterrechte*): The rights are not designed to protect the author's personality but the author's (special) bond to their work.

One of the most important consequences of this conception is that an author cannot transfer or relinquish their copyright.[63] There is even discussion as to whether he or she may relinquish individual exploitation rights.[64] Those who argue against it point out that since both groups of rights were inseparably intertwined, an author would lose parts of their moral rights if they

---

[57]   Ernst Rabel, "Die Übertragbarkeit des Urheberrechts nach dem österreichischen Gesetz vom 26. Dezember 1895" (1900) 27 GrünhutsZ 71–182 (reprinted in 108 UFITA 185–276 (1988)); Philipp Allfeld, *Das Urheberrecht an Werken der Literatur und der Tonkunst* (2nd ed, CH Beck 1928) 18–21; Heinrich Mitteis, *Grundriss des österreichischen Urheberrechts* (Duncker & Humblot 1936) 61–2.

[58]   Cf. Art. 11 German Copyright Act.

[59]   Cf. only Rehbinder and Peukert, *supra* n 25, 154; Schack, *supra* n 25, 343.

[60]   Eugen Ulmer, *Urheber- und Verlagsrecht* (1st ed, Springer Berlin 1951) 69–70. In a later edition, he adds that an author's right might draw its strength exclusively from one of the two roots (3rd ed, Springer Berlin 1980) 116, without, however, explaining when this might be the case.

[61]   Cf. Lucas-Schloetter, *supra* n 17, 811; Sundara Rajan, *supra* n 12, 18.

[62]   Cf. Adolf Dietz, *Das Droit Moral des Urhebers im neuen französischen und deutschen Urheberrecht* (CH Beck 1968) 36–7; Axel Metzger, "Europäisches Urheberrecht ohne Droit moral? Status quo und Perspektiven einer Harmonisierung des Urheberpersönlichkeitsrechts", in Ansgar Ohly and Theo Bodewig (eds), *Festschrift für Gerhard Schricker zum 70. Geburtstag* (CH Beck 2005) 455, 464–6. For a field study on authors' willingness to trade their moral rights, cf. Stefan Bechtold & Christoph Engel, "The Valuation of Moral Rights: A Field Experiment" (2017) 4 Preprints of the MPI for Research on Collective Goods, http://homepage.coll.mpg.de/pdf_dat/2017_04online.pdf; Christopher Jon Sprigman, Christopher Buttafusco and Zachary Burns, "What's a Name Worth?, Experimental Tests on the Value of Attribution in Intellectual Property" (2013) 93 B.U. L. Rev. 1389–435, for an economic analysis of moral rights more generally Henry Hansmann and Marina Santilli, "Authors' and Artists' Moral Rights: A Comparative Legal and Economic Analysis" (1997) 26 J. Legal Stud. 95–143.

[63]   Cf. Art. 29(1) German Copyright Act; Art. 23(3) Austrian Copyright Act. Cf. also German Federal Court of Justice, I ZR 69/93 (23 February 1995) – *Mauerbilder*.

[64]   As to the discussion in Germany, cf. only German Federal Court of Justice, I ZR 69/93 (23 February 1995) – *Mauerbilder*; Ansgar Ohly, *§ 29 UrhG* mn. 18, in Ulrich Loewenheim, Matthias Leistner, and Ansgar Ohly (eds), *Urheberrecht* (6th ed, CH Beck 2020); Schack, *supra* n 25, 362. Cf. also BT-Drucks. IV/270 (23 March 1962) 41.

did so. Expanding on Ulmer's metaphor, Schack states that an author may only allow others to harvest the fruits of the tree but may not give away any of the tree's branches.[65]

Another important difference to the dualist conception is that both groups of rights last equally long:[66] usually for 70 years after the author's death.[67] When the author dies, their copyright passes onto their heirs as a whole.[68] This is true even if the author and their heirs are not related.[69] In Austria, multiple heirs are even treated as co-authors.[70] However, heirs hold the author's moral rights in trust and have to respect the author's wishes while exercising these rights.[71]

3.   BRIDGING THE GAP

Many have taken issue with the Commission's assessment that existing differences between the various Member States do not impair the internal market,[72] and rightly so: Coupled with the territoriality principle upon which copyright is based,[73] the difference in the length of moral rights protection may lead to practical problems.[74] The same is true for the varying extent to which moral rights exist. As seen, some Member States only acknowledge the rights (of attribution and of integrity) provided for by Article 6*bis* of the Berne Convention which all EU

---

[65]   Schack, *supra* n 25, 344.

[66]   However, the German Federal Court of Justice held that moral rights, just like other post-mortem personality interests, do not necessarily hold the same weight after the death of the author as they do during their lifetime, German Federal Court of Justice, I ZR 15/87 (13 October 1988) – *Oberammergauer Passionsfestspiele II*; German Federal Court of Justice, I ZR 216/10 (9 November 2011) – *Stuttgart 21*.

[67]   Art. 64 German Copyright Act; Art. 60 Austrian Copyright Act.

[68]   Art. 28(1) German Copyright Act; Art. 23(1) Austrian Copyright Act.

[69]   By contrast, post-mortem privacy rights do, at least in Germany, generally pass onto the deceased person's closest relatives. Cf. only Art. 22 s. 3 German Art Copyright Act; Haimo Schack, "Das Persönlichkeitsrecht der Urheber und ausübenden Künstler nach dem Tode" (1985) GRUR 352, 354–61.

[70]   Art. 23(4) Austrian Copyright Act. In Germany, this is not the case.

[71]   German Federal Court of Justice, I ZR 15/87 (13 October 1988) – *Oberammergauer Passionsfestspiele II*. Cf. Hauke Sattler, *Das Urheberrecht nach dem Tode des Urhebers in Deutschland und Frankreich* (V&R Unipress 2010) 56–65; Joachim Pierer, "Die Persönlichkeitsrechte des Urhebers nach dem Tod" (2019) GRUR 476.

[72]   Cf. only Torben Asmus, *Die Harmonisierung des Urheberpersönlichkeitsrechts in Europa* (Nomos 2004) 54–86; Hughes, *supra* n 9, 95–108; Marie-Christine Janssens, "Invitation for a 'Europeanification' of Moral Rights", in Paul Torremans (ed.), *Research Handbook on Copyright Law* (2nd ed, Edward Elgar 2017) 200, 211–13; Nadine Klass, "Werkgenuss und Werknutzung in der digitalen Welt: Bedarf es einer Harmonisierung des Urheberpersönlichkeitsrechts?" (2015) ZUM 290, 299–303; Metzger, *supra* n 62, 466–9; Peukert, *supra* n 17, 47; Paul Torremans, "Moral Rights in the Digital Age", in Paul Torremans and Irini Stamatoudi (eds), *Copyright in the New Digital Environment* (Sweet & Maxwell 2000) 97–114; Jacques de Werra, "The Moral Right of Integrity" in Estelle Derclaye (ed.), *Research Handbook on the Future of EU Copyright* (Edward Elgar 2009) 267, 271–8.

[73]   Cf. only Katharina de la Durantaye, "Art. 8 Rome II", in Gralf-Peter Calliess and Moritz Renner (eds), *Rome Regulations* (3rd ed, Kluwer Law International 2020) 2–3.

[74]   Cf. also Carine Doutrelepont, *Le droit moral de l'auteur et le droit communautaire* (Bruylant 1997) 579; De Werra, *supra* n 72, 280–1.

Member States have adopted.[75] Others grant additional rights, such as the right of divulgation and/or of withdrawal.[76]

Even if a moral right is recognized in all Member States, its scope may vary. For example, while most states apply objective criteria in order to determine whether the right of integrity has been violated (e.g. Denmark, Germany, Italy, Netherlands, Portugal, Spain), some apply subjective criteria and allow the author to prohibit any modification of their work which the author determines to be detrimental (Belgium, France, Greece, Poland).[77] Some Member States grant authors of certain groups of works, such as computer programs[78] or movies,[79] a weaker right of integrity than those of other works, some do not.[80] In Ireland, moral rights may be waived, in Continental Europe, they may not.

As a consequence, a work may be distributed in one Member State but not in another, or not in the same way. For example, it is possible that a book may be turned into a movie (and made available) in Germany but not in France, where the same adaptation would violate the author's right of integrity,[81] or that a black and white movie may be colourized[82] or a movie be shown with commercial breaks in some Member States but not in others.[83]

These existing differences matter more than they did a few decades ago because creative practices have changed. Users once were predominantly passive consumers. Nowadays, they have the technical tools necessary to easily change, combine and adapt protected subject

---

[75]   Cf. also Art. 1(4) WCT; Art. 5(1) WPPT.

[76]   Cf. Art. L. 121-4 French Intellectual Property Code; Art. 12, 34(3) s. 2, 41, 42 German Copyright Act; Art. 142(1) Italian Copyright Act.

[77]   Cf. Doutrelepont, *supra* n 21, 299. For a different classification, cf. Agnès Lucas-Schloetter, "Rapport général: le droit moral dans les différents régimes du droit d'auteur", in Fabienne Brison and Séverine Dusollier (eds), *Moral Rights in the 21st Century* (Larcier 2015) 50, 56. Cf. also Tatsuhiro Ueno, "Moral Rights in the Digital Network and 'Cloud' Environment: Subjective or Objective Standard?", in Fabienne Brison and Séverine Dusollier (eds), *Moral Rights in the 21st Century* (Larcier 2015).

[78]   Cf. Art. L. 121-7 French Intellectual Property Code; Art. 69a no. 1, 69d(1) German Copyright Act. For an overview of the breadth of moral rights protection for computer programs throughout the EU, cf. Sirvinskaite, *supra* n 21, 279–84.

[79]   Art L. 121-6 French Intellectual Property Code; Art. 93(1) German Copyright Act.

[80]   Cf. also Art. 6(1) Directive 96/9/EC which allows a lawful user to translate, adapt, arrange, or otherwise alter a database or a copy thereof in order to access and use the database's content.

[81]   Cf. Metzger, *supra* n 62, 465. The decision by Munich's court of appeals in OLG München GRUR 1986, 460, 464 – *Die unendliche Geschichte* serves as one such example.

[82]   Cf. Rolf Platho, "'Colorization' – und die Möglichkeit ihrer Verhinderung durch die Mitwirkenden am Filmwerk" (1987) GRUR 424–431; Sundara Rajan, *supra* n 12, 415–21. Cf. also French Cour de Cassation, Cass. Civ. I (28 May 1991), GRUR Int. 304 (1992) – John Huston II; for an English translation cf. 16 No. 10 Ent. L. Rep. 3 (1995).

[83]   De Werra, supra n 72, 271–4; Mario Franzosi and Giustino de Sanctis, "Moral Rights and New Technology: Are Copyright and Patents Converging?" (1995) EIPR 63, 63–4; Lamberto Liuzzo, "Die Verletzung des Urheberpersönlichkeitsrechts durch Werbeeinblendungen in Fernsehprogrammen" (1989) GRUR Int. 110, 112; Karl-Nikolaus Peifer, "Werbeunterbrechungen in Spielfilmen nach deutschem und italienischem Urheberrecht" (1995) GRUR Int. 25, 25–42; Karl-Nikolaus Peifer, *Werbeunterbrechungen in Spielfilmen* (Nomos 1994) 42–55, 184–6; Jan Rosén, "Werbeunterbrechungen von Spielfilmen nach schwedischem Recht – (immer noch) ein Testfall für das Droit Moral?" (2004) GRUR Int. 1002–10. As to the use of music for commercial purposes cf. Karl Riesenhuber, "Nutzung von Musik für Werbezwecke" (2010) ZUM 137–45; Günter Poll, "Musik in der Werbung" (2008) WRP 1170–4.

matter, and to make the results available to a wide audience. Such creative uses are often socially desirable but might run into conflict with the (original) author's right of attribution and integrity.[84] Moral rights are especially vulnerable in the digital context;[85] protection under EU law might provide some relief for authors.[86] It would also help users[87] and intermediaries: Since the scope and term of moral rights differ between the Member States, EU-wide uses of user generated content, especially making such content available on platforms such as YouTube, are hampered. If the existing differences thus impair intra-Community trade, Article 114 of the Treaty on the Functioning of the European Union (TFEU) grants the European Union authority to enact moral rights legislation.[88] What is more, the European Union does, pursuant to Article 118 TFEU, have authority to create European – as opposed to (harmonized) national – intellectual property rights.[89]

3.1   Harmonization through the Back Door

Five of the copyright directives explicitly state that they do not apply to moral rights. The others do not make mention of moral rights at all. Of the older directives, both the Database and the Information Society Directives declare in their recitals that the moral rights of authors[90] should be exercised in accordance with the Berne Convention (as well as the other pertinent treaties), and that such moral rights remain outside the scope of the directives.[91] For the Term Directive, it was particularly important to clarify whether its rules obliged the Member States to unify the term for all rights granted under copyright. Pursuant to its Article 9, "[t]his Directive shall be without prejudice to the provisions of the Member States regulating moral rights".[92]

Of the directives that were enacted during the past ten years, the Orphan Works Directive affirms in one of its articles that it shall be without prejudice to national provisions on anonymous or pseudonymous works, both of which touch upon the author's (negative) right of attribution.[93] According to the Directive for Copyright in the Digital Single Market, the

---

[84]   Cf. also Janssens, *supra* n 72, 209–11; Klass, *supra* n 72, 298.

[85]   Cf. already Patricia Akester, "Authorship and Authenticity in Cyberspace" (2004) 20 Comp. L. Sec. & Rev. 436–44.

[86]   Interestingly, the German legislature used the transposition of Art. 17 Directive for Copyright in the Digital Single Market to strengthen the right of integrity online: According to Art. 13(3) s. 2 of the German Statute for Providers of Copyrighted Content (Urheberrecht-Diensteanbieter-Gesetz – UrhDaG), an author whose right of integrity is infringed upon may ask for that content to be blocked according to Art. 8 UrhDaG; this is true even if the content is presumed to be legal under Art. 9-11 UrhDaG. As to safeguards against abuse, cf. Art. 18(3) No. 2 UrhDaG. Cf. Axel Metzger and Timm Pravemann, "Die finale Version des UrhDaG – Auf die Plätze, filtern, los?" (2021) ZUM 755, 760.

[87]   For an overview of the ways in which moral rights serve the public interest, cf. only Margaret Ann Wilkinson, "The public interest in moral rights protection" (2006) Mich. St. L. Rev. 193, 212–24.

[88]   In the past, this was less clear. Cf. only Gerhard Schricker, Eva-Marina Bastian and Adolf Dietz, *Konturen eines europäischen Urheberrechts* (Nomos 1996) 122.

[89]   Cf. also Janssens, *supra* n 72, 220.

[90]   The Database Directive uses the phrase "moral rights of the natural person who created the database", while the Information Society Directive misleadingly uses the phrase "moral rights of rightsholders".

[91]   Recital 28 Directive 96/9/EC; Recital 19 Directive 2001/29/EC.

[92]   Art. 9 Directive 2006/116/EC. Cf. Recital 21, Art. 9 Directive 93/98/EEC.

[93]   Art. 2(5) Directive 2012/28/EU.

arrangements for implementing newly mandatory exceptions or limitations established therein may "vary from one Member State to another, to the extent that they do not hamper the effective application of the exception or limitation or cross-border uses. Member States should, for example, remain free to require that the use of works or other subject matter respect the moral rights of authors and performers."[94] The Directive's rules concerning out of commerce works are supposed to allow the use of "never-in-commerce works" but should be "without prejudice to other applicable legal constraints, such as national rules on moral rights".[95]

Despite these statements, some of these as well as some of the other directives which have been enacted over the course of the past decades do, at least implicitly, touch upon moral rights.[96] In some cases, the directives indirectly provide for moral rights protection: The Computer Programs and the Database Directives both grant rightsholders the right to translate, adapt, arrange or otherwise alter computer programs/databases,[97] thereby granting a right of integrity in subject matters where some Member States provide a lower level of moral rights protection.[98] The Enforcement Directive contains a presumption of authorship for the person whose name appears on a literary or artistic work in the usual manner.[99] The Information Society Directive creates, among other things, a certain level of harmonization with respect to exceptions and limitations to copyright. Many of the relevant provisions establish that the author's name be indicated;[100] as such, they consider the right of attribution.[101]

In other cases, directives allow or require Member States to provide for exceptions and/or limitations to exploitation rights which might also create limitations to moral rights: Article 5(3)(d) Information Society Directive grants Member States the option to establish an exception or limitation to the reproduction right and the right of communication to the public in order to enable "quotations for purposes such as criticism or review, provided that ... their use is in accordance with fair practice ...". The provision establishes only a rough framework for what the possible limitation or exception should look like. It is the individual Member States who – enjoying fairly broad discretion – must strike a balance between the relevant interests.[102] In determining whether a use is in accordance with "fair practice", the author's (moral) right of integrity must be taken into account.[103] Similarly, the Directive's Article 5(3)(k) allows Member States to provide for exceptions and limitations that allow a work's reproduction and communication to the public for purposes of "caricature, parody or pastiche". According to the CJEU, the application of such an exception or limitation (for purposes of parody) must strike a fair balance between the rights and interests of the respective author and the freedom

---

[94]   Recital 23 Directive 2019/790/EU.
[95]   Recital 37 Directive 2019/790/EU.
[96]   The same is true for other measures of EU law. For example, provisions that apply to copyright law in general, such as Art. 8 Regulation 864/22007/EC on the Law Applicable to Non-Contractual Obligations (Rome II), are applicable to moral rights; the CJEU has acknowledged that moral rights form part of the subject matter of copyright law. Cf. also Ubertazzi, *supra* n 45, 115.
[97]   Art. 4 lit. b Directive 2009/24/EC; Art. 5 lit. b Directive 96/9/EC.
[98]   Cf. Art. L. 121-7 French Intellectual Property Code (for computer programs).
[99]   Art. 5(a) Directive 2004/48/EC.
[100]   Art. 5(3)(a), (c), (d), (f) Directive 2001/29/EC.
[101]   Cf. also CJEU Case C-145/10 (1 December 2011) – *Painer*.
[102]   CJEU, Case C-469/17 (29 July 2019), mn. 43 – *Funke Medien NRW v. Bundesrepublik Deutschland*.
[103]   Cf. also Peukert, *supra* note 17, at mn. 47.

of expression of the user.[104] In order to determine whether that balance is, in fact, preserved, all circumstances must be taken into account[105] – including the author's right of integrity.[106] While the Information Society Directive only allowed for the creation of the exceptions provided for in its Article 5(3)(d) and (k), the Directive for Copyright in the Digital Single Market now makes their existence mandatory, at least with respect to user generated content on online content-sharing services.[107]

Since there is no EU-wide right of integrity, the application of Article 5(3)(d) and (k) Information Society Directive is difficult – especially for the CJEU. The Court has acknowledged that moral rights form part of the subject matter of copyright.[108] In *Deckmyn*, the CJEU had to decide whether the use of a drawing from a comic book cover featuring one of that comic book series' main characters with a white tunic and throwing coins to people who are trying to pick them up, and where that character was replaced by the Mayor of the City of Ghent, and the people picking up the coins were replaced by people wearing veils and people of colour, constituted a parody under Article 5(3)(k) Information Society Directive. In doing so, the Court could not directly take into account any authorial interests in not being associated with the second drawing's political message. As to be able to weigh such interests anyway, the Court took recourse to anti-discrimination law.[109] It concluded that the specific rightsholders had, "in principle, a legitimate interest in ensuring that the work protected by copyright [was] not associated with such a [discriminatory] message".[110] This line of argument is not convincing: Anti-discrimination law is concerned, first and foremost, with public interests. An author's (moral) right that their work's message is not changed into something he or she does not support is not the domain of anti-discrimination law.[111] Conversely, copyright law is not well suited to suppress discriminatory speech.[112] It is unclear whether the "legitimate interests" are ones of public law or of copyright law.[113]

3.2   Possible Paths Forward

In the future, the CJEU will have to deal with more cases where exceptions and limitations to copyright collide with moral rights – especially now that (most) Member States have fulfilled their duty to transpose the Directive for Copyright in the Digital Single Market into their

---

[104]   CJEU, Case C-201/13 (3 September 2014), mn. 27 – *Deckmyn v. Vandersteen*.
[105]   CJEU, Case C-201/13 (3 September 2014), mn. 28 – *Deckmyn v. Vandersteen*.
[106]   Cf. Peukert, *supra* note 17, at mn. 47.
[107]   Art. 8(7) Directive 2019/790/EU.
[108]   CJEU, Cases C-92/92 and C-326/92 (20 October 1993), 20 – *Phil Collins*. Cf. also CGEU, Case T-69/89 (10 July 1991), 71 – *Magill I*; CGEU, Case T-70/89 (10 July 1991), 58 – *Magill II*; CGEU, Case T-76/89 (10 July 1991), 56 – *Magill III*; Asmus, *supra* n 72, 60–1.
[109]   CJEU, Case C-201/13 (3 September 2014), 28 – *Deckmyn v. Vandersteen*. The Court mentions Council Directive 2000/43/EC of 29 June 2000 (OJ 2000 L 180, p. 22), and Art. 21(1) of the EU Charter of Fundamental Rights.
[110]   CJEU, Case C-201/13 (3 September 2014), 31 – *Deckmyn v. Vandersteen*.
[111]   Cf. also Peukert, *supra* n 17, 47.
[112]   Cf. also European Copyright Society, "Opinion on the Judgment of the CJEU in Case C-201/13 Deckmyn" (2015) 37 EIPR 127, 129; Klass, *supra* n 72, 294; Karl Riesenhuber, "Anmerkung zu EuGH: Parodie als eigenständige Kategorie des Unionsrechts" (2014) LMK 363019.
[113]   Cf. Eleonora Rosati, "Just a Laughing Matter? Why the Decision in Deckmyn is Broader than Parody" (2015) 52(2) CML Rev. 511, 528.

national law.[114] The CJEU will then have to choose whether to stay away from uniformly inter-preting terms that are loaded with moral rights language,[115] or whether to find ways to fill these terms with meaning without being able to rely on an explicit EU moral rights framework.[116] Given its general tendency to actively ensure uniform application of EU law throughout the Union, it is very likely that the Court will take the second route.

If and when it does, the CJEU should consider assessing the various interests at stake through a fundamental rights lens (as opposed to focusing on anti-discrimination law).[117] That task would not be a new one for the Court. Over the past few years, the CJEU has gathered expe-rience in unearthing and weighing the conflicting fundamental rights that underly copyright. It rendered several decisions where it sharpened the contours of copyright by balancing the rightsholders' property interests under Article 17(2) of the Charter of Fundamental Rights of the European Union[118] and the users' freedom of expression and of information as safeguarded by Article 11 of that same Charter as well as Article 10(1) of the European Convention on Human Rights and Fundamental Freedoms – including freedom of the media and of the arts.[119]

When determining the scope of moral rights, the user's freedom of expression and informa-tion may be balanced with a host of different rights. First, since Article 17(2) of the Charter of Fundamental Rights of the European Union grants protection to intellectual property in general, it covers moral rights as well. At the same time, moral rights, especially the right of integrity, can themselves be framed as an element of, or at least be relevant to (the author's) freedom of expression.[120] What is more, under the Continental European concept of moral rights (be it monist or dualist), moral rights are closely connected to the right to privacy as protected under Article 7 of the Charter of Fundamental Rights of the European Union and Article 8 of the European Convention on Human Rights.[121]

---

[114]   The implementing statutes can be found at https://eur-lex.europa.eu/legal-content/EN/NIM/?uri= CELEX:32019L0790.

[115]   According to Peukert, *supra* n 17, 47, that is the only viable option for the CJEU.

[116]   According to Ubertazzi, *supra* n 45, 110–27, moral rights are, in practice, already significantly harmonized.

[117]   Others have long argued for such an approach. Cf. only Christophe Geiger, "The Constitutional Dimension of Intellectual Property", in Paul Torremans (ed.), *Intellectual Property and Human Rights* (1st ed, Kluwer Law Intl 2008) 101–31 with an update as Christophe Geiger, "Reconceptualizing the Constitutional Dimension of Intellectual Property: An Update", in Paul Torremans (ed.), *Intellectual Property and Human Rights* (4th ed, Kluwer Law Intl 2020) 117–67.

[118]   2000/C 364/01.

[119]   Cf. only CJEU, Case C-160/15 (8 September 2016), 31 – *GS Media BV v. Sanoma Media Netherlands B.V.*; CJEU Case C-469/17 (29 July 2019), 55–76 – *Funke Medien v. Bundesrepublik Deutschland*; CJEU C-476/17 (29 July 2019), 31–9 – *Pelham v. Hütter*; CJEU Case C-516/17 (29 July 2019), 40–59 – *Spiegel Online v. Volker Beck*. For an analysis, cf. only Christophe Geiger and Elena Izyumenko, "The Constitutionalization of Intellectual Property Law in the EU and the Funke Media, Pelham and Spiegel Online Decisions of the CJEU: Progress, but Still Some Way to Go!" (2020) IIC 282–306. For a general analysis of the relationship between human rights and IP cf. Gabriele Alì, "Intellectual Property and Human Rights: A Taxonomy of Their Interactions" (2020) IIC 411–45.

[120]   Cf. only Leslie Kim Treiger-Bar-Am, "The Moral Right of Integrity: A Form of Freedom of Expression", in Fiona Macmillan (ed.), vol 2, *New Directions in Copyright* (Edward Elgar 2007) 127–58.

[121]   Cf. also the broader definition in Art. 12 of the Universal Declaration of Human Rights. For a detailed examination of the relationship between authorial autonomy and the rights to privacy and dignity, cf. Hughes, *supra* n 9, 95–108.

The European Court on Human Rights clarified that "private life", as used in Article 8, encompasses "aspects relating to personal identity, such as a person's name … or a person's picture", and "includes a person's physical and psychological integrity; the guarantee … is primarily intended to ensure the development, without outside interference, of the personality of each individual in his relations with other human beings. There is therefore a zone of interaction of a person with others, even in a public context, which may fall within the scope of 'private life'."[122] In a different case, the Court stated that an individual's reputation constitutes "an element of his 'private life'".[123] If the term "private life" is to be construed that way, authorial interests in being associated with one's work, in having one's work not be distorted, and in deciding if and when one's work should be divulged or withdrawn, are akin to or even form part of the right to privacy.[124]

Balancing these different rights might allow the Court to draft tailor-made solutions for different creative contexts.[125] Such sector-specific regulation could take account of today's practical realities. As the European Commission correctly pointed out in its 1988 Green Paper on Copyright and the Challenge of Technology, many protected works are created collaboratively and/or are of a "technical, industrial or commercial character and subject to successive modifications"; it concluded that moral rights in such works should probably be waivable.[126] This is of even greater relevance today, given the collaborative nature of online creative practices.[127] Similar considerations might apply to the many commissioned works and works made for hire. Ghostwriters, for example, might have a strong interest in waiving their moral rights in return for greater remuneration for their labour.[128] Furthermore, the scope and length of the rights of attribution, of integrity, of divulgation and of withdrawal could depend on the nature of the work and the ways in which it is distributed.

Since works are equally marketable under the monist and the dualist approach, and because neither system presets the scope of (moral) rights, the CJEU would not have to choose between the two approaches to copyright law.[129] Even though, it would not be easy for the CJEU to draft a comprehensive moral rights system through case law, and it would take a long time for it to take shape. In addition, from a separation of powers perspective, it is questionable whether the CJEU is the right player for such a task. Instead, the European legislator should use its authority to draft a comprehensive, pan-European copyright system that would replace the existing piecemeal legislation, and that would use fundamental rights considerations as guideposts for bridging the several national moral rights traditions. In 2015, the Commission defined the formation of "a single copyright code and a single copyright title" as long-term

---

[122]   ECHR, Case 59320/00, (24 June 2004), 50 – *von Hannover v. Germany*.

[123]   ECHR, Case 12556/03, (15 November 2007), 38 – *Pfeifer v. Austria*.

[124]   Cf. also Hughes, *supra* n 9, 98–9.

[125]   For such a differentiated set of rules, cf. only Adolf Dietz, "Das Urheberpersönlichkeitsrecht vor dem Hintergrund der Harmonisierungspläne der EU" (1993) ZUM 309, 315–18.

[126]   European Commission, Green Paper on Copyright and the Challenge of Technology (7 June 1988), COM(88) 172 final, 197. Cf. also Doutrelepont, *supra* n 21, 304.

[127]   Cf. also Janssens, *supra* n 72, 230–1, who distinguishes between ex ante waivers, which should only be permissible under certain circumstances, and ex post waivers which should, as a default, be allowed.

[128]   Cf. also Klass, *supra* n 72, 305–6; Ubertazzi, *supra* n 45, 120.

[129]   Cf. also Asmus, *supra* n 72, 124–7.

goals.[130] Now, after the United Kingdom has left the Union, and all Member States except Ireland form part of the Continental legal tradition, such a bold endeavour might have a better chance of succeeding than ever before.

---

[130]   COM(2015) 626 final, 12.

10. Individual and collectively bargained contractual substitutes for moral rights in the US motion picture industry

F. Jay Dougherty

1. INTRODUCTION

In what may be a quintessential understatement, the US Copyright Office stated in its most recent comprehensive study of domestic moral rights, "The landscape of moral rights in the United States is complex."[1] Although US courts and legislatures have historically for the most part[2] refused to recognize explicit moral rights, a complex and changing set of tort laws and unfair competition laws have long protected rights with some similarity to moral rights of attribution and integrity.[3] In addition, copyright law, through recognizing an exclusive right to prepare derivative works, provides a limited right of integrity,[4] although that right is transferable. Additional rights equivalent to certain other rights considered in some jurisdictions to be moral rights are also found in copyright law, e.g., the right of first publication. The limited availability of statutory or judicial protection for moral rights in the US elevates the importance of "private ordering", namely individual and collectively bargained agreements in protecting interests similar to those protected by more explicit moral rights laws in other countries.[5]

The importance of private ordering as part of the US system was discussed without much detail in the US Copyright Office (USCO) Report, so a more detailed overview may be valuable to scholars and practitioners, particularly those who are not familiar with US creative

---

[1] US Copyright Office, Authors, Attribution, and Integrity: Examining Moral Rights in the United States 3 (2019) https://perma.cc/XG2A-XZDT [hereinafter USCO Report].

[2] But see, e.g., Visual Artists Rights Act, Pub. L. No. 101-650, Title VI, 104 Stat. 5089 (1990), (codified as amended at 17 U.S.C. §§ 101, 106A, 113, 301 (1990)); California Art Preservation Act Cal. Civ. Code § 987 (West); Artist's Authorship Rights Act, N.Y. Arts & Cult. Aff. Law § 14.03 (McKinney, 1984). See also USCO Report, *supra* note 1, at 120–7 for additional discussion of VARA and state moral rights statutes, including preemption of the latter by the former.

[3] See generally William Strauss, *Study No. 4: The Moral Right of the Author* (1959), *in* Staff of S. Comm. on the Judiciary, 86th Cong., Copyright Law Revision: Studies Prepared for the Subcomm. on Patents, Trademarks, and Copyrights of the Comm. on the Judiciary, United States Senate: Studies 1–4, at 109 (Comm. Print 1960) (reviewing judicial decisions as of the 1950's, and concluding that "There is considerable body of precedent in the American decisions to afford to our courts ample foundations in the common law for the protection of the personal rights of authors to the same extent that such protection is given abroad under the doctrine of moral right." Ibid. at 142); See also USCO Report *supra* note 1.

[4] 7 U.S.C. §106 (1990); see *Gilliam v. ABC*, 538 F.2d 14, 19-24 (2d Cir. 1976), (pre-1978 common law copyright).

[5] Of course, with only a few exceptions, "equivalent" rights under US law are waivable and transferable, rendering them fundamentally different from true moral rights.

industry practices. Looking primarily at the customs and practices of the US film industry, this chapter will discuss how private ordering through individual contracts and collectively bargained labour agreements may provide substantial, and in some cases un-waivable, rights as to attribution and creative control of changes to works. This complex web of agreements based on market leverage resulting from prior creative and financial success and collective bargaining agreements (CBAs) can furnish robust attribution rights and rights to creative control, at least to some authors.

Although the focus of this chapter will be on the film industry, it is worth noting that, by virtue of custom and practice and the resulting contractual relationships, other entertainment industry segments in the US have varying degrees of copyright control, attribution rights and creative control, in some cases stronger than in the motion picture sector. For example, although live theatre authors have not been permitted to unionize in the US, theatre industry custom and practice, and an influential authors association, The Dramatists Guild, have led to a strong position for live stage authors. It is customary for playwrights (including lyricists and composers for musicals) to retain copyright in their works, and to license specific rights for limited times and markets pursuant to licences that require changes to be approved, and owned, by the author. Those licences also typically require attribution in advertising, playbills, marquees, etc. Literary work authors also customarily retain copyright in their works, subject to limited licences to publish, which may include credit obligations and restrictions on changes to the work. Songwriters with market leverage can contractually restrict changes to and translations of their works, as well as retain approval rights over certain types of use, such as in commercial advertisements. Indeed, songwriters with an established market may retain 50 per cent or even 100 per cent of the copyright in their compositions, licensing to publishers only the right to "administer" certain rights in those copyrights for a fee.

In film, the screenwriter is generally not thought to have much creative control or input into the production process. Film is considered by many to be a "director's medium", as we will see further below. By contrast, in television, the writer who creates the original format for a series and/or the story for the "pilot" episode of a series (or first introductory episode when there is no "pilot") is entitled to "separated rights" and a "created by" credit, which results in certain economic and other benefits. Moreover, that pilot author, if experienced enough, generally becomes the "showrunner", i.e., the chief creative executive producer for the series, where she will continue to write some episodes, but will also supervise the "writers room", assigning episodes to various members of the writing team and overseeing the show creatively.[6] Unlike theatre authors, songwriters and literary authors, the television industry, like the film industry that is the focus of this chapter, is highly unionized in the US, so many protections for the writer *qua* writer are provided in the Writers Guild of America (WGA) Minimum Basic Agreement (MBA). But the executive producing role, although often related to WGA-determined credit, is a matter of custom and practice, as well as market leverage in individual contract negotiations.

---

[6]   See, Ken Basin, *The Business of Television* (Routledge 2018) 100–1. This may be somewhat of an over-simplification of a complex, often multi-writer, creative process. As noted in the text, not all shows have a "pilot", some may have more than one before an exhibitor commits to finance a series. The "pilot" (or "pilots") may not be exhibited at all – ultimately it is important who created the "world" of the show that gets ordered to series. Ultimately, it is the WGA that determines who is entitled to the "created by" credit and separated rights.

Section 2 of this chapter acknowledges the "patchwork" approach to moral rights-type protection in US law. In Section 3, we will explain the interplay between individual and collectively bargained agreements in the highly unionized US film industry. Section 4 will go on to discuss how creative control (which is somewhat equivalent to a right of integrity) and the right to receive credit (equivalent to a right of attribution) arise under individual and CBAs as to some of the main creative contributors to a film: the screenwriter, the director and the actors.

2.   MORAL RIGHTS: THE US PATCHWORK

This chapter is primarily concerned with two moral rights: the right of integrity and the right of attribution.[7] The right of integrity enables authors to prohibit modifications of their works without the author's consent.[8] The original purpose of the integrity right, under Article 6*bis* of the Berne Convention in the Rome revision of 1928, was to give authors the right to protect his or her "honour and reputation".[9] The right of attribution is simply the right to claim "authorship". The Berne Convention sets a minimum and leaves to member countries' legislatures the specifics, so, for example, signatory countries may provide stronger integrity rights, not limited to those that would be harmful to honour or reputation.

Although some scholars have criticized the lack of moral rights protection in US law, in its recent study of the state of protection for rights of attribution and integrity in the US, the Copyright Office concluded that:

> [T]he U.S. moral rights patchwork continues to provide important protections … Title 17 and other federal and state laws, including unfair competition and misappropriation doctrines, combined with a robust private ordering landscape, provide and author with a patchwork of means by which to protect and enforce their interests in being credited as the author of their work and to preserve the integrity of that work. Nonetheless, this patchwork has been narrowly interpreted over the years in ways that could undermine the important rights of individual authors and artists.[10]

The USCO Report went on to suggest certain minimal changes to (1) the Lanham Act (the US federal trademark and unfair competition statute); (2) the Visual Artists Rights Act (the US copyright law's only explicit statute protecting rights of attribution and integrity, which applies only to a limited category of "works of visual art", and which was enacted in 1990, after the US finally acceded to the Berne Convention in 1989); and (3) a section of US law

---

[7]   Some countries recognize various other moral rights. Examples include the "right of divulgation" that allows authors to decide whether, when, and how a work will be displayed to the public; the "right of withdrawal", which allows authors to retract works from public circulation; a right to access the original copy of his or her work; and the right to compel completion of a commissioned work. See USCO Report, *supra* note 1, at 13–14. It should be noted that there may be an interplay between attribution and integrity rights. For example, attributing to the author a work that has been modified substantially from the original author's version (integrity) might also constitute a false attribution. See, *Gilliam, supra*, note 4.

[8]   USCO Report, *supra* note 1, at 6.

[9]   Berne Convention (Rome text), 2 June 1928 Art. 6*bis*, 123 L.N.T.S. 235, 249.

[10]   USCO Report, *supra* note 1, at 5–6. International norms appear to allow great leeway to Berne member countries as to the scope and protection of rights of integrity and attribution. See, Justin Hughes, *American Moral Rights and Fixing the "Dastar Gap"*, 2007 Utah L. Rev. 659, 703–13 (2007), (arguing that the US "patchwork" is consistent with many other member countries' implementation of their obligations under Berne Art. 6*bis*).

enacted as part of the Digital Millennium Copyright Act that prohibits removal or alteration of "copyright management information" including attribution information.[11] The USCO Report further suggested consideration of a Federal right of publicity statute (currently limiting certain uses of names and other subject matter under a patchwork of state laws).[12] This chapter will further explore the "robust private ordering network", at least as to the film industry.

Although the US Copyright Office found the private ordering network to be "robust", it is a common practice in US audiovisual industry contracts for creative talent to waive, and to agree not to assert claims for violation of, moral rights as such. Indeed, such a provision is viewed by many production attorneys as one of the "holy trinity" of provisions that must be included in virtually every contract in connection with the creation of an audiovisual work.[13] Those provisions vary from a fairly simple statement to a much more detailed and lengthy provision.[14]

3.   MORAL RIGHTS PROTECTION IN US: COLLECTIVE BARGAINING AGREEMENTS AND MARKET POWER IN INDIVIDUAL CONTRACTS

3.1   Overview of Motion Picture Labour Relations and Collective Bargaining Agreements

The US motion picture and television industries are highly unionized. Although there are other Guilds and unions representing various categories of workers, including some that make cre-

---

[11]   17 U.S.C. § 1202 (1999).

[12]   USCO Report, *supra* note 1, at 4–5.

[13]   The other two provisions in that "holy trinity" are (1) a provision that the contributions of the creative talent are "works made for hire" and the employer or commissioning party is the author for purposes of copyright law (and including an alternate assignment of all rights to the extent a court might not enforce the work made for hire status); and (2) a waiver of injunctive relief and acknowledgement that in the event of a breach, money damages would be an adequate remedy.

[14]   Here is an example of one of the more thorough moral rights waiver provisions from a major studio's form contract: "Artist, on Artist's behalf and on behalf of Artist's heirs, successors and assigns, hereby waives any so-called 'moral rights of authors' and 'droit moral' rights and any similar or analogous rights under the applicable law of any country of the world (including, without limitation, the so-called right of paternity (*droit de paternité*), right of integrity (*droit au respect de l'intégrité de l'oeuvre*), right of withdrawal (*droit de retrait et de repentir*) and/or right of publication (*droit de divulgation*) which Artist may have in connection with the Picture or the Results and Proceeds [of the Artist's services], and to the extent such waiver is unenforceable, Artist hereby covenants and agrees on Artist's behalf, and on behalf of Artist's heirs, successors and assigns, not to bring any claim, suit or other legal proceeding against Company, its successors, assigns or licensees claiming that any of Artist's 'moral rights' or 'droit moral' rights have been violated ... The parties agree that the United States of America is the country of origin of the Picture." Presumably in order to further support the application of US law to a dispute concerning the moral rights provision, it goes on to state the applicable producer is incorporated in the relevant state in the US. Some other commonly used moral rights waiver provisions also state that the author acknowledges that many parties will contribute to the applicable film and, to the extent the waiver and assignment is not effective, the author agrees to exercise those rights in a manner which recognizes the contribution of and will not have a material adverse effect upon such other parties. For an example of such a conflict, see the Conclusion to this chapter.

ative contributions to films and television programmes as well as non-creative workers, there are three Guilds that represent the interests of the main creative contributors; namely, the WGA (screenwriters),[15] the Directors Guild of American (DGA) (directors and certain members of the directing team), and the Screen Actors Guild – American Federation of Television and Radio Artists (SAG-AFTRA) (actors and some other categories of performers).[16]

All of the major studios, and a large number of other producers, are signatory to CBAs with each of those Guilds. Those CBAs[17] are generally re-negotiated every three years, between representatives of the applicable Guild and the Alliance of Motion Picture and Television Producers (AMPTP), representing the studios and other producers.[18] The CBAs generally include important employment terms, such as minimum wage rates and working conditions, pensions and health programmes. This chapter will explore their provisions regarding credits (attribution) and creative rights.

Two fundamental concepts must be recognized to understand the importance of the CBAs in the US entertainment ecosystem. First, signatories agree that the CBA terms are minimum

---

[15]   Actually, the WGA is comprised of two Guilds, the WGA East and the WGA West. Because there is a single Minimum Basic Agreement between both the WGAe and the WGAw and the Alliance of Motion Picture and Television Producers (the organization that represents the studios and certain other producers in negotiating the film and television CBAs and the Guilds; hereafter, "AMPTP"), this chapter will not distinguish between the two branches.

[16]   The Screen Actors Guild and the American Federation of Television and Radio Artists merged in 2012, and have differing subject matter jurisdiction and different CBAs; this chapter will focus on rights under the Screen Actors Guild collective bargaining agreement (the "Codified Basic Agreement", hereafter "SAG CBA"). Actors and certain other categories of performers for film are covered by the SAG CBA. Note that under most countries' laws, actors/performers are not considered "authors", and that these other Guilds cover most of the primary "authors" of an audiovisual work under EU Directives, other than the film music composer. Film composers are not unionized in the US (although some related functions are under the jurisdiction of the American Federation of Musicians). Although actors are not considered film "authors" under EU law, the WIPO Audiovisual Performers Treaty requires certain moral rights for such performers. Actors clearly contribute creatively to films, and arguably should qualify as "authors" of their contributions under US law (as do musical artists performing on sound recordings), but recent US judicial decisions have rejected a claim that an actor is an author of a copyrightable dramatic work. See *Garcia v. Google*, 786 F.3d 733 (9th Cir. 2015). Using a similar analysis, another US judicial Circuit has also recently rejected a claim that a film director contributes a separately copyrightable work to a film, perhaps demonstrating the weakness of that analysis. Some, including the author of this chapter, have criticized those decisions. See Jay Dougherty, *The Misapplication of "Mastermind": A Mutant Species of Work for Hire and the Mystery of Disappearing Copyrights*, 39 Colum. J.L. & Arts 463 (2016). For an extensive discussion of creative authorship of films, see F. Jay Dougherty, *Not a Spike Lee Joint? Issues in the Authorship of Motion Pictures Under U.S. Copyright Law*, 49 UCLA L. Rev. 225 (2001).

[17]   Generally, hereafter, "CBA" or "MBA" ("Minimum Basic Agreement"); when appropriate, reference to a specific Guild's CBA or MBA will be indicated as such.

[18]   All three of the main CBAs expired in Spring of 2020, all have been renegotiated, and approved by the Guilds' respective memberships. The new agreements will expire in 2023, and will likely be renegotiated in the months preceding their expiration. It does not appear that substantial changes have been made as to the primary topics of this chapter, namely attribution/credit rights and creative controls; however, references to collective bargaining sections in this chapter will refer to the now-expired and replaced 2017 (or, in the case of actors, 2014) agreements. The Guilds and the AMPTP generally take time after the new agreement has been approved by Guild members to make the full new agreements available. The most recent codified minimum basic agreements are generally available in full on each Guild's website. Until the full 2020 agreements are available, there are memoranda and summaries of the most important changes to the prior codified versions available on those websites.

terms applicable to all contracts, and the minimum terms cannot be reduced. In other words, those terms set a floor applicable to all relevant individual contracts; however, individual contract negotiations may provide for terms and conditions more favourable to the talent than the CBA minimums.[19] If an individual contract provided less favourable terms, the CBA would govern.[20] Second, the CBAs require signatories to only hire members (or talent who will become a "member in good standing", as defined by law) of the relevant Guild for work covered by the CBA.[21] Moreover, Guild members may not render covered work for non-Guild signatory producers.[22] Together, these fundamental concepts protect the unionized structure of the industry and secure protections for talent. Of course, as a creative contributor increases in success, stature and market power, more favourable provisions will be negotiated in the individual contract, and the Guild minimums become less important. However, for all but perhaps the most highly compensated creators, collectively negotiated pension and health benefits, credits and residuals payments are substantial benefits that would not have been negotiated in individual contracts.

As to credit/attribution rights and creative controls, the Guild CBAs vary greatly. As noted above, virtually all US film industry talent (and rights) individual contracts contain "waiver of moral rights" provisions. Contractual grants of rights typically include the absolute right to alter the creative contribution. Since readers of this chapter and this *Handbook* (and many US entertainment lawyers) know that a characteristic that distinguishes moral rights from economic rights in creative work is their personal, non-assignable and in many cases non-waivable nature under the laws of countries that have explicit moral rights, those readers will also be aware that the effectiveness of those contractual clauses is potentially limited. Their effectiveness will also depend on private international law concepts, and a given country's courts' emphasis of the importance of moral rights to that country's "public order", its important policy priorities.[23] However, the customary inclusion of the moral rights waiver clause in US talent contracts highlights the importance of the collectively bargained and individual contract credit and creative control provisions, particularly in the US market. For a US

---

[19]   One relevant exception to this concept is with regard to screenwriting credits under the WGA MBA. The form that those credits take is determined by the WGA MBA credit provisions and the WGA credit-determination system. For example, a screenwriter cannot negotiate to receive the only screenwriting credit on a film. Although such a provision would be more favourable to that writer, it would not be permitted under the WGA MBA, presumably because it would diminish the credit rights of other writers on a film. However, the WGA MBA permits all the "participating writers" to agree unanimously on their credits for a film, so long as it complies with the form permitted under the MBA, and subject to some other conditions. WGA MBA, Theatrical Schedule "A", Section 7. Some employers in the individual services agreements preclude certain economic benefits if credits are decided in that manner. Section 7 also contemplates the possibility of complying with different credit obligations to writers if required under foreign laws.

[20]   Only the Guild can waive the minimum provisions required under the CBAs, so a less favourable provision would violate the applicable CBA. See Writers Guild of America, Basic Agreement, Art. 9 (2017) https://www.wga.org/uploadedfiles/contracts/mba17.pdf [hereinafter WGA MBA].

[21]   Each CBA also has its own "geographic scope" provisions. Talent hired for work outside of that geographic scope would not be covered by the CBA and would not be required to become a Guild member.

[22]   This is not in the CBA, of course, since that binds the Guild and the producer. Rather these limitations are found in Guild constitutions, or membership rules and by-laws.

[23]   See *Turner Entertainment Co. v. Huston*, CA Versailles, Civ. Ch., No. 68, Roll 615/92 (1994), *translated in* No. 16 10 Ent. L. Rep. 3 (1995).

court or arbitrator, the waivers would be enforced and the other, contractually created rights and obligations would be applied to determine credit and creative control.

3.2   Creative Controls: Contractual Rights of Integrity

3.2.1   Screenwriters

The US film industry standard is to accord little or no creative control to screenwriters, either by collective bargaining agreement or individual contracts. As is true for other parties rendering services on a film, writers generally work for hire, with the employer or commissioning party deemed the "author" and first owner of copyright in all the results and proceeds of the writer's work. As mentioned above, the contractual grant of rights will include the right to alter the writer's contribution in any manner, at the producer's discretion. It is common for the producer to hire successive writers to re-write prior writers' material, but the writer of the original screenplay sold or optioned generally has a waivable right to do the first re-write, and to do certain rewrites when additional creative elements are added. Although the WGA attempts to increase the creative rights of screenwriters,[24] those creative rights are limited and indirect, more of an opportunity to persuade the producer and director regarding creative matters. For example, the WGA MBA requires the producer to have a discussion with a writer before replacing her.[25] The primary ways a screenwriter preserves creative input in a film include the right to guaranteed payments for as many versions of the screenplay as possible;[26] rights to have meetings and discussions with the producer and in some cases the director; and the right to attend various pre-production and production events and certain screenings. More creative control, as a writer, would be unusual, even where the writer has some market leverage; however, a highly statured screenwriter might also be able to arrange for a production role that might include some further creative consultation or creative controls.

---

[24]   See WGA MBA, *supra* note 20, at Art. 48: (Professional Status of Writers: Writer Participation in the Production Process [General]): "It is mutually recognized that the writer of the screenplay or teleplay, by reason of his/her unique knowledge of the material and creative abilities, can contribute to the translation of the screenplay or teleplay to the screen by participating in other stages of production, including but not limited to discussions with the producer and director during preparation, production and after preview, in relation to changes in the screenplay or teleplay and in the motion picture. It is the policy of the Company to encourage such participation. With respect to discussions not covered under Paragraph A. below, if the writer of the screenplay or teleplay notifies the Company he/she wishes to participate in such discussions, Company shall in good faith invite such participation to such extent as may be feasible under the circumstances, it being understood that the Company shall have the right to determine who shall or shall not be present at a particular conference." See *generally*, Writers Guild of America, *Creative Rights for Writers of Theatrical and Long-Form Television Motion Pictures* (https://www.wga.org/contracts/know-your-rights/creative-rights-for-writers) (last visited 7 November 2020).

[25]   WGA MBA, *supra* note 20, at § 16.A.3.c.

[26]   Virtually all US film talent agreements include a "pay or play" provision, giving the producer the right to terminate the talent's services without any legal justification or excuse (e.g., for "creative differences"), but if there is no legal right to terminate, such as a force majeure, talent default or talent incapacity, the producer will be required to pay guaranteed fees. Thus, although a producer cannot be forced to let the writer write additional drafts of a screenplay, the obligation to pay for further steps creates an incentive to allow the writer to continue to write.

3.2.2   Directors

In the US film industry, the principal film director generally has overall creative supervision on all creative aspects of a film, and therefore, the strongest creative controls, consultation and approval rights,[27] from before being hired, through pre-production, production, and post-production, and distribution in certain media.[28] Director agreements customarily include a provision stating that the employer has the right to "cut" (i.e., edit) the film, subject only to the minimum requirements of the DGA MBA and any specific additional rights accorded the director in the individual contract. Hence, directors' rights of integrity are found in a combination of the minimum creative rights terms of the DGA MBA and any more favourable provisions that may be negotiated by the director in her individual services agreements.

The DGA MBA provides more substantial integrity rights than those discussed above for writers.[29] Most professional directors are members of the DGA and, hence, are entitled to the rights provided under the MBA.[30] In addition, a director with market and creative success will often be able to negotiate more substantial creative rights than the minimums provided in the MBA. Some core principals protecting the director's creative control are the DGA rule that, with very few exceptions for established directing teams, there can be only one director on a film and no one is to direct except the director,[31] and the rule that once employed through the

---

[27]   See Director's Guild of America, Basic Agreement, § 7-101 (2017), https:// www .dga .org/ -/ media/ E9 12CA508ACF 4446BA1C0D EB1B49ED89 .pdf [hereinafter DGA MBA]: "The Director's professional function is unique, and requires his or her participation in all creative phases of the film making process, including but not limited to all creative aspects of sound and picture. The Director works directly with all of the elements which constitute the variegated texture of a unit of film entertainment or information. The Director's function is to contribute to all of the creative elements of a film and to participate in molding and integrating them into one cohesive dramatic and aesthetic whole. No one may direct, as the term direct is generally known in the motion picture industry, except the Director assigned to the picture."

[28]   See generally ibid. at Art. 7 (specifying minimum creative rights through each stage of completion of a film and certain media of distribution).

[29]   See generally Director's Guild of America, *Summary of Directors' Creative Rights under the Directors Guild of America Basic Agreement of 2017 – Features & Long-Form Television*, https://www .dga.org/Contracts/Creative-Rights/Summary---Features.aspx (last visited 7 November 2020) (summarizing the core creative rights of a theatrical film director).

[30]   Of course, it is not "membership" that provides rights, but rather rights of members arise from the signed agreement, often collectively bargained, between the Guild and the production company. A director who directs 100 per cent of the scheduled principal photography of a film may not be replaced, except for "gross willful misconduct". DGA MBA, *supra* note 27, at § 7-503. A director who directs at least 90 per cent of such photography is vested with all of the post-production creative rights, unless the director was responsible for the film going over budget, or the replacement director directs more than 10 per cent of all principal photography (other than to defeat the first director's rights). Ibid. Like all rights under the MBA, they cannot be waived by the director or contracted away in the individual services contract. See ibid. at § 17-115 and 17-117. Although there are some classic examples of directors being replaced, e.g., *Gone with the Wind* and *The Wizard of Oz*, it has generally been unusual for a director to be replaced, for a variety of economic and creative reasons. However, in recent years, with the increasing focus of the major studios on "franchise" films, it has been reported that director replacement has become more common, and the maintenance of the value of the "franchise" outweighs other considerations. See Josh Rottenberg & Daniel Miller, *Directors were Once the Kings of Hollywood, but in the Age of the Franchise, They're Increasingly Interchangeable*, *LA Times*, (13 September 2017, 3:00 AM), https:// www.latimes.com/entertainment/movies/la-et-mn-directors-fired-from-franchises-20170913-story.html.

[31]   Of course, many films utilize a "second unit director" to direct certain supplementary portions of the film, such as an "establishing" shot. DGA directors have the right to approve the second unit director, if there is one. DGA MBA, *supra* note 27, at § 7-205.

completion of the "director's cut", the director must be informed of and consulted on all crea-tive aspects of preparation, pre-production, production and post-production.[32] The DGA MBA requires the producer to consider in good faith the advice and suggestions of the director.[33] Of course, consultation is not control.

Another important core component of a director's minimum creative control over a film is the right to prepare the first "cut" of the film, sometimes referred to as the "DGA cut" or the "director's cut", which is prepared after the film editor prepares an "assembly" of the various scenes and shots for the final film, under the supervision of the director. No one is allowed to "cut behind" the director's DGA cut (i.e., to prepare an edit of the film while the director is preparing her first cut).[34] The producer must view and discuss the director's first cut, and if requested by the director, that cut must be given a public or large private "preview".[35] Ultimately, a rational producer would try to release a film that appeals to the audience, since the larger the audience, the more likely costs will be recouped and profits made. Giving the director the right to require previews of cuts of a film provides the director with the opportu-nity to demonstrate to the person with ultimate cutting authority that her version of the film "works" with the audience.

The preview may also disclose aspects of the film that do not appeal to an audience. The DGA MBA requires that the director be notified of all post-production activities, and that the director is permitted to be present and to be consulted as to each such step, but, with a few exceptions, there is no further right to create additional versions of the film for its initial theat-rical release. Therefore, it is desirable to the director to obtain the right through her individual services contract to prepare cuts of the film beyond that first DGA cut and to require that the producer preview each of those cuts. Those additional rights give the director the opportunity to revise the film as she specifically would like to, in order to address aspects of prior versions that an audience did not like. Producers generally hire directors because of the director's creative abilities and prior success, creatively and in the marketplace, so, arguably, it is also in the producer's interest to allow a director additional cutting and preview rights before finalizing the version to be initially released. A further level of creative control, short of the revered "final cut" right, is for the individual contract to grant the director the rights to prepare additional cuts beyond the DGA cut and to have each of those cuts previewed before an audi-ence. A total of two or three cuts (including the DGA cut) is not unusual for an experienced, successful director. The right to the DGA cut is absolute under the MBA, but additional cutting rights beyond the minimum required by the MBA may be subject to conditions desired by the producer. For example, such further cutting rights are often conditioned on the film not being over budget or over schedule by more than a specified small amount.[36]

---

[32]   Ibid. at § 7-202. To be clear, the creative rights do not end with the completion of the "director's cut". The producer has an obligation to consult throughout the post-production process, and some rights are absolute, such as the right to direct added scenes, re-takes of scenes and voice-over/ADR.

[33]   Ibid. at § 7-202 and 7-1501.

[34]   Ibid. at § 7-504.

[35]   Ibid. at § 7-505.

[36]   It should be noted that a director with market/creative leverage may negotiate provisions that don't deal directly with the editing of the film, but that indirectly reinforce the director's creative vision for the film. For example, a director with sufficient market power may obtain a contractual right to approve (or if the director has substantial leverage, to designate in consultation with the producer) "all creative elements" and possibly "all below-the-line" personnel. This would include elements of the production

The ultimate creative control for a director would be to have the right of "final cut", i.e., to determine the version of the film that is released to audiences in theatres and in other subsequent media. The DGA director does have certain rights under the MBA to be consulted or, in limited circumstances, to personally make or supervise cutting of the film for certain further distribution media, such as home video and television. New media exploitation of films, e.g., digital streaming either through subscription services ("SVOD") or "free"/advertising supported streaming services, is replacing the prior successive "windows" of distribution, e.g., through pay-per-view services, pay television, home video, then free television. The DGA MBA provides that the director has the right to receive certain information about proposed changes, and has the same editing or consultation rights for domestic new media as she would have had as to television.[37]

Article 7-509 of the DGA MBA covers the rights of the director with respect to editing the film for media subsequent to the theatrical release. In the US, television from its earliest days was primarily a commercially sponsored medium. Once the Hollywood studios stopped resisting the then-new medium of television and started licensing theatrical films for television exhibition, it was desirable for television networks to assure that a film was short enough to fit television's timeframes, including a significant amount of time for advertisements, often eight minutes per half-hour of programming. Some directors and other talent challenged such modifications in judicial proceedings, but often without success.[38] Eventually, the DGA was successful in negotiating Article 7-509(b), which limited editing for network television and required that the director be entitled to make changes when required for "Network Standards and Practices" (certain content was customarily not acceptable for broadcast television, either because prohibited by the Federal regulatory agency, the Federal Communications Commission, or because networks believed it would be offensive to audiences). In addition, if the licence to a network permits editing of a film, the DGA MBA requires that the producer obligate the network to consult with the director.[39] As further media for film distribution evolved, further creative rights were negotiated into the DGA MBA. For example, if a film is to be edited at the producer's facilities for "syndicated" television (licensing directly to stations or station groups, customarily after a period of exclusivity for television network

---

team such as the composer/lyricist(s), director of photography and other members of the camera crew, editors and editorial staff, costume designer, production designer/art director, the casting director(s), and others. There is a range as to how robust the right is (e.g., designation vs. only approval) and how extensive it is (which elements are specifically subject to the director's rights). Designation rights, in those rare instances where they are granted, usually have some limitations, such as that the persons designated are available when and where needed and pursuant to budgetary constraints, and that hiring is subject to Guild and state and Federal employment laws or a past negative performance for the producer.

[37]   DGA MBA, *supra* note 27, at § 7-509(g). See also ibid. at 497–510.

[38]   See, e.g., *Autry v. Republic Prods.*, 213 F.2d 667 (9th Cir., 1954) (in a claim by a well-known "Western" movie star, affirming an injunction permitting editing films to 53 minutes to permit incorporation of advertisements, but limiting breadth of injunction because some cutting might exceed the contractual grant of rights to edit and might "emasculate" the films); *Preminger v. Columbia Pictures Corp.*, 49 Misc. 2d 363, 267 N.Y.S.2d 594 (Sup. Ct.), *aff'd*, 25 A.D.2d 830, 269 N.Y.S.2d 913 (1966), *aff'd*, 18 N.Y.2d 659, 219 N.E.2d 431 (1966) (in a litigation over cutting of the classic film *Anatomy of a Murder*, the contract granting final cut rights applied to the theatrical release and the further grant of rights to exhibit on television implied a right to edit the film as required for television exhibition).

[39]   DGA, MBA, *supra* note 27, at § 7-509(c).

exhibition), the director must be given the opportunity to do that editing.[40] There are also limitations on editing for airline exhibition[41] and a right to do the edit under some circumstances.[42] DGA MBA Article 7-509(g) now provides significant rights to the director with respect to editing the film for domestic basic cable services, videodisc/videocassette, in-flight and "New Media", but not a "final cut" right. If a film is licensed for foreign television exhibition with additional shooting, the director is to be hired to do that additional filming and to edit the film.[43] Although the DGA MBA only directly binds the signatories (i.e., the producer/employer and the Guild), the producer is required to obtain an assumption of the creative rights from the buyer or assignee.[44] Hence, while these may not be inalienable rights, the requirement of assumption agreements extends those rights beyond the parties initially in contractual privity.[45]

There are various circumstances where a director could have final creative control over a film.[46] But only a handful of directors are able to secure a form of final cut right as to a film financed by others, especially by studios or other distributors. For a very small number of extremely successful directors, the director may have the right to determine the final cut for initial domestic theatrical release, a right to prepare or supervise preparation of the versions for some of the largest non-US territory theatrical releases (including dubbing and subtitling), various aspects of the version used for home video release, initial domestic pay television, free network television (including placement of commercial breaks), internet platforms, and the initial US airline version. In addition, a director of that stature may contractually have the first opportunity to make other types of necessary changes to the film, such as to achieve rating and length requirements, changes to comply with censorship or matters of local taste, morality or customs (the producer will almost certainly have the final decision as to those), changes to comply with law or address legal claims such as copyright infringement or violations of personal rights, and to comply with broadcaster standards and practices.

3.2.3   Actors

Actors have very few creative controls over a film under the CBAs. The actor does have certain protections as to performing nude or simulated sex scenes, which must be disclosed

---

[40]   See ibid. at § 7-509(d). Of course, the director must be available for that obligation to apply.
[41]   Ibid. at § 7-509(f).
[42]   Ibid. at § 7-509(g).
[43]   Ibid. at § 7-510.
[44]   Ibid. at § 7-511.
[45]   As statute passed with the Digital Millennium Copyright Act requires certain assignees of copyright to comply with Guild residuals provisions under certain circumstances. See, 28 U.S.C. § 4001 (1998) (assumption of contractual obligations related to transfers of rights in motion pictures). Although not among the recommendations of USCO Report, and its desirability can be debated, extending this to include creative rights would go a long way to conforming US contractual rights to the moral right of integrity.
[46]   The individual services contract will generally include a default provision that, except as to rights expressly granted the director, all cutting rights are reserved to the employer/producer. In addition, cutting rights in excess of the DGA minimum rights may be, and are conditioned in a variety of ways; for example, the film delivered must conform to the approved screenplay, achieve a specified MPAA rating level, and not exceed a maximum specified duration. Conditions such as those relating to director availability when and where needed, and the film being not more than a certain amount over budget or over schedule are also common.

and consented to in writing by the actor in advance.[47] If the actor does not consent, "doubles" (actors who resemble and play the part of the actor) cannot substitute for the actor. Of course, if a producer must have one or more nude/simulated sex scenes in the film, it can simply not hire an actor who refuses to consent. But this requirement of written consent gives an economically desirable actor some input on that type of content. In some instances, a star actor may be able to negotiate even stronger limitations on the filming or use of nude/simulated sex scenes.

One important aspect of an actor's creative control is that a star actor will generally not agree to play a role unless he has approved the applicable screenplay, and although the actor would generally not be able to control all potential subsequent changes, it is not unusual that the actor would have the right to approve screenplay changes that "materially affect" the role the actor has agreed to play. Some star actors are able to negotiate the right to view the "dailies", i.e., the various shots of scenes filmed each day, which are generally viewed at the end of each shooting day by a limited group, including the director and one or more producers, through which the actor might influence the director and producer as to which scenes or "takes" are preferable or more effective.

Of course, a star actor might have multiple functions on a film that may involve more substantial creative control. For example, some actors become directors, who would have all the controls of a director, or a producer, with varying degrees of creative control. However, beyond sexual content, additional creative controls by an actor as such would generally relate to the actor's role and appearance, including in the marketing for the film. Because that is not part of the collective bargaining agreement, such approvals, consultations and controls would be negotiated as part of the individual services agreement.

Some examples of individually negotiated creative controls might include: the "look" of the character, hair, makeup and costumes (including the personnel responsible for those aspects of the actor's role). As further discussed below, a statured actor will likely have a set of approval rights over their own photographs and likenesses to be used in marketing, and a star actor may negotiate for other rights that provide some degree of control over how the film is marketed.

3.3   Rights of Attribution: Credits

3.3.1   General
There are some circumstances where giving an inaccurate credit could give rise to a tort or unfair competition/false advertising type claim under US law. Exaggerating an author's contribution to or involvement in a film could give rise to a "passing off" type claim or possibly a defamation claim. However, the US Supreme Court significantly decreased protection for a "reverse passing off" type claim under Federal law,[48] which had previously evolved as a type of unfair competition that would apply where a credit was omitted or a credit was accorded to

---

[47]   Screen Actors Guild – American Federation of Television and Radio Artists, Basic Agreement, § 43 (2014), https://www.sagaftra.org/files/2014_sag-aftra_cba_1.pdf [hereinafter SAG CBA]. It should be noted that the last version of the SAG CBA covering theatrical films that has been "codified" is the 2014 agreement. There are memoranda covering changes and additions made in the 2017 agreement and the 2020 agreement (available at www.sagaftra.org) but as of the writing of this chapter, they have not yet been integrated into the SAG CBA.

[48]   See *Dastar Corp. v. Twentieth Century Fox Film Corp.*, 539 U.S. 23, 123 S. Ct. 2041, 156 L. Ed. 2d 18 (2003).

the wrong party,[49] and that decision has led some courts to interpret state claims in a similarly constricted manner.[50]

Accordingly, in the US film industry, attribution rights arise primarily from individual contracts and CBAs. The relative importance between those two sources of rights varies widely, depending on the particular talent role involved. Screenwriter credits are determined virtually completely by the WGA, under its credit determination process; screenwriter contracts typically say only that credit will be determined according to the WGA.[51] By contrast, the Screen Actors Guild only requires that 50 actors receive credit on-screen in connection with their characters (fewer, if there are not 50 actors in the film). So there is substantial negotiation over numerous details regarding an actor's credits in the individual talent agreement. Directors lie in between those extremes. The DGA has the sole right to determine who is entitled to the "directed by" credit and has controls over placement that cannot be waived by individual contract. The DGA MBA provides significant minimum requirements for a director's credit on-screen and in advertising, but directors with market leverage negotiate additional obligations in the individual contract.

Producers must take these Guild and individual contractual credit obligations seriously. Copies of the proposed credits are generally submitted to the three above-the-line Guilds (WGA, DGA, SAG). Producers prepare detailed credit memos outlining the credits, including their position, size and form. These memos are often prepared or reviewed by attorneys to confirm they comply with the numerous contractual obligations. The size of credits, relative to each other and relative to the size of the title of the film, is carefully measured in mock-ups of the proposed credits. Once the credits for the film are photographed, and advertisements are manufactured, it can be very expensive to make changes, so great effort goes into avoiding errors.

3.3.2   Screenwriters: credit by collectively bargained agreement

It is common practice for a film screenplay to be written and revised by a series of writers and writing "teams". The interest of each writer to receive attribution is sometimes, but not always, consistent with the interests of the producers and distributors. The WGA provides a process for proposing and determining credits, which will appear both on-screen and in various types of advertising and promotion, sets forth specific forms the credits must take, and, to protect the value of writing credits, requires significant writing contributions to qualify and places limi-

---

[49]   See, e.g., *Smith v. Montoro*, 648 F.2d 602 (9th Cir. 1981); *Lamothe v. Atl. Recording Corp.*, 847 F.2d 1403, 1406–8 (9th Cir. 1988); *Cleary v. News Corp.*, 30 F.3d 1255, 1259–62 (9th Cir. 1994).

[50]   See, e.g., *Aquarius Broad. Corp. v. Vubiquity Entm't Corp.*, No. 215CV01854SVWVBK, 2016 WL 6963050 (C.D. Cal. Mar. 4, 2016). See also, USCO Report, *supra* note 1, 44–59. Ironically, the Digital Millennium Copyright Act, which was primarily directed at allocating rights and privileges in the digital system, included a provision that makes it unlawful to remove "copyright management information", which has been applied primarily in a digital network context, but has been extended by some courts to "brick and mortar" contexts. See *Williams v. Cavalli*, No. CV 14-06659-AB JEMX, 2015 WL 1247065 at *2-4 (C.D. Cal. Feb. 12, 2015); *Tiermy v. Moschino S.p.A.*, No. 215CV05900SVWPJW, 2016 WL 4942033 at *4-5 (C.D. Cal. Jan. 13, 2016). See, USCO Report, *supra* note 1, 83–100.

[51]   The WGA process or something similar to it is also often incorporated by reference, or by specific credit exhibits in individual contracts, as to screenwriting not subject to the WGA, for example feature length animated films or independent films written by non-WGA member screenwriters or films written outside of the geographical jurisdiction of the WGA.

tations on the number of writers who may receive credit.[52] It should be noted that the credits ultimately determined not only provide attribution of screen authorship, but also availability of "separated rights" to certain credited writers,[53] bonus payments and contingent compensation, typically tied to the type of credit received, "passive" royalties for certain types of subsequent productions such as sequels or television series, and sometimes rights to be involved in writing such subsequent productions.

Covering the many details of the WGA process exceeds the scope of this chapter, but an overview will illustrate some important elements. Because additional writing can take place during production of a film, screenwriting credits are not determined until after completion of photography. Shortly after completion of principal photography, the producer is required to submit a "notice of tentative writing credits" to the WGA, and to each writer who participated in the writing of the screenplay.[54] Sometimes this is simple, but sometimes more complex; in any event, this notice will set forth the screenwriting credits the producer would like to include. All drafts of the screenplay must also be furnished to the Guild and all the participating writers. There is a short period of time during which the Guild itself or any of the participating writers may challenge the proposed credits. If the dispute cannot be resolved, the MBA sets forth a set of arbitrators and an arbitration procedure that is different from typical arbitrations, focusing almost entirely on the review and assessment of drafts of the script by an anonymous board of three arbitrators. There is an internal appeals process, and the entire procedure has been challenged in court a few times, based on its lack of transparency or unclear norms, for example, but when faced with such a challenge, courts have all affirmed its validity, since it was agreed to by the writer members and the producer signatories.[55] If there is no timely objection to the credits proposed by the producer, or if there is, once the determination has been made, the producer and all the participating writers must abide by the result.

3.3.3   Actors: credit primarily by individual contract

Because of the limited provision for credits in the SAG MBA, most film actor credits derive from their individual services agreements. An actor playing a very minor role who is not a well-known actor will likely receive only the minimum credit required under the SAG MBA, namely a credit on-screen in connection with her character name in the "end titles", which is

---

[52]   See WGA MBA, *supra* note 20, at Theatrical Credit Schedule "A". A more readily understandable resource, and one that sets forth some practices that are not clearly spelled out in Schedule "A", but which guide the arbitrators where there is a dispute as to credits, is the Screen Credits Manual. See Writer's Guild of America, *Screen Credits Manual,* https://www.wga.org/contracts/credits/manuals/screen-credits-manual (last visited 8 November 2020).

[53]   WGA MBA, *supra* note 20, at § 16A. "Separated Rights" are a bundle of rights that are accorded the screenwriters who receive credit for creating an original "story" of the film (if there is one; in some cases the "story" is taken from another source such as an underlying literary work or life story), notwithstanding that most screenplays are works made for hire for the producer.

[54]   See, e.g., *Eddy v. Radar Pictures, Inc.*, 215 F. App'x 575, 577–8 (9th Cir. 2006). In this case, a writer unsuccessfully challenged the Guild's process for making the threshold determination of who qualified as a "participating" writer.

[55]   See *Ferguson v. Writers Guild of Am.*, 226 Cal. App. 3d 1382, 277 Cal. Rptr. 450 (Ct. App. 1991); *Marino v. Writers Guild of Am., E., Inc.*, 992 F.2d 1480 (9th Cir. 1993).

the long rolling list of credits that appears after the film.[56] The Guild provides an arbitration process to resolve billing disputes.[57]

The size and prominence of screen and advertising credits is important to the evolving success of an actor's career. Accordingly, as an actor plays more substantial roles and develops market leverage, substantial additional screen and paid advertising credit requirements are negotiated as part of the actor's personal services contract. The SAG CBA also requires a producer to honour those individual contract obligations.[58] Those provisions can involve a large number of variables, including: placement (e.g., above/before or below/after the film title, whether in main or end titles[59]); position relative to other actor credits; size (height, width and thickness of print, occasionally other, vaguer variables) relative to the title of the film and to other actors or other talent such as the director or producers; the type of advertising and commercial products in which credits will be required, the requirement of the use of an actor's likeness[60] in advertising; its size and position vis-à-vis other actors and the types of advertising in which a likeness will be required; and provisions for correction of an erroneous credit. Because there are often several or even numerous actors negotiating such provisions, the producer also has the difficult task of coordinating all of the various obligations, and negotiating them in a way that will not interfere with subsequent casting decisions made after the negotiation of a given actor's agreement. For example, if a producer agrees that an actor will be in "first position" among the actor credits in the main titles, perhaps because of the importance of the role played or the market value of the actor's name, but later a more highly statured actor takes a lesser role, and demands "first position" credit, the producer is confronted with a conflict to solve. Or where a film features two successful "star" actors, there can be difficult negotiations leading to detailed contractual obligations as to the use of each actor's likeness, e.g., neither will be larger or more "prominent" than the other, and if one is used in an advertisement the other's likeness will also appear (with certain limited exceptions, such as Academy Award congratulatory ads for one of the actors, where no other likenesses appear). The reference to prominence suggests the dignity aspect of these types of provisions. Disputes have arisen as to what it means; for example, is the name or likeness on the left more "prominent" than a name or likeness on the right side of an ad? Ultimately, the credit provisions of the star actor's individual services agreement are highly detailed and can be many pages long.

---

[56]   SAG CBA, *supra* note 47, at § 25.

[57]   Ibid. at § 25.C.(3).

[58]   Ibid. at § 25.C.(1) and (2).

[59]   In this context, "title" means the name of the film and "titles" refers to the long list of credit on-screen.

[60]   The SAG CBA contains a basic agreement that covers all the SAG-covered categories of film performers. In addition, it contains "Schedules" with additional or modified provisions for different categories of performers, e.g., "day players" (hired by the day), "weekly players" (hired by the week), and "deal players" (players who are paid more than $65,000 for all work on a film). Many actors, and particularly deal players (also known as "Schedule F" players, referring to the applicable Schedule to the CBA), negotiate for approval rights of varying levels of rigor over photographic and non-photographic likenesses. Arguably, such approval rights reflect both dignity interests and commercial value. Use of an actor's likeness in advertising for a film can both reflect and enhance the status of the actor (and in some cases, the role played or the film itself).

3.3.4 Directors: a blend of collectively bargained and individually bargained attribution rights

The DGA MBA provides that the Guild ultimately determines who is entitled to the "directed by" credit; requires that it be in that form; and limits almost all other uses of the word "director" in film credits. It also contains minimum requirements affecting both the director's credit on-screen and in paid advertising. In addition, the DGA MBA provides that mock-ups of the screen credits[61] and paid advertising credits[62] must be furnished to the DGA for approval in advance, and that the DGA must be notified of any changes. There are many specific credit requirements in the DGA MBA.[63] For example, generally, there can only be one credit to the director, in the form "directed by ... ". This credit on-screen must be on a "single card" (i.e., on-screen visible with no other credits), and must be the last screen credit seen before the principal photography commences.[64] The MBA prohibits other credits using the term "director" or "direction",[65] except pursuant to certain previously entered into CBAs.[66]

On-screen, in addition to the requirements above, the DGA MBA requires that the directing credit be not smaller than 50 per cent of the size of the title of the film or of any other person.[67] There are numerous detailed requirements as to the director's credit in advertising and publicity, as well as specific detailed limitations and exceptions, for example for particularly large or small ads.[68] The basic principal is that the directing credit will be accorded in all paid advertising prepared or issued by the producer in the US, and the producer will notify its foreign sales and distribution offices of those requirements.[69]

Directors with market or creative leverage will often negotiate improved credit rights, for example, larger size, and most favoured nations-type requirements as to credit size or a requirement to accord credit in advertising or on types of media or related products where the MBA might allow omission or a smaller directing credit. Paid advertising often includes an "artwork title" of the film incorporated into the ad artwork, plus a "billing block" that includes both the film title and the other credits that are required, either contractually or pursuant to the applicable collectively bargained agreements. Most credit size proportions are measured

---

[61] DGA MBA, *supra* note 27, at § 8-201.
[62] Ibid. at § 8-210.
[63] Of course, in accordance with the concept discussed above, the director may negotiate more favourable credit provisions in her individual services agreement, subject to applicable MBA requirements. DGA MBA, *supra* note 27, at § 8-104.
[64] Presumably, this is based on the assumption that the audience may not be seated and paying attention until the film is starting. In more recent times, the "main title" credits often appear at the end of a film, with only the distributor/financier credit and the title at the beginning of the film. In that case, the "directed by" credit must be the first credit at the end of principal photography, again presumably because the audience will still be watching the film at that point. Among professionals, it is considered disrespectful not to sit through the sometimes lengthy credits at the end of a film. As a denizen of Hollywood with an interest in its business and legal practices, this author usually remains seated until the disclaimers and copyright notices at the end of the film, often with virtually no one else seated in the theatre.
[65] DGA MBA, *supra* note 27, at § 8-103.
[66] The permitted other "director/direction" credits are "Art Director" (for the production designer) and "Director of Photography" (for the cinematographer).
[67] DGA MBA, *supra* note 27, at § 8-201. This may be reduced slightly in the rare instances where the Guild permits multiple director screen credits.
[68] See generally ibid. at § 8-203.
[69] Ibid. at § 8-203 (preamble).

by reference to the title in the billing block, with some limitations preventing them from being miniscule relative to the artwork title. Use of a credit in relation to the artwork title is viewed as highly prestigious, usually accorded to well-known actors who will draw an audience, but it is sometimes agreed to for very successful directors.

4. CONCLUSION: CONFLICT BETWEEN AUTHORS

Although detailing the many specifics of creative controls and credits under the collectively bargained and individual contracts exceeds the scope of this chapter, one final concept highlights a problem when contractual "moral rights" of authors conflict in relation to a multi-authored work such as a film and the US approach to addressing that tension. That is the use of a "possessory" or "film by" credit. Such a credit is generally in excess of the Guild minimum credits, but highly desirable. However, it is controversial as between screenwriters and directors (and their respective Guilds). Obviously, the screenwriter feels that a film is her film – for most films would not exist without the story, characters, scenario and dialogue originated by the screenwriter. But the screenplay would not have come to visual life without the director (and the numerous others who expand upon the words to create a visual world). Who should have credit and take creative control of such a work? The existence and variety of approaches to solving that riddle in different cultures perhaps illustrate that there is no one simple answer.

As to the "film by" credit, the US industry leans toward a director, and if the film was "written by" the same person, even more so. Generally,[70] the "possessory" credit (a "film by" or a "so-and-so film" credit, usually before or above the title of the film on-screen and in advertising) is not required by the DGA MBA, but is negotiated by the director in her personal services agreement. The WGA finds such a credit objectionable unless it is given to a screenwriter who directs a film. This agreement puts the producer/employer in the middle of a dispute between the WGA and screenwriters on the one hand and the DGA and directors on the other. The current WGA collective bargaining agreement commences with a preamble, noting that conflict:

> Since its founding, the Writers Guild has opposed the use of the so-called "possessive credit" on-screen and in advertising and promotion when used to refer to a person who is not the sole author

---

[70] But see DGA MBA, *supra* note 27, at § 8-203(d) (requiring credit in the form "a film by" to the director on certain large billboard-size ads where there are numerous other credits). *Contra* ibid. at Sideletter 27 (deleting the sentence requiring that credit, prohibiting the "film by" credit on a director's first film unless the director has brought the literary property on which the film is based to the producer and performed substantial services in the development of the film). Although beyond the scope of this chapter on moral rights, it is worth noting that in US film industry custom, the distributor of a film receives a "presents" credit before the title, and one or more producers and production companies receive a possessory "production" credit. So a group of such credits, all typically before the title of the film might read: "X Presents a Y Production of a Z Film". Needless to say, where there are multiple production companies and distributors, that will become even longer and more complex.

of the screenplay. The Guild's historic, current and ongoing opposition is based upon beliefs and principles which include the following:

Credits should, as far as possible, accurately reflect each individual's contribution.

The granting of a possessive credit to a person who has not both written and directed a given motion picture inaccurately imputes sole or preeminent authorship.

The proliferation of the number of unnecessary credits on-screen and in advertising devalues credits in general.

The widespread use of the credit denigrates the creative contributions of others.[71]

The Preamble concludes by stating that the producers recognize the WGA's long-standing objection and believe that the best way to resolve it is through tri-partite negotiations among the WGA, the DGA and the producing signatories, and they "commit to their full participation" in that process. It has yet to be finally resolved, but illustrates the US approach to attribution in this context. Meanwhile, the complex combination of Guild CBAs and talents' individually negotiated services agreements provide an outcome that reflects pragmatic creative and marketing power as among the creative and financial contributors, on a case-by-case basis, shown best by the multi-faceted solutions that apply to the multitude of motion pictures produced with that system each year.

---

[71]   WGA MBA, *supra* note 20, at 1.

PART IV

CHALLENGES TO MORAL RIGHTS

11. The economic dimension of moral rights

Richard Watt

1. INTRODUCTION

In most countries, copyright law is separated into two streams, or prongs, of protection. On the one hand, the owners of copyright protected material are given property rights in the material itself, so that (outside of any fair use) no other person can produce copies of that material without first obtaining permission from the copyright holder. The property rights that the law provides to copyright holders are often referred to as the "economic" rights, since they provide the foundation upon which economic transactions and agreements can be built, under which the copyright holder can benefit financially from allowing copies to be made and distributed. On the other hand, in many (but not all) countries, there is also a bundle of moral rights in a copyright protected work, which are typically said to be in place to protect the integrity, honour and reputation of the artist or original creator. Thus, the economic rights prong of copyright generally refers to the direct ability of the copyright holder to earn revenue from the work in question, or more to the point, to exclude non-paying users, while the moral rights prong refers to the ability for the original author to be recognized as such and for the work not to be altered in some way that the author would object to.

The Berne Convention[1] clearly places moral rights outside of the economic realm, talking of them being "independent" of the author's economic rights. But, is that perspective strictly correct? It depends on what one means by an "economic" right, and as I will show in this chapter, there are clear economic reasons why moral rights should be in place, and why they have economic value for creators. The present chapter, then, argues that a separation of moral rights from economic value is a reflection of a somewhat flawed understanding of what actually constitutes an economic asset. Indeed, there is a very clear economic dimension to moral rights, and therefore there is also a sound economic argument for the existence and legal protection of moral rights.

The present chapter is certainly not the first to argue that there is an economic dimension to moral rights.[2] Most of the economic theory of moral rights revolves around willingness to pay, willingness to accept, and the initial endowment of rights (a right of the author of integrity and retraction, or a right of purchaser to alter), along with an argument centred on transaction costs and the Coase Theorem.[3] Such a perspective is centred on social welfare maximization and gains from trade. In those settings, if it is efficient for a waiver of rights to occur, it could (if it is permitted by law) be achieved by private contract between the artist (who owns the moral

---

[1]   Berne Convention for the Protection of Literary and Artistic Works, opened for signature on 9 September 1886.

[2]   See, for example, one well-known economist's take on moral rights, W. Landes, "What Has the Visual Artist's Rights Act of 1990 Achieved?" (2001) 25 *Journal of Cultural Economics* 283–306.

[3]   See, for example, the discussion in T. F. Cotter, "Pragmatism, Economics and the Droit Moral" (1997) 76(1) *North Carolina Law Review* 1–96.

rights) and the owner of the work (who wishes to effect some action that would otherwise violate the moral rights).

However, the present chapter focuses on a different aspect of moral rights which is more closely related to efficient allocation of risk, to asymmetric information, and to allowing efficient bargaining to occur. As opposed to the standard economic theory of moral rights, the present chapter will argue that contractual waiver of certain of those rights could be socially inefficient.

2.   OUTLINE OF MORAL RIGHTS

The present chapter reconsiders the economic dimension of moral rights, and as such, there is a need to understand what exactly is meant by "moral rights". However, for the purpose undertaken here it is sufficient that we keep our understanding of moral rights at a somewhat superficial level. In reality, while moral rights include a variety of different legal entitlements,[4] such as rights of disclosure, of retraction, of attribution and of integrity, all that we require for the argument in the present chapter is that all of the works of a given author, works that the author has at some point disclosed (perhaps by having transferred them under economic transactions), be always correctly attributed to that author in the form in which they were originally completed and disclosed. I will therefore not dwell upon the exact legal environment of moral rights, which the interested reader can find in more authoritative sources.[5] Rather, what is important for the superficial perspective that is taken in the present chapter is that our understanding of moral rights retains the essential character of what such rights entail.

Specifically, for the purposes of the present chapter, moral rights are to be understood simply as a mechanism under which a specific work is attributed to a specific author (or artist). The work must be kept in the state in which it was left as a finalized work by the author (i.e., the work cannot be altered in any way), and there is no room for different authors to be added (or removed) as having participated in the creation of the work. In short, moral rights are a one-to-one correspondence between a specific work and a specific author. I will also take the stance that moral rights are publicly observable to anyone who cares to investigate. Perhaps that could rely on some sort of registry or depository, of works, or perhaps it could rely simply upon the identity of the author somehow being attached, visibly, to the work in question (such as when an artist signs their painting or sculpture, or when a literary author places their name at the top of a novel written by them).

In particular, even though much of the literature on moral rights is concerned with visual art, and I will mention the case of visual art throughout the chapter, there is no need at all for my argument and analysis to pertain only to visual art. The argument here can be relevant for any creative endeavour. In many cases, what is important is that the work in question can be commissioned, that is, before the work is actually created a buyer has the opportunity to

---

[4]   See, for example, H. Hansman and M. Santilli, "Authors' and Artists' Moral Rights: A Comparative Legal and Economic Analysis" (1997) 26 *Journal of Legal Studies* 95–143.

[5]   For example, Cotter (n 3) part II offers a historical account of the development and legal underpinnings or the *droit moral*. See also for a discussion of *droit moral* in France; K. Holst, "A Case of Bad Credit: The United States and the Protection of Moral Rights in Intellectual Property Law" (2006) 3(2) *Buffalo Intellectual Property Law Journal* 108–9.

contract with an author to create it. Clearly, this is more often the case for visual art – perhaps a bank might commission a statue or ornament to be displayed on their premises, and portrait paintings are often commissioned – but it can just as easily be the case for other forms of copyrighted creations (songs, written works, movies, etc.). I will also argue that moral rights still retain an important economic element even for works that do already exist, without having been commissioned.

3.   THE ECONOMICS OF MORAL RIGHTS

Whether or not moral rights can be thought to be "economic" in nature depends critically on what one means by an "economic" right. Here, I take the stance that any right is "economic" if it influences or has a direct bearing upon the value of an economic transaction. So, in the strict terms of copyright, if it happens that, when a copyright protected work is somehow used by another person, the amount of payment or fee that is received by the copyright holder (who, for the purposes of this chapter I will assume is also the original author of the work in question) depends in any way on moral rights, then moral rights have a clear economic dimension. Stated differently, if the remuneration received by the copyright holder would be different in a scenario in which moral rights are in place (and enforced) compared to a scenario in which they were not, then moral rights are indeed economic rights in essentially the same way that copyright itself is an economic right. If moral rights do play a part in determining an author's remuneration, then moral rights have a clear economic value to copyright holders.[6] Given that, all that is required is to show how moral rights can, at least in part, determine the amount of remuneration. My intention in this chapter is to argue exactly that.

4.   THE SIGNALLING VALUE OF MORAL RIGHTS

An important insight into the economic value of moral rights is given by Hansman and Santilli, who insist that artistic reputation is based upon the entire body of work that the artist has produced to date, and that each work that has been produced contributes to that reputation. Each work, in effect, has an advertising value for the value of future works.[7] Hansman and Santilli's argument is that modifications of artworks can affect the artist's economic interests by distorting the perception of that artist's general reputation, thereby changing the willingness to pay of potential future purchasers for new works by the same artist. Whenever such modifications

---

[6]   Economists have looked at the effect of moral rights on authors' welfare, with contradictory results. Boyle et al. found that moral rights were damaging to the welfare of artists but did not influence the choice of where artists decide to live, in contrast to Landes who nine years earlier found exactly the opposite (the enactment of moral rights law did not affect artists' earnings, but did affect their choice of place to live). Landes also found that the VARA in the United States may have harmed more than benefited artists, while Bechtold and Engel found that artists value moral rights sufficiently highly so as not to be willing to transact them away. M. Boyle, S. Nazzaro and D. O'Conner, "Moral Rights Protection for the Visual Arts" (2009) 34 *Journal of Cultural Economics* 27–44; Landes (n 2); S. Bechtold and C. Engel, "The Valuation of Moral Rights: A Field Experiment" (Max Planck Institute for Research on Collective Goods, WP Bonn 2017) 4.

[7]   Hansman and Santilli (n 4); Landes (n 2) 452.

result in a depreciation of artistic reputation, the artist him or herself would prefer to be able to assert a moral right that would prevent such modification.

Hansman and Santilli are concerned mainly with the exercise of moral rights to protect artistic reputation from damage caused by distortions of existing works. But in doing so, they do directly recognize the link between the value of past works and the value of future works, which relies upon "artistic reputation". It is then easy to see that moral rights are, in essence, the curriculum vitae of an author or artist. They form the complete registry of the works that a given author has produced in the past. If we take that perspective on the issue, then immediately we can see that moral rights will have as much impact upon the earnings of an author as the CV of any other worker has upon their income and opportunities. So, how does that work? At this point, it is probably worthwhile to separate the discussion between commissioned and non-commissioned works.

4.1   Commissioned Work

The body of existing relevant work that a person has produced in the past is a signal of what sort, and quality, of work they might produce in the future. If that person is in fact a creative author or artist, then their past work provides an indication of what their future work might be like, and a potential buyer of a future work might find some indication in the perceived value of past work of what they should pay for a potential future work. To take this to the extreme, say a movie director wants to hire a song-writer to write material that will be included in a new movie. Then, assume that the song-writer's job is made publicly available, and I myself apply for it along with Paul Simon (the well-known artist and song-writer). As it happens, I have absolutely no prior experience writing songs, so my song-writing CV is empty, whereas Paul Simon's CV is full of works that have proven to be very popular. Why should the movie director choose Paul Simon over me? Obviously, because it is highly probable (actually, since this is an extreme example, it is a sure thing) that Paul Simon will produce a song that is much better than anything I would produce. How does the director know that? He forms his probability priors over the value of the future work of Paul Simon and myself by considering the value of our past work, as set out in our respective CVs. However, those CVs only make reasonable sense if there are moral rights in place, otherwise I could fill my CV with items that I actually had no hand in, and just the same, it might be difficult for Paul Simon to claim authorship over the many very valuable works that he did actually write. This shows that moral rights are an important ingredient in the fee that a song-writer can charge for a commissioned work – Paul Simon can require a high fee, I can require a fee of 0 (or perhaps even a negative fee, as my song-writing work might cause more problems than benefits to anyone silly enough to hire me as a song-writer).

Now, of course, things are much more likely to not be as extreme as that example above. More likely would be a situation in which the set of available authors or artists for any given commission will, in fact, all have some sort of pedigree within the space of creations that is contemplated. So it might not be so clear-cut which author or artist is more likely to produce the sort of work that is being sought. However, the bodies of existing works will still serve as the starting point for the potential commissioning individual to establish a probability prior for the value of the future work of each of the candidates, and based on that, a fee can be worked out to offer to each of them. Again, we see that we rely on moral rights to give us confidence that each candidate artists' CV is a true and credible reflection of the information needed to establish the remuneration for future commissioned work.

4.2   Non-commissioned Existing Works

The above scenario is associated with commissioned works, that is, attempting to put a price on a work that does not yet exist. One might counter with the argument that not too many copyright protected works are commissioned before they exist, and so for works that already exist one can simply observe them directly and infer their quality and therefore their value. However, even if a work is not commissioned, but rather is simply produced by the artist, the price that access to that work can command under a copyright related agreement for use will still depend, at least in part, upon the value of prior works of the same author. For example, it is well known that artists can benefit from high auction prices for their existing works, in that high prices are taken as a signal of high quality,[8] which then may result in equally high (or perhaps even higher) auction prices for future works. But that link is only as strong as the moral rights that tie particular past works to particular authors.

5.   USING MORAL RIGHTS SIGNALLING VALUE TO SOLVE AN EXTERNALITY PROBLEM: THE IMPORTANCE OF NON-WAIVABILITY

The signalling value of moral rights goes beyond their value to the copyright holder (author or artist) alone. Taking the tarnishing argument of Hansman and Santilli mentioned above one step further, Mills points out that a modification that tarnishes an artist's reputation not only affects the economic situation of the artist by lowering the value of future works, but it would also have a negative effect upon any owner of other works by that artist.[9] The value of what they own can be negatively affected as a by-product of the undesirable actions of other owners.[10] This aspect of the issue is important when a contractual waiver of rights by the artist is possible, since it then constitutes an externality that is not taken into account in any contractual waiver agreement between the artist and any given owner (or potential owner) of a work by that artist.[11] While the externality that a modification of a work can have upon the artist's economic situation can be resolved by contracted waiver (assuming that the artist does indeed have a legal moral right that would otherwise prevent modification), there is no way that the externality faced by any other owner (current or future) of works by the artist in question can

---

[8]   Actually, more to the point, a high price signals that the demand curve for the work in question is high, leading to an expectation that the demand curve for other works by the same artist is also high.

[9]   L. A. Mills, "Moral Rights: Well-Intentioned Protection and Its Unintended Consequences" (2011) 90 *Texas Law Review* 443–64.

[10]   Also, other effects exist that alter the signal value of the existing portfolio – the sale of a work by an influential collector, or a larger than normal quantity of works offered for sale as in a "dumping" of works (might signal the artist going out of favour). In any case, moral rights only offer imperfect protection against reputational issues and externalities: ibid.

[11]   Interestingly, Mills (n 9) 456, also points out that destruction of a work of art by an owner might have the effect of increasing the value of the existing stock of works (and, potentially, the value of future works as well), since it would have the effect of increasing the scarcity of works by that artist.

be addressed by a contract between the potential modifier and the artist. Assuming that this is a sufficiently important aspect, there is some economic validity in an argument in favour of moral rights being legally inalienable or non-waivable.

6.   THE SOCIAL ECONOMIC VALUE OF MORAL RIGHTS

For both of the cases considered above, commissioned and non-commissioned work, there is a clear undertone of investment – the actions of an artist or author, as reflected in the efforts they exert in producing high quality works in the present, have a direct influence upon the value of works that the same artist or author produces in the future. However, the investment value would be in danger of being lost if it were not for moral rights which create an inextricable bond between authors and their works. If moral rights were not able to be protected, or more to the point, were simply non-existent, then artists and authors would lose the investment value of current effort, and we should expect to see lower quality of works as a result. We can, therefore, easily appreciate that not only do moral rights have economic value to authors, they also play an important part in generating higher quality works for the consuming public to enjoy. Thus, there is a social value to moral rights as well as an individual value.

There is a second, perhaps equally important social welfare dimension related to the existence (and non-waivability) of moral rights. So far, the discussion has focused on the economic value to authors and artists of enforcement of moral rights. If prior valuable works of a given author are inextricably linked to that author, then the future works of that same author will command a higher price. However, just as high quality past works signal a high probability of high quality future works, low quality past works signal a high probability of low quality future works. With a non-waivable moral rights system in place, not only do authors get to own their high quality works, but they are also forced to own their low quality ones (assuming, of course, that they did in fact make the low quality ones public in the first place). This part of the signal is very valuable to society, and to potential purchasers of future works (e.g., under a commission), since it helps to protect against paying a high price for work that is likely to turn out to be of low quality.[12] Moral rights as a signal of value, therefore, also protect the current or potential owners of a work, helping them to not be misled into paying a higher price than is fair, given the current portfolio of works of the author in question.[13]

To illustrate this, go back to my (futile) attempt to out-bid Paul Simon as a song-writer. Say I realize that my problem is that I have an empty song-writing CV, so I quickly write a few songs to fill that gap. But then, under a strict non-waivable moral rights regime I will not be able to later disown those (very likely) paltry efforts. My low quality past will signal a low quality future.

---

[12]   See Holst (n 5) 115, who also recognizes (in passing) exactly this point.

[13]   Adler also talks about the public interest in moral rights, but from a different perspective. For Adler, it is about preserving works that the public finds value in. Moral rights might stop an artist destroying a work that the public would like to see retained. In the signalling theory in the present chapter, there would be an argument against an artist destroying a work because it would interfere with the signalling mechanism, leading to a distorted price (in detriment of commissioning agents, and the general public) for future works. A. M. Adler, "Against Moral Rights" (2009) 97 *California Law Review* 263–300.

The point to underline here is that it is important that moral rights stick to all works produced by a given artist or author, not just those that are judged to be of a certain quality. The only protection that the creator has against low quality works is to discard them before he or she allows them to go public. Any work that the creator actually makes public, perhaps by displaying it as a commissioned work or by putting it up for auction, should end up becoming a known element in that creator's moral rights CV. Cherry picking by a creator from among the publicly available works would destroy the signalling value to society, along with its social benefits, and it would also destroy the signalling value to the author him or herself (as purchasers would not have confidence in the accuracy of the signal). In short, if moral rights were waivable, then they would carry less signalling value, or what is the same thing, the signal becomes imperfect, leading to a more uncertain situation when the work of a given author or artist is valued. And, as all economists know, risk aversion implies that random is bad! Assuming that potential purchasers or users of the material in question are risk-averse, their willingness to pay will be reduced.

7.   ARROW'S INFORMATION PARADOX

The above discussion of the economic value of moral rights should bring to mind the famous "information paradox", originally ascribed to Ken Arrow.[14] Under the paradox, the true value of information is not known until it is disclosed, and once it is disclosed, there is no incentive to pay for it. The information paradox is certainly relevant for the discussion here of the economic value of moral rights, although the cross-over is not perfect; the information paradox only applies up to half way.

Here, the "information" is the actual (future) work of an artist or author – the work that will fall under copyright protection once it is produced. The information paradox then is more closely related to commissioned work, since it implies that it is difficult to place a value on a work that does not yet exist. However, the paradox then asserts that once the "information" does exist, there is no need to pay for it. That might be true of pure information (like, for example, a weather forecast, or a list of the winning numbers in next week's lottery), but for the case of creative outputs, they will be protected from unlicensed use by the general copyright standard. Given that, being informed (i.e., having seen the work in its final form) is not the same as having the legal ability to use it in any meaningful way. So, the paradox only applies up to the part where information that does not exist is difficult to value. And that is where moral rights come in. Therefore, we can see that in order to get around the information paradox completely, we actually require both copyright and moral rights; copyright solves the second part of the paradox (the need to pay for access to disclosed information), and moral rights solves the first part (valuing information even before it is disclosed).

---

[14]   K. Arrow, "Economic Welfare and the Allocation of Resources for Invention", in R. Nelson (ed.), *The Rate and Direction of Inventive Activity* (National Bureau of Economic Research, Princeton University Press 1962).

8.   AN ILLUSTRATIVE MODEL

At this point, it might be worthwhile to develop a simple but illustrative model of the main points in the above argument. To that end, in this section I will set out how one might envisage the link between moral rights and the value of an existing or future work of a given author or artist, and how that link might be studied. The main point of my argument above is that the signal that past works give for the value of future (or present) works would never be perfect, which directly implies that there is a stochastic element that needs to be analysed.

Assume a situation of two individuals, an "author" and a "buyer". The author offers access to a copyright protected work (e.g. offers a novel to a publisher, offers a film script to a producer, offers to paint a portrait, offers to build a piece of visual art, etc.) to the buyer for a fee, and we are interested in the fee that the buyer would be willing to pay. Assume the buyer's initial wealth is w, and their initial utility is $u(w)$, where the utility function is increasing and either linear or concave. Works by the author have a quality valuation, denoted in general by q, which we assume is measured in monetary terms, so that if, for example, the buyer purchases a work of known quality q at a price of p then his utility would be $u(w - p + q)$. Finally, when the buyer considers a stochastic valuation, then his objective function is the resulting expected utility. If the utility function is linear, then the buyer is risk-neutral, and if the utility function is concave, then the buyer is risk-averse.

On the other hand, the author is known to have produced n individual outputs (of the same or similar type as that of the hypothetical transaction at hand) in the past, and these works make up the observable body of work of the author. Each item is uniquely ascribed to that author by means of the moral rights in those works. Each existing work i has a quality measured by q_i, which we will normalize to be between 0 and 1; $0 \leq q_i \leq 1$ for $i = 1, 2, \ldots, n$. The vector of qualities of the author's works is denoted by $q(n) = (q_1, q_2, \ldots, q_n)$. The quality valuation of each work is a subjective number that is individualized to any given observer, in our case, to the buyer. So, the buyer observes the vector $q(n)$, and uses that observation to decide upon a price, p, to bid for the new or future work.

If we were interested in modelling a regular bargaining situation, we would not only have to work out the price that the buyer will bid for the new work, but also the author's reservation price for the work, that is, the minimum price that the author requires to part with the work. For now, let's only concentrate on the buyer's maximum willingness to pay, which we shall denote by p^*. In doing so, readers will notice that the model proposed here is quite closely related to the way in which financial assets are valued, but where here we are only interested in what is essentially the consumption value of an innovation (rather than a flow of financial returns), and there is no corresponding "risk-free" asset for comparative purposes.

Given the observed vector of qualities, q, the buyer calculates a probability density function for the quality of the new (or future) work, which we shall label as work number $n + 1$, so its expected quality is q_{n+1}^e. That is, we have a probability density $f(x, q(n))$, such that the probability that $q_{n+1} = x$ is $f(x, q(n))$. Then, we end up with the expected value of the quality of the new (or future work), from the perspective of the buyer in question, is $q_{n+1}^e(q(n)) = Ex = \int_0^1 xf(x, q(n))dx$. The buyer's maximum willingness to pay for the new (or future) work, p^*, is calculated from:

$$\int_0^1 u(w - p^* + x)f(x, q(n))dx = u(w) \tag{11.1}$$

The left-hand side is the expected utility from carrying out the transaction at price p^*, and the right-hand side is the utility of not carrying out the transaction. If the buyer is risk-neutral, then $u(w) = w$, and the equation for the maximum willingness to pay is just $w - p_{rn}^* + \int_0^1 xf(x, q(n)) dx = w$, or $p_{rn}^* = \int_0^1 xf(x, q(n)) dx$. So, in the risk-neutral case, the maximum willingness to pay is equal to the expected valuation of the new (or future) work, $p_{rn}^* = q_{n+1}^e$.

On the other hand, and more interestingly, if the buyer is risk-averse, then the expected utility of the stochastic situation of paying for and owning the new or future work is strictly less than the utility of the expected value of the same random variable. Thus, there exists a risk-premium, $\pi > 0$, such that:

$$\int_0^1 u(w - p_{ra}^* + x) f(x, q(n)) dx = u(w - p_{ra}^* + Ex - \pi) \tag{11.2}$$

Substituting from the original equation for the maximum willingness to pay, we see that $u(w - p_{ra}^* + Ex - \pi) = u(w)$, or $p_{ra}^* = Ex - \pi = \int_0^1 xf(x, q(n)) dx - \pi$. Therefore, as is natural, a risk-averse buyer is willing to pay less for the new (or future) work than is a risk-neutral buyer, $p_{ra}^* < p_{rn}^*$. Of course, the amount of discount – the risk-premium π – will depend on all of the parameters of the problem (the perceived quality vector, the amount of initial wealth, and the utility function), and so is individual and specific to the buyer in question.

Now, in general, we might expect to be able to infer a few things about the probability density $f(x, q(n))$ from the observed vector $q(n)$. For example, it seems likely that the higher are the entries in the observed quality vector, the more the density will be skewed right – an observed history of higher qualities leads to a greater likelihood that the new (or future) work will also be of high quality. We would say that an increase in one or more of the elements of the observed quality vector would cause a first-order stochastic dominant shift in the probability density. For example, perhaps the buyer could construct the probability density using Bayes' Theorem from elementary statistics. In that case, the buyer would begin with some initial prior (perhaps a uniform density), and then would go adding the observations, one after another (perhaps in the chronological order in which the works were produced), and with each added quality observation, the prior would be updated according to Bayes' Theorem.

Alternatively, one might simply consider that the important information in the quality vector is all contained within just the mean (or average) and the variance (or, equivalently, the standard deviation), say $\bar{q}(q(n))$ and $\sigma^2(q(n))$ respectively. That is, the buyer's willingness to pay for the new or future work might be able to be expressed in some way as a function of only the mean and variance of the vector q. The greater is the mean, the more the density would be located to the right of the quality domain, while the lower is the variance, the more the estimated quality will be concentrated around its mean. The variance would only be of importance to a risk-averse buyer (as we have already seen – a risk-neutral buyer sets the price at expected value), since it would imply that the new or future work is of lower risk, and this will reduce the risk-premium discount that such a buyer would apply to the expected value. In such a case, we would have $f(x, q(n)) = h(x, \bar{q}, \sigma^2(q))$, and we would end up with

$q_{n+1}^e\left(q(n)\right) = k\left(\overline{q}, \sigma^2(q)\right)$, where h and k are functions.[15] It would be relevant to assume that these two functions are such that the maximum willingness to pay is increasing in the mean for both risk-neutral and risk-averse buyers, and that it is constant in variance for risk-neutral buyers but decreasing in variance for risk-averse buyers.

Regardless of what, exactly, are the characteristics (risk-averse, risk-neutral, etc.) of the buyer, what we can see is that the existence, protection, and non-waivability (inalienability) of moral rights are, in all cases, of the utmost importance to the buyer's valuation of the new or future work, since the observed vector of qualities of past works is the only information that buyers have for working out their maximum willingness to pay. The author is above all interested in the better of his or her past works being included in the vector of past qualities, since that will in general lead to a shift in the calculated density such that buyers will have a higher willingness to pay. And on the other hand, the buyers are interested in both the higher and the lower quality past works being included, since that will allow them to make the most informed decision possible. The only way that all of the past works can be included is if moral rights exist, and are non-waivable.

There is a very clear cross-over between the theory of moral rights outlined here and the economics of insurance, and the economics of self-protection. The author prefers to have moral rights in place (for the past high quality outputs) so as to increase the probability of a high buyer willingness to pay, and so the author will be willing to suffer costs in producing high quality, and in having the moral rights in those high quality works protected. This will reduce the probability of new and future works being valued too low. This is exactly the same as what one finds in the literature on self-protection for losses – people are willing to suffer costs so as to reduce the probability of loss outcomes. On the other hand, from the perspective of buyers, non-waivable moral rights are directly a sort of insurance, since knowing that lower quality works exist among the collection of all works by the author helps a potential buyer from overpaying for a new or future work.

9.   CONCLUSION

In this chapter I have outlined an economic justification for moral rights. The argument rests upon moral rights being an information mechanism that allows markets to work properly, in the sense that they allow an appropriate (albeit stochastic) valuation of a new or future work of a given artist. There is, therefore, economic value in moral rights, for the artist or author him or herself (moral rights in highly valued existing works will increase the value of current and future works), as well as for potential buyers of new and future works (moral rights in low valued existing works removes the risk of overpaying for new and future works), and for society in general (the economic benefit of moral rights to authors will lead to greater effort in producing high valued works for society to enjoy throughout an author's career).

These issues of inalienability or non-waivability, and perpetuity of moral rights have been debated in the legal literature in relation to the Visual Artists Rights Act 1990 (VARA), with no clear consensus falling on either side of the argument. Here, the signalling theory relies on moral rights being both inalienable (non-waivable), and it is sufficient that they be only for the

---

[15]   For example, if the density were normal, then it only depends on the expected value and variance of the underlying vector of qualities.

life of the artist (i.e., until there can be no further new works produced). Thus, while perpetuity would not interfere with the signalling value of moral rights, there is no need for perpetuity in order for the signal to work.

12. Moral rights for corporate entities

Pascal Kamina

The concept of granting moral rights to corporate entities would be viewed with scepticism, if not outright hostility, by many lawyers of author's right or copyright tradition. In most jurisdictions, the general consensus is that moral rights (including the right of divulgation, the right to be identified as author, and the right to object against derogatory treatments of a work) are designed for individual authors, and that corporate entities and, more generally, legal persons, have no need for such or for a similar form of protection, which would be ill-adapted, incongruous, or even dangerous, in the context of business activities. Exceptions exist in several jurisdictions, but they appear limited and do not attract much attention. Perhaps more importantly, publishers, producers and other copyright owners have never really claimed for an extension of moral rights to their benefit. All this certainly accounts for the relative lack of modern legal literature on the subject.

However, positions on this question may be shifting. First of all, the idea of granting copyright owners some kind of additional control over uses of their works has found support in the digital environment. The legal framework of digital rights-management information already implements, in this context, a protection of ownership information,[1] which preserves the interest, if not the right, of copyright owners to be identified as such. More recently, the development of new advertising techniques, such as virtual product placement or behavioural advertising, has highlighted a growing need for copyright owners and service providers to ensure protection of the integrity of their contents and signals.[2] In response, the European directive of 14 November 2018 on audiovisual media services[3] has introduced for the first time a provision aiming at preserving the integrity of such services (so-called "signal integrity"), making it subject to the consent of the media service providers.[4] In a more general perspective, the idea of protecting "non-economic interests" of legal persons is gaining grounds in many legal systems.[5] In some jurisdictions, the recognition of personality rights to legal persons,

---

[1]   World Copyright Treaty (WCT) (1996), Art. 12. See hereunder under Section 2.1.

[2]   On the latter, see European Audiovisual Observatory, New forms of Commercial Communications in a Converged Audiovisual Sector, IRIS Special, 2012.

[3]   Directive (EU) 2018/1808 of the European Parliament and of the Council of 14 November 2018 amending Directive 2010/13/EU on the coordination of certain provisions laid down by law, regulation or administrative action in Member States concerning the provision of audiovisual media services (Audiovisual Media Services Directive) in view of changing market realities, OJ L 303, 28.11.2018, pp. 69–92.

[4]   Article 7b. See hereunder under Section 2.2. The previous directive already provided some protection aimed at protecting the integrity of audiovisual programmes in the field of advertising, for example by providing that the insertion of commercials during must not prejudice "the integrity of the programmes, taking into account natural breaks in and the duration and the nature of the programme concerned, and the rights of the right holders" (Art. 20(1)).

[5]   In Europe, the European Court of Human Rights (ECtHR) has confirmed the right of legal person to a reputation (ECtHR, *Uj v. Hungary*, 19 July 2011, no. 23959/10; however, the Court points out that "there is a difference between the commercial reputational interests of a company and the reputation of

including a right to the respect of their name, a right of consideration and a right of privacy, was proposed.[6] This combination may well pave the way for new claims in the field of copyright, aimed at protecting copyright owners, in the form of moral rights or of pseudo-moral rights.

In what follows we will attempt to define the obstacles to such a protection, and the possible evolutions in this respect. We will suggest that an extension to legal person (copyright owners) of the current protection granted to individual authors is both unnecessary, and would create insuperable technical and practical difficulties (Section 1). We will then address the current perspectives of reinforcement of the protection of copyright owners in this area, relating to their identification and to the protection of the integrity of their works (Section 2).

1.   THE CASE AGAINST AN EXTENSION OF THE MORAL RIGHTS TO CORPORATE ENTITIES

The case against the granting of moral rights, as currently protected, to corporate entities, appears overwhelming, for theoretical and technical reasons (1.1). And the examination of the rare exceptions implemented in certain legal systems would tend to confirm this view (1.2).

1.1   The Rationale for Exclusion

In author's rights systems, the idea that moral rights should be restricted to individual authors is based on firm philosophical and theoretical grounds. For a start, the protection of moral rights consecrates the relationship between an artist and his work, and was inherently associated, from the origins, to natural persons. The strict association of the term "author" to natural persons, which is also deeply rooted in the history and philosophy of *droit d'auteur*, further justifies the strict containment of moral rights to individuals. This position is reinforced by the legal characterization of moral rights. From a civil law perspective, moral rights are "personality rights" or "personal rights" (in French, *droits de la personnalité*, in German, *persönlichkeitsrechten*), or rights that fall, more or less directly, into the broader category of extra-patrimonial (non-economic, unassignable and unwaivable) rights.[7] As such, moral rights have always been

---

an individual concerning his or her social status. Whereas the latter might have repercussions on one's dignity, for the Court interests of commercial reputation are devoid of that moral dimension" pt. 22). Also, the ECtHR has held that a legal person can obtain, under Art. 41 of the European Convention of Human Rights, compensation of moral injury (ECtHR, *Comingersoll SA c/ Portugal*, 6 April 2000, no. 35382/97). For a study under French law, see Ph. Stoffel-Muck, *Le préjudice moral des personnes morales, in Libre droit, Mélanges Ph. Le Tourneau* (Dalloz 2008), p. 959 et seq. For a recent case from the French Supreme Court (*Cour de cassation*), see Cass. 1re civ., 25 nov. 2010, n° 09-15.996, F-D: reputation of a legal person affected by the use of the image of its headquarters.

   6   See, e.g., under French law, H. Martron, *Les droits de la personnalité des personnes morales de droit privé* (LGDJ Paris, 2011). F. Petit, Les droits de la personnalité confrontés au particularisme des personnes morales, D. aff. 1998, n°117, p. 826; L. Dumoulin, "Les droits de la personnalité des personnes morales", Rev. Soc. (2006), p. 1. But see *Cour de cassation*, 1e civ., 17 March 2016, n° 15-14.072 (if legal persons have a right to the protection of their name, domicile, private communications and reputation, only individuals can claim an invasion of privacy under article 9 of the Civil Code).

   7   See P. Kamina, "Author's Right as Property: Old and New Theories", 48 J. Copyright Soc'y U.S.A. 383 (2000–2001). The French Supreme Court has characterized the droit moral as a right of

attached to natural persons, and courts have been, either strongly opposed, or very reluctant, to recognize some sort of vesting or transfer of moral rights to legal persons. Therefore, as a matter of principle, the law makes it clear that legal persons cannot acquire, *ab initio*, but also through contracts or through their status as employers, moral rights.[8] This position of principle is further reinforced by the historical reluctance of most, if not all, civil law systems, to grant "personality rights" to legal persons, or to indemnify their purely moral damages.[9]

In a copyright perspective, philosophical and theoretical barriers to the extension of moral rights to legal entities are less present. But the historical disinclination of copyright systems to implement a protection of moral rights relies on general principles and traditions (contractual freedom, legal certainty and legal security) that would make their extension to legal entities, and more specifically commercial entities, unacceptable. As a result, most copyright countries which have implemented moral rights (often in a diminished form, and subject to broad exceptions) do not extend the protection to legal persons (employers, commissioners, producers and publishers), to the approval of most legal authors and courts. Quite remarkably, in several jurisdictions the exclusion also applies when the latter are "authors" of the work under the copyright act. This is the case in the United Kingdom where, in relation to "films", moral rights have been granted to the film director, and not to the film producer, although both are co-authors of the work under the Act.[10] This is also the case in the United States, where the limited protection offered under the Visual Artists Rights Act (VARA)[11] is restricted to natural persons (it being specified that the protection does not apply when the work is a work-made-for-hire, that is, when the employer or commissioner is the "author" of the work[12]). The fact that the copyright acts, in certain jurisdictions, do not, in this respect, make a distinction between natural and corporate authors, does not necessarily imply an intention of the legislator to extend the protection to legal persons. For example, in the Irish Copyright and Related Rights Act 2000 moral rights are granted to "authors", without further specification.[13] This could well point to the film producer, who is co-author of the film with the principal director under Section 21 of the Act (one of the rare cases in which a legal person can be author of a work, as opposed to copyright owner). However, a reading of the Act suggests that the

---

personality, while specifying that it is different from the other rights of personality protected by the law (*Cour de cassation*, 1re civ. 10 March 1993, no. 91-15.915). In Germany, under the so-called "monistic" theory, the economic and moral rights alike are part of the "sphere of personality".

[8]   For a clear expression under French Law, see *Cour de cassation*, 1e civ., 16 November 2016, no. 15-22723: "[N]either the existence of a contract of employment nor ownership of the material support of the work are likely to confer on the corporation employing the author the enjoyment of that [moral] right". Under German law, Frankfurt Court of appeal, 15 February 1990: [1991] NJW 1839 (a legal person cannot claim a right to be identified under article 13 of the author's right Act on the right of paternity).

[9]   Although the position of courts has evolved in this respect in many countries, so far legal persons have not been recognized full personality rights, similar to those of individuals. See note 5 above.

[10]   UK Copyright, Designs and Patents Act 1988 (CDPA), ss. 77(1) and 80(1).

[11]   Visual Artists Rights Act of 1990, §§ 601-10, 17 U.S.C. §§ 101, 106A, 107, 113, 301, 411, 412, 506.

[12]   See, for the exclusion of works-made for hire, the definition of "work of visual art" in § 101. Although the Act does not expressly characterize the author for the purpose of VARA as a natural person, the provisions, which refer, inter alia, to the "life of the author", would seem to point at the natural person only. Besides, the exclusion of work-made-for-hire prevents corporate authorship in this respect.

[13]   Chapter 7.

protection of legal person was not contemplated by its drafters, as evidenced by references in the text made to the "pseudonym" of the author, to its "employer', or (for the duration of the right against false attribution of authorship) to the "death of the person on whom the right is conferred".[14] Exercises in construction on similarly ambiguous or broad wordings to the effect of granting moral rights to legal persons have been proposed,[15] but do not seem to have been endorsed by courts.[16]

As mentioned, what could be seen as a broad and almost universal principle does not seem to raise concern with copyright owners. The reason for that is quite simple. In fact, most corporate entities, be they publishers or producers of works, have no need for moral rights when they hold the copyright in the work.

In practice, most unauthorized publications or derogatory treatments of a work can be controlled or sanctioned under the exclusive economic rights: for example, first public disclosures covered by the moral right of divulgation also constitute infringements of the right of distribution (when not exhausted) or of the right to communicate to the public; and most unauthorized modifications of a published work are covered by the right of reproduction or the right of adaptation (subject to the application of specially devised exceptions). In addition, the freedom of assignees or licensees to modify a work may be limited by contract, through strictly framed assignments or licences or through the retention of rights of approval. By contrast, most individual authors have lost these possibilities when they assigned their copyright in the work, or just by entering an employment agreement. This is what justified, in the first place, the retention of some degree of control in their favour through moral rights.

In addition, legal entities benefit from alternative forms of protection beside copyright, which may ensure, under certain conditions, the protection of their identification as copyright owners and the respect of the integrity of their works. Most author's rights and copyright acts do not affect rights of action or other remedies, whether civil or criminal, available in respect of certain acts falling under the definition of moral rights. To a limited extent, torts of passing off and unfair competition can be used against false attributions of authorship and mutilations of a work. By contrast, individual authors have limited resources in this respect: in common law jurisdictions, although the tort of unfair competition has been successfully relied upon in cases where a work was falsely attributed to an author, or to object to mutilations of film works,[17] such forms of actions may be ill-adapted to the protection of most authors, in particular those lacking specific goodwill or reputation. This confirms the need for specific forms of actions to the benefit of authors through moral rights (which, in some copyright countries, include, in addition to the rights of paternity and integrity, specific forms of passing off[18]). Commercial entities do not need additional protection in this respect, let alone wide-ranging moral rights.

Beyond these general objections, several technical reasons advocate against the extension of standard moral rights to legal persons. Let us concentrate here on the most relevant moral

---

[14]   S. 115(2).

[15]   See, e.g., for Canada, Emir Aly Crowne Mohammed, Moral Rights and Mortal Rights in Canada, 4(4) Journal of Intellectual Property Law & Practice (April 2009), pp. 261–6.

[16]   See, however, for India, note 34 hereunder.

[17]   See, e.g., in the US, the famous case *Gilliam v. American Broadcasting Companies* 538 F 2d 14 (2nd Cir, 1976) ("Monty Python" case) (protection against the unauthorized editing of a television program).

[18]   See, e.g., the moral right against false attribution of a work under Section 77 of the UK Copyright, Designs and Patents Act 1988.

rights for our purpose, that is, the right of paternity, which would then take the form of a right to be identified as the owner of the copyright in the work, and the right of integrity, that is, the right to object to derogatory treatments of the work.[19] An extension of these protections to corporate entities, especially commercial entities, would create an ocean of problems. Firstly, the principle of non-assignability (and, in many legal systems, of non-waivability) of moral rights, which would result in the first copyright owner retaining the right to object to certain derogatory treatment of the work, would be unacceptable in a commercial environment, especially in the context of complex chains of exploitation. Secondly, the standard test of infringement would be difficult to apply in many systems, in particular in those countries, like France, were the exercise of moral rights is said to be discretionary. In other jurisdictions, the assessment of what could be considered as prejudicial to the honour or reputation of a corporate entity might prove difficult. More generally, there is a strong risk that commercial corporations exercise such rights for purely economic purpose.[20] Thirdly, the "open definition" of the objectionable derogatory treatments adopted in most legal systems would create uncertainties, reinforced in the case of legal persons by the relative lack of predictability of their behaviour in this respect (compared to flesh and blood authors[21]), and by the fact that they will be less restrained in the exercise of these rights.[22] Fourthly, division of the copyright in the chain of exploitation would create additional difficulties if it entails a division of moral rights. This could create conflicts between corporate moral rightholders, it being specified that their respective interests may be far more conflicting and difficult to reconcile than those of individual co-authors. In addition, users would be confronted with the risk of multiple claims coming from holders they cannot identify (the same being true if the moral rights are retained by the initial copyright owner only). Therefore, some sort of identification of the current holder(s) of the moral rights would be needed, and should be regulated. Lastly, granting moral rights to legal persons could give rise to conflicts with authors, unless some kind of hierarchy is provided for, which may prove very delicate to devise and implement.

Some of these problems could be solved by an adaptation of the protection, and in particular through a strict framing of the treatments that could be objected to by a legal person. But clearly, a pure and simple extension of all or part of the protection afforded to individual authors would prove unworkable.

---

[19] We should exclude from our discussion the right of reconsideration, which would lead to absurd results if exercisable by a corporation in a commercial context, and the right of divulgation, which is mostly irrelevant for a copyright owner, for the reasons already exposed.

[20] This risk also exists when moral rights are exercised by authors, and lead, in France, and possibly in other countries, to the dismissal by courts of claims based on moral rights but exercised for purely economic purposes. However, it is submitted that the problem will be more stringent if moral rights are exercised by a commercial entity.

[21] Although this last assertion could be challenged, practising lawyers of civil law jurisdictions who have an experience in dealing with moral rights would certainly agree. At least in France, the reality of the exercise of moral rights by authors is very different to what is generally assumed by foreign lawyers in view of the language of the French IP Code. Pure moral rights cases, consisting solely on a claim based on moral rights, are rare, and in some sectors of the industry the risks associated with manifestly excessive or unreasonable moral rights claims is very limited, due to the implementation of standard practices, to the economic situation of individual authors and to the general attitude of courts.

[22] Many individual authors do not exercise their moral rights for financial reasons or due to their position as employed or commissioned authors. Many corporate copyright owners are in a much better bargaining position.

1.2   The Lack of Relevance of the Few Exceptions

There are two main categories of exceptions allowing the grant or the transfer of moral rights to legal persons. The first ones are broad exceptions, vesting or granting to legal person of all or part of the moral rights otherwise granted to individual authors. These are real exceptions.[23] The second take the form of limited, pseudo-moral rights, granted to certain copyright owners and restricted to certain forms of use. It is submitted that the second category provides a better answer to some legitimate concerns of copyright owners, with regards to the preservation of the integrity of their works. However, their inclusion within the framework of copyright law remains problematic, for the reasons already exposed.

Among the first category, a special case should be made for the various instances in which moral rights, or their exercise, are transferred, *mortis causa*, to legal persons such as authors' societies or public institutions. These exceptions fall under the provisions of Article 6*bis*(2) of the Berne Convention, which provides that the moral rights of the author "shall, after his death ... be exercisable by the persons or institutions authorized by the legislation of the country where protection is claimed". These transfers, which, in practice, concern mostly non-commercial institutions, are designed as ways to preserve the will of the authors and cultural heritage. They cannot serve as a model or justification for the granting of autonomous moral rights to commercial corporate entities.

More directly relevant for our purpose are the exceptions in favour of copyright owners, such as employers, publishers or producers. Surprisingly, the broadest, and most commented on of these exceptions, is found in France, where the protection of moral rights is implemented to its fullest extent, and where the idea of granting moral rights, in general, to legal entities would probably be fought with the utmost energy. This exception is derived from the concept of "collective works", a category of multiple authorship works which grants initial ownership in the works, but also the associated moral right, to the natural or legal person who initiates and publishes the work (in most cases, the publisher-employer).[24] Although the concept of

---

[23]   We do not treat as exceptions the possibility to frame the exercise of moral rights through consents and waivers, when authorized under the applicable law, as they do not transfer the exercise of moral rights. On this question, see A. Kelli, Th. Hoffmann, H. Pisuke, I. Kull, L. Jents, C. Ginter, "The Exercise of Moral Rights by Non-Authors", 6 Journal of the University of Latvia Law (2014), pp. 108–25.

[24]   This category of works was developed by the courts in cases involving dictionaries, and is conceived as a variety of joint or composite works published by an entrepreneur under his name, in which it is impossible to identify the part contributed by each author. Article L.113-2 defines a "collective work" as "a work created at the initiative of a natural or legal person who edits it, publishes it and discloses it under his direction and name and in which the personal contributions of the various authors who participated in its production are merged in the overall work for which they were conceived, without it being possible to attribute to each author a separate right in the work as created". Article L.113-5 of the French IP Code vests author's right directly in the principal under whose name the work is made public, without distinguishing economic and moral rights. For a recent case confirming the vesting of the moral rights, see, e.g., *Cour de cassation*, civ. I, 22 March 2012, Com. com. électr. 2012, comm. no. 61, note Caron, P.I. 2012, no. 44, 329, obs. Bruguière (holding that company for which designer worked, first as an employee and later as an independent contractor, was entitled to moral rights in the series of collective works to which the designer contributed). This moral right in the collective work as a whole does not affect the moral rights of individual authors in their contributions. These rights shall not be exercised so as to compete with the rights in the collective work as a whole. Thus, for example, authors may claim moral rights in their separate works contributed to a collective work, but the courts may limit the exercise of these rights by the need to preserve the overall harmony of the collective work as a whole (See *Cour*

collective works under French *droit d'auteur* is not as broad as similar concepts in other author's rights or copyright systems,[25] this is a significant exception. However, it is interesting to note that this devolution of moral rights to the publisher is not expressly stated in the law, and derives from the general terms of the French IP Code, which vests the author's rights, without distinction between economic and moral rights, in the publisher.[26] Courts and legal authors consequently concluded that moral rights in the collective work, as a whole, vest in the publisher, without much further justification.[27]

In any case, as matter of law, the moral rights granted to the publisher of the collective work are the moral rights of authors, and no specific regime is devised for legal persons.[28] Therefore, standard French rules as to perpetuity and unassignability should apply.[29] And in theory, the publisher could exercise such an incongruous (in a commercial context) moral right as the right of withdrawal from commerce.

However, it is important to note that case law on the subject is scarce.[30] And this is probably the main teaching of the law in this respect, in a country where moral rights are often litigated: they do not seem to be of practical use for publishers. In fact, it could be said that the main practical interest of this "devolution" of moral rights is to deprive individual authors from their exercise.

---

de cassation, civ. I, 8 October 1980, R.I.D.A. 1981, no. 108, 156; *Cour de cassation,* civ. I, 16 December 1986, R.I.D.A. 1987, no. 133, 183).

[25]   Typically, it does not cover works created by single employees, audiovisual works and certain forms of collaborative works.

[26]   Article L.113-5 provides: "A collective work shall be the property, unless proved otherwise, of the natural or legal person under whose name it has been disclosed. *The author's rights shall vest in such person*" (emphasis added). Before the Law of 1957, the category of collective works was instituted by case law, which considered the employer-publisher as "author" of the work. The transfer of moral rights was inferred from this characterization of the employer-publisher as author. For an historical review of the legal doctrine on point, see. C. Blaizot-Hazard, *Les droits de propriété intellectuelle des personnes publiques en droit français* (LGDJ 1991), p. 176 et seq.

[27]   In other terms, the principle of this protection is not justified by philosophical or theoretical reasons, and is best explained by the specifics of collective works under French law.

[28]   Legal authors tend to consider that the regime of the moral rights vested in the legal entities is different from that of authors, but there is no clear evidence of that in case law.

[29]   On the difficulties associated with the application of such rules to corporate entities, see J-M. Bruguière, in *Les grands arrêts de la propriété intellectuelle* (3rd ed, Dalloz, 2020), pp. 312–13 ("La personne morale, auteur"); N. Binctin, note under *Cour de cassation,* civ. I, 22 March 2012, Revue des sociétés (2012), p. 496.

[30]   In addition, the rare reported claims seem accessory to a claim based on copyright infringement, or even "opportunist", such as the claims raised by US producers in France in the famous *Asphalt Jungle* case in order to prevent the exercise by the heirs of film director John Huston of their moral right of integrity, infringed by the colourization of the film *Asphalt Jungle* and to its broadcasting on French television (*Turner Entertainment v. Huston (Asphalt Jungle)*, Paris Court of Appeal, 6 July 1989, *Cour de cassation*, 28 May 1991, noted in (1991) 4 Entertainment Law Review E-55. Versailles Court of Appeal, 19 December 1994, RIDA, April 1995, p. 389, note Kerever).

This broad exception of French law seems to be quite isolated.[31] The US Copyright Office's Report on moral rights of April 2019[32] mentions a similar situation where a protection of moral rights granted to legal persons is inferred from a situation in which the entire copyright in a work (or the "copyright", without an express exclusion of moral rights) is vested *ab initio* in a legal person.[33] However, the report does only mention one Indian case, the scope of which seems limited.[34]

Therefore, the relevance of these "exceptions" in judging whether or not to extend the protection of moral rights to legal persons seems limited at best.

Another approach to the protection of copyright owners takes the form of limited, pseudo-moral rights, granted to certain copyright owners in relation to certain types of uses of treatments of their works. An example of such a protection can be found in Germany and in Austria, in the case of the neighbouring right in the audiovisual recording. Section 94 of the German Copyright Act grants to the producers of such recordings "the right to prevent any distortion or shortening of the visual and sound record which may prejudice his legitimate interest therein". Article 38(2) of Austrian Author's right Act contains a provision to the same effect. This language is interesting as it departs from that used in relation to authors, notably by the reference to the "legitimate interest" of the film producer. The term of this "pseudo-moral rights", as A. Dietz put it,[35] is limited to 50 years running from fixation or publication or communication to the public, as the case may be. However, the German and Austrian Act are surprisingly silent on other aspects of the regime of this right. Here too, case law is rare, which could indicate that the right is not exercised in practice. The interesting aspect of this protection is that it seems to be devised as a substitute to unfair competition. This may have served as an example for the specific protection of the integrity of audiovisual media services consecrated, outside copyright law, by Directive 2018/1808 of 14 November 2018.

---

[31]   Within the European Union, Luxembourg grants authorship in the film to the film producer, without excluding moral rights (Law of 29 March 1972, Art. 27). There does not seem to be case law on point.

[32]   Authors, Attribution, and Integrity: Examining Moral Rights in the United States, A Report of the Register of Copyrights, April 2019.

[33]   "Another area of variation in international approaches to moral rights has to do with how the country's laws treat situations where a work is 'authored' by a corporation or has many 'authors' that all contribute a small piece to a larger whole. In some countries that have adopted copyright ownership rules similar to the work-for-hire doctrine in the United States, corporations are allowed to hold and assert moral rights in such works. For example, South Korea, Japan, and China all designate employers as the default legal author of works created by employees, including for some moral rights purposes, although they allow the parties to contract around this default. Indian courts have also recognized moral rights for corporations" (pp. 16–17).

[34]   *E Sholay Media & Entm't Private Ltd. v. Parag Sanghavi*, Delhi HC, 24 Aug 2015, CS (OS) 1892/2006, 20 (India): infringement of moral rights of a film producer under Section 57 of the Copyright Act, 1957; note, however, that the film producer is "author" of the cinematographic film under Section 2 of the Indian Act. Therefore, the solution does not apply to other copyright owners, including employers (see *Mannu Bhandari v. Kala Vikas Pictures (P) Ltd.* (AIR 1987 Delhi 13)).

[35]   See A. Dietz, Germany in International Copyright Law and Practice, L. Bently (gen. ed), Matthew Bender, annual, §9[1][C].

2. POSSIBLE EVOLUTIONS IN THE DIGITAL ENVIRONMENT

As mentioned, the digital revolution has raised legitimate concerns among copyright owners over certain forms of uses of their works which may occur along the distribution chain, such as the tempering with ownership identification, modifications of technical characteristic of works and advertising techniques. Part of these issues have been legislatively addressed through the protection against removal or alteration of digital rights-management information. But remaining issues, in particular in relation to advertising techniques and technical modification of signals, could justify an evolution of the legislation of point, in the form of a specific, additional, protection for copyright owners. We will address here two possibilities of improvement of the actual situation, in relation to the protection of ownership information associated to a work (2.1), and to the protection of the integrity of works (2.2).

2.1 A General Right to be Identified as Owner of a Work

Corporate entities and, more generally, copyright owners, have a specific, and legitimate interest in their identification as copyright owners: that of being identified as contact for inquiries as to authorization to exploit their works. The mere affixing of a trademark cannot fully satisfy this objective, as the mark does not necessarily identify the copyright owner. And the latter may wish to be more specific, especially if he does not hold all the rights in the work. In addition, the notice of ownership entails an underlying assertion of protection, and may have a dissuasive aspect on potential infringers. This notification also benefits the public in general, and potential re-users in particular.

This legitimate interest in being identified as copyright owner is evidenced in practice by the almost universal (and often erroneous, as far as US Law is concerned) voluntary inclusion of a copyright notice by copyright owner. Although one could claim that the copyright notice was once necessary for protection under local law or in foreign countries, the persistence of such practice cannot be explained by legal concerns anymore. Clearly, most copyright owners want to be identified as such, despite that they are not required by law to do it.

The importance of copyright ownership information has been reinforced with the development of digital uses of works, and was partly consecrated at the international level by the implementation of the regime of digital rights-management information. The definition of rights-management information in Article 12 of the World Intellectual property Organization Copyright Treaty (WCT)[36] includes: "information which identifies ... the owner of any right in the work". Within the European Union, Article 7(2) of Directive 2001/29/CE uses a similar

---

[36] "(1) Contracting Parties shall provide adequate and effective legal remedies against any person knowingly performing any of the following acts knowing, or with respect to civil remedies having reasonable grounds to know, that it will induce, enable, facilitate or conceal an infringement of any right covered by this Treaty or the Berne Convention: (i) to remove or alter any electronic rights management information without authority; (ii) to distribute, import for distribution, broadcast or communicate to the public, without authority, works or copies of works knowing that electronic rights management information has been removed or altered without authority. (2) As used in this Article, "rights management information" means information which identifies the work, the author of the work, the owner of any right in the work, or information about the terms and conditions of use of the work, and any numbers or codes that represent such information, when any of these items of information is attached to a copy of a work or appears in connection with the communication of a work to the public."

language. These certainly cover copyright notices. This mechanism does not create an obligation for the copyright owner to identify itself,[37] but consecrates his "right" to object to (or to consent to) removal of alteration of his notice of ownership. In national legislations, the protection scheme is implemented not as an exclusive right or moral right under copyright law, but through civil remedies, specific criminal sanctions or a combination of both.[38] This form of protection is technically acceptable: the incrimination is narrowly tailored to fit specific acts and is not dependent upon the appraisal of the interest of the copyright owner; it does not impose an obligation to mention the copyright owner if this mention is not included in the work; it is subject to (arguably) carefully defined exceptions; and it does not conflict with the moral rights of authors.

However, this mechanism has serious limitations, and fails to provide a sufficient protection to the public and private interest in the preservation of the identification of the copyright owner. Firstly, it is limited to "electronic rights-management information", leaving unprotected other types of ownership information. Although other rights-management information, such as "information about the terms and conditions of use of the work, and any numbers or codes that represent such information" are mainly relevant in a digital context, this is not the case for ownership information, which should be preserved whatever the media on or in which it is included, and the form of this inclusion. Secondly, and perhaps more importantly, the liability for removal or alteration of rights-management information is restricted to those persons who know or, with respect to civil remedies, have reasonable grounds to know, "that they induce, enable, facilitate or conceal" a copyright infringement.[39] Therefore, the mere removal or alteration of ownership information is not sanctionable in the absence of copyright infringement.

In this respect, the protection of copyright owners could be reinforced, so as to sanction, at the minimum, the voluntary removal of copyright ownership information in any media, irrespective of any copyright infringement of the copyright in the work. A way to do this would be to amend the prohibition of circumventing copyright management information, so as to prohibit the removal or alteration of such information on any media. The protection could also be extended to false attributions of ownership. Note that, under the model of false attribution of authorship, the latter prohibition could also be designed to cover false association, and possibly the use of the notice in relation to an altered work, thus allowing a copyright owner to object to certain forms of derogatory treatments of the work.[40] This would allow a codification, and a simplification, on the rules of unfair competition on point. And could afford to dispense with an additional, specific, protection of the integrity of works.

---

[37]   It is unclear whether this would amount to imposing a formality which is not permitted under the Berne Convention, as this obligation is not an element of copyright law or a condition for protection.

[38]   For the implementation within the EU, see L. Guibault, G. Westkamp and Th. Rieber-Mohn, Study on the Implementation and Effect in Member States' Laws of Directive 2001/29/EC on the Harmonisation of Certain Aspects of Copyright and Related Rights in the Information Society, Report to the European Commission, DG Internal Market, February 2007, Part II. The corresponding provisions of the US DMCA provide both criminal sanctions and civil remedies.

[39]   See also Art. 7 of directive EU 2001/29.

[40]   By analogy with the indirect protection against modifications of works afforded under passing off and similar doctrines in common law jurisdictions.

2.2   A Limited Right to Preserve the Physical Integrity of the Work

As far as moral rights are concerned, the "integrity" of a copyright work can be affected in many ways, including, in many legal systems, through its association with another work or through derogatory or disparaging presentations.[41] For the reasons already exposed, copyright owners do not need an additional protection under a specific moral right against such forms of uses. The same is true for those treatments that can be assimilated to adaptations, such as "fan art", parodies or some user- or AI-generated contents, which are better addressed under copyright or under unfair competition rules.[42]

However, copyright owners, and more generally, authorized professional users, have a legitimate interest in the preservation of the integrity, in the strict sense of physical integrity ("signal integrity" in telecommunications terms), of the works they license and exploit, both for editorial and commercial reasons. In this respect, technological developments have created new risks, through the possibility of insertion of virtual or personalized advertising, modifications of formats, unwanted and uncontrolled exploitations ("piggybacking"), etc. These may affect not only the reputation of the owners/producers, and the value of their works, but also their editorial liability. And some of these treatments would not amount to copyright infringement or tortious liability, or could prove difficult to control under these causes of action. For example, in the American case *Paramount Pictures Corp. v. VBS*,[43] Paramount failed to obtain a preliminary injunction against a company which placed advertisements on the blank section of videotapes of its films rented or sold by retailers. Interestingly, the plaintiff failed on two alternate grounds for the protection of moral rights in the US, false representation under the Lanham Act and infringement of the right to make derivative works.[44] In the same way, the unauthorized insert of (or association with) advertisements does not necessarily constitute a copyright infringement or a civil cause of action. In such cases, the granting of a specific protection of the integrity of a work could be implemented. This idea is reinforced by the fact that there is a strong public interest in the preservation of the integrity of certain works, or at least in the information of the public about the modifications made to a work. Therefore, some kind of prohibition of modifications of a work or of a signal, without the consent of the copyright

---

[41]   In many jurisdictions the right of integrity is not restricted to modifications or alterations of the work, and extends to misleading, disparaging, or derogatory presentations of the work. A mere context for presentation might be sufficient to constitute infringement. For illustrations, see e.g., within the European Union, P. Kamina, *Film Copyright in the European Union* (2nd ed, Cambridge University Press, 2016), p. 378.

[42]   In this respect, it is interesting to note that the debate on transformative art is almost exclusively addressed, on the part of copyright owners, in economic terms (exclusive rights and exceptions). See e.g., White Paper on Remixes, First Sale, and Statutory Damages, US Department of Commerce Internet Policy Task Force, 2016; L. A. Heymann, "Everything is Transformative: Fair Use and Reader Response", 31 Colum. J.L. & Arts 445 (2008); W. M. Landes, Copyright, Borrowed Images and Appropriation Art: An Economic Approach, in Towse Ruth (ed.), *Copyright in the Cultural Industries* (Edward Elgar, 2002), pp. 8–31; R. A. Reese, "Transformativeness and the Derivative Work Right", 31 Colum. J.L. & Arts 467 (2008); P. Samuelson, "Unbundling Fair Uses", 77 Fordham L. Rev. (2009), pp. 2537–621. The same remark applies to parodies, it being specified that even in those countries like France where moral rights are not subject to statutory exceptions, it is generally understood that a parody falling into the exception to the exclusive economic rights would not be held as infringing moral rights.

[43]   11 October 1989, 724 F. Supp. 808 (Kansas District Court).

[44]   See Comment by E. Logeais in [1990] Ent. Law Rev. 184. Comp. with para. 124 and 125.

owner, might prove useful, especially in those jurisdictions when authors have limited moral rights, or waive them in practice. These concerns probably explain the specific moral rights of the producer of film recordings implemented in Germany and Austria, already described.

This idea was consecrated within the European Union, not through an intellectual property instrument, but through media regulation. Directive 2018/1808 of 14 November 2018 on audiovisual media services has introduced for the first time a provision aiming at preserving the integrity of audiovisual media services (an expression which covers, under the Directive, television and on-demand video services). Article 7b of this Directive provides:

> Member States shall take appropriate and proportionate measures to ensure that audiovisual media services provided by media service providers are not, without the explicit consent of those providers, overlaid for commercial purposes or modified.
>
>   For the purposes of this Article, Member States shall specify the regulatory details, including exceptions, notably in relation to safeguarding the legitimate interests of users while taking into account the legitimate interests of the media service providers that originally provided the audiovisual media services.[45]

This provision, aimed at protecting the integrity of the audiovisual media services (the broadcast signals) and, by way of consequence, of the underlying works (but only, for the latter, insofar as the treatment is made through a treatment of the signal), is expressly justified by the need to protect the editorial responsibility of media service providers and the audiovisual value chain.[46] An interesting aspect of the Directive is that the protection is not dependent upon a protection of the signal or of the underlying works under copyright law. Also, the Directive provides a rather detailed and well-devised list of exceptions, which do not require the consent of the media service provider.[47]

It remains to be seen how this mechanism has been implemented and will be enforced by EU Member States.[48] But it seems to offer an interesting example of protection of the integrity of works against some types of derogatory treatments, made by distributors or platforms. This solution could easily be extended to radio and musical services, under the same supervision of broadcasting authorities. It could also serve as a model for a pseudo-moral right of copyright owner (as opposed to media service providers), strictly limited to "signal integrity", with dedicated exceptions. Certain aspects of this extended protection would need to be clarified,

---

[45]   In addition, the Directive provides that "Measures to protect the integrity of programmes and audiovisual media services should be imposed where they are necessary to meet general interest objectives clearly defined by Member States in accordance with Union law. Such measures should impose proportionate obligations on undertakings in the interest of legitimate public policy considerations."

[46]   Directive 2018/1808, Recital 26.

[47]   Which cover, inter alia: overlays solely initiated or authorized by the recipient of the service for private use, such as overlays resulting from services for individual communications, do not require the consent of the media service provider; control elements of any user interface necessary for the operation of the device or programme navigation, such as volume bars, search functions, navigation menus or lists of channels; legitimate overlays, such as warning information, general public interest information, subtitles or commercial communications overlays provided by the media service provider, and data compression techniques which reduce the size of a data file and other techniques to adapt a service to the distribution means, such as resolution and coding, without any modification of the content (ibid).

[48]   In the United Kingdom, corresponding obligations have been introduced in Part 5 of the Audiovisual Media Services Regulations 2020 SI 2020/106, which provides for a penalty scheme and an enforcement by the broadcasting authority, the OFCOM.

and in particular its articulation with the moral right of integrity of authors.[49] However, it is submitted that, as far as signal integrity is concerned, the interests of copyright owners and authors should converge. Which would be an added justification for this protection.

---

[49]   The question being whether the consent given by the service provider or copyright owner prevails over the right of integrity of individual authors. The answer would be negative in most legal systems, but in certain jurisdictions the author cannot exercise his or her moral rights against treatments done by the employer or with its consent (UK CDPA 1988, s. 82(2): "The right conferred by section 80 (right to object to derogatory treatment of work) does not apply to anything done in relation to such a work by or with the authority of the copyright owner … .")

13. Moral rights in cases involving multiple ownership

Tatiana Synodinou

1. INTRODUCTION

Copyright law is dominated by the iconic figure of the romantic author who, working in isolation, expresses their creativity in a unique way by creating works, the control and the fate of which are defined by the creator's will and impulses. Indeed, "the sole author is in a way the splendid, ideal author of copyright law; it is the author as we knew him before the advent of modern complications, the real or fantasy author in the service of the spirit of the arts".[1] Even when the creative process takes a collective form, the individuals involved may still think of themselves and their work in terms of the romantic image of artistic creation.[2] From an ownership perspective, one person holding one exclusive intellectual property (IP) right is the paradigm case of the classical, Western idea of the right to property.[3]

The overwhelming individualistic nature of copyright law does not conjugate well with a plurality of authors. Works deriving from the creative involvement of a plurality of authors can qualify, depending on the jurisdiction, as: works of joint authorship, collective works and compound (composite works). Since there is no harmonized international or EU[4] definition of jointly authored (collaborative), composite (compound) and collective works, the chapter will focus on some fundamental elements common to these types of works, as they appear in several jurisdictions. Multiple authorship and/or ownership are not extensively regulated by copyright laws and the regime of collective enjoyment and administration of rights is often governed by contract. Classic civil law common property regimes that have been designed for tangible property often apply to works deriving from a plurality of authors.

In this context, in a case of jointly authored (collaborative) works and of composite (compound) works, multiple authors are often considered as tenants in common, and therefore they enjoy undivided property rights to the whole of the work.[5]

---

[1]   Benoît Humblot, "The Creator's Independence" (2004) 199 *RIDA* 6.
[2]   Jostein Gripsrud, "Creativity and the Sense of Collective Ownership in Theatre and Popular Music" in Mireille van Eechoud (ed.), *The Work of Authorship* (Amsterdam University Press 2014) 215.
[3]   Alexander Peukert, "Individual, Multiple and Collective Ownership of IPR, Which Impact on Exclusivity?" in Annette Kur & Vytautas Mizaras (eds), *The Structure of Intellectual Property Law* (Edward Elgar 2011) 195–225, available at SSRN: https://ssrn.com/abstract=1563990.
[4]   As stated by Van Eechoud et al., "the European *acquis* does not define derivative works (translations, adaptations), anonymous works, and collaborative works (collective works, joint works, etc.). These aspects are intertwined with the issue of initial ownership and authorship, and by implication with moral rights, both of which are issues that are not generally addressed in the acquis". See: Mireille van Eechoud, P. Bernt Hugenholtz, Stef van Gompel, Lucie Guibault, and Natali Helberger, *Harmonizing European Copyright Law, The Challenges of Better Lawmaking* (Kluwer Law International 2009) 65.
[5]   See for instance, Article L. 113-3 para 1 of the French Intellectual Property Code (*Code de la propriété intellectuelle* – CPI). For UK copyright law see: *Powell v. Head*, (1879) 12 ChD 686, 689–90:

While the application of common property regimes is mostly relevant with regard to the enjoyment of the economic rights conferred by copyright law, their application to authors' moral rights is highly problematic. The personalist and subjective nature of the moral right, coupled with the classic dichotomy between monism and dualism,[6] significantly interfere with the delicate question of the enjoyment and exercise of the moral rights of joint authors. Specifically, the application by analogy of the rule of non-division indicates that one fundamental principle prevails: unanimity. Consequently, as a principle, every author needs to give their consent for every act which interferes with the moral right held over the jointly owned work and every author is authorized to enforce the moral right against anyone (co-author, licensee or user).

It is argued in this chapter that the application of the principle of unanimity poses significant difficulties. These difficulties have increased in the digital era, where new forms of large-scale collaboration schemes have emerged in various contexts. Large-scale digital creative collaboration can take many forms, which have in common the contribution of various authors through digital means and the merger of these contributions into a commonly produced intellectual output which is often freely accessible and lacks commercial profit (such as Wikipedia pages or collaborative non-commercial Internet fanfiction pages,[7] even if there are significant differences between these two collaborative cultures[8]).

Apart from works of joint authorship, plural contributions are also a striking feature of collective works. However, in the case of collective works,[9] the situation is different, as the

---

"where there are two proprietors, the one cannot represent without the consent of the other proprietor". Joint authors are also considered as tenants in common in US copyright law According to 17 U.S.C. § 201(a), "authors of a joint work are co-owners of copyright in the work". See also: *Carter v. Bailey*, 64 Me. 458, 463–4 (1874).

[6]   See: Graham Dutfield and Uma Suthersanen, *Dutfield and Suthersanen on Global Intellectual Property Law* (2nd edn, Edward Elgar 2020) 129.

[7]   The fanfiction community is collaborative and communication between different "fandoms" (communities of fans of original works) facilitates exposure to new creative text. See: M. McCardle. "Fan fiction, fandom and fanfare: What's all the fuss? " (2003) 9(2) *Journal of Science and Technology Law* 1–37. The collaboration can take many forms, such as posting a contribution publicly for other writers to make comments on (writers get feedback from readers that helps them to craft the character and plot through posts or via online forums when the writer directly is communicating with other members) or sharing some writing with other writers in order to work together on manuscripts, take turns writing chapters, or directly edit one another's work. The collaboration practices vary (beta reading, feedback on in-progress work, fanon formation) and the idea that the fanfiction writer or vidder does not produce work alone but with the assistance from the community is relatively uncontroversial. For Stanfill "the model of limited common property is quite useful for fandom: everybody in the community has shared access to everybody else's stories, vids, meta, and other work, but – in part as a result of histories of stigma – there is often a protective attitude in relation to outsiders". "limited common property is not very alienable because, unlike standard property, no one person owns it, such that nobody can really sell it off, and particularly not for individual gain". See: Mel Stanfill, "Fandom Public, Commons" (2013)14 *Transformative Works and Cultures*, https://doi.org/10.3983/twc.2013.0530.

[8]   Even if they are both collaborative, Wikipedia has established standard community-developed policies and norms that have to be followed by the Wikipedia contributors. Internet fanfiction websites are characterized by a variety of policies and offer divergent community engagement options.

[9]   There is no EU or international uniform definition of collective works. In general, a collective work would mean a work that contains the works of several authors created, assembled, harmonized and published under the direction and supervison of a person (the promoter). Regarding copyright ownership, the collective work will often be considered as the property of the promoter under whose name it has

initiator of the work holds the moral right over the work, in parallel with the moral rights held by the multiple contributors over their individual contributions.[10] The situation is not, however, any less complex, because although the courts have affirmed the limitation of the individual moral rights attached to the contribution in favour of the need for their harmonious co-existence within the whole, it remains unclear as to whether individual contributors can still enforce their moral rights against third persons or, alternatively, whether the initiator is the only party who can enforce the moral right over the collective work against third parties.

The aim of this chapter is to analyse, from a comparative viewpoint, the enjoyment and exercise of the moral rights of multiple authors and/or copyright owners in the specific cases of jointly authored works, collective works and composite (compound) works, and also to catalogue and discuss various ways to circumvent the principle of unanimity. It will be demonstrated in the first part of this chapter that the classic co-ownership rules, which have been devised using the model of tangible property and regulate the administration of property as an economic value, provide only an elliptical regulation of the co-existence of multiple moral rights over – and possible conflicts between – multiple rightholders, which often leads to complex situations. This lack of proper regulation has been amplified in the digital era, where variant new forms of large-scale creative collaboration schemes have emerged. For better or worse, no help is available from European copyright law, which, despite recognizing moral rights as part of the specific subject matter of copyright law,[11] still retains its initial position of not intervening in the sphere of moral rights.

---

been disclosed. See for instance: L113-5 of the French Intellectual Property Code (Code de la propriété intellectuelle – CPI); Czech Copyright Act, Article 59(1): "A collective work is a work that is created by more than one author on the initiative and under the management of a natural person or legal person, and is made public under that person's name, provided that the contributions involved in such work are not capable of independent use"; Article 7 of the Italian copyright law "Law No. 633 of April 22, 1941, for the Protection of Copyright and Neighboring Rights": collective works are formed by "the assembling of works or parts of works possessing the character of a self-contained creation resulting from selection and coordination with a specific literary, scientific, didactic, religious, political or artistic aim, such as encyclopaedias, dictionaries, anthologies, magazines and newspapers"; Article 8 of the Spanish Intellectual Property Act: "A work shall be deemed a collective work if it is created on the initiative and under the direction of an individual or legal person, who edits it and publishes it under his name, and where it consists of the combination of contributions by various authors whose personal contributions are so integrated in the single, autonomous creation for which they have been conceived that it is not possible to ascribe to any one of them a separate right in the whole work so created. In the absence of agreement to the contrary, the rights in the collective work shall vest in the person who publishes it and discloses it in his name". Article 5 of the Dutch Copyright Law states that "if a literary, scientific or artistic work consists of separate works by two or more persons, the person under whose guidance and supervision the work as a whole has been made or, if there is no such person, the compiler of the various works, shall be deemed the author of the whole work, without prejudice to the copyright in each of the works separately". See: Christina Angelopoulos, The Myth of European Term Harmonisation: 27 Public Domains for the 27 Member States, Amsterdam Law School Legal Studies Research Paper No. 2012-82, Institute for Information Law Research Paper No. 2012-48.

[10]   See for French law: French Supreme Court, 1st civil chamber [Cour Cass, 1ère ch. civ.]. 22 March 2012 Cour de cassation. See: Arnaud Latil, Droits moraux et oeuvres collectives: une clarification opportune, *Dalloz*, [2012], 1246, hal-02191756.

[11]   Joined cases C-92/92 and C-326/92, Judgment of 20 October 1993, para 20, ECLI:EU:C:1993:847, *Phil Collins v. Imtrat Handelsgesellschaft mbH* and *Patricia Im- und Export Verwaltungsgesellschaft mbH* and *Leif Emanuel Kraul v. EMI Electrola GmbH*.

The second part of this chapter analyses how copyright law has succeeded in limiting, via several legal mechanisms, the power imbalances in enforcing moral rights in joint authorship works. While the general method of balancing interests has been favoured by the German courts,[12] the inherent limitations of moral rights are also enshrined in the Berne Convention. Depending on the national tradition, contract law also plays a role in the "circumvention" of moral rights. The ontological barrier between collective works and derivative works is characterized by a number of uncertainties, and it could also be argued that applying the legal framework of derivative works offers some solutions. Finally, it will be demonstrated that the concept of fairness in its various expressions (such as the theory of abuse of rights[13] or "estoppel" in common law[14]) can also be applied in order to resolve potential conflicts arising around the exercise of moral rights in cases involving a multiplicity of authors.

2.   THE UNANIMITY RULE

This section will explore the principle of unanimity (2.1) by analysing plural creation in the context of jointly authored, composite (compound) and collective works. Then, using a critical approach, it will discuss whether this principle is compatible with new forms of multi-authored creations in the digital era (2.2).

2.1   The Unanimity Rule

The Berne Convention is silent on the status of works created by multiple authors. The only express reference to this category is found in Article 7*bis* of Berne, where, as regards the term of protection of jointly-authored works, it is vaguely stated that for works of joint authorship, the term of protection shall be calculated starting from the death of the last surviving author. A similar provision is found in Article 1(2) of the EU Term Directive.[15]

These provisions appear to support the idea that joint authors are co-owners of the work, given that the death of all the authors is taken into account for the purpose of defining the term of protection. Similarly, Article 2(2) of the Software Directive provides that "in respect of a computer program created by a group of natural persons jointly, the exclusive rights shall be owned jointly".[16] Apart from these scarce and disparate provisions, no further hint is given as regards the administration of rights between copyright co-owners. This is also confirmed by

---

[12]   Agnès Lucas-Schloetter, "Pour une exercice équilibré du droit moral ou le droit moral et la balance d'intérêts" in G. Schricker, C. Heath and P. Ganea (eds), *Urheberrecht gestern –heute –morgen, Festschrift für Adolf Dietz* (Beck 2001) 127–42, 128.

[13]   In favour of the application of the theory even if the author is alive: 1st Civil Chamber [*Civ. 1ère*], 14 May 1991. Against: 1st Civil Chamber [*Civ. 1ère*], 5 June 1984 in *Dalloz* [1985]. IR. 312, obs. Colombet; F. Pollaud-Dulian, "Abus de droit et droit moral" in *Dalloz* [1993] chron 97.

[14]   For moral rights from a comparative perspective: Gillian Davies and Kevin Garnett (eds), *Moral rights* (Sweet & Maxwell/Thomson Reuters 2016). See also: Christophe Caron, *Abus de droit et droit d'auteur* (Litec 1998).

[15]   Directive 2006/116/EC of the European Parliament and of the Council of 12 December 2006 on the term of protection of copyright and certain related rights (codified version) OJ L 372, 27.12.2006, 12–18.

[16]   Directive 2009/24/EC of the European Parliament and of the Council of 23 April 2009 on the legal protection of computer programs (Codified version) OJ L 111, 5.5.2009, 16–22.

Recital 14 of the Term Directive, which provides that "the question of authorship of the whole or a part of a work is a question of fact which the national courts may have to decide".

While most jurisdictions refer to co-ownership or joint authorship, neither international copyright law nor European copyright law regulate the internal structure of such groups of copyright co-owners.[17] National copyright laws have often explicitly stipulated that a jointly authored work is owned indivisibly by the co-authors, either via the application of tenancy in common[18] or via other mechanisms, such as the German *Gesamthandsgemeinschaft* (civil partnership).[19] The application of tenancy in common results in the enjoyment of copyright law indivisibly by all co-authors. In the absence of any contractual arrangements made between the co-owners, this in turn would often appear to necessitate a unanimous decision made by all co-owners in respect of every act of exploitation of the work[20] and of every act which interferes with the moral rights over the jointly authored work.

---

[17]   Peukert, above note 3.

[18]   Article L. 113-3 para 1 of the French Intellectual Property Code (*Code de la propriété intellectuelle* – CPI) provides that a collaborative work is the common property of the co-authors, while Article L. 113-3 para 2 provides that the co-authors shall exercise their rights with a unanimous decision. According to Article 10 of the Italian Copyright Act, "1. If the work has been created with the indistinguishable and inseparable contributions of a plurality of persons, copyright vests commonly in all co-authors. 2. The undivided parts are presumed of equal value, except where there is a written agreement to the contrary. 3. Provisions on tenancy in common are applicable. Moral rights may be invoked by each co-author and the work may not be published, if unpublished, nor may it be modified or used differently from the first publication without the agreement of all co-authors. Nonetheless, in case of unjustified refusal of one or more co-authors, publication, modification, or new usage of the work may be authorized by the judicial authority, and accordingly used". For Italian copyright law, see: Thomas Margoni and Mark Perry, "Ownership in Complex Authorship: A Comparative Study of Joint Works in Copyright Law" (26 January 2012), [2012] 34(1) *European Intellectual Property Review* 22–32, available at SSRN: https://ssrn.com/abstract=1992610 or http://dx.doi.org/10.2139/ssrn.1992610. In UK copyright law, it is also accepted that co-owners are considered as tenants in common and this was understood to necessitate consent on the part of all co-owners to exploitation. See: Elena Cooper, "Joint Authorship in Comparative Perspective: *Levy v. Rutley* and Divergence between the UK and USA" (2005) 62(2) *Journal of the Copyright Society of the USA* 245, 271, with reference to *Powell v. Head*, (1879) 12 ChD 686, 689–90: "where there are two proprietors, the one cannot represent without the consent of the other proprietor". Joint authors are also considered as tenants in common in US copyright law. However, as noted by Cooper, in the US a co-owner is free to exploit the work without the other co-owners' consent. See: Cooper, ibid., with reference to *Carter v. Bailey,* 64 Me. 458, 463–4 (1874).

[19]   In German copyright law, joint creation of a work leads to a so-called *Gesamthandsgemeinschaft* (civil partnership) and there are no distinct assets in the copyright as such, but only one rightholder, composed of several partners. They will, in that sense, become directors of a company in the form of a civil partnership under the Civil Code. In the absence of any agreement to the contrary, the effect of joint authorship is to create a legal entity sharing undivided interests in the intellectual property right – i.e. each party holds a nominal equal share, divided simply per head (*Bruchteilsgemeinschaft*. See: *Peukert*, above note 3. According to Article 718 of the German Civil Code (BGB), the contributions of the partners and the items acquired for the partnership as a result of management are joint assets of the partners (partnership assets). Furthermore, Article 719 of the BGB provides that a partner may not dispose of his/her share in partnership assets and in the individual items that form part of partnership assets, and thus he/she is not entitled to demand division. Regarding the administration of rights, Article 709(1) provides that "the partners are jointly entitled to manage the business of the partnership; for each transaction the approval of all partners is required", while Article 709(2) provides that it can be concluded under the partnership agreement that a majority of votes is required for a decision to be made.

[20]   For joint works, see: Lionel Bently in Dreier/Hugenholtz (eds) *Concise European Copyright Law* (Wolters Kluwer 2006), 218. However, Art. 9 of the Polish Copyright Act states that in cases of joint

However, applying this principle to moral rights involves a number of complications. The principle of unanimity in the context of moral rights is composed of two different elements. First, the principle of unanimity means it is impossible to embark on an activity that would otherwise infringe a moral right without the consent of all of the co-authors concerned. Moral rights must be exercised in concert with the co-authors. A joint author must consult the co-authors before modifying the work or communicating the work to the public for the first time, unless the modification falls under any copyright exceptions or limitations.[21]

The indivisibility of rights also has another significant consequence: the right of each co-owner to initiate court proceedings to protect the undivided work in the event of an infringement committed either by a co-author or a third party.[22] Regarding moral rights, this means that each author has the discretionary right to individually defend the moral rights over the work without needing to consult the co-authors[23] or to defend these rights even against the co-authors,[24] a situation which is justified by the eminently personal nature of the moral right.[25] In this context, *unus pro omnibus* (one for all) is applied, and the reference to "unanimity" is probably ill-named. This individual power is, however, subject to judicial control, since the involvement in a collaborative activity necessarily results in a balancing of interests.[26]

A plurality of authors is also found in the cases of collective works and composite (compound) works, which are recognized and regulated as particular categories of creation in certain jurisdictions. Even though there are national divergences in the definition of collective works, a fundamental element of this type of creation lies in the fact that there is a fusion of multiple authorial contributions within a new work (the collective work), which is created at the initiative of a person in whom both the economic and moral rights over the collective work are vested.[27] The co-existence of multiple authorial contributions which merge into a whole

---

works, each creator may exercise the copyright in the part of the work created by him or her if that part has an intrinsic value, without prejudice to the rights of the other joint creators. A similar provision is contained in Art. 30(3) of the Estonian Copyright Act. See: Van Eechoud et al., above note 4, 241.

[21]   For French law, see André Lucas, Agnès Lucas-Schloetter and Carine Bernault, *Traité de la propriété littéraire et artistique* (5th edn, Lexis Nexis, 2017) 220, no. 198.

[22]   Van Eechoud et al., above note 4, 239.

[23]   Pierre-Yves Gautier, *Propriété littéraire et artistique* (11th edn, PUF 2019) 766.

[24]   See: French Supreme Court [*Cour Cass.*], 15 February 2005, "Communication Commerce Electronique" [2005] no. 61.

[25]   As noted by Lucas, Lucas-Schloetter and Bernault, French case law has admitted that each co-author can initiate proceedings for infringement of the moral right of a jointly-authored work. See: Lucas, Lucas-Schloetter, Bernault, above note 21, 222, no. 199, with reference to a series of court decisions which affirmed this possibility.

[26]   See for France: Paris Appeal Court, 1st Civil Chamber [*CA Paris, 1ére ch. civ.*], 18 April 1976 in *Dalloz* [1957] 108.

[27]   According to Article L.113-2 of the French Intellectual Property Code (*Code de la propriété intellectuelle* – CPI) the Collective work (*oeuvre collective*) shall mean "a work created at the initiative of a natural or legal person who edits it, publishes it and discloses it under his/her direction and name and in which the personal contributions of the various authors who participated in its production are merged in the overall work for which they were conceived, without it being possible to attribute to each author a separate right in the work as created". French case law has affirmed that the moral right over the work is also vested in the legal person who is the author of a collective work: French Supreme Court, 1st Civil Chamber [*Cour Cass, 1ère ch. civ.*], 22 March 2012, appeal [*pourvoi*] no. 11-10132 in *Propriétés Intellectuelles*, July 2012, no. 44, 329, obs. J.-M. Bruguiere. See: Article 7 para 2 of the Greek Copyright Law (Law 2121/1993), which provides that "The term 'collective work' shall designate any work created through the independent contribution of several authors acting under the intellectual direction and coor-

does not completely erase the rights of the authors of these contributions, and the same applies to moral rights. This means that, in principle, the authors of contributions can exercise their moral rights regarding their own contributions (but not the collective work as a whole) in parallel with the moral right of the initiator, who is considered as the author of the work.

Another subcategory of multiple rights or owners concerns the unilateral combination or adaptation of pre-existing subject matter,[28] which has been significantly facilitated by digital technology. Digital compilations or derivative works, such as computer programs, databases, multimedia works or memes, challenge the classic individualistic perception of moral rights, since in cases involving a significant plurality of contributions, it is possible that the name of the author cannot be linked to the work, and in cases involving adaptation of the work or its placing into a different context, the right of integrity may be significantly undermined. In cases of incorporation of separate or pre-existing works into a new "composite" (compound) work, without the collaboration of the author(s) of distinct and/or pre-existing work(s), the situation is much more nuanced, and is amplified by the sometimes subtle delineation of derivative works from jointly authored works and the variant conceptions of "composite work" in national copyright laws.[29]

Depending on the national rules governing "composite works", the work is either considered as belonging to all the authors of the new work, who are then considered as tenants in common,[30] or as belonging only to the person(s) who produced the new work.[31] However, the

---

dination of one natural person. That natural person shall be the initial right holder of the economic right and the moral right in the collective work. Each author of a contribution shall be the initial right holder of the economic right and the moral right in his/her own contribution, provided that that contribution is capable of separate exploitation". Estonian copyright law provides that copyright in a collective work shall belong to the person on whose initiative and under whose management the work was created and under whose name it was published, unless otherwise prescribed by contract (Estonian Copyright Act, Section 31). In Italian copyright law, authorship is deemed to reside in the person or entity undertaking the organization and completion of a collective work, without prejudice to any claims of the contributors in their individual contributions. See: Articles 3 and 7 of Law for Protection of Copyright and Neighbouring Rights (no. 633 of 1941). Article 8 of the Spanish Intellectual Property Act provides that in case of collective works "In the absence of agreement to the contrary, the rights in the collective work shall vest in the person who publishes it and discloses it in his name". For Dutch copyright law. See: Article 5.1 of the Copyright Act 1912.

28   Peukert, above note 3.
29   For France, see: French Supreme Court, 1st Civil Chamber [*Cour Cass, 1ère ch. civ.*], 15 May 2002, appeal [*pourvoi*] no. 99-21090 in *Bull.* [2002] I, no. 130, 100.
30   Article 7 para 2 of the Greek Copyright Law (Law 2121/1993) provides that "the term 'composite work' shall designate a work which is composed of parts created separately. The authors of all of the parts shall be the initial co-right holders of the rights in the composite work, and each author shall be the exclusive initial holder of the rights of the part of the composite work that he has created, provided that that part is capable of separate exploitation." In Italian copyright law, according to Margoni and Perry, the category of composite works is characterized by the fact that contributions are distinguishable, although not separable, such as with regards to the texts and images of a comic. In the view of these authors, a general rule of tenancy in common may be envisioned for the whole category of composite works. See: Margoni and Perry, above note 18.
31   See French copyright law, where according to Article L 113-4 of the French Intellectual Property Code (*Code de la propriété intellectuelle* – CPI), a composite (derivative) work is the property of the person who created it, subject to the rights of the authors of any pre-existing works. According to Danish copyright law (Consolidated Act on Copyright 2014, Act no. 1144 of 23 October 2014, section 5), "A person who, by combining works or parts of works, creates a composite literary or artistic work, shall

permission of the author of the distinct and/or pre-existing work is necessary for any incorporation of this work into the new work, while the exploitation of the composite work must not exceed the contractual framework of the permission granted by the author of the original work.[32] Regarding the exercise of moral rights, applying a tenancy in common regime, which would in general mean that the work is the common property of the multiple authors and is owned by them in notional shares or fractions of the same or different sizes,[33] raises the same issues as in the case of joint authorship, since multiple co-authors enjoy in common the moral right over the work. In the opposite scenario, when copyright over the composite work is owned by the person who produced the new (derivative) work, the moral right of the author(s) of the separate or pre-existing work(s) may be invoked against the author of the composite work, such as when the modification of the pre-existing work is prejudicial to the right of integrity. Furthermore, in cases involving adaptation, the author of the adapted work retains her right to authorship and must be mentioned as such.[34]

The distinction between a jointly authored and a derivative work is crucial since, as previously mentioned, in cases of joint authorship, tenancy in common applies to moral rights. On the other hand, in the case of a composite/derivative work, the moral right is often vested solely in the author of the new work, subject to the rights enjoyed by the author(s) of the pre-existing work(s). In practice, this means that the new work shall be created with the prior authorization of the first author, or without it but falling under one of the exceptions, such parody. The safeguarding of the first author's rights will also mean that the first author will, in some jurisdictions, be able to influence or veto how their work will appear in the new work by exercising the right of integrity.

Certainly, the distinction between jointly authored and compound (composite) works is a delicate one in cases of successive authorial contributions. National copyright laws have often accepted that joint authors can contribute consecutively to the work. In the UK, in the case of *Beckingham v. Hodgens*,[35] the court recognized as a joint author the person who added the introduction to the music of a song. Similarly, in *Brown v. MCASSO Music Productions Ltd*,[36] the person who amended the lyrics to a rap song, which were initially written by another person for a TV commercial, was held to be a joint author of the song. The UK

---

have copyright therein, but the right shall be without prejudice to the rights in the individual works". Article 9 of the Spanish Copyright Act ("Law on Intellectual Property, regularising, clarifying and harmonising the legal provisions in force on the matter" approved by means of the Royal Legislative Decree 1/1996, of 12 April 1996) provides that a new work that incorporates a pre-existing work without the collaboration of the author of the latter shall be considered a composite work, subject to the rights accruing to that author and subject also to the requirement of his/her permission being granted.

[32]   The criterion of intention is expressly provided for in US copyright law for jointly authored works. According to 17 U.S.C. Section 101, "A 'joint work' is a work prepared by two or more authors with the intention that their contributions be merged into inseparable or interdependent parts of a unitary whole."

[33]   For the definition in Germany and UK, see: Andreas Rahmatian, "A Comparison of German Moveable Property Law and English Personal Property Law, in *German Law Review* [2010] https://germanlawarchive.iuscomp.org/?p=340.

[34]   For German law, see: BGH 8 May 2002, *Stadtbahnfahrzeug*: [2002] in *GRUR* 799.

[35]   *Beckingham v. Hodgens* [2003] EWCA Civ 143; [2003] EMLR 18. Specifically, the introduction was not considered to be a separate contribution, since it was found that the introduction depended closely on the rest of the song and would lose its meaning and value without the rest of the song.

[36]   *Brown v. MCASSO Music Productions Ltd* [2005] EWCA Civ 1546; [2006] EMLR 26.

case of *Brighton v. Jones*[37] is illustrative of the intricacies of qualifying work consisting of consecutive authorial interventions by different persons as a jointly authored or a derivative work. Specifically, the court refers to two apparently contradictory principles regarding joint authorship: the collaboration has to be on the creation of the work (implicitly, there is no creation if the work is already completed), but at the same time the collaboration does not need to consist in a joint physical realization of the work.[38] In French law, the express recognition by the French legislator that audiovisual and cinematographic works are works of joint authorship is evidence that the law has acknowledged, at least in the specific case of these works, that joint authorship can derive from persons who collaborate successively on works. In this context, in 2013 the French *Cour de cassation* (Supreme Court) recognized the authors of songs for children, which were incorporated into an audiovisual work, as joint authors of the audiovisual work.[39] Furthermore, it is possible for joint authors to share tasks, in the sense that one intervenes after the other. In this context, it was held in France that the person who makes linguistic corrections to the entirety of a dictionary is a joint author of that work.[40] National case law, therefore, has somehow decided that the place and time of the collaboration between joint authors do not matter. This locational and chronological "neutrality" of co-creation is certainly something not new, but it has been accentuated by the advent of digital communication tools. It has even become the mainstream form of co-creation in certain fields, such as in the collaborative creative schemes of Wikipedia, Internet fanfiction literature or in open-source communities. However, there is a qualitative constraint. Time and place are neutral and are not important insofar as a core, a framework or perspective of cooperation and a shared plan exist. In this context, successive contributions could seemingly hint at the absence of any collaboration.[41] A requirement for "collaboration" in jointly authored works has been either expressly or implicitly applied to national copyright laws, even though – while it appears that "collaboration" requires a "common design" – the degree and intensity of this criterion diverge significantly. On the one hand, some jurisdictions appear to embrace a loose perception of the "common design", such as in the UK,[42] where joint authorship is recognized, even in the absence of a common intention to produce a work of joint authorship.[43] It is noteworthy that the approach taken by the UK courts on this issue is different from other common law jurisdictions such as the US, where intention to create is a fundamental prerequisite of joint authorship.[44] Conversely, in other jurisdictions, the concept of "collaboration" has been construed by courts as implying a stronger requirement for "concerted creative effort undertaken

---

[37]   *Brighton and Another v. Jones* [2004] EWHC 1157 (Ch); [2005] FSR 16.

[38]   The court held that the contribution of a joint author has to be "significant", although not necessarily of the same magnitude as the contributions of the other joint author(s); The contribution must be a contribution to the creation of the work (rather than, for example, to its interpretation); and if the creator's words are physically written down by someone else on the creator's behalf, this will not prevent the creator from being a joint author. For the last point, see also the French case of *Renoir – Guino*: French Supreme Court [*Cour Cass.*] 1, 13 November 1973 in *Dalloz* [1974] Jurisp. 533, note C. Colombet.

[39]   See also Nanterre Court of First Instance [TGI Nanterre], 6 March 1991.

[40]   Paris Appeal Court [*CA Paris*], 27 February 1985 in *Dalloz* [1986]. IR. 181, obs. Colombet.

[41]   Lucas, Lucas-Schloetter, Bernault, above note 21, 215.

[42]   For the criterion in the UK, see: *Levy v. Rutley* (1871) LR 6 CP 523 (Court of Common Pleas) (Keating J, 529).

[43]   *Beckingham v. Hodgens* [2003] EWCA Civ 143; [2003] EMLR 18.

[44]   The Copyright Act defines a joint work as "a work prepared by two or more authors with the intention that their contributions be merged into inseparable or interdependent parts of a unitary whole."

jointly by several authors"[45] and for "common inspiration" (*communauté d'inspiration*[46]) or "mutual control" (*contrôle mutuel*) between the joint authors.[47] Consequently, it is a matter of subtle interpretation, on the basis of the principles governing this issue in national copyright law and on the application of the "collaboration"/common design/intention requirements in each specific context of consecutive co-creation, as to whether the enjoyment of moral rights will take place under a regime of tenancy in common or whether, on the other hand, moral rights will be vested only in one person, with the rights of the authors of pre-existing works being reserved. The question is highly complex, since in some jurisdictions the strongly individualistic nature of moral rights could also influence how the tenancy in common regime will be applied by the courts.

Although the concept of collaborative art creation is inherent to the creation itself, technology now allows the creation of new forms of expression online, where there may be countless contributors but in which collaboration can be said to exist at only the most abstract level,[48] and the qualification of such kind of "productions" as jointly authored, collective or a series of derivative works presents significant challenges. For instance, new forms of creations consisting of multiple authorial contributions, such as Internet non-commercial fanfiction pages and Wikipedia pages, would not be easy to qualify as works of joint authorship in France[49] or in other jurisdictions where a strict criterion of "common inspiration" or "direct collaboration" between co-authors needs to be met. However, a loosely conceived criterion of "collaboration" as common design or the will to contribute to a shared plan or goal might be met, since the entire structure of such works (existence of discussion pages, existence of community culture and norms) supports the existence of a common design, goal or collaboration amongst contributors.[50]

Furthermore, the application or otherwise of the principle of unanimity should be analysed not only via the various existing and often fragmented legal regimes related to the plurality of authors (jointly authored works, collective works and composite works), but also separately with regard to each moral right.

The Berne Convention recognizes only two moral rights: the right of paternity and the right of respect of the integrity of the work.[51] Both rights embody the link between the work and

---

[45]   Paul Goldstein, *International Copyright: Principles, Law, and Practice* (3rd edn, Oxford University Press 2012) 208; *Le Brun v. SA Braesheather*, French Supreme Court, 1st Civil Chamber [*Cour Cass, 1ère ch. civ.*], 18 October 1994, 164 in *RIDA* 304, 308 (1995).

[46]   French Supreme Court, 1st Civil Chamber [*Cour Cass, 1ère ch. civ.*], 21 March 2018, no. 17-14.728 *Sté Ecriture Communication c / Sté Productions Alléluia* and JurisData no. 2018-004135, "Communication Commerce Electronique" [2018] comm. 33, note Caron.

[47]   Lucas, Lucas-Schloetter, Bernault, above note 21, 214, no. 189.

[48]   Sam Ricketson, "Reflections on authorship and the meaning of a 'work' in Australian and Singapore copyright law", [2012] 24 *Singapore Academy of Law Journal* 792–831, 826.

[49]   Christophe Caron, "L'œuvre libre confrontée à quelques aspects du droit commun des biens et du droit d'auteur", "Communication Commerce Electronique"/ no. 7-8, July–August 2018, p. 12, 10–14.

[50]   Daniela Simone, "Copyright or Copyleft? Wikipedia as a Turning Point for Authorship" [2014] 25(1) *Kings Law Journal* 102, available at SSRN: https://ssrn.com/abstract=2330766 or http://dx.doi .org/10.2139/ssrn.2330766, 15, 16.

[51]   Article 6*bis* of the Berne Convention: "(1) Independently of the author's economic rights, and even after the transfer of the said rights, the author shall have the right to claim authorship of the work and to object to any distortion, mutilation or other modification of, or other derogatory action in relation to, the said work, which would be prejudicial to his honor or reputation."

the personality of its creator, and therefore fit well with the unanimity rule. This means that, in principle, any use of the work needs to mention the names of all the authors, but obviously, every author may opt out of exercising this right. The right of the integrity of the work acts *ab initio* as a negative obligation: an extra-contractual obligation not to infringe the integrity of the work. Each author possesses the right to protect the integrity of the whole work, separately and individually. There are several jurisprudential applications of this principle. In this context, the French Supreme Court has affirmed that the person who wrote the lyrics of a song can legitimately exercise his moral right of integrity to stop the music of the song being used by the composer in an advertisement.[52] Conversely, this means that for any use of the work that would interfere with the integrity of the work, the unanimous approval of the joint authors is required.

It could be argued that this controversial principle of unanimity extends to all moral rights, and not only the two moral rights stated in the Berne Convention. Indeed, many countries have established additional moral rights, such as the right of disclosure (*droit de divulgation*) or the right of withdrawal. The exercise of these moral rights is linked to jurisdiction-specific elements and it goes beyond the scope of this chapter to provide a detailed analysis of these rights, which might greatly vary depending on the jurisdiction. Nevertheless, it can be ascertained that the application of these rights might significantly impact the use of the work as whole and, consequently, the rights of other co-authors. Indeed, it is questionable whether other moral rights can be invoked individually by each co-author or whether all the joint authors would first need to be consulted. For instance, in Italian copyright law, the exercise of the right of withdrawal and the right to first unedited publication (*droit de divulgation*) can be activated only with the unanimous approval of the co-authors, since these rights are strongly linked to collaborative creation and their individual activation would significantly influence the usage made by other co-authors, and in some cases, render it impossible.[53] Similarly, in French copyright law, the consent of all the joint authors is needed to exercise the *droit de divulgation*.[54]

The right of access, which is the right of the author to request access to the work when it is materialized in a physical object,[55] is very specific in nature and its exercise is not impacted in case of a plurality of authors. Access to the work must be considered as a personal right enjoyed by each author and could be exercised vis-à-vis any person who is the holder of the tangible object incorporating the work.

---

[52]   French Supreme Court, 1st Civil Chamber [*Cour Cass, 1ère ch. civ.*], 15 February 2005 in *RIDA* 3/2005, 415.

[53]   Margoni and Perry, above note 18.

[54]   Lucas, Lucas-Schloetter, Bernault, above note 21, 220, no. 198; Pierre-Yves Gautier, *Propriété littéraire et artistique* (LGDJ 2019), 701.

[55]   The moral right of access is established in a number of EU Member States: France (Article L.111-3 of the Intellectual Property Code (CPI)), Germany (Article 25 of the Copyright Law), Czech Republic (12 para 3 of the Copyright Act), Greece (Article 4 (1)d of Law 2121/1993), Hungary (Article 69.1 of the Copyright Act), Norway (Section 49 para 2 of the Copyright Act), Finland (Section 52a of the Copyright Act), Spain (Article 14.7 of the Intellectual Property Law).

2.2 The Difficulties of Applying the Unanimity Rule and the Emergence of Massive Collaborative Works

Technological change has inevitably impacted the concept of co-creation. In some instances, collaborative authorship has become the norm. For example, creating a software program or video game usually involves teamwork. At European level, these challenges were pinpointed as early as 1995, in the European Commission's Green Paper on Copyright and Related Rights in the Information Society, which states that:

> The traditional picture of the author as a craftsman working more or less in isolation and using wholly original materials is contradicted by new forms of creation. The new products and services are increasingly the outcome of a process in which a great many people have taken part – their individual contributions often difficult to identify – and in which several different techniques have been used ...[56]

Even though collaborative creativity is not new, advances in digital and communications technology have made it significantly easier for people to work together and have enabled massive collaboration projects to flourish: Wikipedia, creative crowd-writing, open-source software, crowdsourcing of designs, films, etc. Apart from the sense of community spirit shared by the numerous collaborators or contributors, these projects are often based on practices and commons governance rules (which could be considered as disruptive from a classic copyright law perspective) and adherence to community-developed policies and norms, the possibility of anonymity, and constant changes made without direct consultation with other contributors but under the terms and conditions of use.

Exercising the moral rights of multiple co-authors or multiple contributions presents significant difficulties. For instance, in the case of creation of wikis, several questions arise, such as the possibility of waiving the right to object to distortions and mutilations in the case of a wiki over which a multiplicity of authors has editorial rights or the extent to which the right of paternity applies; this is strongly dependent on the variant circumstances of the wiki's creation, either as the product of either a single, named individual or of a single but unnamed individual or of a multiplicity of named or unnamed individuals.[57]

Similarly, in open-source software projects such as Linux and Apache, each contributor can use and further modify the software by adding subject matter that is potentially protected by copyright, while they rely on the permission granted in the open-source licence by all previous contributors, who permit every subsequent contributor to join them as co-contributors.[58] In other words, the licensing question exerts a substantial influence over the exercise of moral rights. There are some key characteristics differentiating open-source software development from traditional coordination of a team-developed software program: "self-identification for roles and tasks; geographically dispersed development groups; and partial merger of the sometimes traditionally separate design, programming, and support functions".[59] Even if moral

---

[56] European Commission, Green Paper on copyright and related rights in the Information Society, Brussels, 19.07.1995 COM(95) 382 final 95, 25.

[57] Jeremy Phillips, "Authorship, Ownership, Wikiship: Copyright in the Twenty-first Century" [2008] 3(12) *Journal of Intellectual Property Law & Practice* 788, 795.

[58] Greg R. Vetter, "The Collaborative Integrity of Open-Source Software", University of Houston Law Center no. 2004-A-11, available at SSRN: https://ssrn.com/abstract=585921, 623.

[59] Ibid. 626.

rights in software are often attenuated due to the inherently functional nature of the software,[60] their potential application is at odds with the structure and goals of open-source projects. Unless their contribution to the code is so minor that it could easily be deleted from the project, hypothetically, each programmer could individually claim that the group's modifications, or even merely the software's use for a purpose they disapprove of (such as when the software is used for disseminating hate speech or in the engineering process for producing nuclear weapons), violates their right of integrity in the software. Such a claim is not compatible with the inherently evolutionary nature of software, as it would obviously have disruptive effects on the developer community associated with the project[61] and would impede the process of efficiently developing new and better versions of existing software.[62] Classic moral rights philosophy and rules were not designed to handle the realities of the software industry. This was already true as regards "traditional software development" and it is more obvious where collaborative authorship may extend to tens, hundreds or even thousands of programmers, each working on specific routines or sub-routines in the final creation.[63]

Accepting the hypothesis that large-scale collaborative intellectual outputs involving multiple creative contributors are not authorless[64] and despite the conundrum of the legal qualification of each collaborative work (jointly-authored, composite, derivative, collective, compilation/database), which is heavily dependent on the modalities and norms of each creative project, the a priori application of a regime of indivisible ownership regarding enjoyment of the moral rights of multiple contributors or the parallel co-existence of multiple moral rights (rights held by the initiator or author of the composite/derivative work and rights held by contributors over their individual contributions) is problematic.

Massive collaborative in the form of intellectual outputs which entail the simultaneous and/or successive participation of numerous contributors, differ substantially from classic joint creation. Participation in the creative process is often a collective engagement in the model of an informal "union" (akin to a "partnership"), which is characterized by its own ethics, practices and attitudes, and serves a variety of specific purposes and values. Furthermore, apart from the specific activities involved in the creative process, it is unclear how much of each contributor's personality is reflected in the final work.[65] These particular circumstances justify limitations placed on the individualistic exercise of moral rights which, depending on the jurisdiction, may be achieved via various legal mechanisms (waiver, contractual limitation, good faith-based restrictions, abuse of rights). Such mechanisms are already applicable in the traditional contexts of co-creation or multiple creation (films, songs, etc.), where a series of principles aimed at establishing a harmonious co-existence of the multiple interests in the work have been either established by legislation or affirmed by case law.

---

[60]   See, for instance, in UK copyright law, where moral rights are denied to authors of computer programs (CDPA Sections 79(2), 81(2)).

[61]   Vetter, above note 58, 665–6.

[62]   Yonatan Even, "The Right of Integrity in Software: An Economic Analysis", [2005] 22 *Santa Clara High Tech. L.J.* 219. Available at: http://digitalcommons.law.scu.edu/chtlj/vol22/iss2/2, 249.

[63]   Ibid. 247.

[64]   See: C. Sunstein, *Infotopia: How Many Minds Produce Knowledge?* (Oxford University Press 2006), 153, where it is suggested that the concept of authorship cannot be applied in Wikipedia,

[65]   Even, above note 62.

3. CIRCUMVENTING THE UNANIMITY RULE

Various mechanisms can be found that are either intended to circumvent and/or result in circumventing the principle of unanimity, in the case of collaborative works. First, it should be emphasized that the exercise of moral rights was never intended to be absolute: a number of inherent limitations exist, which apply even more strongly in the case of a plurality of authors (3.1). Furthermore, a plurality of authors means that the creation of a specific relationship which, depending on the legal system, may translate into contractual obligations preventing an inflexible application of the unanimity rule (3.2). Finally, the chapter argues that the concept of fairness in its variant forms (theory of abuse of rights, estoppel) constitutes the best approach in dealing with an unjustifiable application of the unanimity rule (3.3).

3.1 Inherent Limitations on Moral Rights

The phenomenon of a plurality of authors is not new in itself. What is new is the contemporary magnitude of collaborative creation and multiple authorial contributions. Some flexibility in the application of moral rights has traditionally been accepted, depending on the type of the work and the modes of its exploitation.[66] National copyright laws have introduced several legal mechanisms to solve possible conflicts regarding the exercise of the moral rights of multiple contributors or co-authors.

Regarding collective works, national case law has generally admitted severe limitations to the contributors' moral rights, mainly that the moral rights of multiple contributors over their identifiable contributions are subject to the "natural" limitation of the necessary harmonization of the work as a whole,[67] while in some instances it has been admitted by the courts that the promoter of the work holds both the economic and the moral right over the work.[68] A distinctive feature of the collective work is a limitation of the freedom of contributors in favour of the initiator,[69] which necessarily impacts the exercise of moral rights. In this context, the plurality of contributors and the aim of the collective work, which is to gather these multiple contributions together in a balanced and coherent way, attenuate the moral rights of contributors. This inherent limitation mainly concerns the right of integrity, since the rightholder over the collective work can make any changes which are necessary, either to the creation for the first harmonized version of the work or for updated versions. This does not, however, mean that the authors' moral rights held by multiple contributors are neutralized. The rightholder can update and develop the collective work, whether in terms of its external structure or by modifying the texts of the contributions themselves, provided that these modifications are necessary for the harmonized co-existence of the multiple contributions as parts of the whole. Even though this will generally be easy to prove, it cannot be completely excluded. While the

---

[66] Actes du Congrès d'Anvers de l'ALAI, 1993, 560.

[67] Lucas, Lucas-Schloetter, Bernault, above note 21, 247, no. 227.

[68] French Supreme Court, 1st civil chamber[*Cour Cass, 1ère ch. civ.*]. 22 March 2012 *Cour de cassation*.

[69] Jean Cedras, "La qualification des oeuvres collectives dans la jurisprudence actuelle" in (1995) 2 *Revue Juridique de l'Ouest* 133–47, 134, with reference to the decision of the French Supreme Court [*Cour de cassation*] in the case *Centre nautique de Glénans*, French Supreme Court, 1st Civil Chamber [*Cour Cass, 1ère ch. civ.*], 1 July 1970 in *Dalloz* [1970], 769.

concept of the collective work itself presupposes a merger of the multiple contributions in the whole, the freedom of the promoter to modify the contributions will also depend on the special circumstances of the creation of collective works and on the degree of individualization and the autonomy of each contribution. In this context, if the contributions have been created by closely following the promoter's specific instructions, there might be no room for claiming a violation of the right of integrity of the contributors. Furthermore, the right of paternity can still be invoked by the contributor, at least when the authorial contribution is identifiable,[70] unless the rightholder deletes the contribution from the collective work.

Regarding collaborative works, while as a general principle every collaborator has the right to be mentioned as a co-author,[71] exercising the right of paternity is often subject to limitations when it is not technically or practically possible[72] to list all of the authors' names due to the specific type of communication or exploitation of the work involved.[73] As a result, anyone who engages in commercial exploitation of the work may, under certain conditions, omit the reference to an author. Such a waiver of this specific expression of the paternity right may even result from the practices that exist in a specific branch of activity and have been tacitly agreed.[74] Certainly, an inquiry will be made into how this internal balancing/limiting process takes place. The underlying idea is that, under this internal limitation, for the person who commercially exploits the work, exercising the right of paternity acts in practice like an obligation to act reasonably. This would imply that anyone who engages in commercial exploitation of the work must do whatever is "fair" (and proportionate) in order to respect the author's right of paternity.

The right of disclosure (*droit de divulgation*) is not recognized in the Berne Convention. However, primarily in civil law countries, this is affirmed as one of the author's fundamental moral rights. Traditionally, the right of disclosure is also subject to a number of limitations, the most prominent of them being that it is exhausted after the first publication of the work.[75] The right of disclosure therefore occupies a very specific position in copyright law. It is a sort of "mother right" governing the other rights of the author,[76] since it acts as the preamble to exploitation of the work, and consequently has a strategic role.[77] An orthodox application

---

[70]   See: Paris Court of First Instance, 3rd Civil Chamber [*Tribunal de grande instance de Paris, chambre civile 3*], 7 November 2007, RG no. 07/06925. Available at: https://www.legifrance.gouv.fr/.

[71]   See for Germany: BGH 28 April 1972, *Im Rythmus der Jahrhunderte*: [1972] GRUR 713.

[72]   See for Greece: Multimember First Instance Court of Athens 3141/2015 in *Chronicles of Private Law* (Chronika Idiotikou Dikaiou) 2016/59.

[73]   See Athens Court of Appeal 6520/2008, which held that the author's name must always be mentioned in the way imposed by the type of the work and of its presentation to the public, while customs and practices must be followed, unless regulated otherwise by contract.

[74]   As noted by Lucas-Schloetter, after the seminal decision of the German Federal Court in the case of *Namensnennungsrecht des Architekte* (BGH 16 June 1994: [1995] GRUR 671; [1996] IIC 130), German courts now require not only proof of the existence of the practice invoked by the person who commercially exploits the work, but also its inclusion in the contract between the author and the person who commercially exploits the work. See Agnès Lucas-Schloetter, "Le droit moral en Allemagne" [2013] 25(1) *Cahiers de propriété intellectuelle* 47.

[75]   For the exhaustion of the right in national copyright laws, see for instance: Adolf Dietz and Alexander Peukert, "Chapter 14, Germany" in Davies and Garnett (eds), above note 14, 472.

[76]   Ibid.

[77]   See: Branka Marusic, "Author's Right to Choose: Right of Divulgation in the Online Digital Single Market of the EU" in T. Synodinou, C. Jougleux, P. Markou, and T. Prastitou (eds), *EU Internet law in the Digital Era* (Springer 2019), 137.

of the principle of unanimity of all co-authors for disclosure could therefore lead to a neutralization of the rights enjoyed by the other co-authors if one or more authors objects to the first disclosure of the work to the public. In this context, limitations to this principle are also recognized, though in variant and very diverse forms. In France, it has been recognized that judicial intervention is permitted in order to remove the obstacle of a lack of unanimity.[78] In Germany, in cases involving multiple authors, such as that of a cinematographic work, it has been held that a member of the creative team may not exercise this right in bad faith to obstruct exploitation of the work.[79] Furthermore, special provisions may exist, such as in the case of audiovisual works. Specific mention should be made in this respect of Article 45d of the Dutch Copyright Act, which provides that co-authors of a cinematographic work are deemed to have assigned to the film producer the right to decide to make the film available to the public.[80]

Regarding the right of withdrawal, which is used very restrictively, recognized only in certain countries[81] and seldom used in practice,[82] there is insufficient case law to deduce any common jurisprudential tendencies.[83] In France, it has been held that individual exercising of the right of withdrawal by one of the co-authors, also activates the indemnification rule provided for by Article L.121–4 of the Code de la propriété intellectuelle (CPI), and that the co-author must therefore also indemnify the other co-authors for any prejudice that withdrawal of the work might cause them.[84] Specific limitations may be expressly provided for in specific categories of works, such as in the case of films in German copyright law where, according to Article 90 of the German Act on Copyright and Related Rights (*Urheberrechtsgesetz*) ("UrhG"), application of the right is largely excluded in the film sector, other than where the right to make a film has been granted but shooting of the film has not yet begun.[85]

Significant limitations are also acknowledged in the right of integrity in the case of multiple authorial contributions in the context of audiovisual or cinematographic works. In German law, Article 93 of the UrhG limits the right to integrity of authors and performers who have collaborated on an audiovisual work to cases of serious infringements (*gröbliche Entstellungen*) of their contribution or performance, though this principle was found to also be applicable regarding the moral right of the author of a work which has been adapted.[86] In French copyright law, the right of integrity of co-authors can be exercised only in respect

---

[78]   See, in France: French Supreme Court [*Cour Cass*], 24 November 1993.

[79]   Dietz and Peukert, above note 75, 473, with reference to the "*Dokumentarfilm Massaker*" decision by Cologne OLG (Court of appeal), 10 June 2005 GRUR-RR 2005, 337.

[80]   F. W. Grosheide, "Chapter 18, the Netherlands" in Davies and Garnett (eds), above note 14, 587.

[81]   Such a right is recognized, for example, in Belgium, France, Germany, India, Italy, Spain, and the countries of the Organisation Africaine de la Propriété Intellectuelle (OAPI). See: "Authors, Attribution, and Integrity: Examining Moral Rights in the United States, A Report of the Register of Copyrights", April 2019. Available at: https://www.copyright.gov/policy/moralrights/full-report.pdf.

[82]   Maria Mercedes Fraboni, "Chapter 13, France" in Davies and Garnett (eds), above note 14, 439.

[83]   For instance, as mentioned by Dietz and Peukert, in Germany no relevant case law has been reported since the introduction of the right by the copyright law 1965. See: Dietz and Peukert, above note 75, 475.

[84]   Bordeaux Appeal Court [*CA Bordeaux*], 24 May 1984 in *Dalloz* [1986], 181. In the case of French copyright law Lucas, Lucas-Schloetter and Bernault mention that it is likely that in practice, courts will be vigilant when a co-author of a collaborative work exercises this right individually. See Lucas, Lucas-Schloetter and Bernault, above note 21, 508.

[85]   Dietz and Peukert, above note 75, 475.

[86]   Munich Court of Appeal, 1 August 1985, *Die unendliche Geschichte*: [1986] GRUR 460.

of the completed audiovisual work,[87] which means that this right is temporarily paralysed.[88] Similarly, Cypriot copyright law provides that an author who authorizes the use of his work in a film or television broadcast may not object to any changes which are essential on technical grounds or for the purpose of commercial exploitation of the work.[89]

3.2   The Contractual Approach

The exercise of moral rights in the case of a plural creation is often regulated by contract. Contractual arrangements can either expressly restrict the moral right itself or can be interpreted in a way which restricts one or more moral rights implicitly, provided that this restriction is necessary for the performance of an exploitation contract. The degree and extent of contractual limitations to moral rights depends on the national law concerned. There is no consensus at international or European level regarding the possibility of a contractual waiver of moral rights, and as a result, there are variant approaches on this issue. In any case, the assignment must be distinguished from the waiver, since only the latter is compatible with the personal nature of moral rights. The commentary on the Berne Convention on this point clarifies that:

> [w]hile article 6bis does not specifically rule out transfers of moral rights, their assignment would arguably be inconsistent with the very nature of these rights, which are inherently personal to the author. Moreover, it might seem absurd to accommodate the transfer of "mutilation right", for example. But, in the language of the Convention, the author would not be transferring an affirmative right to mutilate, she would be conveying certain rights of action: to claim authorship, to object to any distortion, etc.[90]

However, even in the civil law tradition, which is more protective of moral rights than common law jurisdictions,[91] interference of contractual law with moral rights is generally recognized.

Contractual restrictions or waivers of moral rights in jurisdictions which are highly protective of moral rights are often recognized as an exception to a general rule of inalienability of

---

[87]   Article L. 121-5 of the French Intellectual Property Code (*Code de la propriété intellectuelle* – CPI) provides that an audiovisual work shall be deemed completed when the final version has been established by common accord between the director or, possibly, the joint authors, on the one hand, and the producer, on the other. However, according to the last paragraph of the same article, the authors' own rights, as defined in Article L.121-1, may be exercised by these authors only in respect of the completed audiovisual work.

[88]   Lucas, Lucas-Schloetter, Bernault, above note 21, 537, no. 639.

[89]   Article 7(4) of Law 59/1976.

[90]   S. Ricketson and J. C. Ginsburg (eds), *International Copyright and Neighbouring Rights: The Berne Convention and Beyond* Volume I (2nd edn, Oxford University Press 2006), 600.

[91]   In the UK, moral rights can be waived by instrument in writing and by informal waiver under general contract or estoppel law. See Section 87 of the Copyright, Designs and Patents Act (CDPA). Under US copyright law, moral rights which are recognized by Visual Artists' Rights Act (VARA) can be waived by the author in a written instrument, while in the case of a joint work created by two or more authors, a waiver of rights made by one author waives such rights for all authors. See: 17 U.S.C. Section 106A(e)(1). Moral rights can also be waived in Australia and Canada. See: Section 195 of the Australian Copyright Act 2000 and Section 12.1. 2 of the Canadian Copyright Act. For moral rights in Canada, see: Ysolde Gendreau, "Moral Rights" in G. H. Henderson (ed.), *Copyright and Confidential Information in Canada* (Carswell 1994) 161.

moral rights, and are subject to significant safeguards which aim to preserve the core of moral rights and to limit the possibility of a waiver only to specific and clear cases which are often justified by the need to execute contractual obligations regarding exploitation of the work. In this context, French case law has admitted a number of limitations to the principle of the inalienability of moral rights, by accepting waivers issued retrospectively, in full knowledge of the consequences,[92] while general blanket renunciations issued a priori (for future uses) are deemed to be void.[93] Similarly, in the German monist conception, Article 29 of the UrhG generally provides that the author's rights are inalienable *inter vivos*, while Article 29 Abs. 2 of the UrhG specifies that conventions on moral rights are prohibited. However, granting the moral rights necessary for the performance of the contract[94] and issuing a waiver[95] continue to be possible, and at the same time the renunciation of moral rights is circumscribed and restrictively interpreted according to the purpose of the contract.[96] As a result, specific and narrowly prescribed waivers of the individual moral rights of paternity and integrity would appear to be permissible, whereas a general waiver of an individual moral right in its entirety and in an unspecified manner will not have any legal effect.[97] Furthermore, Article 39(1) of the UrhG provides that the holder of a right of use of a work shall not be permitted to alter the work, its title or designation of authorship (paternity), unless otherwise agreed, while in some instances the author's consent can be implicit.[98] A waiver of moral rights is also possible in other EU jurisdictions,[99] even if its modalities and its extent present significant variations.

The contractual limitation of moral rights might in some instances concern not the right itself, but the way this right will be exercised or enforced. An interesting example of the influence of a plurality of authors on the individual defence of moral rights can be found in Australian copyright law, where in the case of films, it is especially provided that the authors

---

[92]　Fraboni, above note 82, 444.

[93]　Lucas, Lucas-Schloetter, Bernault, above note 21, 482, no. 545.

[94]　For instance in German copyright law, as mentioned by Lucas-Schloetter, the author implicitly consents to disclosure when he/she grants a publisher the right to reproduce and distribute his/her completed work or when he/she sells the original of a graphic arts work. See: Lucas-Schloetter, above note 74, 42.

[95]　BGHZ 40, 326, 330 and BVerfG, 1 BvR 1520/00.

[96]　The *Bundesgerichtshof* has applied Sections 31. 4 and 5 of the *Urheberrechtsgesetz* (concerning economic rights), to renunciations relating to moral rights, thus restrictively interpreting the agreements according to their purpose. See: BGH GRUR 1997, 551, 554 – *Textdichtersammlung*.

[97]　Dietz and Peukert, above note 75, 478.

[98]　BGH, GRUR Int. 1995, 671, 673.

[99]　In Belgium, waivers can be granted only retrospectively, when the author knows the full extent of the modification and the acts permitted in relation to the work by contractual agreements are clear. See: Paul Torremans, "Belgium" in Davies and Garnett (eds), above note 14, 364. In Greek copyright law, a waiver is not possible (Article 14 of Law 2121/1993) but authors can consent to certain acts or omissions which would otherwise constitute an infringement of the moral right (Article 16 of Law 2121/1993). In Italian copyright law, moral rights are inalienable but an author who is aware of the alterations to the work and has given his/her consent cannot bring an action to prohibit these alterations or ask for the deletion of the altered work. See: Maria Mercedes Fraboni, "Italy" in Davies and Garnett (eds), above note 14, 557. In the Netherlands, contractually consenting to the waiver of certain moral rights (specifically of the right to be mentioned by name, the right to object to the publication of the work under someone else's name and the right to object to modifications of the work and its title) is possible, while a general contractual waiver of moral rights in favour of a third party is not possible. See: Grosheide, "The Netherlands" in Davies and Garnett (eds), above note 14, 595.

may conclude a co-authorship agreement, whereby they undertake not to exercise their right of integrity regarding the film in any way other than jointly with other co-authors.[100] In Greek copyright law, case law has admitted that it is possible to waive the enforcement of copyright law against a person, rather than the moral right itself, while this may also be implied by contract.[101]

Furthermore, apart from the express contractual regulation of the exercise of moral rights, the existence of a plurality of authors could generally imply that a contractual relationship of some sort is informally created between the multiple authors. For instance, in works of joint authorship, this would imply that their joint intention to act in collaboration, by following a common plan or design, results in a mutual understanding that each author is assigned a specific role, task or "duty" in the creative process, while these "duties" are performed on the condition that the co-author will also assume their own part in the creative process. It is, therefore, a matter of interpretation of this informal relationship to distinguish the existence of implicit clauses regarding the reasonable exercise of moral rights between the co-authors. Characteristically, the principle of good faith plays a major role in the legal traditions of civil law jurisdictions, but is also gradually emerging as an autonomous notion in common law countries.[102]

In some instances, good faith is expressly provided by law as a criterion for the assessment of a reasonable exercise of moral rights in plural creation. In this context, Article 8 of the UrhG provides, in relation to jointly authored works, that alterations to a jointly authored work shall be permissible only with the consent of the joint authors, but a joint author may not withhold his consent to publication, exploitation or alteration contrary to the principles of good faith. Good faith is also explicitly provided for as a legal basis for moral rights limitations in general in Article 39(2) of the UrhG, where it is stated that alterations to the work and its title, for which the author cannot withhold his consent based on the principles of good faith, shall be permissible.[103] The role of good faith in the possible limitation of exercising the author's moral right in a way incompatible with its nature and purpose, is also recognized in French copyright law, where it is generally accepted that the author cannot exercise her moral rights in an arbitrary and unjustifiable way that neutralizes contractual good faith.[104] Similarly, in Estonian copyright law, it might be a violation of the principle of good faith if an author has granted permission for a specific use and later exercises his moral rights to prohibit the use of his work (the prohibition of *venire contra factum proprium*).[105]

The contractual waiver of moral rights has taken on a different dimension in the digital era, especially in the context of successive multiple authorial contributions disseminated via open-content licences, such as Creative Commons. Massive digital collaborative projects, such as Wikipedia,[106] are often disseminated with a Creative Commons licence, whereby

---

[100]   Section 195 of the Australian Copyright Act 2000.

[101]   Irini Stamatoudi, "Greece" in Davies and Garnett (eds), above note 14, 503, citing: Athens Court of First Instance, Decision no. 276/2001 (available in the NOMOS database).

[102]   See: Ricketson and Ginsburg, above note 90, 60.

[103]   BGH 16 June 1994, BGHZ 126, 245, 248 = GRUR 1995, 671, 672ff.

[104]   Lucas, Lucas-Schloetter, Bernault, above note 21, 484, no. 549.

[105]   Aleksei Kelli, Thomas Hoffmann, Heiki Pisuke, Irene Kull, Liina Jents, and Carri Ginter, "The Exercise of Moral Rights by Non-Authors" (2014) 6 *Juridiskā zinātne/Law*, 108–25, 117.

[106]   The content of Wikipedia is often co-licensed under the Creative Commons Attribution Sharealike 3.0 Unported Licence and the GNU Free Documentation Licence. See: Simone, above note 50, 91.

the authors agree to enter a net of standardized contracts by accepting a series of limitations regarding the dissemination, re-use and modification of their contribution (work). The "Creative Commons" licensing model generally recognizes the minimum international *acquis* of moral rights protection (Article 6*bis* of the Berne Convention[107]) or excludes moral rights from its scope of application,[108] while the Creative Commons-published CC0, which is a tool used by authors to expressly waive all their rights, even moral ones, will be unenforceable in jurisdictions where the inalienability of moral rights is established.[109]

3.3   The "Fairness"/"Reasonableness" Approach

Fairness and reasonableness have been often recognized in national copyright laws as a source of control of the unjustified exercise of the author's moral rights, something which is of particular significance in cases of multiplicity of moral rights arising in the various contexts of plural creation. Whether conceived, depending on the jurisdiction, as a principle for balancing of interests,[110] as a theory of abuse of right,[111] as "a reasonableness defence"[112] or as an application of the principle of estoppel,[113] fairness in the exercise of moral rights is substantially based on the general notion of reasonableness and the principle of proportionality. Based on

---

[107]   The licences require the licensee to "not distort, mutilate, modify or take other derogatory action in relation to the Work which would be prejudicial to the Original Author's honour or reputation". See: A. Giannopoulou, "The Creative Commons Licences through Moral Rights Provisions in French Law" (2014) 28(1)*International Review of Law, Computers and Technology* Special Issue: BILETA, 60–80.

[108]   In the international/non-ported version of Creative Commons licences 4.0, moral rights are excluded from the scope of the licences.

[109]   Giannopoulou, above note 107.

[110]   As noted by Dietz and Peukert, the method of balancing interests in cases of alleged infringement of the moral right of integrity is a characteristic feature of German moral rights philosophy and practice. See: Dietz and Peukert, above note 75, 468.

[111]   This is the approach used in France and Belgium. See: Agnès Lucas-Schloetter, "Un conflit entre la théorie et la pratique? Le droit moral dans les différents régimes de droit d'auteur – Rapport général" in *Le droit Moral au 21ième Siècle*, ALAI Congress 2014, where it is stated that the responses to the ALAI questionnaire suggest that the question of abuse of moral rights is in fact a Franco-Belgian one and that the use of the concept of abuse actually appears to be superfluous in all systems where moral rights are circumscribed by the concept of reasonableness. For Spain, see: Supreme Court, Decision no. 458/2012. For a comparative perspective on the notion of abuse of rights, see: Loredana Tullio, "La valeur de la théorie de l'"abus de droit"" (2015) 4 *Revue juridique de l'Ouest* 7–49.

[112]   As noted by Bently et al., many legal systems subject the moral right of integrity to such a defence. See: L. Bently, B. Sherman, D. Gangjee, and P. Johnson, *Intellectual Property Law* (5th edn, Oxford University Press 2018), 301, with reference to Australia and Israel. Specifically for Australia, see: Copyright Act 1968, Section 195AS: no infringement of right of integrity of authorship if derogatory treatment or other action was reasonable; Section 195AR: no infringement of right of attribution of authorship if it was reasonable not to identify the author. For Israel, see: Copyright Act 2007, Section 50, which states as follows: "(b) Despite the provisions in sub-section (a), doing an act restricted by section 46(2) shall not constitute an infringement of the said moral right where the act was reasonable in the circumstances of the case. (c) In respect of sub-section (b), the court may take into consideration, *inter alia*, the following: (1) The character of the work in respect of which the act was done; (2) The nature of the act and its purpose; (3) That the work had been made by an employee in the course of his employment or pursuant to commission; (4) Customary behavior in a particular sector; (5) The need for doing the act versus the damage caused to the author by the act".

[113]   See Section 87(3) of the UK Copyright, Designs and Patents Act (CDPA), which states that general law of contract and estoppel applies to informal waiver of the moral right.

the concept of fairness, potential conflicts between the multiple authors and the person who engages in commercial exploitation of the work or between the multiple authors or contributors themselves, will be resolved by evaluating the "legitimacy" of each party's interest. In this context, as with contractual limitations of moral rights, good faith[114] will play a substantial role.

Variant expressions of "fairness" in the exercise of moral rights exist among national copyright laws. In Germany, the courts are competent to weigh the interests of the various parties, in order to determine whether the author is making a legitimate and justified use of their right, on the basis of various criteria, such as the degree of creativity, the functionality of the work, the seriousness of the infringement, the irreversible nature of the infringement, the context and circumstances of creation and the need for the modifications concerned.[115] In France, scholars are still divided on the issue of whether the theory of abuse of rights is also applicable in moral rights or whether the moral right in a specific case cannot be enforced because the conditions for its exercise are not met.[116] However, case law has explicitly affirmed the "abusive exercise" of moral rights when the author invokes their moral right for purely economic reasons,[117] when the exercise of the moral right by the author's heirs is found to be unjustified[118] or when balancing the interests of the author and the owner of the physical object embodying the work,[119] while in some instances, the author's unfair acts are held to be "abusive" not directly but on the grounds of contract law.[120] In Greek copyright law, the general principle of abuse of right as set out in Article 281 of the Civil Code also applies to the exercise of moral rights in cases where the exercise of such a right would be contrary to the protection of personality as the

---

[114]   See: Christophe Caron, "Droit moral et multimédia" [1995/2] (8) *Legicom* 44–53.

[115]   Lucas-Schloetter, above note 74, 52.

[116]   Lucas, Lucas-Schloetter, Bernault, above note 21, 483, no. 548. For French law, see: Frédéric Pollaud-Dulian, "Abus de droit et droit moral" in *Dalloz* [1993], chron 97; Christophe Caron, *Abus de droit et droit d'auteur* (Litec 1998).

[117]   See for instance: French Supreme Court, 1st Civil Chamber [*Cour Cass, 1ère ch. civ.*]. 14 May 2009, (1992) 1 *Revue Internationale du Droit d'Auteur* 273, note P. Sirinelli.

[118]   Paris Court of First Instance, 3rd Chamber [*TGI Paris, 3ème ch.*], 4e Sect., 9 February 2012. See also: Versailles Appeal Court, 1st Chamber [*CA Versailles, 1re ch.*], sect. 1, 16 February 2018, no. 15/08649: JurisData no. 2018-002014; LEPI June 2018, 3, obs. A. Lucas-Schloetter; *Propriétés Intellectuelles* 2018, no. 68, 60, obs. A. Lucas. The Court rejected the complaint based on the abusive nature of the refusal to disclose five posthumous works by a singer's heir, on the grounds that the latter worked for many years alongside his father and was therefore perfectly able to know his intentions regarding these works. For moral rights other than the right of disclosure, see: French Supreme Court, 1st Civil Chamber [*Cour Cass, 1ère ch. civ.*], 11 January 1989, Utrillo (JCP G 1989, II, 21378) note A. Lucas; Paris Appeal Court, 4th Chamber [*CA Paris, 4ème ch.*], 31 March 2004 in *RIDA* 4/2004, 292, note Pollaud-Dulian; Paris Court of First Instance, 3rd Chamber [*TGI Paris, 3ème ch.*], 20 June 2007, Koltès: in "Communication Commerce Electronique" [2007], comm. 116, note Caron.

[119]   For France, see: Case Brit Air, French Supreme Court, 1st Civil Chamber [*Cour Cass, 1ère ch. civ.*] 11 June 2009, "Communication Commerce Electronique" [2009], comm. 75, note C. Caron; Paris Appeal Court [*CA Paris*], 16 October 2013 in *Propriétés Intellectuelles,* January 2014, 70, note J.-M. Bruguière. For an overview, see: Bernard Vanbrabant, "Corpus mechanicum versus corpus mysticum: des conflits entre l'auteur d'une œuvre et le propriétaire du support" [2005] issue 4 *Revue de la Faculté de Droit de l'Université de Liège* 490–562, at 523.

[120]   See Seine Civil Court [*T. Civ. Seine*], 20 March 1895, Paris Appeal Court [*CA Paris*], 2 December 1897 in *Dalloz* [1898] 2. 465; French Supreme Court [*Cour Cass.*], 14 March 1900, Gaz. Pal. 1900. 1. 498 ("Whistler" case); Paris Appeal Court [*CA Paris*], 6 May 2010, Lang c/ Bernard Pascuito in *Propriétés Intellectuelles,* October 2010, 975, obs. A. Lucas.

ultimate purpose of the consecration of moral rights, if it would be contrary to good faith and morality, for example where the composer of a song invokes his moral right in order to prevent the other composer from exercising his economic rights in the song.[121] In Belgium, the notions of "abuse of rights" and "proportionality of the legitimate interests involved" have infiltrated copyright law as corrective mechanisms regarding situations which are legally correct, but are nevertheless perceived as unreasonable.[122] In Dutch copyright law, a specific reference to "reasonableness" for preventing an abusive exercise of moral rights is established in Article 25(1) of the Copyright Act.[123] Furthermore, the strong interconnection between the protection of moral rights and general private law principles favours a possibility of a general defence based on the notion of abuse of right[124] and the application of good faith as a balancing tool between the interests of the parties.[125] As noted in the Netherlands report in the questionnaire of the ALAI 2014 Congress:

> in certain experimental cases, where the courts might be in doubt as to the frontal application of the official doctrine of the "absolute" moral right, they are willing to apply general private law without a shade of hesitation – essentially to the same result as would have been reached under the heading of the authors' moral rights.[126]

A "fairness" approach in exercising moral rights in the context of multiple authorship will necessarily limit a self-centred and unjustified exercise of one author's right to the detriment of the moral and economic rights of other authors. Such an approach will be very valuable in cases of mass collaborative projects, where the large number of known or anonymous authors, and the specific context of creation (free editing, fairly small contributions, etc.) will be taken into consideration to ensure a balanced exercising of each moral right. In this context, the principle of unanimity would give way to a – best fit – principle of majority.

Nonetheless, this approach does not entail only positive outcomes. The concept of fairness is arguably uncertain and unknown in European copyright law. However, it is necessary to highlight the fact that the concept occupies a place both in private law and in international law.[127] In civil law systems, the principle remains an enduring element of private law and is closely linked to the civil wrong rules related to good faith. In common law countries, the references to this principle are certainly less explicit, although it has been argued that the list of torts represents at its essence what society finds to be an abuse of rights.[128] Furthermore, it has

---

[121] Stamatoudi, above note 101, 507, citing: Court of First Instance no. 36247/1999; Supreme Court no. 1009/2007.

[122] Marie-Christine Janssens, "Le droit moral en Belgique" [2013] 25(1) *Les Cahiers de propriété intellectuelle* 91–124, 106.

[123] According to this provision, "Even after assigning his copyright, the author of a work has the following rights: a. the right to oppose disclosure to the public of the work without reference to his name or other indication as author, unless such opposition would be unreasonable".

[124] Grosheide, "The Netherlands" in Davies and Garnett (eds), above note 14, 599.

[125] Antoon Quaedvlieg, "Le théâtre-laboratoire au laboratoire du droit: la liberté du metteur en scène" (2009) 21(3) *Les Cahiers de Propriété Intellectuelle* 673–93, 681.

[126] Report of the Netherlands in the questionnaire of the ALAI 2014 Congress, available at: http://aba -bva.be/IMG/pdf/pays-bas.pdf.

[127] Michael Byers, "Abuse of Rights: An Old Principle, A New Age" (2002) 47(2) *McGill Law Journal* 389, 2002 CanLIIDocs 48, https://canlii.ca/t/2b9k, retrieved on 2021-08-19.

[128] Ibid.

also been noted that common law concepts such as estoppel underly a concept ontologically similar to the concept of abuse of rights.[129]

4.   CONCLUSION

The journey into the practical use of moral rights in cases of a plurality of authors is not an easy one. The plurality of legal systems, of philosophical doctrines, of rights and situations are all obstacles to achieving a single unified approach to the question. There is also an intrinsic contradiction in the existence of moral rights on collaborative works: the "moral" as a general concept could be defined as general principles of right and wrong behaviour, and is therefore a substantial individual and subjective notion.

However, this journey is essential for a multiplicity of reasons. *Mutatis mutandis*, in today's world, there is extensive research into the creative process performed by artificial intelligence and its implications for copyright law. One hypothesis advanced by the doctrine is that the group of programmers and data processors qualify as authors. The next issue would be to find an effective way to manage their rights. Furthermore, as we have seen, on a theoretical level, the discussion on the exercise of moral rights in cases of plural creation, questions the nature of copyright law and how it is balanced. This chapter has described how it is possible to recognize a principle of unanimity as an implicit general principle of international copyright law, and at the same time, how this principle may sometimes be unfit to respond to modern challenges to the creative process.

Three main restrictions have been considered. One approach highlights the inherent limitations of moral rights, another uses a contractual approach to smooth the exercise of the principle of unanimity, while the third one is based on the concept of fairness. Although these three methods lead to similar results, they correspond to very distinct philosophies of copyright law. In the first one, copyright law is interpreted as an autonomous and independent field of law. In the contractual approach, the emphasis is placed on self-regulation and the individual freedom of the sector. In the last approach, there is an implicit acknowledgement that copyright law is founded on an equilibrium of interests and that these interests should be protected by reference to general principles of law. However, to discuss the legitimacy of one approach compared to the others would obviously go beyond the framework of chapter.

---

[129]   Joseph Perillo, "Abuse of Rights: A Pervasive Legal Concept", (1995) 27 *Pac. L. J.* 37. Available at: https://ir.lawnet.fordham.edu/faculty_scholarship/784, 52.

14. "Sharing is caring": Creative Commons, transformative culture, and moral rights protection

Alexandra Giannopoulou

1. INTRODUCTION TO MODERN MORAL RIGHTS PRACTICE

Copyright legislation produces a highly fragmented landscape on a global scale, and moral rights are no exception to that.[1] Modern moral rights application and enforcement on a transnational level, comes in many different shapes, shades and sizes.

Moral rights have long constituted a solid foundation on top of which the defence of authors' rights has been built. This holds true on a European level as well. For instance, the European Court of Justice (CJEU) has held that an author can use moral rights defence arguments to protect the legal monopolies offered by copyright rules. In the Spiegel online case (C-516/17), Advocate General (AG) Szpunar has pointed out that:

> the moral rights flowing from copyright, although they remain outside the scope of the harmonisation carried out by Directive 2001/29, must be taken into account in the interpretation of the provisions of that directive where the application of those provisions may adversely affect those rights.[2]

However, in the midst of an effort to harmonize copyright rules and to create a digital single market, moral rights stand apart.

Historically, moral rights presupposed (at least) one author, and most importantly, a completed, original work. Each author is considered to be able to benefit from these rights independently of how the work was created, and with how many other contributors. The radical shift towards large-scale plurality in creativity, brought by digitization, did not provide an easy path for moral rights towards their digital selves. French law for example, succinctly but substantially, addresses this type of creativity by creating a distinct legal category of "plural works".[3] These are essentially works created by more than one author, as a joint venture or as an assemblage of individual pieces contributed to a larger work. This distinction, even if subtle in theory, would make a difference in putting moral rights in practice. In the first case, the exercise of moral rights by the respective author(s) has to be in accordance with the group

---

[1]   According to an author, "no two countries that give serious thought to moral rights ever produce the same set of provisions": Elizabeth Adeney, "Defining the Shape of Australia's Moral Rights: A Review of the New Laws" (2001) 4 *Intellectual Property Quarterly* 291, 323.

[2]   Opinion of Advocate General Szpunar, 10 January 2019, Case C-516/17, *Spiegel Online GmbH v. Volker Beck*, ECLI:EU:C:2019:16, para 77.

[3]   The plural works (*oeuvres plurales*) are further distinguished in composite works (*oeuvres composites*), collaborative works (*oeuvres collaboratives*) and collective works (*œuvres collectives*).

interests while in the second, each author is free to exercise at will their moral rights on their independent contributions.

The application of an individualistic right carrying significant territorial ties, on the transnational scale of modern (digital) creativity, becomes rather challenging. The advent of the twenty-first century found copyright astounded by the growing need of the public to share, reuse and remix. At the same time, moral rights were regarded as contentious and restricting, even if empowering. Lacking more efficient regulatory tools, private ordering mechanisms were created to facilitate, organize and scale sharing of creative works. Contractual solutions such as those of Creative Commons represent such an approach, which has dominated the sharing collaborative creation field.

This chapter will explore the interaction between moral rights and transformative works, taking the example of Creative Commons licence use. We will first tackle the overall shortcomings of the interaction of moral rights with user-generated content. Then, we will take into consideration the available Creative Commons toolbox in order to examine moral rights compliance and possible ways forward.

2.   MORAL RIGHTS IN USER-GENERATED CONTENT

The public has been traditionally qualified by copyright as simply passive recipients of works. Today, the place of the public at large and of individual users has drastically shifted.[4] Their role in "consuming" culture becomes increasingly more active. Namely, a large part of this public engages in acts of creativity based on pre-existing works. The platform economy and social media incite users to participate in the creation process, and provide the technological tools to publish the products of their expression, online. This type of creativity has become the norm in digital creation.

The claim for the right to reuse protected works without the prior authorization of their respective authors has been at times recognized by courts, using either existing limitations and exceptions to copyright or fundamental rights approaches.[5] However, the reshuffling of author and work legal categorizations is leaving moral rights frameworks perplexed because of the lack of coordination between theory and practice. The conceptual framework in which moral rights have been conceived and developed breaks down with the expansion of user-generated or transformative works.

In civil law countries, the *raison d'être* of the introduction of moral rights appears to be the creation of rights inherent to the author, rights that ensure authorial control and that rebalance negotiating power between artists and third parties. These rights were borne during an era of expansive copyright protections that were responding to the multiple challenges that art was facing. However, the presumption that the author would be considered the weaker party of a negotiated agreement and that regulatory action would ensure the balancing of contractual copyright agreements is taking on a new shape in the last years. While this imbalance is at

---

[4]   Tatiana Eleni Synodinou, "Lawfulness for Users in European Copyright Law: Acquis and Perspectives" (2019) 10 *JIPITEC* 20, para 1.

[5]   Martin Senftleben., "User-Generated Content – Towards a New Use Privilege in EU Copyright Law" in Tanya Aplin (ed.), *Research Handbook on Intellectual Property and Digital Technologies* (Edward Elgar Publishing 2019).

the centre of the European copyright reform, it mostly focuses on the relationship of authors with online intermediaries. So, the balancing exercise involving moral rights in transformative works remains rather under-examined.

In current copyright reform debates these questions are presented through exceptions and limitations to copyright or "user rights". From data mining to user-generated content, and from transformative works to mashups and memes, reuse of existing protected works has formed a new creative category of original works.[6] Copyright exceptions and limitations are facilitating this creative expression, and courts proceed to balance moral rights of the authors of subsisting works with the right to creativity and freedom of expression of the subsequent author. Some national jurisdictions address novel creativity pathways using innovative – even if imperfect – solutions, such as the user-generated works exception in the Canadian copyright legislation.[7] Similarly, during the copyright reform debate in Europe, an exception for transformative use was discussed and put forward, but was not implemented in the final Copyright Directive.

Reliance on the normative instruments has proven to be insufficient due to territorial enforcement and the different national legal regimes. As highlighted by Xalabarder:

> strict territoriality is especially sensitive to the lack of harmonization in the field of moral rights as well as in the field of limitations. Depending on which law applies, some activities may amount to an infringement of moral rights in one country but be considered a lawful use in another. Furthermore, when these acts are done online, its ubiquitous effects make national laws de facto irrelevant.[8]

Addressing moral rights within transformative creativity is twofold: on the one side, respect of moral rights of the author of the transformed work is a *sine qua non* but on the other, the (moral) rights of the author of the transformative (original) work have to be recognized equally and independently. The placement of individualistic rights in plural and non-linear creation is certainly not straightforward. Traditionally, the authorization of the author of the original work is a condition of exercise and not a condition of existence of the subsequent work. An original work made without the authorization of the first author would be infringing, but still subject to copyright protection. So, the author of the transformative work would appear to also have a copyright.

Current balancing of competing rights accounts for the subsisting authorial moral rights of the work undergoing transformation, in both civil law and common law traditions. For instance, the parody exception does not override the right of the author to prevent their work

---

[6]   Jean-Paul Triaille (ed.), Study on the Application of Directive 2001/29/EC on Copyright and Related Rights in the Information Society, Study prepared by De Wolf & Partners in collaboration with the Centre de recherche information, droit et société (CRIDS), University of Namur, on behalf of the European Commission (DG Market), Brussels, 2013, 455–7.

[7]   Ysolde Gendreau, "Highlighting Moral Rights in Exceptions: User-generated Content in the Canadian Copyright Act", in Fabienne Brison, Séverine Dusollier, Marie-Christine Janssens and Hendrik Vanhees, (eds), *Moral Rights in the 21st Century/Le droit moral au 21ième siècle/Los derechos morales en el siglo 21* (Larcier 2015) 223.

[8]   Raquel Xalabarder, "Jurisdiction and Applicable Law Issues for the Protection of Moral Rights Online", in Fabienne Brison, Séverine Dusollier, Marie-Christine Janssens and Hendrik Vanhees, (eds), *Moral Rights in the 21st Century/Le droit moral au 21ième siècle/Los derechos morales en el siglo 21* (Larcier 2015) 172.

from being used in a discriminatory manner.[9] Similarly, fair use accounts for some protection towards the artist's author and reputation, through fundamental rights balancing, even if the moral rights regulations themselves appear to be less influential.[10]

The *droit d'auteur* discourse addresses transformative works as content that has been based on a pre-existing original work where the artist's inspiration is primary and foundational. The presumption is that all transformative works borrow, and all transformed works have not. So, the question is drastically limited to the degree to which the moral rights of the subsisting author would have to be sustained or not.

Finally, global expansion and recognition of transformative works has diversified the intensity of moral rights subsisting for their authors. Moral rights of the transformative artists are rarely safeguarded outside the context of nationally limited jurisdictions with favourable legal frameworks. Also, international availability of an audience makes works subject to platform-orchestrated automated filtering and content moderation. As it is becoming increasingly evident, platform policies appear to be rarely lenient towards transformative creativity especially because heterogenous exceptions according to applicable law make the legal status of the work in question ambiguous.

The lack of international harmonization of transformative culture gave rise, legitimized, and expanded, the use of transnational private ordering mechanisms. Dominant in facilitating the "sharing and reuse" culture, Creative Commons constitutes the most prominent example of these mechanisms.[11] This analysis will focus on Creative Commons, as they were the first international attempt at systematizing a new order of sharing and remixing of non-software works.

3.   CREATIVE COMMONS LICENCES AND MORAL RIGHTS

As authors were starting to question the efficiency and timely application of traditional copyright rules, they moved towards more liberal private ordering mechanisms such as Creative Commons. These legal instruments incorporated a "pick-n-choose" approach in order to facilitate a flexible sharing of works under diverse sets of rules according to the authors' choices.

The term Creative Commons describes an association created in 2001 in the United States by a group of legal academics and prominent actors of the "free movement". Inspired by free software licences, Creative Commons promotes free access, use (and sometimes reuse) of works. Authors can choose from available licence elements that correspond to authorizations

---

[9]   CJEU, 3 September 2014, C-201/13, *Deckmyn v. Vandersteen*. See also Jonathan Griffiths, Christophe Geiger, Martin Senftleben, Raquel Xalabarder, Lionel Bently and The European Copyright Society's, "Opinion on the Judgment of the CJEU in Case C-201/13 Deckmyn" (2015) *EIPR* 37, 3, 127.

[10]   Eugene Lim, "On the Uneasy Interface between Economic Rights, Moral Rights and Users' Rights in Copyright Law: Can Canada Learn from the UK Experience?" (2018) 15(1) *SCRIPTed* 70 https://script-ed.org/?p=3545 DOI: 10.2966/scrip.150118.

[11]   Niva Elkin-Koren, "What Contracts Can't Do: The Limits of Private Ordering in Facilitating a Creative Commons" (2005) 74(2) *Fordham Law Review* 375–422; Niva Elkin-Koren, "Creative Commons: A Sceptical View of a Worthy Pursuit" in Bernt Hugenholtz and Lucie Guibault (eds), *The Future of the Public Domain* (Kluwer Law International 2006) 325–44; Séverine Dusollier, "The Master's Tools v. The Master's House: Creative Commons v. Copyright" (2006) 29 *Columbia Journal of Law and the Arts* 271–93.

and restrictions in order to frame the conditions of use of the work shared. The association juxtaposed the existing system of "all rights reserved" with that of "certain rights reserved".

The licences have been translated and "transposed" (ported) in more than 100 jurisdictions,[12] and in total four successive versions have been published. While the latest 4.0 version has only been translated and not "transposed", the previous three versions are still used, and they can be found with slight linguistic and legal differences depending on the applicable jurisdiction.

Since version 3.0, Creative Commons has systematically altered the language used in its licences to align itself with the Berne Convention terminology. This shift is representative of the organization's aspiration to make the licences legally compatible with international legal norms, and flexible to local interpretations.[13]

Moral rights, absolute by nature,[14] have never been excluded from author contractual transactions with third parties. On the contrary, moral rights can act as a safeguard against excesses in contractual authorizations that the author might (be forced to) concede. For instance, the inalienability principle of moral rights, introduced in civil law jurisdictions with strong moral rights protections, entails the prohibition of a global abdication of moral rights. At the same time, this principle does not incapacitate the authors in making contractual arrangements towards ensuring the practical enforcement of the respect of their moral rights.

The attributes of moral rights that have a quasi-international reach is the right to attribution (*droit de paternité*) and the right of integrity (*droit au respect*) of the work. These two rights have been recognized by the Berne Convention and constitute a *de minimis* protection for all adhering countries. The focus of this chapter will remain on the two "dominant" moral rights aspects, leaving aside the more localized versions of moral rights such as the right of withdrawal (*droit de retrait ou de repentir*) and the right of divulgation (*droit de divulgation*). These rights, previously addressed for their interaction with Creative Commons licences,[15] are producing incompatibilities, but they have provoked very little case law.

The special attention that the rights of attribution and of respect to the work enjoy on an international level, is also due to the diversity in the legal regime, interpretation and enforcement of these rights in different jurisdictions. So, the same hypothetical scenarios, would most likely be subject to variable reasonings and decisions. This lack of interoperability between internationally recognized moral rights makes their interaction with the transnational private ordering mechanisms of Creative Commons, rather problematic. The chilling effects of this legal uncertainty linked to moral rights enforcement could also transform how the law chooses to integrate economic rights of authors of transformative works. As a result, copyright would end up suffering as a whole.

---

[12]   Mélanie Dulong de Rosnay, "Creative Commons Licenses Legal Pitfalls: Incompatibilities and Solutions" (2010) Institute for Information Law, University of Amsterdam.
[13]   Alexandra Giannopoulou, "Les licences Creative Commons", PhD, University of Paris II Pantheon Assas (2016) (L'Harmattan, forthcoming).
[14]   This is the norm for civil law jurisdictions.
[15]   Alexandra Giannopoulou, "The Creative Commons Licenses through Moral Rights Provisions in French Law" (2014) 27(1-2) *International Review of Law, Computers and Technology* 60.

3.1   Paternity Right or Right to Attribution

The moral right to attribution, or paternity right (*droit de paternité*), can be characterized as the cornerstone of moral rights, because of its quasi-worldwide acknowledgement on a both normative and practical level. It is the representation of the inseverable link that ties each protected work to its creator, who remains the main beneficiary of the right until their death. It has been often described as the umbilical cord between the work and its author. Enshrined by the Berne Convention as a right to claim authorship (Article 6*bis*), practice of the moral right to attribution presents itself with great variability. It is the right of the author(s) to receive recognition, which may come even under the use of a pseudonym. In some jurisdictions, the right to remaining anonymous constitutes a lawful exercise of authors' moral right in question.

Naturally, the scope of the right varies. For example, the subject matter of artistic works over which authors can claim their moral right can be limited by national law. The United States moral rights protection is a popular case in that regard. With limited recognition on a federal level, moral rights find only a partial recognition through a combination of federal acts. Enforcement of this fragmented patchwork of national moral rights on an international level becomes a somewhat challenging riddle to solve. As the available functions of exercising the moral right in question is not harmonized, the principle of national treatment prevails. Thus, "an author who is a national of any Berne member country can expect to be treated on par with the nationals of the country where copyright protection is claimed".[16] Enforcement relies predominantly on national implementation with the additional recognition of Article 12 of the World Intellectual Property Organization (WIPO) Copyright Treaty, which requires "effective legal remedies" against infringements on – inter alia – the right to attribution.

The quasi-dominant position of the moral right of attribution did not go unnoticed within Creative Commons, whose licences have rather consistently included clauses adjusting the prerogatives of its respect by third parties, users and subsequent creators. Version 1.0 of the licences included "attribution" as an optional element among others, making sharing sometimes free of the restriction to reference the author creating the work shared. Before this policy could effectively launch a doctrinal discussion among legal scholars, on the conditions and validity of renouncing moral rights protection, Creative Commons launched version 2.0 of the licences, rendering attribution an obligatory element of all available licences.

In the version that did not include the "attribution" element, the licence in itself did not effectively contain a restriction of application of the moral right in question, nor an express abdication of this right. Notwithstanding the extent of the validity of each of these conditions on different jurisdictions, the lack of a direct reference to the fate of the paternity right within the applicable legal text would indicate that the subsisting moral rights legal regime applies. Admittedly, the design process of choosing a licence ensures that the rightsholder makes choices on the elements to include based on key questions, such as whether the author would want to receive attribution to the work in question.[17] Absent a direct waiving clause within the

---

[16]   Mira Sundara Rajan, *Moral Rights: Principles, Practice and New Technology* (Oxford University Press 2011) 235.

[17]   "Announcing (and explaining) our new 2.0 licences", Creative Commons blog, 25 May 2004, https://creativecommons.org/2004/05/25/announcingandexplainingournew20licenses/. "Our web stats indicate that 97–98% of you choose Attribution, so we decided to drop Attribution as a choice from our license menu – it's now standard. This reduces the number of licenses from eleven possible to six and

licence, the legal validity of this process would appear to be weak, and its enforcement questionable, should the author aim to pursue judicial relief on moral rights grounds. More broadly speaking, interpretation of every Creative Commons licence element would have to be based on applicable legislation.

Creative Commons quickly realized that while authors were rather quick to adopt free and open licensing tools, attribution remained a consistent choice among the available elements.[18] This was not due to random or unpredictable elements that affect author choice. On the contrary, it appears that even in the context of making a work freely available to the public with little reuse restrictions, maintaining a "moral" link to the freely shared work is essential both for maintaining some level of control and for creating valuable reputation across different communities.[19] In general, the commons-based peer production communities brought forward a new value to reputation. With trust creation and trust sustenance being the main driver, persistent online identifiers in "social innovation" communities[20] carry a reputation signalling each identified participant's value within the community. One of the drivers for reputation maintenance is to serve as an indicator of expertise, engagement and commitment to the community. Creative Commons strategically placed itself within this ideological field of community creation and governance, even if it showed significant divergences from the dominant discourse and commons practices at the time.[21] The practice of mentioning the author of the work on every instance that the work is being used and reused is perceived as the *de minimis* legal obligation towards the creator in question. According to one author, "recognition, as an end itself and/or as a means to obtaining financial rewards, is the common motivator among creators who use CC licences to share their works".[22]

With the shift from version 1.0 to version 2.0, there was a significant misconception on the compatibility of the licences with moral rights protection across different jurisdictions.[23] In the licences where attribution was required contractually, the respective clause described how an author shall be credited when their work would be shared. According to the Section 2(b) of the licence:

> If you distribute, publicly display, publicly perform, or publicly digitally perform the Work or any Derivative Works or Collective Works, You must keep intact all copyright notices for the Work and

---

makes the license selection user interface that much simpler. Important to remember: Attribution can always be disavowed upon licensor request, and pseudonymous and anonymous authorship are always options for a licensor, as before. If we see a huge uprising against the attribution-as-stock-feature, we'll certainly consider bringing it back as an option."

[18]   Essentially, 98% of the licences used at the time included the "attribution" element.

[19]   Mélanie Clément-Fontaine, "Creative Commons face au droit moral", in Fabienne Brison, Séverine Dusollier, Marie-Christine Janssens and Hendrik Vanhees (eds), *Moral Rights in the 21st Century/Le droit moral au 21ième siècle/Los derechos morales en el siglo 21* (Larcier 2015) 198.

[20]   Samer Hassan and Primavera De Filippi, "Reputation and Quality Indicators to Improve Community Governance" (2015), DOI: 10.2139/ssrn.2725369.

[21]   Mélanie Clément-Fontaine, *L'oeuvre libre* (Larcier, 2014); Alexandra Giannopoulou, "Les licences Creative Commons", PhD, University of Paris II Panthéon Assas (2016) (L'Harmattan, forthcoming).

[22]   Zachary Katz, "Pitfalls of Open Licensing: An Analysis of Creative Commons Licensing", IDEA (2006) 46(3) *The Intellectual Property Law Review* 391–413.

[23]   Because version 1.0 was short-lived due to the rapid deployment of version 2.0 of the licences, the legal ambiguity in the sustenance of moral rights protection for works shared with licences that omitted the "Attribution" element did not have the opportunity to be tested in any court.

give the Original Author credit reasonable to the medium or means You are utilizing by conveying the name (or pseudonym if applicable) of the Original Author if supplied; the title of the Work if supplied; in the case of a Derivative Work, a credit identifying the use of the Work in the Derivative Work (e.g., "French translation of the Work by Original Author," or "Screenplay based on original Work by Original Author"). Such credit may be implemented in any reasonable manner; provided, however, that in the case of a Derivative Work or Collective Work, at a minimum such credit will appear where any other comparable authorship credit appears and in a manner at least as prominent as such other comparable authorship credit.[24]

Since version 2.0 of the licences, the moral right of paternity has been consistently represented by the standard "attribution" restriction found in all Creative Commons licences, with some discrepancies found on the national translations and "ported" versions. For example, while the international version explains the "attribution" element simply by pointing out that "credit must be given to the creator", the French version gives further explanations per that element's role in the licence.[25]

The compatibility exercise of moral rights legislation with the current version (4.0) of the licences is relatively straightforward. Section 3(a) of the licences, entitled "Attribution" describes inter alia how the moral right of paternity will be accommodated with the sharing of the work in question. Specifically, according to Section 3(a)(1)(A)(i) of the licences, "identification of the creator(s) of the Licensed Material and any others designated to receive attribution, in any reasonable manner requested by the Licensor (including by pseudonym if designated)". This restriction translates in contractual terms how the moral right of paternity of the author of the shared work shall be respected. This clause, read in conjunction with Section 3(a)(1) and (2), take into consideration the general difficulties of complying with moral rights obligations in the digital era of sharing, transformation and content generation. In sum, this framing of the moral right of paternity, without an express mention of the specific right in the text of the licences, shows a commitment to standardize and maintain the link between works and authors even in the context of "free culture". According to Rajan, the contractual inclusion of an attribution restriction serves as an incentive for authors to use the Creative Commons licences, as a means to indirectly have a tool for creating a sort of moral rights protection. Rajan notes that:

> in the case of a country where moral rights are not well-protected, the Creative Commons license may offer moral rights protection that is not otherwise available in this form – for example, in the United States.[26]

Whatever the licence chosen, the clause describing the attribution of the author of the work in question presupposes a linear sharing of works. The rightsholder offering the work designates – through the licence – how the author of the work initially shared should be referred to during the sharing and redistribution of the work. However, as the sharing of works becomes

---

[24] Article 4(b) of version on of the licences. See for example, Creative Commons licence "Attribution" version 1.0 available online https://creativecommons.org/licenses/by/1.0/legalcode.
[25] Namely, it points out that "all Creative Commons licenses require those who use your works to give you credit as you request, without suggesting that you approve of their use or give them your endorsement or support".
[26] Mira Sundara Rajan, *Moral Rights: Principles, Practice, and New Technology* (Oxford University Press 2011) 500.

increasingly complex, with modifications, contributions, additions and remixes, the necessary distinction between the initial version of the work and a modification made or a contribution added to it becomes blurry.[27] Attribution of all contributors to the creation of a work shared is not straightforward.

The possibility of differentiating between successive authors and their respective contributions, and the need to demarcate modifications to shared works, are described in version 4.0 of the licences. The section entitled "Attribution" remains the same in all licences with the addition of a simple statement in licences with the restriction "no modifications", which specifies that sharing of the secondary work is not permitted. This is due to standardization concentrated efforts made by the creators of the licenses.

In many jurisdictions, respect for the right of authorship also includes the right of "non-paternity", which gives each author the right to anonymity, as yet another expression of their moral right of paternity. Creative Commons address the possibility of anonymity in an indirect way. The different licence versions specify that the name of the original author (or pseudonym) "if stated" or "if mentioned" must be cited in version 4.0, i.e. the licensor must mention the author "in any reasonable manner requested by him". The question must be asked whether not directly making anonymity an option available to the author is not a conscious choice on the part of Creative Commons to exclude its application. Professor Clément-Fontaine thus proposes that anonymity be considered excluded by free licences, because of the difficulty to identify the author if and when necessary.

The validity of a right to authorial anonymity remains uncertain in the case of Creative Commons licences, because the scope of this choice must be limited. Anonymity is accepted insofar as the author can be identified *a posteriori*. Drawing a parallel with traditional author's contracts, we see that the publisher is aware of the identity of the author and is bound by the contract not to reveal it, but is also responsible for handling any kind of request concerning the work in question. The applicability of these rules to a work that is freely shared and subject to successive modifications seems difficult to ensure. Finally, the introduction of the revocability of anonymity for these licences is not envisaged, which makes it more difficult to assess the author's willingness to remain anonymous or to reverse his choice.

The law does not consider that the author's link with their work is severed even in the case of anonymous works. However, the free circulation of works under a Creative Commons licence on an anonymous basis risks endangering this link. The free circulation of a work does not mean that the author is devoid of their quality. Moreover, the establishment of restrictions on the authorization of non-exclusive exploitation is based on the idea of the possibility of identifying and contacting the author of the shared work. These restrictions are thus incompatible with the exercise of the author's right to remain anonymous.

In the case where authors of secondary works choose to remain anonymous, the risk of misattribution of changes made to the shared work to the downstream author cannot be avoided. In this case, the author of the original work would be able to challenge authorship by claiming an infringement of their moral or personality rights.

Finally, it is important to consider enforcement. The interaction of traditional private international law normative framework, with that of *lex contractus* and the heterogenous copyright

---

27   Mélanie Clément-Fontaine paints the image of a snowflake in order to describe the multiple paths a shared work takes when being reshared, reused, transformed and remixed.

legislations, entrenches the uncertainty of moral rights respect.[28] Thus, the consideration of an anonymity clause or of a waiver of the paternity right, would depend on which rules would be applied by the court. Should the *lex contractus* prevail, then it would be highly probable that jurisprudence would present anomalies depending on the level of protection of moral rights in each jurisdiction and the type of Creative Commons licence used.

3.2   Right to Integrity

Admittedly, the most challenging issue of moral rights compliance for Creative Commons licensing, is the integrity right.

The sharing of a work accompanied by a non-exclusive permission to distribute, use (and often modify), challenges the enforcement of the author's moral right to the integrity of the work. This right is among the quasi-universal moral rights and holds an especially dominant place in the French *droit d'auteur* system.[29] There is abundant case law on the protection of the moral right of integrity, and in multiple jurisdictions. However, due to its versatile nature, the exact scope of the right to the integrity of the work is not unanimously agreed upon. From the high-level protection granted by the Berne Convention to the heterogenous interpretations in national laws and case law, the right to integrity is transnational, but highly fragmented.

Granting different levels of protection depending on the chosen jurisdiction, this moral right is also intrinsically tied to the "lack of discrimination" in protected works. Namely, "the Berne Convention makes little provision for treating different classes of copyright works differently. As long as works fall within the same overall category, they are expected to be treated alike."[30] No type of work is a priori excluded from moral rights or copyright protection, even if some categories of works benefit from special protection or specific rights. This affirmation extends to original transformative works, which would benefit from the same level of protection as their constituting parts.

From the available implementations of integrity rights in different jurisdictions, there are two elements identified in the scope of application, a distinction made between two types of infringements: an objective infringement, which concerns any material alteration, and a subjective infringement, which concerns any exploitation that is not in keeping with the spirit of the work. Thus, there is absolute respect when the use of the work does not bring about any modification and relative respect when a modification is observed in the work.

According to Section 2b§1 of the Creative Commons licences:

> moral rights, such as the right of integrity, are not licensed under this Public License, nor are publicity, privacy, and/or other similar personality rights; however, to the extent possible, the Licensor waives and/or agrees not to assert any such rights held by the Licensor to the limited extent necessary to allow You to exercise the Licensed Rights, but not otherwise.

---

[28]   Raquel Xalabarder, "Jurisdiction and Applicable Law Issues for the Protection of Moral Rights Online", in Fabienne Brison, Séverine Dusollier, Marie-Christine Janssens and Hendrik Vanhees (eds), *Moral Rights in the 21st Century/Le droit moral au 21ième siècle/Los derechos morales en el siglo 21* (Larcier 2015) 172.

[29]   Alexandra Giannopoulou, "The Creative Commons Licenses through Moral Rights Provisions in French Law" (2014) 27(1-2) *International Review of Law, Computers and Technology* 60.

[30]   Mira Sundara Rajan, *Moral Rights: Principles, Practice, and New Technology* (Oxford University Press 2011) 249.

Thus, moral rights of the author, especially the moral right of integrity, are placed outside the scope of the authorization granted by the licence by the promise not to act against any possible infringement of the licence during the exercise of the rights granted. The limits of this promise are somewhat unclear. Section 2a§4 of the licences clarifies that simply making technical modifications in media and formats "never produces Adapted Material" according to the given definition of "Adopted Material". So, there is an a priori contractual distinction that disregards the nuances of contemporary creativity and most importantly, established case law on originality.

This mixture of contractual agreements of moral rights respect, and applicable jurisdiction, all in the context of international digital transformative creativity, make enforcement relatively problematic if not practically impossible.[31] Some authors have brought forward the idea of extending the concept of abuse of rights in the event of a conflict between the authorization granted and the rights judicially claimed.[32] This solution, while it has merit in the jurisdictions where abuse of rights is recognized, does not appeal to a transnational moral rights application. Overall, reconciling the right to the integrity of the work with Creative Commons licences raises different questions depending on the licences that allow the sharing of a work with (3.2.2) or without (3.2.1) the freedom to modify it.

3.2.1 Sharing without permission to modify the licensed work

There are two Creative Commons licences which contain the "no modifications" element, thus restricting permission only to the verbatim sharing of the original work, without permission to publish transformative or any other secondary works. The applicable restriction relates to, what the licence defines as "Adapted material". However, and as noted above, the restriction is not absolute, since technically necessary modifications are expressly permitted by all licences. Furthermore, the same restriction cannot prohibit the incorporation of the entire shared work into a collection.

Depending on the applicable jurisdiction, the scope of moral right of integrity could affect this restricted authorization to pursue technical modifications to the shared work. Would the contractual agreement be able to override this right? For instance, while the processing of a work may be qualified as a technically necessary modification permitted by the licences, it could be viewed as lowering the quality of the work in question. Case law in France has concluded, for example, that streaming "allows only poor quality viewing, in particular because of a very small frame, unsuitable for a feature film, and the jerky effect of which the unity of the film is furthermore disturbed by splitting it into two parts; that the infringement on the integrity of the work is therefore constituted".[33] Further issues arise, pertaining to the possibility of

---

[31] Raquel Xalabarder, "Jurisdiction and Applicable Law Issues for the Protection of Moral Rights Online", in Fabienne Brison, Séverine Dusollier, Marie-Christine Janssens and Hendrik Vanhees (eds), *Moral Rights in the 21st Century/Le droit moral au 21ième siècle/Los derechos morales en el siglo 21* (Larcier 2015) 172.

[32] Philippe Gaudrat, "L'abus du droit moral", in Fabienne Brison, Séverine Dusollier, Marie-Christine Janssens and Hendrik Vanhees (eds), *Moral Rights in the 21st Century/Le droit moral au 21ième siècle/Los derechos morales en el siglo 21* (Larcier 2015) 98.

[33] "*ne permet qu'une visualisation de mauvaise qualité du fait notamment d'un cadre très réduit, inadapté pour un film de long métrage et de l'effet saccadé dont l'unité du film est par ailleurs troublée du fait d'un découpage en deux parties; que l'atteinte à l'intégrité de l'œuvre est donc constituée*" Tribunal

the courts to exercise a balancing exercise between fundamental rights and the moral rights of the authors[34] so as to discern infringement.

The extent of the infringement of the integrity of a work is determined by the author; no legal limit is usually put forward. Although placed outside the scope of the permissions granted by the licence, the integrity right may be contractually restricted for the purpose of facilitating these authorizations. So, if the right to the integrity of the work cannot be restricted in compliance with the authorization granted by the author, then it could risk losing its substance. Also, the *raison d'être* of the licences in question would be misguided if the system of prior authorizations to any use of the shared work is imposed for fear of infringement of moral rights.

3.2.2 Sharing with permission to modify the licensed work

The licences that do permit modifications of the shared work, by omitting the "no derivatives" element, contain no specific substantial moral rights clauses. Instead, the generic exclusion of the moral right of integrity from the scope of the licence is repeated. The authorization to modify the work subject to the respect of the integrity right is limited to a "formality clause" which recalls a principle of "reasonable and non-abusive" application of the moral right without practically contributing to the development of the moral right within the context of this generic authorization in question.

The creation of derivative works constitutes a form of legitimate infringement of the right to the integrity of the work of the first author. Namely, it constitutes a circumvention of that right for the benefit of the creative freedom of the author of the derivative work. Traditionally, and in order to accommodate this moral right with the freedom of creation, adaptation contracts describe the authorized modifications, i.e., modifications that the author does not consider as an infringement of his moral right. Reconciling *ex ante* authorizations to create derivative works with the right to the integrity of the work is not a new problem, but it is becoming more acute in the open licences in question. The reason for this is that this pre-emptive authorization to modify is large enough to accommodate all changes, amendments, contributions and remixes to the shared work. These interventions may lead to the creation of new, separate original transformative work or to the mere evolution of the shared work without adding a layer of originality. In both cases, the secondary author benefits from the licence to modify, but still risks a moral rights objection from the licensor, depending on the jurisdiction on which protection will be claimed.

Firstly, it should be stressed that the qualification of the authorization to modify as a simultaneous abandonment or express renunciation of the right to the integrity, would not be a generalizable solution nor an interpretation appropriate to the licences in question. For instance, if the licences expressly mention the renunciation of the moral right, this clause would not be applicable in French law because of the inalienable nature of this right. In this example, the narrowest interpretation of licences that authorize the creation of derivative works would lead to the conclusion that the only modifications authorized are those not interfering with the integrity of the work. Swiss law contains a provision in that regard. According to Article 11

---

de Grande Instance Paris, 3e ch., 13 July 2007, Christian C., Nord Ouest Production/Dailymotion, UGC Images.

[34]   This balancing exercise is dominant in other features of copyright, mainly related to exercise of economic rights and to the application of exceptions and limitations to copyright.

para. 2 of the Loi fédérale sur le droit d'auteur et les droits voisins (Loi sur le droit d'auteur, LDA), the author retains the right to oppose infringements of integrity rights even in the case of a contractual authorization to modify the work in question.

With the addition that "to the extent possible, the Licensor waives and/or agrees not to assert any such rights held by the Licensor to the limited extent necessary to allow You to exercise the Licensed Rights, but not otherwise", Creative Commons describes a total waiver of moral rights and in the case that this is not possible, then the waiver turns into a (contractual) promise not to enforce them. Naturally, this limited waiver of moral rights would find different inter- pretations in various jurisdictions. From French law, where this clause would be considered null and void due to the inalienability of the right, to common law traditions where it would be applicable to its full force, the same clause finds two entirely different sets of obligations. It becomes thus clear that among the various licences and their versions, Creative Commons recognizes also that the same licence would carry different rights for the parties and it would have different enforcement depending on applicable law.

Admittedly, the compliance of right to integrity with new forms of creativity and culture is not specific to Creative Commons and open licensing in general. The right's application compared to current practices of adaptation is rather limited. However, the specificity running within the open licensing field is the fact that it is also the author that actively participates in open culture creation, by contributing their work within communities of sharing. In that regard, the licences go beyond a simple adaptation contract but rather adhere to a system that incorporates a specific ideology formed by either communities or specific organizations (in this case, Creative Commons). In a similar vein, the French precursor to Creative Commons – *Licence Art Libre* – acknowledged that the traditional view towards the integrity right would render free and open licensing impossible in countries with a high level of protection towards moral rights. The compromise they proposed was to partially waive that right but only when the work concerned would be transformed into a free, and evolutive work.[35] This proposal of a new doctrinal category of protected works, the *oeuvres evolutives*, carries a more balanced approach towards moral rights protection and the public interest, all within the broader frame- work of the commons.

Finally, although with few use cases to date, enforcement of the moral right of integrity in Creative Commons-licensed works authorizing modifications should not be a strict exercise of legal compliance. Rather, it would have to be placed within the broader copyright management system of Creative Commons,[36] which includes an organization that guides the shape of the licences and most importantly, an ideology depicted in each of them. Finally, it is important to stress that authorial autonomy, empowerment and control are guiding principles behind moral rights protections and also commons. However, the depiction and prioritization of these principles in the private tools created by Creative Commons cannot be left unchecked to fit a liberal approach of "choose what you want" without ensuring that proper safeguards are in place. In continental Europe with strong moral rights tradition at least, this would require a deep uprooting of fundamental *droit d'auteur* principles.

---

[35]   Mélanie Clément-Fontaine, *L'oeuvre libre*, (Larcier 2014).
[36]   Alexandra Giannopoulou, "Les licences Creative Commons", PhD, University of Paris II Pantheon Assas (2016) (L'Harmattan, forthcoming).

4.   CC0 OR TOWARDS A VOLUNTARY PUBLIC DOMAIN

The expansions of Creative Commons licences, open sharing and remix-inspired innovation inevitably led to the question of what is the minimum threshold of rights an author can keep and, ultimately, can a work be shared completely free of all rights? The legal parallel made, was the concept of the public domain. In copyright terms, the public domain is constituted by the intellectual elements that have never been protected by copyright or whose term of protection has expired.

While the concept in itself suffers from jurisdictional differences that make it largely fragmented, the legal interest towards enriching a global knowledge and creativity "pool" was undertaken under policy actions towards supporting the (informational or knowledge) commons in order to specifically emphasize both the free and open use of such works but also the collective and shared character of this use and maintenance.[37]

The concept of the "voluntary public domain" where rightsholders and authors can willingly place their words towards benefiting the public interest and common good, was highlighted in copyright reform and policy discussions. With the community interest rising, and the legal uncertainty surrounding these concepts, came the Creative Commons private ordering instrument. CC0 was the tool developed to create a space where authors relinquish all rights related to their shared work.[38] The intent was to create this "artificial" public domain space, not by the effect of the law but by the simple will of the authors themselves.[39] The obvious issue quickly became moral rights. Are there legal instruments to facilitate a waiver of moral rights, and, if so, to what extent can this be done according to applicable law?

The legal framework of CC0 is that it is not intended to be a licence but a waiver. In that sense, a unilateral act from the author renouncing all possible rights that they hold to the work in question. There are multiple legal ambiguities related to this construct, but the most relevant for our discourse would be the effect this tool has on moral rights. According to Creative Commons, CC0 is the "no rights reserved" option, contrasted to the "some rights reserved" of the rest of the licences. Its aim is to bring protected works "as close as possible to the public domain". Naturally, civil law and common law traditions would give very different answers to this rather unclear legal statement.

For example, French law seems a priori to be poorly adapted to the CC0 tool, not recognizing a waiver of copyright, in particular because of the inalienability of the author's moral rights. In contrast, commons law jurisdictions such as the United States were more suited for an "overt act" of copyright abandonment.

Specifically, Article 2 of CC0 constitutes the waiver:

---

[37]   Séverine Dusollier, Scoping Study on Copyright and Related Rights and the Public Domain, WIPO, Committee on Development and Intellectual Property (CDIP), (2010), CDIP/4/3/REV./STUDY/INF/1.

[38]   The precursors to this tool were the Public Domain Dedication and the Founders' Copyright. But these tools were short-lived. For an overview of these tools, see: Alexandra Giannopoulou, "Les licences Creative Commons", PhD, University of Paris II Pantheon Assas (2016) (L'Harmattan, forthcoming; and Mélanie Dulong de Rosnay, "Creative Commons Licenses Legal Pitfalls: Incompatibilities and Solutions" (2010) Institute for Information Law, University of Amsterdam.

[39]   Professor Clément-Fontaine calls this *"domaine public consenti"*: Mélanie Clément-Fontaine, *L'oeuvre libre* (Larcier 2014).

to the greatest extent permitted by, but not in contravention of, applicable law, Affirmer hereby overtly, fully, permanently, irrevocably and unconditionally waives, abandons, and surrenders all of Affirmer's Copyright and Related Rights and associated claims and causes of action, whether now known or unknown (including existing as well as future claims and causes of action), in the Work (i) in all territories worldwide, (ii) for the maximum duration provided by applicable law or treaty (including future time extensions), (iii) in any current or future medium and for any number of copies, and (iv) for any purpose whatsoever, including without limitation commercial, advertising or promotional purposes (the "Waiver"). Affirmer makes the Waiver for the benefit of each member of the public at large and to the detriment of Affirmer's heirs and successors, fully intending that such Waiver shall not be subject to revocation, rescission, cancellation, termination, or any other legal or equitable action to disrupt the quiet enjoyment of the Work by the public as contemplated by Affirmer's express Statement of Purpose.

Certainly, there is a lot to untangle in this clause, even to the limited extent of a moral rights angle.

4.1   The Scope of the Moral Rights Waiver

The copyright abandonment envisaged by CC0 appears to be intended as a global renunciation of copyright. As the statement of purpose implies, this abandonment is done for the benefit of the public interest. It is a rather audacious text, because it seems to reject not only a bundle of rights, but a whole legal system related to copyright.

This overall dissatisfaction with the copyright system, which becomes apparent in reading the CC0 text, is not used to place the works outside of this system but, rather, to subvert it as much as possible so that "the public can reliably and without fear of later claims of infringement build upon, modify, incorporate in other works, reuse and redistribute as freely as possible in any form whatsoever and for any purposes, including without limitation commercial purposes".

According to US law (and other common law jurisdictions), a waiver seems like the appropriate tool to do that. Specifically, and as far as moral rights are concerned, the US Copyright Act specifies that while the right of attribution and the right to the integrity of the work cannot be transferred, they may be waived by the authors.[40] However, it should be stated that the application of this provision to a general *ex ante* waiver in the form of the CC0 is not evident. The clarity of the waiver, according to the law, is one of the conditions of its validity. Namely, this is due to the importance of distinguishing between a waiver of rights and a "covenant not to sue". Although the latter is only a promise, it may be enforced under US contract law. In the case of CC0 and according to its "statement of purpose", the tool's purpose and the author's intention appear to be sufficiently clear. Evidently, the text does not attempt to establish a unilateral promise towards an unspecified party to not exercise the rights mentioned. Rather, the language in the text remains consistent to that of waivers of rights. However, waiver of rights does not necessarily mean extinguishment of rights, and this becomes evident in the doctrinal

---

[40]   According to Title 17 United States Copyright Act §106A(e), moral rights "may be waived if the author expressly agrees to such waiver in a written instrument signed by the author. Such instrument shall specifically identify the work, and uses of that work, to which the waiver applies, and the waiver shall apply only to the work and uses so identified. In the case of a joint work prepared by two or more authors, a waiver of rights under this paragraph made by one such author waives such rights for all such authors."

ambiguity around the legality of terminating the revocation.[41] As one of the "instruments that seek to express, with maximum clarity, an author's attempt to abandon copyright and dedicate a work to the public domain",[42] CC0 implements of the author's willingness to waive their rights but in favour of a commons. So, in this underexamined legal field, question remains if moral rights can be "resuscitated" in favour of an author and if so, on what grounds? It is unclear whether the danger of recapture of the shared work from proprietary copyright powers justify a termination to try to re-enforce moral rights of integrity in the future. These issues might become more prevalent with the growing needs for training machine learning algorithms with quality datasets, and CC0 works could be ideal in that regard.[43]

In French law (and most civil law jurisdictions in general), the abandonment of moral rights is prevented by their inalienable nature. Article L.121–1 of the Intellectual Property Code states that authors cannot renounce on their moral rights in principle because of this inalienability. According to the concept of renunciation of rights in French law, when permitted, it constitutes an absolute and permanent alienation from those rights. For this reason, the French legislator appears to be rather reluctant to remove the veil of inalienability from moral rights. However, the doctrine has long been in favour of an adjustment of moral rights at the clear initiative of the authors, especially in the digital content. With case law trying to fill the gap between theory and practice of moral rights, this arrangement has not yet been instituted and for this reason the applicability of CC0 by French moral rights standards remains limited. It has never been tested in court, but it is quite likely that the clause would a priori be declared void and thus, unenforceable.

Recent efforts at reform have tried to enlarge and clarify policy around public domain and the commons, in order to introduce a more attenuated approach towards the absolutist approach to moral rights in France. However, the final legislative text of the Law of the Digital Republic in 2016 included none of the proposed amendments that would contribute to creating a positive space legally recognized and safeguarded so that a dedication to the public domain could be properly framed both from an economical and moral rights perspective.

4.2   The Balancing Act

Since moral rights waivers are unenforceable under civil law tradition, the fallback provision would apply,[44] effectively transforming the waiver into a licence. The effect of the licence would be to retain only the inalienable moral rights to the licensed work. This could be also

---

[41]   Lydia Pallas Loren, "Building a Reliable Semicommons of Creative Works: Enforcement of Creative Commons Licenses and Limited Abandonment of Copyright" (2007) 14 *Geo. Mason L. Rev.* 271.

[42]   Timothy Armstrong, "Shrinking the Commons: Termination of Copyright Licenses and Transfers for the Benefit of the Public" (2010) 47 *Harvard Journal on Legislation* 359–423.

[43]   Recently, IBM obtained Flickr CC-licensed datasets to train facial-recognition software. This use, while legal according to the Creative Commons licence terms, was frowned upon by open content and commons activists and lawyers. See Andres Guadamuz, "Using Creative Commons Images to Train Artificial Intelligence", 13 March 2019, https://www.technollama.co.uk/using-creative-commons -images-to-train-artificial-intelligence.

[44]   "In the event that any part of the Waiver is held to be legally invalid or ineffective for any reason under applicable law, the Waiver shall be preserved to the maximum extent permitted by law, so as to allow the fullest possible consideration of the Declarant's Declaration of Intent."

perceived as a promise not to exercise any of the rights in question.[45] However, this strict interpretation does not fit well with the effort of creating a voluntary public domain, where works can be freely reproduced, but also adapted at will by the public. Indeed, according to this interpretation, each act of adaptation or modification associated with the work would still remain subject to the control of the author of the original work. The importance of proceeding in a balancing act of moral rights protections against, for example, the public interest and freedom of expression presents as a way out of the dissonance between absolute moral rights and digital creativity.

For example, the singularity of the CC0 act lies in its implementation, which is both legal and ideological in nature. The author's declaration of intention, which is a kind of prelude to the coming waiver, is a reaction to the reluctance of copyright law to include means of extinguishing copyright other than by the passage of time. CC0 is described as a tool contributing "to a common pool of creative, cultural and scientific works (the 'commons')" that the public has the opportunity to develop, modify and incorporate into other works in a reliable manner. In this sense, the clear objective of authors is to revolutionize copyright through the instrumentalization of the waiver. Since the voluntary extinction of moral rights is impossible, the combination of the intentional element expressed in the statement of purpose and the legal framework surrounding CC0 could serve as a mitigation of the enforcement of these rules. Thus, the positive action of placing a work in a non-protection regime for the benefit of all could be interpreted as an author-empowering act and not as a decision against which they must be protected.

In terms of free works, Professor Clément-Fontaine has put forward the following analogy. The law provides that, on the death of the author, almost all moral rights persist and that their exercise is entrusted to the author's heirs. Similarly, as rights aiming to maintain the life of works, Mélanie Clément-Fontaine proposes a similar "*reasonable*" application for works voluntarily placed in the public domain.[46] With the expressed will of the author as a guiding principle, the act of dedicating the work to the public domain without any constraint could allow case law to develop in a way that approaches moral rights protection after the balancing act with the intended service to the public interest. To that end, CC0's statement of purpose may serve as a framework for the author to describe the guiding principles of the sharing of the work in the commons.

5.   CONCLUSION

Whether as a part of technology-mediated user creative expression, or as private legal instruments, sharing and transformability are here to stay. Moral rights enforcement in these cases would have to find its place and frame of application. There is no contradiction in varying the enforcement of moral rights according to type of creative content, making it modulable. So,

---

[45]   A waiver of the exercise of moral rights exists in copyright practice but only under the condition that it is specifically framed, precise and freely revocable. The most well-known example of a waiver of the exercise of a moral right would be "ghostwriting" where the original author consents that their creation be attributed to a third party. The author thus does not renounce on their moral right, but promises not to exercise it.

[46]   Mélanie Clément-Fontaine, *L'oeuvre libre* (Larcier 2014).

a relative and modular application to copyright-protected creative works could be a welcome correction to the expansive application of its scope.

Critically applied, moral rights legislation could be used as a valid defence mechanism against aspects of open content licensing that promote little in the public or the author's interest. Most importantly, it is essential to test the applicability of this tool against automated filtering mechanisms and machine learning processing of big data. In this regard, moral rights could enhance their scope of application, and reimagine where the authors' interests would lie in modern platform-dominated digital creativity.

15. Artificial intelligence and moral rights
Sérgio Branco and Beatriz Nunes

1. INTRODUCTION

"Humans created art, humans created machines, and now machines create art."[1] However, can a machine or, more specifically, an artificial intelligence (also known as AI) be considered an artist? And, as such, sell paintings and be subject to moral and economic rights?

The year is circa 1973. Harold Cohen, a painter and professor at the University of California, San Diego, has been collaborating with a program called AARON, which has been able to create pictures autonomously for decades.[2] Are the pictures the program has created over the last four decades really works by Harold Cohen,[3] or should they be considered independent creations by AARON itself? To whom should authorship be attributed? Would the possibility of co-authorship be viable?

Fast forward to October 2018. An artificial intelligence artwork is sold for $432,500, making Christie's, a fine art auction house, the first to auction off a work of art created by an algorithm: The *Portrait of Edmond de Belamy*. The portrait depicts a gentleman wearing a dark frockcoat and plain white collar, possibly a man of church, although the facial features are indistinct and there are blank areas on the canvas,[4] it looks as though it is constantly in motion. At the bottom of the work is the artist's signature: an algorithmic formula.

The *Edmond Belamy* painting was created and developed by Obvious,[5] a Paris-based art collective headed by Hugo Caselles-Dupré, Pierre Fautrel and Gauthier Vernier, having been assisted by a young coder, Robbie Barrat. Obvious is known for exploring the interface between art and artificial intelligence using a *machine learning*[6] method called GAN

---

[1] Olivia Hicks, "Art-ifical Intelligence: The Curious Case of Edmond de Belamy" (*Isis Magazine*, 1 March 2019) https://isismagazine.org.uk/2019/03/art-ifical-intelligence-the-curious-case-of-edmond-de -belamy/ accessed on 24 June 2020.

[2] BBC, MIT and FORBES, "Timeline of AI Art" (*AIArtists.org*, 2019) https:// aiartists .org/ ai -timeline-art accessed on 29 June 2020.

[3] Harold Cohen, "The Harold Cohen Trust" http://www.aaronshome.com/aaron/index.html accessed on 29 June 2020.

[4] *CHRISTIE'S*, "Is Artificial Intelligence Set to Become Art's Next Medium?" (*Christie's*, 12 December 2018) https://www.christies.com/features/A -collaboration -between -two -artists -one -human -one -a -machine-9332-1.aspx accessed on 9 June 2020.

[5] Obvious, "La famille de Belamy" (*Obvious Artwork*, 2018) https:// obvious -art .com/ page -collection-obvious/ accessed on 29 June 2020.

[6] Ethem Alpaydin, "Machine Learning" [2016] The MIT Press, 17, 39. "Machine learning is not just a database or programming problem: it is also a requirement for artificial intelligence. A system that is in a changing environment should have the ability to learn; otherwise, we would hardly call it intelligent. If the system can learn and adapt to such changes, the system designer need not foresee and provide solutions for all possible situations"; "… the aim of machine learning is rarely to replicate the training data but to the correct prediction of new cases".

(Generative Adversarial Network).[7] Essentially, GAN is a system that pits algorithms against each other to improve the quality of the results. Therefore, while one algorithm generates data, the other competes with it, discriminating between the real and the false data produced.[8] In the *Edmond de Belamy* case, the dataset consisted of a collection of 15,000 pre-twentieth century portraits previously selected by the humans involved in the project.

What makes the *Edmond de Belamy* case unique is the fact that it was signed, although not with a human name, and, further, it was auctioned, thus touching upon the economic sphere, raising the same questions which surfaced back in 1973 regarding attribution and authorship.

Artificial intelligence is a broad term usually applied to describe an elaborate software with the capacity of learning and storing information, later applying the knowledge gathered to a certain environment or context to solve problems or to create something new, possibly original. It replicates human intelligence and cognitive processes through various computational, mathematical, logical, mechanical, and even biological principles and devices.[9] Consequently, the term *artificial intelligence* is used to designate both a field of study and the ability of software to imitate, replicate and improve human cognitive exercise.

It is safe to establish that artificial intelligence has progressed substantially in recent decades and is no longer just the stuff of science fiction movies. Instead, it plays an increasingly evident role in our society impacting a wide range of sectors, namely that of technology and intellectual property. As such, since artificial intelligence creates works endowed with aesthetic elements, we can speculate on how copyright and its ramifications will henceforth be constantly challenged. And the million-dollar question is: who owns copyright in works created by machines?

Although copyright is viewed as a somewhat recent concept, it was internationally forged in the nineteenth century, with the 1886 Berne Convention, which is still the single-most important international legal instrument in the field.

Copyright is divided into two groups: economic rights, which grants rights of reproduction, distribution, adaptation, among others, and moral rights, which include a series of non-economic privileges.[10] For the purposes of this chapter, greater emphasis will be given to the moral rights and, while copyright laws may differ according to each country, most recognize that moral rights translate into the right of attribution and the right to integrity and are solely applicable to individuals.

It is safe to state that the importance of moral rights has increased considering our technological context: machine learning is becoming commonplace as is its varied forms of application. Moral rights have thus emerged as an area of interest and one with several implications

---

[7]   Olivia Hicks, "Art-ificial Intelligence: The Curious Case of Edmond de Belamy" (*Isis Magazine*, 1 March 2019) https://isismagazine.org.uk/2019/03/art-ificial-intelligence-the-curious-case-of-edmond-de -belamy/ accessed on 29 June 2020.

[8]   Amanda Turnball, "The Price of AI Art: Has the Bubble Burst?" (*The Conversation*, 6 January 2020) https://theconversation.com/the-price-of-ai-art-has-the-bubble-burst-128698 accessed on 29 June 2020.

[9]   Florian De Rouck, "Moral Rights & AI Environments: The Unique Bond between Intelligent Agents and Their Creations" (2019) 14 (4) Journal of Intellectual Property Law & Practice https://doi .org/10.1093/jiplp/jpz010 accessed 7 July 2020.

[10]   J. Carlos Fernández-Molina and Eduardo Peis, "The Moral Rights of Authors in the Age of Digital Information" (2001) J. Assoc. Inf. Sci. Technol. http://hera.ugr.es/doi/15003176.pdf accessed 2 July 2020.

once the element of artificial intelligence is included in the equation. What is the impact of artificial intelligence on the creation of copyrightable works? Or should we be questioning whether copyright can even accommodate artificial intelligence?

Section 2 of this theoretical chapter provides a global view of moral rights and its connection to the concept of authorship, considering the already mentioned Berne Convention. Other examples of existing legislations on the subject will also be examined, touching upon the fact that in Brazil, as in other countries, an author is defined as a natural person, meaning that machines would not qualify for copyright protection for they are not qualified as individual persons, and moral rights are non-negotiable. Section 3 addresses the requirements for a work be protected by copyright and its connection to ownership and moral rights. Finally, Section 4 analyzes the connection between artificial intelligence, creative works and possible legal answers to the questions asked throughout this chapter.

2.   AUTHORSHIP AND MORAL RIGHTS

While the emergence of sophisticated artificial intelligences with the ability to learn and improve has paved the way for new artistic opportunities, it has also led to a variety of new legal challenges, especially where copyright laws and ideals are concerned.

The Berne Convention of 1886 provides for the protection of works and the rights of their authors, containing a series of provisions determining the minimum protection to be granted, among other specifications.[11] More than 130 years after its enactment, the Berne Convention is still the most important international document concerning copyright regulation, having been ratified under the 1994 TRIPS Agreement (Agreement on Trade-Related Aspects of Intellectual Property Rights).[12]

In Brazil, copyright is regulated under Law No. 9.610/98, the Brazilian Law on Copyright and Neighboring Rights (hereinafter referred to BCL). According to its Article 11,[13] *author* is defined as an *individual person*, creator of literary, artistic, or scientific work, as is established by law in other countries. In Brazil, legal entities cannot be considered authors, even if they retain authorship rights on a specific work, as determined by Article 11's *sole* paragraph.

As to what copyright consists of in terms of rights, it can be thought of as divided into two parts: moral rights and economic rights. The moral rights are those identified in Article 24 of the BCL.[14] In contrast to economic rights, moral rights have a non-economic nature and are, as expressly determined by law, inalienable and irrevocable rights,[15] thus meaning they cannot be subject of a legal business act. In other words, they cannot be transferred, by the author,

---

[11]   WIPO, Summary of the Berne Convention for the Protection of Literary and Artistic Works (1886). https://www.wipo.int/treaties/en/ip/berne/summary_berne.html#:~:text=The%20Convention %20also%20provides%20for,the%20author"s%20honor%20or%20reputation. accessed on 7 July 2020.
[12]   TRIPS (Agreement on Trade-Related aspects of Intellectual Property Rights) [1994] Article 9 *Relation to the Berne Convention* https://www.wto.org/english/docs_e/legal_e/27-trips_04_e.htm accessed on 7 July 2020.
[13]   Law No. 9610 (1998) Article 11: The author of a literary, artistic, or scientific work is the natural person who created it. *Sole paragraph*: The protection conferred on the author may be conferred on legal entities in the cases provided for in this Law.
[14]   Law No. 9610 (1998) Article 24 on *Moral Rights of the Author*.
[15]   Law No. 9610 (1998) Article 27: *Moral rights are inalienable and irrevocable*.

to a third party. The Berne Convention also provides for moral rights which, in short, encompasses the right to claim authorship of the work and the right to object to any mutilation, deformation, or other modification of, or other derogatory action in relation to the work that would be prejudicial to the author's honor or reputation. Hence allowing for a right of attribution and the right of integrity, both provided for in Article 6*bis* of the Berne Convention.[16]

Economic rights, on the other hand, allow for the economic exploitation of the intellectual creation by its owner, if by prior authorization provided by the author of the intellectual work in question, as determined by Article 29[17] of the BCL. In short, economic rights allow the owner of the intellectual work to sell access to said work or otherwise exploit it for profit.

From this initial exposure to what the BCL determines, it is possible to grasp the fact that if *authorship* is solely attributed to an individual, to a person, therefore it is only logical that the same applies to moral rights. Would it then be possible to assume that if there is no personality, no *author*, the works created by machines, by artificial intelligence would be devoid of copyright and thus belong to the public domain?[18]

Prior to the *Edmond de Belamy* case, the most emblematic example involving the creation of artistic works by means of algorithms had occurred in 2016: *The Next Rembrandt*.[19] Although *new*, the painting was created by an artificial intelligence. This painting was generated through the process of *machine learning* trained to recognize the technical and aesthetic standards of 346 paintings by the Dutch artist Rembrandt.[20] The machine conducted a thorough analysis of the lighting, coloring and geometric patterns used by the artist and, with the help of a 3D printer, produced a portrait based on the styles found in Rembrandt's other works. This painting was not considered an imitation, but something unique and that could have been created by the actual Rembrandt.

The development process of the painting is indeed impressive. There is, however, one lingering question – which is, in truth, the most important issue for us to legally analyze the effects of the production of works by artificial intelligence regarding the ownership of copyrights. To what extent did the algorithms act independently in the elaboration of the new work? Or, in other words, what is the degree of human interference involved in the result of the painting? That was one of the many questions raised regarding the *Edmond de Belamy* case. There were those who claimed that the artwork had been made without any human interference. However, that was not the case for the creative process of the *Edmond de Belamy*

---

[16]   Berne Convention for the Protection of Literary and Artistic Works [1886], Article 6*bis*(1): "Independently of the author's economic rights, and even after the transfer of the said rights, the author shall have the right to claim authorship of the work and to object to any distortion, mutilation or other modification of, or other derogatory action in relation to, the said work, which would be prejudicial to his honor or reputation."

[17]   Law No. 9610 (1998) Article 29: "The express prior authorization of the author of a literary, artistic, or scientific work shall be required for any kind of use, such as … ."

[18]   Andrés Guadamuz, "Do Androids Dream of Electric Copyright? Comparative Analysis of Originality in Artificial Intelligence Generated Works" (2017) (2) Intellectual Property Quarterly 169 https://ssrn.com/abstract=2981304 accessed 7 July 2020.

[19]   ING, "The Next Rembrandt" (2016) https://www.nextrembrandt.com/ accessed 8 July 2020.

[20]   Microsoft Reporter, "Blurring the Lines between Art, Technology and Emotion: The Next Rembrandt" (13 April 2016) https://news.microsoft.com/europe/features/next-rembrandt/ accessed 8 July 2020.

portrait involved a human artist, who oversaw the collection of images that would be fed to the algorithm.[21]

The discussion, thus, is once more connected to the concept of author. In addition to the requirement that we have a natural person creating the work, the BCL, in its Article 7, establishes that the work, to be protected, comprises a "creation of the spirit", clearly meaning a creation of the intellect. The law does not support copies or reproductions, being necessary, to some extent, an original creation, an original addition to the realm of intellectual, aesthetic works. It seems that the concept of authorship is closely related to the existence of an intent to create, meaning that for an AI to be solely attributed with authorship, it would need to have some degree of an intent to create something original, however small this originality is.

In short, knowingly interfering in the result of a work seems to be of utmost importance to define who is its author. The Brazilian and Portuguese laws require that the authorship be the result of an act of intellectual creation and cannot be the result of chance or nature. Therefore, it would mean that if there is no intellectual contribution by a human being, the work would be in the public domain. However, what has been argued in the *Edmond de Belamy* case is in fact that there was some degree of intellectual contribution by a human being. But *how much* contribution is necessary to guarantee copyright protection?

The use of artificial intelligence in the production of intellectual works takes place in various ways and at different intensities. Someone can use artificial intelligence as an instrument of creation, just as a painter uses brushes or a writer uses a computer. In this case, then we can consider that there is an author behind that creation thus meaning that depending on the degree of intervention of the individual or individuals operating the artificial intelligence, copyright may be granted. The question remains as to whom and in what degree.

On the other hand, because of the massive production and collection of data provided by the Internet (big data), the development of more efficient algorithms and the evolution of hardware, the world today presents a very favorable scenario for the development of *machine learning*. In a nutshell, machine learning is a type of artificial intelligence that allows software applications to become more accurate at predicting outcomes without being explicitly programmed to do so.[22]

And some applications of this phenomenon have been dedicated to the elaboration of works supposedly susceptible to authorial protection. Comprehending this process is crucial in characterizing what AI-generated art really is. If we consider the creative process overall, and not just the resulting images, an AI-artwork could arguably be more than just its outcome.[23]

Nevertheless, if, ultimately, copyright protection as provided for by the BCL and by other existing international and national legislations is not compatible with AI-generated works for they would not fall under the concept of author, nor would they be considered a legal entity, how should the world deal with the fact that we will increasingly witness works created by artificial intelligence? If the works created by *machine learning* are devoid of copyright, will

---

[21]   Ahmed Elgammal, "What the Art World is Failing to Grasp about Christie's AI Portrait Coup" (29 October 2018) https://www.artsy.net/article/artsy-editorial-art-failing-grasp-christies-ai-portrait-coup accessed 8 July 2020.

[22]   Ed Burns, "Machine Learning" (March 2021) https://searchenterpriseai.techtarget.com/definition/machine-learning-ML accessed 10 July 2021.

[23]   Ahmed Elgammal, "What the Art World is Failing to Grasp about Christie's AI Portrait Coup" (29 October 2018) https://www.artsy.net/article/artsy-editorial-art-failing-grasp-christies-ai-portrait-coup accessed 8 July 2020.

there be any economic incentive for producing AI-generated works? To whom would moral rights belong in this case?

3.   WORKS PROTECTED BY COPYRIGHTS

Not every creation will be protected by copyrights. First, it is necessary to distinguish works of aesthetic nature from those of utilitarian and technical nature. Copyright covers the former, while Industrial Property, notably trademarks and patents, concerns creations of a utilitarian nature. A brand, for example, is expected to have an aesthetic and attractive component. However, its main function is not related to art, entertainment, or human delight, but rather to identify products and services. Patents, in turn, must solve technical problems, essentially involving rights that guarantee the exclusive use of inventions and utility models.

The protection of a work by copyright will be dependent to the fulfillment of some requirements. It is important to note that the international copyright system excludes any formality for the granting of rights, as is predicted by the Berne Convention, in its Article 5(2): "the enjoyment and the exercise of these rights shall not be subject to any formality".[24] For this reason, the registration of the work in official or governmental entities is not mandatory.

Although scholars diverge in regard to which aspects of copyright law should be observed to grant any given work copyright protection, it seems safe to assert that "the most basic requirements to acquire copyright that apply in most jurisdictions are subject-matter, originality, fixation and qualification".[25]

In relation to the *subject-matter* requirement, the Berne Convention establishes, in its Article 2, to which works copyright protection can be granted under the international system. According to item (1), literary or artistic works should be considered:

> … every production in the literary, scientific and artistic domain, whatever may be the mode or form of its expression, such as books, pamphlets and other writings; lectures, addresses, sermons and other works of the same nature; dramatic or dramatico-musical works; choreographic works and entertainments in dumb show; musical compositions with or without words; cinematographic works to which are assimilated works expressed by a process analogous to cinematography; works of drawing, painting, architecture, sculpture, engraving and lithography; photographic works to which are assimilated works expressed by a process analogous to photography; works of applied art; illustrations, maps, plans, sketches and three-dimensional works relative to geography, topography, architecture or science.

In addition to this list, we can include "translations, adaptations, arrangements of music and other alterations of a literary or artistic work shall be protected as original works without prejudice to the copyright in the original work" (mentioned in item 3 of the same article) and "collections of literary or artistic works such as encyclopedias and anthologies which, by reason of the selection and arrangement of their contents, constitute intellectual creations shall be protected as such, without prejudice to the copyright in each of the works forming part of such collections" (item 5 of the same article). On the other hand, item (8) excludes from

---

[24]   All references to Berne Convention for the Protection of Literary and Artistic Works [1886] https://www.wipo.int/edocs/lexdocs/treaties/en/berne/trt_berne_001en.pdf accessed 21 July 2020.
[25]   Jan Oster, *European and International Media Law* (Cambridge University Press 2017) 392.

copyright protection "news of the day or to miscellaneous facts having the character of mere items of press information".

In short, we have presented the international framework for the protection, through copyright, of intellectual works. They include, but are not limited to texts, music, audiovisual works, works of photographic arts etc. However, not all types of creations within this realm will be automatically viable for copyright protection and intrinsic requisites will be demanded for the application of such protection.

The first requirement is that of the concept of *originality*. "There is broad agreement that copyright protection requires originality, although this is expressed in different ways among international and domestic legal documents", declares Jan Oster.[26] He continues, commenting the European perspective on the topic:[27]

In *Painer*,[28] the Court went on to explain that an intellectual creation is an author's own "if it reflects the author's personality. That is the case if the author was able to express his creative abilities in the production of the work by making free and creative choices". On several occasions the Court applied its "own intellectual creation" formula, and came to the conclusion, for example, that newspaper articles, computer manuals, portrait photographs and graphic user interfaces can fulfil this criterion, whereas sporting events cannot. In practice, the required level or originality is fairly low, as has been demonstrated by the *Infopaq* judgements.[29]

A close look at the originality requisite framework reveals that it is connected to the idea that the author is a person. "Author's own intellectual creation", "author's personality", "express his creative abilities" and "free and creative choices" are expressions we would use to address the intellectual activity of a human being. This makes sense if we consider that two of the major theories used to justify copyright protection aim at ensuring compensation for the authors' labor or a defense of her/his personality.

Although "different jurisdictions have developed their own version of originality, and furthermore, the level of originality may vary in one jurisdiction depending on the nature of the work",[30] Professor William Fisher mentions that:

In all countries, a work must be "original" to be entitled to copyright protection. Two distinct requirements are encompassed by that principle. First, the work must be independently created – in other words, not copied from another work. Second, the work must embody a modest degree of something extra – what might be described, intentionally vaguely, as a "contribution" by the author.[31]

Depending on how we define originality, it may arise from a non-human creation. If an animal or a machine, for instance, creates something new (in the sense that it is not a copy of another

---

[26]   Ibid. 394.

[27]   Ibid. 394–5.

[28]   *Eva-Maria Painer v. Standard VerlagsGmbH and Others* [2011] European Court Reports 2011-00000. Judgment of the Court [Third Chamber].

[29]   *Infopaq International A/S v. Danske Dagblades Forening* [2009] European Court Reports 2009 I-06569. Judgment of the Court [Fourth Chamber].

[30]   Andres Guadamuz, "Do Androids Dream of Electric Copyright? Comparative Analysis of Originality in Artificial Intelligence Generated Works" (2017) (2) Intellectual Property Quarterly 169 https://papers.ssrn.com/sol3/papers.cfm?abstract_id=2981304 accessed 20 July 2020.

[31]   William Fisher, "Recalibrating Originality" (2016) Houston Law Review https://houstonlawreview .scholasticahq.com/api/v1/articles/3912-recalibrating-originality.pdf accessed 29 July 2020.

work) and added a "modest degree of something extra", it seems that originality can lie on non-human creations. However, if originality is necessarily considered an extension of the "*author's personality*", then there would be an obstacle to overcome if our goal is to grant copyright protection to non-human creations, considering the lack of personality rights granted to non-humans in most of the countries (at least, for now).

France, for example, "traditionally retains a subjective conception of originality, such as the imprint of the personality of its author. This apprehension again excludes all non-human creation."[32] On the other hand, however,

> Some doctrine writers also offer a different reading of the originality criterion, such as "novelty in the universe of forms". In any case, shouldn't the originality of the work be sought in the work precisely, and not by reference to its author? Besides, how to demonstrate this originality when the author is deceased or anonymous? Also, the criterion of originality should remain intrinsic to the work, as a sort of minimum creative manifestation.[33]

Fixation, in turn, is not a mandatory requirement for attaining copyright protection of a creative work. The Berne Convention establishes, in its Article 2(2) that: "It shall, however, be a matter for legislation in the countries of the Union to prescribe that works in general or any specified categories of works shall not be protected unless they have been fixed in some material form." This means that protection will be dependent upon the establishment of conditions imposed by each national law. According to the BCL, for example, the intellectual works that are protected are creations of the mind, whatever their mode of expression or the medium, tangible, or intangible, that is, notwithstanding their fixation or medium.

The last requirement, *qualification*, is not only important for the purpose of this chapter but is probably the most sensitive of the four. "The work will be copyright-protected only if the author qualifies for such protection at the material time."[34] In other words, we must have authorship or be a rightsholder. Since international treaties do not set forth any definition of authorship or even determine if a human author is mandatory, this issue will be left for national laws to decide.

Although it might be easy to assume that there must be an individual involved if a work is deemed to be protected by copyright, that is not always true and can be illustrated by the notorious case which involved a photographer, a selfie and, well, a monkey.

In July 2011, British photographer David Slater was photographing nature sights in Indonesia's National Park. After several attempts at close-up shots of the monkeys' faces, he

---

[32]   Free translation by the author. In the original, we can read: "*La France retient traditionnellement une conception subjective de l'originalité, comme l'empreinte de la personnalité de son auteur. Cette appréhension exclut à nouveau toute création non humaine*". Alexandra Bensamoun and Grégoire Loiseau, *Droit de l'intelligence artificielle* (LGDJ Éditions 2019) 256. The same reasoning can be found in Nathalie Nevejans, *Traité de droit et d'éthique de la robotique civile* (LEH Edition 2017) 279.

[33]   Free translation by the author. In the original, we can read: "*Certains auteurs de doctrine proposent également une lecture différente du critère d'originalité, comme la 'nouveauté dans l'univers des formes'. Dans tous les cas, l'originalité de l'oeuvre ne devrait-elle pas être recherchée dans l'oeuvre justement, et non par référence à son auteur? D'ailleurs, comment faire la démonstration lorsque l'auteur est décédé ou anonyme? Aussi, le critère d'originalité devrait rester intrinsèque à l'oeuvre, comme une sorte de manifestation créative minimum*". Alexandra Bensamoun and Grégoire Loiseau, *Droit de L'Intelligence Artificielle* (LGDJ Éditions 2019) 256.

[34]   Jan Oster, *European and International Media Law* (Cambridge University Press 2017) 395.

eventually gave up, believing that the animals were feeling somewhat threatened or intimidated. He then placed the camera on a tripod and waited for the monkeys to reach out and handle the camera themselves, which ultimately happened. According to the photographer, although many photos were useless, at least one was good enough to be displayed on the cover of National Geographic.[35]

According to Slater, he sent the photo to his agent and it reached the *Daily Mail*. At that point, the mentioned photograph had gone viral and was also featured in Wikipedia. The photographer asked the digital encyclopedia to remove and promptly delete the photo because he had not authorized its publication. However, Wikipedia officials refused. As a result, an intriguing legal dispute arose in which the photographer David Slater was sued in California by the PETA (People for the Ethical Treatment of Animals) organization. He was accused of violating *Naruto*'s (as the monkey was referred to during the lawsuit) copyrights. In other words, Slater was accused of copyright infringement.

Slater eventually won the case,[36] which is not surprising. Although animals have gained more rights,[37] it does not seem reasonable to grant them copyrights. Unfortunately, the lawsuit did not touch upon the question of ownership and, as such, it did not determine whether David Slater owned, to some extent, the copyrights of the photo in question.

At this point, an analysis of historical details is essential. Though one of the versions of the notorious *Naruto* case (the one reported above) pointed out that Slater had intentionally placed the camera on a tripod and waited for the monkey to approach it to take pictures, its accuracy remains a matter of controversy. An alternative version states that *Naruto* could have acted without the photographer's participation, even against his will, because the camera would have been taken by the monkey and later recovered by the photographer.[38] It is precisely in the space residing between a set tripod and a stolen camera that the legal developments on the photograph reside.

We are well aware that in the world of facts, the monkey *Naruto* is the author of this photo. But what about the legal world? Who will be attributed with authorship and ownership? It depends on the version of the David Slater's story that we chose to accept.

If Slater sets up a tripod and expects the monkey to take a picture of himself, he can (but not without controversy) be considered an author. After all, he will oversee and interfere in the creative work, since he has adjusted the equipment and intentionally left it where the monkey can reach it. There is an intention to create a work and a creative technical mechanism pre-

---

[35] Andres Guadamuz, "Can the Monkey Selfie Case Teach Us Anything about Copyright Law?" (*WIPO Magazine*, February 2018) https://www.wipo.int/wipo_magazine/en/2018/01/article_0007.html accessed 14 July 2020.

[36] BBC, "British Photographer Wins Two-year Legal Fight over Monkey Selfie" (*Newsround*, 12 September 2017) https://www.bbc.co.uk/newsround/41239954/ accessed 14 July 2020.

[37] David Chazan, "Pets No Longer Just Part of Furniture in France" (*The Telegraph*, 16 April 2014) https://www.telegraph.co.uk/news/worldnews/europe/france/10771361/Pets-no-longer-just-part-of-furniture-in-France.html accessed 14 July 2020.

[38] "Monkey Steals Camera to Snap Himself" (*The Telegraph*, 4 July 2011) https://www.telegraph.co.uk/news/newstopics/howaboutthat/8615859/Monkey-steals-camera-to-snap-himself.html accessed 14 July 2020; "Cheeky monkey! "Macaque Borrows Photographer's Camera to Take Hilarious Self-portraits" (*Daily Reporter Mail*, 4 July 2011) https://www.dailymail.co.uk/news/article-2011051/Black-macaque-takes-self-portrait-Monkey-borrows-photographers-camera.html accessed 14 July 2020; Olivier Laurent, "Monkey Selfie Lands Photographer in Legal Quagmire" (*Time*, 6 August 2014) http://time.com/3393645/monkey-selfie-lands-photographer-in-legal-quagmire/ accessed 14 July 2020.

scribed by the photographer in advance. Therefore, Slater could be determined as the author of the work because, according to some laws, he is the natural, individual person behind it. This is a possible argument, although the extent of his actual work is debatable.

However, if the camera was actually taken by the monkey without the photographer's intention, it seems that, at least according to the Brazilian law, he cannot be considered an author for he did not contribute intellectually to the creation of the photo. In this case (which would be Wikipedia's understanding), due to the lack of authors, the photo would enter the public domain.

In effect, the result of the intervention appears to be particularly important in determining who the author is – and if there is an author. Some laws determine that authorship is a consequence of intellectual creation and thus, cannot be accidental or the result of natural forces. Consequently, it is not a matter of who the camera belongs to or even if the monkey is on Indonesian land. If there is no intellectual contribution from an individual, the work would belong to the public domain.

4.   ARTIFICIAL INTELLIGENCE AND ARTISTIC CREATION

The purpose of this section is not to point out how some of the national laws potentially regulate copyright ownership resulting from works created by artificial intelligence[39] or how they are preparing for the inevitable challenge. Its aim is rather to evidence in which axis lies the imminent decision-making on how we can regulate the issue in discussion and what are the possible results.

With the constant technological evolution, not only concerning artificial intelligence, but other technologies as well, it is more than likely that national and regional initiatives will take a stand in regard to regulating this issue, which could, in a short time, substantially alter the conclusions proposed here. Therefore, what is intended is to identify the dilemmas that need to be faced so that the decision on how to regulate such works is made possible.

Let us go back for a moment to the *Naruto* case. A photograph depicting a monkey is, in theory, protected by copyright because it belongs to the realm of arts and is encompassed by the Berne Convention spectrum of *protected works* (see Article 2(1), as mentioned above). The *fixation* of such photograph in not indispensable, but in this case the requirement was fulfilled. Given that the level of *originality* requested for the purpose of granting copyright protection is not usually high, we can uphold that the picture of *Naruto* was original in the sense that it consisted of an independent creation and there was something new – a "contribution",

---

[39]   Two of the best papers written on the topic are mentioned here: Andres Guadamuz, "Do Androids Dream of Electric Copyright? Comparative Analysis of Originality in Artificial Intelligence Generated Works" (2017) (2) Intellectual Property Quarterly 169 https://papers.ssrn.com/sol3/papers.cfm?abstract _id=2981304 accessed 20 July 2020; and Ana Ramalho, "Will Robots Rule the (Artistic) World? A Proposed Model for the Legal Status of Creations by Artificial Intelligence Systems" (2017) https:// papers.ssrn.com/sol3/papers.cfm?abstract_id=2987757 accessed 29 July 2020: "All the jurisdictions examined – EU, US, Australia – have two things in common. First, they still equate the author with a human being. That makes sense if nothing else because rights need to have a subject – rights arising from authorship need to be ascribed to human beings, as machines are not subjects of rights. Second, they intertwine authorship with requirements for protection in a way that the former appears to be embedded in the latter."

a "modest degree of something extra", as mentioned by Professor William Fisher in the quote above. We know the definition of originality can be deeper and more complex, including those who claim that originality derives from human attributes. However, let us stick to the broader theory that defends that originality is intrinsic to the work, not to the author. Still, even more troublesome when analyzing copyright protection over the monkey's picture is the remaining requisite: *qualification*.

Who qualifies as the author of the picture? Is it the monkey or is it the photographer?

According to the BCL, neither. The photographer is not the creator of the picture (even if the equipment was his, which is not a criterion for granting copyright) and the monkey, who created the picture in the world of facts, cannot hold any kind of right, including copyrights, because to monkeys – as to any animal – rights cannot be granted. In general, animals are the object of rights, not the subject of rights. This is the reason for which the photograph was considered to be in public domain by Wikimedia Commons, "the reasoning being that the monkey was the author of the photo and because monkeys aren't legally capable of being authors under copyright law, the photo cannot be copyrighted".[40]

The notorious case involving the *Naruto* can be quite instructive in understanding how the creations made by artificial intelligence and copyright are connected. After all, we are presented with a work potentially protected by copyright (a photograph) that was not created by a human being. Therefore, the first question that needs to be asked when there is an artificial intelligence involved is whether it can create works regardless of the performance and interference of a human being.

According to Ana Ramalho:[41]

> Besides intelligence, AIs also presupposes autonomy. Autonomy implies that the work produced by the AIs results from it acting alone, independently from the constant input of a human operator. Autonomy can be defined as a matter of scale, according to the level of human involvement, and not necessarily in the binary state autonomous–non autonomous. In the low end of the spectrum of autonomy, machines are mere tools, whereas at the high end they will be an AIs capable of autonomously creating works, with little to no human input. The middle of the scale blends human and AIs participation, and it is arguably where the grey area and most problems for now lie.

This distinction between autonomous/non-autonomous artificial intelligence is of paramount importance for us to understand the problem we are attempting to tackle. When artificial intelligence works as a tool for intellectual creation developed by an individual, it seems reasonable to believe that the individual behind the creation can be considered the author of the work. In such cases, the use of artificial intelligence will be analogous to that of a brush by a painter or, perhaps more appropriately, the use of any software to create a work. If the author uses artificial intelligence to any extent while he has intellectual control over the result, he or she will be considered the author for legal purposes. After all, the fulfillment of the originality

---

[40]   Sarah Jeong, "The Monkey Selfie Lawsuit Lives" (*The Verge*, 13 April 2018) https:// www .theverge .com/ 2018/ 4/ 13/ 17235486/ monkey -selfie -lawsuit -ninth -circuit -motion -to -dismiss -denied accessed 19 July 2020.

[41]   Ana Ramalho, "Will Robots Rule the (Artistic) World? A Proposed Model for the Legal Status of Creations by Artificial Intelligence Systems" (2017) https://papers.ssrn.com/sol3/papers.cfm?abstract_id =2987757 accessed 29 July 2020.

prerequisite, necessary for copyright protection of a work, will be a consequence of the intellectual performance of an individual.

However, understanding the creative process and the role artificial intelligence plays in the decision-making of a work is crucial for purposes of attributing any kind of ownership rights. If it is determined that the artificial intelligence acts alone, making all the decisions throughout the creative process, it is arguable that the individual's intellectual contribution to the creation is null. Therefore, he or she will not be the one responsible for complying with the requirement of a minimum degree of originality, as was the case with the photograph taken by *Naruto*.

Considering this premise, the first difficulty to be addressed concerns the relationship between the work created and the copyright holder of the software or program. It has already been established that the creator of a computer program will enjoy a specific right over the developed program – either by copyright or by patents. There is no doubt about that. However, would the programmer also be entitled to the copyrights pertaining to the work created using the artificial intelligence, which was ultimately also developed by him?

The answer is not necessarily. The central point of the discussion is to know who, in the decision-making chain of the work's creation, is responsible for adding that minimum of novelty and originality that, as a consequence, makes it a work that can be protected by copyright. Who has creative control over the work?

UK 1988 Copyright, Designs and Patents Act has a provision concerning the authorship of a work that might be useful if examined. Section 9(3) determines that: "In the case of a literary, dramatic, musical or artistic work which is computer-generated, the author shall be taken to be the person by whom the arrangements necessary for the creation of the work are undertaken." The definition of "computer-generated" work is in Section 178 and is "the work … generated by computer in circumstances such that there is no human author of the work".

When analyzing the scope UK's legislation, Andres Guadamuz, in his article "Do Androids Dream of Electric Copyright? Comparative Analysis of Originality in Artificial Intelligence Generated Works", makes the following comments:[42]

> In that context, Lord Beaverbrook usefully commented that "[m]oral rights are closely concerned with the personal nature of creative effort, and the person by whom the arrangements necessary for the creation of a computer-generated work are undertaken will not himself have made any personal, creative effort." This suggests that the law recognizes that there is no creative input in computer-generated works, and therefore s 9(3) has been framed as an exception to the creativity and originality requirements for the subsistence of copyright. It is precisely this divorce with creativity what makes the UK"s computer-generated clause so different to other jurisdictions.

In addition to that, he mentions:

> Some commentators seem to be concerned about the ambiguity present both in the law and in *Express Newspapers*. Dorotheu goes through the options of who owns a work produced by an artificial intelligent agent, weighing the merits of giving ownership to the programmer, to the user, to the agent itself, or to no one at all. However, this apparent ambiguity could be solved simply by reading the letter of the law and applying it on a case by case basis. If the artificial agent is directly started by the programmer, and it creates a work of art, then the programmer is clearly the author in accordance to s

---

[42]   Andres Guadamuz, "Do Androids Dream of Electric Copyright? Comparative Analysis of Originality in Artificial Intelligence Generated Works" (2017) (2) Intellectual Property Quarterly 169 https://papers.ssrn.com/sol3/papers.cfm?abstract_id=2981304 accessed 20 July 2020.

9(3) CDPA. However, if a user acquires a program capable of producing computer-generated works, and uses it to generate a new work, then ownership would go to the user.

Thus, one of the apparent criteria to define the authorship of a work created by artificial intelligence would be to understand who, within the production chain, would have a determining role in the creative control of the work, who would be the person to contribute with originality to the emergence of that work. It could be the user, it could be the programmer, or even both. Even so, in some situations we could be facing an independent, autonomous creation, without the contribution of an individual. In this case, perhaps another solution is needed.

Apart from the situation brought up by UK law,[43] if the computer program acts in an absolutely independent manner, leaving no margin for any human interference in the final result of the work, then we would be probably facing a work without an author. On the other hand, if the software acts according to aesthetic choices defined by the programmer or the user that will add the minimum originality required for the work to be protected, then we may have a copyright holder. In any case, for there to be any copyright holder, whoever s/he is, we need an individual responsible for an *independent creation* and who offers a *minimally original contribution*.

Ana Ramalho addresses this situation arguing that:[44]

> By contrast, in AIs creations that are completely autonomous from any human input, it might be hard to discern a human being who would be responsible for the arrangements further up the chain. In fact, the scale of autonomy of AIs seems to work in inversely proportionate terms to the applicability of the regime of computer-generated works: the more autonomous the AIs, the less likely the applicability of the regime would be, due to the lack of human intervention. The provisions on computer-generated works do not therefore seem to be a solution for (increasingly autonomous) AIs, and even where they are a solution to less autonomous AIs, it is unclear who the person responsible for the arrangements is.

Consequently, it is possible to establish the relationship between artificial intelligence autonomy and the probability of having a copyright holder, whoever she or he might be (the programmer or the user, or both) shown in Figure 15.1.

The second issue to be faced is even more difficult to solve. With technological advances, AI-generated works, especially between the two extremes of autonomy (autonomous x non-autonomous), will become more and more common. They will be done by the thousands, by the millions – daily. How to know, with precision, the level of participation of an individual in its production chain to the point that we can say that a specific work has a human author,

---

[43]   A possible criticism towards the UK solution comes from Alexandra Bensamoun and Grégoire Loiseau, *Droit de l'intelligence artificielle* (LGDJ Éditions 2019) 260–1: "Indeed, [the law] invests the quality of author in a person who suffices to 'commission' the creation, to organize the generation, far from any idea of originality or creative choices. How could the sponsor of a work be its author? The frescoes in the Sistine Chapel are by Michelangelo and not by Pope Julius II, as Jane Ginsburg writes, not without provocation" (translated by the author). In the original we can read: "*En effet, elle investit de la qualité d'auteur une personne qui se contente de 'commander' la création, d'en organiser la génération, loin de toute idée d'originalité ou de choix créatifs. En quoi le commanditaire d'une oeuvre pourrait-il en être l'auteur? Les fresques de la chapelle Sixtine sont bien de Michel-Ange et non du pape Jules II, comme l'écrit, non sans provocation, Jane Ginsburg.*"

[44]   Ana Ramalho, "Will Robots Rule the (Artistic) World? A Proposed Model for the Legal Status of Creations by Artificial Intelligence Systems" (2017) https://papers.ssrn.com/sol3/papers.cfm?abstract_id =2987757 accessed 20 July 2020.

Figure 15.1   Copyright protection vs AI autonomy

who was responsible for giving it a minimum of originality, and who can, thus, be considered a copyright holder?

If national laws come to understand that works created by autonomous artificial intelligences are not protected by copyright (as is seemingly the current conclusion, considering the repercussions of the *Naruto* case), would this mean a lack of encouragement when it comes to business investments for the creation of autonomous works by artificial intelligence? This is a tough call. Intellectual creation does not depend exclusively on legal protection, although it is true that the monopoly created by copyright serves as an incentive.

If we consider Queen Anne's Statute of 1710 as a legal framework for the emergence of copyright in the world, it is evident that many works were created prior to its enactment, devoid of any kind of legal protection. Shakespeare, for example, did not need a legislative incentive to produce his plays. And even today, with the international copyright system consolidated in almost every country in the world, there are several initiatives that give up copyright protection and, even so, are successful, such as Wikipedia. There are many reasons for producing works that would be protected by copyright but waiving such rights: creation of public goods; desire for fame and recognition; amateurism are a few reasons. Accordingly, although it may be possible that the consolidated understanding that works created by autonomous artificial intelligences are in the public domain may indeed lead to a disincentive to the entrepreneurial production of such works, it does not seem sufficient to fully eliminate it.

It appears that in a scenario of imprecision on the extent to which a given work was created by artificial intelligence, companies will naturally claim relevant human participation in the design of their works generated with the aid of artificial intelligence. Thus, it would be possible to guarantee that the works are protected, preventing them from falling into the public domain.

All things considered, one or maybe a few final questions are called for: Will there be transparency in the future about the production of intellectual works using artificial intelligence tools? Will these works be audited? Will it be considered ethical to publish works created by autonomous machines as if they were created by humans? Will human works be more expensive and prestigious? Or otherwise, as exemplified with the *Edmond de Belamy* case?

Considering all the elements necessary for the protection of a work by copyright, *attribution* is perhaps the most relevant in the analysis of works created by artificial intelligence. If there is an author who can be qualified as such, we will have someone to whom we confer moral rights. The absence of an individual who created the work does not seem to be compatible with the granting of moral rights.

5.   CONCLUSION

Although international treaties do not stipulate that authorship stems from the existence of a human author, the copyright system seems to lean in that direction, since the Berne Convention determines that the initial term of copyright-protected works will go on for a specific number of years after the author's death and also confers moral rights to authors.

The creation of works using artificial intelligence is an inescapable reality. There are already many notorious examples among us, including some that demonstrate economic interests to be protected, and there will be increasingly more creations made by means of these technologies.

For a work to be endowed with copyright, it is necessary that some requirements are fulfilled, such as the subject-matter, its fixation in tangible medium, a minimum degree of originality, and the attribution of authorship to someone, as in an individual. In this last aspect, lies all the difficulty in protecting copyrighted works created by artificial intelligence.

Artificial intelligence encompasses a varied and heterogeneous series of technologies. As far as this work is concerned, the most relevant element concerns the possibility of artificial intelligence acting autonomously in the creation of a work subject to copyright protection due to complying with the other three requirements (subject-matter, fixation and originality). However, in this case, once the work is created, is it possible to attribute its authorship to someone?

The more autonomous the creative decisions of an artificial intelligence, the less probable that the work will be protected. After all, the international copyright protection system seems to demand the existence of a human for the work to be protected. If the aesthetic and original decisions were taken without the contribution of a human being, one of the fundamental requirements for the protection of the work by copyright would be absent. In this case, there would be no author. Therefore, there would be no moral rights to be protected.

Could an artificial intelligence hold moral rights? It seems highly unlikely. Firstly, because rights are attributed to human beings. Moral rights are precisely connected to the personal rights of the authors. The Berne Convention associates moral rights with ideas such as "honor or reputation" of the author (Article 6*bis*(1)) and death of the author (Article 6*bis*(2)), demonstrating a clear connection between moral rights and individuals. In fact, it will not be uncommon for authors who dedicate themselves to the analysis of personality rights to include the moral rights of authors among them, even if the classification is controversial.

From what has been discussed throughout the present chapter, it seems to us that moral rights of authors can never be conferred to third parties other than the author herself or himself. The concept of authorship may become blurred in the face of works created by artificial intelligence, but the safest theoretical criterion that seems to exist at the moment is to define who is responsible for the aesthetic decisions that provide originality to the work created through artificial intelligence.

If the artificial intelligence program is used as a tool by an artist and it is s/he who controls it, and therefore is responsible for providing it originality, s/he will be the author – and to the author will be granted moral rights. If, on the other hand, the work is the result of the performance of an autonomous artificial intelligence, which elaborated the work without the participation of an individual responsible for aesthetic decisions, then we must consider that this work lacks an author – in which case no one can hold moral rights. Therefore, it must be considered as a work in public domain.

16. Exceptions and limitations to moral rights
Johan Axhamn

1. INTRODUCTION

Much has been written about the need to balance the economic rights of the author and other rightsholders in relation to other, sometimes competing, private and public rights and interests.[1] This balancing act may take different forms, such as the prerequisites for protection, the scope of the economic rights, the term of protection and available enforcement measures. The main vehicle for balancing economic rights in relation to other rights and interests are generally held to be provisions on exceptions and limitations.[2] In recent years, much policy making at national,[3] regional[4] and international[5] level, as well as discussions in legal scholarship,[6] have been devoted to exceptions and limitations to economic rights.

---

[1]   See, for example, the proceedings from the ALAI Study Days, University of Cambridge, 14–17 September 1998: Libby. Baulch, Michael Green and Mary Wyburn (eds), *The Boundaries of Copyright: Its Proper Limitations and Exceptions* (Australian Copyright Council 1999).

[2]   Cf. Paul Goldstein and P Bernt Hugenholtz, *International Copyright: Principles, Law, and Practice* (4th edn, Oxford University Press, 2019) chapter 11.

[3]   See, for example, the recently (July 2022) set up investigation by the Swedish government on a complete review of the provisions on exceptions and limitations in the Swedish Copyright Act.

[4]   See, for example, Communication from the European Commission, Copyright in the Knowledge Economy, COM/2009/0532 final.

[5]   The issue of limitations and exceptions has been discussed by the WIPO Standing Committee on Copyright and Related Rights (SCCR) since its 12th session in 2004.

[6]   See, for example, P Bernt Hugenholtz and Martin Senftleben, Fair Use in Europe: In Search of Flexibilities, Amsterdam Law School Research Paper No. 2012-39; Ruth L Okediji (ed.), *Copyright Law in an Age of Limitations and Exceptions* (Cambridge University Press 2017); P Bernt Hugenholtz and Ruth L Okediji, Conceiving an International Instrument on Limitations and Exceptions to Copyright, Amsterdam Law School Research Paper No. 2012-43; L Guibault, "The Nature and Scope of Limitations and Exceptions to Copyright and Neighbouring Rights with Regard to General Interest Missions for the Transmission of Knowledge: Prospects for Their Adaptation to the Digital Environment", UNESCO-Copyright Bulletin, October–December 2003; T Rendas, *Exceptions in EU Copyright Law: In Search of a Balance between Flexibility and Legal Certainty* (Kluwer Law International 2021); Christophe Geiger and Franciska Schönherr, "Limitations to Copyright in the Digital Age", in Andrej Savin and Jan Trzaskowski (eds), *Research Handbook on EU Internet Law* (Edward Elgar 2014) 110–42; Christophe Geiger and Franciska Schönherr, "Defining the Scope of Protection of Copyright in the EU: The Need to Reconsider the Acquis Regarding Limitations and Exceptions", in Tatiana-Eleni Synodinou (ed.), *Codification of European Copyright Law, Challenges and Perspectives* (Kluwer Law International 2014) 133–67; Jonathan Griffiths, Christophe Geiger, Martin Senftleben, Raquel Xalabarder and Lionel A F Bently, "Limitations and Exceptions as Key Elements of the Legal Framework for Copyright in the European Union – Opinion on the Judgment of the CJEU in Case C-201/13 Deckmyn" (2015) 45(1) EIPR 93–101.

An example of this trend is the World Intellectual Property Organization (WIPO) Marrakech Treaty from 2013,[7] which requires contracting parties to introduce a standard set of limitations and exceptions to copyright rules in order to permit reproduction, distribution and making available of published works in formats designed to be accessible to visually impaired persons, and to permit exchange of these works across borders by organizations that serve those beneficiaries. Another example is the European Union (EU) Directive on copyright in the Digital Single Market from 2019,[8] which includes mandatory exceptions and limitations for the purpose of text and data mining.

In addition, the WIPO Development Agenda, adopted in 2007 by the General Assembly of WIPO,[9] provides a mandate and impetus for this international policy shift, emphasizing the importance of flexibilities, exceptions and limitations in intellectual property norm-setting and recognizing the benefits of a rich and accessible public domain. Also, the policy and scholarly debate on exceptions and limitations has been intensified in recent years with the recognition in case law, for example by the Court of Justice of the European Union (CJEU),[10] of so-called users' rights.[11]

In comparison, less, or almost no, focus has recently been devoted to the question on whether there is a need to further "balance" moral rights. The reason for this is not entirely clear. A fair assumption is that moral rights are not considered to be of similar "economic" importance as the economic rights, and that the precise scope of moral rights – and their relationship with economic rights, i.e. the distinction between monistic and dualistic traditions[12] – differs at national level and is often considered to reflect national copyright traditions. This could be related to, for example, the purposes and nature of copyright protection at national level and the relationship between economic and moral rights. The international minimum standard for protection of moral rights, the rights of paternity and integrity set out in Article 6*bis* of the Berne Convention,[13] may also have lost some importance by being excluded from the Agreement on Trade-Related Aspects of Intellectual Property Rights (TRIPS Agreement)[14] and its dispute settlement mechanism.

---

[7]   Marrakesh Treaty to Facilitate Access to Published Works for Persons Who Are Blind, Visually Impaired, or Otherwise Print Disabled.

[8]   Directive (EU) 2019/790 of the European Parliament and of the Council of 17 April 2019 on Copyright and Related Rights in the Digital Single Market and Amending Directives 96/9/EC and 2001/29/EC.

[9]   See Report adopted by the WIPO General Assembly, WIPO document WO/GA/34/16.

[10]   See, for example, case C-469/17 *Funke Medien NRW*, ECLI:EU:C:2019:623.

[11]   On the concept of "users' rights", see for example, Pascale Chapdelaine, *Copyright User Rights* (Oxford University Press 2017).

[12]   Other contributions to this *Handbook* go more in depth on the distinction between monistic and dualistic traditions.

[13]   Some countries provide for additional moral rights, such as rights of divulgation (disclosure), withdrawal and access. For an overview, see e.g., Sam Ricketson, *The Berne Convention for the Protection of Literary and Artistic Works: 1886–1986* (Centre for Commercial Law Studies, Queen Mary College 1987) para 8.95.

[14]   Agreement on Trade-Related Aspects of Intellectual Property Rights, 15 April 1994, Marrakesh Agreement Establishing the World Trade Organization, Annex 1C, 1869 UNTS 299, 33 ILM 1197 (1994) (hereinafter TRIPS Agreement). According to Article 9(1) of the TRIPS Agreement, "Members shall comply with Articles 1 through 21 of the Berne Convention (1971) and the Appendix thereto. However, Members shall not have rights or obligations under this Agreement in respect of the rights conferred under Article 6bis of that Convention or of the rights derived therefrom."

Against this background, this chapter will focus on exceptions and limitations to the moral rights set out in Article 6*bis* of the Berne Convention. On its face, Article 6*bis* does not seem to recognize a possibility to introduce exceptions and limitations to the rights recognized in that article. As questions of exceptions and limitations to moral rights relate directly to the scope of the rights as such, this chapter begins with a short and general description of Article 6*bis*.[15] This approach also provides the opportunity to describe the nature of moral rights and their relationship to economic rights; a relationship that, as mentioned, varies between different jurisdictions and, as will be shown, is connected to the occurrence of limitations to moral rights at national level.

The chapter is structured as follows. The next section, Section 2, provides a general overview of Article 6*bis* of the Berne Convention. Section 3 sets out the exceptions and limitations that are permissible in relation to economic rights, and discusses whether they are also relevant for the moral rights set out in Article 6*bis* of the Berne Convention. Section 4 describes the existence of exceptions and limitations to moral rights in some jurisdictions. Section 5 analyses the permissibility of exceptions and limitations to moral rights at national level in relation to 6*bis*. Section 6 includes a concluding discussion.

2. ARTICLE 6BIS OF THE BERNE CONVENTION

Article 6*bis* of the Berne Convention sets out minimum protection for moral rights at international level. The article was introduced at the Rome Conference for the revision of the Convention in 1928, and has been subject to revisions at subsequent revision conferences in Brussels (1948) and Stockholm (1967). The origins, or roots, of the article can be traced back to French case law and German scholarship during the nineteenth century.[16] In its English version, the article sets out the following:

(1) Independently of the author's economic rights, and even after the transfer of the said rights, the author shall have the right to claim authorship of the work and to object to any distortion, mutilation or other modification of, or other derogatory action in relation to, the said work, which would be prejudicial to his honour or reputation.

(2) The rights granted to the author in accordance with the preceding paragraph shall, after his death, be maintained, at least until the expiry of the economic rights, and shall be exercisable by the persons or institutions authorized by the legislation of the country where protection is claimed. However, those countries whose legislation, at the moment of their ratification of or accession to this Act, does not provide for the protection after the death of the author of all the rights set out in the preceding paragraph may provide that some of these rights may, after his death, cease to be maintained.

(3) The means of redress for safeguarding the rights granted by this Article shall be governed by the legislation of the country where protection is claimed.

---

[15]   Other contributions to this *Handbook* go more in depth on the scope of the moral rights of paternity and integrity, as set out in Article 6*bis* of the Berne Convention.

[16]   See Stig Strömholm, *Le droit moral de l'auteur* (Norstedt & Soeners 1966).

The main underlying rationale for the recognition of moral rights is the view that the work is the spiritual child of the author.[17] The development of new technologies and related possibilities to exploit works in new technological environments have made it necessary to safeguard the authors' interests with a set of rights that supplemented the economic rights.[18] The contents of Article 6*bis* do not refer explicitly to "moral rights"; it is only mentioned in its heading. In any case, the predominant view is that "moral rights" is the common label for these rights.[19]

Obligations to protect moral rights have subsequently been recognized in international and legal instruments and conventions on human rights, such as the Universal Declaration on Human Rights[20] and the International Covenant on Economic, Social and Cultural Rights.[21] Both of these international agreements state that authors, creators, and inventors should have some form of recognition and benefit deriving from their intellectual products. In comparison, the European Convention on Human Rights (ECHR), does not hold a specific provision on protection of property or intellectual property. This is cured by Protocol 1 to the ECHR,[22] which encompasses the right to property. Also, Article 17(2) of the Charter of Fundamental Rights of the European Union[23] holds that "Intellectual property shall be protected".[24]

Article 6*bis* of the Berne Convention is commonly held to reflect a dualistic perspective on copyright in the sense that the moral rights must be protected in addition to and independent of the economic rights.[25] The precise relationship between economic rights and moral rights may however differ at national level. Some countries – notably Germany – belong to a monistic tradition where the moral and economic rights are intertwined and are considered to constitute a unity. Conversely, some countries – for example France – adhere to a dualistic tradition that separates the two sets of rights. In addition, the preparatory works to the Berne Conventions states that contracting states are provided with great leeway on how to protect moral rights; protection does not have to be provided within copyright law proper.[26] This is a result of the

---

[17]   Claude Masouyé, *Guide to the Berne Convention for the Protection of Literary and Artistic Works (Paris Act, 1971)* (WIPO 1978) 41, Sam Ricketson and Jane C Ginsburg, *International Copyright and Neighbouring Rights: The Berne Convention and Beyond*, vol 1 (2nd edn, Oxford University Press 2006) para 10.02.

[18]   Elizabeth Adeney, *The Moral Rights of Authors and Performers: An International and Comparative Analysis* (Oxford University Press 2006) para 6.09.

[19]   General Report of the Drafting Committee, by Edoardo Piola Caselli, Vice-President and Rapporteur-General of the Conference, Records of the Conference, in *The Berne Convention for the Protection of Literary and Artistic Works from 1886 to 1986* (WIPO 1986) 171 n. 3. See also Gillian Davies and Kevin Garnett, *Moral Rights* (2nd edn, Sweet & Maxwell 2016) ix.

[20]   Universal Declaration of Human Rights, adopted 10 December 1948, GA Res. 217A(III), 3 UN GAOR (Resolutions, Part 1) at 71, UN Doc. A/810 (1948).

[21]   International Covenant on Economic, Social and Cultural Rights, adopted 16 December 1966, 993 UNTS 3 (entered into force 3 January 1976), GA Res. 2200(XXI), 21 UN GAOR Supp. (No. 16) at 49, UN Doc.A/6316 (1966).

[22]   Council of Europe, Protocol 1 to the European Convention for the Protection of Human Rights and Fundamental Freedoms, 20 March 1952, ETS 9.

[23]   OJ C 326, 26.10.2012, pp. 391–407.

[24]   For a discussion, see Martin Husovec, "The Essence of Intellectual Property Rights under Article 17(2) of the EU Charter" (2019) German Law Journal 840–63.

[25]   Sam Ricketson and Jane C Ginsburg, *International Copyright and Neighbouring Rights: The Berne Convention and Beyond*, vol 1 (2nd edn, Oxford University Press 2006) para 10.16.

[26]   See General Report of Main Committee 1 of the Stockholm Conference, Doc. S/247: Records 1967, Vol 1, p. 1159, Records of the Intellectual Property Conference of Stockholm, 1967, Report of

negotiations on 6*bis*, as moral rights where deemed by representatives of common law countries to be inconsistent with their legal traditions.[27] The question of the relationship between economic and moral rights can thus be said to reflect an underlying view on the hierarchy or structural conflict between the two types of protection.[28]

The perceived leeway, or flexibility, on how to implement Article 6*bis* makes it difficult to determine whether a particular country is complying with its obligations under the Convention. This pragmatic approach made it possible for the United States to ratify the Berne Convention in 1988 without amending its law to provide specific moral rights coverage. The United States took the position that a "patchwork" of common law actions and other federal statutory claims together afforded the rough equivalent of formal moral rights provisions.[29]

Moral rights have subsequently been recognized at international level also for performers. Article 5 of the 1996 WIPO Performances and Phonograms Treaty (WPPT)[30] provides international recognition for moral rights of paternity and integrity in favour of performers as regards their live aural performances or performances fixed in phonograms. In comparison, the Beijing Treaty on audiovisual performances,[31] which entered into force in 2020, does not include a similar provision on moral rights.

3.   LIMITATIONS AND EXCEPTIONS TO MORAL RIGHTS

3.1   General

As regards economic rights, it was held already at the negotiations that led to the Berne Convention that "limits to absolute protection are rightly set by the public interest".[32]

---

the Work of Main Committee 1, para 170. See also Gillian Davies and Kevin Garnett, *Moral Rights* (2nd edn, Sweet & Maxwell 2016) 29, 50; and Wilhelm Nordemann, *International Copyright and Neighboring Rights Law: Commentary with Special Emphasis on the European Community* (VCH Publishers 1990) 85.

[27]   Elizabeth Adeney, *The Moral Rights of Authors and Performers: An International and Comparative Analysis* (Oxford University Press 2006) para 6.20.

[28]   Gerald Dworkin, *The Moral Right of the Author: Moral Rights and the Common Law Countries* (ALAI 1993) 111 et seq.

[29]   Sam Ricketson and Jane C Ginsburg, *International Copyright and Neighbouring Rights: The Berne Convention and Beyond*, vol 1 (2nd edn, Oxford University Press 2006) para 10.36; Cf. William A Tanenbaum, "US Copyright Law after the Berne, Moral Rights and 1990 Amendments" (1991) EIPR 449–65; Gerald Dworkin, "The Moral Right of the Author: Moral Rights and the Common Law Countries" (1995) Columbia-VLA Journal of the Law and Arts 229–68.

[30]   WIPO Performances and Phonograms Treaty, adopted by the Diplomatic Conference on 20 December 1996 (WPPT).

[31]   Beijing Treaty on Audiovisual Performances, adopted by the Diplomatic Conference on the Protection of Audiovisual Performances in Beijing, on 24 June 2012.

[32]   Numa Droz, the Swiss official who presided over the first diplomatic conference on the (forthcoming) Berne Convention in 1884, submitted in his closing speech that "limitations on absolute protection are dictated, rightly in my opinion, by the public interest". See Actes de la Conférence international pour la protection des Droits d'auteur réunie à Berne du 8 au 19 septembre 1884 (International Office 1884) 67, also in WIPO 1886: Berne Convention Centenary 1986 (Geneva, 1986) 105. Cf. Sam Ricketson, *The Berne Convention for the Protection of Literary and Artistic Works: 1886–1986* (Centre for Commercial Law Studies, Queen Mary College 1987) para 9.1.

However, the exact meaning of "exceptions" and "limitations" is not entirely clear. In general, one can speak of subject matter limitations (or exceptions) and use limitations. Subject matter limitations include provisions that excludes protection altogether in the case of particular categories of works. Use limitations takes aim at provisions that provides immunity from infringement proceedings for particular kinds of use, for example, for private use, quotations or news reporting. Some use limitations require payment of remuneration or compensation, such as provisions on compulsory licences.[33]

At present, the Berne Convention includes both a general provision on permissible exceptions and limitations to the economic right of reproduction, in the form of the so-called three-step test (Article 9(2)), as well as more specific exceptions and limitations to the economic rights. This latter category includes exceptions for the purposes of quotations and illustrations for teaching (Article 10), as well as certain articles and broadcast works and of works seen or heard in connection with current events (Article 10*bis*). The Convention also includes provisions that permit contracting states to, in their national legislation, decide on the exercise of certain forms of broadcasting and communication to the public (Article 11*bis*) and the right of recording of musical works (Article 13) – for example in the form of statutory or compulsory licences.

Most countries around the world that are parties to the Berne Convention are also parties to the TRIPS Agreement. Article 9(1) of the TRIPS Agreement requires adherence to Articles 1 to 21 of the Berne Convention (with the exception of Article 6*bis*), including the outer limits on permitted exceptions and limitations set out in the Berne Convention. However, Article 13 of the TRIPS Agreement sets out a more general wording of the three-step test that applies to the limitations and exceptions that are permitted under Berne.[34]

In addition, Article 2(2) of the TRIPS Agreement holds that "nothing in Parts I to IV of this Agreement shall derogate from existing obligations that Members may have towards each other under … the Berne Convention". Thus, to the extent that Article 13 of the TRIPS Agreement might permit further limitations or exceptions to the exclusive rights protected under the Berne Convention than are presently allowed under that text, Article 2(2) of the TRIPS Agreement would require that Article 13 should not be applied in this way.

A further limiting factor is to be found in Article 20 of the Berne Convention, which is incorporated into TRIPS by virtue of Article 9(1) of that Agreement. This provides that Berne Members can make "special agreements among themselves" insofar as such agreements grant to authors "more extensive rights than those granted by the Convention or contain other provi-

---

[33]   See, for example, Sam Ricketson and Jane C Ginsburg, *International Copyright and Neighbouring Rights: The Berne Convention and Beyond*, vol 1 (2nd edn, Oxford University Press 2006) para 13.01; Silke von Lewinski, *International Copyright Law and Policy* (Oxford University Press 2008) para 5.150; Johan Axhamn, "Exceptions, Limitations and Collective Management of Rights as Vehicles for Access to Information", in Dana Beldiman (ed.), *Access to Information and Knowledge: 21st Century Challenges in Intellectual Property and Knowledge Governance* (Edward Elgar Publishing 2013) 164–86.

[34]   Cf. Report of the WTO Panel, 15 June 2000, document WT/DS/160/R, 30. The three-step test has received increased interest among legal scholars. See, for example, Martin Senftleben, *Copyright, Limitations and the Three-Step Test: An Analysis of the Three-Step Test in International and EC Copyright Law* (Kluwer Law International 2004); and Reto M Hilty, Christophe Geiger and Jonathan Griffiths, "Towards a Balanced Interpretation of the 'Three-Step Test' in Copyright Law" (2008) EIPR 489–96.

sions not contrary to this Convention". On the basis that TRIPS is such a "special agreement", the second limb of Article 20 is particularly relevant in the case of limitations and exceptions to exclusive rights other than the reproduction right. Thus, exceptions to any of the rights protected under Berne will need to find a basis under that Convention, rather than in the general language of Article 13 of the TRIPS Agreement.[35]

In a similar manner, the 1996 WIPO Copyright Treaty (WCT)[36] is also a "special agreement" within the meaning of Article 20 of Berne (see Article 1(1) of the WCT). This means that the WCT may only grant authors more extensive rights than those granted in the Berne Convention.[37]

In addition, with reference to discussions during revisions of the Berne Convention, it is the dominant view that the Berne Conventions permits "minor reservations" to the economic right of public performance. This includes uses for the purposes of "musical performances made in the course of religious worship, concerts given by military bands, charitable performances, public concerts organized on the occasion of particular festivals or holidays", although this is not reflected in the treaty text. The argument is that such reservations are of a *de minimis* nature and thus fall outside of the scope of the Convention.[38] The permissibility of the "minor reservations" has been questioned, especially in the light of subsequent legal developments such as the adoption of the TRIPS Agreement. The World Trade Organization (WTO) Panel in *United States – Section 110(5) of the US Copyright Act* concluded that the possibility of providing minor reservations has been incorporated into the TRIPS Agreement.[39]

The predominant view is that the provisions on permitted exceptions and limitations to the economic rights, as set out in the Berne Convention, are not relevant for moral rights. This also includes the so-called "minor reservations" doctrine. This interpretation follows from the fact that the provisions permitting exceptions and limitations to the economic rights are specifically related to the economic rights, in combination with the position that the Berne Conventions is based on a dualistic view of copyright.[40] This view is, however, blurred by the fact that some provisions in the Berne Conventions make explicit reference to the need to respect the moral rights of the author, an aspect that is further developed in the next section.

---

[35]   Cf. Daniel J Gervais, *The TRIPS Agreement: Drafting History and Analysis* (3rd edn, Sweet & Maxwell 2008) para 2.116 et seq.

[36]   WIPO Copyright Treaty (WCT), adopted in Geneva on 20 December 1996.

[37]   See, for example, Mihály Ficsor, *The Law of Copyright and the Internet: The 1996 WIPO Treaties, Their Interpretation and Implementation* (Oxford University Press 2002) para C1.10.

[38]   Sam Ricketson and Jane C Ginsburg, *International Copyright and Neighbouring Rights: The Berne Convention and Beyond*, vol 1 (2nd edn, Oxford University Press 2006) para 13.79.

[39]   United States – Section 110(5) of the US Copyright Act, document WT/DS160/R, para 6.63. Cf. Daniel J Gervais, *The TRIPS Agreement: Drafting History and Analysis* (3rd edn, Sweet & Maxwell 2008) para 2.127.

[40]   See, for example, Silke von Lewinski, *International Copyright Law and Policy* (Oxford University Press 2008) para 5.107 et seq; Sam Ricketson and Jane C Ginsburg, *International Copyright and Neighbouring Rights: The Berne Convention and Beyond*, vol 1 (2nd edn, Oxford University Press 2006) para 13.46; Gillian Davies and Kevin Garnett, *Moral Rights* (2nd edn, Sweet & Maxwell 2016) para 4.008. Cf. Paul Goldstein and P Bernt Hugenholtz, *International Copyright: Principles, Law, and Practice* (2nd edn, Oxford University Press 2010) para 10.5.2.

3.2   Reference to Moral Rights in Other Articles of the Berne Convention

In addition to the rights of attribution (paternity) and integrity mentioned in Article 6*bis*, other articles of the Berne Convention also refer to moral rights. Such references are found in Articles 10(3), 10*bis*(1) and 11*bis*. The application of Article 6*bis* has also been discussed in the context of Article 13.

Articles 10(1) and 10(2) set out provisions on certain free uses of works for the purposes of quotation and illustrations for teaching. According to Article 10(3), where use is made of works in accordance with the preceding paragraphs of the article, "mention shall be made of the source and of the name of the author if it appears thereon". The predominant view in the legal literature is that these "moral rights" referred to in Article 10(3) are distinct, rather than derivative, from Article 6*bis*.[41] Different views have been expressed on whether this means that Article 6*bis* still applies to lawful quotations and uses for illustrations for teaching. In the first edition of his commentary to the Berne Convention, Ricketson held – with references to recordings from the revision conferences – that the references in Article 10(3) to certain "moral rights" implied that Article 6*bis* did not apply to the uses mentioned in this Article. The argument was that it had been stressed at the revision conferences that modifications and alterations to a work are often necessary where it is quoted or utilized for teaching purposes.[42] In the second (and latest) version of the Commentary, authored by Ricketson together with professor Ginsburg, it is however submitted that Article 6*bis* applies also to the uses mentioned in Article 10.[43] The latter interpretation should be preferred as it is in line with wording of Article 6*bis* and the dualistic structure of the Berne Convention. Disagreements during the revision conferences on whether to include an article that re-iterates that Article 6*bis* apply to the uses mentioned in Article 10, does not remove the content of Article 6*bis*. Indeed, a statement in the report of Main Committee I notes that delegates were generally agreed that Article 6*bis* applies in respect of exceptions authorized by the Convention, including Article 10.[44] Thus, in summary, the rights of paternity and integrity in Article 6*bis* apply in addition to the requirement to "mention the source and the name of the author" set out in Article 10(3). The reference to "mention the name of the author" is thus redundant, and the text should be subject to legal scrubbing.[45]

Article 10*bis*(1) includes provisions on possible free uses of works of certain articles and broadcast works. The last sentence of this provision holds that when use is based on this article, "the source must always be clearly indicated". This reference is narrower than the reference in Article 10(3) to both the name and the source. The uncertainties that Article 10(3) gave rise to as regards the application of Article 6*bis* is thus not present for Article 10*bis*(1):

---

[41]   See, for example, ibid.

[42]   Sam Ricketson, *The Berne Convention for the Protection of Literary and Artistic Works: 1886–1986* (Centre for Commercial Law Studies, Queen Mary College 1987) para 9.28.

[43]   Sam Ricketson and Jane C Ginsburg, *International Copyright and Neighbouring Rights: The Berne Convention and Beyond*, vol 1 (2nd edn, Oxford University Press 2006) para 13.46. The same interpretation has been submitted by Silke von Lewinski, *International Copyright Law and Policy* (Oxford University Press 2008) para 5.107.

[44]   Records of the Intellectual Property Conference of Stockholm, June/July 1967 (Geneva: WIPO 1971) 1165.

[45]   Although any such possibility seems, at the time of writing, quite improbable due to the political stalemate in WIPO.

the moral rights set out in Article 6*bis* apply in addition to the requirement in Article 10*bis*(1) of indicating the source.[46]

With regard to broadcasting licences in Article 11*bis*, the situation is different. Article 11*bis* provides authors with the exclusive right to authorize the broadcasting of their works. However, according to the first sentence of Article 11*bis*(2), national legislation in the Union countries is given the task of regulating "the conditions under which the rights ... may be exercised". Such regulation might lead to the granting, by national rules, of statutory or compulsory licences that would undermine the author's control over the form in which the work was made known to the public. The second sentence of Article 11*bis*(2) thus holds that such national conditions on the exercise of the right "shall not in any circumstances be prejudicial to the moral rights of the author". Against the starting point that the Convention reflects the dualistic view of copyright, this reference to "moral rights" appears superfluous.[47] Nevertheless, it was thought appropriate to insert such a requirement in paragraph (2) at the time of its adoption by the Rome Conference.[48] The predominant view is that the expression "moral rights" refers to the rights mentioned in Article 6*bis*, i.e. the rights of paternity and respect.[49] In summary, the requirements of Article 6*bis* also apply to the uses mentioned in Article 11*bis*.

The application of Article 6*bis* has also been discussed at revision conferences in relation to Article 13, which deals with possible limitations of the right of recording of musical works (and any words pertaining thereto). The article provides contracting states with the possibility to place restrictions on this exclusive right, for example by providing for statutory or compulsory licensing. The flexibility provided by Article 13 to contracting states, gave rise to concerns among delegates at the Rome and Brussels conferences, since such removal of control from the author opened the way to exploitations of the work that were inimical to the author's moral interests. The matter was discussed in a special sub-committee, which came to the conclusion that when it came to Article 13 "a reservation of the droit moral went without saying and there was no reason to include it expressly as had been done in art 11bis, para 2".[50] The conclusions of the sub-commission should be supported. However, the fact that it was at all deemed necessary to discuss the application of Article 6*bis* in relation to Article 13 is, together with the references to moral rights in Articles 10(3), 10*bis*(1) and 11*bis*(2), an indication that it was not apparent that Article 6*bis* applied also in the context of exceptions and limitations to economic rights.

---

[46]   Cf. Silke von Lewinski, *International Copyright Law and Policy* (Oxford University Press 2008) para 5.158.

[47]   Wilhelm Nordemann, *International Copyright and Neighboring Rights Law: Commentary with Special Emphasis on the European Community* (VCH Publishers 1990) 55, 128.

[48]   See Actes de la Conférence réunie à Rome: du 7 mai au 2 juin 1928: Union internationale pour la protection des oeuvres littéraires et artistiques, also in WIPO 1886: Berne Convention Centenary 1986 (Geneva: WIPO 1986) 174.

[49]   Sam Ricketson and Jane C Ginsburg, *International Copyright and Neighbouring Rights: The Berne Convention and Beyond*, vol 1 (2nd edn, Oxford University Press 2006) para 13.71; Silke von Lewinski, *International Copyright Law and Policy* (Oxford University Press 2008) para 5.19.

[50]   For a discussion, see, for example, Claude Masouyé, *Guide to the Berne Convention for the Protection of Literary and Artistic Works (Paris Act, 1971)* (WIPO 1978) 80; Elizabeth Adeney, *The Moral Rights of Authors and Performers: An International and Comparative Analysis* (Oxford University Press 2006) para 7.45; Silke von Lewinski, *International Copyright Law and Policy* (Oxford University Press 2008) para 5.197.

In conclusion, the references to "moral rights" etc. in Articles 10(3), 10*bis*(1) and 11*bis*(2) are not only superfluous, but also misleading. They are misleading because they could lead to the erroneous conclusion that no attention needs to be paid to the moral rights of the author, as set out in Article 6*bis*, in cases where no explicit reference to moral rights is made. This should be subject to legal scrubbing at eventual future revision conferences.[51] As will be further described and analysed in Sections 4, 5 and 6, the wording of Articles 10(3), 10*bis*(1) and 11*bis*(2), and related discussions at the revision conferences, might have contributed to the retention or implementation of national rules on exceptions and limitations to moral rights that might not be fully compatible with the obligations of Article 6*bis* of the Berne Convention.

3.3   The Police Power under Article 17

In addition to the limited scope of permitted exceptions and limitations to the moral rights of integrity and paternity set out in Article 6*bis* of the Berne Convention, the Convention itself also permits exceptions and limitations on conditions set out in its Article 17.

Article 17 is based on the recognition that, in particular circumstances, sovereign states have the undisputed power to limit or deny private rights as part of their obligation to maintain "public order". In the context of literary and artistic works, this could take the form of, for example, censorship for the purposes of state security and the protection of public morals.[52] Article 17 has remained unaltered since the Berne Act:

> The provisions of this Convention cannot in any way affect the right of the Government of each country of the Union to permit, to control, or to prohibit by legislation nor regulation, the circulation, presentation, or exhibition of any work or production in regard to which the competent authority may find it necessary to exercise that right.

The article is generally held to be concerned with matters of "public order", rather than matters relating generally to the public interest. At the Stockholm Conference, however, there was considerable debate on the provision, in the light of a proposal from the United Kingdom to delete the words "to permit". The reason for this was to remove any implication that a member nation might, in the absence of the author's consent, authorize the exploitation of a work, or to invoke the article as a justification for the imposition of compulsory licences. This received the support of all delegates, except the South African delegate. This delegate took the view that, under Article 17, Union Members, as sovereign states, were "free to 'permit' the dissemination of the work, even against the will of the author, if that were necessary as a matter of public policy in the country".[53] However, Main Committee I recorded in its report that the

---

[51] Cf. Wilhelm Nordemann, *International Copyright and Neighboring Rights Law: Commentary with Special Emphasis on the European Community* (VCH Publishers 1990) 55, 128.

[52] Sam Ricketson and Jane C Ginsburg, *International Copyright and Neighbouring Rights: The Berne Convention and Beyond*, vol 1 (2nd edn, Oxford University Press 2006) para 13.90; Silke von Lewinski, *International Copyright Law and Policy* (Oxford University Press 2008) para 5.205 et seq.

[53] See General Report of Main Committee I of the Stockholm Conference, Doc. S/247: Records 1967, vol 1, p. 1173 et seq.

"overwhelming majority" of the Committee interpreted Article 17 in another sense, even with the inclusion of the words "to permit".[54] The scope of Article 17 is thus not entirely clear.

4.   EXCEPTIONS AND LIMITATIONS TO MORAL RIGHTS AT REGIONAL AND NATIONAL LEVEL

4.1   General

Whereas Sections 2 and 3 have focused on the scope of Article 6*bis* of the Berne Convention, this section will describe and analyse national norms on exceptions and limitations to moral rights at regional and national level: United Kingdom (4.2), France (4.3) and Germany (4.4). Section 4.5 sets out the current level of harmonization within the EU, and Section 4.6 describes the situation in the United States. Section 4.7 includes a summary and assessment.

4.2   United Kingdom

The current UK provision on moral rights of authors came into force in August 1989, via provisions in the UK Copyright, Designs and Patents Act 1988 (CDPA 1988).[55] Chapter IV Moral Rights of the 1988 Act grants the following specific moral rights: (i) the right of attribution (i.e. paternity right, set out in Sections 77 to 79 of the CDPA 1988); (ii) the right to object to derogatory treatment of work (Sections 80 to 83 CDPA 1988); (iii) the right to object to false attribution Section 84 CDPA 1988); and the right of privacy in certain films and photographs (Section 85 CDPA 1988). The first two are in implementation of the Berne Convention, whereas the third protects against passing off, and the fourth deals with particular situations concerning initial ownership of copyright.[56]

The UK legislators have used limitations on the definition of works, and of authors, to narrow the ambit of the moral rights.[57] Only copyright works and films can attract the rights of attribution and integrity. In addition, within the range of copyright works, the right of attribution and the right of integrity are limited by a detailed listing of the copyright works to which they do not apply, such as works made to report current events, periodicals, newspapers or encyclopaedias. In addition, the right of attribution needs to be asserted before it applies.

Section 81(6) of the CDPA 1988 includes three exceptions whereby the right of integrity is not infringed by anything done for the purposes: (1) of avoiding the commission of an offence; (2) of complying with a duty imposed by or under an enactment; or (3) in the case of the British Broadcasting Corporation, of avoiding the inclusion on a programme broadcast by it of

---

[54]   Ibid. For a discussion, see Sam Ricketson and Jane C Ginsburg, *International Copyright and Neighbouring Rights: The Berne Convention and Beyond*, vol 1 (2nd ed, Oxford University Press 2006) para 13.89; Silke von Lewinski, *International Copyright Law and Policy* (Oxford University Press 2008) para 5.205 et seq.

[55]   Previously, moral rights in copyright had received limited protection under the 1956 Copyright Act. For a discussion, see, for example, Simon Newman, "The Development of Copyright and Moral Rights in the European Legal Systems" (2011) EIPR 682 ff.

[56]   Cf. William Rodolph Cornish, "Moral Rights Under the 1988 Act" (1989) EIPR 449 ff.

[57]   For a discussion, see, for example, Simon Newman, "The Development of Copyright and Moral Rights in the European Legal Systems" (2011) EIPR 688.

anything which offends against good taste or decency or which is likely to encourage or incite to crime or to lead to disorder or to be offensive to public feeling.

As regards the paternity right, the CDPA 1988 provides for a large number of exceptions. The way this has been done is to provide that the paternity right is not infringed in cases where copyright "would not be" infringed because the act falls within certain of the permitted acts (Section 79(4) CPDA 1988). There is also an exception for incidental inclusion, for example if an artwork appears in an unplanned way in a film or broadcast. There are further exceptions relating to computer programmes and computer-generated artwork and artworks used in examinations.

In summary, the protection of moral rights in the UK is comparatively weak. It is a reflection of the sceptical approach towards moral rights in a common law tradition.[58] It is sometimes held that the protection of moral rights in the UK since 1988 merely codifies previous protection according to common law.[59] Although the protection of moral rights in UK law is limited in several ways, it is generally held to belong to a dualist perspective on the relationship between economic and moral rights. This is so because the two types of protection are clearly separated.[60]

4.3   France

France adheres to a dualistic view on the relationship between economic and moral rights. The protected work is treated as an extension of the personality of the author. The French copyright law (*droit d'auteur*) protects the following moral rights: (i) the right of disclosure (Article L121–2 of the Intellectual Property Code, IPC); (ii) the right of attribution or paternity (Article L121–1 IPC); (iii) the right to the respect of the work's integrity (Article L121–1 IPC); and (iv) the right of withdrawal (Article L121–4 IPC).

The characteristics and prerogatives of the moral rights in French law are remarkably strongly protected. The moral rights are perpetual, inalienable and imprescriptible (Article L121–1 IPC). In addition, the right of integrity is broader than what is required by Article 6*bis* of the Berne Convention. Article L121–1 of the Intellectual Property Code holds that "the author enjoys the right to respect for his ... work". Under French law, the author only needs to show that the integrity of the work has been violated, by way of alteration in form or spirit. He does not need to prove that he has suffered any prejudice as result of such alteration.

In general, the moral rights are not subject to limitations. In some instances, the limitations to the economic rights may give rise to a potential conflict between the protection of moral rights and limitations to the economic rights. This is, for example, the case concerning the limitation for the purpose of creating parodies (Article L122–5(4)). The strong protection of

---

58   Simon Newman, "The Development of Copyright and Moral Rights in the European Legal Systems" (2011) EIPR 683; William Rodolph Cornish, "Moral Rights Under the 1988 Act" (1989) EIPR 449; Paul Hughes, "Painting on a Broader Canvas – The Need for a Wider Consideration of Moral Rights under EU Law" (2018) EIPR 101; Gerald Dworkin, "The Moral Right of the Author: Moral Rights and the Common Law Countries" (1995) Columbia-VLA Journal of the Law and Arts 229.

59   See William Rodolph Cornish, "Moral Rights Under the 1988 Act" (1989) EIPR 449.

60   See Simon Newman, "The Development of Copyright and Moral Rights in the European Legal Systems" (2011) EIPR 688 ff. and William Rodolph Cornish, "Moral Rights under the 1988 Act" (1989) EIPR 449. Cf. Irini Stamatoudi, "Moral Rights of Authors in England: The Missing Emphasis on the Role of Creators" (1997) 4 IPQ 478.

moral rights may also give rise to conflicts with other rights. For example, the moral rights of the author may conflict with the property rights of the owner of the work, for example an architect who tries to prevent modifications to a building he designed.

Conflicts are resolved on a case by case basis, taking into account for example the type of use and work.[61] In situations where the author has granted a right of adaptation or translation of his work, the author is normally considered to have accepted that the work is modified accordingly. Even if modifications are necessary, the spirit, the character and the substance of the original work must be respected. In addition, a work's level of originality may be a factor in the assessment of a potential infringement. If the work is of limited originality, this may reduce the scope of the right of integrity. In addition, certain categories of works of a utilitarian nature, such as architecture, applied art and computer programs, are provided with a weaker protection for the integrity right.

4.4   Germany

Germany adheres to the monist view of copyright, according to which copyright is a single right under which the author's economic and moral interests are intertwined. The protection of moral rights is granted for the same term as that of economic rights, moral rights cannot either be transferred or waived; only upon the death of the author can they be transferred as part of the copyright to a third person by way of hereditary succession or can their exercise be assigned to an executor (Section 28 of the German Copyright Act, *Urheberrechtsgesetz* – UrhG).

The UrhG provides for three different moral rights of authors. The right of disclosure, set out in Section 12 UrhG, holds that the author has the right to determine whether and how his work shall be disclosed. The right of paternity is recognized in Section 13 of the UrhG, as the right to be identified as the author of the work, and also the right to determine whether the work shall bear a designation of authorship and which designation should be used. The right of integrity is recognized in Section 14 UrhG: the author has the right to prohibit the distortion or any other derogatory treatment of his work which is capable of prejudicing his legitimate intellectual or personal interests in the work.[62]

The term "legitimate" involves a balancing of interests between author and the defending party. In most situations where a use of a work is permitted in relation to the economic rights on the basis of an exception or limitation, the right to integrity still applies. However, the exercise of the right of integrity is subject to certain limitations.

According to Section 62(1)1 UrhG, use of limitations pursuant to §§ 44a UrhG et seq. may lawfully only be made without any alterations of the work. This prohibition of alterations is closely linked to the author's right of integrity provided for in Section 14 UrhG. According to Section 62(1)2 UrhG, the provision of § 39 UrhG on alterations of a work that are necessitated by performing a contractual licences use applies. This means that any alterations which are

---

[61]   See, for example, Paul Hughes, "Painting on a Broader Canvas – The Need for a Wider Consideration of Moral Rights under EU Law" (2018) EIPR 102; Simon Newman, "The Development of Copyright and Moral Rights in the European Legal Systems" (2011) EIPR 684; Elizabeth Adeney, *The Moral Rights of Authors and Performers: An International and Comparative Analysis* (Oxford University Press 2006) para 8.97; Gillian Davies and Kevin Garnett, *Moral Rights* (2nd edn, Sweet & Maxwell 2016) 429 et seq. with references.

[62]   In addition, German copyright law also recognizes the right of access (Section 25 UrhG). This right equally serves moral as well as economic interests of the author.

necessitated by the individual exemptions and do not conflict with moral rights of the author will be allowed. In addition, Section 62(2) UrhG allows for translations and alterations which merely amount to extracts or to transpositions of music into another key or pitch. Likewise, with respect to works of fine arts and photography, Section 62(3) UrhG allows for alterations which are necessitated by the method of reproduction being used, encompassing in particular the change of scale. Furthermore, § 62(4) UrhG provides for specific lawful alterations necessary for the use of works of language within collections for schools, religious services and instruction.

In any case, users as well as licencees must explain why the alteration of the work is justified in a particular case. The "core" of the right of integrity is, however, always preserved; the author can always prohibit severe distortions even if he has granted the right to alter his work.[63]

Special limitations apply for film works and the works used in the making of such works (Sections 83 and 93 UrhG). The authors of a film work and of the works used in the film's production can prohibit only gross distortions or other gross impairments of their works or achievements, with appropriate regard taken for each other and for the film producer.

The German Federal Supreme Court has held that destruction of a work would fall within the scope of application of the right of integrity.[64] However, to find infringement of the right against distortion, a balancing of interests with the legitimate interests of the proprietor (and his right to freely use his property) has to be undertaken. According to the Federal Supreme Court, within the scope of this balancing of interests it is necessary to take into account whether the destroyed work is the only copy and the level of originality of the work. It may also be relevant whether the author has had the opportunity to take back the work or to make copies. In most cases, the balancing of the right of integrity against the rights of the proprietor would lead to the result that the author's interests do not prevail.

4.5   European Union

4.5.1   General

Copyright has been the subject of extensive harmonization within the EU. There are currently over ten directives in force, covering most dimensions of copyright; subject matter, exclusive rights, permissible exceptions and limitations, and term of protection. The case law of the CJEU has clarified or increased ("gap filling") the scope of harmonization.

One area of copyright where there currently is no explicit EU harmonization is moral rights. At present, some articles and recitals in some EU directives include references with the content that the directive does not apply, or is without prejudice, to provisions on moral rights in the member states.[65] The question of whether to harmonize these rights within the EU have been discussed by the European Commission[66] and by legal scholars,[67] especially taking into

---

[63]   See, for example, BGH GRUR 1971, 269 – Das zweite Mal.
[64]   See ref.: I ZR 98/17 and I ZR 99/17.
[65]   See, for example, Article 9 and Recital 21 of the Term Directive, Recital 28 of the Database Directive, and Recital 19 of the Information Society Directive.
[66]   See, for example, European Commission, Green Paper Copyright and the Challenge of Technology – Copyright Issues Requiring Immediate Action, COM(88) 172 final, Brussels, 7 June 1988, paras 1.4.9 and 1.4.10.
[67]   See, for example, Adolf Dietz, *Copyright Law in the European Community* (Sijthoff & Noordhoff 1978) paras 193, 194, Alain Strowel and Marjut Salokannel, *Moral Rights in the Context of the*

account the development of digital technology and the online environment,[68] but so far there is no political support for direct harmonization. National divergences on the protection of moral rights have – so far – not been deemed to disturb the functioning of the internal market. The CJEU has referred to the protection of moral rights as a recognized area of copyright that is not (yet) subject to EU harmonization.[69] There is also a common perception that any harmonization of this area may lead to a weakening of protection in some countries, to an extent that would be unacceptable for some member states with a tradition of strong protection of moral rights.[70]

The fact that moral rights have so far not been subject to explicit harmonization within the EU also means that there has been no explicit harmonization of any exceptions and limitations to such rights. However, what could maybe be labelled as "partial" or "quasi" harmonization of the moral right of paternity is reflected in some of the provisions in the closed list of exceptions and limitations to the economic rights in Article 5.3 of Directive (2001/29) on copyright in the information society.

Article 5(3)(a) of the directive permits member states to provide for an exception or limitation for use for the sole purpose of illustration for teaching or scientific research, as long as the source, including the author's name, is indicated, unless this turns out to be impossible and to the extent justified by the non-commercial purpose to be achieved. Article 5(3)(c) holds that member states may provide for an exception or limitation for reproduction by the press, communication to the public or making available of published articles on current economic, political or religious topics or of broadcast works or other subject matter of the same character, in cases where such use is not expressly reserved, and as long as the source, including the author's name, is indicated, or use of works or other subject matter in connection with the reporting of current events, to the extent justified by the informatory purpose and as long as the source, including the author's name, is indicated, unless this turns out to be impossible. Article 5(3)(d) permits member states to provide for an exception or limitation for quotations for purposes such as criticism or review, provided that they relate to a work or other subject matter which has already been lawfully made available to the public, that, unless this turns out to be impossible, the source, including the author's name, is indicated, and that their use is in accordance with fair practice, and to the extent required by the specific purpose. Article 5(3) (f) allows member states to provide for an exception or limitation to permit use of political speeches as well as extracts of public lectures or similar works or subject matter to the extent justified by the informatory purpose and provided that the source, including the author's name, is indicated, except where this turns out to be impossible.

Exploitation of Works through Digital Technology: Final Report (European Commission 2000) (Study contract No ETD/99/B5-3000/E 28).

[68]   See, for example, "Commission Staff Working Paper on the Review of the EC Legal Framework in the Field of Copyright and Related Rights" (2004) SEC 995, 17 July 2004 para 3.5; See also G Lea, "Moral Rights: Moving from Rhetoric to Reality in Pursuit of European Harmonisation", in Eric Barendt and Alison Firth (eds), *Yearbook of Copyright and Media Law* Volume VI (Oxford University Press 2002) 61, 62.

[69]   See Case C-55/80, *Musik-Vertrieb Membran GmbH v. GEMA*, ECLI:EU:C:1981:10, para 12: "copyright comprises moral rights".

[70]   Gillian Davies and Kevin Garnett, *Moral Rights* (2nd edn, Sweet & Maxwell 2016) 1257. Cf. Paul Hughes, "Painting on a Broader Canvas – The Need for a Wider Consideration of Moral Rights under EU Law" (2018) EIPR 95 ff.

The references to "the name of the author" in the referred exceptions and limitations is in line with the obligation according to some of the similar provisions on exceptions and limitations in the Berne Convention (see Section 3.2 above) on the requirement to indicate the name of the author.

Notwithstanding this "quasi" harmonization of the right of paternity within the scope of application of exceptions and limitations, it is difficult to see how the EU can avoid harmonization of moral rights in the long term.[71] There are references in the recently adopted EU Directive (2019/790) on copyright in the digital single market (DSM Directive),[72] that indicates a movement towards at least an indirect harmonization in this area. This aspect will be discussed in the next section.

4.5.2   EU Directive on Copyright in the digital single market

Similar to previous EU directives, the DSM Directive sets out to harmonize aspects of economic rights rather than moral rights. The directive includes no general references to moral rights, although Recitals 23 and 37 in the preamble to the directive refers to the freedom of the member states to require that the use of works or other subject matter based on an exception or limitation set out in the directive respect the moral rights of authors and performers.

However, Article 17 in the directive includes provisions that might have an impact – at least indirect – on moral rights in the EU member states. The article creates an obligation on information society service providers storing and giving access to large amounts of works and other subject matter uploaded by their users – so-called online content-sharing service providers (OCSSPs) – to take measures to ensure the functioning of agreements concluded with rightholders and to prevent the availability on their services of content identified by rightholders in cooperation with the service providers.

To achieve this, Article 17(1) holds that member states shall provide that an OCSSP performs an act of communication to the public or an act of making available to the public when it gives the public access to copyright-protected works or other protected subject matter uploaded by its users. An OCSSP needs to obtain an authorization from the rightholders, for instance by concluding a licensing agreement, in order to lawfully communicate to the public or make available to the public works or other subject matter. Article 17(2) holds that where an OCSSP obtains an authorization according to Article 17(1), that authorization shall also cover acts carried out by users of the services. In addition, Article 17(3) provides that when the service providers carry out an act of communication to the public according to Articles 17(1) or 17(2), the limitation of liability established in Article 14(1) of the e-commerce Directive 2000/31/EC4 does not apply.

Where no authorization is granted under Article 17(1) and (2), Article 17(4) provides for a specific regime that allows the OCSSPs to avoid liability, under specific conditions, for the act of communication to the public within the meaning of Article 17(1). Article 17(5) provides that the assessment of whether OCSSPs comply with the conditions set out in Article 17(4)

---

[71]   Cf. Paul Hughes, "Painting on a Broader Canvas – The Need for a Wider Consideration of Moral Rights under EU Law" (2018) EIPR 95 ff.

[72]   Directive (EU) 2019/790 of the European Parliament and of the Council of 17 April 2019 on copyright and related rights in the Digital Single Market and amending Directives 96/9/EC and 2001/29/EC.

needs to be done in light of the principle of proportionality. Article 17(6) provides for a different liability regime for new service providers, under certain conditions.

Article 17(7) stipulates that when OCCSPs cooperate with rightholders under Article 17(4) to avoid unauthorized content, such cooperation shall not result in the unavailability of works and other subject matter uploaded by users, which do not infringe on copyright and related rights, including where such works or other subject matter are covered by an exception or limitation.

What is of interest for this chapter, concerning Article 17, is the content of the second paragraph of Article 17(7). This paragraph holds that member states shall ensure that users are able to rely on any of the following existing exceptions or limitations when uploading and making available content generated by users on online content-sharing services: (a) quotation, criticism, review; and (b) use for the purpose of caricature, parody or pastiche.

It thus seems as if Article 17(7) makes these limitations mandatory; both for the member states to introduce in their national legislation, but also to make them mandatory in relation to any contractual conditions between rightholders and the service providers (according to Article 17(1)). The novelty here is that exceptions and limitations have, so far, in general been voluntary for the member states to introduce in their national legislation. The most important provision in EU law on exceptions and limitations (to the economic rights) is Article 5 of the Infosoc Directive (see Section 4.5.1 above), which includes a closed list of permitted and voluntary exceptions to economic rights. In contrast, the particular exceptions and limitations in Article 17(7) are mandatory for the member states to implement. In addition, they apply specifically and only to the online environment and to all users when uploading and making available content generated by users on OCCSPs.

The question appears whether Article 17(7), second paragraph, has any impact on the protection of moral rights in the member states. The wording of Article 17(7) is quite general and does not refer explicitly to exceptions and limitations to "economic rights". The relevant recitals, related to Article 17, in the preamble to the directive does not refer to moral rights, whereas recitals related to articles in the directive harmonizing other exceptions and limitations include such references.[73] However, the context is Article 17 which is directly related to the economic rights of communication to the public and making available to the public, as referred to in Articles 17(1) and 17(2). It is thus a fair interpretation that Article 17(7), second paragraph, does not intend to harmonize any exceptions and limitations to moral rights at member state level.

There might be pronounced – and possibly legitimate – expectations that use of existing works for the purposes of quotations, caricature, parody and pastiche, should be permitted on a cross-border, pan-European level without any concerns related to protection for the right of integrity in some member states.

4.6   United States of America

The United States signed up to the Berne Convention in 1988. The main reason for the delay was the protection of moral rights in Article 6*bis* of the Convention. This provision, with its

---

[73]   See Recitals 23 (related to Article 5 on use of works and other subject matter in digital and cross-border teaching activities), and 37 (related to Article 8 on use of out-of-commerce works and other subject matter by cultural heritage institutions).

dualistic approach to the relationship between economic and moral rights, was deemed by the United States to constitute a challenge for the exploitation of copyright-protected content.[74]

There is at present no general statutory provision on the protection of moral rights that fully reflect the content of Article 6*bis*. The US is sometimes held to fulfil its international obligations through case law and legislation in the individual states,[75] and a federal statute on moral rights for certain categories of works – the Visual Artists Rights Act of 1990 (VARA). It is, however, doubtful whether these in combination fully reflects the requirements of Article 6*bis* of the Berne Convention.[76] The US was also influential in the exclusion of Article 6*bis* from the scope of the TRIPS Agreement.[77]

VARA protects original "works of visual art", which essentially means certain paintings, drawings, prints, sculptures, or still photographic images that can be considered "fine art" (cf. Section 101 of the Copyright Act). In addition, to be eligible for protection under VARA, the works must only exist in a single copy or be works produced in signed and numbered editions of 200 or less. VARA grants artists limited rights of paternity and integrity (see Section 106A of the Copyright Act of 1976).

Numerous exclusions and qualifications severely limit VARA's scope. For example, protection does not extend to visual art that is utilitarian in nature or is reproduced in books, magazines, newspapers, motion pictures and other commercial contexts that otherwise would be infringing. Works created by employees and in other "work for hire" contexts are excluded from protection.

Section 106A of the Copyright Act provides limited moral rights of attribution and integrity. With respect to the right of attribution, the author of a work of visual art has the right to claim authorship of that work and to prevent the use of his or her name as the author of any work of visual art that he or she did not create. The author of a work of visual art also has the right to prevent the use of his or her name as the author of a work of visual art that has been distorted, mutilated, or otherwise modified so as to be "prejudicial to his or her honor or reputation". With respect to the right of integrity, the author of a work of visual art has the right "to prevent any intentional distortion, mutilation, or other modification of that would be prejudicial to his or her honor or reputation", a right that would be violated by "any intentional distortion, mutilation, or modification of that work". The author of a work of visual art also has the right "to prevent the destruction of a work of recognized stature", a right that would be violated by "any intentional or grossly negligent destruction of that work".

The author's rights of attribution and integrity provided by Section 106A are subject to significant statutory exceptions. In particular, the right of attribution "does not apply to any reproduction, depiction, portrayal, or other use of a work" in, upon, or in connection with

---

[74] See, for example, Gerald Dworkin, "The Moral Right of the Author: Moral Rights and the Common Law Countries" (1995) Columbia-VLA Journal of the Law and Arts 229–68; William A Tanenbaum, "US Copyright Law After the Berne, Moral Rights and 1990 Amendments" (1991) EIPR 449–65.

[75] Some individual states in the United States have enacted legislation which provides some form of moral rights. In addition, state and common law provide causes of action for misappropriation, unfair competition, breach of contract etc. which may be of some relevance.

[76] See, for example, Gerald Dworkin, "The Moral Right of the Author: Moral Rights and the Common Law Countries" (1995) Columbia-VLA Journal of the Law and Arts 229–68; William A Tanenbaum, "US Copyright Law After the Berne, Moral Rights and 1990 Amendments" (1991) EIPR 449–65.

[77] See, for example, Daniel J Gervais, *The TRIPS Agreement: Drafting History and Analysis* (3rd edn, Sweet & Maxwell 2008) para 2.87 et seq.

a work made for hire, motion pictures, books, magazines, advertising, any other item excluded from the definition of a "work of visual art".

The right of integrity does not apply to the "reproduction, depiction, portrayal, or other use of a work" in, upon, or in connection with a work made for hire, motion pictures, books, magazines, advertising, or any other item excluded from the definition of a "work of visual art". The right of integrity provided by Section 106a also does not apply to modifications of a work of visual art that are "the result of the passage of time or the inherent nature of the materials" of the work or to modifications that are "the result of conservation efforts, including lighting and placement, unless the modification is caused by gross negligence". Finally, the right of integrity is subject to the specific limitations that are applicable to exclusive economic rights in pictorial, graphic and sculptural works.

4.7   Summary and Assessment

The description of the protection of the moral rights of attribution (paternity) and integrity, as required by Article 6*bis* of the Berne Convention, in the selected jurisdictions (United Kingdom, France, Germany, the EU and the United States), shows that there are great differences in how and to which extent these rights are recognized, and the availability of exceptions and limitations.

Whereas Article 6*bis* of the Berne Convention seems to encompass most literary and artistic works, some jurisdictions exclude moral rights protection for some categories of works. In addition, some jurisdictions exclude certain modifications or alterations from the scope of the right of integrity. To a large extent these exclusions seem to be based on utilitarian or economic interests. However, not all of these exclusions are incompatible with Article 6*bis*. First of all, the Convention does not oblige contracting states to provide protection for applied art (cf. Article 2(7) of the Convention).[78] Thus, it seems as if it is permissible, according to the Convention, to exclude moral rights protection for works of applied art.

Even though Article 6*bis* provides some leeway to the contracting states when it comes to the contours of moral rights protection at national level, including how moral rights should be protected, the provision undoubtedly sets out a minimum "core" for the rights of integrity and paternity.

As regards the right of integrity, even countries with a "strong" protection for this right usually also acknowledge the need for a balance between the interests of the author and the user of the work or owner of the physical embodiment of the work, particularly in the case of works with a utilitarian aspect, such as works of architecture. Differences emerge in the approach to questions of repair or destruction of a work.

The exceptions and limitations to the moral rights of attribution and integrity that are reflected – to a small or greater extent – in all the studies jurisdictions, do not seem to find explicit support in the Berne Convention. The assessment is, however, complex as some jurisdictions, such as France, provide for broader rights of attribution and integrity than what is required by the Convention. A use which falls within an exception or limitation to the right

---

[78]   According to Article 2(7) of the Convention, "it shall be a matter for legislation in the countries of the Union to determine the extent of the application of their laws to works of applied art and industrial designs and models, as well as the conditions under which such works, designs and models shall be protected".

of integrity may in some instances fall completely outside the "core" of the right as recognized by Article 6*bis*. Thus, an assessment has to be made not only based on the existence and scope of an exception or limitation, but rather based on the recognition that a specific use might not even fall within the "core" of the right as recognized in Article 6*bis*.

The fact that some articles on exceptions and limitations to the economic rights in the Berne Convention make references to the moral rights is confusing (see Section 3.2). This should be adjusted during any future revision of the Berne Convention. In any case, it cannot be ruled out that some countries may have based some of their exceptions and limitations on non-traditional interpretation of the mentioned articles in the Berne Convention. In addition, the scope of exceptions or limitations based on the "*ordre public*" provision in Article 17 of the Convention is not clear. At the same time, it seems far-fetched that some of the broad exceptions and limitations to moral rights set out in some jurisdictions should be permissible on the basis of Article 17. Article 17 concerns matters of "public order", not "the public interest" in general.

This said, there might be room to base a national exception or limitation to moral rights on other sources of international law such as state practice.

5.   EXCEPTIONS AND LIMITATIONS TO MORAL RIGHTS – COMPATIBLE WITH INTERNATIONAL LAW?

5.1   Customary International Law

Previous sections have indicated that it is doubtful whether exceptions and limitations to the right of paternity and the right of integrity, are permitted according to the wording, context and purpose of the Berne Convention, especially its Article 6*bis*. There may, however, be a legal basis in international law for such national provisions: subsequent state practice and customary international law. This will be explored in the following.

The question of whether national exceptions and limitations to the moral rights set out in Article 6*bis* of the Berne Convention may be permitted on the basis of "customary international law" touches on fundamental questions in international law on the relationship – or hierarchy – between treaty law and customary international law.

Article 38(1) of the Statute of the International Court of Justice (ICJ) sets out the sources of international law. The article requires the Court to apply, among other things: (a) international conventions, whether general or particular, establishing rules expressly recognized by the contesting states; (b) international custom, as evidence of a general practice accepted as law; (c) the general principles of law recognized by civilized nations; and (d) judicial decisions and the teachings of the most highly qualified publicists of the various nations, as subsidiary means for the determination of rules of law.

In the words of Article 38(1)(b) customary international law requires "a general practice accepted as law". This entails both sufficiently widespread and consistent practice and *opinio juris* accompanying it.[79] *Opinio juris* refers to belief by the states engaging in the practice that it is legally required or permitted.[80]

The relationship between treaty law and customary law is not entirely settled. Is there a hierarchical relationship in the sense that one source is to be given priority over the other? Article 38(1) of the Statute of the ICJ lists the sources of international law, but does not indicate specifically whether the order in which they are mentioned also indicated the order in which they are to be applied.[81] The predominant view, also expressed in case law from the ICJ, is that Article 38 does not establish a rigid hierarchy of sources, in particular when it comes to the relationship between customary law and treaties; these can supersede each other and also exist alongside each other.[82]

However, a conflict is not necessarily the result. Rather, it is a generally accepted principle that when several norms bear on a single issue they should, to the extent possible, be interpreted so as to give rise to a single set of compatible obligations; and that it may be found that one norm simply "assists in the interpretation of the other".[83] It could be the case, for example, that a practice among parties to a treaty establishes the agreement. That such a situation could appear is reflected in the Vienna Convention on the Law of Treaties.

Articles 31 and 32 of the Vienna Convention on the Law of Treaties set forth, respectively, the general rule of interpretation and the recourse to supplementary means of interpretation. These rules also apply as customary international law.

Article 31, paragraph 1 provides that a treaty shall be interpreted in good faith in accordance with the ordinary meaning to be given to its terms in their context and in the light of its object and purpose. Article 31, paragraph 3, provides, inter alia, that there shall be taken into account, together with the context: (a) any subsequent agreement between the parties regarding the interpretation of the treaty or the application of its provisions; and (b) any subsequent practice in the application of the treaty which establishes the agreement of the parties regarding its interpretation. Recourse may be had to other subsequent practice in the application of the treaty as a supplementary means of interpretation under Article 32.

A practice "which establishes the agreement" means a practice on the basis of which the assumption can arguably be made that an agreement exists. Thus, a practice "which establishes the agreement of the parties" regarding the treaty's interpretation will not necessarily be a practice to which all parties themselves have contributed. All parties must have acquiesced in the interpretation. However, if the circumstances allow for the assumption that a party has

---

[79]   See, for example, 1985 Continental Shelf Case, and 2012 Jurisdictional Immunities of the State judgment. For a discussion, see Brian D Lepard, "Introduction", in Brian D Lepard (ed.), *Reeaxamining Customary International Law* (Cambridge University Press 2017) 9; Michael Wood, "Foreword", in Brian D Lepard (ed.), *Reeaxamining Customary International Law* (Cambridge University Press 2017) xiv.

[80]   Brian D Lepard, "Introduction", in Brian D Lepard (ed.), *Reeaxamining Customary International Law* (Cambridge University Press 2017) 9; Jan Klabbers, *International Law* (2nd edn, Cambridge University Press 2017) 29.

[81]   Hugh Thirlway, *The Sources of International Law* (2nd edn, Oxford University Press 2019) 10, 152.

[82]   Jan Klabbers, *International Law* (2nd edn, Cambridge University Press 2017) 27 ff. Cf. Hugh Thirlway, *The Sources of International Law* (2nd edn, Oxford University Press 2019) 153.

[83]   Hugh Thirlway, *The Sources of International Law* (2nd edn, Oxford University Press 2019) 152.

consented, even though the party itself did not contribute to the practice, then this shall be sufficient.[84]

A subsequent practice is used, either to make the ordinary meaning appear more precise or to determine which one of the two possible ordinary meanings is correct and which one is not. A subsequent practice in the application of a treaty can be said to establish an agreement between the parties regarding the treaty's "interpretation" insofar as practice is consistent with "the ordinary meaning to be given to the terms of the treaty".[85]

However, the Vienna Convention on the Law of Treaties does not specify how much practice is needed to establish an agreement. It is therefore unclear how many states parties need to engage in this practice, how agreement can be established and whether state practice needs to be uniform.[86]

Since practice as an objective element is only one aspect of Article 31(3)(b) of the Vienna Convention, it is necessary to show also the agreement of those states parties who do not participate in the practice (voluntary element). In general, a common understanding regarding the interpretation of the treaty, which the parties are aware of and accept, is required.

If state practice lacks the necessary agreement by all states or is insufficiently consistent and thus does not meet the threshold of Article 31(3)(b) of the Vienna Convention, it can still be relevant as a subsidiary means of interpretation. As such, subsequent practice can contribute to the clarification of the meaning of a treaty if it remains within the limits of treaty interpretation.

5.2   State Practice

When considering the question whether (and to what extent) state practice may have an impact on international treaties, interpretation in light of subsequent practice is only one aspect. An additional and even more controversial issue is the question whether treaties may be modified by way of state practice. This aspect was discussed already at the Vienna Conference where the originally proposed draft Article 38 on the modification of treaties by subsequent practice was later withdrawn from the Convention. The main argument against the proposed rule was that any practice incompatible with a treaty generally constituted a violation rather than a new rule. Practice itself seemed to be insufficient to legalize a new situation. Rather, the conclusion of a new agreement was required in order to comply with the principle of *pacta sunt servanda*.[87]

---

[84]   Ulf Linderfalk, *On The Interpretation of Treaties* (Springer 2007) 167.
[85]   Ulf Linderfalk, *On The Interpretation of Treaties* (Springer 2007) 168 ff.
[86]   Anja Seibert-Fohr, "The Effect of Subsequent Practice on the European Convention on Human Rights: Considerations from a General International Law Perspective", in Anne van Aaken and Iulia Motoc (eds), *The ECHR and General International Law* (Oxford University Press 2018).
[87]   In addition, several constitutional issues were raised because in some states the principle of formal parallelism required that treaty modifications followed the same procedure as the original text. Modification by practice would give rise to unconstitutional modifications without parliamentary approval. Delegates also argued that the draft article would deprive specific provisions for revision contained in many treaties of their meaning. Finally, modification by subsequent practice raised issues of legal certainty and security. See UN Conference on the Law of Treaties, "Summary Records of the Plenary Meetings and of the Meetings of the Committee of the Whole" (Vienna 26 March–24 May 1968) (1969) UN Doc A/CONF.39/11, para 208 et seq. See further Anja Seibert-Fohr, "The Effect of Subsequent Practice on the European Convention on Human Rights: Considerations from a General International Law Perspective", in Anne van Aaken and Iulia Motoc (eds), *The ECHR and General International Law* (Oxford University Press 2018), 76.

Thus, in general, the threshold for modification is higher if it leaves the realm of textual limits. In other words, for the modification of a treaty, it is insufficient to consider subsequent practice alone; it is also necessary to establish a corresponding *opinio juris*, comparable to customary international law.

5.3   Summary and Assessment

It was described in Section 4 that some states applied exceptions and limitations to moral rights in their national legislation. In some instances full categories of works were excluded from copyright protection, and in some instances the limitations took aim at specific uses. It was discussed in Section 4.7 whether such exceptions and limitations are compatible with the text of the Berne Convention. The conclusion was that it is doubtful whether such broad exceptions and limitations are compatible with the Convention.

This section has described that in addition to the text of the Berne Convention, it may be possible for states to provide such exceptions and limitations on the basis of another source of international law – customary international law and/or state practice.

It follows from Article 31 of the Vienna Convention that customary international law may serve as means for interpretation of a treaty if such custom constitutes "subsequent state practice". For this, it is required that there is both sufficiently widespread and consistent practice and *opinio juris* accompanying it. *Opinio juris* refers to belief by the states engaging in the practice that it is legally required or permitted. Even though this study is not based on a global investigation of exceptions and limitations in all countries around the world, it is fair to say already based on the description of the jurisdictions in Chapter 4 it is very doubtful whether current the state practice fulfils these requirements. There does not seem to be any (coherent) state practice, and in any case the practice of several states has been questioned and criticized. Hence, there does not seem to be any support for the current practice based on *opinio juris*.

It is more controversial whether customary international law may alter the international obligations between states, as set out in (Article 6*bis* of) the Berne Convention. In any case, as with state practice, the general criteria for "customary international law" to be present does not seem to be fulfilled as the "custom" to include exceptions and limitations to moral rights seems to be made in different ways at national level, and the current practice is not supported by *opinio juris*.

6.   DISCUSSION AND CONCLUSIONS

The purpose of this contribution (see Section 1) is to describe and analyse the permissibility of exceptions and limitations to the moral rights of integrity and paternity, as set out in Article 6*bis* of the Berne Convention, both in relation to the text of Convention itself (as a source of international law) and in relation to customary international law as a means for interpreting the Convention as well as an independent source of international law.

The possibility to use and exploit copyright-protected content has – over time – led to expansions of the scope of the economic rights. The broadening of the economic rights has, in turn, led to increased demands for the "balancing" of copyright, for example via exceptions and limitations. Much research and policy discussions in the area of copyright in the last decades has been devoted to the question on whether, to what extent and how copyright should be balanced.

A recent example of the expansion of the economic rights is Article 17 of the recently adopted EU DSM Directive. The article sets out obligations on certain online intermediaries – so-called OCSSPs – to obtain a licence covering internet content that is uploaded on the platform by its users. This licence will also cover the uploading by the users of the platform. Article 17 thus provides a complementary (*lex specialis*) liability and obligation for internet platforms. Article 17 is also novel in that it establishes "user rights" – users of internet protected content shall be able to rely on some exceptions or limitations when uploading and making available content generated by users on online content-sharing services: (a) quotation, criticism, review; and (b) use for the purpose of caricature, parody or pastiche.

Whereas much focus has targeted the economic rights and exceptions and limitations to those rights, less focus has been devoted to the protection of moral rights in the digital environment, and the impact of digital technology on those rights (and vice versa). There are several possible explanations for this. One explanation is that moral rights are to a large extent regulated at national level, although Article 6*bis* of the Berne Convention provides a minimum level of protection for such rights. To some extent, it could also be the case that moral rights are deemed not to be important from an "economic" perspective.

However, as copyright-protected content is increasingly accessed, used and often modified by internet users, the scope of protection of moral rights may become a new "battlefield". Article 17 of the DSM Directive reflects this. The article includes mandatory exceptions to the economic rights – exceptions that are deemed important for internet users, such as making parodies based on existing works. Article 17, however, only harmonizes exceptions to economic rights – not moral rights. The implementation of Article 17 may thus not lead to the desired "level playing field". Future developments may lead to increased requests for the harmonization of moral rights within the EU. This will, in turn, put the finger on the possibility of exceptions and limitations to the moral rights. The topic of this chapter can contribute to these discussions.

Sections 2 and 3 described and analysed the text of Article 6*bis* in the Berne Convention. At face value, it seems as if the Convention does not permit any exceptions or limitations to moral rights. However, the scope of the minimum "core" rights in Article 6*bis* is not sharp: the Convention provides some flexibility but at the same time Article 6*bis* has general and broad language. Supposedly all works[88] are covered and no forms of exploitation are excluded per se. The text of the Convention is, however, somewhat ambiguous, for example as several provisions on exceptions and limitations to the economic rights include references to moral rights. As submitted by legal scholars, the content of these articles should be clarified at any future revision conference.

Section 4 explored that several states that are parties to the Berne Convention, have – in their national legislation – introduced exceptions and limitations to the right of paternity and integrity. At first glance, and in line with the conclusions from Section 2 and 3, such exceptions and limitations appear not to be consistent with the Berne Convention. Article 6*bis* does not seem to permit such exceptions and limitations. It is also doubtful whether some of these exceptions and limitations may be permitted on the basis of Article 17 of the Berne Convention, which

---

[88]   With the possible exception of works of applied art, see Section 4.7.

provides for the possibility to introduce exceptions and limitations to copyright protection for the protection of "*ordre public*" and not "public interest" in general. Article 17 is to be understood a narrow provision.

Section 5 explored the permissibility of exceptions and limitations to moral rights on the basis of subsequent state practice and customary international law. It was submitted that it is improbable that the state practice described in Section 4 fulfils these requirements. There does not seem to be any (coherent) state practice, and in any case the practice of several states has been questioned and criticized. As with state practice the general criteria for "customary international law" to be present does not seem to be fulfilled as the "custom" supported by *opinio juris* to include exceptions and limitations to moral rights seems to be made in different ways at national level.

In summary, many jurisdictions seem not to be in line with their international obligations when it comes to Article 6*bis* of the Berne Convention. At the same time, we can expect that the moral rights, especially the right of integrity, will gain importance. If not from an economic, so at least from a practical perspective – for example related to user-generated content etc. This will, in turn, raise the question of the permissibility of exceptions and limitations to moral rights.

17. Designing a freedom of expression-compliant framework for moral rights in the EU: challenges and proposals

Christophe Geiger and Elena Izyumenko

1. INTRODUCTION

In the discussions on copyright and freedom of expression, it is common to concentrate on copyright's economic rights and their preventive effects on the exercise by users of their freedom of creativity, freedom to express criticism or freedom to receive and impart information.[1] By

---

1 The literature on the intersection of the protection of copyright's economic rights with freedom of expression is abundant. Among many sources covering this topic in the European context, see, e.g., F. MacMillan Patfield, "Towards a Reconciliation of Free Speech and Copyright", in: E. Barendt (ed.), *The Yearbook of Media and Entertainment Law 1996* (Oxford University Press, 1996), p. 199; J. Griffiths, "Copyright Law and Censorship: The Impact of the Human Rights Act 1998", in: E. Barendt and A. Firth (eds), *Yearbook of Copyright and Media Law* (Oxford University Press, 1999), p. 4; A. Strowel, "Droit d'auteur et accès à l'information", in: S. Dusollier (ed.), *Copyright: A Right to Control Access to Works?* (Bruylant, 2000), p. 5; P.B. Hugenholtz, "Copyright and Freedom of Expression in Europe", in: R.C. Dreyfuss, D.L. Zimmerman and H. First (eds), *Expanding the Boundaries of Intellectual Property* (Oxford University Press, 2001), p. 343; J. Griffiths, "Copyright Law and the Public's Right to Receive Information: Recent Developments in an Isolated Community", in: E. Barendt and A. Firth (eds), *The Yearbook of Copyright and Media Law 2001/2* (Oxford University Press, 2002), p. 29; D. Voorhoof, "Freedom of Expression, Parody, Copyright and Trademarks", in: J.C. Ginsburg and J.M. Besek (eds), *Adjuncts and Alternatives to Copyright* (ALAI 2001/Kernochan Center for Law Media and the Arts, 2002), p. 636; M.D. Birnhack, "Acknowledging the Conflict between Copyright Law and Freedom of Expression under the Human Rights Act", 14(2) *Entertainment Law Review* 24 (2003); C. Geiger, *Droit d'auteur et droit du public à l'information: approche de droit comparé* (Litec, 2004); H. Cohen Jehoram, "Copyright and Freedom of Expression, Abuse of Rights and Standard Chicanery: American and Dutch Approaches", 26(7) *EIPR* 275 (2004); S. Balganesh, "Copyright and Free Expression: Analyzing the Convergence of Conflicting Normative Frameworks", 4 *Journal of Intellectual Property* 45 (2004); J. Griffiths and U. Suthersanen (eds), *Copyright and Free Speech* (Oxford University Press, 2005); R. Danay, "Copyright vs. Free Expression: The Case of Peer-to-Peer File-Sharing of Music in the United Kingdom", 8 *Yale Journal of Law & Technology* 32 (2005); P. Akester, "The Political Dimension of the Digital Challenge – Copyright and Free Speech Restrictions in the Digital Age", 1 *IPQ* 16 (2006); A. Strowel and F. Tulkens (eds), *Droit d'auteur et liberté d'expression* (Larcier, 2006); C. Geiger, "Author's Right, Copyright and the Public's Right to Information: A Complex Relationship", in: F. Macmillan Patfield (ed.), *New Directions in Copyright Law* (Edward Elgar, 2007), p. 24; J. Rosen, "Copyright and Freedom of Expression in Sweden – Private Law in a Constitutional Context", in: P. Torremans (ed.), *Copyright Law: A Handbook of Contemporary Research* (Edward Elgar, 2008), p. 355; C.J. Angelopoulos, "Freedom of Expression and Copyright: The Double Balancing Act", 3 *IPQ* 328 (2008); U. Suthersanen, "Copyright as an Engine of Free Expression: An English Perspective", in: R. Xalbarder (ed.), *Copyright and Freedom of Expression: Proceedings of the ALAI Study Days* (Huygens Editorial, 2008), p. 167; G. Smith, "Copyright and Freedom of Expression in the Online World", 5(2) *JIPLP* 88 (2010); A. Strowel, "Pondération entre liberté d'expression et droit d'auteur sur internet: de la réserve des juges de Strasbourg à une concordance pratique par les juges de Luxembourg", 100 *Revue*

contrast, moral rights of the authors (such as the right of divulgation, the right of attribution and the right of integrity) are much less thought of in terms of the conflict with users' freedom of expression.[2] Without doubts, moral rights are at the core of copyright protection, in particular in systems following the so-called "civil law" tradition shared on the European continent and many other parts of the world. However, by contrast to the international human rights law instruments,[3] an elaborated and balanced clause for intellectual property (IP) protection which includes moral rights is lacking at European level.[4] Nevertheless, their protection represents an important interest that can claim foundations in several different fundamental rights. On a more general level, moral rights are said to emanate from the need to protect the authors' dignity and personality[5] – the values underlying a number of fundamental rights in the human

---

Trimestrielle des Droits de l'Homme 889 (2014); C. Geiger and E. Izyumenko, "Copyright on the Human Rights' Trial: Redefining the Boundaries of Exclusivity through Freedom of Expression", 45(3) *IIC* 316 (2014); D. Voorhoof, "Freedom of Expression and the Right to Information: Implications for Copyright", in: C. Geiger (ed.), *Research Handbook on Human Rights and Intellectual Property* (Edward Elgar, 2015), p. 331; A. Lucas and J. Ginsburg, "Droit d'auteur, liberté d'expression et libre accès à l'information (étude comparée de droit américain et européen)", 249 *RIDA* (2016); E. Izyumenko, "The Freedom of Expression Contours of Copyright in the Digital Era: A European Perspective", 19(3-4) *Journal of World Intellectual Property* 115 (2016); B.J. Jütte, "The Beginning of a (Happy?) Relationship: Copyright and Freedom of Expression in Europe", 38(1) *EIPR* 11 (2016); C. Geiger and E. Izyumenko, "Freedom of Expression as an External Limitation to Copyright Law in the EU: The Advocate General of the CJEU Shows the Way", 41(3) *EIPR* 131 (2019); C. Geiger and E. Izyumenko, "The Constitutionalization of Intellectual Property Law in the EU and the Funke Medien, Pelham and Spiegel Online Decisions of the CJEU: Progress, But Still Some Way to Go!", 51(3) *IIC* 282 (2020).

2   For a few existing studies on this issue, see, in the European context, A. Lucas-Schloetter, "Pour un exercice équilibré du droit moral ou le droit moral et la balance des intérêts", in: P. Ganea, C. Heath and G. Schricker (eds), *Urheberrecht, Gestern-Heute-Morgen, Mélanges A. Dietz* (Beck, 2001), p. 127; G. Pessach, "The Author's Moral Right of Integrity in Cyberspace – A Preliminary Normative Framework", 34(3) *IIC* 250 (2003); J. Griffiths, "Not Such a 'Timid Thing': The United Kingdom's Integrity Right and Freedom of Expression", in: J. Griffiths and U. Suthersanen (eds), *Copyright and Free Speech* (Oxford University Press, 2005), p. 211; J. Groffe, "Droit moral et liberté de creation", 253 *RIDA* 5 (2017); E.C. Lim, "On the Uneasy Interface between Economic Rights, Moral Rights and Users' Rights in Copyright Law: Can Canada Learn from the UK Experience?", 15(1) *SCRIPTed* 70 (2018). For the US context, see C.H. Settlemyer III, "Between Thought and Possession: Artists' 'Moral Rights' and Public Access to Creative Works", 81 *Georgetown Law Journal* 2291 (1993); K.A. Kelly, "Moral Rights and the First Amendment: Putting Honour Before Free Speech?", 11 *University of Miami Entertainment & Sports Law Review* 211 (1994); G.J. Yonover, "The Precarious Balance: Moral Rights, Parody, and Fair Use", 14 *Cardozo Arts & Entertainment Law Journal* 79 (1996); P. Masiyakurima, "The Trouble With Moral Rights", 68(3) *The Modern Law Review* 411 (2005); J.M. Beck, A.M. Scott and K.M. Sullivan, "Moral Rights and Wrongs: Conflicts in the Digital World", 57 *Journal of the Copyright Society of the USA* 587 (2009).

3   See Article 27(2) Universal Declaration of Human Rights (UDHR) and Article 15(1) of the International Covenant on Economic, Social and Cultural Rights (ICESCR). On these articles see Section 5.

4   C. Geiger, "Building an Ethical Framework for Intellectual Property in the EU: Time to Revise the Charter of Fundamental Rights", in: G. Ghidini and V. Falce (eds), *Reforming Intellectual Property* (Edward Elgar, 2022,).

5   See, e.g., P.B. Hugenholtz, "Copyright and Freedom of Expression in Europe" (*supra* note 1), at 346 (pointing to the German case law and doctrine that recognize implied constitutional underpinnings for moral rights by situating the interest in their protection in the German Constitution's rights to dignity and self-fulfillment); J. Drexl, "Constitutional Protection of Authors' Moral Rights in the European Union – Between Privacy, Property and the Regulation of the Economy", in: K.S. Ziegler (ed.), *Human*

rights treaties. More specifically, certain scholars allocate the interest in the protection of the authors' moral rights in the right to privacy, personal integrity and even property,[6] others – in the so-called "negative" aspect of the right to freedom of expression – the right not to speak and to be free from unwanted associations.[7] Either one way or another, however, the interest of the author in the protection of her personality via moral rights should not be accorded absolute

---

Rights and Private Law: Privacy as Autonomy (Hart Publishing, 2007), p. 159, at 159 (highlighting that, according to the continental copyright tradition of author's rights, "the copyrighted work is considered an emanation of the creator's personality"). See also P. Hughes, "Painting on a Broader Canvas: The Need for a Wider Consideration of Moral Rights under EU Law", 40(2) *EIPR* 95 (2018) (exploring the concept of moral rights with reference to the fundamental right to human dignity); C. Geiger, *Droit d'auteur et droit du public à l'information: approche de droit comparé* (*supra* note 1), p. 129 sq. and from the same author: "Reconceptualizing the Constitutional Dimension of Intellectual Property – An Update", in: P. Torremans (ed.), *Intellectual Property and Human Rights*, (4th ed., Kluwer Law International, 2020), p. 117, at 137 (in particular fn. 79).

[6]   See, e.g., L.K. Treiger-Bar-Am and M.J. Spence, "Private Control/Public Speech", in: K.S. Ziegler (ed.), *Human Rights and Private Law: Privacy as Autonomy* (Hart Publishing, 2007), p. 177, at 180 (contending that privacy understood as autonomy and not as secrecy can ground the moral right of integrity); C. Bohannan, "Copyright Infringement and Harmless Speech", 61 *Hastings Law Journal* 1083 (2010), at 1154 (claiming that "[in] copyright cases in which the defendant free-rides on a copyrighted work but the copyright holder cannot show any economic harm … the copyright holder might argue a privacy-based interest in metering or controlling the precise amount of exposure that her copyrighted work receives"); S. Balganesh, "Privative Copyright", 73 *Vanderbilt Law Review* 1 (2020), at 3 (suggesting the privacy grounds for the moral right of divulgation by contending that "the publication (or distribution) [that] compels the author to publicly accept authorship of the work against her own will … produces a form of dignitary harm that melds considerations of privacy, personality, and autonomy"). Exploring the possibility of grounding authors' moral rights in Article 8 (private life) of the ECHR, see C. Geiger and E. Izyumenko, "Intellectual Property before the European Court of Human Rights", in: C. Geiger, C.A. Nard and X. Seuba (eds), *Intellectual Property and the Judiciary* (EIPIN Series Vol. 4, Edward Elgar Publishing, 2018), p. 9, at 67–8. Under a personalist approach to the right to property, as deducted from Locke's understanding of the right to property as the precondition for individual freedom and the guaranty of his or her autonomy, moral rights could also be derived from the right to property (for a discussion, see C. Geiger, *Droit d'auteur et droit du public à l'information: approche de droit compare* (*supra* note 1), p. 128. For a discussion of the protection of moral rights by a balanced constitutional property clause, see below Section 4.

[7]   For a detailed treatment of the issue of grounding authors' moral rights in freedom of expression, see C. Leonard, "Copyright, Moral Rights and the First Amendment: The Problem of Integrity and Compulsory Speech", 35 *Columbia Journal of Law & the Arts* 293 (2012); A. Dimmich, "Copyright as a Human Right under the European Convention on Human Rights", in: J. Gaster, E. Schweighofer and P. Sint (eds), *KnowRight 2008: Knowledge Rights – Legal, Societal and Related Technological Aspects* (Conference Proceedings, Kraków, Poland, 18–19 September 2008), p. 21. Highlighting the links between – specifically – the right of attribution and free speech, see N.W. Netanel, *Copyright's Paradox* (Oxford University Press, 2008), at 216 (arguing that "a requirement that creative appropriators take reasonable steps to accord authorship credit for underlying works and ensure that audiences understand the source of the modified version can help to protect authors' interest in avoiding 'forced speech'"); C.G. Stallberg, "Towards a New Paradigm in Justifying Copyright: An Univeralistic-Transcendental Approach", 18 *Fordham Intellectual Property, Media and Entertainment Law Journal* 333 (2008), at 371 (claiming that "the attributing act performed by a plagiarist must be qualified as a defective speech"). On the right of integrity and the similarity of its rationales for protection with those of freedom of expression, see L.K. Treiger-Bar-Am, "The Moral Right of Integrity: A Form of Freedom of Expression", in: F. Macmillan Patfield (ed.), *New Directions in Copyright Law* (Edward Elgar, 2007), p. 127, at 143–8; J. Hughes, "The Philosophy of Intellectual Property", 77 *Georgetown Law Journal* 287 (1988), at 359; T.-I. Lee, "A Battle between Moral Rights and Freedom of Expression: How Would Moral Rights Empower

and hence unqualified protection.[8] In particular, competing freedom of expression interests of users (including derivative creators) must not be neglected as a result of such protection. Establishing clear and fundamental rights-compliant guidelines for the use of moral rights is thus crucial since certain (otherwise permitted) uses such as parodies or pastiches entail per se an alteration of the integrity of the work.

The argument of this chapter is that, despite the relative lack of attention towards this issue, moral rights (in Europe in particular, but not solely) have a potential to disproportionately impede users' freedoms to even a greater extent than economic rights of copyright holders. This is largely due to two factors. First, because of a traditionally higher relevance of moral rights in so-called "continental" copyright laws of a majority of European countries, the level of protection for moral rights in this region is also higher than in other regions that follow common law traditions. Second, by contrast to economic rights, no exceptions to moral rights of the authors allowing for the freedom of expression uses of copyright-protected works are prescribed explicitly by the relevant national copyright legislation. Furthermore, the recent developments in the case law of the Court of Justice of the European Union (CJEU or "Luxemburg Court") are likely to have triggered this speech-threatening potential of the moral rights protection to the maximum, significantly constraining freedom of expression in the EU.

The discussion proceeds as follows. The chapter first outlines the unharmonized status of moral rights in the EU and ambiguities as to the availability in their context of the so-called "exceptions" to the exclusive rights of copyright holders (Section 2).[9] The chapter then turns to the discussion of the two sets of cases from the CJEU that, arguably, have significantly reduced users' freedoms against the claims of moral rights holders. The first set concerns one single judgment, *Deckmyn*, rendered by the Court of Justice in 2014, wherein, apart from clarifying the standards of application of the parody exception in the EU, the CJEU had also pronounced on inapplicability of copyright exceptions when the holders of moral rights claim violation of their quasi-integrity right (construed by the CJEU as a right to be free from unwanted associations) (Section 3). The second set of cases concerns the recent copyright/ freedom of expression triad of *Funke Medien*, *Pelham* and *Spiegel Online*, all decided in July

---

the 'Charging Bull' Against the 'Fearless Girl'?", 17 *John Marshall Review of Intellectual Property Law* 672 (2018), at 684.

[8]   K.A. Kelly, "Moral Rights and the First Amendment: Putting Honour before Free Speech?", 11 *University of Miami Entertainment & Sports Law Review* 211 (1994), at 215, 249–50; J. Griffiths, "Not Such a 'Timid Thing'" (*supra* note 2), at 226; L.K. Treiger-Bar-Am, "The Moral Right of Integrity" (*supra* note 7), at 156; T.-I. Lee, "A Battle between Moral Rights and Freedom of Expression" (*supra* note 7), at 685, 689.

[9]   As argued by the authors of this chapter elsewhere, copyright exceptions and limitations in the EU might need to be more properly conceptualized as "user rights", all the more so in view of the recent developments in the CJEU case law to this effect – see, notably, *Funke Medien NRW*, C-469/17, 29 July 2019, EU:C:2019:623, at para. 70 (hereinafter "Judgment in *Funke Medien*"); and *Spiegel Online*, C-516/17, 29 July 2019, EU:C:2019:625, at para. 54 (hereinafter "Judgment in *Spiegel Online*"), with further references to CJEU, Judgment in *Ulmer*, C-117/13, 11 September 2014, EU:C:2014:2196, at para. 43. For this reason, the term "exceptions" is referred to sometimes in the quotes throughout this chapter. For further discussion, see C. Geiger and E. Izyumenko, "The Constitutionalization of Intellectual Property Law in the EU and the Funke Medien, Pelham and Spiegel Online Decisions of the CJEU" (*supra* note 1). On the legal realities behind the "limitations" and "exceptions" terminology used in the EU copyright legislation, see also C. Geiger, "Promoting Creativity through Copyright Limitations: Reflections on the Concept of Exclusivity in Copyright Law", 12(3) *Vanderbilt Journal of Entertainment and Technology Law* 515 (2010), at 520 et seq.

2019, in which the CJEU expressly excluded applicability of any external freedom of expression limitation on top of exceptions already available to copyright users by virtue of Article 5 of the InfoSoc Directive (Section 4).[10] This chapter argues that the possibility of excluding both exceptions and freedom-of-expression-grounded limitations in the moral rights context produced significant unbalances in the (nearing absolute) protection of the moral rights of the authors when contrasted with the freedom of users to use the works of authorship for the purposes of criticism, artistic expression or for other goals traditionally ranking highly on the freedom of expression balancing scale. After a detailed assessment, the final part of the chapter suggests a number of alternatives by which the requisite balance between the rights of authors and copyright users can be re-established in the EU insofar as the delicate area of unharmonized moral rights protection is concerned, which might be important to consider when designing a freedom of expression-compliant legal framework for moral rights protection in the EU (Section 5).

2.   UNHARMONIZED STATUS OF MORAL RIGHTS IN THE EU AND AMBIGUITIES AS TO THE AVAILABILITY OF TRADITIONAL COPYRIGHT EXCEPTIONS IN THEIR CONTEXT

In accordance with Article 6*bis* of the Berne Convention, creators of the works of authorship hold, independently from economic rights, moral rights over their creations.[11] Berne defines these moral rights as the right of attribution (paternity) – referred to as "the right to claim authorship of the work"[12] – and the right of integrity that allows the author "to object to any distortion, mutilation or other modification of, or other derogatory action in relation to, [his or her] work, which would be prejudicial to his [or her] honor or reputation".[13] In addition, many EU states recognize the moral right of divulgation conceived as the right of first publication or of disclosure of the work that has never previously been made public.[14]

The claim has sometimes been made in the literature that these moral rights, and in particular the right of integrity (defined as "the central tenet of moral rights jurisprudence"[15]), are

---

[10]   Directive 2001/29/EC of the European Parliament and of the Council of 22 May 2001 on the harmonization of certain aspects of copyright and related rights in the information society, OJ L 167, 22 June 2001, p. 10 (hereinafter "InfoSoc Directive"). For further discussion, see C. Geiger and E. Izyumenko, "Copyright on the Human Rights' Trial" (*supra* note 1).

[11]   Article 6*bis*(1) of the Berne Convention for the Protection of Literary and Artistic Works (9 September 1886, 828 UNTS 221) (as amended on 28 September 1979), available at: https://wipolex.wipo.int/en/text/283693 (accessed February 2020) (hereinafter "Berne Convention").

[12]   Article 6*bis*(1) of the Berne Convention.

[13]   Ibid.

[14]   See, e.g., Article L. 121-2 of the French Loi relative au code de la propriété intellectuelle (partie législative) (French Intellectual Property Code), No. 92–597 of 1 July 1992, as last amended by Laws Nos 94-361 of 10 May 1994 and 95-4 of 3 January 1995, available (in English translation by the International Bureau of WIPO) at: https://internet-law.ru/law/int/nation_cleo/france/fr003en.pdf (accessed March 2020) (hereinafter "French Code de la propriété intellectuelle").

[15]   N.W. Netanel, "Copyright Alienability Restrictions and the Enhancement of Author Autonomy: A Normative Evaluation", 24 *Rutgers Law Journal* 347 (1993), at 387.

capable of curtailing the freedom of expression of copyright users to an even greater extent than copyright's economic rights.[16]

In the EU, moral rights in copyright, unlike economic rights, were left unharmonized. As stated in the Recital 19 of the InfoSoc Directive,

> The moral rights of rightholders should be exercised according to the legislation of the Member States and the provisions of the Berne Convention for the Protection of Literary and Artistic Works, of the World Intellectual Property Organization (WIPO) Copyright Treaty and of the WIPO Performances and Phonograms Treaty. *Such moral rights remain outside the scope of this Directive.*[17]

Because of the harmonization of only economic rights in the EU and because of the independence of moral rights from the latter,[18] a fair amount of uncertainty persists on whether exceptions to economic rights set forth, EU-wide, in Article 5 InfoSoc are also applicable to moral rights. Such exceptions include, among others, the use for the purposes of quotation,[19] news reporting,[20] parody[21] and many other valuable freedom of expression uses.

In principle, nothing in the wording of Article 5 InfoSoc precludes applying copyright exceptions also to the moral rights of the authors, except when the wording of an exception explicitly precludes it from overriding a certain moral right. One example is the quotation exception of Article 5(3)(d) InfoSoc that "relate[s] to a work or other subject-matter *which has already been lawfully made available to the public*".[22] This wording of the quotation exception unambiguously precludes it from being applied as an exception to the author's right of first publication.[23] Insofar as the moral right of attribution is concerned, a number of exceptions including, again, quotation[24] but also illustration for teaching or scientific research[25] and reporting of current events[26] cannot be applied in defence to an alleged violation of the right of attribution as the InfoSoc Directive conditions the exercise of these exceptions to the requirement that "the source, including the author's name, is indicated" "unless this turns out to be impossible".[27]

Except these specific examples, however, InfoSoc leaves open the possibility, in principle, to extend the reach of its Article 5 exceptions also to the (unharmonized) moral rights. Much in line with this interpretation, it appears that the CJEU had "tacitly accepted",[28] originally, availability of copyright exceptions in the moral rights context. Thus, in *Painer*, the Court of Justice

---

[16]   See the sources cited *supra* in note 2.
[17]   Emphasis added.
[18]   Highlighting the independent nature of authors' moral rights and copyright holders' economic rights, see Article 6*bis*(1) of the Berne Convention.
[19]   Article 5(3)(d) of the InfoSoc Directive.
[20]   Article 5(3)(c) of the InfoSoc Directive.
[21]   Article 5(3)(k) of the InfoSoc Directive.
[22]   Article 5(3)(d) of the InfoSoc Directive (emphasis added).
[23]   See also CJEU, Opinion of Advocate General Szpunar in *Spiegel Online*, C-516/17, 10 January 2019, EU:C:2019:16 (hereinafter "Opinion of Advocate General Szpunar in *Spiegel Online*"), at para. 55 stating that "the work obviously cannot be made available to the public for the first time as a result of the quotation itself."
[24]   Article 5(3)(d) of the InfoSoc Directive.
[25]   Article 5(3)(a) of the InfoSoc Directive.
[26]   Article 5(3)(c) of the InfoSoc Directive.
[27]   See the wording of Article 5(3)(a), (c) and (d) of the InfoSoc Directive.
[28]   CJEU, Opinion of Advocate General Szpunar in *Spiegel Online*, at para. 55.

considered an exception of Article 5(3)(e) InfoSoc safeguarding the use for the purposes of public security acceptable as an exception to the moral right of divulgation.[29]

The copyright legislation of individual EU Member States is often likewise ambiguous on the question of applicability of copyright exceptions to moral rights. Article L. 122–5 of the French *Code de la propriété intellectuelle*, for instance, states merely that, "[o]nce a work has been disclosed, the author may not prohibit" the acts qualifying as copyright exceptions listed in that article, without specifying which rights of the author this provision targets.[30] The wording of the German Act on Copyright and Related Rights is much less ambiguous in this sense, as it explicitly casts copyright exceptions as exceptions to *economic* rights.[31] This did not prevent German judges from at times applying other provisions such as the German "free use"[32] in order to protect derivative creativity from the claims of also moral rights violation.[33] In a similar fashion, Dutch courts have occasionally applied exceptions to economic rights (parody in particular) to the moral rights of the author.[34] Insofar as the UK is concerned, copyright exceptions (as exceptions to economic rights) appear to be inapplicable to the claims of the moral rights violation.[35]

In addition to the ambiguities related to the question of applicability of copyright exceptions to moral rights, no legal certainty exists as to whether an *external* freedom of expression limitation can be invoked by the alleged infringers of authors' moral rights either.

The lack of clarity as to the exceptions and limitations applicable in the moral rights context coupled with the almost sacred status of moral rights in many European countries (France specifically) resulted in a situation in which national courts at times accorded a particularly strong protection to the moral rights of authors, having refused to weigh these rights against competing freedom of expression interests of derivative creators and other users.[36] This

---

[29]   See CJEU, Judgment in *Painer*, C-145/10, 1 December 2011, EU:C:2011:798, at paras 144–6. In *Painer*, the national security authorities themselves were the cause of the making available to the public of the contested photographs which were the subject of subsequent use by the defendants in the main proceedings.

[30]   See Article L. 122-5 of the French Code de la propriété intellectuelle.

[31]   See Para. 44a-53 of the German Act on Copyright and Related Rights (*Urheberrechtsgesetz – UrhG*) of 9 September 1965 (Federal Law Gazette I, p. 1273), as last amended by Article 1 of the Act of 28 November 2018 (Federal Law Gazette I, p. 2014), available (in unofficial English translation) at: https://www.gesetze-im-internet.de/englisch_urhg/englisch_urhg.html (accessed March 2020) (hereinafter "German Act on Copyright and Related Rights").

[32]   Para. 24 of the German Act on Copyright and Related Rights.

[33]   See, e.g., Bundesgerichtshof (German Federal Supreme Court), *Alcolix*, no. I ZR 263/91, 11 March 1993, *GRUR* 206 (1994). See also J. Griffiths, "Not Such a 'Timid Thing'" (*supra* note 2), at 226; and D. Jongsma, "Parody after Deckmyn – A Comparative Overview of the Approach to Parody under Copyright Law in Belgium, France, Germany and the Netherlands", 48(6) *IIC* 652 (2017), at 663.

[34]   See, e.g., Gerechtshof Amsterdam (Court of Appeals of Amsterdam), *Mercis B.V. v. Punt.nl B.V.*, 13 September 2011, NL:GHAMS:2011:BS7825, at 4.16, available (in Dutch) at: https://uitspraken.rechtspraak.nl/inziendocument?id=ECLI:NL:GHAMS:2011:BS7825&showbutton=true (accessed March 2020).

[35]   Griffiths explains the decision of the UK legislator to immunize the moral right of integrity from copyright exceptions by the believe that "alteration of a work [can] never be justified where such alteration cause[s] prejudice to the creator". See J. Griffiths, "Not Such a 'Timid Thing'" (*supra* note 2), at 224, with further references.

[36]   See, e.g., M. Hahn, "Digital Music Sampling and Copyright Policy – A Bittersweet Symphony? Assessing the Continued Legality of Music Sampling in the United Kingdom, the Netherlands, and the United States", 34 *Georgia Journal of International and Comparative Law* 713 (2006), at 723 (contend-

mostly concerned the right of integrity, although the right of attribution had been occasionally engaged too.

One example of such a rigorous European approach towards protecting the authors' moral rights is the French case decided at the beginning of 1990s that concerned the staging of a theatrical play *Waiting for Godot* with exclusively female cast involved, contrary to the original intention of the play's late author Samuel Beckett.[37] During his lifetime, Samuel Beckett was actively opposing his play being performed by female actors as he considered women incapable of accurately portraying the play's two lead characters.[38] The *Tribunal de grande instance de Paris* respected the late playwright's view on his creation and found that the right of integrity exercised by Samuel Beckett's estate trumped the right of the theatre stage director to replace male performers by women on stage.[39]

Around the same time, the *Cour d'appel de Versailles* held, following instructions by the French *Cour de cassation*, that colourization of a black and white film violated the right of integrity of the film's director.[40]

More recently, in the case from 2012, the French *Cour de cassation* found that reduction by the Google Images search service of the original photographs to the thumbnails violated the right of integrity of the photographer, despite Google's claim that such a use was required by the search engine's proper functioning and that it was furthermore crucial for the exercise of the Internet users' freedom to receive information.[41] The right of attribution was likewise found infringed in that case as the thumbnails failed to mention the photographer's name.[42]

It has to be mentioned, however, that, until recently, this restrictive approach to freedom of expression of secondary users in the moral rights context did not form an established practice. Furthermore, especially beginning from 2000s, European judges, including French ones, started to increasingly recognize the necessity of balancing not only economic rights of copyright holders but also authors' moral rights with freedom of expression of derivative creators, other secondary users and the public in general.

---

ing that, "in most cases, particularly in civil law jurisdictions, which place a greater emphasis on moral rights, it is likely that the rights of the original author will trump the rights of the new creator"). See also J. Griffiths, "Not Such a 'Timid Thing'" (*supra* note 2), at 212 (noting that, in civil law jurisdictions in particular that provide for a strong protection of the integrity right, there is "a clear possibility of conflict" between this moral right and the free speech of secondary users).

[37]   Tribunal de Grande Instance de Paris (The High Court of Paris), *"Godot"*, 15 October 1992, 155 *RIDA* 225 (1993). For commentary, see J. Griffiths, "Not Such a 'Timid Thing'" (*supra* note 2), at 212.

[38]   D. Valjak, "Samuel Beckett Objected to Female Theatre Groups Staging His Play 'Waiting for Godot' because 'Women Don't Have Prostates and Couldn't Portray the Characters Accurately'" [Blog post], *The Vintage News*, 7 March 2017, available at: https://www.thevintagenews.com/2017/03/07/samuel-beckett-objected-to-female-theater-groups-staging-his-play-waiting-for-godot-because-women-dont-have-prostates-and-couldnt-portray-the-characters-accurately/ (accessed March 2020).

[39]   Tribunal de Grande Instance de Paris, *"Godot"* (*supra* note 37).

[40]   See Cour de cassation (French Supreme Court), 28 May 1991, 149 *RIDA* 197 (1991) and Cour d'appel de Versailles (Versailles Court of Appeal), *Turner Entertainment Company v. Huston*, 10 December 1994, 164 *RIDA* 256 (1995). For commentary, see J. Griffiths, "Not Such a 'Timid Thing'" (*supra* note 2), at 212.

[41]   Cour de cassation (French Supreme Court), *La société Google France and Others v. La société Aufeminin.com and Others*, nos. 11-15.165 and 11-15.188, 12 July 2012, available (in French) at: https://www.courdecassation.fr/jurisprudence_2/premiere_chambre_civile_568/827_12_23881.html (accessed March 2020).

[42]   Ibid.

Absent any explicit internalization, in the moral rights context, of the freedom of expression interest within the copyright law's own structure, national courts generally took three alternative approaches. They either interpreted, first, the scope of moral rights restrictively – an approach that had led, in many cases, to a simple denial of an existence of the moral right interest[43] – or accepted, second, application of copyright exceptions to the moral rights sphere.[44] The majority of the courts had taken, however, the third route – the route of applying freedom of expression externally in order to trump excessiveness of the moral rights protection in each particular case. The freedom of expression argument had also frequently featured in the reasoning of the courts adopting the first two approaches, in particular when the restrictive interpretation of the scope of the right of integrity was considered commanded by the freedom of expression.

One example in the line of these freedom of expression-informed cases on moral rights is the 2007 judgment by the French *Cour de cassation* in which the Court dismissed the claims by Victor Hugo's heirs, who had argued that the publication of the sequels to the work "Les Misérables" was an infringement of the author's moral rights although the work had already become part of the public domain.[45] Citing Article 10 (freedom of expression) of the European Convention on Human Rights (ECHR), the French highest court criticized the lower court's failure to demonstrate concretely the manner in which the sequels altered Victor Hugo's famous novel or to show that there was confusion as to the work's authorship.[46] According to the *Cour de cassation*, "subject to respect of the right to paternity and of integrity of the adapted work, freedom of creativity hinders the author of the work or his heirs preventing the making of a sequel after the exploitation monopoly [has] expired".[47]

Freedom of expression was likewise relied upon by the Italian *Tribunale di Roma* (court of first instance) in the case with the same factual setting as that of the French "*Godot*" case

---

[43]   Exploring, within the framework of the legal system of the UK, the different options for "reading down" the right of integrity by interpreting the scope of this right in a manner that minimizes any conflict with freedom of expression of users (thereby compensating for the absence of relevant statutory exceptions), see J. Griffiths, "Not Such a 'Timid Thing'" (*supra* note 2), at 230–43.

[44]   For an example of a judicial "internalization" of the defences to the moral rights infringement by extending the applicability of exceptions to economic rights to the moral rights context, see Gerechtshof Amsterdam (Court of Appeals of Amsterdam), *Mercis B.V. v. Punt.nl B.V.*, 13 September 2011, NL:GHAMS:2011:BS7825, at 4.16, available (in Dutch) at: https://uitspraken.rechtspraak.nl/inziendocument?id=ECLI:NL:GHAMS:2011:BS7825&showbutton=true (accessed March 2020). In that case, the Gerechtshof Amsterdam considered, notably, that the fact that the derivative use at issue met the parody exception criteria precluded the primary author's ability to rely on the protection of the right of integrity in order to stop the use at issue. By doing so, the Gerechtshof Amsterdam had effectively internalized, judicially, the parody exception within the scope of the moral rights protection. For commentary on this judgment, see L. Guibault, "The Netherlands: Darfurnica, Miffy and the Right to Parody!", 3 *JIPITEC* 236 (2011).

[45]   Cour de cassation (French Supreme Court), *Société Plon SA and Others v. Pierre Hugo and Others*, no. 04-15.543, 30 January 2007, available (in French) at: https://www.legifrance.gouv.fr/affichJuriJudi.do?oldAction=rechJuriJudi&idTexte=JURITEXT000017627153&fastReqId=1110318844&fastPos=1 (accessed March 2020). For a summary of this case in English, see D.W., "Copyright Law: France – Victor Hugo II", 38(6) *IIC* 736 (2007). For commentary, see C. Geiger, "Copyright and the Freedom to Create – A Fragile Balance", 38(6) *IIC* 707 (2007).

[46]   Cour de cassation, *Société Plon SA and Others v. Pierre Hugo and Others* (*supra* note 45).

[47]   Ibid., translation from French by C. Geiger in "Copyright and the Freedom to Create" (*supra* note 45), at 710.

discussed above. According to the *Tribunale di Roma* that reached the opposite conclusion to that of the *Tribunal de grande instance de Paris*, freedom of expression supported the all-female *Godot*.[48]

More recently, the French *Cour de cassation* had once again shown a more favourable approach towards the freedom of expression rights of derivative creators in the situation of their clash with the moral rights protection. At issue this time was the 2010 staging of the opera *Les dialogues des carmélites* in Munich based on the screenplay by Georges Bernanos, with music and libretto by Francis Poulenc.[49] The staging was made by the Russian theatre director Dmitri Tcherniakov, who, while changing neither the dialogues nor the music, situated the play in a completely different factual background – namely, that of modern times (instead of the times of The Terror during the French Revolution originally at stake in Georges Bernanos' screenplay). Dmitri Tcherniakov modified likewise the final scene: in his reading of *Les dialogues des carmélites*, the main heroine was saving the Carmelites, who all, in the original libretto, end up being guillotined.

The heirs of Georges Bernanos and Francis Poulenc objected to such a profound, in their opinion, alteration of the original work and sued Dmitri Tcherniakov, the Munich Opera and the companies that co-produced the audiovisual recording of the Munich staging of *Les dialogues des carmélites* for the violation of the moral right of integrity of the original composite work.

Contrary to the *Cour d'appel de Paris*,[50] the French *Cour de cassation* ruled in favour of the creative reuse of the work at issue.[51] It drew attention to the *Cour d'appel*'s own finding that Dmitri Tcherniakov's staging had modified neither the dialogues nor the music, and that the end of the story respected the themes of hope, martyr, grace and communion of the saints cherished by the authors of the original composite work.[52] On that basis, the *Cour de cassation* ruled that the *Cour d'appel* had failed to draw legal consequences from its own conclusions, having thereby violated the provision of the French *Code de la propriété intellectuelle* on the

---

[48]   Tribunale di Roma (Rome District Court), *Fondazione Pontedera Teatro v. SIAE (Società Italiana Autori ed Editori and Ditta Paola D'Arborio Sirovich di Paola Perilli)*, 2 December 2005, reported in L. McDonagh, "Two Questions for Professor Drassinower: (i) What Is the Meaning of Communication in the Context of Theatre and (ii) When Is Music Speech?" [Book Review], 29 *Intellectual Property Journal* 71 (2016), at 73.

[49]   Cour de cassation (French Supreme Court), *"Dialogues des carmélites"*, nos. 15-28.467 and 16-11.759, 22 June 2017, available (in French) at: https://www.legifrance.gouv.fr/affichJuriJudi .do?oldAction=rechJuriJudi&idTexte=JURITEXT000035004718&fastReqId=765344921&fastPos=1 (accessed March 2020). For commentary, see M.-A. Weiss, "France's Highest Court Rules in Favor of Freedom of Expression of Director over Heirs' Droit Moral" [Blog post], *The 1709 Blog*, 29 June 2017, available at: http://the1709blog.blogspot.com/2017/06/frances-highest-court-rules-in-favor-of.html (accessed March 2020). See also C. Geiger, "Appropriation créative et droit d'auteur, Réflexions sur les évolutions récentes de la jurisprudence française à la lumière du droit de l'Union et du droit comparé", in: *Mélanges en l'honneur du Professeur Claude Witz* (LexisNexis, 2018), p. 325, at 336.

[50]   Cour d'appel de Paris (Paris Court of Appeal), 13 October 2015. For commentary on this judgment, see M.-A. Weiss, "The Paris Court of Appeals Gives Freedom of Expression the Ax in Favor of Droit Moral" [Blog post], *The 1709 Blog*, 13 November 2015, available at: http://the1709blog.blogspot .com/2015/11/the-paris-court-of-appeals-gives.html (accessed March 2020).

[51]   Cour de cassation, *"Dialogues des carmélites"* (*supra* note 49).

[52]   Ibid.

rights in the composite work.[53] The *Cour de cassation* had also concluded that, by banning any further dissemination of the recordings of the Munich staging of *Les dialogues des carmélites*, without nevertheless examining, as it was required, how the search for a fair balance between the protection of the moral rights of the composer and the author of the libretto and the freedom of creativity of the director justified the prohibition in question, the *Cour d'appel* divested its decision of the legal basis in the light of the second paragraph of Article 10 (freedom of expression) of the ECHR that requires balancing of the right to freedom of expression with the rights of others.[54]

An approach of the national courts in Europe that favours the balancing of the protection of moral rights of the authors with freedom of expression of secondary users, however, could be endangered by the CJEU's recent endorsement of quite an absolutist position towards the protection of the right of integrity in its judgment on the case of *Deckmyn*,[55] while rejecting, at the same time, applicability of an external freedom of expression limitation to copyright in the EU in the yet more recent judgments on *Funke Medien*, *Pelham* and *Spiegel Online* cases.[56]

3.   THE *DECKMYN* DECISION OF THE CJEU: INAPPLICABILITY OF COPYRIGHT EXCEPTIONS IN THE CONTEXT OF MORAL RIGHTS?

In *Deckmyn*, which mainly concerned interpretation of the parody exception in the EU, the CJEU had also set a quasi-moral rights standard of protection.[57] According to the Court of Justice, original creators "have, in principle, a legitimate interest in ensuring that the work protected by copyright is not associated"[58] with the message those creators oppose, even if that message complies otherwise with the requirements set forth by the Court for a parody exception.[59]

Of course, the overall conclusion by the Court on the non-protection of hate speech (that was, arguably, at stake in that case) by means of a parody exception was totally correct as hate speech cannot benefit from the freedom of expression protection in Europe, and the author of a copyright-protected work should be free to oppose the use of her works for spreading the

---

[53]   Ibid., with further references to Article L. 113-4 on the rights in the composite work of the French Code de la propriété intellectuelle.

[54]   Cour de cassation, *"Dialogues des carmélites"* (*supra* note 49). The Cour d'appel de Versailles to which the case was remitted by the French *Cour de cassation* for a fresh consideration ruled in favour of Dmitri Tcherniakov and the companies that co-produced the audiovisual recordings of the Munich staging of *Les dialogues des carmélites*. See Cour d'appel de Versailles (Versailles Court of Appeal), *Gilles B. and Others v. Dimitri T., Sarl Bel Air Media, Sa Mezzo, Le Land de Bavière (Dialogues des Carmélites)*, no. 17/08754, 30 November 2018. For commentary (in French), see J. Boireau, "Dialogues des Carmélites: suite et fin?", 4 *Les MÀJ IRPI* 1 (2019), available at: http://www.irpi.fr/upload/pdf/maj/ Num%C3%A9ro%204%20janvier%202019/maj_4_janvier_2019_2.pdf (accessed March 2020).

[55]   CJEU, Judgment in *Deckmyn*, C-201/13, 3 September 2014, EU:C:2014:2132, at para. 31 (hereinafter "Judgment in *Deckmyn*").

[56]   CJEU, Judgments in *Pelham*, C-476/17, 29 July 2019, EU:C:2019:624, at para. 65 (hereinafter "Judgment in *Pelham*"); *Funke Medien*, at para. 64; and *Spiegel Online*, at para. 49.

[57]   CJEU, Judgment in *Deckmyn*, at paras 28–31.

[58]   Ibid., at para. 31.

[59]   Ibid.

racist messages.[60] Indeed, the balancing between fundamental rights in this particular context leads to privilege the right not to speak of an original author or her personality right that can be derived from Article 8 (right to privacy) of the ECHR over the alleged freedom of expression interest of a racist parodist. It is more the reasoning that the CJEU used in *Deckmyn* in order to reach this conclusion that is controversial as it could create potential dangers of an absolutist construction of moral rights of authors in the EU, even *beyond* the situations in which such authors rely on the protection of their moral rights in order to prevent the use of their works in hate speech.

The overbroad nature of a message sent by the CJEU in *Deckmyn* could in fact open the door for interpreting the scope of moral rights protection in the EU as a sort of absolute entitlement of an original creator to oppose *any* derivative uses with which she disagrees, *even if* such secondary uses do not constitute racist or other forms of hate speech not protected by the freedom of expression guarantees. Subsequently, the CJEU's Advocate General Szpunar endorsed the CJEU's somewhat ambiguous pronouncement on non-applicability of copyright exceptions to the moral rights of the author in a more explicit manner. In his opinion on the *Pelham* case, the Advocate General stated, relying explicitly on *Deckmyn*, that "[m]oral rights, particularly the right to the integrity of the work, may legitimately preclude use of that work, *even where that use is covered by an exception*".[61] The same was repeated in the Advocate General's subsequent opinion on the *Spiegel Online* case where the Advocate General Szpunar once again specified – now in a more general manner with a potential effect for *all* moral rights – that "exceptions provided for in Article 5(1) to (3) of Directive 2001/29 [InfoSoc] derogate only from the economic rights of authors and should not in principle adversely affect their moral rights".[62]

Deckmyn has sometimes been interpreted in the literature as requiring to consider the interest of the author in the protection of her moral rights *within* and not *on top of* the proportionality assessment of the application of a parody exception.[63] The above pronouncements of the Advocate General might, however, have dispelled such ideas. It appears that the Advocate General had explicitly endorsed a much more restrictive interpretation, which has, since then, been shared by a number of domestic courts in Europe.

One of the most recent examples of the national courts endorsing this restrictive approach is the case decided by the Commercial Court of Brussels in May 2019.[64] The case concerned

---

[60]   The parodic use at stake in *Deckmyn* concerned the calendar reproduction by a member of the far right Belgian political party (*Vlaams Belang*) of a drawing resembling one of the covers in *Suske en Wiske* comic books (known in English as *Spike and Suzy* and in French as *Bob and Bobette*). With an aim and result of conveying a message forming a part of the *Vlaams Belang*'s ideology, one of the comic book's main characters depicted on the drawing was replaced by the Mayor of the City of Ghent throwing coins to people who, in the original work, were trying to pick them up and who were replaced in the drawing by people wearing veils and people of colour.

[61]   CJEU, Opinion of Advocate General Szpunar in *Pelham and Others*, C-476/17, 12 December 2018, EU:C:2018:1002, at para. 97 (emphasis added) (hereinafter "Opinion of Advocate General Szpunar in *Pelham*"), with further references to CJEU, Judgment in *Deckmyn*, at paras 27–31.

[62]   CJEU, Opinion of Advocate General Szpunar in *Spiegel Online*, at para. 55.

[63]   See D. Jongsma, "Parody after Deckmyn" (*supra* note 33), at 663–4, 677.

[64]   Nederlandstalige   Ondernemingsrechtbank   Brussel   (Commercial   Court   of   Brussels (Dutch-speaking)), *Studio 100 nv en Waldemar-Borsens Stiftung v. Greenpeace Belgium vzw*, 4 April 2019, reported and commented (in Dutch) by D. Voorhoof in "Studio 100 en Greenpeace beide tevreden met Maya de Bij-vonnisat" [Blog post], *Apache/ inhoud heerst*, 2 May 2019, available at: https://

a video campaign launched by Greenpeace in May 2018 in which the famous kids character Maya the Bee was depicted advertising cigarettes. The purpose of the campaign was to criticize the fact that the production company of animated series about Maya the Bee, Studio 100, was marketing products harmful for children (meat notably). Concerned with the adverse effects of the campaign at issue for its reputation, Studio 100 sued Greenpeace for copyright and trademark infringement. It also invoked the claim of an alleged violation of the moral right of integrity of the original designer of an animated image of Maya the Bee.

On the copyright side of the case, Greenpeace relied in its defence, inter alia, on the domestic implementation of the copyright's parody exception and on the external freedom of expression provision.

Insofar as the parody exception was concerned, the Commercial Court of Brussels held that the *Deckmyn*-established criteria for parody (i.e., "first, to evoke an existing work while being noticeably different from it, and, secondly, to constitute an expression of humour or mockery"[65]) were complied with by the use at issue. The Court considered, however, that the use at stake did not satisfy the *Deckmyn* standard of protection for the quasi-integrity right by harming the reputation and kids-friendly image of Studio 100. The Commercial Court of Brussels also reasoned that the fact that Greenpeace used the images of Maya the Bee in an unmodified form created an impression that Studio 100 itself produced the cigarettes advertisement. All these considerations necessitated, in the opinion of the Court, the conclusion on inapplicability of the exception for parody to Greenpeace.

Similar logic permeated the Brussels Court's reasoning on the potential external applicability of the freedom of expression limitation on copyright to the case of Greenpeace. Pursuant to the Commercial Court of Brussels, the video campaign by Greenpeace had failed to preserve a fair balance between the environmental organization's freedom of expression and the need to duly respect the carefully built kids-friendly image of the Studio 100 company.

The Brussels Court's reasoning thus presented – insofar as the parody exception was concerned – a direct consequence of the restrictive practice established in *Deckmyn*. On the (external) freedom of expression side, the Brussels Court's reasoning can be criticized for its failure to proportionately balance the free speech rights with the protection of copyright,[66] as well as for (mis)using the copyright's mechanisms of the moral rights protection in order to reach, essentially, the goal of securing the reputation of a commercial enterprise.[67] There is, however, one positive free speech aspect that is nevertheless present in this judgment. It concerns the Brussels Court's acknowledgement of the possibility, in principle, for the secondary

---

www.apache.be/gastbijdragen/2019/05/02/studio-100-en-greenpeace-beide-tevreden-met-maya-de-bij-vonnis/ (accessed March 2020). For other commentaries on this case, see I. Verschueren and C. Benson, "Parody and Trade Mark Infringement in Belgium: No Cigarettes for Maya the Bee" [Blog post], *Lexology*, 28 June 2019, available at: https://www.lexology.com/library/detail.aspx?g=73aaaa54-9e21-47df-9b0c-236ea0176f52 (accessed March 2020); T. D'hulst, "Belgium: Greenpeace's Use of Maya the Bee Infringes Copyright" [Blog post], *Mondaq*, 11 July 2019, available at: http://www.mondaq.com/x/824638/Copyright/Greenpeaces+Use+Of+Maya+The+Bee+Infringes+Copyright (accessed March 2020).

65   CJEU, Judgment in *Deckmyn*, at para. 20.

66   For such detailed critique, see D. Voorhoof, "Studio 100 en Greenpeace beide tevreden met Maya de Bij-vonnisat" (*supra* note 64).

67   Detailed on the issue of inadmissibility of misusing copyright for the purposes not corresponding to its rationales (social function), see C. Geiger and E. Izyumenko, "Freedom of Expression as an External Limitation to Copyright Law in the EU" (*supra* note 1), at 136.

user of a copyright-protected work to rely on an external free speech limitation even when the claim of a moral right infringement is made.

This last freedom of expression "shelter" might, however, not any longer be available to copyright users in the EU in view of the most recent pronouncements of the CJEU in *Funke Medien*, *Pelham* and *Spiegel Online* cases decided in July 2019.

4.   EXTERNAL FREEDOM OF EXPRESSION LIMITATION NOT APPLICABLE EITHER? *FUNKE MEDIEN*, *PELHAM* AND *SPIEGEL ONLINE* AND THEIR POTENTIAL IMPACT ON THE MORAL RIGHTS PROTECTION IN THE EU

In *Funke Medien*, *Pelham* and *Spiegel Online*, the CJEU explicitly rejected the possibility for copyright users to rely on an external freedom of expression limitation beyond the list of copyright exceptions set exhaustively in Article 5 InfoSoc.[68] According to the Court of Justice, to allow each Member State to derogate from an author's exclusive rights beyond the exceptions and limitations set out in Article 5 InfoSoc would have endangered both the effectiveness of the harmonization of copyright and related rights and the objective of legal certainty and would have been, in addition, contrary to the requirement of consistency in the implementation of exceptions and limitations in the EU.[69]

The combined reading of the *Funke Medien*, *Pelham* and *Spiegel Online* trilogy and *Deckmyn* creates a danger of significant impediments to the freedom of expression of copyright users when a violation of the right of integrity (and possibly of other moral rights) is alleged by the original work's author or her heirs. Taken together, *Deckmyn* and *Funke Medien*, *Pelham* and *Spiegel Online* trilogy allow for the conclusion on inadmissibility of either copyright "exceptions" or external freedom of expression limitation in the moral rights context.

Although it is true that *Funke Medien*, *Pelham* and *Spiegel Online* concerned only economic rights, it is not impossible to envisage the national courts extending analogous reasoning on the dangers of external freedom of expression limitations for harmonization, legal certainty and consistency also to the moral rights context.

Such a restrictive approach would present serious dangers not only for the more conventional ways of creativity and expression of criticism, but also for the contemporary artistic production and informational exchanges in the digital era.[70]

---

[68]   CJEU, Judgments in *Pelham*, at para. 65, *Funke Medien*, at para. 64, and *Spiegel Online*, at para. 49.

[69]   CJEU, Judgments in *Funke Medien*, at paras 62–3, *Pelham*, at paras 63–4, and *Spiegel Online*, at paras 47–8. For further detailed discussion of the CJEU's pronouncement on inapplicability of the freedom of expression external limitations on copyright in EU and its consequences for the protection of the rights of copyright users, see C. Geiger and E. Izyumenko, "The Constitutionalization of Intellectual Property Law in the EU and the Funke Medien, Pelham and Spiegel Online Decisions of the CJEU" (*supra* note 1). See more generally also B.J. Jütte, "Finding the Balance in Copyright Law: Internal and External Control Through Fundamental Rights", in: P. Torremans (ed.), *Intellectual Property Law and Human Rights*, (4th ed., Kluwer Law International, 2020), p. 481.

[70]   For a detailed treatment of the free speech problems posed by the protection of the right of integrity in the digital era, see G. Pessach, "The Author's Moral Right of Integrity in Cyberspace" (*supra* note 2); J.M. Beck, A.M. Scott and K.M. Sullivan, "Moral Rights and Wrongs: Conflicts in the Digital World", 57 *Journal of the Copyright Society of the USA* 587 (2009); O. Kotila, "Respektioikeus uusien haastei-

Insofar as the artistic sphere and cultural production are concerned, music sampling, for instance, can be compromised by the absolutist approach towards the protection of the moral right of integrity.[71] In the *Pelham* judgment, devoted specifically to the issue of music sampling and its permissibility under the current EU rules on copyright and related rights, the CJEU set certain safety valves for the protection of the free speech of samplers.[72] At least one such safety valve demanded applicability of the quotation exception to certain ("dialogic") practices of music sampling.[73] This safety valve might, however, be inoperational in the moral rights context considering the recent stance of the courts in Europe (started in *Deckmyn*) on inapplicability of exceptions to economic rights to the claims of the moral rights infringement.

An absolutist reading of the moral rights of original creators can also compromise the freedom of information on the Internet.[74] The claim of a violation of the moral right of integrity can be advanced, for instance, on the basis of the digitization of an analogue work that is almost inevitably accompanied by the reduction in the work's quality.[75] Embedding a work in a different web page can also become problematic as the original author may claim that placing the work in a new context disrupts her message or is in any other way degrading to her.[76]

Such an unlimited protection of moral rights of the authors capable of causing a disproportionate impairment of the freedom of expression of secondary creators and other users[77] is hard to reconcile with the requirements of a balanced and proportionate application of any restrictions on freedom of expression established in the second paragraph of Article 10 ECHR and associated case law of the European Court of Human Rights (ECtHR or "Strasbourg Court"). Notably, it is a well-established practice in the Strasbourg Court's application of Article 10 ECHR that limitations on freedom of expression "must be narrowly interpreted and the necessity for any restrictions must be convincingly established".[78]

---

den edessä" [Blog post], *IPRinfo* 3/2007, 23 October 2017, available (in Finnish) at: https://iprinfo.fi/artikkeli/respektioikeus_uusien_haasteiden_edessa/ (accessed March 2020). More generally on the difficult interface of copyright and freedom of artistic creativity, in particular in the context of the creation of derivative works, see C. Geiger, "Freedom of Artistic Creativity and Copyright Law: A Compatible Combination?", 8(3) *UC Irvine Law Review* 413 (2018).

[71]   On music sampling and protection of the moral rights of original creators, see M. Hahn, "Digital Music Sampling and Copyright Policy" (*supra* note 36).

[72]   CJEU, Judgment in *Pelham*.

[73]   See, notably, CJEU, Judgment in *Pelham*, at para. 72: "[W]here the creator of a new musical work uses a sound sample taken from a phonogram which is recognisable to the ear in that new work, the use of that sample may, depending on the facts of the case, amount to a 'quotation', on the basis of Article 5(3)(d) of Directive 2001/29 read in the light of Article 13 [freedom of the arts] of the Charter, provided that that use has the intention of entering into dialogue with the work from which the sample was taken, … and that the conditions set out in Article 5(3)(d) are satisfied."

[74]   O. Kotila, "Respektioikeus uusien haasteiden edessä" (*supra* note 70); G. Pessach, "The Author's Moral Right of Integrity in Cyberspace" (*supra* note 2), at 253.

[75]   O. Kotila, "Respektioikeus uusien haasteiden edessä" (*supra* note 70); G. Pessach, "The Author's Moral Right of Integrity in Cyberspace" (*supra* note 2), at 254.

[76]   O. Kotila, "Respektioikeus uusien haasteiden edessä" (*supra* note 70); G. Pessach, "The Author's Moral Right of Integrity in Cyberspace" (*supra* note 2), at 253.

[77]   Contending that, absent any freedom of expression limitation on the right of integrity, this right can provide for an excessive protection even in those common law jurisdictions that traditionally provide for quite a "timid" level of protection for moral rights, see J. Griffiths, "Not Such a 'Timid Thing'" (*supra* note 2), at 223.

[78]   See, among many other authorities, ECtHR, *Handyside v. the United Kingdom*, no. 5493/72, 7 December 1976, CE:ECHR:1976:1207JUD000549372, at para. 49; ECtHR, *Jersild v. Denmark* [GC],

Whereas the protection of moral rights of authors can – and should – in itself benefit from the protection of human and fundamental rights, and notably of the right to human dignity, the rights to privacy and to the protection of personal integrity, as well as of the right not to speak and to be free from unwanted associations (the "negative" aspect of the right to freedom of expression), the competing freedom of expression rights of users should not be neglected as a result of such protection. In other words, although it is without doubt important to protect the personality interest of an original creator, it is equally important leaving some free spaces for balancing this interest with the freedom of expression rights of derivative creators and the latter's interest in autonomy of expression.

5.   PROPOSALS FOR IMPROVEMENT: DESIGNING A FREEDOM OF EXPRESSION-COMPLIANT LEGAL FRAMEWORK FOR MORAL RIGHTS

A more preferable solution would have been for the CJEU, in *Deckmyn*, without denying the authors' interest in the protection of their works from unwanted associations, to construct this interest in not absolutist, but rather in qualified terms by requiring a proportionate balancing of this interest with the free speech of users. Importantly, again, such a balancing by no means demands prioritizing the freedom of expression of secondary users – it only instructs accounting for such interests in a proportionate manner.[79] Balancing in a more nuanced manner with the opposing fundamental rights of the users would imply, among others, that the authors claiming moral rights protection would need to substantiate their claims by demonstrating in what way the use in question affects their personality interests. This is even more important considering that creators are also often on the users' side when they are re-using copyright-protected material in an artistic or otherwise innovative manner.

In view of the unharmonized nature of the moral rights protection in the EU, the Court of Justice could then have left it to the domestic legislative authorities and judges to decide on the manner in which such a proportionate balancing can be reached.[80]

One way of doing so would have been to explicitly admit availability of exceptions for the economic rights also in the moral rights context. It might, however, be the case that the "opening-up" of such exceptions would still be needed in order to ensure that all competing

---

no. 15890/89, 23 September 1994, CE:ECHR:1994:0923JUD001589089, at para. 37; ECtHR, *Wille v. Liechtenstein* [GC], no. 28396/95, 28 October 1999, CE:ECHR:1999:1028JUD002839695, at paras 61–3; ECtHR, *Stoll v. Switzerland* [GC], no. 69698/01, 10 December 2007, CE:ECHR:2007:1210JUD006969801, at para. 101. For the CJEU adhering likewise to the restrictive interpretation of limitations on freedom of expression, see, e.g., CJEU, Judgment in *Connolly v. Commission*, C-274/99 P, 6 March 2001, EU:C:2001:127, at para. 41.

[79]   See J. Griffiths, "Not Such a 'Timid Thing'" (*supra* note 2), at 212.

[80]   Favouring a judicial case-by-case approach in the context of a conflict of copyright with freedom of artistic expression, see C. Geiger, "'Fair Use' through Fundamental Rights in Europe, When Freedom of Artistic Expression Allows Creative Appropriations and Opens up Statutory Copyright Limitations", in: S. Balganesh, W.L. Ng-Loy and H. Sun (eds), *The Cambridge Handbook of Copyright Limitations and Exceptions* (Cambridge University Press, 2021), p. 174; C. Geiger, "Contemporary Art on Trial – The Fundamental Right to Free Artistic Expression and the Regulation of the Use of Images by Copyright Law", in: T. Dreier and T. Andina (eds), *Digital Ethics: The Issue of Images* (Bloomsbury Publishing, 2022).

freedom of expression interests of copyright users are sufficiently accounted for in the context of such protection. In this sense, the freedom of expression-grounded European "fair use" provision discussed elsewhere by the authors of this chapter in the copyright's economic rights context could be envisaged for the moral rights alike.[81] As the discussion in Section 1 demonstrated, European judges already engage occasionally in the multi-factor free speech balancing of the interests of secondary users with the protection of moral rights of original creators. In this sense, introduction of the freedom of expression-grounded "fair use" in the moral rights context in Europe would simply internalize this already existing balancing within copyright law's own framework.

Apart from extending copyright "exceptions" to the sphere of moral rights protection, another, second avenue for securing the freedom of expression of users can be the creation of a specific exception or limitation to the claims of the moral rights infringement capable of safeguarding the free speech of users. One could draw inspiration in this respect from the Australian Copyright Amendment (Moral Rights) Act of 2000 that incorporates a provision on "[n]o infringement of right of integrity of authorship if derogatory treatment or other action was reasonable".[82]

Examples of limiting the right of integrity internally can also be found in Article 2(b) of the Marrakesh Treaty,[83] in accordance with which "[t]he accessible format copy [for blind,

---

[81]   See C. Geiger and E. Izyumenko, "Towards a European 'Fair Use' Grounded in Freedom of Expression", 35(1) *American University International Law Review* 1 (2019), arguing in favour of an introduction of an open-ended copyright exception in the EU legal framework based on the balancing factors of Article 10 (freedom of expression) ECHR. Importantly, "fair use" for moral rights is not something completely unusual. Section 195AS of the Australian Copyright Amendment (Moral Rights) Act 2000, No. 159, 2000, C2004A00752 (hereinafter "Australian Copyright Amendment (Moral Rights) Act"), for example, sets a multi-layered factor analysis akin to the fair use types of defences in order to establish whether the interference with the right of integrity was reasonable. According to paragraph 2 of Section 195AS, notably, "[t]he matters to be taken into account in determining … whether it was reasonable in particular circumstances to subject a literary, dramatic, musical or artistic work to derogatory treatment include the following: (a) the nature of the work; (b) the purpose for which the work is used; (c) the manner in which the work is used; (d) the context in which the work is used; (e) any practice, in the industry in which the work is used, that is relevant to the work or the use of the work; (f) any practice contained in a voluntary code of practice, in the industry in which the work is used, that is relevant to the work or the use of the work; (g) whether the work was made: (i) in the course of the author's employment; or (ii) under a contract for the performance by the author of services for another person; (h) whether the treatment was required by law or was otherwise necessary to avoid a breach of any law; (i) if the work has 2 or more authors – their views about the treatment." Analogously, in the US, the limited moral rights protection granted under the Visual Artists Rights Act is subject to fair use limitations of Section 107 of the US Copyright Act (see the Visual Artists Rights Act of 1990 (VARA), codified in Section 106A of the US Copyright Act). For further discussion and positive assessment of the Australian and US provisions as allowing the fair balance to be achieved between the protection of the moral rights of the authors and any competing public interest, see J. Griffiths, "Not Such a 'Timid Thing'" (*supra* note 2), at 224–6. See also G. Pessach, "The Author's Moral Right of Integrity in Cyberspace" (*supra* note 2), at 258 describing Australian limitation of reasonableness on the reach of the right of integrity as "a mechanism under which the moral right of integrity can be balanced and shaped in accordance with all the other values and interests that should be taken into account, including other constitutional values such as freedom of speech".

[82]   Section 195AS of the Australian Copyright Amendment (Moral Rights) Act.

[83]   Marrakesh Treaty to Facilitate Access to Published Works for Persons Who Are Blind, Visually Impaired, or Otherwise Print Disabled, 27 June 2013, TRT/MARRAKESH/001.

visually impaired, or otherwise print disabled people] … must respect the integrity of the original work, *taking due consideration of the changes needed to make the work accessible in the alternative format and of the accessibility needs of the beneficiary persons*".[84]

Finally, explicit admittance of an external freedom of expression limitation to the moral rights infringement claims could serve as an alternative to the two above-discussed avenues or it could also work in combination with them.

Importantly, admitting an external freedom of expression limitation would not go contrary to the *Deckmyn* judgment (because an external free speech limitation cannot, arguably, be treated the same way as the exceptions to the economic rights of copyright holders which the CJEU in *Deckmyn* held inapplicable to the moral rights context). Nor would such admittance contradict the *Funke Medien*, *Pelham* and *Spiegel Online* trilogy. With regards to the latter, it can be claimed that the Court of Justice had disallowed in those cases an external free speech limitation *only insofar as* the economic rights were concerned and that, hence, such a limitation can still be admitted in the moral rights context. In fact, one of the arguments advanced by the CJEU in the *Funke Medien*, *Pelham* and *Spiegel Online* trilogy in support of its position on inadmissibility of an external free speech limitation to the economic rights infringement was that the freedom of expression interest of users was *already* accounted for internally through the operation of copyright exceptions.[85] Due to the absence of such an internalization in the moral rights context (as admitted by *Deckmyn* and its subsequent readings by the Advocate General of the CJEU and national courts), an external freedom of expression limitation should still be allowed there.

It is essential, however, that the national judges, when resolving the claims based on an external Article 10 ECHR, account for all relevant balancing factors and assess their weight in full compliance with the ECtHR case law on freedom of expression and information.[86]

Despite the lack of harmonization of the moral rights in the EU, the principles for the protection of the right to freedom of expression in Europe already establish a sort of harmonization that binds not only the Member States of the EU, but also (as a minimum) all Council of Europe Member States that are all parties to the ECHR and are thus bound to respect its Article 10 (freedom of expression).

The potential of seeing moral rights in the context of the human right to freedom of expression and/or of the somewhat derivative from it right to freedom of arts and culture is already reflected in the international instruments for the human rights protection. In this regard, it is instructive that, notably, the Universal Declaration of Human Rights (UDHR)[87] states, in its Article 27(1), that everyone has "the right freely to participate in the cultural life of the community, to enjoy the arts and to share in scientific advancement and its benefits", while Article 27(2) continues by stating that everyone has "the right to the protection of the moral and material interests resulting from any scientific, literary or artistic production of which he

---

[84]   Emphasis added.

[85]   CJEU, Judgments in *Funke Medien*, at paras 58 and 70, *Pelham*, at para. 60, and *Spiegel Online*, at paras 43, 54.

[86]   For further discussion of these factors and the methods of their balanced interpretation, see C. Geiger and E. Izyumenko, "Copyright on the Human Rights' Trial" (*supra* note 1) and C. Geiger and E. Izyumenko, "Towards a European 'Fair Use' Grounded in Freedom of Expression" (*supra* note 81).

[87]   UN General Assembly, Universal Declaration of Human Rights, 10 December 1948, Resolution 217 A, UN Doc. A/810.

is the author".[88] Article 15(1) of the International Covenant on Economic, Social and Cultural Rights (ICESCR),[89] which, unlike the UDHR, has a direct binding effect, adopts the wording of Article 27 of the UDHR almost verbatim.[90]

The classical foundations of intellectual property are placed in a stable balance in these internationally recognized instruments for the human rights protection: on the one hand, the foundation of natural law by acknowledging an exploitation right and a "*droit moral*" for the creator; and, on the other hand, the utilitarian foundation, because this acknowledgement has the promotion of intellectual variety and the spread of culture and science throughout the society as a goal.[91] In addition, neither the UDHR nor the ICESCR determine *the way* in which the protection of the relevant material and immaterial interests has to be achieved. This leaves countries a good deal of room for manoeuvre, including for accommodating the freedom of expression interests of derivative creators and other users of copyright-protected works, while at the same time guaranteeing the creators, apart from just remuneration for their work, the protection of their moral rights. This makes the relevant provisions of the UDHR and the ICESCR particularly modern and flexible means for regulating intellectual property matters, including in the sphere of the moral rights protection.[92]

Importantly, the wording of Article 27 UDHR and of Article 15(1) of the ICESCR was adopted in many national constitutions in Europe and elsewhere.[93]

Because the moral and cultural values behind human rights are undisputed and represent the outcome of a worldwide agreement, incorporation of both the authors' rights protection (in its economic and moral aspects) and the protection of freedom of expression of users in the concept of freedom of arts and culture and the right to freedom of expression and information can be beneficial for the balanced IP laws and policies.

One, perhaps more "conservative" way for preserving the values behind the freedom of arts and culture and the freedom of expression in the IP clauses can be taking the positive wording

---

[88]   For the further analysis of Article 27 UDHR, see, inter alia, E. Stamatopoulou, *Cultural Rights in International Law: Article 27 of the Universal Declaration of Human Rights and Beyond* (Martinus Nijhoff Publishers, 2007), p. 110.

[89]   UN General Assembly, International Covenant on Economic, Social and Cultural Rights, 16 December 1966, 993 UNTS 3.

[90]   See, for further discussion of this provision, C. Sganga, "Right to Culture and Copyright: Participation and Access", in: C. Geiger (ed.), *Research Handbook on Human Rights and Intellectual Property* (*supra* note 1), p. 560; L. Shaver and C. Sganga, "The Right to Take Part in Cultural Life: On Copyright and Human Rights", 27 *Wisconsin International Law Journal* 637 (Winter 2010); C. Geiger, "Taking the Right to Culture Seriously: Time to Rethink Copyright Law", in: C. Geiger (ed.), *Intellectual Property and Access to Science and Culture: Convergence or Conflict?* (CEIPI/ ICTSD publication series on "Global Perspectives and Challenges for the Intellectual Property System", Issue No. 3, Geneva/ Strasbourg, 2016), p. 84.

[91]   For further discussion of the classical foundations of IP law, see C. Geiger, "'Constitutionalising' Intellectual Property Law?, The Influence of Fundamental Rights on Intellectual Property in Europe", 37(4) *International Review of Intellectual Property and Competition Law* 371 (2006), at 377 et seq.

[92]   See also in this sense, T. Mylly, "Intellectual Property and Fundamental Rights: Do they Interoperate?", in: N. Bruun (ed.), *Intellectual Property Beyond Rights* (WSOY, 2005), p. 197; C. Geiger, "'Constitutionalising' Intellectual Property Law?" (*supra* note 91).

[93]   For further detailed discussion and overview of such provisions, see C. Geiger, "Implementing Intellectual Property Provisions in Human Rights Instruments: Towards a New Social Contract for the Protection of Intangibles", in: C. Geiger (ed.), *Research Handbook on Human Rights and Intellectual Property* (*supra* note 1), p. 661.

Table 17.1   *(First Alternative): IP protection under the right to property: revision of Article 17 of the EU Charter*

Current Clause	Suggested Clause
1. *Everyone has the right to own, use, dispose of and bequeath his or her lawfully acquired possessions. No one may be deprived of his or her possessions, except in the public interest and in the cases and under the conditions provided for by law, subject to fair compensation being paid in good time for their loss. The use of property may be regulated by law in so far as is necessary for the general interest.* 2. *Intellectual property shall be protected.*	1. *Everyone has the right to own, use, dispose of and bequeath his or her lawfully acquired possessions. No one may be deprived of his or her possessions, except in the public interest and in the cases and under the conditions provided for by law, subject to fair compensation being paid in good time for their loss. The use of property may be regulated by law in so far as is necessary for the general interest.* 2. *In order to promote the progress of science, creativity, learning and culture, everyone shall have the right to the protection of the moral and material interests resulting from his or her scientific, literary or artistic production. The guarantees laid down in paragraph 1 apply.*

of the UDHR and the ICESCR, as well as of certain national constitutions, and implementing it within the protection of property, thereby extending the social function of property to intellectual property.[94] The objectives and conditions of the exercise of intellectual property should therefore always be examined in the light of the general interest. The proposal for implementing such a balanced vision of IP within the concept of the right to property on the EU level is reflected in the Table 17.1, which takes Article 17 (right to property) of the EU Charter as a starting point.[95]

The second, alternative way of a balanced construction of an IP clause in the EU is reflected in Table 17.2, which advocates the revision of Article 13 of the EU Charter that protects the freedom of the arts and sciences. This second proposal has a visible advantage of situating intellectual property in the category of cultural rights. In this manner, the social function of IP is placed at the very core of protection. In fact, it must be stressed that it is of substantial importance whether IP is understood as a cultural or an economic right. In the first case, the main emphasis is on the aspect of the "intellectual" enrichment of the society, whereas in the second, it is on "material" or "economic" enrichment. In the first case, a diversity of opinions and democratic dialogue with as many different works as possible is to be enabled, while in the second case the exploitation of a work, meaning the monetary realization of profits, is at centre stage. Of course, both aspects are often very closely linked and ideally converge. Nevertheless, the distinction can be relevant, because cultural policy goals can help to counterbalance the current "absolutist", investment-tailored tendencies of IP protection.[96] In addition, incorpora-

---

[94]   C. Geiger, "The Social Function of Intellectual Property Rights, or How Ethics can Influence the Shape and Use of IP Law", in: G.B. Dinwoodie (ed.), *Intellectual Property Law: Methods and Perspectives* (Edward Elgar, 2013), p. 153; C. Geiger, "Copyright as an Access Right: Securing Cultural Participation through the Protection of Creators' Interests", in: R. Giblin and K. Weatherall (eds) *What if We Could Reimagine Copyright?* (ANU Press, 2017), p. 73.

[95]   The tables are extracted and the following development draw from: C. Geiger, "Implementing Intellectual Property Provisions in Human Rights Instruments" (*supra* note 93), p. 685 sq.

[96]   Indeed, as has been aptly pointed out with regards to the European context, "the continuing trend towards ever stronger" IP protection was partly "supported by the fact that some Member States referred

*Table 17.2   (Second Alternative): IP protection under the freedom of arts and sciences:
revision of Article 13 of the EU Charter*

Current Clause	Suggested Clause
The arts and scientific research shall be free of constraint. Academic freedom shall be respected.	*1. Everyone has the right to benefit from the achievements of scientific progress, to enjoy the arts and to participate in the cultural life of the community.* *2. Creators of scientific, literary or artistic production shall have the right to the protection of the moral and material interests resulting from their creative activity. The rights granted are regulated by law in so far as is necessary to guarantee the rights in the preceding paragraph and the general interest.* *3. The arts and scientific research shall be free of constraint. Academic freedom shall be respected.*

tion of IP within the "freedom of arts and sciences" provision would help to balance creators' rights against the core values of human dignity and the right to freedom of expression and information.[97]

Finally, the third alternative reflected in Table 17.3 underpins the strong social limits of protection by linking IP to the freedom of expression and information. Under this mode of IP-clause construction, it is the freedom of use that has to be considered as the principle and exclusivity as the exception, which has to be justified,[98] – the principle from which IP law currently deviates. Moreover, the third alternative dovetails with the recent tendency of the ECtHR to examine copyright disputes within the framework of Article 10 (freedom of expression) of the Convention[99] (to which Article 11 of the EU Charter corresponds).[100]

Interestingly, the Spanish Constitution of 1978 explicitly situates IP protection within the framework of the right to freedom of expression and information in Article 20, paragraph 1(b)

---

to the legal protection of copyright as 'property' under their national Constitutions" (A. Kur and T. Dreier, *European Intellectual Property Law: Text, Cases and Materials* (Edward Elgar, 2013), at 248). See further C. Geiger, "The Construction of Intellectual Property in the European Union: Searching for Coherence", in: C. Geiger (ed.), *Constructing European Intellectual Property: Achievements and New Perspectives* (EIPIN Series, Vol. 1, Edward Elgar, 2013), p. 5.

[97]   Note from the Praesidium, *Draft Charter of Fundamental Rights of the European Union*, Text of the Explanations Relating to the Complete Text of the Charter as set out in CHARTE 4487/00 CONVENT 50 (Brussels, 2000), at 15 stating that the right under Article 13 "is deduced primarily from the right to freedom of thought and expression. It is to be exercised having regard to Article 1 (Human Dignity) and may be subject to the limitations authorized by Article 10 of the ECHR." See also, more recently, CJEU, Judgment in *Pelham*, at para. 34 (interpreting Article 13 of the EU Charter is a *lex specialis* in relation to Article 11 of the EU Charter that protects freedom of expression).

[98]   C. Geiger, "Fundamental Rights, a Safeguard for the Coherence of Intellectual Property Law?", 35(3) *IIC* 268 (2004), at 272.

[99]   See ECtHR, *Ashby Donald and Others v. France*, no. 36769/08, 10 January 2013, CE:ECHR:2013:0110JUD003676908; ECtHR, *Neij and Sunde Kolmisoppi v. Sweden* (dec.), no. 40397/12, 19 February 2013, CE:ECHR:2013:0219DEC004039712. For commentary, see C. Geiger and E. Izyumenko, "Copyright on the Human Rights' Trial" (*supra* note 1).

[100]   See Note from the Praesidium, *Draft Charter of Fundamental Rights of the European Union* (*supra* note 97), at 13–14.

Table 17.3   *(Third Alternative): IP protection under the freedom of expression and information: revision of Article 11 of the EU Charter*

Current Clause	Suggested Clause

1. *Everyone has the right to freedom of expression. This right shall include freedom to hold opinions and to receive and impart information and ideas without interference by public authority and regardless of frontiers.*
 	
2. *The freedom and pluralism of the media shall be respected.*
	1. *Everyone has the right to freedom of expression. This right shall include:*
	
	  a) *freedom to hold opinions and to receive and impart information and ideas without interference by public authority and regardless of frontiers;*
	
	  b) *the right to the protection of his or her moral and material interests resulting from literary, artistic or scientific production, subjected to the aim of promoting the progress of science, creativity, learning and culture.*
	
	2. *The freedom and pluralism of the media shall be respected.*

of the Constitution.[101] Arguably, this provision reflects the origins of IP, in particular of copyright, which since its inception has maintained a close relationship with the freedom of expression and its corollary, the public's right to information.[102] In fact, one can infer from Article 20 of the Spanish Constitution that the goal of IP is, at least partly, to guarantee freedom of expression and the public's right to information.

6.   CONCLUSION

Without doubt, a desired constitutional paradigm on IP would not automatically trigger an immediate recalibration of the conflicting interests between copyright holders, including in their moral rights dimension, and derivative creators and society at large: there are many other factors which should come into play in order to achieve this aim. Those include enormous legislative and judicial efforts accompanied by effective implementation and enforcement measures.

However, any of these endeavours would prove futile should the legislators draft and the courts apply the laws guided by "wrong" rationales. In this light, to rely on a balanced fundamental law guarantee of IP would mean giving shape and weight to the de facto fair approach by both safeguarding the moral link between the creators, their production and the people, and in addition enabling the creators to receive a fair remuneration for their creative input. Providing for the protection of the economic and moral interests of copyright holders that is

---

[101]   For further discussion of this provision, see J.M. Otero, "La protección constitucional del derecho de autor: Análisis del artículo 20.1 b/ de la Constitución española de 1978", Part 2 *La Ley* 370 (1986).

[102]   See C. Geiger, *Droit d'auteur et droit du public à l'information* (*supra* note 1), C. Geiger, "Author's Right, Copyright and the Public's Right to Information: A Complex Relationship", in: F. Macmillan (ed.), *New Directions in Copyright Law*, Vol. 5, 24 (Edward Elgar Publishing, 2007). See also F. Bondia, *Propiedad intelectual. Su significado en la Sociedad de la Información* (Trivium, 1988), at 94 and 105; J. Rodriguez, "A Historical Approach to the Current Copyright Law in Spain", 28(7) *EIPR* 389 (2006), at 393.

capable of demonstrating that copyright is intrinsically linked to the interests of society would bring copyright closer to people, and thus contribute to restore its public acceptance.[103]

---

[103]   C. Geiger, "'Humanising' the Intellectual Property System – Securing a Fair Balance of Interests through Fundamental Rights at European and International Level", 33 *The Quarterly Review of Corporation Law and Society (Waseda University)* 291 (September 2012); C. Geiger, "Implementing Intellectual Property Provisions in Human Rights Instruments" (*supra* note 93).

18. Protection of moral rights in Greece, limitations and issues of abuse

Irini A. Stamatoudi

1. COPYRIGHT PROTECTION IN GREECE

1.1 Historical Background

The first law which was enacted in the area of copyright, after the foundation of the modern Greek State in 1830,[1] was the Penal Law of 1834. This law provided for criminal sanctions against the illegal reprinting of printed works.[2] No provisions concerning moral rights were included. Act No. 3483 of 1909 was subsequently adopted, especially to protect copyright in dramatic works. Again, no provisions on moral rights were introduced. Act No. 2387 of 1920 was then enacted to provide the first complete protection of copyright. Although this Act did not deal with moral rights comprehensively, it introduced, for the first time in Greek law, the right of disclosure (Art. 1 of the Act), the right of paternity (Art. 13 of the Act), and the right of integrity (Art. 15 of the Act). This 1920 Act was amended many times up until 1944 and was supplemented by many further provisions on specific matters in separate laws even after that.

The present Copyright Act came into effect on 2 March 1993, the date of its publication in the Official Gazette of the Greek Government and has been amended since then on several occasions. The 1993 Act supersedes all prior provisions in statutes and decrees concerning copyright and covers the whole field of copyright and neighbouring rights alike. The 1993 Act also implemented almost all the provisions of the directives which the European Union was contemplating or had adopted in the field of copyright and neighbouring rights at the time the

---

[1]   The modern Greek State was founded in 1830 after the Liberation War against the Turkish occupation.

[2]   Penal Law of 1834 Arts 432 and 433. This law was abolished in 1950, being then superseded by a new Penal Code, which does not contain any provisions on copyright.

Act was passed. Further amending legislation has since been passed,[3] largely implementing EU directives.[4]

Greece is also a member to the international conventions in the area of copyright and related rights providing for moral rights protection.[5]

Greek copyright law follows the monistic theory,[6] belongs to the civil law tradition and offers a strong moral rights protection.

---

[3]   See Act No. 2173/1993; Act No. 2218/1994; Act No. 2435/1996; Act No. 2557/1997; Act No. 2819/2000; Act No. 3049/2002, Art. 14; Act No. 3057/2002, Art. 81; Act No. 3524/2007; Act No. 3905/2010 (also amending Presidential Decree No. 311/1994 on the Statutes of the Hellenic Copyright Organization [OPI]); Act No. 4212/2013, implementing the amended Term Directive and the Orphan Works Directive into Greek law; Act No. 4481/2017, implementing the Collective Rights Management (CRM) Directive; Act No. 4514/2018; Act No. 4531/2018, under which the institutions of the Commissioner for Reorganization and of the Special Service of exceptional rights management have been established; Act No. 4540/2018; Act No 4605/2019; Act No. 4672/2020 implementing into Greek law the provisions of EU Directive 2017/1564 (on certain permitted uses of certain works and other subject matter protected by copyright and related rights for the benefit of persons who are blind, visually impaired or otherwise print-disabled and amending Directive 2001/29/EC on the harmonization of certain aspects of copyright and related rights in the information society); Act No. 4761/2020 amending certain provisions concerning online copyright infringements; Act No. 4829/2021 also amending certain provisions concerning online copyright infringements; Act No. 4961/2022 regarding emerging computer technologies and especially 3D printing (Arts. 53–57); Act No. 4996/2022 implementing Directive 2019/790 of the European Parliament and of the Council of 17 April 2019 on copyright and related rights in the Digital Single Market and amending Directives 96/9/EC and 2001/29/EC (hereinafter: the DSM Directive) and Directive 2019/789 of the European Parliament and of the Council of 17 April 2019 laying down rules on the exercise of copyright and related rights applicable to certain online transmissions of broadcasting organisations and retransmissions of television and radio programmes, and amending Council Directive 93/83/EEC (hereinafter: the Online SatCab Directive); Act No 5039/2023 (Art. 117) amending certain provisions regarding private copy levy; Act No 5043/2023 (Art. 67) amending certain provisions regarding public lending.

[4]   For systematic treatises in Greek, identified here by translating their titles into English, see George A. Koumantos, *Copyright Law* (Athens, Ant. Sakkoulas, 8th ed, 2002); Michalis D. Marinos, *Copyright Law* (Athens, Ant. Sakkoulas, 2nd ed, 2004); Lambros Kotsiris, *Copyright Law* (Athens and Thessaloniki, Sakkoulas Editions, 4th ed, 2005); Dionissia Kallinikou, *Copyright Law and Related Rights* (Athens, P.N. Sakkoulas, 3rd ed, 2008); Lambros Kotsiris and Irini Stamatoudi (eds), *Commentary on the Greek Copyright Act* (Athens and Thessaloniki, Sakkoulas Editions, 2009); C. Christodoulou, *Copyright Law* (Athens, Nomiki Vivliothiki, 2018); Irini Stamatoudi (eds), *Collective Management of Copyright* (Athens, Nomiki Vivliothiki, 2020).

[5]   By Act No.5257/1931 Greece ratified the Berne Convention as revised in 1928 in Rome, with certain reservations, which did not relate to moral rights. It also ratified the Berne Convention as revised in 1948 in Brussels and in 1971 in Paris, with no reservations whatsoever, by the Presidential Decree 3565/1956 and by Act No.100/1975 respectively. Greece also ratified the 1952 Geneva Convention by Law Decree 4254/1962. It also ratified the 1996 WIPO Copyright Convention and the 1996 WIPO Performances and Phonograms Treaty by Laws 3184/2003 and 3183/2003 respectively. Greece has also ratified other Conventions in the area such as the TRIPs Agreement and the 1971 Geneva Convention, which, however, do not contain any moral rights provisions. For Greek legislation see I. Stamatoudi (ed.) (in Greek), Copyright Law, National and Community Legislation and International Conventions (Athens: Nomiki Vivliothiki, 2007).

[6]   Although Greek copyright law follows the monistic theory, according to which copyright forms one right with two sets of (sub-) rights, economic rights and moral rights, it has, however, maintained the position that moral rights are absolute rights, non-transferable inter vivos and – though separate – still closely linked to the right to one's personality: L. Kotsiris, in L. Kotsiris and I. Stamatoudi (eds), Commentary on the Greek Copyright Act (Athens and Thessaloniki: P.N. Sakkoulas, 2009), pp. 9–10.

1.2   The Greek Copyright Act (No. 2121/1993)

According to the principle which underlies Greek copyright law, namely that a creator of a work can only be a natural person and that copyright initially vests in the author (or director of a film), moral rights, forming part of copyright, can only be vested in the natural person who created the work. They cannot be vested in legal entities such as companies. This is by reason of the fact that moral rights are there to indicate and protect the particular personal bond existing between the author and his work. In that sense, an author has as many moral rights as works.[7]

Foreign authors whose countries of origin are members of the Berne Convention are given the same protection in Greece as Greek authors or Greek works (the principle of national treatment). Such protection is independent of the existence of protection in the country of origin of the work (the principle of the independence of protection).[8] Thus, even if the work of an English author is not protected by a particular moral right in the UK (e.g. right of retraction),[9] its author may still invoke the right under Greek law for acts having taken place in Greece. Performers are also entitled to moral rights in relation to their performances, which are, however, more limited in scope and duration as compared to those of authors.[10]

1.3   Prerequisites for Copyright Protection

As regards the prerequisites for copyright protection, Art. 1 of the 1993 Act makes it clear that "copyright" within the meaning of Greek law must be understood in the continental European sense of "author's right".[11] To start with, it declares that copyright includes two types of rights: economic rights, that is, the author's prerogatives to control the exploitation of his work, and moral rights, that is, the author's prerogatives with regard to his personal interests in the work. Furthermore, copyright initially vests only in the author, that is, the natural person who created the work, without his having to satisfy any formalities. Finally, both economic and moral rights are exclusive in that the author may assert them against anyone who violates them.[12]

Greek law imposes no formalities as preconditions of copyright.[13] Nor does it impose any requirement that a work be fixed.

The Copyright Act, according to Art. 2(1), protects as a work "any original creation". The statute, however, does not define the notions or criteria either of "originality" or of "creativity". Traditionally, a work that expresses the personality of its author has been considered to be original. A current formulation of the traditional criterion calls for originality to be assessed

---

[7]   Court of First Instance, Iraklio, Decision No. 553/2003, Commercial Law Review, 2000, p. 805.

[8]   If, however, a Member State to the Berne Convention provides for a longer term than the minimum prescribed by the Convention and the work ceases to be protected in the country of origin, protection may be denied in that Member State.

[9]   Either because such moral right does not exist in the UK (as it is the case with the right of retraction) or because the scope of this moral right differs in the UK from that in Greece.

[10]   Copyright Act, Art. 50. Greek law introduced moral rights for performers well before they were introduced at international level by the WIPO Performances and Phonograms Treaty (1996).

[11]   See the contrast with UK law on the issue of moral rights. I. Stamatoudi, "Moral Rights of Authors in England: The Missing Emphasis on the Role of Creators" (1997) 4 Intellectual Property Quarterly 478.

[12]   This is discussed further in Section 3.

[13]   Copyright Act, Art. 6(2).

on the basis that statistically unique elements present in the work are indices of creativity.[14] As one decision puts it, a work meets the requisite criteria of protectability if another author, under similar circumstances and with the same aim in mind, would not reasonably reach the same creative outcome or if the work at issue presents an individual particularity or a modicum of creativity such that the work can be distinguished from everyday productions or from other similar and known works.[15] Yet, according to the Court of Justice of the EU recent case law, the notion of originality has been interpreted in a uniform and autonomous manner throughout the EU.[16] In this context a work is protected insofar it is original, originality being the sole prerequisite for protection. A work is original if it is its author's own intellectual creation, i.e., if the author has made upon its creation free and creative choices and has stamped the work with his personal touch.[17]

2.   PRESENT NATIONAL LEGISLATION ON MORAL RIGHTS

2.1   Nature of Rights, Beneficiaries and Duration of Protection

2.1.1   Nature of rights
The Copyright Act, in Art. 1(1), starts by explicitly declaring that copyright is made up of both economic and moral rights. This approach has been preferred although these distinct

---

[14]   See, e.g., Supreme Court, Decision No. 118/2006, Legal Tribune, 2006, p. 1140 (finding originality in a study submitted to a contest on the basis of its ostensibly creative elements).

[15]   Court of First Instance (Multimember Panel), Athens, Decision No. 2028/2003, Nomos (online). I. Stamatoudi, in L. Kotsiris and I. Stamatoudi (eds), Commentary on the Greek Copyright Act (Athens and Thessaloniki: P.N. Sakkoulas, 2009), pp. 31, et seq.

[16]   Case C-5/08 *Infopaq International* (2009) ECR I-6569 [27]; Case C-34/10 *Brüstle* (2011) ECR I-09821 [25]; and Case C-510/10 *DR and TV2 Danmark* (published in the electronic Reports of Cases: https://curia.europa.eu/jcms/jcms/P_106320/en/?rec=RG&jur=C&anchor=201204C0076 #201204C0076) [33], as referred to in Case C-128/11 *UsedSoft GmbH v. Oracle International Corp.* [39] (published in the electronic Reports of Cases: https://curia.europa.eu/jcms/jcms/P_106320/en/?rec =RG&jur=C&anchor=201207C0127). See also, Case C-357/98 *Yiadom* (2000) ECR I-9265 [26]; Case C-245/00 *SENA* (2003) ECR I-1251 [23]; and Case C-306/05 *SGAE* (2006) ECR I-11519 [31]. See also I. Stamatoudi and P. Torremans (eds), EU Copyright Law (Cheltenham (UK) and Northampton (USA): Edward Elgar Publishing, 2014, and 2021, 2nd ed), pp. 1102–4.

[17]   Case C-5/08 *Infopaq International A/S v. Danske Dagblades Forening* (2009), judgment of 16 July 2009 ECR I-656; Cases C-403/08 and C-429/08 *Football Association Premier League Ltd and Karen Murphy*, judgment of 4 October 2011, (2011) ECR I-9083; Case C-145/10 *Eva-Maria Painer v. Standard VerlagsGmbH and others* (2013), judgment of 7 March 2013 (2011) ECR I-12533; Case C-604/10, *Football Dataco Ltd and Others v. Yahoo! UK Ltd and Others* (2012), judgment of 1 March 2012 (published in the electronic Reports of Cases: https://curia.europa.eu/jcms/jcms/P_106320/en/ ?rec=RG&jur=C&anchor=201203C0031); Case C-393/09, *Bezpečnostní softwarová asociace – Svaz softwarové ochrany v. Ministerstvo kultury* (2010) ECR I-13971, judgment of 22 December 2010, (2010) ECR I-13971; Case C-406/10, *SAS Institute Inc. v. World Programming Ltd* (2012), judgment of 2 May 2012 (published in the electronic Reports of Cases: https://curia.europa.eu/jcms/jcms/P_106320/en/ ?rec=RG&jur=C&anchor=201205C0081#201205C0081). For the notion of originality in the EU see I. Stamatoudi, "Originality under EU Copyright Law" in P. Torremans (ed.), *Copyright Law: A Handbook of Contemporary Research* (Cheltenham (UK) and Northampton (USA), Edward Elgar Publishing, 2017), p. 57; and I. Stamatoudi, "'More' Originality for Cypriot Copyright Law according to the CJEU's Case Law" (Spring 2018) 30(1) *The Cyprus Review* 207–31.

rights manifest many differences between them: for instance, economic rights are contractually transferable, whereas moral rights are not. The legislative intent was to ensure national
treatment for foreign authors, as provided by the Berne Convention, also with regard to moral
rights.

Generally, moral rights protect the personal interests of the author in his work. These rights
are, therefore, of the same nature, though not of the same content, as the "right in one's own
personality", which Art. 57 of the Greek Civil Code recognizes and which, inter alia, includes
the rights to privacy and to personal reputation.[18] It is not clear whether one can invoke simul-
taneously the protection afforded by the "right in one's own personality" and that of moral
rights. The jurisprudence, as well as the academic literature, are divided in this respect.[19] The
prevailing view is that the two rights are entirely separate and in many respects different and,
as a result, the "right in one's own personality" can only be invoked in those instances where
the prerequisites for the application of the moral rights protection are not met.[20] No other
causes of action apply to moral rights protection, as Law 2121/1993 provides for a specialized
and comprehensive protection in this area.

The Greek Copyright Act in Art. 4[21] refers to five illustrative, but not exhaustive, moral
rights vested in authors: the right of disclosure, the right of paternity, the right of integrity,
the right of retraction and the right of access to the work. Moral rights (i.e., a limited right of

---

[18]   For a general review of the Greek case law concerning the right to respect for personality, see
Georgiades and Stathopoulos, Annotated Civil Code, vol 1, notes 2–10 to Art. 57 (Athens: Sakkoulas,
1978).

[19]   See Supreme Court, Decision No. 171/1957, Journal of Greek Lawyers, 1958, Vol. 25, p. 265. But
cf. Court of Appeal, Athens, Decision No. 8138/2000, Business and Company Law, 2001, pp. 60–70,
English translation in European Copyright and Design Reports, 2002, p. 75 (holding that the prerequisites for the application of the "right to one's personality" do not always coincide with those of authors'
moral rights).

[20]   M.D. Papadopoulou, in L. Kotsiris and I. Stamatoudi (eds), Commentary on the Greek Copyright
Act (Athens and Thessaloniki: P.N. Sakkoulas, 2009), pp. 143–5.

[21]   Art. 4 (Moral Rights): "(1) The moral rights shall confer upon the author notably the following
rights: a) to decide on the time, place and manner in which the work shall be made accessible to the public
(publication) b) to demand that his status as the author of the work be acknowledged and, in particular,
to the extent that it is possible, that his name be indicated on the copies of his work and noted whenever
his work is used publicly, or, on the contrary, if he so wishes, that his work be presented anonymously
or under a pseudonym c) to prohibit any distortion, mutilation or other modification of his work and any
offence to the author due to the circumstances of the presentation of the work in public d) to have access
to his work, even when the economic right in the work or the physical embodiment of the work belongs to
another person; in those latter cases, the access shall be effected with minimum possible nuisance to the
rightholder e) in the case of a literary or scientific work, to rescind a contract transferring the economic
right or an exploitation contract or license of which his work is the object, subject to payment of material
damages to the other contracting party, for the pecuniary loss he has sustained, when the author considers
such action to be necessary for the protection of his personality because of changes in his beliefs or in
the circumstances. (2) With reference to the last case of the preceding paragraph, the rescission shall
take effect after the payment of the damages. If, after the rescission, the author again decides to transfer
the economic right, or to permit exploitation of the work or of a like work, he must give, in priority, the
former other contracting party the opportunity to reconstitute the old contract with the same terms or
with terms similar to those which were in force at the time of the rescission. (3) The moral rights shall
be independent from the economic rights and shall remain with the author even after the transfer of the
economic rights."

paternity and a limited right of integrity in their works compared to authors) in relation to performers and their performances are set out exhaustively in Art. 50 of the Greek Copyright Act.

The list of five moral rights in the Greek Copyright Act is only indicative and by no means exhaustive. This means that the author may invoke aspects of his personal interests in his work even if these aspects do not come expressly within the scope of moral rights set out in the Act. Such an example might be false allegations as to the circumstances of creation of a work.[22] Moral rights are absolute in the sense that they may be asserted against anyone and may be violated by anyone and are exclusive in the sense that they belong only to the author. As explicitly provided in the first sentence of Art. 12(2) of the Copyright Act, the author may not, in principle, transfer them, although they may be subjected to contractual limitations.[23]

Although moral rights descend to an author's heirs, they may not, in principle, be transferred *inter vivos*. They also cannot be waived. This limitation results from the character of the right as protecting interests that intimately concern the personality of the author. In particular, moral rights are independent of the economic copyright and remain vested in the author even after all the economic rights have been transferred to others.[24]

2.1.2   Beneficiaries of protection

Moral rights, of course, vest in the author as the natural person who has created a work of the mind. Even authors of computer software, which are assimilated to literary works, are granted moral rights just like any other author. In the case of an anonymous or pseudonymous work, where under Greek law[25] the publisher of such a work initially holds the copyright, the publisher may exercise some moral rights, for example, the right of integrity and the right to prevent a third party from falsely claiming to be the author, but only to the extent justified by the publisher's capacity as a fictive author.[26]

Just as they have neighbouring rights, performing artists have limited moral rights as regards their performances.

The Copyright Act provides the same civil remedies against violations of moral rights as for infringement of economic copyright, while some violations may also trigger criminal penalties.

2.1.3   Duration of moral rights

The duration of moral rights is equal to that of copyright, namely generally for 70 years after the death of the author calculated from the 1 January of the year following the event of his death.[27]

---

[22]   G.A. Koumantos, Copyright Law, 8th ed, 2002, p. 248.

[23]   This is discussed in more detail in Section 3 below.

[24]   Copyright Act Art. 4(3). See also Court of Appeal, Athens, Decision No. 5866/2003, Business and Company Law, 2003, p. 1330; Court of Appeal, Athens, Decision No. 7458/1999, Commercial Law Reports, 2000, p. 750.

[25]   Copyright Act, Art. 11.

[26]   Copyright Act, Art. 11(2).

[27]   Copyright Act, Art. 29(1).

After the author's death, the right to assert moral rights devolves on his heirs,[28] who may exercise the rights subject to certain limitations.[29] Most notably, the heirs are bound to exercise the rights in accordance with the intent of the author, as expressed in his lifetime or will.[30] After the end of the term of protection, the state, represented by the Minister of Culture, may exercise some of the component rights included in moral rights, namely the right of attribution of authorship and the right to safeguard the integrity of the work.[31] These two rights are perpetual.

The duration of performers' moral rights is disputed. Greek law is rather ambiguous on this point, since it does not clarify what the exact duration is.[32] Hence, different views have been asserted. The prevailing view, however, is that performers' moral rights last at least as long as the performer's lifetime. After their death[33] their rights devolve on their immediate[34] heirs for as long as their heirs live.[35]

2.2   The Five Types of Moral Rights

2.2.1   Right of disclosure

Article 4(1)(a) provides that an author has the right "to decide on the time, place and manner in which the work shall be made accessible to the public (publication)". The author thus has the right to determine the time, place, and way in which a work will be made accessible to the public for the first time and any subsequent time after that[36] as well as whether the work should be published in the first place.[37] The publication of a work without the author's authorization

---

[28]   This is also the only possibility where moral rights as a whole can be transferred according to the Greek Copyright law: Court of First Instance, Athens, Decision No. 5743/2000, Nomos (online); Court of First Instance, Athens, Decision No. 32992/1997, Commercial Law Review, 1999, p. 409.

[29]   Copyright Act, Art. 12(2): "The moral rights shall not be transferable between living persons. After the death of an author, the moral rights shall pass to his heirs, who shall exercise the rights in compliance with the author's wishes, provided that such wishes have been explicitly expressed."

[30]   See, e.g., Court of First Instance, Athens, Decision No. 5743/2000, Nomos (online) (holding that the heirs of a music composer could preclude the public performance of the composer's compositions in a theatrical play where there was the danger that these compositions could be mixed with others' compositions of a style regarding which the dead author had expressed reservations). But cf. Court of First Instance, Athens, Decision No. 36247/1999, Private Law Annals, 2001, pp. 465–7.

[31]   Copyright Act, Art. 29(2).

[32]   Art. 50 (Moral right): "(1) During their lifetime, performers shall have the right to full acknowledgment and credit of their status as such in relation to their performances and to the right to prohibit any form of alteration of their performances. (2) After the death of a performer that person's moral right shall pass to his heirs. (3) The provisions of Article 12(2) and Article 16 of this Law shall be applicable *mutatis mutandis* to the moral right of performers".

[33]   Even if the 50-year term of protection of their performances has expired.

[34]   That is, the first generation of heirs.

[35]   N. Kyprouli, in L. Kotsiris and I. Stamatoudi (eds), Commentary on the Greek Copyright Act (Athens and Thessaloniki: P.N. Sakkoulas, 2009), pp. 890–1.

[36]   It includes any new publication of the work which takes place in a new form or in a different way. See Supreme Court, Decision No. 1010/2002, Greek Justice, 2003, p. 1357 Court of First Instance (Multimember Panel), Athens, Decision No. 1669/2003, Nomos Database.

[37]   See Court of Appeal, Athens, Decision No. 8138/2000, Business and Company Law, 2001, p. 62; Court of First Instance, Athens, Decision No. 2122/2004, Mass Media, Information and Communications Law, 2005, p. 100; Court of First Instance, Athens, Decision No. 20669/1998, Commercial Law Review, 1999, p. 152; Court of First Instance, Athens, Decision No. 11923/1998, Legal Tribune, 1998, p. 1476;

or consent does not exhaust the author's right of disclosure.[38] In this context, the 1993 Act uses the Greek term usually translated by "publication" and understood in the broad sense of making the work accessible to the public in any way[39] with the author's consent.[40] The publication of the work does not form a necessary prerequisite in order for a work to be protected, i.e. unpublished works are also protected. Thus, the publication of a work (finished or unfinished) or extracts of it on the Internet is not permitted without the author's consent. The same applies in relation to the publication of a work in a printed format or the republication of a work in a printed format via an electronic medium such as a DVD. Thus, the reproduction of an artistic work, which was created for the purposes of an advertising poster, on phonecards was found to infringe the author's right of disclosure[41] as was also the sporadic publication on the Internet of a book without the author's consent.[42]

The notion of "public" is understood as encompassing any circle of persons larger than the narrow circle of family and friends, or larger than the immediate social environment. Some examples from the jurisprudence are as follows: the showing of an advertising film for the purposes of a contest amongst a closed circle of persons was not considered to constitute publication of the work;[43] the reproduction of a work by way of 50 sample copies, in order for the final version of the book to be approved for publication, the sample copies not being made available for sale in bookshops and which people could not buy and read, was also not considered to constitute publication.[44] Generally, for this purpose it is irrelevant whether the work is made available to a large or a small group of people; even the possibility of the public having

---

Court of First Instance (Multimember Panel), Athens, Decision No. 32992/1997, Commercial Law Review, 1999, p. 409.

[38]   M.D. Papadopoulou, in L. Kotsiris and I. Stamatoudi (eds), Commentary on the Greek Copyright Act (Athens and Thessaloniki: P.N. Sakkoulas, 2009), p. 151.

[39]   Publication can take place in a number of ways, such as publication in print, digital publication, lecture, announcement, broadcast through television or radio, by performing the work, showing it in a gallery and so on. In other words, all the modes of the economic exploitation of the work constitute publication within the meaning of the moral right of disclosure.

[40]   It goes without saying that it is either the author who makes the work available to the public or a third person or entity which has acquired the author's consent (e.g., a publisher): Court of Appeal, Athens, Decision No. 8138/2000, Business and Company Law, 2001, p. 62; Court of First Instance, Athens, Decision No. 11923/1998, Legal Tribune, 1998, p. 1476. The author's consent may be found expressly in a contract or may be derived from the circumstances, e.g. the handing by a composer of a demo CD over to a phonogram company in order for the latter to listen to a new work does not give the company the right to make it available to the public (Supreme Court, Decision No. 238/1995, Legal Tribune, 1996, p. 801). On the contrary, if a film director hands over to the producer of the film a copy containing the final cut of his work, then it is presumed that the producer can proceed with its publication (KG NJW--RR 1986, 608—Paris--Texas by Wim Wenders LG München I, ZUM 2000, 416—Down under). In any case the transfer of ownership in a medium (e.g. CD, DVD, book) cannot be taken as the transfer of any rights in its contents unless there is an express provision to this effect between the author and the new owner of the medium (Court of First Instance, Athens, Decision No. 32992/1997, Commercial Law Review, 1999, p. 409).

[41]   Court of First Instance, Athens, Decision No. 2122/2004, (Mass Media, Information and Communications Law, 2005, p. 100.

[42]   Court of First Instance, Athens, Decision No. 1639/2001, Business and Company Law, 2001, p. 858.

[43]   Court of First Instance, Athens, Decision No. 24610/2004, Private Law Annals, 2006, p. 929.

[44]   Court of First Instance, Athens, Decision No. 20669/1998, Commercial Law Review, 1999, p. 153.

access to the work suffices for the purposes of the law (e.g. where a film is shown on television but no one watches it).[45] It is further argued that the reconstruction and subsequent publication of a work, which has been discarded (or dismantled and thrown away) by its author, may also infringe the author's moral right.[46] The right of disclosure also encompasses the right of the public announcement of the work. This is particularly important with regard to films where the producer[47] usually wants to choose the precise time when to announce the film (by way of presenting small extracts of it) to the public for advertising purposes before the film is made available to the cinemas.[48]

2.2.2   Right of paternity

(a)   Authors
Article 4(1)(b) provides that the author has the right "to demand that his status as the author of the work be acknowledged and, in particular, to the extent that it is possible, that his name be indicated on the copies of his work and noted whenever his work is used publicly, or, on the contrary, if he so wishes, that his work be presented anonymously or under a pseudonym". Thus, the author has the right to have his creative contribution to his work recognized. In particular, the author is specifically entitled to have his name mentioned on published copies or the original of the work and in connection with any public showing or display of the work or, in the alternative, to keep the work anonymous or to use a pseudonym. If the author chooses not to reveal his identity, then the term of protection of the work cannot be calculated as usual, i.e., 70 years from the death of the author. In this case, Art. 11(1) applies, according to which "any person who lawfully makes available to the public anonymous or pseudonymous works is deemed as the initial holder of the economic and moral right towards third parties. When the true author of the work reveals his identity, he shall acquire the above-mentioned rights in the condition they are in, as a result of the actions of the fictitious rightholder". In this event, the moral rights belong to the fictitious rightholder to the extent justified by his actual capacity (Art. 11(2)).[49] If so, the term of protection of the work will be calculated based on the date the work was lawfully made available to the public.[50]

---

[45]   M.D. Papadopoulou, in L. Kotsiris and I. Stamatoudi (eds), Commentary on the Greek Copyright Act (Athens and Thessaloniki: P.N. Sakkoulas, 2009), p. 146.

[46]   L. Kotsiris, Copyright Law (Athens: Sakkoulas, 4th ed, 2005), p. 124, and Cour d'appel de Paris, 6 March 1931, D.P.1931.88 – Camoin· Cour de Cass. 13 December 1995, RIDA 169/1996, 307 – Colette Granier de Cassagnac.

[47]   According to Art. 9 of the Greek Copyright Act, the principal director of an audiovisual work is considered to be the author.

[48]   M.D. Papadopoulou, in L. Kotsiris and I. Stamatoudi (eds), Commentary on the Greek Copyright Act (Athens and Thessaloniki: P.N. Sakkoulas, 2009), p. 147 and TGI de Paris, 17 January 1999, RIDA 181/1999, p. 331.

[49]   This latter prerequisite ("justified by its actual capacity") means that the fictitious rightholder cannot exercise those rights which are linked to the author of the work (e.g., claim to be acknowledged as the author of work) since he is not the author. He can only exercise moral rights for the benefit of the work and not his own benefit. A. Papadopoulou, in L. Kotsiris and I. Stamatoudi (eds), Commentary on the Greek Copyright Act (Athens and Thessaloniki: P.N. Sakkoulas, 2009), p. 311.

[50]   Art. 31(1): "In the case of anonymous or pseudonymous works, the term of copyright shall last for seventy (70) years calculated from 1st January of the year after that in which the work is lawfully made available to the public. However, if, during the said period, the author discloses his identity or when the pseudonym adopted by the author leaves no doubt as to his identity, then the general rules shall apply."

The Greek Copyright Act also refers explicitly to a number of cases where specific provisions in relation to a right of attribution apply, such as in cases of translation (where the translator's name must be clearly indicated on the main title page of the work),[51] publication of photographs (where the name of the photographer should always be mentioned on the work),[52] and authors of theatrical plays (whose name should always be indicated in relation to the advertising of their works).[53] This right should be distinguished from the author's right to deny the paternity of a work on the basis of artistic or personal reasons or generally to have his name removed from a work that is not his work.[54] This latter right is not considered under Greek law to form part of the paternity right. It is rather considered to be an aspect of one's right to one's personality and as such can be invoked on the basis of the provisions of the Greek Civil Code.

The name of the author should be indicated on the work (or copies of the work) whenever the work is used publicly to the extent that this is possible and in the appropriate manner depending on the type of work in question and the mode of disclosure of the work (e.g., if a work is announced on the radio, the name of the author should be mentioned by the announcer). If the work is presented in a digital format without being attached to any medium, then the acknowledgement of the author's name should take place orally or in some other manner which is appropriate in the circumstances.[55] The name of the author should be announced in a comprehensible manner or be easily readable (e.g., an indication of the author's name with very small letters in a hidden part of the work does not suffice).[56]

(b)   Performers
The act of paternity is also provided for performers. The Act provides that "[d]uring their lifetime, performers shall have the right to full acknowledgement and credit of their status as such in relation to their performances".[57] As with authors, this right is also subject to the dictates of logic, practice and customs in the field. That means that the names of the actors participating in a film should be mentioned in the opening and closing titles and the names of singers should be given in a concert programme. On the other hand, it is not usual for the names of the members of an orchestra to be mentioned on the cover of the CD or during a broadcast: such a claim on the part of the performers would be considered abusive.

---

[51]   Copyright Act, Art. 34(2). See also Court of First Instance (Multimember Panel), Athens, Decision No. 1322/1997, Legal Tribune, 2000, p. 285; Court of First Instance (Multimember Panel), Athens, Decision No. 66/1995, Legal Tribune, 1996, p. 232; Court of First Instance (Multimember Panel), Athens, Decision No.8753/1995, Commercial Law Review, 1995, p. 708.
[52]   Copyright Act, Arts 38(4) and 72(5). Court of First Instance, Athens, Decision No. 2122/2004, Mass Media, Information and Communications Law, 2005, p. 100. For more details see I. Stamatoudi, "Photographers' Rights in Photographs Published in Mass Media", in I. Stamatoudi (ed.), Journalists and Mass Media Publishers: Copyright Issues (Athens and Thessaloniki, P.N. Sakkoulas, 2009), p. 263.
[53]   Copyright Act, Art. 72(2).
[54]   Court of First Instance, Athens, Decision No. 1478/1997, Jurisprudence Archive, 1998, p. 237.
[55]   G.A. Koumantos, Copyright Law, 8th ed, 2002, p. 259; L. Kotsiris, Copyright Law (Athens: Sakkoulas, 4th ed, 2005), p. 126. See also Court of First Instance, Athens, Decision No. 3343/1999 (not reported); Court of First Instance, Athens, Decision No. 1357/1997, Business and Company Law, 1997, p. 1166. Court of First Instance, Athens, Decision No. 1478/1997, Jurisprudence, 1998, p. 236.
[56]   Court of First Instance, Athens, Decision No. 1293/1987, Legal Tribune, 1987, p. 1424.
[57]   Copyright Act, Art. 50(1).

2.2.3 Right of integrity

(a)   Authors
Article 4(1)(c) provides that an author has the right "to prohibit any distortion, mutilation or other modification of his work and any offence to the author due to the circumstances of the presentation of the work in public". Thus, the author has the right to object to any distortion, mutilation, or other modification of a work, as well as in respect of any prejudice arising out of the conditions of dissemination or presentation of the work to the public.[58] There are no limitations on the kind of modifications (distortions or mutilations) that fall within the scope of the relevant provision (Art. 4(1)(c)) and the impact these modifications may have on the author's image. This means that any modification, even if it may be considered to be favoura-ble as regards the author or his work, is not permissible under the right of the integrity. In this respect, the integrity right of authors under Greek law is much wider than the integrity right guaranteed under Art. 6bis of the Berne Convention since prejudice to the author's honour or reputation is not required.

Examples of infringement of various types of works are set out below.

Musical works – Some examples of infringement of the right of integrity in relation to musical works are the following: the shortening of musical works, a change of title, a change of rhythm,[59] and the use of parts of the musical work in a documentary film[60] or in an adver-tisement, if the work was initially commissioned for another purpose.[61] However, it is not considered an infringement of the integrity rights of either the composer of the music, the author of the lyrics or the original performer if the same musical work is performed by another performer with a different instrumentation.[62]

Photographs – Photomontage may also be considered an infringement of the photogra-pher's integrity right.[63]

Works of architecture – With reference to works of architecture, there is often a clash between the rights of the owner of the building and the architect's integrity right. This clash is solved by a weighing of the interests of the relevant parties in each case, taking into account a number of factors such as the extent to which the character of the work is utilitarian, the customs in the field, the good faith of the parties,[64] financial considerations (including changes which have been made in order for the owner to diminish the costs of the construction), public order, security, and technical reasons or changes, which are dictated by necessity or practice.[65] However, the guiding principle (which is derived from the spirit of the law and the case law

---

[58]   Copyright Act, Art. 4(1)(c). See Court of First Instance (Multimember Panel), Athens, Decision No. 276/2001, Legal Tribune, 2001, p. 1332.

[59]   Court of First Instance, Athens, Decision No. 1293/1987, Legal Tribune, 1987, p. 1423.

[60]   Court of Appeal, Athens, Decision No. 7458/1999, Commercial Law Review, 2000, p. 749.

[61]   Court of Appeal, Athens, Decision No. 143/2004, Business and Company Law, 2004, p. 415; Court of Appeal, Patras, Decision No. 352/2005, Commercial Law Reports, 2005, p. 1017.

[62]   Court of First Instance, Athens, Decision No. 14751/1996, Business and Company Law, 1998, p. 843.

[63]   Court of First Instance, Athens, Decision No. 2122/2004, Mass Media, Information and Communications Law, 2005, p. 100.

[64]   Court of First Instance, Athens, Decision No. 276/2001, Legal Tribune, 2001, p. 1332.

[65]   Court of First Instance (Multimember Panel), Thessaloniki, Decision No. 13300/2004, Armenopoulos, 2005, p. 723; Court of First Instance (Multimember Panel), Athens, Decision No. 2028/2003, Jurisprudence Archive, 2004, p. 210; Court of First Instance, Athens, Decision No.

in the area) is that the particular character of the building should be maintained whilst any changes or modifications should cause the least possible dilution of this character.[66] A few examples from the case law are as follows: the addition of an extra floor to a hotel was not found to spoil the style of the building and was also considered necessary for financial reasons, as it would increase the owner's income and save him from financial disaster.[67] In the case of the Olympic Village built for the 2004 Games, it was held that the Olympic Committee owning the buildings of the Village could make changes dictated by practical needs, even though such changes would constitute substantial alterations, which were subject to the architect's right of integrity.[68] It is also argued that even the destruction of a building is allowed if there are important reasons dictating it.[69] Such decisions are fact-specific, and the courts have decided both for and against architects.[70]

Deterioration or destruction of work – A controversial issue is the extent to which a third party-owner of the medium/carrier of the work (e.g., the painting, the statue, the photograph, etc.) may without the creator's consent let it deteriorate or even destroy it if he so wishes. In these cases, a weighing of the interests of the parties applies. In cases where multiple copies of a work already exist, e.g., books, copies of statues, etc. the owner's interests should prevail. If unique works of art are in question, the creators' interests will probably prevail. Such cases are when the work is of a very significant cultural value or when its preservation and care are provided for by the letter or the purpose of the contract between the creator and the owner of the work. In these cases, it is argued that the right to ownership (in favour of the owner of the medium) prevails over the right of integrity; the latter is limited by the provisions on abuse of rights.[71] It could also be argued that the destruction of a work is not a "modification" within the scope of the relevant article. In any case, the owner of any work (in the sense of the medium) may always make changes or modifications to the work, no matter how extensive they are, as long as the work remains in his private sphere and is not published or communicated to third parties. According to the Greek law, anyone is allowed to produce derivative works by carrying out changes to an original work. It is, however, the exploitation of such derivative work (if the original author's consent is not there), which is prohibited.

The situation is different if someone chooses to create a work on someone else's property (e.g., graffiti on someone's walls). The illegal character of the creation does not affect the

---

276/2001, Legal Tribune, 2001; Court of First Instance, Athens, Decision No. 4714/1971, (1971) ArhN 425.

[66]   Court of First Instance (Multimember Panel), Athens, Decision No. 2028/2003, Jurisprudence Archive, 2004, p. 210.

[67]   Court of First Instance (Multimember Panel), Thessaloniki, Decision No. 13300/2004, Armenopoulos, 2005, p. 723; Court of First Instance, Athens, Decision No. 4714/1971, Commercial Law Review, 1971, p. 462.

[68]   Court of First Instance, Athens, Decision No. 276/2001, Legal Tribune, 2001, p. 1332.

[69]   G.A. Koumantos, Copyright Law, 8th ed, 2002, p. 265.

[70]   Compare Court of First Instance (Multimember Panel), Thessaloniki, Decision No. 13300/2004, Nomos (online) (not accepting changes to a work that violated the architect's moral right), with Court of First Instance (Multimember Panel), Thessaloniki, Decision No. 2028/2003, Nomos (online) (accepting changes to the work by reason of the functional needs of the owners).

[71]   M.D. Papadopoulou, in L. Kotsiris and I. Stamatoudi (eds), Commentary on the Greek Copyright Act (Athens and Thessaloniki: P.N. Sakkoulas, 2009), p. 163.

act of creation as such.[72] In these cases, the owner of the property has the right to wipe off or otherwise destroy the work whereas he has no right to exploit it or make changes to it.[73]

Use in different context – The notions of "distortion, mutilation and modification" refer not only to an actual tampering with the content of the work itself but also encompass instances where the work is presented in a context which is prejudicial to the author's image or does not meet his beliefs. As can be seen from what follows, the circumstances of the presentation of a work (with regard to time, place, context, etc.) play a significant role.

The right against prejudicial dissemination has been found to be violated where a work was used for publicity purposes without the author's consent; where a musical composition was executed badly;[74] where, in cases of the public performance of a work during a theatrical play, other musical works of a different style were performed, which the deceased composer had expressly stated should not be performed alongside his music. The integrity right may equally be violated where an art work is placed at a site which contradicts its purpose or spirit, or where the work is unjustifiably transferred to a place other than its original site.[75] Other examples include the use of a religious song in an erotic scene,[76] or the use of a musical work in a pornographic film or in an inappropriate context such as the entrance of a boxer into an arena,[77] the publication of musical works together with works of musical groups belonging to the neo-fascist or extreme right wing,[78] the publication of a scientific work in a pornographic magazine,[79] the use of a work for advertising purposes,[80] the publication of a work on the Internet in a context which was insulting to the author's personality and reputation,[81] the removal of a statue to a place other than the one for which it was initially intended (site-specific art),[82] and so on. If the work is exhibited in a public place, the public interest and the interest of the state will also be taken into consideration.

Audiovisual works – The law provides for a specific regime of protection for audiovisual works and related rights. According to Art. 34(1), the creation of an audiovisual work is deemed to be completed when the master from which copies for exploitation are to be made

---

[72]   TGI Paris, 13 October 2000, RIDA 195/2003, 280.
[73]   M.D. Papadopoulou, in L. Kotsiris and I. Stamatoudi (eds), Commentary on the Greek Copyright Act (Athens and Thessaloniki: P.N. Sakkoulas, 2009), p. 164. See also BGH NJW 1995, 1556 – Mauer Bilder, 1997 IIC, 282.
[74]   See, respectively, Court of First Instance, Athens, Decision No. 7642/1977, Commercial Law Review, 1977, pp. 654–5; Court of Appeal, Athens, Decision No. 7545/1982, Commercial Law Review, 1983, p. 165.
[75]   See Counsel of State, Decision No. 1465/1954, Themis, 1955, p. 174; Court of Appeal, Dodoni, Decision No. 47/1956, Legal Tribune, 1956, p. 861.
[76]   TGI Paris, 5 May 1991, JCP 92 II 21919, Daverat. Note that a Greek court is likely to follow the decisions of other EU courts.
[77]   LG München, ZUM 1993, 289, o Fortuna.
[78]   OLG Frankfurt GRUR 1995, 215.
[79]   OLG München NJW 1996, 135, Herrenmagazin.
[80]   Court of Appeal, Athens, Decision No. 143/2004, Business and Company Law, 2004, p. 415; Court of Appeal, Athens, Decision No. 9040/2002, Greek Justice, 2002, 217; Court of First Instance, Athens, Decision No. 7642/1977, Journal of Greek Lawyers, 1977, p. 454.
[81]   Court of First Instance, Athens, Decision No. 1639/2001, Business and Company Law, 2001, p. 860.
[82]   Counsel of State, Decision No. 1465/1954, Journal of Greek Lawyers, 1955, p. 78; Court of First Instance, Athens, Decision No. 15489/1992, not reported, Court of Appeal, Dodoni, Decision No. 47/1956, Legal Tribune, 1956, p. 861.

is approved by the author. No alteration, abridgement or other modification should be made to this definitive form of the audiovisual work without the author's prior consent. Authors of individual contributions to an audiovisual work may exercise their moral rights only in relation to the definitive form of the work, as approved by the author.

(b)   Performers
As for performers, Art. 50(1) stipulates that they "have the right ... to prohibit any form of alteration of their performances". When comparing the wording used for authors and the one used for performers, the performer's right of integrity is more limited. More specifically, in the case of performers, the words "distortion, mutilation or other modification" and "any offence to the author due to the circumstances of the presentation of the work in public" are not used. It is only alterations which are prohibited. The notion of alteration seems to include distortions, mutilations or modifications of the performance as long as they are severe, harm the work or reduce its importance or aesthetic style. These alterations may also be made to the medium containing the performance.[83] By way of illustration, an actress' right of integrity was held to be infringed where pornographic scenes from another film were added to a DVD containing a film in which she participated, whilst the cover of the DVD mentioned the words "Greek Erotic Cinema"; in this way her acting was misrepresented.[84]

2.2.4   Right of retraction/withdrawal
Article 4(1)(e) provides that the author has the right "in the case of a literary or scientific work, to rescind a contract transferring the economic right or an exploitation contract or licence of which his work is the object, subject to payment of material damages to the other contracting party, for the pecuniary loss he has sustained, when the author considers such action to be necessary for the protection of his personality because of changes in his beliefs or in the circumstances". The author thus has the right to rescind contracts that transfer or licence[85] economic rights in literary or scientific works, when this is necessary to protect his personality in the event of subsequent significant changes[86] in his own personal convictions (e.g., scientific, religious, political or ethical convictions) or in other relevant external circumstances. "External circumstances" means objective circumstances, which do not relate to the idiosyncrasy of the author, such as a war, a political crisis or a new discovery.[87] In such a case, the rescission comes into effect as soon as the author pays the holder of the rights in question for any resulting damage. However, if the author later intends to exploit the same or a similar work himself or to transfer rights in it, he must first offer this prior holder of rights the opportunity of entering a contract similar to the one he rescinded.[88] The change in conviction or in

---

[83]   Court of Appeal, Athens, Decision No. 7458/1999, Commercial Law Reports, 2000, p. 749. See also N. Kyprouli, in L. Kotsiris and I. Stamatoudi (eds), Commentary on the Greek Copyright Act (Athens and Thessaloniki: P.N. Sakkoulas, 2009), p. 889.

[84]   Court of First Instance, Athens, Decision No. 9090/2006, Business and Company Law, 2007, p. 792.

[85]   Both exclusive and non-exclusive licences are covered.

[86]   Small or unimportant changes in convictions are not covered by this provision. These changes should also be able to be perceived by the public. In other words, only changes which would substantially affect the author's personality if the work were to be exploited or continued to be exploited are covered.

[87]   Personal disputes between the author and the other contacting party as well as financial reasons relating to the exploitation of the work are not covered.

[88]   Copyright Act, Art. 4(1)(e).

external circumstances required by law must be proved by the author. He may, for instance, submit the new discovery which renders his work outdated or scientifically wrong, or submit prior and later works of his own which demonstrate the changes in his convictions and so on.

The rescission takes effect after the payment of damages and it takes effect ex nunc. The author has to pay all the expenses the other contracting party has incurred up to that time (known in Greek civil law as "positive damage") but not the earnings the latter would have obtained in the future from the exploitation of the author's work. Any income incurred in the past from the exploitation of the work cannot be claimed by the author, since the rescission has effect only for the future. The use of the work, as so far published, communicated to the public or otherwise exploited, is subject to the usual copyright exceptions provided in the law (e.g., one may use short extracts of the work for criticism purposes).

2.2.5 Right of access

Article 4(1)(d) provides that the author notably has the right "to have access to his work, even when the economic right in the work or the physical embodiment of the work belongs to another person; in those latter cases, the access shall be effected with minimum possible nuisance to the rightholder". The author thus has the right to obtain access to unique embodiments of a work even if other persons own the economic copyright in the work or have personal property interests in these embodiments. In such a case, access must take place in a way which causes the smallest possible inconvenience to the owner of rights or of the embodiments.[89]

Although the law does not expressly restrict the right to works of unique embodiment, it is presumed that this is the case, given that the author can easily have access to works reproduced in multiple copies. In such cases, the exercise of this right would be considered abusive. Works considered to be of unique embodiment are essentially works of visual arts such as paintings, sculptures and so on. However, these provisions seem to apply to other works as well, such as works of architecture, musical works or works of literature, if they are contained in unique manuscripts. Works in multiple copies are, however, also covered to the extent that the author no longer has any copies in his possession.[90]

The law does not specify the reasons for which a creator may require access to his work. In this sense, any reason would be considered legitimate, including access for personal pleasure, enjoyment or inspiration or for the economic exploitation of the work. The creator may require access to the work for himself or for a third party, e.g., the creator sends a photographer to take a picture of his work.

Access, as mentioned above, must take place in a way that causes the least possible inconvenience to the owner of the economic rights or of the embodiments. This, in turn, means that it should be done at a time which is convenient to both the owner and the creator, and even that the creator may have to wait a substantial time, for example, where the work has been moved to another place, is undergoing preservation or the owner is ill. The creator cannot use his right abusively, e.g. by visiting the place where the work is situated too often, staying too long or bringing with them a large working crew. What is more, the creator cannot require access to

---

[89]   Copyright Act, Art. 4(1)(d) and 4(2).
[90]   M.D. Papadopoulou, in L. Kotsiris and I. Stamatoudi (eds), Commentary on the Greek Copyright Act (Athens and Thessaloniki: P.N. Sakkoulas, 2009), p. 166.

parts of the work he has not created himself (for instance, an interior decorator cannot require access to the rooms he has not decorated himself).[91]

3.   EXERCISE OF MORAL RIGHTS

The general scope of moral rights does not, in itself, mean that these rights are not subject to limitations. We have already looked into some examples in the sections where the various moral rights were explained. These limitations may arise from general law, from contracts or other concurrent rights. In Greek law moral rights are also limited by the purpose of the exploitation contract or the employment contract, by the application of the provisions on abuse of rights, as well as by reason of a weighing of interests.

3.1   The Theory of the Purpose of the Contract

According to Art. 15(4):

> If the extent and the means of exploitation which the transfer concerns or for which the exploitation or the exploitation licence is agreed are unspecified, it shall be deemed that the said acts refer to the extent and the means that are necessary for the fulfilment of the purpose of the contract or licence.

This provision reflects the theory of the purpose of the contract according to which only those rights are transferred to the licensee as necessary for the fulfilment of the contract.

An equivalent provision exists in the Greek Copyright Act that deals with works that employed authors create on the job. With regard to such works, the law draws a distinction between employment in the private sector and employment by the state or other public entities. In the case of private employment, economic copyright in works created by the employee on the job is *ipso iure* transferred to the employer only to the extent necessary to fulfil the aim of the employment contract.[92] In the other case, the whole economic component of copyright in works created by civil servants in fulfilment of their duties is transferred to the employer. The employment contract may, by its own terms, increase or decrease the scope of the rights to exploit the work that are reserved by the author or vested in the employer.[93] A similar but broader rule is provided in accordance with the Software Directive. The entire economic copyright in a computer program made by an employee in the execution of his duties or following

---

[91]   L. Kotsiris, Copyright Law (Athens: Sakkoulas, 4th ed, 2005), p. 133.

[92]   Copyright Act, Art. 8, as amended by Act No. 2557/1997. *See also* Court of First Instance (Multimember Panel), Athens, Decision No. 1701/2015, Nomos (online) (the unauthorized republication of an instruction manual for disease prevention written by a publishing company's employee infringed the employee's copyright for while the copyright was automatically transferred to the employer this was only to the extent necessary to fulfil the purpose of the economic exploitation of the work, and the further acts exceeded those determined as "necessary" for the fulfilment of the contractual mandate and were without the employee's authorization).

[93]   *See* Supreme Court, Decision No. 498/2019, Nomos (online) (concerning the extent of the rights transferred to the employer in the case of an employment contract; more specifically, the Court confirmed that – as provided under Art. 8 of the Greek Copyright Act – only those economic rights that are necessary for the fulfilment of the purpose of the contract shall be transferred to the employer, unless otherwise provided by the contract).

his employer's instructions are to be exercised by the employer absent an agreement to the contrary.[94]

Although the theory of the purpose of the contract is relevant for economic rights only, since moral rights cannot be transferred, it is alleged in the literature[95] that it has repercussions on moral rights, too, as otherwise it would have been impossible for one to exercise the economic rights transferred to her or to him by operation of the law or by contract if this exercise is blocked on the basis of the moral rights' protection. For example, one gets rights to certain designs, and although it is a designs museum, it cannot exhibit them without the designer's consent. One could come to an equitable legal solution not only on the basis of the purpose of the contract but also on the basis of the interpretation of it in good faith[96] or on the legal basis of abuse of rights, that we shall discuss later on.

3.2   Consent and Contractual Limitations

One cannot waive his moral rights under Greek law.[97] However, as has already been seen, it is possible to *consent* to certain acts or omissions,[98] which otherwise would be considered as an infringement of their moral rights. Yet, in order for this consent to be valid, it should be express, specific and it should be only in writing.[99] *Custom and practice* may also form a basis for limiting moral rights.[100] A particular example is set out below in relation to the paternity right. Examples in relation to the five types of rights are also set out below.

---

[94]   Copyright Act, Art. 40.

[95]   M-D. Papadopoulou, "The Exercise of Moral Rights in Digital Libraries", (2007) *Chronicles of Private Law* 173; O. Garoufalia, *Infringement of Moral Rights and the Right to Personality in the Digital Environment* (Athens: Nomiki Vivliothiki, 2009), at pp. 20 et seq.; Despotidou, Art. 15, in L. Kotsiris and I. Stamatoudi (eds), Commentary on the Greek Copyright Act (Athens and Thessaloniki: P.N. Sakkoulas, 2009); Court of Appeal, Athens, Decision No. 631/1990, Greek Justice, 1991, p. 207; Court of First Instance, Athens, Decision No. 11923/1998, Legal Tribune, 1998, p. 1476.

[96]   Arts 200 and 288 Greek Civil Code (on good faith and business usages).

[97]   Although it has been argued that waiver in relation to some of the rights in relation to some of the works, existing or future ones, is possible. See O. Garoufalia, *Infringement of Moral Rights and the Right to Personality in the Digital Environment* (Athens: Nomiki Vivliothiki, 2009), at pp. 25 seq. and M. Marinos, Copyright Law (Athens: Ant. Sakkoulas, 2nd ed, 2004), p. 202.

[98]   Copyright Act, Arts 14 and 16. Art. 16 (Consent of the Author as Exercise of the Moral Right): "The granting of consent by an author for an action or an omission which would otherwise constitute an infringement of his moral right shall be deemed to be a form of exercise of his moral right, and shall be binding upon him". See Court of Appeal, Athens, Decision No. 631/1990, Greek Justice, 1991, p. 207. Waiver of the enforcement of a moral right against a particular person, rather than of the moral right itself, is allowed or may be implied from a contract: Court of First Instance, Athens, Decision No. 276/2001, Nomos (online). See also Court of First Instance (Multimember Panel), Thessaloniki, Decision No. 5872/1997, Business and Company Law, 1998, p. 147.

[99]   Article 14 (Form of Contracts and Licenses): "Acts dealing with the transfer of economic rights, with the assignment or licensing of the right of exploitation *and with the exercise of the moral right* shall be null and void, unless they are concluded in writing. Nullity may be invoked only by the author". Consent in relation to performers' moral rights should also be given in writing. Copyright Act, Art. 50(a) (emphasis added).

[100]   Where musical compositions and lyrics may be performed by any performer. Court of First Instance DEE 1998, p. 843, where an author cannot prevent a performer from executing his works on the basis of his moral rights.

3.2.1   Right of disclosure

Although Greek Copyright Law permits contracts in relation to the exploitation of future works as long as these contracts are limited in time or scope,[101] such contracts may not contain provisions regarding the exercise of the right of disclosure (i.e., where, when and how the work will be disclosed); this right remains with the author.

Once the author has agreed with a third party how, when and where his work will be exploited and thus disclosed (by way of a transfer of copyright or an exclusive licence), he is then bound by it. The same applies for the third party who has undertaken to exploit the author's work on the basis of a transfer of rights or an exclusive licence. If he fails to do so, the author has the right either to request the third party to proceed with the publication of his work or to withdraw from the contract. He may also ask for compensation if the other party fails intentionally to proceed with the publication or exploitation of the work.[102] There has also been a case where despite the fact that an author failed (and did not respond to the publisher's invitations) to come and sign the copies of his book, as he was entitled by the law, he then decided to turn legally against the publisher for distributing these copies without his signature. Such a claim was found to be abusive although it did not strictly speaking pertain to the right of disclosure.

3.2.2   Right of paternity

As the Greek Copyright Act has been interpreted by the courts, there also may be limitations to the paternity right dictated by the custom and practices in a particular commercial domain. Examples are advertising spots, operating instructions, utensils and mass production products (e.g. chairs, lamps, cars[103] and so on).[104]

As with other moral rights, the exercise of the paternity right may also be limited on the basis of the author's consent or agreed contractual limitations. However, these limitations should not impinge on the central core of this right. Even though it is not entirely clear what this central core is, it is accepted that the author's moral and personal bond with his work should not be seriously jeopardized or irreparably infringed.[105] An example would be the case where the author leaves it up to the publisher to decide how his name should be indicated on the book and the publisher decides to mention the author's name on the back cover with very small, almost illegible letters. This would clearly infringe the author's paternity right. As regards "ghostwriters", it is not entirely clear whether a "ghostwriter" may legally renounce his right to have his name mentioned on a work, which he writes in the name of a third party.[106]

---

[101]   See Art. 13(5), which prohibits exploitation contracts in relation to all future works: "The contract or licence may under no circumstance confer any right over all the future works of the author, and shall never be deemed to also refer to forms of exploitation which were unknown on the date of the contract."

[102]   G.A. Koumantos, Copyright Law, 8th ed, 2002, p. 322; M.D. Marinos, Copyright Law (Athens: Ant. Sakkoulas, 2nd ed, 2004), p. 264; L. Kotsiris, Copyright Law (Athens: Sakkoulas, 4th ed, 2005), p. 124.

[103]   In relation to cars, see Cour d'appel, Paris, 22 November 1983 – Barrault v. Citroen. A Greek court may take such decisions into consideration when deciding a case.

[104]   This conclusion could also be reached solely on the basis of the application of the provisions on the abuse of rights (i.e., Art. 281 Greek Civil Code) without referring to the customs in a particular field (Court of First Instance, Athens, Decision No. 14751, Commercial Law Review, 1996, p. 858).

[105]   Court of First Instance, Athens, Decision No. 1444/1935, Themis, 1936, p. 33.

[106]   Some commentators consider it as infringing public policy. See G.A. Koumantos, Copyright Law, 8th ed, 2002, p. 257; L. Kotsiris, Copyright Law, (Athens: Sakkoulas, 4th ed, 2005), p. 126.

The prevailing view is that such a contract is valid, based on the author's consent.[107] It can also be compared to those cases where a Minister's or Prime Minister's consultant drafts all of his speeches and public announcements for him.

3.2.3   Right of integrity

The integrity right may be limited as a result of the author's consent.[108] Such consent may be expressed (e.g., given in writing in relation to a particular act) or arise implicitly out of a contract for the exploitation of the work, as when a particular mode of exploitation has been agreed between the author and a third party such that the author allows certain acts for the exploitation to become possible[109] (e.g., the publication of a story in a newspaper in parts selected by the editor of the newspaper), or be derivable from the particular circumstances of the case (i.e. the kind of the use and the work). Any limitations, even if contractually agreed, must, however, be very specific and will be interpreted according to customs in the field, good faith and competing interests. Not all modifications are permitted. The factors taken into account include the utilitarian nature of the work, whether it was created by a freelance or a dependent author,[110] the economic rights involved, the form of exploitation at issue and so on.

The right of integrity also applies in relation to uses of the work, which are permitted on the basis of the exceptions to copyright. Thus, for example, where people with visual disabilities are allowed to use a work without the author's consent, they still have to respect the author's moral rights. Limitations apply in these cases only in so far as to make the exception operative.

Other examples are where an author may agree to allow alterations to his work or to make use of his right of access to a work only under certain conditions (e.g., a writer may allow his publisher to omit parts of his work before publication or a buyer of a painting may enter a contract with the painter preventing him from having access to his work more often than once every two years). That means in practice that although an author cannot waive his moral rights, he can, however, consent to use of his work in such a way and to such an extent that in some (rare) cases this may in practice amount to a waiver with regard to particular aspects of moral rights.[111] For instance, an author, in effect, partially renounces the moral right to determine

---

[107] Court of Appeal, Athens, Decision No. 6478/1981, Armenopoulos, 1982, p. 515. See also CA, Paris, 10 June 1986, RIDA 133/1987, p. 193; CA, Paris D. Jur. 1993, p. 442; Cour de cass. RIDA 174/1997, p. 205.

[108] Art.16: "The granting of consent by an author for an action or an omission which would otherwise constitute an infringement of his moral right shall be deemed to be a form of exercise of his moral right, and shall be binding upon him."

[109] Court of First Instance (Multimember Panel), Athens, Decision No. 5606/1963, Copyright and Industrial Property Review, 1963, p. 64.

[110] In relation to journalists see, A. Papadopoulou, "The Journalist as an author and moral rights protection", in I. Stamatoudi (ed.), Journalists and Mass Media Publishers: Copyright Issues (Athens and Thessaloniki: P.N. Sakkoulas, 2009), p. 11.

[111] Article 16 (Consent of the Author as Exercise of the Moral Right): "The granting of consent by an author for an action or an omission which would otherwise constitute an infringement of his moral right shall be deemed to be a form of exercise of his moral right, and shall be binding upon him." See Court of Appeal, Athens, Decision No. 631/1990, Greek Justice, 1991, p. 207. Waiver of the enforcement of a moral right against a particular person, rather than of the moral right itself, is allowed or may be implied from a contract: Court of First Instance, Athens, Decision No. 276/2001, Nomos (online). See also Court of First Instance (Multimember Panel), Thessaloniki, Decision No. 5872/1997, Business and Company Law, 1998, p. 147.

when and how to disseminate a work when they enter a contract with a publisher allowing the publication of the work.

Although contractual limitations on the exercise of moral rights are allowed, these permitted limitations are not unlimited, i.e., they cannot reach the point where the core of the author's moral rights is touched upon. It is not clear from the academic literature or the jurisprudence precisely what this "core" is. Nevertheless, commentators agree that a contractual limitation relating to moral rights which goes beyond this limit will be null and void, as infringing public morality.[112] For example, the author may ask that a work may be published without any mention of his name, although a contractual term obligating him not to reveal his name after publication would in principle be void.

3.2.4   Right of retraction

As with any other moral right, the author cannot waive his right of retraction of the work. Neither can he accept contractual limitations as to how and when and in which cases or on the basis of what prerequisites to exercise his right, nor any provisions substantially increasing the compensation due, if such limitations are considered to render the right difficult to exercise.[113]

3.2.5   Right of access

The same applies for the right of access, where an author cannot waive this right although she or he may accept conditions under which to exercise it. These conditions are also dictated by the law, which provides that "access shall be effected with minimum possible nuisance to the right holder" (Art. 4(1)(d)). That means that the right of access should be exercised in such a way so as not to cause undue inconvenience to the proprietor of the embodiment of the work.[114]

3.3   Abuse of Moral Rights

Article 281 of the Greek Civil Code states that: "The exercise of a right shall be prohibited if such exercise obviously exceeds the limits imposed by good faith or morality or by the social or economic purpose of the right."[115] This prohibition of the "abuse of right" would apply if the exercise of a specific moral right was attempted contrary to the purpose for which it was

---

[112] For "public morality" see Arts 178–170 of the Greek Civil Code. See also M.D. Papadopoulou, in L. Kotsiris and I. Stamatoudi (eds), Commentary on the Greek Copyright Act (Athens and Thessaloniki: P.N. Sakkoulas, 2009), p. 139, with references to G.A. Koumantos, Copyright Law, (Athens: Ant. Sakkoulas, 8th ed, 2002), p. 251; M.D. Marinos, Copyright Law (Athens: Ant. Sakkoulas, 2nd ed, 2004), p. 203; D. Kallinikou, Copyright Law and Related Rights, (Athens: P.N. Sakkoulas, 3rd ed, 2008), p. 158; L. Kotsiris, Copyright Law, (Athens: Sakkoulas, 4th ed, 2005), p. 121, and others.

[113] G.A. Koumantos, Copyright Law, 8th ed, 2002, p. 271; M.D. Marinos, Copyright Law, (Athens: Ant. Sakkoulas, 2nd ed, 2004), p. 199.

[114] See, e.g., Court of First Instance, Athens, Decision No. 36247/1999, Private Law Annals, 2001, p. 465.

[115] Article 25(3) of the Greek Constitution can be invoked to the same end. See Georgiades in Georgiades and Stathopoulos, Annotated Civil Code, p. 268 (Athens: Sakkoulas, 1978). There is also a specific provision in the Greek Copyright that refers to abusive conduct in relation to films. Article 23: Reproduction of Cinematographic Works: "In cases where the holder of the economic right abusively withholds consent for the reproduction of a cinematographic work of special artistic value, for the purpose of preserving it in the National Cinematographic Archive, the reproduction shall be permissible without his consent and without payment, subject to a decision by the Minister of Culture, taken in

originally provided for in the law, most notably, contrary to the purpose of maintaining respect for the author's personality (e.g., the exercise of the moral right of disclosure to prevent the publication of a work by a publisher to whom the author has already provided a licence to publish).[116] Thus, an abuse of right is invoked mainly when moral rights are invoked by the author or his heirs for reasons other than the ones, they are supposed to serve, e.g. for economic or financial reasons rather than for the protection of the author's personal interests in the work. In general, any exercise of the (moral) right that does no abide with its social[117] and economic purpose,[118] goes well above the limits set by good faith and morals, and is invoked with a view to inflict damage on the other party, should be reviewed as being abusive. Examples of abusive conduct are the ones examined below.[119]

It should be noted here that in the area of moral rights the exercise of a right is assessed both on subjective as well as on objective grounds meaning that on the one hand the view of the author (since it is his work that is at issue) is taken into account, e.g. when an act is considered as impinging on his right of integrity.[120] On the other hand, abusive conduct needs to be assessed on an objective basis, too, so that one may be capable of conceiving the act as a conduct that goes beyond good faith, morals and defies the socioeconomic purpose of the right.

3.3.1 Contradictory behaviour and weakening of rights

By contradictory behaviour we mean any behaviour that does not logically follow from a person's previous behaviour on the same matter, and which for this reason impinges on the other party's rights, as these rights have been in the meantime acquired on the basis of the first person's behaviour.[121] Such a behaviour may have as a further consequence the weakening of the holders' rights.

This is a case where one (although he was entitled by law) he did not take any legal action against someone for a considerable amount of time so as to create to that other person the impression that he would not enforce or invoke his rights. This applies in cases where one by invoking his rights overturns a situation with negative consequences for the other party.[122] Here

---

conformity with the prior opinion of the Cinematography Advisory Council." Although this refers to the reproduction of cinematographic works, it has repercussions on the moral right of divulgation.

[116] These provisions also apply to performers' moral rights.

[117] A characteristic example in this respect is the denial of an author for his works to be published in a collection for works for the benefit of the public (under Governmental Order) since this was supposed to defy the social interests. Court of First Instance of Athens 6678/1969 (1969) Nomiko Vima 693.

[118] Court of First Instance of Athens 25686/1995 (1996) DEE 490 where the termination of a publishing contract by an author was found to be abusive since the book was still on the market and her monies were paid with no problem.

[119] See A. Georgiades and M. Stathopoulos, Annotated Civil Code, Art. 281 (Athen: Sakkoulas 1978). For French law see C. Caron, "Abus de droit d'auteur. Une illustration de la confrontation du droit special et du droit commune en droit civil français" 1998 RIDA 35.

[120] I. Spyridakis, *Papers on Civil Law*, 3rd ed, 2004, at 67.

[121] A. Papadopoulou, *Author's Integrity Right*, (Athens: Sakkoulas Publications, 1997), at p. 120. See also Court of Appeal 931/2000 (2001) Chronicles of Private Law 171 (this case concerned related rights); Court of First Instance of Patras 2885/2008 (2008) Chronicles of Private Law 749.

[122] Court of Appeal of Athens 8263/2007 (2008) DIMEE 1115 where the Court came to the conclusion that failing to enforce your right for an extended period alone does not suffice for your action to be held abusive. See also Court of Appeal of Athens (Multimember Panel), 606/2003 (2004) DIMEE 395, and Supreme Court 2101/1984 (1985) NoB 648, Supreme Court 971/1998 ElD (1999) 278, Supreme

again the situation created should be due to the first person's (now invoking his rights) prior behaviour.[123] An example has been where one has created an advertising spot for a company and has been paid for that. Although the company was using the film for two years and he was in full knowledge of it, he then decided to turn against the company for not having concluded with him a written contract (as the law provides in these instances). The Court found that the author's conduct was abusive.[124]

3.3.2   Useful/utilitarian works

When an action is assessed for abusiveness the nature of the work is also taken into account. The more artistic the work is the less intrusion in the work is tolerated. That means that utilitarian, functional and useful works are approached taking into account third parties' rights (i.e., the possessors of the embodiments of the works, the users and so on).

A characteristic example in this respect are works of architecture, databases and software. An architect's request to have all names of all co-authors mentioned in each and every use of the work was found abusive since the co-authors could have invoked their rights themselves.[125] Also changes in the facet of the building were allowed despite the architect's opposite view and his claim that his integrity right had been infringed. The Court found that the building was not meant as a work of art but rather as a work to cover practical needs. Therefore, in a weighing of interests the rights of the owners prevailed as the changes were made to meet practical needs that emerged after the building was constructed. Usages and good faith were also taken into account.[126] In another interesting case the architects of the Olympic Village in Greece were against the change of use of the buildings that were originally built to accommodate the athletes of the Olympic Games 2004. The state decided to transform the buildings into houses and give them to families. The Court found that the architects' allegations were abusive since (a) when they decided to participate in the original competition they accepted all terms and conditions; (b) they also accepted the term that their plans could be used by the organizers as they saw fit and in combination with other plans and ideas; and (c) the fact that they were fully remunerated.[127] In another case changes to the building for aesthetical reasons were found to have gone beyond good faith, morals and the socioeconomic purpose of the right and therefore the architect's right of integrity was found to be infringed. This was not the case for changes dictated for practical reasons.[128] In all these cases the legal basis of "abusiveness" was found as a means of a weighing of interests and led to the general (but not formal) rule that changes in architectural buildings dictated by need and practicability are allowed. Yet, no changes are allowed for aesthetical reasons alone.

Court 502/1996 (1997) 83, Supreme Court 190/1993 (1994) NoB 654, and Supreme Court 1569/1983 (1984) 1955.
[123]   Supreme Court 7/2002 (2003) Nomiko Vima 648; Supreme Court 1142/2002 (Nomos), Court of Appeal of Patras 1019/2004 (2005) AhaiaNom 25.
[124]   Supreme Court 1009/2007 (2008) DIMEE 77.
[125]   Court of First Instance of Athens 276/2001 (2001) DEE 599.
[126]   Court of First Instance of Athens 2028/2003 (2004) ArhN 210.
[127]   Court of First Instance of Athens 276/2001 (2001) DEE 599.
[128]   Court of First Instance (Multimember Panel), Thessaloniki, Decision No. 13300/2004, Armenopoulos, 2005, p. 723; Court of First Instance (Multimember Panel), Athens, Decision No. 2028/2003, Jurisprudence Archive 2004, p. 210; Court of First Instance, Athens, Decision No. 276/2001, Legal Tribune, 2001; Court of First Instance, Athens, Decision No. 4714/1971, (1971) ArhN 425.

As regards works of the visual arts, in the case of a statue that was ordered for a particular Athenian central square (Omonoia) (site specific art) and which had to be transferred to another square, a lot smaller and not central, the Court found that the removal, which was due to construction work for the Metro, was justified on grounds of the public interest.[129]

3.3.3   Co-authors' rights

Abusive conduct has also been found in the case of co-authored works. A characteristic example in this respect are collaborative works. In principle, licensing or other transfers of copyright in a collaborative work as a whole require the unanimous consent of all co-authors of the work. However, Article 281 of the Civil Code prohibits abusively exercising any right, that is, asserting it outside "the limits imposed by good faith or morality or by the social and economic purpose of the right",[130] while Articles 200 and 288 of the Greek Civil Code impose good faith in contractual and similar dealings. Thus, if a co-author abusively or otherwise in bad faith refuses to consent to a transfer agreed to by another or other co-authors, a court may provide appropriate relief.[131] Special provisions of the Copyright Act govern the allocation of rights in audiovisual works, a special case of joint works. Article 281 of the Civil Code may apply to cases in which such works are at issue as well.[132] Other examples are where a composer of a song invokes his moral right in order to prevent the lyricist from exercising his economic rights (i.e. exploiting) in the song[133] and where one co-author of a literary work prevents on the basis of his moral rights the other one from exploiting the work both as a hard copy as well as in a digital manner.[134]

---

[129] Court of First Instance, Athens, Decision No. 15489/1992, not reported.

[130] See, e.g., Court of First Instance, Athens, Decision No. 36247/1999, Commercial Law Review, 2001, vol. 52, p. 120 (finding abuse where the exercise of one co-author's moral right prevented the other co-author from exercising his moral and economic rights in the work); Supreme Court, Decision No. 1009/2007, Mass Media, Information and Communications Law, 2008, p. 75 (finding abuse where a person who had written the scenario, directed and produced a film for a chain of restaurants and had delivered copies to them for their promotional purposes, subsequently sought to prevent them using the film for such purposes on the basis of the lack of an agreement in writing as Greek law normally requires for valid licensing agreements). See also Court of First Instance, Athens, Decision No. 11923/1998, Legal Tribune, 1998, p. 1476 and Supreme Court 1251/2003, (2004) EEmpD 174.

[131] See, e.g., Court of First Instance, Thessaloniki, Decision No. 39982/2005, Mass Media, Information and Communications Law, 2006, pp. 71–5 (finding to be in bad faith, and disallowing, such refusal to consent by a student who had co-authored a book with a university professor, given that both had orally agreed to publish it with a specific publishing house and, as well, to have the student's name follow the professor's in the credits for the authors).

[132] See, e.g., Court of First Instance, Athens, Decision No. 36247/1999, Private Law Annals, 2001, pp. 465–7 (where the heir of a film composer invoked a dead composer's moral right in order to prevent the public performance of his music in a theatrical play as part of extracts of the film to be included in the play, the Court found that such a refusal was abusive because, on the one hand, it prevented the joint owner of copyright in the film from exercising his economic rights in it and, on the other, the composer had never objected to the inclusion of his songs in a theatrical performance).

[133] See Court of First Instance No. 36247/1999, Private Law Annals, 2001, p. 465. See also Supreme Court, Decision No. 1009/2007, Private Law Annals, 2008, p. 21; Court of Appeal, Athens, Decision No. 931/2000, Private Law Annals, 2001, p. 170; Court of First Instance (Multimember Panel), Athens, Decision No. 276/2001, Hronika Idiotikou Dikaiou, 2003, p. 63.

[134] Court of Appeal of Athens 8263/2007 (2008) DEE 1115 (the fact that two years went by without the rightholder invoking his rights does not suffice as such for his conduct to be held abusive. There should have been additional circumstances that have led the other party believe that the rightholder will

4.   CONCLUSIONS

The moral rights system is particularly strong in Greece and it confers on authors a rather comprehensive protection in relation to their personal interests in their works. In the context of this regime, moral rights are absolute and exclusive rights, some of which never expire, and none of which can be waived, contracted out of or transferred *inter vivos*. On the face of it, it looks like an inflexible regime of protection when it comes to users of works. However, moral rights are subject to limitations, which are dictated either by the author's consent (which may take the form of a contractual provision) or by reasons of practice, customs in the field,[135] the purpose of the exploitation contract or the employment contract, application of the provisions on abuse of rights, as well as by reason of a weighing of interests. In this perspective, the strictness of Greek copyright law in this area is in practice relaxed, while the judicial or other final outcome is suitable both to deal with everyday realities and to serve the interests of authors and performers.

---

not invoke his right so as when he invokes it a situation would have to be overturned, which was however created under specific circumstances and applied for a long period of time so that the change of this situation is damaging for the other party and clearly goes against the principles of good faith, morals and the social and the economic purpose of the right). Court of First Instance of Thessaloniki 39982/2005 (2006) DIMEE 71 (where a work has been created in collaboration between the professor and the student whereas the student was denying authorization).

[135]   Court of First Instance of Athens 14751/1996 (1998) DEE 843, where the putting into the market of a musical performance of the original song by another producer on the basis of a licence provided by the original authors of the song (although the rights in them had been transferred to another producer and he had not consented to this musical performance) was not found to be abusive as it was dictated by a custom in the field. Court of First Instance of Athens 36247/1999 (2001) Chronicles of Private Law 465 where a heir's conduct of preventing the public performance of songs having been performed in known films and theatrical plays was found abusive.

19. Moral rights and alternative dispute resolution

Brigitte Lindner

1. INTRODUCTION

International law leaves the determination of the means of redress for safeguarding moral rights to the national legislator.[1] Thus legislators are free to opt for a variety of legal tools to solve moral rights disputes. Alongside traditional court litigation, alternative, more consensus-based forms of dispute resolution as well as arbitration have been encouraged by both regional and national lawmakers for solving disputes in the field of copyright law. This is not as recent a phenomenon as one might think; already in 1894, the Congress of the Association Littéraire et Artistique Internationale (ALAI) was called upon to debate and vote on a proposal on arbitration as a means for settling disputes on literary and artistic property.[2]

This chapter explores the role of alternative dispute resolution (ADR) in the area of moral rights. The risk of moral rights disputes is growing in tandem with technological advancement, in particular with the arrival of new players such as online platforms and the rise of existing players, principally users. By way of an illustrative and non-exhaustive typology of moral rights disputes, this chapter identifies traditional and novel case scenarios and explores the different tools for solving such disputes, including the strengths and weaknesses of individual forms of ADR and potential legal obstacles on the road to ADR.

2. THE CHANGING LANDSCAPE OF MORAL RIGHTS DISPUTES

Moral rights concern the personal relationship of authors with their works and of performers with their performances. Thus, a violation of moral rights, whether as a result of a breach of contract or a tort, is likely to affect the soul of the creation in question with the consequence that the dispute can be highly emotional. Moral rights can also clash with the artistic freedom of other creators, as well as with rights of others, for example personality and privacy rights of persons who feature in a work. Moral rights disputes therefore often involve a balancing of

---

[1]   Cf. Article 6*bis* (3) Berne Convention; Article 5(3) WIPO Performances and Phonograms Treaty; Article 5(3) Beijing Treaty on Audiovisual Performances.

[2]   Bulletin de l'Association Littéraire & Artistique Internationale, Deuxième Série, No. 22, Août 1894, 16e Congrès International Anvers 1894: discussion at pp. 21–3, Rapport par MM. Lucien Layus et Maurice Maunoury, 'De l'arbitrage en matière de propriété littéraire et artistique' in the annex. More than 100 years later, ALAI devoted parts of its 2002 Study Days in Neuchâtel to copyright and arbitration, see *ALAI Copyright Internet-World*, Report on the Neuchâtel study session, 16/17 September 2002, Paul Brügger (ed.), (Groupe Suisse de l'ALAI et des auteurs, Lausanne/Berne 2003) 223–371 ('ALAI Study Days 2002').

the different rights and interests that may be affected by the exercise of a moral right.[3] Another aspect of moral rights disputes, in particular regarding the integrity right, is the fact that the establishment of an infringement, and especially a derogatory treatment, is often a matter of opinion, which can be a fertile ground for disagreements.

2.1   Traditional Moral Rights Case Scenarios

Disputes over moral rights can arise out of a contract or a tort and concern all common types of moral rights which a national law may protect, the most prominent examples being the divulgation right, the paternity or attribution right, the integrity right or the right to withdraw a work.[4]

Although moral rights are in general inalienable, the contractual exercise of moral rights in individual scenarios is usually allowed, at least to a certain extent, even in civil law countries where assignments and waivers are usually not permitted.[5] For example, authors may agree to concrete uses or modifications of their works which may interfere with moral rights.[6] Common law systems often permit the waiver of moral rights,[7] while Scandinavian laws allow waivers only with regard to uses that are limited in character and extent.[8] Disputes may therefore arise over the scope of a waiver or consent to a specific use, particularly as there can be a fine line between a permitted simple modification and an actual derogatory treatment of a work which may not be covered by the author's consent. Disputes may also arise between an author and other creative contributors to a production or performance, including other co-authors, performers, directors, producers, publishers or broadcasters regarding the timing of the divulgation, the attribution of author- or performer-ship, the integrity and/or withdrawal of a work or performance. Where a work has been commissioned, tensions may arise between the author and the owner of the material object over alterations or the destruction of the work embodied

---

[3]   For some commentators this balancing act has grown out of proportion: see the discussion by Pierre-Yves Gautier, *Le droit moral* [2018] 256 RIDA 43, 46–55; Julie Groffe, 'Droit moral et liberté de création' [2017] 253 RIDA 11–27.

[4]   For an overview see J.A.L. Sterling and Stavroula Karapapa, in J.A.L. Sterling and Trevor Cook (eds), *Sterling on World Copyright Law* (5th edition, Sweet & Maxwell 2018) paras 8.12–8.25 ('Sterling, *WCL*').

[5]   Cf. Agnès Lucas-Schloetter, 'Rapport général: le droit moral dans les différents régimes du droit d'auteur', in F. Brison, S. Dusollier, M.-C. Janssens and H. Vanhees (eds), *Moral Rights in the 21st Century, The Changing Role of the Moral Rights in an Era of Information Overload* (Larcier 2015) 50–68, 60–1, ('*ALAI Report 2014*'). For French law cf. André Lucas, Agnès Lucas-Schloetter and Carine Bernault, *Traité de la propriété littéraire et artistique* (5th edition, LexisNexis 2017) paras 545, 548–9, 644 ('Lucas/Lucas-Schloetter/Bernault').

[6]   Cf. for French law: Lucas/Lucas-Schloetter/Bernault, ibid., para. 644; for German law: Peukert in Loewenheim/Leistner/Ohly (eds), Schricker/Loewenheim, *Urheberrecht* (6th edition, C.H. Beck 2020) Vor §§ 12ff., paras 11–19 ('Schricker/Loewenheim'); Dustmann in Axel Nordemann, Jan Bernd Nordemann and Christian Czychowski (eds), Fromm/Nordemann, *Urheberrecht* (12th edition, Kohlhammer 2018) Vor §§ 12–14 UrhG, paras 9–10 ('Fromm/Nordemann').

[7]   E.g. UK, Sec. 87(2) and (3) CDPA for moral rights of authors and Sec. 205J (2) and (3) CDPA for moral rights of performers.

[8]   Article 3(3) Copyright Acts of Denmark, Finland, Norway and Sweden.

in the material object, which is often the case with works of architecture and other works of art combined with fixed objects.[9]

Tort-based disputes are usually moral rights violations by third parties who are unrelated to the author or performer, including acts by subsequent licensees of the original producer or publisher who engage in derogatory treatment or omit credits. Such disputes can include the alteration of a work without a licence or the publication of an unpublished work without the authorisation of the author. There may also be disputes about the reach of statutory limitations and exceptions, e.g. parody or quotation, which a user may invoke as a defence against a claim for a moral rights infringement.

Disputes regarding the divulgation right come in various forms. The divulgation right may interfere with the author's contractual obligation to deliver a commissioned work at a certain point in time, as in the famous *Whistler* case.[10] Other scenarios include unpublished manuscripts that are stolen and subsequently published against the will of the author[11] or heirs who are reluctant to publish a work posthumously after the death of the author.[12]

Disputes concerning the paternity right can consist in questioning the manner of attribution of a work to the author. For example, in *Sawkins v. Hyperion*, the English Court of Appeal held that thanking the author for preparing materials was not sufficient for attribution of authorship.[13] Questions regarding attribution can also arise in ghostwriting scenarios.[14]

Disputes regarding the integrity right have generated abundant case law. Cases in this area often concern the change of the context in which a work is used. This can be a particular challenge when works are staged in a manner which disregards the intention of the author. The staging of Samuel Beckett's all male play *Waiting for Godot* by an all-female cast is a good example for the different perspectives regarding derogatory treatment: while a Paris Court held that the change infringes Beckett's integrity right,[15] a Dutch court saw in this particular way of staging the exercise of artistic freedom by the director.[16] Change of context may also involve parodies and quotations. Moreover, the reproduction of sound recordings in bad quality was held to be an infringement of the integrity right by courts in France[17] and Italy[18]

---

[9] For an overview of illustrative cases see Sterling/Karapapa in Sterling, *WCL*, (n 4), paras 8.95–8.127.

[10] *Whistler v. Eden*, Cass. civ., 14 March 1900, Dalloz Jurisprudence Générale 1900, 497: Whistler could not be forced to deliver the work as agreed in the contract as long as he was not satisfied with the creation.

[11] *Bouvier v. Cassigneul*, Cass. crim., 13 December 1995, [1996] 169 RIDA 307.

[12] According to Article L. 121-3 French Intellectual Property Code a court may take into account the public interest and order publication where heirs refuse posthumous publication. See also Philippe Gaudrat, 'L'abus du droit moral' in *ALAI Report 2014*, (n 5), 98–126, paras 18–21.

[13] *Sawkins v. Hyperion* [2005] EWCA Civ 565, [66]–[69].

[14] German courts do not necessarily see an infringement of the paternity right (OLG Frankfurt/Main, 1 September 2009, [2010] NJW 780 – *Ghostwriter-Vereinbarung*); French courts have not yet had to address ghostwriting scenarios *strictu sensu*, cf. the discussion in Lucas/Lucas-Schloetter/Bernault, (n 5), para. 614.

[15] TGI Paris, 15 October 1992, [1993] 155 RIDA 225, 229–30.

[16] Rechtbank Haarlem, 29 April 1988, reported in Matthijs Engelberts,'Stiltes rond Godot: het Nederlandse debat over de vrouwelijke rolbezetting van Wachten op Godot' [1989] Forum der Letteren, 174.

[17] Cass. civ. 1re, 24 September 2009, [2009] Bull. Civ. I, No. 184 – *Jacky Boy Music*.

[18] Corte d'Appello di Milano, 3 June 2003, N.S. Srl v. L.B., Il Diritto di Autore 2004, N.2, Aprile-Guigno.

as was the unauthorised shortening of a sound recording for use as a ringtone by the German Federal Supreme Court.[19] Courts were further occupied with questions regarding the destruction or displacement of architectural works or sculptures by the owner of the physical object.[20]

The integrity right plays a particularly important role in the audiovisual sector.[21] Disputes in this field may concern questions regarding the colourisation of black and white films,[22] the shortening of films,[23] cinematographic adaptations of novels,[24] advertising breaks[25] or particular practices of film restoration.[26]

2.2   Impact of the Changing Technological Environment

While the described traditional moral rights scenarios remain relevant today, the changing technological environment has added a further dimension. The potential created by the Internet and other emerging forms of technology to transform and manipulate works and to use them for purposes not originally contemplated by the author or performer across borders represents a major challenge for the protection of moral rights, particularly in view of the diverse moral rights concepts and traditions around the world.[27]

The de-contextualisation of a work is already a catalyst for traditional moral rights disputes. The Internet has increased considerably the potential for the use of works out of context in ways which may interfere with moral rights.[28] Works may be easily placed in a new setting, voices of performers may be isolated and used in entirely different ways as may be nude scenes from films.[29] Hyperlinks can associate works and other creative productions against the intentions of their creators, as can advertising, which is already a critical aspect in the offline environment.[30] The same is true for user-generated content on blogs, social media and other

---

[19]   BGH [2009] GRUR 395, 397 and BGH [2010] GRUR 920 – *Klingeltöne für Mobiltelefone I and II.*

[20]   See cases in Sterling, *WCL*, (n 4), paras 8.116–8.126.

[21]   Hubert Tilliet, 'La pratique collective: le cas du secteur de l'audiovisuel' in *ALAI Report 2014*, (n 5), 139, 143–4.

[22]   *Turner Entertainment Co v. Huston*, Cass. civ 1re, 28 May 1991 [1991] 149 RIDA 197 regarding the film Asphalt Jungle.

[23]   *Schoendoerffer v. ModFilms*, TGI Paris, 23 March 1994, [1995] 164 RIDA 401, 405: the unauthorised reduction of a film from 131 to 119 minutes held to be infringement of the director's moral right. Compare with KG Berlin, 23 March 2004, [2004] GRUR 497 – *Die Schlacht um Berlin*, where the shortening of a documentary from 80 to 40 minutes was not held to infringe the director's integrity right.

[24]   Cass., 22 November 1966, Recueil Dalloz Sirey 1967 (2) 485 – *Bernanos*: a screen adaptation which required changes to a literary work was held not to denature the spirit of the literary work.

[25]   Cour d'Appel de Paris, 1re ch. A, 26 November 1990: advertising breaks violate integrity right.

[26]   Cour d'Appel de Paris, 5 October 1994, Recueil Dalloz Sirey 1996 (2) Jurisprudence 53.

[27]   Sterling, *WCL*, (n 4), paras 8.17 and 8.18; for an in-depth discussion see Guy Pessach, 'The Author's Moral Right of Integrity in Cyperspace – A Preliminary Normative Framework' [2003] IIC 34 250–70.

[28]   On de-contextualisation see Nikolaus Kraft, 'Der Raub der Persönlichkeit – Veröffentlichungen und Einbettungen von Werken wider den Willen des Urhebers', in M. Weller, N. Kemle, K. Kuprecht and T. Dreier (eds), *Neue Kunst – Neues Recht*, Schriften zum Kunst- und Kulturrecht (Nomos 2014) 18, 153–65.

[29]   Dominick Luquer, 'Position of the FIA', in *ALAI Report 2014*, (n 5), 133.

[30]   Cf. Case C-392/19, *VG Bildkunst v. Stiftung Preußischer Kulturbesitz*, Opinion of Advocate General Szpunar delivered on 10 September 2020, paras 87 and 89 for moral rights aspects in the context of the use of framing.

platforms in forms of parodies, memes and the like, which may distort works and/or use them out of context against the wishes of their authors. In the online environment, these challenges are no longer confined to a particular territory, but are likely to have an effect across borders. Paired with differences in moral rights concepts and protection in legal systems around the world, these challenges require pragmatic solutions.

3.   LEGAL TOOLS FOR SOLVING MORAL RIGHTS DISPUTES

The question arises whether, compared with traditional court proceedings, ADR could represent a more pragmatic approach for solving moral rights disputes.

3.1   General Observations

There is no official definition of ADR, which is a portmanteau term covering a variety of procedures for solving disputes with the assistance of independent and impartial third-party neutrals. Compared with traditional court litigation, ADR is flexible and leaves room for more unconventional forms of dispute settlement.

While ADR is often seen as an alternative outside the judicial system, such procedures are increasingly linked to court proceedings in one way or another. Sometimes, ADR can be a prerequisite in court procedures,[31] whereas in other cases ADR is encouraged but not compulsory.[32] However, even when ADR is voluntary, the unreasonable refusal of an invitation to mediate can lead to a wasted cost order in court proceedings.[33]

ADR is not a novelty in the copyright field, where it has long been a popular means for solving disputes in the area of collective rights management.[34] ADR also plays a role in disputes regarding the interface between technological measures and limitations or exceptions to copyright.[35] The EU continues to be an enthusiastic supporter of ADR, with a directive devoted entirely to the promotion of mediation in certain cross-border civil and commercial disputes[36] and specific rules on ADR in various directives concerning copyright, the latest example being Directive (EU) 2019/790 of 17 April 2019 on Copyright in the Digital Single Market.[37]

---

[31]   E.g. § 278 of the German Civil Procedure Code provides for an attempt to 'mediate' ('*Güteverhandlung*') before the actual hearing of the case; the court can also propose extra-judicial mediation (§ 278a). An ADR procedure is compulsory in certain civil proceedings in France, Article 750-1 of the Civil Procedure Code. Article 5 of the Mediation Directive 2008/52/EC also encourages mediation in the context of judicial proceedings before the ordinary courts.

[32]   Civil Procedure Rules (England & Wales), Overriding Objectives, para. 1.4(2)(e).

[33]   So in the UK: *Dunnett v. Railtrack* [2002] EWCA Civ 302; *Halsey v. Milton Keynes General NHS Trust* [2004] EWCA Civ 576; *DSN v. Blackpool Football Club* [2020] EWHC 670 (QB).

[34]   E.g. in the EU Articles 34 and 35 of Directive 2014/26/EU which address independent and impartial ADR mechanisms in the field of collective management.

[35]   Further details in Brigitte Lindner, 'Alternative Dispute Resolution – A Remedy for Soothing Tensions between Technological Measures and Exceptions' in Paul Torremans (ed.), *Copyright Law – A Handbook of Contemporary Research* (Edward Elgar Publishing 2007), 426–48.

[36]   Directive 2008/52/EC of the European Parliament and of the Council of 21 May 2008 on certain aspects of mediation in civil and commercial matters, [2008] OJ L 136/3.

[37]   Directive (EU) 2019/790 encourages ADR for certain contractual disputes regarding remuneration (Article 21) as well as for settling disputes regarding the take-down of works and other protected

The proponents of ADR usually point to a number of benefits over court litigation,[38] such as efficiency in terms of time and cost, the confidentiality of the procedure, particular expertise of the neutrals, greater party autonomy than in a court procedure, beneficial effects on ongoing business relationships between the parties, taking into account cross-cultural aspects and, most importantly, cross-border solutions and enforcement, in the case of international arbitration on the basis of the New York Convention,[39] and for international settlement agreements concluded as a result of a mediation the Singapore Convention.[40] In the EU, cross-border enforcement is facilitated for settlement agreements that fall under the scope of the Mediation Directive 2002/58/EC (Article 6).

Yet, despite these advantages, ADR has not escaped criticism. ADR is not always an appropriate, faster or more cost-efficient tool. In addition, ADR, which is sometimes labelled as a 'private justice system', has been accused of lack of transparency, absence of proper judicial review, disadvantaging weaker parties or pressurising parties into settlement by using ADR as a case management tool.[41] Indeed, legislators are often charmed by ADR as a means to reduce the caseload in their national courts. As such, the public value of ADR has been questioned; in particular, there have been rule of law concerns with regard to the fundamental right to a fair trial, which is protected under international and European human rights instruments, particularly where ADR is mandatory.[42] This being said, the right to a fair trial, which includes the right of access to a court, is not absolute and does not therefore, in principle, preclude the recourse to ADR.[43] In particular, according to the European Court of Human Rights, access to a court does not necessarily require a court of law in the classic sense which is integrated

---

subject-matter on online content-sharing platforms (Article 17(9)). For an overview of ADR featuring in other EU directives on copyright, cf. Brigitte Lindner, 'European Union, Part A', in Carlo Scollo Lavizzari and René Viljoen (eds), *Cross-border Copyright Licensing* (Edward Elgar Publishing 2018), paras 2.112–2.115 ('Lavizzari/Viljoen').

[38]   Heike Wollgast, 'WIPO Alternative Dispute Resolution – Saving Time and Money in IP Disputes', WIPO Magazine November 2016/Special Supplement, 32–35; Miriam R. Arfin, 'The Benefits of Alternative Dispute Resolution in Intellectual Property Disputes' [1995] 17 Hastings Comm. & Ent. L.J. 893 at 898–901 ('Arfin'); Theophile Margellos, Sophia Bonne, Gordon Humphreys and Sven Stürmann, *Mediation: Creating Value in International Intellectual Property Disputes* (Wolters Kluwer 2018) 54–61 ('Margellos, *Mediation*'). For the pros and cons of international arbitration see Nigel Blackaby and Constantine Partasides QC with Alan Redfern and Martin Hunter, *Redfern and Hunter on International Arbitration* (6th edition, Oxford University Press 2015) paras 1.94–1.134 ('Redfern and Hunter'); Trevor Cook and Alejandro I. Garcia, *International Intellectual Property Arbitration* (Wolters Kluwer 2010) 48 ('Cook and Garcia').

[39]   Convention on the Recognition and Enforcement of Foreign Arbitral Awards, New York, 10 June 1958 (New York Convention).

[40]   United Nations Convention on International Settlement Agreements Resulting from Mediation, Singapore, 7 August 2019, effective from 12 September 2020 (Singapore Convention on Mediation).

[41]   For an overview of the different arguments see Lorna Mc Gregor, 'Alternative Dispute Resolution and Human Rights: Developing a Rights-Based Approach through the ECHR' [2015] EJIL 26(3) 607–34, 610–17.

[42]   Cf. Article 10 Universal Declaration of Human Rights; Article 14(1) International Covenant on Civil and Political Rights (1966); Article 6 European Convention of Human Rights; Article 47 European Charter of Fundamental Rights.

[43]   European Union Agency for Fundamental Rights and Council of Europe, Handbook on European Law relating to access to justice, 2016, 50–5; European Court of Human Rights, Guide in Article 6 of the European Convention of Human Rights, Right to a fair trial (civil limb), Updated to 31 August 2019, 31–2, 45.

in the standard judicial system of a country, but may also be an alternative body, subject to appropriate guarantees and safeguards, meaning that in the case of mandatory arbitration, the fundamental principles in Article 6(1) ECHR must be respected.[44] Likewise, the European Court of Justice has accepted out-of-court settlement procedures, even where mandatory, provided that appropriate safeguards are respected.[45]

3.2   Forms of ADR

A variety of forms of ADR exist:[46] mediation and conciliation are facilitative forms of ADR where the parties themselves reach a consensus on the settlement of their dispute with the help of a third-party neutral. Depending on the role given to the mediator by the parties, the third-party neutral may either guide the parties through the negotiation process (mediation) or provide a non-binding evaluation of the situation together with a settlement proposal which the parties may or may not accept (conciliation).

The more evaluative forms of ADR, such as (early) neutral evaluation and expert determination, give the third-party neutral a more determining role; whereas in the case of a neutral evaluation, the third party neutral provides a non-binding assessment of the case which the parties can accept, expert determination comes closer to adjudication, particularly where the parties agree for the determination to be legally binding.

Arbitration differs from these forms of ADR insofar as the parties agree to refer their dispute to one or more arbitrators with the aim of obtaining a binding and final decision. In view of these aspects, which are closer to court procedures, arbitration is sometimes perceived as being outside ADR.[47] Nevertheless, for the purposes of this chapter, a broad understanding of the term ADR is pursued and arbitration is treated as an adjudicative form of ADR.

Different elements of ADR can be combined into hybrid forms of ADR.[48] For example, mediation can be used in the context of an arbitration to facilitate the settlement of a dispute. Arbitration can follow an unsuccessful mediation instead of an ordinary court procedure. Early neutral evaluation or fact-finding may be useful in the context of a mediation to ease the negotiations between the parties. Thus, the flexibility of ADR allows parties to opt for the most suitable form of dispute settlement.

3.3   Providers of ADR

ADR can be provided either with the help of a specialised institution or independently in an ad hoc procedure. At the international level, the most prominent example is the World Intellectual Property Organization's Arbitration and Mediation Center, which was established in 1994 and offers support for mediation, arbitration, expedited arbitration and expert determination,[49] including services dedicated to specific areas, such as film, media and entertainment, arts and

---

[44]   *Mutu and Pechstein v. Switzerland*, Applications nos. 40575/10 and 67474/1 (ECHR, 2 October 2018) [93]–[96]; *Suda v. Czech Republic*, Application no. 1643/06 (ECHR, 28 October 2010) [48], [49].

[45]   Joined cases C-317/08 to C-320/08, *Rosalba Alassini v. Telecom Italia SpA*, (European Court of Justice (4th Chamber), 18 March 2010) [61]–[67].

[46]   For more detail consult: Margellos, *Mediation*, (n 38), 22–54; Arfin, (n 38), 901–8.

[47]   See the discussion at *Redfern and Hunter*, (n 38), paras 1.137–8.

[48]   Cf. the overview at Margellos, *Mediation*, (n 38), 52–4.

[49]   For details see http://www.wipo.int/amc/en/ (accessed 8 March 2022).

cultural heritage or fashion.[50] There has been a steady increase of cases handled in the copyright field, which now amount to 24 per cent of the overall case load of the Center.[51]

There are other institutions at the international level which serve specific copyright sectors, such as the Court of Arbitration for Art (CAFA), whose aim is 'to resolve disputes in the wider art community through mediation and arbitration'.[52] Another example is IFTA Arbitration, an initiative by the Independent Film and Television Alliance, whose focus is on the resolution of international disputes arising out of entertainment-related production, finance, and distribution agreements.[53] At the national level, dispute resolution services in the area of copyright and/or specific sectors are often offered by public or private institutions.[54]

In view of the increasingly important role of moral rights in online uses, it is worth pointing out that some online providers have their own dispute resolution procedures.[55] In the EU, Article 17(9) of Directive (EU) (2019/790) on Copyright in the Digital Single Market requires certain online platforms to provide redress mechanisms to deal with issues arising out of user-generated content, particularly in order to enable users to invoke defences where their content has been blocked or removed. While moral rights are not harmonised at EU level, they can be affected by parodies, quotations, criticism and the like. Whether the required redress mechanisms would be apt to embrace also the complexity of moral rights issues that may occur on such platforms is, however, questionable.[56]

4.   THE SUITABILITY OF ADR FOR MORAL RIGHTS DISPUTES

ADR can provide helpful tools for solving moral rights disputes. While the nature of each individual case will determine whether a particular form of ADR, an ordinary court procedure or a combination of both is best suited to solve the dispute, there may be legal obstacles to embarking on an ADR procedure which are a threshold issue.

4.1   Potential Legal Obstacles to ADR

A number of legal obstacles may be encountered on the road to ADR, which may vary in degree depending on whether the chosen procedure is domestic or international.

---

[50]   https://www.wipo.int/amc/en/center/specific-sectors/ (accessed 8 March 2022).

[51]   https://www.wipo.int/amc/en/center/caseload.html (accessed 8 March 2022).

[52]   https://www.cafa.world/ (accessed 8 March 2022).

[53]   https://ifta-online.org/ifta-arbitration/ (accessed 8 March 2022)

[54]   By way of example: UK Intellectual Property Office Mediation Service (https://www.gov.uk/guidance/intellectual-property-mediation; AMAPA, a French association for dispute settlement in the audiovisual sector (https://lamapa.org); IP Panel at the Hong Kong International Arbitration Center (https://www.hkiac.org/news/panel-arbitrators-intellectual-property-disputes). See also the information in the Arbitration Country Guides published by the International Bar Association at https://www.ibanet.org/LPD/Dispute_Resolution_Section/Arbitration/Arbcountryguides.aspx (all accessed 8 March 2022).

[55]   Cf. for example YouTube: https://support.google.com/youtube/answer/2797454?hl=en&ref_topic=9282678# (accessed 8 March 2022).

[56]   See also the critique by Jacques de Werra, 'Moral Rights, A View from Continental Europe' in *ALAI Report 2014*, (n 5), 69–82, 80 regarding dispute resolution by online platforms.

4.1.1   Jurisdictional issues

Jurisdictional issues may be encountered where copyright disputes are reserved by law to the national courts or administrative authorities, such as specific panels or bureaus.[57] In such cases, the question arises whether the exclusive competence of a court or other adjudicative body could bar a particular ADR procedure.

For example, in Germany, disputes arising out of the Law on Author's Right are referred by law to the ordinary courts (§ 104 German Law on Author's Right). The objective of the exclusive competence of the ordinary courts in copyright matters is to exclude competence conflicts and to allow for a harmonised case law in copyright.[58] Nevertheless, it is generally accepted that parties may opt for arbitration even in copyright matters in accordance with the specific provisions in § 1029 et seq. of the German Civil Procedure Code; these provisions allow for arbitration proceedings as long as the claim is arbitrable.[59] Facilitative forms of ADR should not be affected, since the exclusive competence of the ordinary courts only becomes relevant if the matter reaches the courts, i.e. where the parties could not settle the case themselves.[60] In any event, even if a dispute reaches the ordinary courts, efforts to settle the dispute by way of mediation in the context of a court procedure must be made as a matter of law before the trial can begin.[61]

The French Intellectual Property Code in Article L. 331–1, first subsection, provides for the exclusive competence of the '*tribunaux judiciaires*' (regional courts) in copyright matters. However, Article L. 331–1, 4th subsection specifically allows for arbitration in copyright matters, provided the conditions under Articles 2059 and 2060 of the Civil Code are respected. This provision was introduced in 2011 in order to clarify that arbitration is a possible route in copyright disputes, which hitherto was doubtful.[62] Thus, arbitration is possible as long as the claims are arbitrable, which could be problematic in view of the inalienability and public policy nature of moral rights under French law.[63]

The Indian Copyright Act of 1957 also contains a specific provision governing the jurisdiction of Indian courts in copyright disputes. Pursuant to Section 62(1), all copyright disputes under the Act shall be instituted in the district court having jurisdiction. Nevertheless, in *Eros International v. Telemax Links India Pvt. Ltd.*, the Bombay High Court decided that the jurisdiction clause in Section 62(1) of the Indian Copyright Act of 1957 did not rule out arbitration.[64] According to the Court, the rule in Section 62(1) only defines the entry level of such actions in the judicial hierarchy.[65] Thus, the provision prevents cases from being brought to

---

[57]   See the discussion by Anna P. Mantakou, 'Arbitrability and Intellectual Property Disputes', in Loukas A. Mistelis and Stavros L. Brekoulakis, *Arbitrability – International and Comparative Perspectives* (Kluwer Law International 2009) 263–71, 265 ('Mistelis & Brekoulakis').

[58]   Amtliche Begründung (Motives), BT-Drs. IV/270, 106.

[59]   Wimmers in Schricker/Loewenheim, (n 6), § 104 UrhG para. 2 and § 105 UrhG, para. 25; Haberstumpf in Mestmäcker/Schulze, *Urheberrechtskommentar*, Vol. 1.2, (Luchterhand 2011) § 104 UrhG, para. 16 ('Mestmäcker/Schulze'). On arbitrability see below at 4.1.2.

[60]   Although there could be subject matter issues arising out of EU law, cf. below at 4.1.2.

[61]   Cf. above under Section 2.1, note 30.

[62]   Pierre-Yves Gautier, *Propriété Littéraire et Artistique* (10th edition, PUF 2017), para. 814 ('Gautier, *Propriété Littéraire et Artistique*').

[63]   Cf. discussion below under 4.1.2.

[64]   *Eros International Media Limited v. Telemax Links India Pvt Limited*, Bombay High Court, Decision of 12 April 2016.

[65]   Ibid. [16].

lower courts than the district courts. The Court also clarified that the provision does not define whether or not a copyright claim is arbitrable. Rather, this depends on the nature of the claim that is made.[66] As such, the provision would not per se rule out arbitration proceedings. The arbitral tribunal is hence a forum for dispute resolution which is available in parallel with the courts, unless arbitration is expressly barred and/or the claim is not arbitrable.[67]

The Canadian Supreme Court also had to address jurisdictional issues in *Les Editions Chouette (1987) inc. and Christine L'Heureux, v. Hélène Desputeaux et al.*, a dispute arising out of a licensing agreement regarding the use of the fictitious character 'Caillou'.[68] The Supreme Court had to opine, inter alia, on the question whether the – now repealed – Section 37 of the Canadian Copyright Act, which provided for concurrent jurisdiction of the Federal Court with provincial courts to hear all proceedings relating to the Act, could be an obstacle to arbitration in copyright cases. The Supreme Court held in a unanimous decision that this was not the case, pointing to the trend in legislation and case law which had accepted and encouraged civil and commercial arbitration.[69] In addition, 'if Parliament had intended to exclude arbitration in copyright matters, it would have clearly done so'.[70] Thus, the Supreme Court confined the former Section 37 narrowly by singling out the two objectives of the provision: to affirm the role of provincial courts in copyright cases and to avoid fragmentation of trials concerning copyright, hence aspects which have also played a role in the German and Indian situation discussed earlier in this section.[71] While subsequent decisions have cast a doubt over the Supreme Court's arbitration-friendly attitude,[72] the Court affirmed in a case opposing Uber and some of their drivers that 'arbitration is endorsed and encouraged as a means for resolving disputes', pointing specifically to *Desputeaux v. Editions Chouette*.[73]

As these examples demonstrate, jurisdictional hurdles are not necessarily insurmountable. This is even more so in international arbitration where Article II(3) New York Convention instructs a court seized with the matter to refer the case to arbitration at the request of one of the parties unless the arbitration agreement is null and void, inoperational or incapable of being performed.[74]

---

[66]   Ibid.
[67]   Kshama A. Loya and Gowree Gokhale, 'Arbitrability of Intellectual Property Disputes: A Perspective from India' [2019] JIPLP 14(8), 632, 639 ('Loya and Gokhale').
[68]   [2003] 1 SCR 178.
[69]   Ibid. [38].
[70]   Ibid. [46].
[71]   Ibid. [39].
[72]   *Seidel v. Telus Communications Inc.* [2011] 1 SCR 531: arbitration is not the appropriate forum for enforcing a public interest remedy in the context of a consumer contract ([33]–[40]); see also the criticism regarding arbitration in *Hryniak v. Mauldin*, [2014] 1 SCR 87 [26]: 'In some circles, private arbitration is increasingly seen as an alternative to a slow judicial process. But private arbitration is not the solution since, without an accessible public forum for the adjudication of disputes, the rule of law is threatened and the development of the common law undermined.'
[73]   *Uber Technologies v. Heller*, 2020 SCC 16 [116]. Despite this endorsement of arbitration in a majority decision with two judges dissenting, the Court declared the arbitration clause invalid under the doctrine of unconscionability as a result of the particular circumstances of the case.
[74]   Cf. Cook and Garcia, (n 38), 57–8.

4.1.2 Substantive issues

From an international perspective, it is generally accepted that disputes on intellectual property, including copyright, may be solved with the help of ADR.[75] Nevertheless, caution is called for in moral rights disputes.[76] In view of their personal dimension, authors and performers cannot dispose over moral rights, at least not in the same way as would be the case for economic rights. In some jurisdictions moral rights may be a matter of public policy, which may have implications for ADR procedures. Subject matter and public policy issues are often interconnected. While these issues are most often discussed in the context of arbitration, they can also arise in other forms of ADR.

For example, Article 1(2) of the EU Mediation Directive (2008/52/EC) allows for mediation in cross-border civil and commercial matters 'except as regards rights and obligations which are not at the parties' disposal under the relevant applicable law'. According to Recital 10, these are rights and obligations on which the parties are not free to decide themselves. As moral rights are usually inalienable and often unwaivable, this could be a potential obstacle to mediation. On the other hand, under some national civil procedure laws mediation is a step in proceedings before the ordinary courts, which remains unaffected by the EU Mediation Directive (Article 5(2)).

Arbitrability and public policy issues play a particular role in the enforcement of an arbitral award. Under Article V(2) of the New York Convention, the enforcement of an award may be refused in the country where recognition or enforcement is sought because:

(a) the subject matter of the dispute is not capable of settlement by arbitration under the law of that country; or
(b) the recognition or enforcement of the arbitral award would be contrary to the public policy of that country.

Thus, the enforcement of an award in a moral rights dispute could be rejected on the grounds of arbitrability or public policy depending on the applicable law in the country of enforcement. Similar grounds of refusal may be found in Article 5(2) of the Singapore Convention on Mediation. Prior risk-assessment is therefore particularly important in moral rights cases in order to avoid disappointment at the stage of enforcement.[77]

While case law is sparse, the Canadian Supreme Court has shown support for the arbitrability of moral rights. In the already mentioned case *Les Editions Chouette v. Desputeaux*, the Supreme Court had to confront the question whether claims with regard to the author's paternity right are arbitrable.[78] Under the Civil Code of Québec (Article 2639 CCQ), where the case originated, parties are free to submit disputes to arbitration, except for disputes over a matter of public order or the status of persons. The Supreme Court confirmed that courts enjoy a considerable amount of discretion to define the notion of public order, given the variable, shifting or

---

[75] Jacques de Werra, 'Global Policies for Arbitrating Intellectual Property Disputes' in Jacques de Werra (ed.), *Research Handbook on Intellectual Property Licensing* (Edward Elgar Publishing 2013) 353, 357 with further references ('de Werra, *Handbook*'); Redfern and Hunter, (n 38), para. 2.132.

[76] de Werra, ibid.; Mantakou in Mistelis & Brekoulakis, (n 57), 266; World Intellectual Property Organization (WIPO) (2021). *Alternative Dispute Resolution Mechanisms for Business-to-Business Digital Copyright-and Content-Related Disputes.* Geneva: WIPO Publication No. 969E, p. 25.

[77] For further details in the field of arbitration see de Werra, *Handbook*, (n 75), 373–5.

[78] [2003] 1 SCR 178, [47]–[69].

developing nature of the concept. Nevertheless, a broad interpretation of public order had been expressly rejected by the legislature. Therefore, the nature of a rule as public order was not in itself a ground for denying arbitration.[79] More specifically with regard to the arbitrability of moral rights the Court drew attention to the fact that, while moral rights may not be assigned, they are waivable, which pointed to an overlap between economic rights and moral rights.[80] The Supreme Court also stressed the importance placed on economic aspects in the Canadian copyright system. The objective of the Copyright Act was primarily the economic management of intellectual property, with copyright being foremost a mechanism for protecting and transmitting the economic values associated with that type of property.[81] This was reflected in the fact that artists could earn remuneration from the exercise of their moral rights and even charge for waivers.[82] Consequently, arbitration over copyright, including moral rights, was not held to be against the public order. Thus, the overlap of moral and economic rights, as reflected in the waivability of moral rights, coupled with the economic objectives underlying the Canadian Copyright Act, paved the way for the Supreme Court to accept arbitration as a means for solving a moral rights dispute.

The approach by the Canadian Supreme Court was favourably received by some commentators. According to Professor de Werra, moral rights should be arbitrable in view of the fact that the exercise of such rights can be the object of contractual arrangements which renders them at least partly disposable.[83] This, he submits, is further supported by the close interrelationship between moral and economic rights and the economic value of moral rights, referring specifically to the decision of the Canadian Supreme Court.[84] Others have also pointed to the symbiotic relationship between moral rights and the grant of economic rights[85] or taken the view that moral rights cannot be dissociated from money.[86]

Such an approach appears less likely in a *droit d'auteur* system with a strong moral rights protection, such as France, where moral rights are inalienable, imprescriptible and perpetual as well as unwaivable (Article L. 121–1 Intellectual Property Code).[87] While the Intellectual Property Code expressly allows for arbitration in the case of copyright disputes (Article L. 331–1, 4th subsection), this is subject to the general rules on arbitration in Articles 2059 and 2060 of the Civil Code. As a result, arbitration is only allowed where the parties can freely dispose over the right in question and the matter does not relate to *ordre public*. Moral rights under French law are not only inalienable and unwaivable, but are also a matter of public policy.[88] It therefore does not come as a surprise that Professor Lucas and his co-commentators have called for the respect of the special nature of moral rights where recourse to arbitration is

79   Ibid. [53].
80   Ibid. [57].
81   Ibid.
82   Ibid. [58].
83   de Werra, *Handbook*, (n 75), 357–8.
84   Ibid.
85   Dominick Luquer, 'Position of the FIA' in *ALAI Report 2014*, (n 5), 133.
86   Michael F. Flint, 'Moral Rights in the Theatre and Some Comments on Moral Rights and Audiovisual Works', in *The Moral Right of the Author*, ALAI, Congress of Antwerp, 19–24 September 1993, 469, 472.
87   Mantakou in Mistelis & Brekoulakis, (n 57), 266 referring to Bruno Oppetit, 'L'arbitrabilité des litiges du droit d'auteur et droits voisins, Arbitrage et Propriété Intellectuelle' (1994) 121–31.
88   *Turner Entertainment Co v. Huston*, Cass. civ 1re, 28 May 1991, [1991] 149 RIDA 197 where moral rights provisions were characterised as '*lois d'application impérative*'.

sought, however not without the concession that the consequences of a moral rights violation may well be arbitrable.[89] Professor Gautier equally points out that while moral rights may not be disposed of, disputes on moral rights nonetheless exist and must be solved; for him, it is not apparent that arbitrators would be less competent to deal with such cases than a judge.[90] Despite the inability of the author to freely dispose of moral rights, the Paris Court of Appeal accepted the arbitrability of moral rights in the case *Zeldin v. Sté Editions Recherches*.[91] Under the particular circumstances, moral rights were only one aspect of the contractual dispute between the parties in an international arbitration and the Court saw some merit in keeping all the aspects of the case together in the arbitration procedure. The decision was criticised by Professor Kerever, who considered that the arbitration clause came close to a waiver of moral rights as a result of withdrawing from the jurisdiction of the French courts.[92] Under what conditions moral rights claims may ultimately be the subject of an arbitration under French law, therefore remains a matter of speculation.[93]

Under German law, a civil law system following the monist approach with a generally non-transferable broad author's right encompassing both personality and economic rights components, ADR, including arbitration, can play a role in the resolution of copyright disputes.[94] In accordance with the general provisions governing arbitration in §§ 1029 et seq. Civil Procedure Code, the arbitrability of author's rights claims depends on the nature of the claim: while pecuniary claims are in general arbitrable, unless arbitration is expressly excluded or subject to specific conditions, an arbitration agreement regarding non-pecuniary claims has legal effect only insofar as the parties to the dispute are entitled to conclude a settlement agreement regarding the subject matter of the dispute.[95] Consequently, where pecuniary claims, such as a claim for damages for a moral rights violation as a result of a breach of contract or tort are at issue, the arbitrability of the claim should not be problematic. On the other hand, the arbitrability of non-pecuniary claims is not automatically excluded simply because moral rights are not transferable. This is so because it is generally recognised that legal transactions concerning moral rights are possible in certain cases, which is partly reflected in § 39 of the Law on Author's Right with regard to agreements on the alteration of a work, its title or designation of authorship.[96]

The nature of the claim matters also under Indian law. Following the decision of the Indian Supreme Court in the *Booz Allen* case, a distinction is made between claims regarding rights *in rem* and rights *in personam*.[97] Only claims regarding rights *in personam* are arbitrable.[98]

---

[89]   Lucas/Lucas-Schloetter/Bernault, (n 5), para. 1183.
[90]   Gautier, *Propriété littéraire et artistique*, (n 62), 876, note 1.
[91]   Cour d'Appel de Paris, 1re, 26 May 1993, [1994] 159 RIDA 292–3.
[92]   Ibid.
[93]   Maxence Rivoire, 'L'arbitrabilité du droit d'auteur: le cas du droit français' [2017–2018] McGill Journal of Dispute Resolution, 4, 43, 53–9, 64.
[94]   Wimmers in Schricker/Loewenheim, (n 6), § 104 UrhG para. 2 and § 105 UrhG, para. 25; Haberstumpf in Mestmäcker/Schulze, (n 59), § 104 UrhG, para. 16.
[95]   Cf. § 1030 (1) German Code of Civil Procedure.
[96]   Cf. Peukert in Schricker/Loewenheim, (n 6), Vor §§ 12ff. UrhG, paras 12 and 17; Ohly, ibid., § 29 UrhG, paras 35/36; Dustmann in Fromm/Nordemann, (n 6), Vor §§ 12-14, paras 9 and 10.
[97]   *Booz-Allen & Hamilton Inc v. Sbi Home Finance Ltd. & Ors*, Judgment of the Supreme Court of India of 15 April 2011.
[98]   Ibid. [22], [23].

This distinction applies also in copyright cases.[99] However, as a result of contradictory court decisions, it is not entirely clear what exactly amounts to a right *in rem* and a right *in personam* in the field of copyright. In the *Eros* case, which concerned a dispute arising out of a copyright licensing agreement, the Court held that:

> Where there are matters of commercial disputes and parties have consciously decided to refer these disputes arising from that contract to a private forum, no question arises of those disputes being non-arbitrable. Such actions are always actions in personam, one party seeking a specific particularized relief against a particular defined party, not against the world at large.[100]

Conversely, in a licensing dispute between the *Indian PRS and Entertainment Network India*, the Bombay High Court decided that the question whether or not a licence must be obtained was a dispute over a right *in rem* and therefore had to be referred to the public courts.[101]

There is, as far as one can see, no equivalent case on moral rights. In view of the case law on the licensing of economic rights, it is questionable how an Indian court would treat a moral rights claim – as a right *in rem* or as a right *in personam*. While under Indian law, moral rights may not be assigned or licensed, they may be waived.[102] If one therefore applies the rationale of the decision in the *Eros* case, disputes over a waiver of moral rights in a commercial agreement may well be arbitrable. However, where questions regarding the substance of moral rights are concerned, and in particular where they would have an *erga omnes* effect, courts may be tempted to turn to the *Indian PRS* case as a precedent.

Additional aspects must be considered in the context of international arbitration. Some countries have made use of the facility provided for in Article I(3) of the New York Convention and restrict the recognition and enforcement to foreign awards that concern commercial relationships between parties.[103] The personal nature of moral rights is therefore also of importance in this context and an additional threshold issue to be taken into account in international arbitration. Moreover, in cross-border cases, complex applicable law questions may be encountered which are, however, outside the scope of this chapter.[104]

In conclusion, the preceding examples from case law demonstrate that it is not always a given that a dispute on moral rights is solvable with the help of ADR, especially in arbitration proceedings. In practice, such uses therefore require careful consideration.

4.2   Which Form of ADR for Which Case Scenario?

One of the key benefits of ADR is the ability of the parties to select a suitable process for resolving their dispute and to customise the chosen process to the case rather than forcing

---

[99]   Loya and Gokhale, (n 67), 638.

[100]   *Eros v. Telemax*, Bombay High Court, (n 64). [19].

[101]   *IPRS v. Entertainment Network (India) Ltd.*, Bombay High Court, Judgment of 31 August 2016, [140].

[102]   Binny Kalra, Tanvi Misra and Suzanne Rab, 'India' in Lavizzari/Viljoen, (n 37), paras 3.54 and 3.175.

[103]   For the list of Contracting States together with declarations and reservations: https:// www .newyorkconvention.org/countries (accessed 8 March 2022).

[104]   For further information on this subject please consult Redfern and Hunter, (n 38), Chapter 3; Cook and Garcia, (n 38), 54–7 and Chapter 5.

a case into an existing mould.[105] While there is no particular recipe, a successful choice will need to match the particularities of the case and the goals of the parties with available ADR options. This being said, ADR may not always be the best approach. If a precedent or a review of the decision is desired, a procedure before a court may be preferable. Likewise, where remedies are sought which can only be obtained before the ordinary courts, ADR is not an option. By way of example, where a test case is to achieve legal certainty with regard to the application and/or interpretation of existing legislation in the wake of technological advances, court procedures may be more likely to achieve that result.[106] Conversely, where the focus of a case is on the interpretation of an existing contract against new developments, ADR may be an option, depending on the circumstances of the case.

4.2.1   Consensus-based forms of ADR

Where the common goal of the parties is to settle the dispute in a friendly manner and to defuse hostilities, consensus-based forms of ADR in form of mediation, conciliation or binding or non-binding expert determination may be an option. As we have already seen, consensus-based forms of ADR do not need to be used in isolation, but can also play a role in the context of an adjudicative form of ADR or in conjunction with court proceedings.

These procedures do not only offer the general advantages of consensus-based ADR like speed, cost-control, confidentiality and the guiding hand of an expert. They also offer creative settlement possibilities, which can be built into and thus preserve the existing business relationship of the parties.[107] In addition, such forms of ADR allow for the resolution of cross-border disputes in a single forum where cross-cultural aspects may be taken into account, which is of increasing importance in the area of online exploitation.

Since moral rights disputes often touch the soul of the work, consensus-based ADR may be particularly helpful in bridging controversies between the parties. Disagreements can exist between a contractual party who has acquired economic rights to a work or performance and an author and/or performer who retains moral rights. As has been pointed out, a rigorous enforcement of moral rights in such a case can be a double-edged sword[108] and consensus-based ADR may help bring the quarrelling parties closer together. Divergences may also occur in the context of complex works where a multitude of authors and other creative contributors to a production may quarrel about alterations, credits, timing of divulgation or the withdrawal of a work. In such a case, guidance by a mediator or conciliator may facilitate discussions between the parties.

In view of the fact that interferences with moral rights can often be a matter of opinion, consensus-based ADR can be a tool for easing differences, particularly regarding the character of a potentially derogatory treatment, which can be a particular challenge in the online environment.

Thus, consensus-based ADR can be of use in all those case scenarios where harmony between the parties could potentially be restored with the help of a third-party neutral.

---

[105]   Arfin, (n 38); cf. in particular the Chart in Appendix A, 914 showing how to select an ADR process.

[106]   Cf. the discussion of this question at the ALAI Study Days Neuchâtel, 2002, (n 2), 326–8, 338–40, 350–71.

[107]   Margellos, *Mediation*, (n 38), 54–61.

[108]   Pessach, (n 27), 256.

4.2.2   Adjudicative forms of ADR

Adjudicative forms of ADR, and in particular arbitration, may be of use where the goal of the parties is to achieve legal certainty over a complex legal issue and/or to obtain an enforceable decision. Such issues may, for instance, concern the validity of a waiver of moral rights across borders or the interpretation of a contract with regard to the scope of the exercise of a moral right. Thus, an adjudicative form or ADR is called for where it is the goal of the parties to establish whether or not a particular use affecting moral rights is lawful.

In such cases, arbitration offers parties expert decision-making by third-party neutrals who can be chosen by the parties with a view to their familiarity with moral rights as well as the jurisdictions and specific sectors concerned. Like consensus-based forms of ADR, arbitration allows the resolution of cross-border and multi-jurisdictional cases in a single forum. Compared with court procedures, arbitration has the added benefit of international, cross-border enforcement on the basis of the New York Convention, subject, however, to the already discussed potential legal obstacles in the country of enforcement, which should be considered as a threshold issue.

While arbitration will most often be based on an existing arbitration clause in a contract, such a clause is not always necessary. Arbitration can also be embarked upon in the absence of a pre-existing contract if a submission agreement can be concluded and the dispute as such is arbitrable.[109] Thus, arbitration is not per se excluded in the case of a tort, but could be considered, for example, concerning a claim for damages arising out of a moral rights violation.

4.2.3   Institutionalised or ad hoc ADR?

Apart from selecting the appropriate form of ADR, parties will have to determine whether or not the assistance of an ADR institution should be sought. Whether a dispute should be solved in an institutionalised or an ad hoc procedure depends first of all on the ADR clause in the contract, if any, and secondly on the individual circumstances of the case. While an institutionalised procedure may offer a sound structure and welcome support for the proceedings, it is also more rigid and may diminish the creativity and flexibility which is the essence of ADR. As with the choice of the appropriate form of ADR, the decision depends on the particular circumstances of the case and the goal of the parties.[110]

5.   CONCLUSION

Alternative dispute resolution can be a powerful tool for solving disputes over moral rights provided that recourse to ADR for moral rights is not barred by law and a particular case scenario and the goals of the parties can be matched with a suitable dispute resolution process. Nevertheless, there may be instances where moral rights disputes are better left to the courts. In the absence of a specific recipe and at the peril of repetition, the choice of the most suitable option for solving a moral rights dispute ultimately depends on the particulars of each individual case scenario and the intentions of the parties.

---

[109]   Mantakou in Mistelis & Brekoulakis, (n 57), 265.
[110]   For more details regarding ad hoc and institutionalised arbitration cf. Redfern and Hunter, (n 38), paras 1.140–1.181.

20. Private international law issues of moral rights

Paul L. C. Torremans

INTRODUCTION

In this chapter I will look at moral rights from a private international law perspective. Rather than look at the scope and exact content of moral rights I will look at issues of jurisdiction and choice of law. It is important to note that from a private international law perspective one needs to determine first of all the court that will have jurisdiction or, if a case is brought before a court, the court will have to check whether it has indeed jurisdiction to hear the case. That will also happen in a case that involves moral rights. Once the court has established its jurisdiction to hear the case involving moral rights it will then, under its own rules of private international law, determine the law applicable to the moral rights issue before it.

The chapter will therefore look at jurisdiction in a first stage, before moving on to choice of law. The analysis will be conducted from a European Union perspective, but it is fair to say that most private international law systems around the world adopt a very similar approach. In the jurisdiction area that can be explained by the use of the same basic rules that are firmly based on fundamental principles of justice, whilst in the choice of law area there is the harmonizing influence of Article 5 of the Berne Convention and its principle of national treatment.[1]

1. MORAL RIGHTS AND THE JURISDICTION ISSUE

1.1 Normal Jurisdiction Rules Apply to Moral Rights Cases

Jurisdiction *in personam* in the courts of the domicile of the defendant
Intellectual property lawyers tend to forget this, or at least they tend to dismiss its applicability too easily, but when one thinks about jurisdiction in intellectual property cases one needs to turn first of all to the general rule on jurisdiction. Admittedly, there is not even the faintest hint of intellectual property in it, but that should not surprise anyone, as the general rule is linked to the person of the defendant and provides jurisdiction *in personam*, rather than to put a focus on a link between the facts and the courts of a certain jurisdiction. The latter is much closer to our familiar territory in intellectual property, where we almost automatically think about infringing acts and damage making up infringement and being linked to an identifiable single location. Instead the general rule, found in almost every single system of private international law around the world, links to the person of the defendant and grants jurisdictions to the courts of the country where the defendant has his or her domicile, habitual residence or place of business. That jurisdiction is broad in scope and covers any civil and commercial case that is

---

[1]   J.J. Fawcett and P. Torremans, *Intellectual Property and Private International Law*, Oxford University Press (2nd ed, 2011), Ch. 13.

brought against the defendant. That general rule reflects a basic principle of fairness. The court needs the respect of both parties if it is to play its role in resolving disputes and the best way to achieve this is to act as a neutral arbiter between the parties. Another aspect of such a system is that there needs to be a level playing field for the parties when they have access to the arbiter. The claimant chooses the attack in the sense that he or she decides to bring the case, as well as the grounds on which the case is brought. The defendant cannot undo that and is obliged to defend the case as it is brought by the claimant. In order to get the balance right the system will allow the claimant to play at home, or in jurisdiction language it will oblige the claimant to bring the case in the domicile, habitual residence or place of business of the defendant. The rule also promotes the values of predictability and legal certainty that always figure prominently in a private international law setting. Or as the Court of Justice of the European Union (CJEU) put it: 'That jurisdictional rule is a general principle, which expresses the maxim actor sequitur forum rei, because it makes it easier, in principle, for a defendant to defend himself.'[2]

This approach is found in Article 4 of the Brussels I Regulation.[3] Intellectual property falls squarely within the broad scope of the Regulation as it is clearly a civil and commercial matter. There is therefore no reason at all to question the applicability of Article 4 Brussels I Regulation in cases that involve copyright, including cases about moral rights. These cases can be brought in the courts of the country where the defendant has his or her domicile, habitual residence or place of business.[4] That is always an option and one that should not be neglected in a moral rights setting. One can bring a single global case against the defendant. The court with jurisdiction under the rule will be able to deal with the whole moral rights infringement by the defendant, irrespective of the place around the world where it takes place. At least in an Internet environment, but not limited to such an environment, infringements of the rights of paternity and integrity tend to have an impact in multiple jurisdictions as they affect, as it were, the standing of the author who is not identified as such or the integrity of whose work is affected. The option to bring a single case with a global scope is therefore an attractive one.

Tort or infringement grounds for jurisdiction

The general principles
The alternative to the general rule for jurisdiction *in personam* is to move away from the link between the person of the defendant and the country where the court is based and to focus instead on the facts of the case at issue and their link with the country where the court is based. In an intellectual and moral rights setting these cases are cases concerned with infringement. The case is brought as a result of the (alleged) disrespect for, or infringement of, moral rights, such as the right of paternity if the author is not identified as such or the right of integrity when the integrity of the work is put in issue. From a private international law perspective infringement of intellectual property rights in general, or of moral rights in particular, is seen as a form

---

[2]   Case C-256/00 *Besix v. WABAG* [2002] ECR I-1699, para 52.
[3]   Regulation (EU) No. 1215/2012 of the European Parliament and of the Council of 12 December 2012 on jurisdiction and the recognition and enforcement of judgments in civil and commercial matters [2012] OJ L 351/1.
[4]   See Article 2:101 Principles for Conflict of Laws in Intellectual Property, European Max Planck Group on Conflict of Laws in Intellectual Property, *Conflict of Laws in Intellectual Property: The CLIP Principles and Commentary*, Oxford University Press (2013) for the specific application of the rule to intellectual property.

of tortious liability.[5] The link with the facts of the case to determine a court that is well placed to deal with the matter is found through the determination of the place where the harmful event occurs. Or, for our specific purposes, the place where the alleged infringement of the moral rights takes place or the place where the event that allegedly amounts to an infringement of the moral rights takes place. Article 7.2 Brussels I Regulation is a typical example of such a rule. That rule is well underpinned as the court of the place where the harmful event occurs will typically have easy access to witnesses and factual evidence, as well as to other circumstances that are of relevance for the decision that is to be made.[6]

The cases that form the basis for the application of Article 7.2 Brussels I Regulation are unrelated to intellectual property, let alone to moral rights, but they are nevertheless of critical importance in the understanding of how this article will apply to moral rights. First of all, one needs to be clear about what is meant by the concept of the place where the harmful event occurs. This concept was clarified in a case where pollutants were dumped in the river in one country and where trees irrigated with the polluted water died in another country. The CJEU held in *Handelskwekerij G.J. Bier BV v. Mines de Potasse d'Alsace SA*[7] that both the acts leading to the damage and the damage itself were part of the concept of the place where the harmful event occurs. Article 7.2[8] therefore gives jurisdiction to the court of the country where the act leading to the damage took place and to the court of the country where the damage resulting from that act occurred. Only direct damage, i.e. damage resulting directly from the act, is taken into account. With the *Shevill* case[9] we came closer to intellectual property, and maybe even more to moral rights, as the case involved the tort of defamation. The CJEU ruled that under Article 7.2 Miss Shevill could sue the newspaper publisher either in France at the place where the defamatory article had been published or in the UK at the place where the damage to her reputation had arisen. On the latter basis she could sue wherever there was damage to her reputation as a result of the defamatory publication, but on each of these occasions the jurisdiction of the local court was limited to the local damage, i.e. the damage in the jurisdiction. At first some doubt remained as to whether this case law could be applied to intellectual property,[10] but the recent case law from the CJEU has taken that doubt away and has also set out in more detail how Article 7.2 should be applied.

---

[5]   J.J. Fawcett and P. Torremans, *Intellectual Property and Private International Law*, Oxford University Press (2nd ed, 2011), Chs 4 and 5.

[6]   See Article 2:202 Principles for Conflict of Laws in Intellectual Property, European Max Planck Group on Conflict of Laws in Intellectual Property, *Conflict of Laws in Intellectual Property: The CLIP Principles and Commentary*, Oxford University Press (2013).

[7]   Case 21-76 *Handelskwekerij G.J. Bier BV v. Mines de Potasse d'Alsace SA* ECLI:EU:C:1976:166. The case is often referred to as the Bier or Beer case, but there is no alcohol involved. The gentleman growing the trees was simply called Bier, which means beer in Dutch. And as a Belgian, I will refrain from commenting further on the oddities of Dutch surnames if you just allow me to salute what started as an act of civil disobedience in Napoleonic times.

[8]   Or Article 5.3 as it then was.

[9]   Case C-68/93 *Fiona Shevill, Ixora Trading Inc., Chequepoint SARL and Chequepoint International Ltd v. Presse Alliance SA* ECLI:EU:C:1995:61.

[10]   J.J. Fawcett and P. Torremans, *Intellectual Property and Private International Law*, Oxford University Press (2nd ed, 2011), Ch. 5.

A factual basis approach and the risks associated with it

The CJEU has indeed in recent years delivered a number of key judgments in relation to Article 7.2. The doctrine that emerges from these judgments makes perfect sense at first glance, especially in the context of the original case that was completely unrelated to intellectual property rights. As we will see, complications do, however, arise when it is applied to intellectual property cases, but the question needs to be asked whether these complications also apply to moral rights.

In the context of Article 7.2 one needs to identify the place where the infringing act takes place and the place where the damage that flows directly from that act occurs. Once that has occurred the court which has jurisdiction to hear the case on the basis of Article 7.2 is easily identified and that court can then deal with the matters of substantive law that arise in the case. It makes, therefore, perfect sense to reserve points of substantive law for the substantive case and therefore leave them out of the jurisdiction debate. Places where acts take place and where damage arises are much more fact related. The CJEU therefore grounds its jurisdiction approach under Article 7.2 in a purely factual analysis and refuses to involve points of substantive law. That should improve the level of predictability and legal certainty and, most importantly, it should avoid the jurisdiction stage turning into a mini-trial on substance, only for the substantive proceedings to double up with another substantive law analysis. The approach should therefore also save time by disposing quickly and efficiently of the jurisdiction point. The original decision in the *Melzer* case[11] demonstrates that clearly. Mr Melzer and the investment company with whom he dealt are based in Germany, but the money was invested (and subsequently largely lost) by an associate of the latter based in London. Mr Melzer wanted to bring his case for compensation in tort on the first leg of Article 7.2, i.e. the place where the act leading to the damage was committed. That was logically speaking London, but Mr Melzer argued on the basis of German national tort law that it could also be in Germany. German tort law contains a rule that states that each of the parties involved is liable for unlawful acts undertaken in common. That rule would cover the German company and its London affiliate and on the basis of it Mr Melzer wanted to impute the unlawful behaviour of the London affiliate, who clearly was the perpetrator who committed the act on the German defendant and on that basis bring his Article 7.2 case in Germany. That was, after all, the more cost-efficient option for him. The CJEU refused to consider elements of substantive German tort law and interpreted Article 7.2 in the sense that it does not allow the courts of the place where a harmful event occurred which is imputed to one of the presumed perpetrators of damage, who is not a party to the dispute, to take jurisdiction over another presumed perpetrator of that damage who has not acted within the jurisdiction of the court seised.[12] Only purely factual elements could be taken into account and these all pointed to London. In a case with several perpetrators Article 7.2 does not allow one of them to be sued in a country where he or she did not act.[13]

Shortly after the court rendered its judgment in *Melzer* the *Pinckney* case[14] turned the attention to the second limb of Article 7.2, i.e. the place of the damage, in a copyright context. In

---

[11]   Case C-228/11 *Melzer v. MF Global UK Ltd* ECLI:EU:C:2013:305.

[12]   Case C-228/11 *Melzer v. MF Global UK Ltd* ECLI:EU:C:2013:305, para. 41.

[13]   Case C-387/12 *Hi Hotel HCF SARL v. Uwe Spoering* ECLI:EU:C:2014:215; Case C-360/12 *Coty Germany GmbH, formerly Coty Prestige Lancaster Group GmbH v. First Note Perfumes NV* ECLI:EU:C:2014:1318.

[14]   Case C-170/12 *Peter Pinckney v. KDG Mediatech AG* ECLI:EU:C:2013:635.

a previous life Mr Pinckney had been a singer and much to his surprise he saw, now that he lived years later in the south-west of France, CDs that contained recordings of his music for sale via a website accessible from his home in France. He bought these and they were duly delivered to his home, but the royalty payment for the use of his music and the recordings did not follow. By the time the case reached the courts the website had disappeared in thin air, leaving Mediatech, the Austrian company who had physically produced the CDs, as the sole defendant. The basis for the jurisdiction of the French court was therefore the fact that the website was accessible in France and that delivery without royalty payment took place there, i.e. the place of the damage in the second limb of Article 7.2 was in France. The CJEU endorsed that approach, as it is a logical application of its factual approach with access to the website and failure to pay royalties both located in France. That conclusion applied despite the fact that Mediatech had in no way acted in France, but the somewhat peculiar aspects of copyright liability can be left to one side here.[15] The CJEU applied its *Shevill* doctrine here too and limited the jurisdiction of the court to local damage,[16] but that does not avert the risk that factual access to the website as a basis for jurisdiction potentially grants such 'local damage' jurisdiction to courts in any country around the world. The *Pinckney* case merely dealt with a 'poor' individual musician who wanted to bring a case in a single court, but the impact of the decision is potentially much wider … and much more risky, as Advocate-General Jääskinen pointed out to no avail in the trademark/unfair competition case *Coty Germany*.[17] It is in that respect worth adding that the French Supreme Court applied that same approach at global level outside the Brussels I Regulation when it based the jurisdiction of the French courts over a US company on the fact that its website, on which it sold T-shirts with a copyright protected photograph printed on them, was accessible in France.[18]

The real danger of the CJEU's approach became apparent in the *Hejduk* case.[19] In this case any hard copy element, such as the delivery of CDs in one location, disappears and the alleged infringement takes place entirely on the Internet through a website that is accessible in every single country. Ms Hejduk is an Austrian photographer who specializes in photographs of buildings and the work of specific architects. She had granted EnergieAgentur, a German company, a licence to use some of her photographs in an exhibition, but later found out that they were or remained available on the website of EnergieAgentur without her consent. The question arose whether she could use Article 7.2 to sue EnergieAgentur in the courts in Austria. The CJEU gave an affirmative answer.[20] In doing so it repeated that the place of the damage (where a claim for local damage can be brought) is every place where the website is accessible. In this case both the architect and the photographer were Austrian and, if one leaves the concerns surrounding the fact that this is a kind of a *forum actoris* to one side, one is bound to conclude that there is a strong link between the case and Austria, which makes the Austrian

---

[15] See the decision of the Cour de Cassation in case No. 10-15.890 at http://www.courdecassation.fr/jurisprudence_2/premiere_chambre_civile_568/33_22_28276.html.

[16] Case C-170/12 *Peter Pinckney v. KDG Mediatech AG* ECLI:EU:C:2013:635, at para. 47. See also case C-387/12 *Hi Hotel HCF SARL v. Uwe Spoering* ECLI:EU:C:2014:215.

[17] Case C-360/12 *Coty Germany GmbH, formerly Coty Prestige Lancaster Group GmbH v. First Note Perfumes NV* ECLI:EU:C:2014:1318.

[18] Cour de Cassation, Cass. 1re Civ., 22/01/2014, case 11-26822 *Korda v. Onion/The Onion*, ECLI:FR:CCASS:2014:C100060.

[19] Case C-441/13 *Pez Hejduk v. EnergieAgentur.NRW GmbH* ECLI:EU:C:2015:28.

[20] Ibid.

courts suitable courts to hear the case. But Ms Hejduk could have sued EnergieAgentur anywhere on the basis of this approach. This turns the CJEU's argument of legal certainty and predictability into a weird form of certainty and predictability, to say the least. One must hope that the claimant will only sue in a jurisdiction where there is sizeable local damage, but the risk of harassment from the side of a claimant who takes a punitive approach cannot be ruled out and the defendant may be forced to defend cases on substance in jurisdictions that have an almost non-existent link with the case. One is almost obliged to ask whether it does not make more sense to require that there is targeting of the jurisdiction by the defendant or serious damage in the jurisdiction before jurisdiction can be established on this basis (whilst that will then in copyright/ubiquitous circumstances allow one to drop the restriction to local damage only).[21] Or one may wish to be reminded of the French case *Samuel v. BBC*, where the Cour de Cassation held that access in the jurisdiction to programs that another party had put on line via Youtube, despite the fact that the BBC was only accessible via a subscription service, was sufficient to grant the French courts jurisdiction as the mere factual requirement of access to the website (one way or another and by whichever party) had been met.[22]

Application to moral rights
Where does that leave us in relation to moral rights? In the first place we will have to accept that the Article 7.2 jurisdiction analysis is a factual analysis and that this approach applies to both the act and the damage limb. There is no place for a substantive law analysis whether a certain act really infringes the integrity right in the conditions described in any national copyright law or whether a certain reference to an author, or the lack of it, fall short of the substantive law requirements of the right of paternity. Instead one focuses on the allegedly infringing act and, more particularly on the factual location where that act took place. If a book was published in France without mentioning the name of someone who sees him- or herself as a (co-)author and who sues on the basis of the right of paternity one looks at France as the place of the act. The French court will locate the act of publication (without mentioning the name of the claimant) in France and will take jurisdiction on that basis. There is no reason to look at substantive law and risk having a mini substantive trial at the jurisdiction stage. The same analysis can be made for the right of integrity when comments that destroy the reputation of the author are inserted in a certain location. The place of the damage is then the place where the copies of the work in which the paternity of the author is not acknowledged are distributed or where the work is on that basis communicated to the public. Or it is the place where the copy that affects the author's reputation is distributed or where that version of the work is communicated to the public.

Taken on its own, the factual approach can be applied to moral rights. It is by no means a hurdle that cannot be overcome. There is, of course, the argument that intellectual property in general, and moral rights in particular, have the peculiarity that infringement necessarily involves an act and damage in the same location. Maybe this is a logical consequence of the principle of territoriality[23] that in turn flows from the principle of national treatment in the

---

[21]   See Article 2:203 Principles for Conflict of Laws in Intellectual Property, European Max Planck Group on Conflict of Laws in Intellectual Property, *Conflict of Laws in Intellectual Property: The CLIP Principles and Commentary*, Oxford University Press (2013).

[22]   Cass. 1re Civ., 22/01/2014, case 11-24019, *Samuel v. BBC* ECLI:FR:CCASS:2014:C100039.

[23]   European Max Planck Group on Conflict of Laws in Intellectual Property, *Conflict of Laws in Intellectual Property: The CLIP Principles and Commentary*, Oxford University Press (2013), pp. 38–41.

Berne Convention.[24] That needs to be confronted with the reality that a version of the work without the name of the author or with distorting alterations may be realized on the Internet in one place and can and will be accessed anywhere else in the world. Does that mean that there is an act leading to damage in one country and damage (at least potentially) in any country in the world (with an Internet connection)? It is submitted that the answer does not really matter if one takes a merely factual approach to jurisdiction. In the country of release or upload there is arguably also damage, as a result of the upload and as a result of the fact that the work is now available in that jurisdiction and that the website can be accessed there. And in all the other countries of the world a website that is accessible does not merely lead to the presence of damage. On a factual basis, without the need to look at the substantive law requirements of whichever local or applicable law, there is also an act of communication to the public whenever the website is accessed.

That means that in the second place the risk that the claimant can potentially (or abusively) sue the defendant anywhere in the world if mere possible access to the website is the factual criterion for jurisdiction is also present in cases that deal with moral rights. Perhaps it feels less abusive in these moral rights cases, as we take for granted that anywhere in the world the author has a minimal right to paternity and to the integrity of his or her work. We almost intuitively see these minimal rights of paternity and integrity as global rights or rights whose content or essence does not depend on the detail of national (applicable) laws. One finds a parallel in the recent CJEU case on (derogatory) content that was harmful to a person's reputation and where an injunction was requested to oblige a service provider to remove the comment on a global basis.[25] The court goes along with that and finds no problem with such a global obligation and what is important for our current purposes, the court does at no stage discuss the applicable law or more precisely whether the claimant has in each country a right to object to derogatory comments and whether the particular (type of) derogatory comments are covered by it in each case. The judgment seems to assume that the claimant has a global right to object to the derogatory comments and ask for their removal.

Interim conclusion on jurisdiction
That leads logically to the conclusion that the normal jurisdiction rules apply to moral rights cases, but that they present the same problems in these moral rights cases as in intellectual property cases in general. There is, however, another line of cases in relation to defamation and privacy/personality right that we should look at, as these areas of law show a certain affinity with moral rights. They relate to the person involved and this has given rise to a jurisdictional focus on the centre of interests of the person involved. It is to that centre of interests approach that we now turn.

1.2 The Centre of Interests Approach and Its Value for Moral Rights Cases

The centre of interests approach can be seen in EU insolvency law. Jurisdiction over an insolvency is based on the concept that each insolvent debtor is anchored in the community in a certain place. This is the place where they do business, have their main establishment, the majority of their assets, as well as their reputation and business goodwill. The Insolvency

---

[24] Article 5.1 Berne Convention 1886.
[25] Case C-18/18 *Eva Glawischnig-Piesczek v. Facebook Ireland Limited* ECLI:EU:C:2019:821.

Regulation defines it succinctly in its Article 3.1 as 'the place where the debtor conducts the administration of its interests on a regular basis and which is ascertainable by third parties',[26] but for our current purposes the wider approach gives an idea of where all this comes from and where it can lead. Another example can be seen in the facts of the *Shevill* case.[27] Fiona Shevill was a jobstudent from Yorkshire. The whole defamatory story in the newspaper unfolded in Paris and that was where the newspaper was published and had its main distribution, but she wanted to sue in the UK and not merely for financial/legal aid reasons. Her reputation merely existed and could be damaged by the story in the region where she lived. People knew her there and she was operating in the community there. The UK, and Yorkshire in particular, was her centre of interests.

The CJEU turned its attention to the centre of interests approach in a privacy/right of personality context in *E-date and Martinez*.[28] Dancer Olivier Martinez had been in a relationship with singer Kylie Minogue and despite the relationship having ended he came to her assistance when she developed cancer. He objected to these aspects of his private life being made public by the defendants. The CJEU added a third ground of jurisdiction in this context to the place of the act leading to the damage and the place of the damage in Article 7.2. Olivier Martinez could also bring the case in his centre of interest. This was the place where he leads his private life and where the substance of his right to privacy is located. In other words, he could sue in his centre of interests. The CJEU admits that the place of the centre of interests is in most cases the place of the habitual residence of the claimant, even if it could be elsewhere as a result of the very significant professional activity of the claimant in the latter place. By way of example one could think of a TV presenter from the Netherlands with a habitual residence there, but who becomes famous as a result of his shows on German television.[29] That gives rise to a strong argument that he has his centre of interests in Germany. More importantly though, we are dealing here with a *forum actoris*, whereby the claimant can both choose the course of action and sue at home, thus distorting the normal balance between the claimant choosing the course of action and the defendant having the benefit of the home jurisdiction. The CJEU justifies this exceptional departure with the strong link between the facts in such a case and the person of the claimant. The Court puts this case in the context of the personality rights of the claimant, which not only involves his or her privacy, but also his or her voice or image. The concept of the personality right is, of course, closely related to the concept of the moral right of paternity. A right to be identified is in a sense a right to a signpost to one's personality. That personality is also reflected in the work and its integrity. The link with moral rights is therefore made quite easily and one could argue that the centre of interests approach could also be used to identify the court that has jurisdiction under Article 7.2 in cases concerning moral rights.[30]

---

[26]   Regulation (EU) 2015/848 of the European Parliament and of the Council of 20 May 2015 on insolvency proceedings (recast) [2015] OJ L 141/19.

[27]   Case C-68/93 *Fiona Shevill, Ixora Trading Inc., Chequepoint SARL and Chequepoint International Ltd v. Presse Alliance SA* ECLI:EU:C:1995:61.

[28]   Joined Cases C-509/09 and C-161/10 *e-Date Advertising GmbH v. X and Olivier Martinez, Robert Martinez v. MGN Limited* ECLI:EU:C:2011:685.

[29]   Such as the late Rudi Carrell.

[30]   Hanan Mohamed Almawla, *Moral rights in The Conflict-of-Laws: Alternatives to the Copyright Qualifications* Doctoral thesis Queen Mary, University of London (2012).

1.3 Personality Rights or Intellectual Property: An Issue of Classification/Are Moral Right the Exception to the Intellectual Property Approach?

It is on the other hand clear from the *Winstersteiger* case[31] that the CJEU is not prepared to apply the centre of interests approach to intellectual property cases. *Winstersteiger* was a trademark case, but the CJEU has never distinguished between the various intellectual property rights in relation to Article 7.2 Brussels I Regulation. One must therefore assume that the refusal to apply the centre of interests approach does also extend to copyright. Not surprisingly for those who are familiar with private international law we do end up here with an issue of classification.[32] Does one classify moral rights issues as copyright issues for the purposes of private international law in general, and jurisdiction in particular, or does one classify them as issues related to the personality right? Despite the fact that moral rights are clearly very close to the personality right it is submitted that a copyright classification is in the end more suitable. Irrespective of whether one adheres to the monist or dualist theory, moral rights are part and parcel of copyright. Both the economic and moral rights are part of a package of rights and protection that is given to the author with the overall aim in the words of the US Constitution: 'To promote the progress of science and useful arts, by securing for limited times to authors and inventors the exclusive right to their respective writings and discoveries.'[33] Guaranteeing authors the right to be identified as authors of their works and guaranteeing the integrity of their works is as much part of this promotion effort as giving them economic rights to make a living out of the exploitation of their works. There is also a close relationship to the right of integrity as the ultimate stick behind the door in extreme cases and the right for the author to authorize of prohibit an adaptation of his or her work, to take just that example of the inter-relationship between moral and economic rights. It is therefore advisable to use a copyright classification and to apply the same jurisdiction (and maybe choice of law rules) to each aspect of copyright. Handing the whole case to a single court on the same basis is the best guarantee for a consistent outcome in those cases where not only moral rights, but also other aspects of copyright are involved. It is therefore submitted that there is no scope for the application of the centre of interests approach in relation to more rights.

2. MORAL RIGHTS AND THE CHOICE OF LAW ISSUE

2.1 Classification (Again)

The classification issue also arises when it comes to choice of law. One can, once more, link moral rights to the person of the author and to personality rights and then use a centre of interests approach to determine the applicable law.[34] Or one can prefer a unitary approach to copyright and apply the same law to moral rights and to economic rights. In terms of classifi-

---

[31] Case C-523/10 *Wintersteiger AG v. Products 4U Sondermaschinenbau GmbH* ECLI:EU:C:2012:220.

[32] Paul Torremans (general editor), James J. Fawcett (consulting editor) et al, *Cheshire, North & Fawcett: Private International Law*, Oxford University Press (15th ed, 2017), Ch. 3.

[33] Article I Section 8 | Clause 8, US Constitution.

[34] Hanan Mohamed Almawla, *Moral Rights in The Conflict-of-Laws: Alternatives to the Copyright Qualifications* Doctoral thesis Queen Mary, University of London (2012).

cation it makes sense to apply the same approach both to jurisdiction and to choice of law. On most occasions the same arguments apply and it guarantees consistency. It is submitted that that logic also applies to the moral rights cases for the reasons highlighted above in relation to jurisdiction. That, of course, leaves open the question which choice of law rule will be used to determine the applicable law.

2.2   Moral Rights as Part of the '(Copy-)Right as Such'

Often reference is made to the principle of territoriality in a copyright context, but that principle is not '*expressis verbis*' to be found in any international legal instrument. It does, however, form the consequence of the way in which national treatment is construed in Article 5 of the Berne Convention. National treatment as such already tells us there is not a single harmonized copyright law at international level. Access to international protection for authors and their copyright works is handled at national level and foreign authors are given access to these various national systems. That leads to a territorial country-by-country approach, but it does not quite determine the applicable (national) law. Article 5.2 Berne Convention draws, however, a consequence from the national treatment principle that sounds strange in our current legal systems even if it may have been less strange in 1886. Be that as it may, the so-called consequence refers to choice of law in the following terms:

> Article 5
> (1)   Authors shall enjoy, in respect of works for which they are protected under this Convention, in countries of the Union other than the country of origin, the rights which their respective laws do now or may hereafter grant to their nationals, as well as the rights specially granted by this Convention.
> (2)   The enjoyment and the exercise of these rights shall not be subject to any formality; such enjoyment and such exercise shall be independent of the existence of protection in the country of origin of the work. *Consequently, apart from the provisions of this Convention, the extent of protection, as well as the means of redress afforded to the author to protect his rights, shall be governed exclusively by the laws of the country where protection is claimed. ...*[35]

Whatever is classified as the extent of protection and the means of redress, the two being sides of the same coin in the context of private intellectual property rights that are effectively negative rights to stop others from doing things, such as communicating the work to the public in the copyright setting, without the permission of the rightholder, will come under the application of the law of the country where protection is claimed. If I claim to have copyright in my work in Germany, e.g. in an attempt to make a user take a licence, German law will apply. And national treatment means that that exercise will be repeated country by country. One will therefore get a jigsaw of national copyright laws that apply on a country-by-country basis. Or, in other words, this is territoriality in practice as a result of national treatment.[36] One applies the *lex loci protectionis* or the law of the country for which protection is sought on a country-by-country (or a territorial) basis.[37]

---

[35]   My italics.
[36]   J.J. Fawcett and P. Torremans, *Intellectual Property and Private International Law*, Oxford University Press (2nd ed, 2011), Ch. 9.
[37]   See Judgment of 22 December of the French Cour de Cassation, *Société Fox-Europa v. Société Le Chant du Monde* (1960) 28 RIDA 120, annotated by Holleaux at 121 et seq.

The next issue that needs to be addressed is, of course, what is included in the concept of the extent of protection (and the means of redress). The essence here is that the extent of protection refers to the rights 'as such', thereby leaving the contractual exploitation or transfer of the intellectual property right to one side. The aspects of the right as such are then governed (each time) by the law of the country for which protection is sought, which is the conclusion that is also arrived at by modern private international law codifications.[38] In more detail, we are looking at issues such as the creation of the right, the scope of the right, the duration of the right,[39] the assignability of the right, etc. Creation of the right[40] also includes the question whether[41] and, if so, which moral rights arise when a work attracts copyright protection (as a result of its creation). The scope of the right also applies to the scope of the moral rights. How broad or narrow the protection offered by the right of integrity is defined, for example, as a matter of the scope of the right. Duration of the right includes the question whether or not the moral rights are perpetual or the determination of the term of protection for each of the moral rights that are granted under a particular national law. Assignability addresses, on the other hand, the question whether moral rights are transferable. A clear example of the latter point is found in the case between Michael of Greece and Anne Bragance.[42] Anne Bragance had signed a contract to act as the ghostwriter for the autobiography of Michael of Greece. That contract was governed by the law of the state of New York and stipulated a transfer of all rights to Michael of Greece. When the French translation was published by Olivier Orban, Ann Bragance sued for the infringement of her right of paternity (and for more royalties). The French court argued that the moral rights point was governed by the law of the country for which protection was sought, i.e. France. Under French copyright law the right of paternity cannot be assigned, so she could have her name on the cover of the book and the contract (as the actual transfer or assignment) never entered the picture. And for reasons of completeness, French law as the law of the country for which protection is sought allowed for the economic rights to be assigned, which in turn allowed the contract to be considered under the law of the state of New York. That contract was held to involve a valid and global transfer of rights and hence her claim for additional royalties was denied.

2.3   Scope in a Bit More Detail and Applied to Moral Rights

Once copyright has been created it is important to know what the content of the exclusive right will be. How far will the protection extend? Logically speaking, this issue is inextricably linked with the decision to grant copyright, as it determines what exactly is being granted. The issue should, therefore, be decided under the same applicable law. The law of the country for

---

[38]   See the Belgian code on private international law, Wet van 16 juli 2004 houdende het wetboek van international privaatrecht, [2004] Belgisch Staatsblad-Moniteur belge 57344 (27 July 2004), Art. 93. For an English translation see Torremans and Clijmans [2006] RabelsZ 358–97.

[39]   In a wide-ranging approach that can be used as a first starting point Von Bar, 108 (1988) UFITA 27, refers for the three latter issues to the law of the country where the right has been used, which is also the approach of the Austrian Private International Law Statute.

[40]   Oberlandesgericht Munich (6th Civil senate) judgment of 10 January 2002, [2002] MMR 312, [2003] ZUM 141.

[41]   See Siehr's argument in 108 (1988) UFITA 9 at 18 in relation to the question whether rights exist.

[42]   *Anne Bragance v. Olivier Orban and Michael of Greece*, Cour d'appel de Paris, 1 February 1989, (1989) 142 RIDA 39.

which protection is sought should apply.[43] The law of the place where the right is used has to decide whether the right exists and what its content is.[44]

This choice of law point is important, in practice, as the Berne Convention does not define the scope of protection in a rigid way. It rather sets minimum standards. Suffice it to refer here to the fact that some countries merely grant a right of paternity and a right of integrity that mirror exactly the narrow contours of Article 6*bis* Berne Convention, whilst other countries combine a broad definition of these rights, that is, for example, triggered as soon as the work is modified, with other additional moral rights, such as the right of divulgation. The exact scope of the economic and moral rights granted depends on the national law and is therefore different on a country-to-country basis. Hence the importance of determining the applicable law of the country for which protection is sought.[45]

Whether one sees moral rights as an integral part of copyright or as separate rights, the precise content of the moral rights that are granted is determined by the law of the country for which protection is sought.[46] Either they are just part of the scope of the copyright that has been granted, or, if they are seen as independent rights, they come into being automatically through the creation of the copyright. It is logical, in these circumstances, to accept that they are governed by the same rule, for reasons of uniformity. The applicability of the law of the country for which protection is sought is confirmed by Article 6*bis*(3) of the Berne Convention, which states explicitly that the means of redress in relation to moral rights are governed by the law of the country for which protection is sought. The specific means of redress for each moral right are linked so strongly to the moral right concerned that it would make no sense to separate them in terms of the applicable law. Moral rights, i.e. their content and who can exercise them, before and after the death of the author, and how, are therefore governed by the law of the country for which protection is sought.[47]

---

43   See *Novello & Co Ltd v. Hinrichsen Edition Ltd and Another* [1951] 1 Ch 595.

44   See Walter (1976) 89 RIDA 45 at 51, and, for an example, see the judgment of 1 March 1989 of the Arrondissementsrechtbank (Dutch Court of first instance) in *Leewarden, United Feature Syndicate Inc v. Van der Meulen Sneek BV* [1990] Bijblad Indutriële Eigendom 329, the scope of copyright in the Garfield dolls in the Netherlands was determined by Dutch law (law of the country for which protection is sought), rather than under US law.

45   The view that the scope of copyright and the extent of the rights granted is governed by the law of the country for which protection is sought or *lex loci protectionis* was confirmed by the German Bundesgerichtshof (German Supreme Court) in its *Spielbankaffaire* judgment of 2 October 1997, [1998] GRUR Int 427. See also in the same sense the judgment of 4 February 1997 of the Court of Appeal of Milan, [1998] GRUR Int 503.

46   The term 'rights' in the Berne Convention includes both pecuniary and moral rights, see Ginsburg 17 (1993) Columbia-VLA Journal of Law and the Arts 395, at 405 and see also the analysis of the *John Huston* case below.

47   This was confirmed by the French courts in the *Giacometti* case that went all the way to the Supreme Court, *LP v. BG and Others*, Cour d'appel de Paris (première chambre), judgment of 23 September 1997, (1998) 176 RIDA 418; confirmed by the judgment of 6 July 2000 of the Cour de Cassation (first civil chamber), *Mrs Lisa Palmer v. Roland Dumas q.q., B Giacometti and Others* [2001] RCDIP 329.

2.4   Overriding Mandatory Rules

Moral rights are also a topic certain legal systems care a lot about and that brings us to consider public policy and overriding mandatory rules issues. We have argued elsewhere that moral rights should be seen as fundamental rights that protect the author against the abuse of his work.[48] Let us look at the consequences of this point from a UK perspective, by way of example. From that point of view, the UK's approach to moral rights should form part of its public policy. This would have important implications in a situation where the case is litigated in the United Kingdom, but where the law of the country for which protection is sought is not the Copyright, Designs and Patents Act 1988. Rather than applying the law of the country for which protection is sought, the court would be obliged to apply the UK's provisions on moral rights, if the standard of moral rights protection in the law of the protecting country would be lower than the one in the Copyright, Designs and Patents Act 1988. It needs to be stressed that this approach does not replace the choice of law rules and the law of the country for which protection is sought altogether. Public policy considerations, and eventually the application of the law of the forum, can only be considered at a later stage.[49]

Overriding mandatory rules, however, operate in a slightly different way. These rules are directly applicable[50] and the choice of law process is not followed at all. The provisions on moral rights of the forum are directly applicable, irrespective of the content of the law of the protecting country, if they are mandatory rules. This is the approach that was taken by the French Cour de Cassation[51] in the *John Huston* case.[52] It is submitted that the nature of moral rights, as rights that come only into operation when the copyright work is used abusively, does not justify the latter approach. The traditional law of the protecting country, plus public policy of the forum in exceptional cases, is far more suitable.[53] The same law would then also be applied to all issues that form part of the scope of copyright.

It is clear that the applicability of the UK's substantive provisions on moral rights has certain interesting implications, if we continue with the UK example. A foreign author, who is not resident in the United Kingdom and whose work is first published abroad, will not have the right to be identified, unless he asserts that right in the format prescribed by Section 78 of

---

[48]   P. Torremans, *Holyoak and Torremans Intellectual Property Law*, Oxford University Press (9th ed, 2019), Ch. 14.

[49]   See Ginsburg and Sirinelli, (1991) 15 Columbia-VLA Journal of Law and the Arts 135 at 139.

[50]   In French legal terminology these rules are referred to as 'règles d'application immédiate', which characterizes them very well.

[51]   Different decisions were reached at first instance and upon appeal, see Judgment of 23 November 1988 of the Tribunal de grande instance de Paris, [1989] Recueil Dalloz Sirey 342 (Jurisprudence), annotated by Audit and [1989] Revue critique de droit international privé 372, annotated by Gautier; Judgment of 6 July 1989 of the Cour d'appel de Paris, [1990] Recueil Dalloz Sirey 152 (Jurisprudence), annotated by Audit and [1989] Revue critique de droit international privé 706, annotated by Gautier; Judgment of 28 May 1991 of the Cour de Cassation, [1991] Revue critique de droit international privé 752, annotated by Gautier.

[52]   For an in-depth analysis of the case see Ginsburg and Sirinelli, above (an English translation of the judgment is attached as an appendix); Ginsburg and Sirinelli [1991] 150 RIDA 3; see also Ginsburg (1988–1989) 36 Journal of the Copyright Society of the USA 81, and Ginsburg (1993) 17 Columbia-VLA Journal of Law and the Arts 395.

[53]   See Ginsburg and Sirinelli (1991) 150 RIDA 3 at 21.

the Copyright, Designs and Patents Act 1988.[54] The fact that a similar assertion requirement is unheard of in the author's country, or in the country of first publication, is irrelevant in this respect. This conclusion, though correct, could seem rather bizarre, especially as it may be doubted whether the UK's assertion requirement is in compliance with the no-formalities rule in the Berne Convention.[55]

CONCLUSION

For the purposes of private international law the main question concerning moral rights is whether they are very tightly linked to the person of the author and therefore to the personality right and the centre of interests approach. But that is a deceptive question. Yes, there is a strong link with the person of the author and there are strong similarities between the rights of paternity and integrity on the one hand and the right of personality on the other hand, but that strong link with the author is first of all part and parcel of copyright. Copyright is centred around the author, i.e. it is an author's right or *droit d'auteur*. Moral rights are an integral part of copyright and they cannot be separated from it. That also applies in a private international law setting. It is therefore submitted that moral rights follow the copyright approach for the purposes of private international law, even if that approach is not without its complications or problems.

---

[54]   The exceptions to moral rights will also apply, see Copyright, Designs and Patents Act 1988, ss 79 and 81.

[55]   English courts are not entitled to verify this point, but see Art. 5(2) Berne Convention.

PART V

MORAL RIGHTS OUTSIDE EUROPE

21. Moral rights and the protection of traditional knowledge

Susy Frankel

1.   INTRODUCTION

When scholars from either a European or Anglo-American copyright tradition hear the claims of those seeking to protect their traditional knowledge (which is also an embodiment of their culture and identity) from offensive treatment, the scholars' first thoughts might be that sounds like a moral rights claim. Traditional knowledge claimants note that harmful uses of their knowledge can occur in many ways, including uses without attribution to the source and the culture from which the knowledge comes and that the knowledge has not been treated with integrity. The use may even be derogatory or offensive. Thus, some of the key concerns about the protection of traditional knowledge echo two major moral rights: the right to attribution and the right to integrity, which is sometimes called the right to object to derogatory treatment.[1] Although some aspects of claims to traditional knowledge resemble moral rights claims, the overlap is partial and complicated by jurisdictional variations in the scope of protection for both moral rights and traditional knowledge.[2] In some countries, where moral rights are strongly protected and traditional knowledge protection is legally lacking but is a growing social concern, those moral rights may provide a vehicle to protect some aspects of traditional knowledge. In contrast, in jurisdictions where moral rights are not a strong tradition, those who seek protection of traditional knowledge might be foolhardy to attach their claims to moral rights which are thinly protected and weakly enforced.

To explain the overlap of traditional knowledge and moral rights this chapter first discusses what is traditional knowledge and what protection claimants of that knowledge aspire to. The second part of this chapter details the overlap between traditional knowledge and moral rights claims and, in particular, those relating to attribution, integrity and divulgation. The third part analyses how moral rights can be a complementary but small part of the ambit of desired protection of traditional knowledge. Consequently, moral rights are not enough to protect traditional knowledge.

---

[1]   Berne Convention for the Protection of Literary and Artistic Works, 1161 UNTS 30 (adopted on 9 September 1886), as revised at Paris (24 July 1971) (Berne Convention), Art. 6*bis*(1).
[2]   Susy Frankel, "Towards a Sound New Zealand Intellectual Property Law" (2010) 32 VUWLR 47–74, at 70. See also Michael Brown, *Who Owns Native Culture* (Harvard University Press, 2003) at 73, stating, "In principle, [moral rights] could provide a powerful screen of protection for indigenous cultural productions" and "At first glance native concerns seem tailor made for a moral-rights strategy."

2.   UNDERSTANDING TRADITIONAL KNOWLEDGE CLAIMS

When sitting in a movie theatre watching the blockbuster film, *The Revenant*, a young man is surprised how familiar the voice is that is reciting a poem in the soundtrack. He tells his mother that it is her on the soundtrack. She is surprised but he turns out to be correct. The woman receives no payment at all for the use of her recorded voice.[3] Intellectual property law might effectively condone such a use as it seems the work was licensed by the person who created the recording that was incorporated into the film. The woman whose voice was on the recording said that she was unsure about any agreement she may have made with those who recorded her. In addition to exploiting a recording without compensation – such an action is not merely financial but is an effect of colonization – this could easily form the basis of a traditional knowledge claim for several reasons, but particularly the use of the traditional song in a commercial film in a context that the traditional knowledge holders may consider inappropriate.

Another example that I have outlined elsewhere involves a western band, Deep Forest, exploiting a lullaby sung by a woman from the Solomon Islands and recorded in the first instance by the United Nations Educational, Scientific and Cultural Organization (UNESCO). As I explain:[4]

> The two Frenchmen, who are Deep Forest, never seem to have had anyone's permission to use the recording. Money has not been paid to UNESCO for its recording and neither was the woman, known as Afunakwa, whose voice is heard in Deep Forest's recording ever paid or acknowledged.[5] UNESCO perhaps lacked the motivation to pursue any claim and Afunakwa may have lacked the means and even the possibility of an enforceable cause of action.

The song and even the recording of it were not protected by copyright for one reason or another.[6] Thus, intellectual property becomes the means by which the traditional knowledge

---

[3]   *The Guardian*: "Woman whose voice was used in The Revenant got no screen credit or money", stating that "A little more than halfway through the Oscar-winning Leonardo DiCaprio movie The Revenant, a voice recites a poem in a Native American language. In the scene, Hikuc, a Pawnee portrayed by Arthur Redcloud, is building a shelter for DiCaprio's frontiersman, Hugh Glass. But the lines of poetry are recited not in the Plains Indian Pawnee dialect, but in the Inupiaq language of Arctic Alaska, and the voice, it has emerged, is that of Doreen Nutaaq Simmonds, a Fairbanks, Alaska, resident who had no inkling that a recording of her would be used in the film – which has grossed millions and earned 12 Oscar nominations, winning best director and best actor", see http://www.theguardian.com/film/2016/mar/14/the-revenant-womans-voice-used-without-screen-credit.

[4]   Susy Frankel, "Traditional Knowledge, Indigenous Peoples, and Local Communities", in Rochelle Dreyfuss and Justine Pila (eds), *The Oxford Handbook of Intellectual Property Law* (Oxford University Press, 2018).

[5]   Don Niles, "Stealing Music from/in Papua New Guinea", in Kathy Whimp and Mark Busse (eds), *Protection of Intellectual, Biological and Cultural Property in Papua New Guinea* (ANU epress, 2013) 116–24, at 119–20.

[6]   The Solomon Islands is a member of the World Trade Organization and as a least developed country it not obliged yet to comply with intellectual property obligations of the Agreement on Trade-Related Aspects of Intellectual Property Rights, Marrakesh Agreement Establishing the World Trade Organization, 15 April 1994, 33 ILM 81 (1994) ("TRIPS Agreement"), Art. 66.1 provides a transition period of 10 years for least developed country members. There have been successive extension of this times; the latest is until 2034. *See* Council for Trade-Related Aspects of Intellectual Property Rights, *Extension of the Transition Period under Article 66.1 for Least Developed Country Members*, Decision of the Council for TRIPS, IP/C/64 (12 June 2013) now extended until 2034, see *WTO members agree*

embodied in that song is exploited. The injustice of allowing the exploitation of one culture for the benefit of another, without allowing for sufficient recourse to approve relevant uses or even benefit from them, lies at the heart of claims for the protection of traditional knowledge.

Calls from both Indigenous peoples and developing countries (including India and Peru, for example) for the protection of traditional knowledge has accelerated as global trade has increased. In the global world what is "exotic" and therefore sells, in the marketplaces of the developed world, may very well be extracted from a place where the object or knowledge is not exotic but is a matter of tradition and cultural identity. The world is global, but knowledge of cultures is asymmetric. Majority cultures are known to many, whereas details or even the existence of many minorities can often be unknown to those outside of their location or country. The intellectual property system exploits this asymmetry by treating the supposedly unknown as something to be extracted from in order to build the new.[7]

The uses of traditional knowledge by those not associated with the origin or tradition of that knowledge can cause many grievances, which can be categorized as two broad harms. Those harms are the disassociation from origin and changes in the function of the knowledge in a way that counters against uses by those from whom the knowledge originates and can even impact their identity. As Patterson and Karjala have said:[8]

> the cognitive heritage that gives indigenous peoples their identity is under assault from those who would gather it up, strip away its honored meanings, convert it to a product, and sell it. Each time that happens, the heritage and knowledge die a little, and with them, the people.

Kapa Kingi argues that this kind of extractive use of traditional knowledge, his focus is on mātauranga Māori, is a kind of modern colonization.[9] For Indigenous peoples who still feel the effects of colonization this is extremely problematic. Those seeking protection of traditional knowledge are often members of communities that need economic development and in many cases whose culture has been eroded.[10]

---

to extend TRIPS transition period for LDCs until 1 July 2034, at https://www.wto.org/english/news_e/news21_e/trip_30jun21_e.htm. The Solomon Islands is not a member of the Berne Convention at WIPO but is via the TRIPS Agreement, which incorporates the Berne Convention, TRIPS Agreement, Art. 9. Although at one stage the Solomon Islands was a British Protectorate, neither the Solomon Islands nor Papua New Guinea, its near neighbour, have local copyright legislation, see Niles, above n 5.

[7]   For a discussion of the extractive nature of intellectual property see Peter Drahos, *Intellectual Property, Indigenous People and their Knowledge* (Cambridge University Press, 2014) 1–14.

[8]   Robert K Paterson and Denis S Karjala, "Looking beyond Intellectual Property in Resolving Protection of the Intangible Cultural Heritage of Indigenous People" (2003) 11(2) Cardozo J of Int'l and Comp L 634–70.

[9]   Eru Kapa-Kingi, "Kia Tāwharautia Te Mātauranga Māori: Decolonising the Intellectual Property Regime in Aotearoa New Zealand" (2020) 51(4) VUWLR 643–72, available at https://doi.org/10.26686/vuwlr.v51i4.6701.

[10]   It is beyond the scope of this chapter to discuss fully the scope of economic development rights in relation to traditional knowledge. Many such rights are more directly connected to other areas of intellectual property than copyright. Of course copyright and authors' rights can be characterized as rights which may enable creators to live from their creative works (at least ideally even if not always). Economic development in the context of traditional knowledge may have a role as a form of distributive justice in order to "repair" relationships and address past wrongs. For a discussion of the issues in the protection of traditional knowledge, see generally Susy Frankel and Peter Drahos, "Indigenous Peoples'

The existence of this problem, that is exacerbated by increased cross-border activity both by trade and the internet, is recognized by international institutions, such as the World Intellectual Property Organization (WIPO).[11] While debate about whether and how traditional knowledge should or should not be protected continues at WIPO and in various other fora, the impacts of non-protection on the holders of the knowledge remain. Even where jurisdictions provide some protection in their national laws that may not be enough to address the international issues. Traditional knowledge users cannot enforce that protection in other jurisdictions where the extracted knowledge, language or object has the appearance of the exotic or, in copyright terms, something original.

WIPO continues to grapple with finding norms to include in a treaty, the finalization of which seems to be politically fraught. Even though a final agreed text remains to be completed the debate and negotiations have illuminated many of the issues and even a broader understanding of what traditional knowledge is. WIPO uses the following broad definition to explain what traditional knowledge is:[12]

> …intellectual activity in a traditional context, and includes the know-how, skills, innovations, practices and learning that form part of traditional knowledge systems, and knowledge embodying traditional lifestyles of indigenous and local communities, or contained in codified knowledge systems passed between generations and continuously developed following any changes in the environment, geographical conditions and other factors. It is not limited to any specific technical field, and may include agricultural, environmental and medicinal knowledge, and any traditional knowledge associated with cultural expressions and genetic resources.

The benefit of this definition is its breadth and explanatory nature.[13] The danger of this sort of definition is also its breadth and, as a result, such wide definitions become the basis of some countries seemingly intractable negotiating position that the matter is too broad and therefore is unprotectable. Definitions can bring a kind of comfort to those who are looking for what is sometimes called, perhaps erroneously, legal certainty. Definitions are useful but subject matter definitions are often not definitive and can be inclusive or open-ended. Intellectual property is riddled with definitions that are less than legally certain and, in fact, their existence forms a kind of parameter to litigation rather than any certainty about their application. The scope of copyright originality, for example, is not defined in the Berne Convention[14] and is instead left to members to frame at national law. The parameters of originality are often not

---

Innovation and Intellectual Property: The Issues", in Peter Drahos and Susy Frankel (eds), *Indigenous Peoples Innovation: Intellectual Property Pathways to Development* (ANU epress, 2012).

[11] For WIPO's work see generally see http://www.wipo.int/tk/en/tk/.

[12] The Protection of Traditional Knowledge: Revised Objectives and Principles, WIPO Document WIPO/GRTKF/IC/18/5 (10 January 2011), annex 18. This definition appears also in subsequent drafts.

[13] A similarly broad definition is found in Article 31 of the United Nations Declaration on the Rights of Indigenous Peoples, which provides: "Indigenous peoples have the right to maintain, control, protect and develop their cultural heritage, traditional knowledge and traditional cultural expressions, as well as the manifestations of their sciences, technologies and cultures, including human and genetic resources, seeds, medicines, knowledge of the properties of fauna and flora, oral traditions, literatures, designs, sports and traditional games and visual and performing arts. They also have the right to maintain, control, protect and develop their intellectual property over such cultural heritage, traditional knowledge, and traditional cultural expressions." Available at https://www.un.org/development/desa/indigenouspeoples/declaration-on-the-rights-of-indigenous-peoples.html.

[14] Berne Convention, above n 1.

a result of statutory definition alone but are contoured by ever-developing case law. The definition of patentable subject matter, both internationally and in many jurisdictions, is another example of a wide and litigious definition.[15] It comes, usually, with exceptions or exclusions and uses terms that are disputable. The United States is a perfect illustration of this.[16] There the debate on patentable subject matter has led to the inclusion and then exclusion of computer programs[17] and gene sequences,[18] for instance. Thus, the desire to have very detailed certainty around a definition of traditional knowledge is a false standard. Focusing on the definition seems to primarily be used as a tool for a political argument that is predominantly motivated by a desire not to recognize minority rights.

When definitions are required to do too many tasks, combined with taking on a formalist role then they become like "quicksand".[19] They are not just definitions but are ways to control, or worse to silence, a debate. It is complex to create a subject matter definition that is applicable to all cultures that seek the protection of their traditional knowledge, most obviously because the cultures will be variable and, in some cases, extremely so. Commonalities may be broad, but it only makes sense to have commonalities form the basis of an international norm and specifics are found in customary, national or regional laws. In reality many cultures can identify and explain the knowledge, expressions of that knowledge and innovations that they seek protection for. Even western cultures do this, they just usually claim the protection without referencing the notion of traditional knowledge. The framework of copyright law, for example, reflects a western culture of authorship that requires an individual or named collaborators who might be treated as joint authors or co-authors. Traditional knowledge does not ignore the individual but focuses on the how the knowledge is holistic (not isolated but part of a system) and relevant to all.

Further an important feature of much Indigenous knowledge is that it is uncodified and cannot always be captured by rules or subject to limited definitions. The transmission of this sort of knowledge involves teaching and tradition. The difference between this approach and copyright law, for example, has become even more stark with copyright ownership (especially

---

[15]   The TRIPS Agreement, above n 6, Art. 27.1, entitled patentable subject matter, provides that "patents shall be available for any inventions, whether products or processes, in all fields of technology, provided that they are new, involve an inventive step and are capable of industrial application". None of the terms used in in this Article are defined in the Agreement leaving it to national legislatures and courts to frame the definition's scope.

[16]   The relevant definition provides "Whoever invents or discovers any new and useful process, machine, manufacture, or composition of matter, or any new and useful improvement thereof, may obtain a patent therefor, subject to the conditions and requirements of this title", 35 U.S.C. § 101.

[17]   *Alice Corp. v. CLS Bank International*, 573 U.S. 208 (2014), finding that computer programs were not patentable subject matter.

[18]   See, *Association for Molecular Pathology v. Myriad Genetics, Inc.*, 569 U.S. 576 (2013), finding that isolated gene sequences were not patentable subject matter.

[19]   See Drahos and Frankel, above n 10, pp. 9–13 and see also J Russell-Smith et al., "Challenges and Opportunities for Fire Management in Fire-prone Northern Australia", in J Russell-Smith, P Whitehead and P Cooke (eds), *Culture, Ecology and Economy of Fire Management in North Australian Savannas: Rekindling The Wurrk Tradition* (CSIRO Publishing, 2009) 1; and Raukawa and the Raukawa Settlement Trust and the Sovereign in Right of New Zealand, "Deed in Relation to a Co-Management Framework for the Waikato River" (17 December 2009) 1.34; Alex Steenstra, The Waikato River Settlement and Natural Resource Management in New Zealand, at http:// www .nzares .org .nz/ pdf/ The %20Waikato %20River%20Settlement.pdf.

corporate ownership and creative industries) rather than authorship being the focus.[20] Some are critical, however, that authorship has not been the focus of much copyright law and debate about its scope.[21]

Localized or national understandings and practices of traditional knowledge do not necessarily lend themselves to a wholly prescriptive international definition because, as noted above, cultures differ. This means that an international definition must be broad enough to be relevant to all and as such functions as a minimum standard that requires more precision at domestic law. This is exactly how the international system of intellectual property is broadly structured.[22] Members of the Agreement on Trade-Related Aspects of Intellectual Property Rights (TRIPS) Agreement, for example, must enact domestic laws that meet the Agreement's minimum standards.[23] They are free to increase the standard and most often, for it to be effective, prescribe more detail in their domestic law.

The phrase "traditional knowledge" does not reflect that Indigenous peoples' knowledge is often used developmentally and as a tool for innovation. Some broader definitions capture aspects of this. If a community has knowledge about the flora and fauna and lands that have been their home for generations then this knowledge can be useful for a variety of purposes relating to that environment.[24] Such uses often involve innovation, such as to control and fight bush fires or to remove pollution from waterways.[25] In fact, if the knowledge was not useful for such dynamic processes others would not extract it for their own intellectual property uses, or possibly at all.

Much of what is labelled as traditional knowledge is more than just knowledge. It can embody learnings (collections of information across generations) that are useful for innovation. For knowledge that is not used for innovation or developmental purposes but is more static, and possibly also sacred or even iconic, there is a glaring mismatch in levels of available protections. Doctrines such as trade secret protection or breach of confidence are ill-fitting for culturally based secrecy. Trade secrets law, as its nomenclature reveals, is about protecting secrets where they relate to trade. Cultural matters that are secret are not foremostly, if at all, trade related. Some jurisdictions (such as New Zealand and Australia) do not have a trade secrets law to protect confidentiality but do so on the basis of the doctrine of breach of confidence. That doctrine is not framed to address the needs of traditional knowledge owners, even if some traditional knowledge is held confidentially. The framework of the doctrine, which

---

[20]   The TRIPS Agreement, above n 6, Art. 9 incorporates the Berne Convention but otherwise only refers to authors in connection with the rental right, Art. 11. Otherwise, the TRIPS Agreement adopts the language of "right holder", Art. 13.

[21]   Jane C Ginsburg, "The Concept of Authorship in Comparative Copyright Law", (2003) 52 DePaul L Rev 1063.

[22]   Substantive international intellectual property treaties are structed to proscribe the minimum levels of protection that members must enact in their domestic laws. The treaties do not prescribe the law but frame the standard that must be met.

[23]   Members can also provide greater protection, see for example TRIPS Agreement, above n 6, Art. 1.1.

[24]   See for example, Rosemary J Coombe, "Protecting Traditional Environmental Knowledge and New Social Movements in the Americas: Intellectual Property, Human Right or Claims to an Alternative Form of Sustainable Development?" (2005) 17 Florida J of Int'l L 115–35.

[25]   See discussion of these examples in Drahos and Frankel, above n 10.

has been more geared towards individual privacy,[26] does not simply translate to the goals of protecting traditional knowledge.

Further inequality is observable as the icons of western society are protected in a variety of ways, including when flag and emblem status is afforded to them.[27] Having this status removes the need to show reputation, goodwill or substantial use as a means to gain protection. It also prevents their commercial exploitation except by permission.[28] Flags, emblems and icons of Indigenous groups are usually not protected by the same means as the flags and emblems of the states in which those groups reside. The flags of the Indigenous peoples of Canada, Australia and New Zealand, for example, are not official government flags.

Trademark law and common law doctrines, such as passing off, also protect fame and icons of pop culture.[29] But icons of smaller groups, particularly Indigenous or local communities, remain accessible for all to use.[30] If one strips back the legally refined distinctions as to why fame (sometimes the term well known is used) is the yardstick for protection and as a consequence the often less famous traditional knowledge is less protected, we see a political rather than purely legal problem.

It is predominantly politically motivated that certain cultural icons receive protection and others do not.[31] Outside of the culturally embedded framework of intellectual property, there is no discernible reason other than political hegemony to provide extensive protection for some cultural icons but to eschew it for others. Why should a pop-star be able to stop her image being used on a tee-shirt, but an elder Indigenous person (who is not famous) not be able to prevent the use of her image on, for example a tourist souvenir? The only difference between the two is fame. In some cultures dignity is more important. Understanding these factors opens the possibility of understanding that the legal distinctions that are used to exclude traditional knowledge from effective protection or to block related negotiations are not the main barriers to achieving that effective protection.

Traditional knowledge evolves as it is passed from generation to generation. One of the key purposes of passing on knowledge in this way is to develop that knowledge for current needs as well as guarding the knowledge for future generations. This does not mean that the relevant

---

[26]   For the scope of breach of confidence, see Megan Richardson, *Breach of Confidence: Social Origins and Modern Developments* (Edward Elgar, 2012).

[27]   Article 6(1)(a) of the Paris Convention states that: "The countries of the Union agree to refuse or to invalidate the registration, and to prohibit by appropriate measures the use, without authorization by the competent authorities, either as trademarks or as elements of trademarks, of armorial bearings, flags, and other State emblems, of the countries of the Union, official signs and hallmarks indicating control and warranty adopted by them, and any imitation from a heraldic point of view."

[28]   See for example, Guidance on the Use of Royal Arms, Names and Images, at https://www.royal .uk/sites/default/files/media/royal_arms_blue_booklet20152.pdf.

[29]   See for example, *Robyn Rihanna Fenty v. Aracadia Brands* [2013] EWHC 2310 (Ch), [2015] EWCA Civ 3.

[30]   See discussion in Waitangi Tribunal, *Ko Aotearoa Tēnei: A Report into Claims Concerning New Zealand Law and Policy Affecting Māori Culture and Identity* (2011), http:// www .waitangi -tribunal .govt .nz/ news/ media/ wai262 .asp, ("*Ko Aotearoa Tēnei*"). For further discussion see Susy Frankel, "Traditional Knowledge as Entertainment", in Megan Richardson and Sam Ricketson (eds), *Research Handbook on Intellectual Property in Media and Entertainment* (Edward Elgar Publishing, 2017) pp. 446–64. See also, Lee Ann Tong, "Protecting Traditional Knowledge – Does Secrecy Offer a Solution?" (2010) 13(4) Potchefstroom Electronic Law Journal (PELJ) 159–80, at http://www.scielo .org.za/scielo.php?script=sci_arttext&pid=S1727-37812010000400008.

[31]   *Ko Aotearoa Tēnei*, above n 30, discusses this point.

traditions and the knowledge system from which they come are entirely elastic. There may well be principles that are core and do not change. For example, mātauranga Māori is a knowledge system which continues to evolve but retains core principles that govern that evolution. As the Waitangi Tribunal explains:[32]

> Mātauranga' derives from "mātau," the verb "to know". "Mātauranga" can be literally translated as "knowing" or "knowledge". But "mātauranga" encompasses not only what is known but also how it is known – that is, the way of perceiving and understanding the world, and the values or systems of thought that underpin those perceptions. "Mātauranga Māori" therefore refers not only to Māori knowledge, but also to the Māori way of knowing.

Traditional knowledge and intellectual property are distinct but both can be seen as knowledge systems. The frameworks of those systems are very different and so is the detail, although the two may overlap.

3.   TRADITIONAL KNOWLEDGE OVERLAPS AND DISCONNECTION WITH MORAL RIGHTS

One similarity between traditional knowledge claims and moral rights is a relationship between the claimant (individual or collective) with that knowledge and a desire to not have that relationship denigrated but to maintain its integrity.

The divulgation moral right has some aspects which are closely analogous to the goals of protecting traditional knowledge if that knowledge is secret. In other words, the right not to disclose knowledge is analogous to the right of an author to choose to divulge their work. That said, what might be described as secret traditional knowledge,[33] which holders of that knowledge would not want to divulge, is not at the forefront of the aim of achieving economic development through the protection of traditional knowledge that can be used for commercial purposes.

Both moral rights and traditional knowledge claimants seek attribution and respect for their works.[34] At first blush, the moral right to be identified as the author of a work may appear similar to the aspiration of traditional knowledge owners to be identified as the source of traditional knowledge. The difference lies in the traditional knowledge claim being motivated by more than attribution, but also having the aim of protecting the customs and culture that is the traditional knowledge and the relationship between the people and their knowledge. The framing of separate moral rights of attribution and integrity tends to split its goals into

---

[32]   *Ko Aotearoa Tēnei*, above n 30, The Tribunal details how mātauranga Māori incorporates language, whakapapa, technology, systems of law and social control, systems of property and value exchange, forms of expression, and much more it includes, for example, traditional technology relating to food cultivation, storage, hunting and gathering it includes knowledge of the various uses of plants and wildlife for food, medicine, ritual, fibre, and building, and of the characteristics and properties of plants, such as habitats, growth cycles, and sensitivity to environmental change it includes systems for controlling the relationships between people and the environment. And it includes arts such as carving, weaving, tā moko (facial and body tattooing), the many performance arts such as haka (ceremonial dance), waiata (song), whaikōrero (formal speechmaking), karanga (ceremonial calling or chanting).

[33]   Sacred traditional knowledge may not be secret if it is openly available.

[34]   See *Ko Aotearoa Tēnei*, above n 30.

a complementary series of rights, whereas traditional knowledge claimants see these matters are more directly linked and indivisible.

As far as copyright is concerned, it is well established that the embodiment of some traditional knowledge may attract copyright. This is because those embodiments may be works of art or culture which fit the definition of artistic and literary work, both under the Berne Convention and at national law where the categorization of works is usually more nuanced.[35] Literary and artistic works are, in the parlance of the WIPO draft treaties for the protection of traditional knowledge, traditional cultural expressions (TCEs).[36] Other embodiments of traditional knowledge may not qualify as original works and would, therefore, not attract copyright. An example is where a customary practice requires skilful replication of an art form and the knowledge of how to replicate that is a kind of traditional knowledge. Even where uses of traditional knowledge do create something which qualifies as a copyright work, copyright does not last forever[37] and it does not protect the embodied knowledge from subsequent inappropriate use. In other words, copyright is not designed to protect the integrity of the knowledge or any customary norms or practices surrounding its use.

The categorization of traditional knowledge into categories such as TCEs uses a framework which is convenient for those with a focus on intellectual property, but that is viewed by many as problematic. The approach appears to be trying to fit traditional knowledge into a western paradigm of intellectual property, which many Indigenous peoples see as a modern form of colonialism.[38] To those seeking protection for their knowledge system, the separation of traditional knowledge into outputs which may fit into intellectual property categories is not the right approach. If intellectual property categories were effective then they would have been used. Instead, they have often become effective in enabling others to extract traditional knowledge for their own intellectual property gains. The goals of intellectual property creation tend to focus on the commodification of the knowledge (whether economic or individualistically driven). In contrast, traditional knowledge focuses on the nature of the knowledge, its connections and the customary law associated with that knowledge and its people.

Importantly, this should not set up a dichotomy of intellectual property always being tradable and traditional knowledge not being commodified. Neither is completely true. The protection of traditional knowledge may or may not permit its commodification using that knowledge, but that may not be the central goal of the protection. As WIPO has noted:[39]

> Traditional knowledge holders do not separate "artistic" from "useful" aspects of their intellectual creations and innovations; rather, all such aspects emanate from a single belief system which is expressed in daily life and ritual.

---

35   Berne Convention, above n 1, Art. 2.

36   "TCEs are integral to the cultural and social identities of indigenous and local communities, they embody know-how and skills, and they transmit core values and beliefs. Their protection is related to the promotion of creativity, enhanced cultural diversity and the preservation of cultural heritage." See "Traditional Cultural Expressions" at http://www.wipo.int/tk/en/folklore/.

37   Under the TRIPS Agreement, above n 6, Art. 12, copyright is protected for life of the author plus 50 years or 50 years form creation of the copyright work. Protection of traditional knowledge requires a form of continuous protection.

38   Kapa-Kingi, above n 9.

39   WIPO Doc, Roundtable on Intellectual Property and Traditional Knowledge, WIPO/IPTK/RT/99/2, 1999: 51.

The use of "single" in the above passage might be better understood by the notion of holistic. Examples are useful to explain what drives the calls for the protection of traditional knowledge. One example is the use of tā moko; an ancient art form of marking the skin. Today's practitioners of this artistic skill use both traditional and modern tools and practices. As the Waitangi Tribunal has explained:[40]

> Māori people today are increasingly choosing tā moko as a sign of their own commitment to Māori culture and values, just as Mataora did. [A witness in the claim] said that a handful of tohunga tā moko are working full time to meet this demand. They use both traditional and modern tools, and their work is either wholly traditional or derived from tradition. In all cases, these tā moko reflect the whakapapa of the bearer, or kōrero of relevance to his or her iwi, hapū or whānau life. This work requires exceptional knowledge of iwi history and whakapapa, as well as rigid adherence to the values and protocols of the art form. It is not tattoo.

Copyright cannot usually assist with protecting the art of tā moko because it may be deemed unprotectable as it involves exact copying of the original work. Also, it may have fallen out of protection because it is older than any possible copyright term. Even if term is not an issue, in a particular instance, copyright may protect some expression of tā moko, as each one is "unique and personal", but copyright was not designed to protect the knowledge and traditions and rules that accompany various tā moko. This has consequences such as people offering tattooing to those without complete knowledge of tā moko thinking it looks like the real thing or that they can pass it off as the real thing. Such a situation is analogous to the drinker of champagne like products that are not champagne, but the consumer not necessarily knowing the attributes of what makes champagne "champagne" and not just sparkling wine. Although there is an analogy there is also an important difference. The traditional knowledge related objection is not one of false competition, as is the key part of the rationale of the protection of names like champagne, whether that protection is through the use of geographical indications or passing off.[41] The objection is use that is detached from the traditional knowledge holder and their culture, or worse, the use is offensive in some way including offence to identity. So, for example, when Sony appropriated specific tā moko and rearranged them to use in a video game because it looks "warrior like", it detached tā moko from the customary norms and traditions that maintain and develop it. Such uses may even cause offence because of the way in which tā moko are used. And the offence cannot be addressed through any moral rights claim because in New Zealand (and other countries) the absence of copyright means an absence of moral rights protection.

When copyright works and traditional knowledge claims interact, in modern contexts, the nexus to moral rights is starkly apparent. When presenting on this topic at the ALAI conference, in Brussels in 2014, I used an example of a ceramic tile mural that was designed and painted by a prominent New Zealand artist. The Crown commissioned the mural as an exhibit in the entranceway of for a public building, which at the time was the site where a major tele-

---

40   Waitangi Tribunal, *Ko Aotearoa Tēnei*, above n 30, 39.

41   Champagne is a protected geographical indication in many countries. Some jurisdictions that do not have a geographical registration system have protected "champagne" through the use of passing off. See for example, *Wineworths Group Ltd v. Comité Interprofessionel du Vin de Champagne* [1992] 2 NZLR 327 (NZCA). Since that dispute New Zealand has enacted a geographical indications registration system for wines and spirits.

communications cable emerged from the ocean and landed in New Zealand.[42] The mural was both created by a Māori artist and depicted his interpretation of a Māori legend. As telecommunications technology developed it was necessary to relocate those public offices and during that process the mural was dismantled. Some years later another artist located the dismantled mural and then restored each piece of the mural and reconstructed the whole.[43] She did this in consultation with the artist's family. As the restoration progressed, she made digital images of each tile from the mural and placed them online, so that others can view the rebuilding of the mural.[44] The family of the original artist were involved in the restoration process. As a result no issues of cultural appropriation or misuse of mātauranga Māori arose. But it is equally easy to conceive of an analogous situation where relevant family are not consulted and, in such circumstances, there might be questions about whether the reconstruction and digitization is a violation of the integrity of the traditional knowledge or, if such a moral right were available, a violation of an integrity right and possibly a divulgation right. Further details around the mural's original creation and destruction were a bit hazy. As it was housed in a public building and commissioned by the Crown it could have been subject to Crown copyright (and thus no moral rights would exist[45]) but the Crown did not make any claim to the mural.[46]

Imagined as a moral rights problem the above example shows how the features of moral rights claims, that protect predominantly non-economic interests,[47] resemble claims to the protection of traditional knowledge. If, for example, a traditional knowledge claimant does not want a sacred artefact to be decorated with Christmas decorations this is potentially analogous to the claim of a Canadian sculptor to prevent the adorning of his avian work with seasonal red ribbons.[48] The difference will be that the artefact may not attract moral rights in some jurisdictions if it is out of copyright[49] and in other jurisdictions the problem may be there is no single owner to claim any moral right, which are seen as necessary to protect the author's personality rather than any direct collective cultural interest. This structure of moral rights is effective for some cultural interests, where those are recognized via the individual artist or creator, but not for any collective cultural or identity interest, particularly where that collective nature is the starting point. Something analogous to a divulgation right would be in issue if the traditional knowledge claimant(s) did not want the work displayed.

---

[42]   Susy Frankel, "The Nexus and Disconnect of Moral Rights and the Protection of Traditional Knowledge", in F Brison, S Dusollier, M-C Janssens and H Vanhees (eds), *Moral Rights in the 21st Century: The Changing Role of Moral Rights in an Era of Information Overload* (Larcier, 2015) 164–71.

[43]   Bronwyn Holloway-Smith (ed.), *WANTED: The Search for the Modernist Murals of E. Mervyn Taylor* (Massey University Press, 2018).

[44]   See "Te-Ika-Akoranga – A Story about the Southern Cross Cable and a Mural 1962 – 2014", at http://lettingspaceorgnz.squarespace.com/blog/2014/9/14/te-ika-akoranga-a-story-about-the-southern-cross-cable-and-a.html.

[45]   Copyright Act 1994 (NZ), Section 97(7)(a) provides there is not right to be identified as the author of a work if the Crown owns copyright and Section 100(8)(b) provides that there is no right to integrity where the Crown owns copyright.

[46]   Copyright Act 1994 (NZ), Section 26(1) provides works commissioned for the Crown are owned by the Crown. Crown copyright lasts for 100 years, Section 26(3).

[47]   The non-economic nature of moral rights is underscored by the exclusion of them from the TRIPS Agreement, above n 6, Art. 9.1.

[48]   *Snow v. Eaton Centre Ltd* (1982) 70 CPR (2d) 105.

[49]   In many common law jurisdictions moral rights terminate when copyright does.

There are further difficulties with slotting aspects of traditional knowledge into moral rights categories, particularly where moral rights themselves are somewhat constrained and limited in a legal system. In common law systems the right of integrity, where it exists, is narrow in scope. In the United Kingdom and New Zealand law, for example, the integrity right is a right based on the notion of offensive or derogatory treatment of the copyright work.[50] This makes it less adaptable to traditional knowledge protection for at least two reasons. First, offensive or derogatory treatment is not as wide as integrity. Second, the focus on the copyright work is different from a focus on the integrity of any traditional knowledge and related customary practices and norms.

It is possible to see overlaps between moral rights and traditional knowledge, but those overlaps do not make the two areas equivalent or interchangeable in any way. Further, a closer examination shows that the areas are not well aligned and that moral rights laws are not a solution to protect traditional knowledge.

4.   MORAL RIGHTS ARE NOT ENOUGH TO PROTECT TRADITIONAL KNOWLEDGE

Overall, the similarities between moral rights and traditional knowledge claims are limited. And certainly, to the extent there is an overlap, in some situations that is predominantly an overlap in some circumstances (depending on a given set of facts) rather than one of substantive policy. Further the goals of protection of traditional knowledge cannot be fully answered by moral rights, particularly as such rights have a different cultural underpinnings and differing rationales.

One of the key drivers behind the protection of traditional knowledge is the use of that knowledge for economic development. The issue of protection fundamentally to incentivize economic development points to another important difference between moral rights and claims for the protection of traditional knowledge. If moral rights are used to protect traditional knowledge then a limitation is that moral rights are often framed as distinct from economic rights, particularly in common law countries where it is often stated that moral rights are separate from economic rights and should not be used for economic goals. One of the reasons for this distinction is to separate the rights of authors from copyright owners so they complement rather than interfere with each other. The concern of interference is why moral rights are labelled as non-economic, but they can have considerable economic importance. Protecting integrity can be to ensure that the artist's work also has a future income stream. The fact that moral rights can have economic consequences is part of why common law countries have limited moral rights and are often accompanied by the well-established practice that authors waive their moral rights in favour of the copyright owner.[51]

---

[50]   Copyright Act 1994 (NZ), Section 98(1)(b) provides "the treatment of a work is derogatory if, whether by distortion or mutilation of the work or otherwise, the treatment is prejudicial to the honour or reputation of the author or director".

[51]   See for example, Copyright Act 1994 (NZ), Section 107 and Copyright, Designs and Patents Act 1988, Section 87 (UK).

Using moral rights as a means to control the economic exploitation of traditional knowledge would certainly change the rationale of moral rights.[52] Such an approach seems somewhat untenable, especially in common law countries with Indigenous minority populations that seek the protection of their traditional knowledge such as New Zealand, Australia and the United States. Although these countries have very different approaches to Indigenous rights they do not have strong moral rights regimes.

Australia amended its moral rights regime within its copyright law, arguably making it stronger than the equivalents in the United Kingdom and New Zealand, but any strength is not its applicability to Indigenous rights and the protection of traditional knowledge.[53] Australia has some well-known cases regarding Aboriginal traditional knowledge,[54] but it has no real protection of traditional knowledge. The suggestion that the protection of traditional knowledge be included in the moral rights regime was specifically rejected in the legislative process. This is hardly surprising for a country that does not provide strong protection of Indigenous rights in general. In contrast, in New Zealand where the protection of Indigenous peoples' rights is relatively strong, particularly when compared to the other common law jurisdictions, the moral rights regime is relatively weak. The United Kingdom model of moral rights is found in New Zealand's law.[55] New Zealand is, however, often regarded as leading the way on the protection of Indigenous rights and the protection of traditional knowledge.

Also, using moral rights as a means to protect traditional knowledge may embed intellectual property law categories into the framework for the protection of traditional knowledge. As noted above, the slotting of traditional knowledge into intellectual property law-related categories is an approach that those seeking protection fundamentally object to.[56] Part of that objection is that traditional knowledge claimants seek recognition of collective rights to their knowledge and cultural heritage and see the use of intellectual property law as too focused on individual rights. Moral rights systems (and copyright and other intellectual property rights) derive from the belief that individual rights create a common public good. The traditional knowledge claim is that individual rights are not an effective mechanism to achieve the collective need for protection of traditional knowledge. Thus, the frameworks of moral rights applying to individuals and the potential model of protection of traditional knowledge as collective rights to cultural heritage are not frameworks that can be merged into one.

5.   CONCLUSION

The underlying concerns of moral rights and the protection of traditional knowledge have commonalities, but they also have substantial differences in their rationales and, thus, their frameworks. It seems unlikely that internationally those commonalities will be developed to

[52]   Any such changes must be in accordance with international obligations in the Berne Convention and TRIPS Agreement.
[53]   Copyright Amendment (Moral Rights) Act 2000.
[54]   See *Bulun Bulun v. R&T Textiles (Pty) Ltd* (1998) 41 IPR 513, which concerned sacred images reproduced on fabric, and *Milpurrurru & Ors v. Indofurn Pty Ltd and Ors* (1994) 30 IPR 209, about culturally significant images reproduced on carpets. These are not moral rights cases.
[55]   For a discussion of moral rights in New Zealand law see, Frankel, above n 4, pp. 68–70.
[56]   See *Ko Aotearoa Tēnei*, above n 30.

provide greater linkages, but some national legislatures may have the option of building on the relationship between moral rights and traditional knowledge.

The degree of nexus between moral rights and the protection of traditional knowledge depends very much on the extent of moral rights protection in the jurisdiction. However, the existence of moral rights does not guarantee the protection of traditional knowledge. In countries which have strong moral rights regimes and an interest in protecting traditional knowledge, moral rights are potentially a strong vehicle and ally of the protection of traditional knowledge. But there are very few places where this is a likely alliance. This could be the situation in some developing countries with civil law traditions. For Indigenous minorities in common law jurisdictions, where moral rights are thinly protected, they are a weak vehicle through which to protect traditional knowledge. These jurisdictions include the United States, Australia and New Zealand, where claimants of traditional knowledge protection in these countries are minority Indigenous populations.[57]

Where moral rights are a good fit to provide an avenue for protection, for some aspects of traditional knowledge, they should be used. But it seems that moral rights will only protect some parts of the greater claims for the protection of traditional knowledge. The expansion of moral rights, however, to address collective integrity claims and attribution interests has practical limits. This is particularly so in countries where moral rights are not strongly protected in the legal system and are thus not a good vehicle to protect traditional knowledge interests.

---

[57]   See generally, Christoph Graber, Karoline Kuprecht and Jessica C Lai (eds), *International Trade in Indigenous Cultural Heritage: Legal and Policy Issues* (Edward Elgar, 2012).

22. Moral rights in Japan – 'moral rights' of juridical persons?

Tatsuhiro Ueno

1. MORAL RIGHTS IN JAPAN

The Japanese Copyright Act (hereinafter referred to 'JCA')[1] provides for three moral rights, the right to make the work public (Art. 18), the right of paternity (Art. 19) and the right of integrity (Art. 20).[2]

1.1 Right to Make the Work Public (Art. 18)

1.1.1 Details
Article 18(1) of the JCA stipulates, '[t]he author of a work not yet made public (this includes a work made public without the author's consent ...) has the right to make available or present that work to the public'. Accordingly, the right to make the work public is the right of the author to determine whether or not to make his unpublished work publicly available.

The right to make the work public covers only those works which have 'not yet been made public' (Art. 18(1) of the JCA). Under Article 4(1) of the JCA, 'a work has been "made public" when it has been published or when ... it has been made available to the public', which is, from Article 3(1) of the JCA:

> when copies of it have been made and distributed in reasonably sufficient quantities to meet public demand ... given the nature of the work, by a person entitled to the right provided for in Article 21 or with the authorization of such person ... or by a person in favor of whom the right of publication provided for in Article 79 has been established ...

In one precedent regarding a poem written by a famous soccer player (Hidetoshi Nakata) in his secondary school days and incorporated by the school into a collection of student compositions, which was later published by a third party in a book without authorization, the poem was

---

[1]   Act No. 48 of 6 May 1970. Translations of the Japanese Copyright Act are available at https://www.cric.or.jp/english/clj/ and http://www.japaneselawtranslation.go.jp/law/detail/?id=3379&vm=02&re=02&new=1. Regarding the outline written in English of the JCA and major cases, *see* Tatsuhiro Ueno, 'Chapter 22 (Japan)' in Silke von Lewinski (ed.), *Copyright throughout the World* (Thomson Reuters, annually updated); Teruo Doi and Tatsuhiro Ueno, 'Chapter (Japan)' in Lionel Bently (ed.), *International Copyright Law and Practice* (Lexis-Nexis, annually updated); Peter Ganea, Christopher Heath, and Hiroshi Saito (eds), *Japanese Copyright Law, Writings in Honour of Gerhard Schricker* (Kluwer Law International, 2005).

[2]   *See also* Tatsuhiro Ueno, 'Moral Rights' in Peter Ganea, Christopher Heath, and Hiroshi Saito (eds), *Japanese Copyright Law, Writings in Honour of Gerhard Schricker* (Kluwer Law International, 2005) pp. 41–9.

held to have been reproduced and distributed in a quantity sufficient to satisfy the requirements of the public (roughly 300 copies), and determined to have been made public.[3]

1.1.2 Limitation

The right to make a work public is subject to certain limitations. In the following cases, the making public of a work which has not yet been made public does not constitute an infringement of the right to make the work public.

Firstly, where an author carries out any of the following acts, he is presumed to have consented to making the work available to or offering the same to the public, to a certain extent (Art. 18(2) of the JCA). Thus, where an author has transferred his copyright in a work, he is presumed to have consented to making the work available to or offering the same to the public by the exercise of the transferred copyright (Art. 18(2)(i) of the JCA). Where an author has transferred the ownership of the original of an artistic or photographic work which has not been made public, the author is presumed to have consented to making the work available to the public by exhibiting the original (Art. 18(2)(ii) of the JCA). Furthermore, where the copyright in a cinematographic work has vested in the film producer in accordance with the provisions of Article 29 of the JCA, the author is presumed to have consented to the making available or offering to the public of the work by the producer's exercise of the transferred copyright (Art. 18(2)(iii) of the JCA). However, since these are presumptive provisions, provisions to the contrary between the parties concerned will mean that the author can still claim his right to make the work public.

Secondly, where an author has offered a work to an administrative agency, an independent administrative body, etc., or a local public entity and has made no declaration that she does not consent to its disclosure by the time of the decision to disclose the same, the author is deemed to have consented to its disclosure under the relevant Information Disclosure Act (Art. 18(3) of the JCA).

Thirdly, it is provided that, in certain cases, including where public interest is perceived to necessitate disclosure, where a work not yet made public is disclosed by the head of an administrative agency, an independent administrative body, etc., or an organ of a local public entity, unauthorized disclosure does not constitute an infringement of the author's right to make it public (Art. 18(4) of the JCA).

1.2 The Right of Paternity (Art. 19)

1.2.1 Details

Article 19(1) of the JCA stipulates:

> The author of a work has the right to decide whether to use the author's true name or pseudonym to indicate the name of the author on the original work or in connection with the work at the time it is made available or presented to the public, or to decide that the author's name will not be indicated in connection with that work.

---

3 Tokyo District Court, 29 February 2000, 1715 Hanrei-Jihô 76 [Hidetoshi Nakata Case]. A translation is available at http://www.ip.courts.go.jp/app/files/hanrei_en/220/002220.pdf.

Accordingly, the right to determine the indication of the author's name (hereinafter referred to 'the right of paternity') is the right of the author to determine whether or not to indicate the author's name on any of the works and, if so, what name is to be indicated.

This right protects the author's personal interest in the indication of the author's name. It follows that if, for instance, a third party makes an author's works public without indicating the author's name in spite of the author's desire to indicate the true name, that party is infringing on the right of paternity. As this protection similarly applies to the indication of the author's name on a derivative work deriving from the original work, the author of the original work can exercise the right of paternity when a derivative work is to be offered or made available to the public.

The right of paternity can be invoked 'at the time it is made available or presented to the public' (Art. 19(1) of the JCA). It follows that if a person publicly announces that the person is the author of another person's work without making the work available to the public, the right of paternity is not infringed.

In one precedent, 'made available or presented to the public' in Article 19(1) does not necessarily refer to the act covered by copyrights. In this case, the Court held that a retweet in the Twitter of another person's tweet containing another photographer's image without authorization constituted the infringement of the photographer's right of paternity, on the ground that the author's name on the original image was not shown in the automatically cropped image incorporated in the retweet, although an inline hyperlinking in a retweet might not constitute an infringement of copyrights.[4]

1.2.2   Limitation

The right of paternity is subject to certain limitations, and it is provided that none of the following cases constitutes an infringement of the right of paternity.

Firstly, a person exploiting a work of an author may indicate the name of the author in the same manner as that already adopted by the author, in the absence of any declaration of the intention of the author to the contrary (Art. 19(2) of the JCA). It follows that a work already made public under the author's pseudonym (pen name) can be made available or offered to the public with an indication of that pseudonym without infringing on the author's right of paternity.

Secondly, it is permissible to omit the name of the author where it is found that there is no risk of damage to the interests of the author in the light of the purpose and the manner of exploitation and insofar as such omission is compatible with fair practice (Art. 19(3) of the JCA). For instance, where many works of music are played in a bar as background music, omission of the indication of the composer's name for each work is not construed as an infringement of the right of paternity.

Thirdly, where the head of an administrative agency, an independent administrative body, etc., or an organ of a local public entity is to offer or make available a work to the public under the relevant Information Disclosure Act, the author's name may be indicated in the manner already adopted by the author in respect of the work, or omitted, without infringing on the right of paternity (Art. 19(4) of the JCA).

---

[4]   Supreme Court, 21 July 2020, Case No. 1412 (ju) of 2018 [Retweet Case]. The translation is available at https://www.courts.go.jp/app/hanrei_en/detail?id=1776. *See also* Tatsuhiro Ueno, 'The Infringement of the Right of Attribution by "Retweet"', 71(1) GRUR Int. 60 (2012).

1.3   Right of Integrity (Art. 20)

1.3.1   Details

Article 20(1) of the JCA stipulates, '[t]he author of a work has the right to preserve the integrity of that work and its title, and is not to be made to suffer any alteration, cut, or other modification thereto that is contrary to the author's intention'. This means that the author can object to any modification of the work.

Article 20(1) of the JCA prohibits any modification against the author's intention or will. This means that the author may even proceed against modifications which enhance the value of the work.[5] For example, the unauthorized modification of a manuscript by a publisher constitutes an infringement of the right of integrity, even if the modification does not prejudice the author's honor or reputation.[6]

In this regard, Article 20(1) of the JCA goes beyond the standard set by Article 6*bis* of the Berne Convention,[7] which stipulates that 'the author shall have the right ... to object to any distortion, mutilation or other modification of, or other derogatory action in relation to, the said work, which would be prejudicial to his honor or reputation'. Hence, Article 20(1) of the JCA may also be regarded as a 'Berne plus' provision.[8]

1.3.2   Limitation

Article 20(2) of the JCA initially lists three specific provisions defining the types of modifications which do not constitute an infringement of the right of integrity (items (i) through (iii)) and additionally provides a general basket clause for 'other unavoidable modification' (item (iv)). In any of the following cases, modifications do not infringe the right of integrity.

Firstly, following the application of provisions on copyright exceptions, changes in ideographs or words or other modifications deemed unavoidable for the purpose of school education in the case of the exploitation of works in textbooks or the like or in the broadcasting of school education programs do not constitute an infringement of the right of integrity (Art. 20(2)(i) of the JCA). For instance, when a novel is to be included in an elementary school textbook, replacement of difficult words with simpler terms does not infringe on the right of integrity of the novelist.

Secondly, the modification of an architectural work by means of extension, rebuilding, repairing, or remodeling does not constitute an infringement of the right of integrity (Art. 20(2) (ii) of the JCA). For instance, modifying a dilapidated building for the purpose of repair would not constitute an infringement of the right of integrity. There is one precedent where the Court held that the relocation of a building onto the third floor of a newly erected building for the

---

5   *See* Tatsuhiro Ueno, 'Moral Rights in the Digital Network and "Cloud" Environment – Subjective or Objective Standard?' in Fabienne Brison and Séverine Dusollier (eds), *Moral Rights in the 21st Century: The Changing Role of the Moral Rights in an Era of Information Overload* (Bruylant Larcier, 2015) p. 216.

6   *See* Tokyo High Court, 19 December 1991, 1422 Hanrei-Jihô 123 [Hôsei University Case].

7   The Berne Convention for the Protection of Literary and Artistic Works (as amended on 28 September 1979).

8   *See* Ueno *supra* note 5 at 218–19.

purpose of maintaining the old structure did not infringe the right of integrity of the architect (Isamu Noguchi).[9]

Thirdly, a modification which is necessary for debugging or updating a computer program does not constitute an infringement of the right of integrity (Art. 20(2)(iii) of the JCA).

Fourthly, a modification which is considered unavoidable in the light of the nature of a work as well as the purpose and the manner of exploitation does not constitute an infringement of the right of integrity (Art. 20(2)(iv) of the JCA). This provision is intended to supplement the foregoing specific provisions (items (i) through (iii)) as a basket clause. For instance, failure to perfectly reproduce colors in publishing an illustration of a painting or to perfectly perform a work of music on account of the performer's immaturity does not constitute an infringement of the right of integrity. Although this provision had been restrictively applied in case law, it is flexibly applied for the purpose of striking a proper balance between the authors' moral rights and the interest of the public in recent court cases and the current major theories.[10]

1.4   Acts Deemed to Infringe on Moral Rights (Art. 113(11))

In addition to three moral rights, Article 113(11)[11] of the JCA stipulates, '[t]he exploitation of a work in a way that is prejudicial to the honor or reputation of the author is deemed to constitute an infringement of the author's moral rights'. It follows that, if an act which involves no modification of a work and would not otherwise infringe on the right of integrity is prejudicial to the honor or reputation of the author, the act will be deemed to infringe on moral rights. For instance, if an artistic nude photograph is reproduced for the billboard of a nude revue, or a very solemn work of religious music is played as background music in a brothel, the author's moral rights may be deemed to have been infringed.

There is a precedent where the Court held that the unauthorized posting to the Twitter of an image of drawing which a famous manga artist had drawn along with the misleading explanations concerning the political philosophy or ideological position of the manga artist constituted an infringement of his moral rights.[12]

The wording 'honor or reputation' is construed as the social reputation and honor of an author, meaning the objective evaluation by society of an author's personal values including character, virtue, reputation and trustworthiness.[13]

---

[9]   Tokyo District Court, 11 June 2003, 1840 Hanrei-Jihô 106 [Noguchi Room Case]. A translation is available at http://www.ip.courts.go.jp/app/files/hanrei_en/168/002168.pdf.

[10]   *See* Tatsuhiro Ueno, 'Chosakubutsu no kaihen to chosakushajinkakuken womeguru ichikôsatsu (1) (2)' [Modification of Works and Moral Rights: Suggestion from 'Balance of Interests' Approach in the German Copyright Law], (1999) 120-4/5 Minshôhôzasshi 748, 120-6 Minshôhôzasshi 925 (in Japanese).

[11]   This provision was first provided for as Article 113(2) in the original version of the JCA in 1970 and is currently Article 113(11) since 1 January 2021 (after the enactment of the 2018 Amendment).

[12]   *See* IP High Court, 11 December 2013, Case No. 24571 (wa) of 2012 [Majesty Project Case].

[13]   *See* Supreme Court, 30 May 1986, 40-4 Minshû 725 [Parody Case].

1.5   Posthumous Protection of Author's Personal Interests (Art. 60)

The JCA has no term of protection provided for moral rights. Since the moral rights are, however, provided to 'be personal and exclusive to the author' (Art. 59 of the JCA), they are understood to expire upon the death of the author.

Nevertheless, even after the author ceases to exist (dies if the author is a natural person or is liquidated if the author is a juridical person), no person who offers or makes available a work to the public 'may commit an act which would constitute an act of infringement of the moral rights of an author if the author were alive' (Art. 60 of the JCA).

Certain members of the author's bereaved family (the surviving spouse, children, parents, grandchildren, grandparents, brothers, and sisters of the deceased author) may make a demand for injunction against those who commit or are likely to commit such an act (Art. 116(1) of the JCA). The author may appoint a person who can make such demands on behalf of the bereaved family only in the author's will (Art. 116(3) of the JCA).[14]

In one precedent regarding a novel written by the defendant, who quoted undisclosed letters from the late Yukio Mishima, the famous novelist, addressed to the defendant, without authorization, the Court held that this was an act which would have infringed Yukio Mishima's right to make the works public, if he had still been alive.[15]

It is also provided, however, that 'this does not apply if that conduct is found not to contravene the will of the author in light of the nature and extent of the conduct as well as changes in social circumstances and other conditions' (the proviso to Art. 60 of the JCA). For instance, altering terminology to keep up with changes in the times, or the disclosure of a work in response to changes in socially accepted values will be permissible, if it is considered no longer prejudicial to the intent of the author.

An act in violation of Article 60 of the JCA is punishable as a criminal offense. A person who has prejudiced the moral interests of an author or a performer after the author or performer's death is punishable by a fine of up to 5 million Japanese Yen (JPY) (Art. 120 of the JCA).

1.6   Remedy: Demand for Apology (Art. 115)

As civil remedies, an author whose moral rights have been infringed may demand for injunction against the infringer (Art. 112(1) of the JCA) and claim damages against a person who has intentionally or negligently infringed the author's moral rights (Art. 709 of the Japanese Civil Code).

Additionally, it is unique under the JCA that an author whose moral rights have been infringed may demand for 'apology' as civil remedy. Article 115 of the JCA stipulates, '[t]he author or the performer may demand the person who has infringed his moral rights intentionally or negligently to take measures necessary to identify him as the author or the performer, to correct distortions, mutilations, or modifications or to recover his honor or reputation either in place of or together with indemnification of damages'.

---

14   There is a precedent where the Court rejected a claim on the ground that the Isamu Noguchi Foundation had not been appointed in the sense of Article 116(3) of the JCA. *See* Tokyo District Court, 11 June 2003, 1840 Hanrei-Jihô 106 [Noguchi Room Case]. Regarding the translation, *see supra* note 9.

15   *See* Tokyo High Court, 23 May 2000, 1725 Hanrei-Jihô 165 [Yukio Mishima Case]. A translation is available at http://www.ip.courts.go.jp/app/files/hanrei_en/997/001997.pdf.

According to precedent, the 'honor or reputation' in the context of this provision refers to social honor. Likewise, in order for a claim under Article 115 of the JCA to be upheld, it is not sufficient that merely the author's subjective sense of honor has been prejudiced; prejudice to the author's social honor is required.[16]

When an author's moral right has been infringed and the author's honor or reputation has been prejudiced, the author may demand for apology and thus the Court may order the infringer to make a publication of an apology in major newspapers. The demand for apology is also available in the case of defamation under Article 723 of the Japanese Civil Code, which stipulates that 'the court may order a person that has defamed another person to take appropriate measures to restore the reputation of the victim in lieu of or in addition to compensation for loss or damage, at the request of the victim'.

The following is the translation of one example of the publication of an apology in newspapers in the case where the Court ordered to the defendants who were a broadcast company etc., on the ground that the dramatization and broadcast without authorization of a novel created by the plaintiff infringed the right of integrity.[17]

BOX 22.1 PUBLICATION OF APOLOGY

To: Ms. Kimiko Tanaka

The TV drama 'Akusai Monogatari', which we produced and broadcasted between 9:00 pm and 9:54 pm on 9 February 1987, was unauthorized copy of the first episode 'Mezame' of the book 'Tsumatachi wa Garasunokutsu wo nugu' written by you and modified your work without your authorization. I hereby apologize for infringing your moral rights and for causing a tremendous inconvenience.

(date/month/year)

Susumu Kondo (producer & screenwriter)

IVS TV Production

TV Tokyo Corporation

It is true that a demand for 'apology' as civil remedy is not common and might sound strange to you or even unconstitutional in European countries. However, there had been some court cases in Japan, where the Court ordered the infringers of moral rights to make a publication of an apology in newspapers, although it should be noted that the Court very rarely admits the order to publish an apology in recent decades, even in the case where the author's social honor would be prejudiced.[18]

---

[16]   *See* Supreme Court, 30 May 1986, 40-4 Minshû 725 [Parody Case].
[17]   *See* Tokyo High Court, 16 April 1996, 28-2 Chizai-Saishû 271 [Akusai Monogatari Case].
[18]   *See in detail* Tatsuhiro Ueno, 'Mediation and Arbitration in Copyright Disputes' in Ysolde Gendreau (ed.), *Copyright in Action: International Perspectives on Remedies* (Éditions Thémis, 2019) pp. 392–5, 398.

2.   'MORAL RIGHTS' OWNED BY JURIDICAL PERSONS

Under the JCA, it is unique that moral rights shall be vested in not only natural persons as human creators but also juridical persons, since the authorship of a work can be attributed to juridical persons under the Japanese work-for-hire system.

2.1   Japanese Work-for-Hire (Art. 15)

The JCA defines an 'author' as 'a person who creates a work' (Art. 2(1)(ii) of the JCA) and provides that an 'author' shall enjoy the moral rights and copyrights (Art. 17(1) of the JCA). On the other hand, the JCA provides for a unique work-for-hire system (Art. 15 of the JCA), where the authorship of a work shall be attributed to employers including juridical persons.[19]

As a result, for instance, if a staff writer who is an employee at a newspaper company has written a news article in the course of the staff writer's duty, the authorship of the article is ascribed not to the staff writer who actually wrote the article but to the company under the Japanese work-for-hire system.

2.1.1   Requirements
Article 15(1) of the JCA stipulates:

> For a work (except a work of computer programming) that an employee of a corporation or other employers (hereinafter in this Article such a corporation or other employers are referred to as a 'corporation, etc.') makes in the course of duty at the initiative of the corporation, etc., and that the corporation, etc. makes public as a work of its own authorship, the author is the corporation, etc., so long as it is not stipulated otherwise in a contract, in employment rules, or elsewhere at the time the work is made.

Hence, the Japanese work-for-hire system is basically subject to the requirement (for any work except computer programs[20]) that a work is made public as a work of the employer's own authorship, in other words, under its own name as the author. Therefore, for instance, if a company makes a publicity brochure created by its employee and publishes it under the company's own name as the author, the authorship of the work shall be attributed to the company.

It should be noted that this requirement has been broadly construed in case law and according to the major theories.[21] As a result, even though a newspaper (bylined) article bears the name of an employee who actually wrote it, it can be regarded as not having been published by the newspaper company as a work under its own name, because this byline is not necessarily considered as the writer's personal identification of authorship, but merely an indication of in-house responsibility; and accordingly, the news article shall be regarded as being published

---

[19]   *See in detail* Ueno in Lewinski (ed.), *supra* note 1.
[20]   Article 15(2) of the JCA stipulates, '[f]or a work of computer programming that an employee of a corporation, etc. makes at the initiative of the corporation, etc. in the course of duty, the author is the corporation, etc., so long as it is not stipulated otherwise in a contract, in employment rules, or elsewhere at the time the work is made'.
[21]   *See* Moriyuki Kato, *Chosakukenhô Chikujôkôgi* [Commentary on the Copyright Act], (CRIC, 7th revised ed. 2021) pp. 153 (in Japanese). Regarding case law, *see e.g.* Tokyo District Court, 18 December 1995, 1567 Hanrei-Jihô 126 [Last Message in Saishûgô Case]; IP High Court, 4 August 2010, 2101 Hanrei-Jihô 119 [Kitami Kôgyô University Case].

under identification of authorship by the newspaper company, and, consequently, the authorship of the work shall be attributed to the newspaper company.

That means that the Japanese work-for-hire system has a wide application. In reality, a large number of works including most news articles, news photos, magazines, TV programs, video games, and character goods are considered as works-for-hire and thus the authorships of such works are attributed to the companies and, accordingly, not only economic rights but also moral rights are *ab initio* vested (not transferred[22]) in the companies who are the 'authors' under the JCA, while no rights of any kind are granted to the employee who actually creates the work.

2.1.2   Justification?

What is the justification for the Japanese work-for-hire system?

The record of the law-making process of the current JCA (1970) implies that the Japanese government decided to introduce the unique system, after exploring several foreign laws including the 'collective work' under French law (1957), the 'contract of service' under UK law (1956), the 'works made for hire' under US law (1909), the works-for-hire under Turkish law (1951), and so on.[23] There seems to be an idea that, when an employee creates a work which is to be published under the company's name as the author, the employee creates the work on behalf of the company, and, on the other hand, the company undertakes social responsibility for the work published under the company's name. Hence, it has been considered appropriate that moral rights shall be vested in the company for the purpose of guaranteeing its own 'non-economic' interests in relation to the work and that the company can invoke the moral rights on behalf of the employees.[24]

2.2   Court Cases on Juridical Persons' Moral Rights

It is true that not only Japan but also a few of other civil law countries, South Korea,[25] and the Netherlands,[26] provides for a similar work-for-hire system where the authorship shall be

---

[22]   Article 59 of the JCA provides for, 'moral rights are exclusive to that author, and are inalienable'.

[23]   *See in detail* Takakuni Yamane, Chosankukenhô 15 jô 1 kô womeguru Keifutekikôsatsu [Historical Examination on Article 15(1)], 39 Nihonkôgyôshoyûkenhôgakkainenpô 57 (2016).

[24]   *See* Kato *supra* note 21 at 152. *See also* the statement of Moriyuki Kato in (1997) 23 Chosakukenkenkyû 68 (in Japanese).

[25]   The South Korean Copyright Act (Act No. 432 of 28 January 1957) has a work-for-hire provision (Art. 9), which was originally modelled from Article 15 of the JCA. The translation of the Korean Copyright Act is available at https://wipolex.wipo.int/en/legislation/details/16953.

[26]   The Dutch Copyright Act (1912) provides for Article 7, which stipulates, '[w]here labour carried out by an employee consists in the making of certain literary, scientific or artistic works, the employer shall be deemed the author thereof, unless otherwise agreed between the parties', and Article 8, which stipulates, '[a] public institution, association, foundation or company which communicates a work to the public as its own, without naming any natural person as the author thereof, shall be regarded as the author of that work, unless it is proved that the communication to the public in such manner was unlawful'. The translation is available https://dutch-law.com/copyrightact.pdf. *See also* Jacqueline Seignette, *Challenges to Creator Doctrine, Authorship, Copyright Ownership* (Kluwer Law International, 1994) p. 45 (stating 'pragmatic mixture'); J. Seignette, 'Authorship, Copyright Ownership and Works made on Commission and under Employment', in Bernt Hugenholtz et al. (eds), *A Century of Dutch Copyright Law* (DeLex, 2012), p. 115.

attributed to employers including juridical persons and thus, theoretically speaking, not only economic rights but also moral rights can be vested in juridical persons. Nevertheless, it seems unlikely in practice that the Court upholds juridical persons' claim for injunction or awards damages for infringement of moral rights in these countries.

On the other hand, in Japan, it is normal that juridical persons as 'authors' invoke their moral rights. In fact, there are a number of court cases mainly relating to video game companies, book publishers, broadcast companies, and religious organizations, where the Court not only upheld the claim for injunction[27] but also awarded damages for infringement of moral rights owned by juridical persons to compensate for the 'non-economic' loss.[28] Table 22.1 shows the amount of damages for infringement of moral rights,[29] the rights infringed, and the plaintiffs as the 'authors' of such works. Among the cases mentioned in Table 22.1, this chapter introduces some cases in which the Court awarded damages for infringement of the companies' moral rights.

2.2.1 Tokimeki Memorial Case[30]

The Supreme Court held that the distribution of a memory card which contains data altering parameters defining the character constituted a tort (Art. 709 of the Japanese Civil Code) on the ground that the use of the memory card results in the development of the story of the game beyond its planned scope and thus constituted the infringement of the right of integrity.[31] The plaintiff in this case is not a human creator but a business company, whose 'moral rights' were infringed.

(a)   Facts
The plaintiff is a video game company (KONAMI) who created a computer game software titled 'Tokimeki Memorial', which is a dating simulation game, where a player becomes an imaginary high school student who over a period of three years makes accumulating efforts to acquire capabilities sufficient to earn a confession of love from the female high school student who is the target of his passions.

---

[27]   *See* Tokyo High Court, 26 May 1999, Case No. 5223 (ne) of 1998 [SMAP Daikenkenkyû Case]; Tokyo District Court, 30 August 1999, 1696 Hanrei-Jihô 145 [Dogimagi Imagination Case]; Tokyo High Court, 29 November 2004, Case No. 1464 (ne) of 2003 [Seikyô Graph Case]; IP High Court, 28 December 2007, Case No. 10049 (ne) of 2006 [HRD Textbook Case]; Tokyo District Court, 8 July 2010, Case No. 23051 (wa) of 2009 [Nyûmon Kampô Igaku Case]; Tokyo District Court, 26 March 2015, Case No. 19494 (wa) 2013 [Gensô Naming Jiten Case]; IP High Court, 28 May 2015, Case No. 10103 (ne) of 2014 [Kaichô Jisatsu Case].
[28]   *But see* the judgment of Tokyo District Court on 18 September 2019, Case No. 14843 (wa) of 2018 [Andante Case] which dismissed the claim for damages by the plaintiff (a company which sold music-related products) who claimed for compensation for the 'economic' loss caused by the infringement of the right of paternity, on the ground that the infringement of moral rights did not cause any economic loss.
[29]   JPY refers to Japanese Yen. 1 US dollar is roughly equivalent to about 100 JPY.
[30]   Supreme Court, 13 February 2001, 55-1 Minshû 87 [Tokimeki Memorial Case]. Regarding the translation, *see* https://www.courts.go.jp/app/hanrei_en/detail?id=1524. *See in detail* Tatsuhiro Ueno, 'Intellectual Property Liability of Consumers, Facilitators and Intermediaries: The Position in Japan', in Christopher Heath and Anselm Kamperman Sanders (ed.), *Intellectual Property Liability of Consumers, Facilitators and Intermediaries* (Kluwer Law International, 2012), p. 160.
[31]   After this decision, there is another court case concerning a fighting game software. *See* Tokyo High Court, 31 March 2004, 1864 Hanrei-Jihô 158 [Dead or Alive 2 Case].

Table 22.1   Cases awarding damages for infringement of juridical persons' moral rights

1	Tokyo District Court, 16 May 1995, 27–2 Chizai-Saishû 285 [Derujun Takken Case]	
	350,000 JPY	Right of paternity & right of integrity (a preparatory school which published a textbook)
2	Tokyo District Court, 25 June 1999, Case No. 20088 (wa) of 1998 [Chugakusei nimo Wakaru Case]	
	400,000 JPY	Right of integrity (a foundation which published a textbook)
3	Tokyo District Court, 30 August 1999, 1696 Hanrei-Jihô 145 [Dogimagi Imagination Case]	
	2,000,000 JPY	Right of integrity (a video game company)
4	Supreme Court, 13 February 2001, 55–1 Minshû 87 [Tokimeki Memorial Case][a]	
	1,000,000 JPY	Right of integrity (a video game company)
5	Tokyo High Court, 31 March 2004, 1864 Hanrei-Jihô 158 [Dead or Alive 2 Case]	
	2,000,000 JPY	Right of integrity (a video game company)
6	Tokyo High Court, 29 November 2004, Case No. 1464 (ne) of 2003 [Seikyô Graph Case]	
	500,000 JPY	Right of paternity & right of integrity (a religious organization which took a photo of the founder)
7	Tokyo District Court, 12 April 2007, Case No. 15024 (wa) of 2006 [Sôkagakkai Case][b]	
	50,000 JPY	Right of integrity (a religious organization which took a photo of the founder)
8	IP High Court, 28 December 2007, Case No. 10049 (ne) of 2006 [HRD Textbook Case]	
	100,000 JPY	Right of paternity & right of integrity (consulting companies which created a textbook)
9	Tokyo District Court, 18 April 2008, Case No. 26738 (wa) of 2006 [Network Basic Case]	
	500,000 JPY	Right of paternity & right of integrity (a technical expert training company which created a textbook)
10	Tokyo District Court, 25 June 2008, Case No. 33577 (wa) of 2007 [CCNP 100% Enrollment Guarantee Case][c]	
	500,000 JPY	Right of paternity (a technical expert training company which created a textbook)
11	Tokyo District Court, 8 July 2010, Case No. 23051 (wa) of 2009 [Nyûmon Kampô Igaku Case][d]	
	300,000 JPY	Right of integrity (a publishing company which published a textbook)
12	Tokyo District Court, 12 September 2014, Case Nos 29975 & 10544 (wa) of 2012 [Kaichô Jisatsu Case]	
	300,000 JPY	Right of paternity & right of integrity (newspaper publishing company)
13	Tokyo District Court, 29 January 2015, Case No. 8146 (wa) of 2013 [Kenkô Matsushita 21 Case]	
	50,000 JPY	Right of integrity (an advertising company which created a character)
14	Tokyo District Court, 26 March 2015, Case No. 19494 (wa) 2013 [Gensô Naming Jiten Case]	
	500,000 JPY	Right of paternity & right of integrity (a publishing company which published a dictionary)
15	IP High Court, 28 May 2015, Case No. 10103 (ne) of 2014 [Kaichô Jisatsu Case]	
	300,000 JPY	Right of paternity & right of integrity (a newspaper publishing company)
16	Tokyo District Court, 16 February 2016, Case No. 22603 (wa) of 2014 [KOHLER Catalog Case]	
	300,000 JPY	Right of paternity & right of integrity (an import agent company which published a product catalog)
17	Tokyo District Court, 4 March 2016, Case No. 37302 (wa) of 2015 [Sôkagakkai Case][e]	
	500,000 JPY	Right of integrity (a religious organization which took a photo of the founder)
18	Tokyo District Court, 21 February 2018, Case No. 37339 (wa) of 2016 [Urizun no Ame Case][f]	
	200,000 JPY	Right of paternity (a broadcast company which created a video film)
19	IP High Court, 23 August 2018, Case No. 10023 (ne) of 2018 [Urizun no Ame Case][g]	
	200,000 JPY	Right of paternity (a broadcast company which created a video film)
20	Tokyo District Court, 28 February 2019, Case No. 16958 (wa) of 2018 [Speed Leaning Case]	
	100,000 JPY	Right of integrity (a company which develops English materials)
21	IP High Court, 10 October 2019, Case No. 10028 (ne) of 2019 [Speed Leaning Case]	
	100,000 JPY	Right of integrity (a company which develops English materials)
22	Tokyo District Court, 23 April 2021, Case No. 27196 (wa) of 2020 [Sôkagakkai Case]	
	40,000 JPY	Right of integrity (a religious organization publishing newspapers)

Notes: [a] The translation is available at https://www.courts.go.jp/app/hanrei_en/detail?id=1524. [b] The translation is available at https://www.ip.courts.go.jp/app/files/hanrei_en/246/001246.pdf. [c] The translation is available at https://www.ip.courts.go.jp/app/files/hanrei_en/307/001307.pdf. [d] The translation is available at https://www.ip.courts.go.jp/app/files/hanrei_en/556/001556.pdf. [e] The translation is available at https://www.ip.courts.go.jp/app/files/hanrei_en/084/002084.pdf. [f] The translation is available at https://www.ip.courts.go.jp/app/files/hanrei_en/541/002541.pdf. [g] The translation is available at https://www.ip.courts.go.jp/app/files/hanrei_en/359/002359.pdf.

The defendant imported and sold a memory card titled 'X-TERMINATOR for PS Ver.2 Tokimemo Special' containing thirteen sets of high degree of parameters used in the plaintiff's video game (Blocks 1 to 13), and players could load the data into a block of their choice onto the game hardware and use it. If the data in Blocks 1 to 11 of the Memory Card is used, almost all the apparent parameters rise to an extremely high value immediately after the player enters high school and female high school students, who should not appear at this early stage, appear. Further, if the data in Blocks 12 and 13 is used, the game jumps to a point just prior to graduation when the game is started and at that point the parameter values are such that the player will definitely be able to obtain a confession of love from the female student of his dreams.

The plaintiff filed a lawsuit seeking damages on the grounds of an infringement of the right of integrity of the plaintiff's video game. After the Osaka High Court upheld the plaintiff's claim and awarded damages (1 million JPY) for infringement of the right of integrity,[32] the defendant appealed to the Supreme Court.

(b)   Findings
The Supreme Court dismissed the appeal holding as follows. The use of the memory card at issue is to modify the plaintiff's video game and infringes the right of integrity (Art. 20(1) of the JCA). This is because the parameters in the plaintiff's video game are the means by which a player expresses his personality and the story develops in accordance with changes in the same. The use of the memory card means that the player's personality, which is expressed through parameters authorized by the game software, is modified and, as a result, the storyline in the game software develops beyond the envisaged boundaries, bringing about a modification of the storyline.

The defendant imported and sold the memory card with the sole objective of modifying the game software and numerous people actually purchased the memory card with the same objective. This being the case, the defendant distributed the memory cards in the expectation that there would actually be people who would use them, and people presumably did actually purchase and use the memory cards. It follows that the right of integrity of the plaintiff's video game was infringed by the use of the memory card. If the defendant's acts had not taken place, the infringement of the plaintiff's right of integrity would never have taken place.

Accordingly, the defendant, who imported, sold and distributed the memory card envisaging others to use it, with the sole objective of modifying the game software, infringed the plaintiff's right of integrity through the users' use and should be held liable for damages to the plaintiff.

2.2.2   Gensô Naming Jiten Case[33]
The plaintiff is a publishing company who has published a book titled 'Gensô Naming Jiten', which is a dictionary containing 1,234 words and the (ten languages[34]) translations of each word and is helpful for fantasy authors who writes works of fantasy including fantasy novel, manga, video game, and animation in the naming of their characters.

---

[32]   Osaka High Court, 27 April 1999, 1700 Hanrei-Jihô 129.
[33]   Tokyo District Court, 26 March 2015, Case No. 19494 (wa) 2013 [Gensô Naming Jiten Case].
[34]   English, French, Italian, German, Spanish, Russian, Latin, Greek, Arabic, and Chinese.

On the other hand, the defendant published a book titled 'Gensô Sekai 11– Kakokugo Naming Jiten', which is a dictionary containing 1,213 words and the (11 languages[35]) translations of each word. The plaintiff filed a lawsuit seeking an injunction and damages on the grounds of an infringement of copyright and moral rights (the right of paternity and the right of integrity).

The Court upheld the plaintiff's claim, holding that the defendant had committed an infringement of the right of adaptation (Art. 27 of the JCA), the right of paternity (Art. 19 of the JCA) and the right of integrity (Art. 20 of the JCA) on the ground that the defendant's dictionary was substantially similar to the plaintiff's one which was regarded as a copyrighted work of compilation by reason of the selection or arrangement of its contents (Art. 12(1) of the JCA), and the defendant modified the title and the contents of the plaintiff's dictionary and the defendant's book did not bear the plaintiff's name (the company name). The Court upheld the plaintiff's claim for injunction and awarded damages (500,000 JPY) for infringement of moral rights in addition to damages for infringement of economic right, holding that the plaintiff has suffered non-economic damage by the defendant's modification of the title and contents of the plaintiff's dictionary against the plaintiff's will and by the failure to indicate the plaintiff's name in the defendant's book, and considering the extent of the defendant's modification and the number of copies sold of the defendant's book, it is reasonable to award 500,000 yen as damages to compensate for this damage.[36]

2.2.3   Nyûmon Kampôigaku Case[37]

The plaintiff is a publishing company in the field of medicine who has published a book titled 'Nyûmon Kanpôigaku' (meaning 'Introduction to Chinese medicine'). The plaintiff commissioned a design company A, who was not a party in this lawsuit, to make the design of the front cover of the plaintiff's book, which was created by an employee of the company A as work-for-hire. Hence, the company A is the 'author' of the design and transferred the copyright of the design to the plaintiff.

The defendant is another publishing company in the field of medicine who has published a book titled 'Nyûmon Shikatôyôigaku' (meaning 'Introduction to Oriental dental medicine') bearing another front cover.

The plaintiff filed a lawsuit seeking an injunction, damages, and apology on the grounds of an infringement of copyright and the right of integrity, in relation to the front cover. It is true that the author of the front cover of the plaintiff's book is not the plaintiff but the company A. However, under Article 118(1) of the JCA, in case of an anonymous or pseudonymous work, a publisher of the work who is not the author may demand for injunction, damages, and apology for infringement of moral rights of the work on behalf of the author.[38]

---

[35]   Portuguese was added to ten languages contained in the plaintiff's dictionary (*see supra* note 34).

[36]   The amount of damages for infringement of economic right is not disclosed, probably due to trade secret of the plaintiff.

[37]   Tokyo District Court, 8 July 2010, Case No. 23051 (wa) of 2009 [Nyûmon Kampôigaku Case]. Regarding the translation, *see* https://www.ip.courts.go.jp/app/files/hanrei_en/556/001556.pdf.

[38]   Article 118(1) of the JCA stipulates, '[t]he publisher of an anonymous or pseudonymous work may file the claim referred to in Article 112, Article 115, or Article 116, paragraph (1) or may claim damages or the return of the benefit of any unjust enrichment in that person's own name, on behalf of the author or the owner of the copyright to the work; provided, however, that this does not apply if the

The Court upheld the plaintiff's claim, holding that the defendant had committed an infringement of the right of adaptation (Art. 27 of the JCA), the right of transfer (Art. 26–2 of the JCA) and the right of integrity (Art. 20 of the JCA) on the ground that the front cover of the defendant's book was substantially similar to the front cover of the plaintiff's book, which was regarded as a copyrighted work, and the defendant modified the front cover. The Court upheld the plaintiff's claim for injunction and awarded damages (300,000 JPY) for infringement of moral rights in addition to damages for infringement of economic right (150,000 JPY), while it dismissed the plaintiff's claim for apology on the ground that the author's honor or reputation was not prejudiced.

3. CONSIDERATIONS

The above-mentioned Japanese unique 'moral rights' system and its practice might sound strange to you.[39] In fact, despite the lack of the explicit definition of 'author' in the Berne Convention, only the natural person who created the work can be 'author' in the meaning of the Convention according to the dominant theories.[40] Moreover, I guess that, if such system were to be introduced in Europe, it could perhaps be regarded as unconstitutional, because such employees who actually create works are deprived of not only economic rights but also moral rights under such system.[41]

In fact, not a few Japanese scholars have been criticizing the Japanese work-for-hire system that deprives a human author of the economic rights as well as moral rights and even the authorship.[42] However, realistically speaking, it seems unlikely for the Japanese government to revise the existing work-for-hire system for the time being, because it must be very much convenient for business companies in Japan and it seems that the Constitution of Japan is not

---

pseudonym is the name by which the author is commonly known or if the true name of the author has been registered as referred to in Article 75, paragraph (1)'.

[39] Regarding the basic concept of 'authorship' in international copyright law, *see* Jane C. Ginsburg, 'The Concept of Authorship in Comparative Copyright Law', 52 DePaul L. Rev. 1063 (2003); Tatiana Eleni Synodinou, 'Authorship in International Copyright Law', in Tatiana Eleni Synodinou (ed.), *Pluralism or Universalism in International Copyright Law*, (Kluwer Law International, 2019), p. 563.

[40] *See* WIPO Guide to the Copyright and Related Rights Treaties Administered by WIPO and Glossary of Copyright and Related Rights Terms (2004), p. 31; Sam Ricketson and Jane C. Ginsburg, *International Copyright and Neighbouring Rights: The Berne Convention and Beyond*, 2nd edition (Oxford, 2006), Vol. 1 p. 369; Sam Ricketson, 'People or Machines: The Berne Convention and the Changing Concept of Authorship', 16(1) Columbia-VLA Journal of Law and the Arts, 8, 11 (1991); Adolf Dietz, 'The Concept of Authorship under the Berne Convention', 155 Revue internationale du droit d'auteur (RIDA) 3, 16, 26 (1993); Silke von Lewinski, *International Copyright Law and Policy*, (Oxford University Press, 2008), p. 129.

[41] *See* Tatsuhiro Ueno, 'Jinken' toshiteno Chosakuken? [Copyright as 'Human Right'?], 722 Kopiraito 2 (2021) (in Japanese).

[42] *See e.g.* Masao Handa, *Chosakukenhôgaisetsu* (Hôgakushoin, 16th edition, 2015) p. 66; Tatsuki Shibuya, *Chosakukenhô* (Chûôkeizaisha, 2013) p. 112; Tatsuhiro Ueno, Kokusaishakai niokeru Nihon no Chosakukenhô: Creator-shikô Approach no Kanôsei [Japanese Copyright Law in International Society: Possibility of Creator-oriented Approach], 613 Kopiraito 2 (2012); Hisayoshi Yokoyama, Shokumujôsôsakusareru Sôsakubutsu no Kenri no Kizoku nitsuite [Ownership of Copyright of Works Made for Hire], 39 Nihonkôgyôshoyûkenhôgakkainenpô 200 et seq. (2015) (in Japanese).

capable of playing a strong enough role to guarantee the fundamental rights of human creators in Japanese legislation so far, unfortunately.[43]

I, nevertheless, am one of the critics against the Japanese work-for-hire system and do believe that it should be revised at least on a long-term basis for the purpose of guaranteeing the fundamental rights of human creators.

4.   CONCLUSION

Under the JCA, it is unique that moral rights shall be vested in not only natural persons as human creators but also juridical persons, since the authorship of a work can be attributed to juridical persons under the Japanese work-for-hire system, although the JCA basically adheres to the *droit d'auteur* system.

Moreover, there are many court cases in Japan where the Court not only upheld the claim for injunction but also awarded damages for infringement of juridical persons' moral rights to compensate for the 'non-economic' loss.

Such unique Japanese 'moral rights' might sound strange to you and could perhaps be regarded as unconstitutional in your jurisdictions. In fact, I am one of the critics against the Japanese work-for-hire system, although it seems unlikely for the Japanese government to revise the existing work-for-hire system for the time being. I hope that such unique Japanese 'moral rights' could be somehow meaningful for you.

---

[43]   *See in detail*, Ueno *supra* note 41 at 7 et seq.

23. Moral rights in China
Yong Wan

1.   INTRODUCTION

On 7 September 1990, the People's Republic of China promulgated its first Copyright Law (1990 Copyright Law), which entered into force on 1 June 1991. Out of question, the 1990 Copyright Law helped promote the creation and dissemination of works and fulfil China's aspirations for the growth of its economy.[1] However, after ten years since the enactment of the 1990 Copyright Law, significant social and economic changes had taken place in China[2] and in order to make the Chinese Copyright Law compliant with the Agreement on Trade-related Aspects of Intellectual Property Rights (TRIPs Agreement) to pave the way for China's accession to the World Trade Organization (WTO), in 2001, China amended the 1990 Copyright Law. Although the 2001 Amendment made significant changes to the 1990 Copyright Law, it did not touch upon the moral rights provisions. In 2010, the Copyright Law was revised in order to implement the WTO panel report's recommendations.[3] The scope of this revision was limited: only one article was revised, one article was added, and the provisions on moral rights remained unchanged.

China has acceded to a few international copyright conventions, including (but not limited to) the Berne Convention for the Protection of Literary and Artistic Works (Berne Convention), the TRIPs Agreement, the World Intellectual Property Organization (WIPO) Copyright Treaty (WCT) and the WIPO Performances and Phonograms Treaty (WPPT). In the international copyright treaties, specific moral rights provisions are only present in the Berne Convention (Article 6*bis*) and the WPPT Article. In the TRIPs Agreement, moral rights are explicitly excluded from that Agreement's scope. The WCT requires compliance with Article 6*bis* of the Berne Convention and specifies no additional protections.[4] Article 6*bis* of the Berne Convention recognizes two categories of moral rights: the right to claim authorship and the right to protect the integrity of the work. Since the Berne Convention and the WPPT adopts a minimum of protection, plenty of scope is left for each Contracting Party to give full rein to its conception of moral rights, provided that they apply the minimum standards required by the international conventions.[5] In this regard, the Berne Convention or the WPPT may affords generously worded guidance as to the interpretation of moral rights in national laws, the specific application and interpretation should be based on domestic statutory laws and case

[1]   Lulin Gao, "China's Intellectual Property System in Progress", in Frederick M. Abbott (ed.), *China in the World Trading System: Defining the Principles of Engagement* (Springer 1998) 127, 128.
[2]   Kangsheng Hu et al., *Zhonghua Renmin Gongheguo Zhuzuoquanfa Shiyi* (*Interpretations on the Copyright Law of the P. R. China*) (Law Press 2002) 2.
[3]   WTO, China-Measures Affecting the Protection and Enforcement of Intellectual Property Rights paras 7.145–7.192 (WT/DS362/R) (26 January 2009).
[4]   Sam Ricketson and Jane C. Ginsburg, *International Copyright and Neighboring Rights: The Berne Convention and Beyond* (2nd edn, Oxford University Press 2006) 619.
[5]   Ibid 231.

laws. As regards the moral rights system in China, it is difficult for the Western readers to understand, not only because the absence of the records of the conferences adopting and revising the Chinese Law, but also because the complex nature of the Copyright Law itself: China follows the *droit d'auteur* tradition, but also adopts the drafting technique of the common law countries, with the characteristics of socialist and developing countries.

The first article of the Chinese Copyright Law makes an express recognition that "this Law is enacted in accordance with the Constitutional Law", which means that China has adopted a positive law approach, under which moral rights and economic right are granted solely as a matter of statute. In this regard, the natural law justification for copyright protection is refused by China.[6]

It is understood that Article 47 of the Constitutional Law establishes a solid basis for the Copyright Law,[7] which provides as follows: "[t]he State encourages and assists creative endeavors conducive to the interests of the people that are made by citizens engaged in education, science, technology, literature, art and other cultural work". Along with Article 1 of the Copyright Law, which reflects the objectives of the Copyright Law, it may be said that the Copyright Law was crafted to "encourage the creation and dissemination of works which would contribute to the construction of socialist spiritual and material civilization", and to "promote the development and prosperity of the socialist culture and science".[8] In addition, it is also implied from Article 1 of the Chinese Copyright Law the need to maintain a balance between the rights of authors, related rightsholders and the larger public interest.[9]

From the above analysis, it is understood that China adopts the utilitarian justification for copyright protection, instead of natural law justification. It is interesting to note that, in principle, the natural law justification is the founding philosophy in the civil law countries and the utilitarian justification is adopted by the common law countries. On the other hand, Chinese lawyers take it for granted that China belongs to the civil law system and shall follow the *droit d'auteur* tradition.[10] This contradiction partly interprets some controversial provisions and ambiguities in the Copyright Law.

2.   THE NATURE OF MORAL RIGHTS IN CHINESE COPYRIGHT LAW

2.1   Dualism or Monism?

Moral rights and economic rights are treated as separate in France, which leads to the description of the French system of authorial protection as dualist. In contrast, a single author's right protects the author in relation to the personal interests in the work and the author's interests in

---

6   In fact, although the principle of national justice has always been a hot topic in Chinese literature, it has never been adopted by Chinese legislature or courts.

7   Muwen Song, "Report on the Draft of the Chinese Copyright Law (Draft)" (1990) 4 Zhonghua Renmin Gongheguo Quanguo Renmin Daibiao Dahui Changwu Weiyuanhui Gongbao 14, 14.

8   Copyright Law Art. 1.

9   Song (n 7) 16; Mingde Li and Chao Xu, *Zhuzuoquan Fa* (*Copyright Law*) (Law Press 2003) 10.

10   Hu et al. (n 2) 41.

the work's commercial exploitation in Germany, which leads to the description of the German system as monist.[11]

In the Chinese Copyright Law, the moral rights are generally perpetual and un-transferrable, while the economic rights are limited in time and transferable.[12] This separation is similar to the French system as dualism.

Since the theory of dualism is adopted, the question of ranking may arise. Although Article 10 mentions the moral rights firstly, it does not necessarily mean that the moral rights are pre-eminent in China. Different from the French Intellectual Property Code,[13] the Chinese Copyright Law, which insists on a reciprocity requirement, does not make a distinction between the moral rights and the economic rights for the protection of foreign works.[14]

2.2 Alienable or Inalienable?

2.2.1 Assignment

The 1990 Copyright Law is silent on the issue whether economic rights or moral rights can be transferred.[15] Some commentators argue that the assignment of moral rights is permissible since the Copyright Law does not specifically rule out assignment of moral rights.[16] Others are of the view that it means a simple and total assignment of the copyright, including the moral rights, is not possible.[17] In order to resolve this ambiguity, the 2001 Copyright Law expressly recognizes (only) the transferability of economic rights.[18] It flows from the *a contrario* principle that moral rights are not assignable. Some commentators are of the view that moral rights in China cannot be transferred *inter vivos nor mortis causa*.[19] The reason for this controversial conclusion seems to lie in the fact that these commentators misunderstood the moral rights as property rights which expire with the death of the person. In this author's opinion, the moral rights in China cannot be transferred *inter vivos*, but can be transferred upon the author's death. However, not all parts of the moral rights pass to the heirs; only the negative parts pass to the heirs.

---

[11] For a detailed analysis of French dualism and German monism, please see Adolf Dietz, "The Moral Right of the Author: Moral Rights and the Civil Law Countries" (1994–1995) 19 Columbia-VLA Journal of Law and the Arts 199, 206–13.

[12] Li and Xu (n 9) 71–2, 82–5.

[13] Code de la propriété intellectuelle [Intellectual Property Code] Art. L121-1, http://195.83.177.9/code/liste.phtml?lang=uk&c=36&r=2497 accessed 7 January 2020. In accordance with Art. L 111-4 of the French Intellectual Property Code, for the economic rights, French insists a reciprocity requirement, which will deny protection to foreign works if their country of origin does not provide adequate protection for French works. However, neither the integrity nor the authorship of such works may be impaired.

[14] Chinese Copyright Law Art. 2.

[15] It should be noted that the inalienable nature of moral rights was expressly recognized in the Statement of Muwen Song, the then Director of NCAC, before the Standing Committee of the National People's Congress (NPC). See Song (n 7) 18.

[16] Laijun Suo, "Zhuzuoquan Zhuanrang Zhiyi" ("Query the Validity of the Statement of the Transferability of Moral Rights") (1992) 5 Zhuzuoquan 28, 28.

[17] Zongshun Tang, *Zhuzuoquan Fa Yuanli* (*Principles of Copyright Law*) (Zhishichanquan Press 2005) 61.

[18] 2001 Copyright Law Art. 10(2).

[19] See Zhi Wei, *Zhuzuoquan Fa Yuanli* (*Principles of Copyright Law*) (Peking University Press 1998) 35.

2.2.2   Consent

It is always stated in the Copyright Law[20] and judgments[21] that the infringement has consisted in acting without authorization. Therefore, it seems that consent to an infringing act precludes infringement.

2.2.3   Waiver[22]

Although an author or a performer may consent to acts that would otherwise infringe his moral rights, it is not clear in the Chinese Copyright Law whether he can enter into an enforceable agreement not to change his mind in the future and seek a remedy for the infringement. In this author's opinion, a person may waive any benefit conferred upon him by statute, unless to do so would be contrary to public policy or is expressly or implicitly prevented by the statute creating the benefit. Since the Copyright Law does not explicitly forbid waiver of moral rights, waiver may be permissible, provided that it is not contrary to the public policy.

2.3   Perpetual or Definite?

Three of the moral rights – the rights of attribution, alteration and integrity – are granted an indefinite term of protection.[23] In contrast, the right of divulgation is dealt with separately, whose term of protection is the lifetime of the author plus 50 years, the same as that of economic rights, since this right also has a commercial nature.[24]

It should be noted that the Regulations on Computer Software Protection introduce an exception for the term of protection of moral rights in software, which is definite and the same as that of economic rights.[25] This specific norm, however, is consistent with the Article 6*bis*(2) Berne Convention, which establishes the basic principle that the duration of moral rights is to be for at least the duration of the economic rights.[26]

---

[20]   See e.g. 2001 Copyright Law Art. 46(1), (2).

[21]   See e.g. *Daxuesheng Magazine v. Beijing Jingxun Public Information Tech. Co., Ltd.*, Decision Document No. 18 Erzhongzhichuzi (The Second Intermediate Court of Beijing, 2000); *Jiahe Shen v. Beijing Publishing House*, Decision Document No. 77 Gaozhizhongzi (Beijing Higher Court, 2001); *Zhenyu Gu v. China Academic Journal Electronic Publishing House*, Decision Document No. 27898 Chaominchuzi (Chaoyang District Court of Beijing, 2008).

[22]   Waiver is different from consent in that the latter is short term and relates to a specific act, but the former is long term and does not necessarily relate to any particular acts. However, some commentators believe that such distinctions between waiver and consent are artificial, and whether the rights are retained or given up seems to be central to the distinction. See e.g., Elizabeth Adeney, *Moral Rights of Authors and Performers: An International and Comparative Analysis* (Oxford University Press 2006) 423–4.

[23]   2001 Copyright Law Art. 20.

[24]   Hu et al. (n 2) 93.

[25]   The term of protection for a natural person's software copyright shall be the lifetime of the natural person plus 50 years; in the case of joint authorship, the term shall be calculated according to the date of the death of the last surviving author. In the case of a legal person or other organization's software copyright, the term of protection shall be 50 years after the software is divulged for the first time, provided that any such software that has not been divulged within 50 years after the completion of its development shall no longer be protected under the Regulations. See Article 14(2), (3) of Regulations on Computer Software Protection.

[26]   Ricketson and Ginsburg (n 4) 610.

3. MORAL RIGHTS OF AUTHORS IN CHINESE COPYRIGHT LAW

The author is defined as the citizen who creates a work.[27] The term "citizen" in the provisions of the Copyright Law should be understood as a synonym of "natural person", extending also to a person without nationality.[28] Creation, the corresponding noun format of "create",[29] is defined as "intellectual activity from which literary, artistic and scientific works are directly derived".[30] In this regard, it seems that only natural persons can be authors in the Chinese Copyright Law, since no other entity is considered capable of intellectual activity. However, the controversial provisions of Article 11(3) of the Copyright Law make this issue complex.

In the case of a work created as representing the will of a legal person or other organization[31] (hereinafter legal entity) which directs and bears full responsibility for the work, such a legal entity is considered the author,[32] and such a work is called "*faren zuopin*" ("legal entity's work") in Chinese literature.[33] Under this circumstance, since the legal entity is considered the author, such an entity is entitled to all moral rights and economic rights.

In Chinese Copyright Law, authors enjoy four moral rights: right of divulgation, right of attribution, right of alteration and right of integrity.[34]

3.1 Right of Divulgation

The right of divulgation is defined as the right to decide whether the work in question should be made available to the public.[35] It should be noted that "divulgation" (*fabiao*) has been mistranslated as "publication".[36] In fact, "divulgation" is broader than the concept of "publication", since it can arise from the public performance, exhibition or broadcasting of the work.[37]

The definition does not expressly mention whether the author has the right to determine the manner of divulgation (for example, through publication or broadcasting). Some commentators argue that the right of divulgation covers the right to determine the manner of divulgation

---

[27] 2001 Copyright Law Art. 11(2).

[28] See Chuntian Liu, *Zhishichanquan Fa* (*Intellectual Property Law*) (RUC Press 2007) 117.

[29] In Chinese, there is no difference between the term "create" and its noun format "creation" as in the English language, which use the same characters "chuang zuo".

[30] Art. 3 of 2002 Implementing Regulations of the Copyright Law (hereinafter "2002 Implementing Regulations").

[31] Other organizations are those organizations not possessing legal personality but lawfully established and possessing certain organizational structure and property. They have the ability to enter into contracts and to conduct litigation, but they are not able to assume obligations independently. It means that if those organizations are unable to perform their legal obligations, the court may enforce their obligations against the assets of the legal or natural persons who undertake obligations to those organizations. See Art. 272 of the Supreme People's Court Opinions on Certain Questions Concerning the Application of the P. R. China Civil Procedure Law.

[32] 2001 Copyright Law Art. 11(3).

[33] Peter Feng, *Intellectual Property Law in China* (2nd edn, Sweet & Maxwell 2003) 19.

[34] 2010 Copyright Law Art. 10(1)(1)-(4).

[35] 2001 Copyright Law Art. 10(1)(1).

[36] Xue Hong, "China", in Paul Edward Geller (ed.), *International Copyright Law and Practice* (Lexis Nexis 2009) § 7[1][a].

[37] Tang (n 17) 64.

by implication under the Copyright Law.[38] The opposing view is that the protection provided by the right of divulgation in Chinese Copyright Law is narrower than that by other countries (e.g., France or Germany).[39] This ambiguity needs to be clarified, since it is related to the establishment of infringement. For example, if an author authorizes another person to divulge his/her work in traditional newspaper media, but such a person transmits the work via the internet. Does it constitute infringement of the right of divulgation? If the right of divulgation also includes the right to determine the manner of divulgation, the person in question infringes. If the answer is negative, the person does not infringe.

The right of divulgation may also be exercised by implication. It is submitted that, from the point of view of Article 18 of the 2001 Copyright Law, the transfer of the original of a work of fine art[40] will mean that the new owner is permitted to divulge the work.[41] It is also a usual practice in China that the divulgation right is exercised by implication when an author permits another to exploit the work in one of the ways provide for by the Copyright Law.[42]

In the case of a collaborative work of which the contributions of the authors are inseparable, any co-author may not invoke his rights to preclude other co-authors from using his contribution (excluding the transfer of his economic rights in his contribution) without his agreement, even his moral rights to control divulgation of his contribution.[43]

It should be noted that the right of divulgation is a negative right, not a right to have the work published or otherwise exploited. It does not allow an author to demand of another person that divulgation take place.[44]

3.2   Right of Attribution

Right of attribution means the right to claim authorship and to have the author's name mentioned in connection with the work.[45] This right has two facets: the author can not only claim recognition of his/her authorship, but also determine whether and how his/her name shall be affixed to the work (he/she can choose an artistic name, a pseudonym, or insist on anonymity).[46] To be unnamed does not mean waiver of the right of attribution. However, under this circumstance, the copyright, except the right of attribution, shall be exercised by the owner of the original of the work; the author can only exercise his/her copyright, after he/she discloses his/her identity.[47]

---

[38]   See e.g., Li and Xu (n 9) 74; Tang (n 17) 64.

[39]   See e.g., Chengsi Zheng and Michael Pendleton, *Copyright Law in China* (CCH International 1991) 89; Qian Wang, *Zhuzuoquan Fa (Copyright Law)* (PKU Press 2007) 72.

[40]   Works of fine art are two-dimensional or three-dimensional works created in lines, colours or other media which, when being viewed, impart aesthetic effect, such as works of painting, calligraphy and sculpture. See 2002 Implementing Regulations Art. 4(8).

[41]   Tang (n 17) 65.

[42]   Zheng and Pendleton (n 39) 89; Handong Wu et al., *Zhishichanquan Fa (Intellectual Property Law)* (2nd edn, Law Press 2007) 71.

[43]   See 2002 Implementing Regulations Art. 9.

[44]   *Lijun Xie v. Cixi-Zhongxing Network Information Media Co., Ltd.*, Decision Document No. 1005 Ciminerchuzi (Cixi District Court 2007).

[45]   2001 Copyright Law Art. 10(1)(2).

[46]   Tang (n 17) 65.

[47]   2002 Implementing Regulations Art. 13.

In most cases, this right operates where the work is issued to the public, or where it is commercially exploited (for example, the author must be named when the work is advertised[48] and the attribution must be made orally upon radio transmission of the work), and includes the right to be identified as the author of a work from which any adaptation is made (for example, the original author of a novel from which a dramatic work is derived must be named).[49] However, no credits are required if it is impractical and unreasonable to identify the author due to the special characteristic of the manner of the use of the work.[50]

It was one of the most passionately discussed issues, during the preparatory work of the 1990 Copyright Law, whether the right of attribution gives the author a right to object if his/her name is used in relation to a work that is not his/her own. There were two opposing views. The first one is that the right to object to the false attribution of authorship is not a moral right and should not be dealt with in the Copyright Law, since the false attribution of someone's work to another person does not require the latter to be the author of any work; it belongs to the right of name which has been included in the General Principles of the Civil Law.[51] The other is that false attribution should be regarded as violations of the moral right. At last, a compromise was adopted: on the one hand, the 1990 Copyright Law does not expressly recognize the attribution right as preventing false attribution; on the other hand, Article 46(7) of the 1990 Copyright Law states that making, selling a work of fine art[52] with the forged signature of another person should be regarded as an infringement of copyright.[53] However, such a compromise is questioned by some commentators, that there is no basis to regard the false attribution as an infringement under the Copyright Law without the incorporation of the right to object to false attribution into the right of attribution.[54]

In the first Chinese copyright case concerning false attribution: *Wu Guanzhong v. Duoyunxuan Company and Co.*,[55] it seems that the compromise was adopted by the courts of both first and second instances. The courts found that the law protected the right of citizens to claim authorship, and at the same time the law prohibited the making and selling of works of fine art with counterfeiting signature. However, in a number of subsequent cases, the Chinese courts expressly recognized that the right to prevent false attribution of authorship is covered by the attribution right.[56] Interestingly, a court found that the right to prevent false attribution is covered by the rights provided for in the open-ended clause in Article 10(1) (17) of the Copyright Law: "any other rights a copyright owner is entitle to enjoy", and the infringement liability under Article 47(8) of the 2001 Copyright Law (the counterpart of Art.

---

[48] *Jianliang Yao v. Shanghai Guanhe Industrial Co., Ltd.*, Decision Document No. 59 Huerzhongzhichuzi (The Second Intermediate Court of Shanghai 2001).

[49] Chengsi Zheng, *Banquan Fa* (*Copyright Law*) (2nd edn, RUC Press 1997) 144; Tang (n 17) 66.

[50] 2002 Implementing Regulations Art. 19.

[51] Civil Law Art. 99 states: "[c]itizens shall enjoy the right of personal name … usurpation of and false representation of personal names shall be prohibited".

[52] In 2001 Copyright Law Art. 47(8), the term "a work" replaces the term "a work of fine art" in 1990 Copyright Law Art. 46(7).

[53] Zheng and Pendleton (n 39) 90–1.

[54] See e.g., Wang (n 39) 77.

[55] *Guanzhong Wu v. Duoyuanxuan Company and Co.,* Decision Document No. 48 Hugaominzhongzi (Shanghai Higher Court, 1995).

[56] See e.g., *Guoping Zhou v. Zhou Ye & Shihua Li,* Decision Document No. 17913 Haiminchuzi (Haidian District Court of Beijing, 2005); *Han Han v. Suzhou Guwuxuan Publishing House and Co.,* Decision Document No. 15285 Erzhongminzhongzi (The Second Intermediate Court of Beijing, 2005).

46(7) of the 1990 Copyright Law) is derived from the infringement of the right provided for in Article 10(1)(17).[57] At first glance, it sees that this reasoning may establish a foundation for Article 47(8) of the 2001 Copyright Law to regard the false attribution as an infringement of copyright. Nevertheless, such a view is wrong, after Articles 10(2)[58] and (3)[59] are also read together, which state that the rights provided for in Article 10(1)(5)-(17) may be licensed and transferable. From this regard, it seems that although Article 10(1)(17) is open ended, it must be economic rights as the other rights provided for in Article 10(1)(5)-(16), thus excluding the right against false attribution. Even if the economic nature of the rights provided for in Article 10(1)(5)-(16) is neglected, since the right against false attribution is a negative right, the conclusion is also that it cannot be covered by Article 10(1)(17), otherwise it will conflict with Article 10(2). The judicial divergence from this view appears to be based on the compromise mentioned above: on the one hand, the Copyright Law does not expressly recognize the right against false attribution as a part of the attribution right; on the other hand, the false attribution is regarded as an infringement of copyright by that Law.

Another controversial issue is the question of how far contractual arrangements concerning not naming the real author but naming another person are enforceable and whether the attribution right can be waived. The Chinese Copyright Law explicitly forbids one who did not participate in the creation of the work to claim authorship.[60] In addition, a contract in violation of "the compulsory provisions of the laws and administrative regulations" is void.[61] However, a specific exception appear in the judicial interpretation: if a report, speech or other works drafted by other person but reviewed and finalized not by such other person and not published in the name of such other person, the copyright (including the attribution right) belong to the report maker or the speech maker.[62] Under such a circumstance, the waiver is deemed valid since the public is aware that the work is always a compilation by anonymous authors (in other words, "the object of the waiver is not deception of the public"[63]). If the waiver has the deception of the public as its sole object (for example, in an academic thesis written for others), the waiver will be void.[64] It seems that the Chinese Law does not prohibit the waiver of the attribution right in general; the validity of the waiver must depend on the public interest case by case. In fact, the Chinese practice allows waiver within certain limits, determined partly by reasonable usage and partly by a balancing of interests.[65]

---

[57] *Feng Jiang v. Guangdong University of Finance,* Decision Document No. 241 Suizhongfaminsanzhichuzi (Guangzhou Intermediate Court, 2005).

[58] 2001 Copyright Law Art. 10(2) states that "[a] copyright owner may license another person to exercise the rights under the preceding paragraphs (5) to (17), and receive remuneration pursuant to an agreement of this Law".

[59] 2001 Copyright Law Art. 10(3) states that "[a] copyright owner may assign, in part or in whole, the rights under the preceding paragraphs (5) to (17), and receive remuneration pursuant to an agreement of this Law".

[60] 2001 Copyright Law Art. 13(1), 46(3).

[61] Art. 52(5) of Contract Law of P. R. China.

[62] Art. 13 of Interpretation by the Supreme Court of Several Issues Relating to Application of Law to Trial of Copyright Cases (2002).

[63] Martin A. Roeder, "The Doctrine of Moral Right: A Study in the Law of Artists, Authors and Creators" (1940) 53 Harvard Law Review 554, 564–5.

[64] Ibid 565.

[65] Zheng (n 49) 280–1.

It is not clear whether the attribution right entitles the anonymous or pseudonymous author to prevent a third party from disclosing the author's real name. However, some commentators hold that the answer is positive.[66]

In the case of reproductions of the work statutorily permitted (for example, where the work is quoted or where the work is reproduced for teaching purpose), the source of the reproduction is to be named, including the name of the author.[67] In other words, the acts covered by the free use or the statutory licence for which the right of attribution is also to be respected. In China, some commentators argue that in such a case, there is still an obligation to mention the source. In this author's opinion, under such a circumstance, the obligation shall disappear after the user makes reasonable efforts to ascertain the name of the author but fails.

3.3   Right of Alteration

This right provides an author with the right to alter or authorize others to alter his/her work.[68] It seems that this right is quite a unique one, which is absent in the Berne Convention and many countries' copyright laws.[69] From the above definition, it appears as a right to preserve the work's integrity, thus overlapping with the right of integrity provided for in Article 10(1)(4) of the Copyright Law. In fact, most commentators regard this right as redundant.[70] However, some commentators interpreted this right as a quasi-right of withdrawal in the sense that this right enables an author to sue a publisher if the publisher reprints the work and objects to the author amending the original edition where the copies of the first edition of the work are sold out and the author hopes to update the original edition or make other amendments before reprints.[71] Nevertheless, the practice in China does not support this interpretation.[72] It is of interest to note that several courts in China interpret the right of alteration as the right to have the work maintained in a physically undistorted form (and interpret the right of integrity as the right not to have the spirit of the work impaired) (the right of integrity will be discussed below in detail (Section 3.4)).[73] In relation to literary works, a question may arise: whether alterations to the title infringe the right of alteration? One court held that this right is violated since the title is a part of the work.[74] However, another court found that such an act does not constitute infringement of the alteration right, since the title cannot be classified as a literary work in its

---

[66]   See e.g., Wang (n 39) 75.

[67]   See 2001 Copyright Law Arts 22, 23, 32.

[68]   2001 Copyright Law Art. 10(1)(3).

[69]   Zheng and Pendleton (n 39) 90–1; Peter Ganea et al., *Intellectual Property in China* (Kluwer Law International 2005) 237.

[70]   See e.g., Wang (n 39) 79; Chen Li, "Beiwudude Xiugaiquan" ("The Misunderstood Attribution Right") (2004) 78 China Patent & Trademarks 69, 69.

[71]   Zheng and Pendleton (n 39) 91–2; Zheng (n 49) 147–50; Li and Xu (n 9) 79–80.

[72]   Feng (n 33) 118.

[73]   See e.g., *Deheng Yang v. Beijing Wentelai Hotel Co., Ltd.* Decision Document No. 12 Erzhongminzhongzi (The Second Intermediate Court of Beijing, 2009); *Guo Chen v. People's Education Publishing House,* Decision Document No. 11715 Haiminchuzi (Haidian District Court of Beijing, 2008).

[74]   *Guo Chen v. People's Education Publishing House* (n 73).

own right, thus excluded from copyright protection, and alterations to the title do not constitute infringement of the alteration right.[75]

It should be noted that there are several statutory limitations on the alteration right. Firstly, in the case of a work submitted to a newspaper or periodical publisher, such a publisher may make editorial modifications and abridgements in the work in question, but shall not make modifications in the substantial content of the work.[76] Secondly, an author, who has authorized others to make cinematographic works to which are assimilated works expressed by a process analogous to cinematography, can prohibit only (gross) distortions or mutilations of his/her work.[77]

3.4   Right of Integrity

Right of integrity is defined as the right to object to any distortion or mutilation of the work.[78] Unlike Article 6*bis* of the Berne Convention, the integrity right in Chinese Copyright Law is expressed in a more absolute way since there is no express requirement that the honour or reputation of the author be prejudiced. The lack of prejudice to the authors in the wording of the Copyright Law has led to uncertainty and a substantial divergence in the practical application of the right of integrity. Some courts found that a prejudice to the author's honour or reputation should not be deemed a prerequisite for infringement of the right of integrity, while it could be an important factor when determining the resulting damages. Consequently, the courts determine whether the effect of the act is to betray the spirit or denature the ethic of the work.[79] However, some courts are of the view that this element is implied in the Chinese Copyright Law that the right of integrity is only confined to control prejudicial distortion or mutilation of an author's reputation.[80]

Compared with Article 6*bis* of the Berne Convention, the provisions of the Chinese Law also miss the words "other derogatory action in relation to (the said work)". These words were added at the 1948 Brussels Revision Conference,[81] since it was felt that distortion, mutilation and modification were insufficiently inclusive. The rights of the author could be infringed by actions that did not involve any change to the work at all, but elements surrounding the work cause a prejudicial effect to the author (for example, when the work is placed in a milieu

---

[75]   *Bibo Jiang v. Sichuan Fine Arts Institute*, Decision Document No. 342 Yuyizhongminchuzi (The First Intermediate Court of Chongqing 2001).

[76]   2001 Copyright Law Art. 33.

[77]   2002 Implementing Regulations Art. 10.

[78]   2001 Copyright Law Art. 10(1)(4).

[79]   See e.g., *Deheng Yang v. Beijing Wentelai Hotel Co., Ltd.*, Decision Document No. 12 Erzhongminzhongzi (2009) (The Second Intermediate Court of Beijing); *Ruyun Ding v. Wuxi Daily*, Decision Document No. 0123 Suminsanzhongzi (Jiangsu Higher Court, 2005).

[80]   See e.g., *Muye Zhang v. China Film Co. Ltd et. al.*, No. 83 Minchu (2016) (Xicheng District Court of Beijing).

[81]   In the original Rome version, the right of integrity read as follows: [the right] "to object to any distortion, mutilation or other modification of the said work, which would be prejudicial to his honour or reputation". See Ricketson and Ginsburg (n 4) 592; WIPO, *Guide to the Copyright and Related Rights Treaties Administered by WIPO and Glossary of Copyright and Related Rights Terms* (WIPO Publication 2004) 44.

which is not that which the author would desire for it).[82] After the inclusion of the new phrase, it was clarified that "the protection of honour and reputation should extend not only to the honour and reputation of the author as an author, but also to his/her honour and reputation as a human being".[83] In this regard, it seems that the scope of the right of integrity provided for in the Chinese Law is narrower than the Berne Convention. However, some Chinese courts interpreted the integrity right more broadly to cover contextual modifications in addition to actual modification, and found the following acts infringed the integrity right: the publication of a book with an offensive cover and the performance of a musical work in a teasing tune.[84] Nevertheless, there are also courts refusing to interpret the integrity right in such a broader manner.[85]

It is uncertain (once a work has been divulged) whether parody is tolerated; if such a parody is intended to criticize an author's work, then almost an author's honour or reputation is at stake. This issue has never been dealt with by statutes nor by case law. In fact, parody is an important genre of literature and arts, which always "adds something new, with a further purpose or different character, altering ... with new expression, meaning or message" the original work,[86] and thus furthers the goal of the Copyright Law to promote the development and prosperity of the culture and science, and thus shall be exempted from the infringement of the integrity right, provided that no confusion should arise between the parody and the original work.

4. MORAL RIGHTS OF PERFORMERS IN CHINESE COPYRIGHT LAW

In Chinese Copyright Law, performers' rights are a category of "rights related to copyright".[87] "Rights related to copyright" means the rights enjoyed by publishers in the typographical design of their publications, the rights enjoyed by performers in their performances, the rights enjoyed by the producers of sound and video recordings in their respective recordings and the rights enjoyed by radio and television broadcasters in their broadcasts.[88] In all of the rights related to copyright, only performers' rights include moral rights.

Performers are actors, performing organizations or other persons who perform literary or artistic works.[89] It is a curious provision to include "performing organizations" under the coverage of the definition of performers, since Article 37(1) and (2) grants performers the "right to claim performership" and the "right of respect", which can only be enjoyed by natural persons,

---

[82] Adeney (n 22) 136; Thomas Heide, "Reinterpreting the Right of Integrity under Article 6bis of the Berne Convention" (1997) 31 Copyright Bulletin 5, 7.
[83] WIPO (n 81) 45.
[84] Wei (n 19) 62–3.
[85] See e.g., *Shanghai Weicali Machine Knives Co., Ltd., v. Shanghai Zhan Shi Machinery Blades Ltd.*, Decision Document No. 301 Huerzhongminwu(zhi)chuzi (The Second Intermediate Court of Shanghai, 2006).
[86] *Campbell v. Acuff-Rose Music, Inc.*, 510 U.S. 569, 579 (1994).
[87] In China, the term "neighboring rights" is commonly used in academic circles, not used in the Copyright Law.
[88] See Art. 26 of the 2013 Implementing Regulations of the Copyright Law of P. R. China.
[89] 2002 Implementing Regulations Art. 5(6).

instead of legal persons as "performing organizations". The reason for this mistake, from this author's opinion, is that the drafters misunderstood the difference between the rightsholders and the representatives who can claim rights on behalf of rightsholders.

The WPPT is the first multilateral treaty on moral rights of performers.[90] Article 5(1) WPPT obliges Contracting Parties to provide for performers the right to claim performership[91] and the right of integrity.[92] However, the moral rights are limited to apply in respect of live aural performances or performances fixed in phonograms. Article 37(1) of the Copyright Law provides that a performer has the right to claim to be identified as the performer of his performances. In Chinese Copyright Law, performance extends to audiovisual performances. In this regard, the scope of moral rights of performers in Chinese Copyright Law is broader than that under the WPPT. In addition, compared with Article 5 of the WPPT, we can find that the Chinese Copyright Law misses the phrase "except where omission is dictated by the manner of use of the performance". It is not clear whether the performers' names must always be indicated even if the manner of use of the performance makes this impossible or at least highly impractical.

Article 37(2) grants a performer the right to prevent distortions of the image inherent in the performance. This provision is criticized by some commentators, since the right of respect under this provision is not confined to distortions prejudicial to a performer's reputation, and consequently it "goes far beyond the standards set by the majority of foreign laws and by Article 5(1) of the WPPT".[93] However, some commentators are of the view that it is implied in the 2001 Copyright Law that the right of respect is only confined to control prejudicial distortion of a performer's reputation.[94]

5.   LATEST DEVELOPMENTS

It is understood that certain gaps and ambiguities exist in the moral rights provisions of the Chinese Copyright Law. Many Chinese lawyers noticed this problem and some lawyers suggested to improve the moral rights provisions by the opportunity of the amendment of the Copyright Law.[95]

---

[90]   Jorg Reinbothe and Silke von Lewinski, *The WIPO Treaties 1996: The WIPO Copyright Treaty and the WIPO Performances and Phonograms Treaty: Commentary and Legal Analysis* (Butterworths 2002) 294.

[91]   The right to claim performership is the right "to claim to be identified as the performer of his performances". The exception to this right exists in the circumstances where the omission of names is "dictated by the manner of the use of the performance". See Art. 5(1) of the WPPT.

[92]   The right of integrity is the right to object to any distortion, mutilation or other modification of the performance that would be prejudicial to the performer's reputation. See Art. 5(1) of the WPPT.

[93]   Ganea et al., (n 69) 261.

[94]   Li and Xu (n 9) 188.

[95]   On 13 July 2011, the 3rd Revision of the Copyright Law was launched. It was believed that this revision will make substantial revisions on the Copyright Law. Mingfang Lai, "The 3rd Revision of the Copyright Law Commenced", http://www.ncac.gov.cn/cms/html/309/3517/201107/737276.html accessed 7 January 2020.

5.1   Draft Amendments of the Copyright Law

On 31 March[96] and 6 July[97] 2012, the National Copyright Administration of the Peoples Republic of China (NCAC) released the First and Second Draft Amendment of the Copyright Law for public comments respectively. On 6 June 2014, the State Council Legislative Affairs Office (SCLAO) released the Revised Draft.[98] Since then, there was no substantial progress in the process of legal revision of the Copyright Law.

The three drafts do not make any change to the moral rights of performers. In contrast, there are substantive changes in the moral rights of authors. Since the three drafts contained practically identical provisions on the moral rights of authors, although there are minor changes in the wording, the following will discuss the substantive changes together. Under the drafts, the right of divulgation of an author is extended to cover the right to determine the manner of divulgation; in the current Chinese Copyright Law, the right of divulgation is only the right to determine whether or not to divulge. As regards the right of alteration, it is deleted and the substantive content of the right of alteration is incorporated into the right of integrity, in order to avoid any overlap with the right of integrity that adversely affects the clarity of the law.

5.2   Guidelines Issued by Beijing Higher Court

The Guidelines or Guiding Opinions issued by a Higher Court have no *de jure* binding effect, but *de facto* binding effect on the basic and intermediate courts and the Higher Court of the province or the municipality directly under the Central Government where the Higher Court is located.[99] Since Beijing is the capital of China, Beijing Higher Court has played a very important role in the Chinese intellectual property (IP) legal system. In 2018, Beijing Higher Court issued the Guidelines for the Trial of Copyright Infringement Cases (hereinafter "Guidelines"). The Guidelines make certain necessary clarifications in the interpretation of moral rights.

Despite the absence of specific provisions concerning the issue on the exhaustion of the divulgation right in the Copyright Law, it is agreed among the lawyers that once the author has exercised the right and divulgation has taken place, the right is exhausted.[100] In practice, the controversial issue is whether the right of divulgation will be exhausted if the work is divulged without the author's consent. The Guidelines give the answer: yes.[101]

---

[96]   NCAC, "Circular on Solicitation of Public Comments on the Draft Amendment of the Copyright Law", http://www.ncac.gov.cn/cms/html/309/3502/201203/740608.html accessed 7 January 2020.

[97]   NCAC, "Circular on Solicitation of Public Comments on the Second Draft Amendment of the Copyright Law", http://www.ncac.gov.cn/cms/html/309/3502/201207/759779.html accessed 7 January 2020.

[98]   SCLAO, "Circular on Solicitation of Public Comments on the Revised Draft Amendment of the Copyright Law", http://www.chinalaw.gov.cn/article/cazjgg/201406/20140600396188.shtml accessed 7 January 2020.

[99]   Although China adopts a two-tier trial system, there are four levels of courts in China: Basic courts, Intermediate courts, Higher courts and Supreme Court. A Higher court is the highest court in a province (for example, Anhui Province, Hubei Province) or a municipality directly under the Central Government (for example, Beijing, Shanghai).

[100]   See e.g., Tang (n 17) 64; Wu (n 42) 71; Li and Xu (n 9) 74; *Yunfeng Liang v. Zhongshan Wanglong Computer Co., Ltd.*, Decision Document No. 219 Yuegaofaminsanzhongzi (Guangdong Higher Court, 2007).

[101]   See Point 4.3 of the Guidelines.

In *Muye Zhang v. China Film Co. Ltd et al.*, Beijing Intellectual Property Court found that the right of adaptation is an economic right, while the right of integrity is a moral right, which is supposed to be independent of the transfer of one's own economic rights. Thus, whether economic rights are transferred or not does not affect the scope of an author's right of integrity.[102] However, the Guidelines take the opposite view: if an author has assigned or licensed the copyright in his/her work to another person, the user may make reasonable modifications to the work according to the nature, purpose and method of the use of the work.[103]

The Guidelines enumerate the following elements in deciding whether the right of integrity is infringed or not: (1) whether the defendant has been authorized to use the work; (2) the degree of modification to the work by the defendant; and (3) whether the act of the defendant has caused damages to the work or the author's reputation.[104]

As regards the moral rights of performers, the Guidelines recognize the following methods as claiming performer status: (1) a performer's name is set out on the performance advertisement, bulletin board, programme schedule or stage photos published on the relevant publication; (2) a performer's name is introduced by the host before or after his/her performance; (3) a performer's name is broadcast by the radio or TV station; or (4) a performer's name is indicated in the captions on the screen.[105]

---

[102]   *Muye Zhang v. China Film Co. Ltd et. al.*, Decision Document No. 587 Minzhong (Beijing Intellectual Property Court, 2016).
[103]   Point 4.8 of the Guidelines.
[104]   Point 4.8 of the Guidelines.
[105]   Point 6.1 of the Guidelines.

24. A reinforced protection for the constitutional fundamental right to authors' moral rights in Latin America

Jhonny Antonio Pabón Cadavid

From Mexico to Chilean and Argentinian Patagonia, including countries in the Caribbean such as Cuba and the Dominican Republic, Latin America extends as a political and historical construction of nations and territories that share a colonial history, a common linguistic cultural heritage (mainly the Castilian/Spanish language, and Portuguese in Brazil), the influence of the Catholic religion and a legal tradition of constant confluence and dialogue. The objective of this chapter is to highlight some characteristics of authors' moral rights in Latin America. The first section of this chapter explores how moral copyright in Latin America is framed by the strong influence of French and Spanish legislation and jurisprudence on the intellectual property system implemented in these nations. Each Latin American country has legal, political, and economic peculiarities so it would be inaccurate to speak of a uniform system of moral rights in the region. However, there are multiple elements in common in the ways that moral rights of authors are enshrined and protected in this region. The second section of the chapter explores the copyright legislation of the Andean Community (Andean Decision 351 of 1993) to which Colombia, Peru, Ecuador, and Bolivia belong. The Andean legislation recognizes the moral right of disclosure, the right of integrity, and the right of paternity. In addition, it established that moral rights are perpetual and that each country can recognize protection for other moral rights. The third section of this chapter analyses authors' moral rights in Colombia from a constitutional perspective. In Colombia, the Constitutional Court has declared moral rights as fundamental rights, providing a special legal status to these rights. Furthermore, the Court has understood that international norms relating to moral rights are part of the constitutional block. In this context, the third section explores different decisions from the Constitutional Court and from the Supreme Court dealing with the relationship between authors' moral rights and children's rights, the constitutional analysis for establishing exceptions to authors' moral rights, the relationship between freedom of expression and moral rights, and the moral rights protection by criminal law. The chapter ends with a series of conclusions.

1. AUTHORS' RIGHTS IN LATIN AMERICA

Authors' rights in Latin America are especially influenced by the Spanish and French legal traditions. The new republics of Latin America started gaining independence from the Spanish Empire from 1811. The political constitutions of the new countries included provisions relating to granting privileges to the creators of literary and artistic works.[1] With the Chilean legislation of 1834 the protection of literary property began in the region by following French post-revolutionary legislation.[2] By the end of the nineteenth century most of Latin American countries had laws for literary and artistic property following the European discussions regarding these rights in natural law. Mexico for example in 1870, inspired by some of the radical French stances on natural law, established the perpetuity of authors' rights.[3] The Spanish copyright legislation of 1879 would become influential for Latin American countries, for example, the Colombian legislation of 1886 copied much of it, including the term of protection of 80 years *post mortem auctoris*.[4]

First, provisions in the nineteenth century related to authors' moral rights punished fraudulent reproduction, specifically linked to the rights of integrity and paternity. For example, the Colombian literary property law of 1886 enacted as an aggravating criminal factor the importation of illegal works when the text had been adulterated and other changes made maliciously to the detriment of the author.[5] Likewise, in the same law, in a provision that mixes authors' rights and patents, it was an offence when a person claimed as their own a method or system invented by another. The law refers to the author having the right to go to court and obtain a ruling "that his name be cited, and the honour of the invention be returned to him".[6]

International law in Latin America recognized authors' moral rights from the first half of the twentieth century. In 1910 in Buenos Aires (Argentina) during the Fourth American International Conference, various Latin American countries signed the Convention on Literary and Artistic Property,[7] whose purpose was to create a multilateral intellectual property treaty at the continental level. At the Sixth American International Conference of 1928 in Havana (Cuba) the protection of moral rights was incorporated explicitly in the Literary Property Convention. Article 13*bis* established that the authors of literary and artistic works have an inalienable right to oppose any reproduction or public exhibition of their works when they are altered, mutilated, or modified.[8]

Spanish speaking Latin American countries only began to sign the Berne Convention in the second half of the twentieth century, unlike Brazil which signed the Berne Convention in 1922.[9] Mexico and Uruguay were the first to sign it in 1967 and in the following years other Latin American countries followed. They are currently signatories to the main intellectual property treaties, and to human rights instruments, implementing the obligations of the Berne

---

[1]   See Jorge Mahú, "Apuntes sobre la evolución histórica del derecho de autor en América Latina (desde la perspectiva de las normas constitucionales)", Seminario Conmemorativo de los 120 años de la Dirección Nacional de Derecho de Autor sobre el TLC y el Derecho de Autor, (29 November – 1 December 2006). Bogotá, Pontificia Universidad Javeriana.

[2]   Law of Literary Property, 1834 (Chile).

[3]   Civil Code, 1870 (Mexico).

[4]   Article 15, Law 32 of 1886 (Colombia).

[5]   Article 67, Law 32 of 1886 (Colombia).

[6]   Article 71, Law 32 of 1886 (Colombia).

[7]   Argentina, Brazil, Chile, Colombia, Costa Rica, Cuba, República Dominicana, Ecuador, Guatemala, Haiti, Honduras, Mexico, Nicaragua, Panama, Paraguay, Peru, El Salvador, Uruguay, Venezuela.

[8]   Convención de Buenos Aires sobre protección a la propiedad literaria y artística, revisada por la Sexta Conferencia Internacional Americana (Sexta Conferencia Internacional Americana, La Habana, 1928).

[9]   Decree 4541, 6 February 1922 (Brazil).

Convention for moral rights and develops a framework of robust authors' moral rights following European civil law.

In recent years, the strong tradition of civil law on authors' rights in Latin America has been confronted by the increasing influence of the Anglo copyright system. Free trade agreements signed between the United States and Latin American countries have accelerated the convergence of legal traditions, incorporating legal innovations for Latin America intellectual property, for example in statutory damages. Furthermore, in the context of globalized education, it is common for Latin American lawyers to carry out their postgraduate education in intellectual property in English-speaking countries, which is gradually having effects on the legal culture of the region. However, authors' moral rights have been strengthened, as we will analyse in the final part of this chapter regarding the constitutional development in Colombia. To get there, next, let us study the moral rights of authors in the Andean Community.

2. GENERAL VIEW OF MORAL COPYRIGHT IN THE ANDEAN COMMUNITY

The Cartagena Agreement of 1969 created the Andean Community as a block for economic integration and regional development. The Andean Community is a legal political transplant of the European Community and similarly has a Court of Justice that produces preliminary interpretations.[10] The Andean Community nowadays consists of Colombia, Peru, Bolivia, and Ecuador. The Cartagena Agreement made explicit mention of the creation of one regional common framework for trademarks, patents, licences, and royalties.[11] No reference was made to copyright, so while in 1970 the first regional industrial property provisions were enacted,[12] it was not until 1993 that a regional copyright and related rights regime was created.[13]

Decision 351 of 1993 established a detailed copyright framework for the region. Chapter IV of the Decision is dedicated to moral rights. It recognizes the right of paternity, the right of disclosure, and the right to integrity. Each country can legislate extending the rights and developing in detail the regional legislation. Article 12 of Decision 351 recognizes that domestic law of the Andean Community countries may enact additional moral rights different to the ones granted by the regional legislation.

2.1 Perpetuity of Moral Rights

The regional legislation adopts a dualistic model of rights, enacting the perpetuity of authors' moral rights. According to the Andean law once the economic right expires the State or other

---

[10] Laurence R. Helfer and Karen J. Alter, "The Andean Tribunal of Justice and Its Interlocutors: Understanding Preliminary Reference Patterns in the Andean Community", 41 New York University Journal of International Law and Politics 871–930 (2009).

[11] Article 55, Cartagena Agreement (Andean Pact) Agreement of Subregional Integration, 1969 (Andean Community).

[12] Decision 24, Common regime of treatment of foreign capital and on trademarks, patents, licences and royalties, 1970 (Andean Community).

[13] Decision 351, Common regime of Copyright and Related Rights, 1993 (Andean Community).

designated institutions will assume the defence of the moral rights of paternity and integrity.[14] Perpetuity is also based on the understanding that copyright works are part of the cultural heritage of each country, therefore, perpetuity is an intersection between copyright and cultural heritage policies. For example, the Peruvian copyright law explicitly acknowledges that the purpose of this perpetual protection is to safeguard Peruvian cultural heritage.[15] The Colombian Constitutional Court has interpreted copyright law as part of "a humanistic, cultural and integrationist philosophy" and "not a sui generis form of property but a mechanism to protect the cultural heritage of people and the nation as a whole, in order to promote and perpetuate Colombian cultural identity, within the framework of mutual respect within the international community".[16]

National legislation of each Andean country differs substantially in how it adopts perpetuity. In Peru, although Article 21 of the Copyright Act explicitly establishes that all moral rights are perpetual, the law only develops perpetual protection for the rights of paternity and integrity, the same as the Andean Decision. Article 29 of Peruvian Copyright Act allows the heirs of the author, the State, collecting management organizations or any natural or legal person who proves a legitimate interest on the work to exercise these moral rights. In Bolivia, similarly to Peru, the heirs, the State, any municipality or any natural or legal person are allowed to enforce actions against the violation of moral rights.[17] It is worth noting that Bolivia has a paying public domain (*dominio público pagante, domaine public payant*) policy, which means that after the copyright term of protection expires users must pay the government when using works with a commercial purpose.[18] In a more restricted manner, in Colombia, the Ministry of Culture is the entity in charge of defending the rights of paternity, integrity, and authenticity when the works have entered the public domain.[19] In another direction, the new Ecuadorian Copyright Act of 2016 enacts that after the death of the author, moral rights will be exercised by the heirs, but does not mention anything about the exercise of moral rights after the work falls in the public domain.[20] In this sense, in Ecuador there is no clarity about which agency could exercise the defence of the rights of paternity and integrity once the works enter the public domain.

2.2   The Right of Disclosure

In Bolivia and Colombia, the length of the right to retain the work unpublished is for the life of the author and can only be extended by the will of the author.[21] In Peru, the legislation is more flexible and the author may prevent publication, either in a will or by other written form. This right applies while the work is not in the public domain.[22] In Colombia the legislation is not

---

[14]   Article 11, Decision 351, Common regime of Copyright and Related Rights, 1993 (Andean Community).
[15]   Article 29, Legislative Decree 822 of 1996 (Peru).
[16]   Judgment C-334 of 1993, Colombian Constitutional Court.
[17]   Article 7, Supreme Decree 23907, Regulation of the Copyright Act, 1994 (Bolivia).
[18]   Article 60, Law 1322 of 1992 (Bolivia).
[19]   Article 30, Law 23 of 1982 (Colombia).
[20]   Article 119, Organic Code of the Social Economy of Knowledge, Creativity, and Innovation, 2016 (Ecuador).
[21]   Article 14, Law 1322 of 1992 (Bolivia).
[22]   Article 23, Legislative Decree 822 of 1996 (Peru).

clear about whether this right can be extended indefinitely even after the work is in the public domain. By contrast to Bolivia, Colombia, and Peru, in Ecuador this right can be exercised until the economic rights expire without the need of requirements after the death of the author, and when the work is in the public domain, this right is not enforceable.[23]

In Peru, there are special rules in the civil code for epistolary and personal or family memoirs. These rules seek to protect confidentiality and privacy. Epistolary, confidential communications of any kind, voice recordings or communications that refer to intimate personal and family life, may not be disclosed without the consent of the author and the recipient. It is the heirs who have the right to grant permission for publication when the author or the recipient are dead. In the case of disagreement, the court will have to decide. The prohibition of posthumous publication by the author or the recipient cannot be extended beyond 50 years from the author's death.[24]

2.3 The Right of Paternity (Right to Anonymity and Right to a Pseudonym)

The right of paternity allows the author to decide how she will be identified in relation to her work. The Andean legislation does not include any reference to anonymous or pseudonymous works within its moral rights provisions. However, the Justice Tribunal of the Andean Community has recognized that the right of paternity includes the protection for the author to use a pseudonym or keep her anonymity.[25] National legislation explicitly includes the right to anonymity and the right to a pseudonym connected with the right of paternity. The right to a pseudonym is exercised when a pseudonymous work is published. A pseudonymous work is defined as one in which the author hides behind a pseudonym that does not identify her.[26] Here the word pseudonym should be interpreted in a broad sense, which allows the author to use her right to a pseudonym with full freedom; that means that no conditions should be imposed on the use of a pseudonym and the author can use as many pseudonyms as desired. For example, in Colombia, a restrictive interpretation on the registration of pseudonymous works requires a declaration from a public notary stating that the pseudonym is registered according to the provisions for the civil register. The requirement for any document, such as a certification of the pseudonym, by the inscription of the pseudonym in the birth register is an unjustified restriction on the free exercise of the moral right of paternity.[27]

Peruvian law includes the right to use a sign as identification of authorship in addition to using a pseudonym, orthonym, or publishing the work anonymously.[28] The right to keep the work anonymous or pseudonymous expires when the work falls into the public domain.[29] In Bolivia the right to keep the work anonymous or pseudonymous continues after the death of

---

[23] Article 118, Organic Code of the Social Economy of Knowledge, Creativity, and Innovation, 2016 (Ecuador).

[24] Article 16, Civil Code (Peru).

[25] Case 110-IP-2007, Official Gazette of the Cartagena Agreement, 1588, 20 February of 2008 (Andean Community).

[26] Article 8(f), Law 23 of 1982 (Colombia).

[27] For an example of the problems of an author to register a work using his pseudonym see: Piper Valca, "Cómo registrar mi seudónimo" https://www.antronarrativo.com/2015/10/mi-desventura-con-el-seudonimo.html.

[28] Article 24, Legislative Decree 822 of 1996 (Peru).

[29] Article 23, Legislative Decree 822 of 1996 (Peru).

the author;[30] her real identity can only be revealed when the author authorizes it in her will.[31] In Colombia, by contrast, the author's right to keep the work anonymous operates until her death, and can be extended only by a testamentary provision.[32] In Ecuador, a right to keep the work anonymous is not included as part of author's moral rights.

National laws establish a shorter term of protection for anonymous or pseudonymous works than when the author reveals her name. These national regulations follow the guidelines of the Berne Convention in Article 7.3.[33] A practical reason for this is to define the copyright term of these works from the date of publication, which makes it easier to determine when they enter the public domain. Nonetheless, this seems to be a negative incentive for authors to exercise their right to use a pseudonym and their right to anonymity.

In Colombia, anonymous works are protected for a period of 80 years from the date of their publication.[34] In Bolivia, 50 years after its disclosure;[35] in Ecuador 70 years since the works have been lawfully made accessible to the public.[36] In Bolivia, if the author reveals her identity during her life or by will, the term of *post mortem auctoris* protection will be applied,[37] without affecting the rights acquired by third parties.[38] In Ecuador, if the author of an anonymous or pseudonymous work reveals her identity or when the pseudonym adopted by the author leaves no doubt about her identity, the term of protection will be *post mortem auctoris*. If the identity of the author of the work disclosed under a pseudonym is unknown, it will be considered an anonymous work.[39]

In Peru, anonymous and pseudonymous works are protected for a term of 70 years after their disclosure, unless the author reveals her identity before the end of that period, in which case the copyright term is counted from the death of the author.[40] In addition, the right to keep the work anonymous or pseudonymous expires when the work falls in the public domain.[41]

2.4   Right of Integrity

The Andean Decision states that the author has the right to oppose any deformation, mutilation, alteration, or modification of the work that causes damage to the author's honour or

---

[30]   Article 14, Law 1322 of 1992 (Bolivia).
[31]   Article 14(c), Law 1322 of 1992 (Bolivia).
[32]   Article 30(c), Law 23 of 1983 (Colombia).
[33]   Article 7.3, Berne Convention for the Protection of Literary and Artistic Works (Adopted on September 28, 1979, entry into force: 19 November 1984).
[34]   Article 25, Law 23 of 1983 (Colombia).
[35]   Article 19, Law 1322 of 1992 (Bolivia).
[36]   Article 201, Organic Code of the Social Economy of Knowledge, Creativity, and Innovation, 2016 (Ecuador).
[37]   Article 18, Law 1322 of 1992 (Bolivia).
[38]   Article 19, Law 1322 of 1992 (Bolivia).
[39]   Article 203, Organic Code of the Social Economy of Knowledge, Creativity, and Innovation, 2016 (Ecuador).
[40]   Article 53, Legislative Decree 822 of 1996 (Peru).
[41]   Article 23, Legislative Decree 822 of 1996 (Peru).

reputation.[42] In Ecuador, protection is also extended when the decorum of the work is altered[43] and in Colombia when the merit of the work is affected.[44] On the other hand, Bolivia[45] and Peru[46] provide a wider right to oppose any modification, alteration, mutilation, or deformation of the work without limiting the right to damaging the honour and reputation of the author.

The Justice Tribunal of the Andean Community in one of its few cases dealing with moral rights has analysed the conflict between the right of integrity and property rights. In this case an artist was hired in 2006 to paint a mural in a shopping mall in Medellin (Colombia). In 2013 the shopping mall erased the mural due to the need to repair the construction where the mural was located. The artist claimed that his right of integrity was infringed by the shopping mall. The Tribunal reasoned that in conflicting cases what is established in the contracts between the author and the owner of the construction should prevail. The Tribunal provided some criteria for balancing rights and to solve conflicts when the contract does not say anything about modifications, restorations, or any effects on the construction and its relation to the integrity to the work. First, when the copyright work is made without the consent of the owner of the construction, the former can destroy or change the work. The same applies to a work for hire when the author does not follow the precise instructions of the commissioner. Second, it should be analysed if the work was created to last for a limited time due to the materials, purpose, function, contractual agreement, or any other reason. Third, public interest and public safety should prevail over the moral right of integrity. Fourth, the owner of the construction that needs repair or alteration should give the opportunity to the author to withdraw her artwork when that is possible, or to take photographs or use other methods to keep a record of the artwork. Fifth, when the work affects rights of third parties, such as privacy or the right of publicity, it can be modified. Sixth, the owner of the construction has the duty of diligent care to protect and preserve the work.[47]

In addition to the development of these rights enshrined in the regional copyright system, some countries in the community have established exceptions to moral rights and additional authors' moral rights.

2.5 Exceptions to Moral Rights

In Colombia, Ecuador, and Peru there are exceptions to the right of paternity and integrity in relation to architectural works.[48] In these works, the author may not oppose modifications during construction or after it, nor oppose demolition. If the modifications are made without the author's consent, the author has the right to repudiate the paternity of the modified work,

---

[42] Article 11, Decision 351, Common regime of Copyright and Related Rights, 1993 (Andean Community).

[43] Article 118, Organic Code of the Social Economy of Knowledge, Creativity, and Innovation, 2016 (Ecuador).

[44] Article 30, Law 23 of 1982 (Colombia).

[45] Article 14(b), Law 1322 of 1992 (Bolivia).

[46] Article 25, Legislative Decree 822 of 1996 (Peru).

[47] Case 47-IP-2017, Official Gazette of the Cartagena Agreement, 3118, 20 October of 2017 (Andean Community).

[48] Article 43, Law 23 of 1982 (Colombia); Article 156, Organic Code of the Social Economy of Knowledge, Creativity, and Innovation, 2016 (Ecuador); Article 80, Legislative Decree 822 of 1996 (Peru).

prohibit his name from being associated with the altered work, and the owner will be prohibited from using the name of the original author of the project.

In Colombia there is a general limitation on the exercise of moral rights of works belonging to public entities. When the works are created by public servants as part of their legal duties the copyright belongs to the government. In relation to these works, authors' moral rights cannot be exercised when they are incompatible with the rights and obligations of public entities.[49]

In addition, Ecuador adopts a reasonable requirement stating that the right of paternity is enforceable only when the normal use of the work allows the identification of the author.[50]

2.6   Other Rights in the National Legislation

In addition to the rights of paternity, disclosure, and integrity, in some of the countries of the Andean region there are moral rights of access to the work, the right of modification, and the right of withdrawal. Among the Andean countries Bolivia has no additional moral rights to those found in the regional legislation.

2.6.1   Right of access

In Peru and Ecuador, the right of access is understood to be the power to access the unique or rare copy of the work when it is held by another person so that the author or heirs can exercise their moral or economic rights. In Ecuador, the law highlights the usefulness of this right mainly to exercise the right of disclosure.[51] This right does not impose an obligation for the displacement of the work and access to it will take place in the place and form that causes least inconvenience to the owner.[52]

2.6.2   Right of modification or variation

In Peru, the author has the right of modification, also called variation, which grants a right to modify her work before or after disclosure of the work, respecting the rights acquired by third parties, who must be indemnified for any damages related to the exercise of this right.[53] In Colombia, the right to modify the work before or after its publication[54] can be exercised as long as any damage that may be caused by that action is paid.[55]

In addition, in Colombia the rules relating to publishing contracts state that the publisher is obligated to print the work without making any modification that the author has not authorized.[56] In Ecuador the moral right of modification is found in the articles related to publishing contracts. The author has the right to make any corrections, amendments, additions, or improvements to her work that she believes appropriate before printing begins. When the modifications make the edition more expensive, the author is not obliged to pay the additional

---

[49]   Article 91, Law 23 of 1982 (Colombia).
[50]   Article 118, Organic Code of the Social Economy of Knowledge, Creativity, and Innovation, 2016 (Ecuador).
[51]   Article 118, Organic Code of the Social Economy of Knowledge, Creativity, and Innovation, 2016 (Ecuador).
[52]   Article 28, Legislative Decree 822 of 1996 (Peru).
[53]   Article 26, Legislative Decree 822 of 1996 (Peru).
[54]   Article 30(d), Law 23 of 1982 (Colombia).
[55]   Article 30(4), Law 23 of 1982 (Colombia).
[56]   Article 99(a), Law 23 of 1982 (Colombia).

expenses to the publisher, unless otherwise agreed. The work will be withdrawn from publication when the publisher does not accept modifications that involve fundamental changes in the content or form of the work. In those circumstances the author must compensate for the damages caused to the publisher and third parties. The above also apply to reprints during the term of the contract.[57]

Furthermore, in Ecuador the publisher cannot publish the work with abbreviations, additions, deletions or any other alterations without the consent of the author.[58] A similar prohibition is found in Colombian copyright law, but with an exception in the case of works that due to their nature must be updated. In those cases, the preparation of the updated version must be done by the author, but if she cannot or does not wish to do so the publisher may contract a suitable person, indicating it in the edition and highlighting in different size or style the parts of the text that are added or modified, without affecting the remuneration to the author, unless otherwise agreed.[59]

2.6.3   Right of withdrawal

In Peru, the author has the right to suspend any form of use of the work, after compensating third parties for any damages that may be caused.[60] The right is limited to withdrawing the work from the commercial field. In Colombia this right is more comprehensive because the author can withdraw the work from circulation,[61] or suspend any form of use, even if it had been previously authorized, which for example would also apply to withdrawing the work from cultural institutions such as libraries, archives, and museums. In Peru, the right of withdrawal expires after the death of the author. Once the work is in the public domain it may be freely published or disclosed, but it should be stated that it is a work that the author had rectified or repudiated.[62] In Ecuador the only right of withdrawal is that indicated in the provisions regarding publishing contracts in relation to the right of modification, as already mentioned.

3.   MORAL RIGHTS IN COLOMBIA: A CONSTITUTIONAL PERSPECTIVE

From the earliest years of Colombian independence some authors have claimed their moral rights, especially regarding paternity. Some infringements have stayed in absolute impunity and others have generated conflicts that were solved in different ways to the legal one. For example, the writer, politician, and diplomat Anibal Galindo made the first translation into Spanish of John Milton's *Paradise Lost*, which he published in Ghent, Belgium, in 1868. A few years later his translation was published in Barcelona (Spain) without giving him any

---

[57]   Article 177, Organic Code of the Social Economy of Knowledge, Creativity, and Innovation, 2016 (Ecuador).
[58]   Article 176, Organic Code of the Social Economy of Knowledge, Creativity, and Innovation, 2016 (Ecuador).
[59]   Article 125, Law 23 of 1982 (Colombia).
[60]   Article 27, Legislative Decree 822 of 1996 (Peru).
[61]   Article 30(e), Law 23 of 1982 (Colombia).
[62]   Article 27, Legislative Decree 822 of 1996 (Peru).

type of acknowledgement. Galindo described in his memoirs how in Spain his paternity right was infringed along with his economic rights, and he could not initiate any legal action.[63]

In a memorable incident in 1845 in Panama (part of Colombia in that time), Justo Arosemena thought that Louis Lewis, a British citizen, plagiarized his writing about developing the Panama channel between the Atlantic and Pacific oceans. In an exchange of pamphlets, Arosemena and Lewis defended the originality of their writings, and in addition, there were testimonies before a judge of the Circuit of Panama to vouch for the accuracy of the explanations given in the pamphlets. At that time, it was understood that the charge of plagiarism affected both the honour of the victim and the perpetrator, so the matter was resolved as was every problem associated with honour at that time: Arosemena and Lewis went to a duel and, following the rules, with sponsors and guns, solved their conflict. Justo Arosemena in his first pamphlet denouncing the plagiarism explained that he did not trust the courts of law and instead he believed that public opinion was an impartial jury.

At the end of the nineteenth century, Miguel Antonio Caro, one of the main drafters of the Political Constitution of 1886 and later president of the country, was a strong defender of literary property. He publicly denounced the pirate practices by the French publishers Garnier, and reported they had reprinted without authorization the work of Francisco Torres Amaya entitled *Delicias al Pie del Altar*.[64] Caro drafted the literary property law of 1886, based on his ideas of natural law and Spanish legislation of 1879. However, moral rights were only recognized in the Copyright Act of 1946 (Law 86). This law granted inalienable authors' moral rights of integrity, paternity, and disclosure.

Integrity in the 1946 Copyright Act referred to the right to demand of the publisher integrity of the text and the title in printed works; and for all other works the right to oppose any reproduction or public exhibition of the work, altered, mutilated, or modified.[65] The right of paternity was restricted to being able to demand the acknowledgement of the author's name or pseudonym to identify the authorship.[66] These rights were protected even after the term of protection of the work had expired. Thus, it was established that in the publication or reproduction of works that are in the public domain, the author's name could not be erased or insertions made without the clear distinction between the original text and editorial modifications or additions.[67]

The 1946 legislation was replaced by the 1982 Copyright Act, which is currently in force in Colombia, enacting the moral rights discussed in the section above. In 1991 Colombia adopted a new constitution, which replaced that of 1886. Since its creation in 1991, the Constitutional Court of Colombia has gained an international reputation for the development of case law characterized by judicial activism, theoretical sophistication, and guaranteeing human rights.[68] In terms of copyright, the Court has constructed moral rights as fundamental rights, placing these rights on a higher level of constitutional protection than economic rights.

---

[63]   Anibal Galindo, *Recuerdos Históricos de 1840 a 1895* (Editorial la Luz, Bogotá, 1900).
[64]   Miguel Antonio Caro (Gualberto Roca i Montiano). "A caza de anónimos", Papel Periódico Ilustrado, Bogotá, 1 October 1884.
[65]   Article 49, Law 86 of 1946 (Colombia).
[66]   Article 49(b), Law 86 of 1946 (Colombia).
[67]   Article 7, Law 86 of 1946 (Colombia).
[68]   Rosalind Dixon and Tom Ginsburg, *Comparative Constitutional Law in Latin America* (Edward Elgar, 2017).

3.1   Moral Rights as Fundamental Rights

In 1998 the Constitutional Court examined a claim of unconstitutionality against Articles 33 and 34 of the Law 397 of 1997 (General Law of Culture) declaring the moral and economic rights of the author as inalienable and establishing that royalties cannot be waived. In its decision, the Court declared the unconstitutionality of the inalienability of the royalties related to the exploitation of economic rights. Regarding moral rights, the Court considered that these are fundamental rights. The Court stated that the creative faculty of human beings, the possibility of expressing ideas or feelings in a particular way, the capacity for invention, ingenuity, and all forms of manifestation of the spirit are inherent characteristics of human nature, its rational condition, its individuality, and freedom. For this reason, authors' moral rights are fundamental and must be protected as rights that emanate from the condition of being human. Economic rights are not fundamental, but also deserve the protection of the State.[69]

The Constitutional Court giving moral rights the status of fundamental rights has several consequences within the Colombian legal system. On one hand, only statutory laws can restrict the exercise and regulate the essential core of a fundamental right. The approval, modification, or repeal of statutory laws have a special and much more rigid legislative procedure than that of ordinary laws. Statutory laws require an absolute majority of the members of Congress and their approval must be within one session of the Congress. Statutory laws have prior constitutional review by the Constitutional Court and in this process any citizen can intervene to defend or challenge this kind of law.[70]

On the other hand, fundamental rights in Colombia are protectable through the *tutela*, which is a writ of protection of basic rights and an appeal for immediate relief. Since 1991 the *tutela* has become one of the most useful tools for access to justice in a country of immense inequality, judicial corruption, and systematic violation of human rights.[71] The *tutela* can be filed before any judge of the country for the protection of fundamental rights. The judge has a ten-day time limit for deciding and can take any temporary or permanent measure, even before reaching a final decision, to prevent violation of fundamental rights.[72]

3.2   Children's Rights and Moral Rights

Four months after declaring moral rights as fundamental, the Constitutional Court resolved a *tutela* for the protection of the moral rights of a child. This was the first time in Colombia that copyright rights were protected by means of a *tutela* and the first decision in Colombia regarding the relationship of children's rights and copyright.[73]

The facts of the case were the following. In 1997 the University of Caldas published the book *The Magical Dimension of Mass Communication* by Euclides Arboleda Hernandez. The author's son, Juan Pablo Arboleda, made six drawings, one for the cover and five to illustrate and separate the book's chapters. The drawings were published without acknowledging the

---

[69]   C155, 28 April of 1998, Constitutional Court (Colombia).

[70]   Article 153, Colombian Constitution, 1991.

[71]   See: Whitney K. Taylor, "Ambivalent Legal Mobilization: Perceptions of Justice and the Use of the Tutela in Colombia", 52(2) Law and Society Review 337–67 (2018).

[72]   Decree 2591 of 1991 (Colombia).

[73]   T-409, 11 August 1998, Constitutional Court (Colombia).

authorship of the child. Furthermore, the originals of the drawings were not returned to the child. The child considered the violation of his moral right of paternity and the arbitrary retention of his work as an abuse, so through a *tutela* he decided to request that the university make the appropriate corrections to the book mentioning his name as the author of his published works.

The Colombian Constitution establishes, among other rights for children, fundamental rights to education and culture, freedom of expression, and that children will be protected against all form of labour or economic exploitation (Article 44). The analysis of the Court did not directly focus on the paternity right, but it asserted that the infringement of authors' moral rights of the child is a form of exploitation prohibited by the Constitution. The court reasoned that the Constitution protects the results of artistic or literary creativity of children which cannot be used for editorial purposes without their consent, even if it is only for academic or didactic purposes, or be published without the explicit acknowledgement of the minor to whom authorship belongs. In addition, in the decision, Justice José Gregorio Hernández Galindo, stressed that in the protection of their fundamental rights children are not required to be represented by their parents or by guardians or by any State official, a position already clearly established in the Constitution and developed by the Court since 1993.[74] Furthermore, the Court ratified that the fundamental rights of children prevail over the rights of any other person. In these cases, the judge has to play an active role in the investigation and effective protection of children's fundamental rights. The Court highlighted that the intellectual activity of children is often not properly appreciated and respected, giving as an example that the publisher of the book respected the right of paternity in other cases when the illustrator was an adult, but in this case the publisher did not take care to verify the identity of the artist or acknowledge the authorship of the child.

In its decision, the Constitutional Court protected the moral right of paternity of the child ordering the publisher to acknowledge the child as the author of the drawings. The Court also stated that the author's economic rights are not protectable using the *tutela*, which the child can protect by ordinary legal actions.

3.3   Moral Rights as Part of the Constitutional Block

The decision that declared moral rights as fundamental rights led the Constitutional Court to interpret that the moral rights provisions of the regional copyright legislation (Andean Decision 351) are part of the Colombian constitutional block.[75] In accordance with Article 93 of the Constitution, international treaties that deal with human rights and that prohibit their limitation in states of emergency are part of the constitutional block. For the Court, the constitutional block:

> is made up of those principles and norms that have been normatively integrated into the Constitution by various means and by express mandate of the Charter, for which reason they then have constitutional rank, such as humanitarian law treaties. In principle, they make up the constitutional block in the broad sense: (i) the preamble, (ii) the articles of the Constitution, (iii) some international human rights treaties and conventions (CP art. 93), (iv) organic laws and (v) statutory laws.[76]

---

[74]   T-341, 25 August 1993, Constitutional Court (Colombia).
[75]   C-1490, 2 November 2000, Constitutional Court (Colombia).
[76]   C-1490, 2 November 2000, Constitutional Court (Colombia).

The Court has defined the constitutional block as a set of norms that are used as a parameter for the legal creation and constitutional control of laws. The Court, considering the nature of authors' moral rights as fundamental rights, decided to incorporate the moral rights provisions of the Andean Community into the Colombian Political Constitution. Following this line of interpretation of the Court, all moral rights provisions of international law to which Colombia is a party could be part of the Colombian constitutional block. In practical terms, this has meant that the Constitutional Court must declare the unconstitutionality of any law contradicting moral rights provisions of any international treaty. In addition, these moral rights provisions in international treaties are a constitutional source when interpreting any national law or regulation.

It is interesting to highlight the concurring opinion of the constitutional Justice Martha Victoria Sáchica Méndez. For Justice Sáchica, provisions of the Andean Community should not be considered part of the constitutional block since they are intended to harmonize regulatory mechanisms of foreign trade for regional integration. The Constitutional Court in a 1998 ruling had clearly and explicitly declared that legislation of the Andean Community was not part of the constitutional block.[77] For Justice Sáchica, moral and economic authors' rights should not be treated as human rights. The Court confuses freedom of expression and authors' moral rights. The Court justifying the importance of recognizing authors' rights as the result of creativity, exclusive manifestation of human spirit and ingenuity, is nothing more than a statement of freedom of expression in the broad sense. For Justice Sáchica, the lack of protection of fundamental rights of people limits their ability to act and, ultimately, subjugate a human being to a treatment that strips them of its human condition, but the same consequence cannot be said of the lack of protection for authors' moral rights.

3.4 Criminal Law and Moral Rights

The constitutional doctrine of recognizing authors' moral rights as fundamental rights has had consequences in the field of criminal law.[78] The title VIII of the Criminal Code establishes offences against copyright. Article 270 is related to moral rights, punishing with penalties of two to five years in prison violations of the right to integrity, the right of disclosure through publication, and the fraudulent registration of a work. Colombia's Criminal Code does not criminalize plagiarism, however a decision by the Supreme Court of Justice created the crime of plagiarism in the country.

The facts of the case were the following. The literature professor at the Pontificia Javeriana University Luz Mary Giraldo was convicted for violating paternity and disclosure rights. She published in Mexico claiming as her own some parts of an unpublished thesis for a master's degree in literature on the Colombian poet Giovanni Quessep written by Rosa María Londoño Escobar. The professor was sentenced by the Criminal Court of Bogotá to two years in prison and to one small fine. The decision was confirmed by the Criminal Decision Chamber of the Superior Court of Bogotá. The Supreme Court of Justice confirmed the conviction. The court criminalized the violation of the paternity right based not on the Criminal Code but on an interpretation that considered that moral rights are fundamental rights. In its *ratio decidendi*,

---

[77] C-256, 27 May 1998, Constitutional Court (Colombia).
[78] Karen Isabel Cabrera and Marcela Palacio, "Los Derechos de Autor en Colombia: Objeto de Constitucionalización y Sujeto Constitucionalizante", 13(1) Revista Jurídicas 116–31 (2016).

in a judgment of more than 100 pages, Justice Sigifredo Espinosa Perez reasoned that there should be a broad interpretation of criminal protection for moral rights. The court adopted the *pro homine* principle, which "is a criterion for the interpretation of human rights law, according to which the broadest possible construction should be given to provisions, that is, their extensive interpretation should be favoured".[79] Then the Court notes that Article 270 of the Criminal Code must be construed to include as criminal sanction the infringement of a paternity right. In addition, the court extended the reach of the crime related to the violation of the right of disclosure not only to the publication but to any kind of divulging of an unpublished work.[80]

The Court called its argument a "constitutional interpretation". However, it seems quite the opposite, it could be argued that it was an unconstitutional interpretation under the values and principles promoted by the Constitution. The Colombian Congress has the exclusive power to define by law what behaviours are considered crimes.[81] In this case, the Supreme Court acted contrary to the principle of legality of Colombian criminal law, by creating a criminal offence of plagiarism through judicial channels to protect the moral right of paternity without the participation of the democratic bodies that constitute the Colombian Congress. In addition, the Court took a position of criminal expansionism that is contrary to the principles of minimum intervention and *ultima ratio* of criminal law.

3.5   Exceptions to Moral Rights

The Constitutional Court studied a claim of unconstitutionality against the limitation to the author's moral rights regarding architectural works (a provision that was analysed in a previous section). The claimant argued that treating architectural works with an inferior protection in moral rights compared to other protected works is discriminatory. The Court made a comparative study regarding copyright exceptions for architectural works in other Latin American countries and, following the scholarship of Argentinian academic Delia Lipszyc, analysed the Colombian exception.[82] Then, in a rather strange analysis, the Constitutional Court applied the three-steps test to finally decide that this exception is acceptable according to the test. Although the Court mentions the possible conflict between authors' moral rights and property rights over constructions, it does not elaborate which criteria and principles should be applied to solve the tension of these rights. However, in relation to the discussion about discrimination, the Court clarified that exceptions could be established for different types of work since each kind of work has special characteristics that deserves a particular regulation, that is, according to the study of each kind of work the lawmaker must provide the appropriate limitations. The Court reasoned that it is not acceptable to apply by analogy an exception that the lawmaker has created regarding the use of a different kind of work. The Court claimed that the legislator cannot establish the same limitations and exceptions for all kind of works, since each kind of work can have specificities in their creation and exploitation demanding different treatment,

[79]   Decision 31403, 28 May 2010, Supreme Court of Justice, Criminal Chamber (Colombia), citing C-355, 10 May 2006, Constitutional Court (Colombia).
[80]   Decision 31403, 28 May 2010, Supreme Court of Justice, Criminal Chamber (Colombia).
[81]   Article 29, Colombian Constitution, 1991.
[82]   C-871, 4 November 2010, Constitutional Court (Colombia).

which is why the lawmaker established a regime of limitations and exceptions that cannot be analysed on equal grounds.[83]

One issue that was not discussed in this decision is the need for a statutory law for creating exceptions to moral rights.

3.6   Freedom of Expression and Moral Rights

The Constitutional Court has analysed the relationship between freedom of expression and the moral right to integrity. In 1994 the renowned Colombian writer Germán Castro Caicedo released the book *La Bruja: Coca, Politica y Demonio*, a literary work based on real events around the first years of cocaine trafficking in Colombia. The work was quite controversial and the subject of several legal actions against him. The daughter of one of the individuals mentioned in the book filed a *tutela* action requesting, among other things, that the work be withdrawn from circulation and modifications be made to a couple of pages where her late mother was mentioned. The grounds of the claim were based on protecting her privacy and personal and family reputation. The Fredonia's court ordered the removal from the market of editions of the book where sections alluding to Mrs Domitila appeared and ordered the suppression of such sections in future editions or the changing of the names to fictitious ones. On appeal, the Court of Antioquia confirmed the decision. In the third edition of the book Germán Castro Caicedo changed the names of the people specified in the *tutela* to fictitious names. On the other hand, two other people mentioned in the book (one of them, Margarita María Vásquez Arango, an influential politician and later a senator) filed another *tutela* requesting the removal of the book from the market, rectifications and changes in the work.

The Constitutional Court reviewing the *tutela* annulled the decisions ordering changes in the names and other measures relating to censorship of the book.[84] In addition to ruling out the violation of the right to privacy, one of the main arguments of the Constitutional Court was the need to respect the authors' moral right to integrity. For the Court, the change of the names of the people who are mentioned and described in the book and ordering the rectifications to the information contained in the work would alter the narrative and is an affront to the rights and intellectual creation of the author. For the Court:

> the book that is the object of censorship through the *tutela* actions, even though it uses the genre of journalistic testimony, is a literary work that cannot be understood as news. For this reason, it is not feasible to introduce modifications to its narrative content, because authorizing them would alter the material essence of the work, apart from the fact that it would make the judge a critic of its intellectual creation, which, being a meta-legal issue, that goes beyond the judges competence.[85]

In addition, the Court reasoned that judge's orders to change essential aspects of the work would force the author to rewrite his work not according to his free expression, but in accordance with that of the judge.[86] In this way, safeguarding the right to the integrity of the work aims to preserve the essential elements of the work and no person or authority, either deliberately or for lack of understanding, can alter its content.

---

[83]   C-871, 4 November 2010, Constitutional Court (Colombia).
[84]   SU-056, 16 February 1995, Constitutional Court (Colombia).
[85]   SU-056, 16 February 1995, Constitutional Court (Colombia).
[86]   SU-056, 16 February 1995, Constitutional Court (Colombia).

4.   CONCLUSION

Authors' moral rights in Latin American countries share their grounds based on common legal traditions and colonial history. However, there is not a standard approach to moral rights among these countries or such a thing as Latin American moral rights. The only regional legislation is that of the Andean Community, which also in each country differs in implementation and local approaches to moral rights.

French and Spanish authors' rights legislation and scholarship have been the most influential sources in relation to authors' moral rights in Latin America. An apparent dualistic approach to authors' rights is prevalent in Latin America. However, there is not a strong theoretical framework behind the legislation and in many ways in each country some provisions developing moral rights are part of a dualistic approach and others are from a monistic approach. The legislation of the Andean Community established that the right of paternity and integrity are perpetual, but there are several examples of national provisions that limit these rights going against the regional legislation.

From a constitutional perspective the Colombian approach to authors' moral rights epitomizes a dualistic approach. Authors' moral rights in Colombia have been declared fundamental rights by the Constitutional Court, and therefore can only be limited by statutory laws and for their protection the special right of the *tutela* action can be used. The *tutela* action for the protection of children's rights in relation to moral rights is an original development that could be further developed in the theory of moral rights. However, the constitutional approach of moral rights as fundamental rights has been overused and misused. The criminal expansionism supported by the Colombian Supreme Court violating the principle of legality of criminal law is an example of the dangers of courts misinterpreting the relationship between human rights and authors' rights.

25. Moral rights of the author under Brazilian law: importance and challenges in the communication society and in the digital era

Silmara Juny de Abreu Chinellato

1. THE IMPORTANCE OF MORAL RIGHTS

The awareness about the importance of moral rights of the author appeared for the first time in Morillot's work dated 1878, a time that coincides with the foundation of the International Literary and Artistic Association (ALAI) in France. Its president at that time was Victor Hugo, who emphasized the deep connection between the author's personality and his work, in which such personality is projected. For this reason, he recognized the nature of personality rights to the moral rights of the author. However, this origin has been pushed into the background over the years. Moral rights of the author represented and still represents today great fear, an unwanted restriction for some producers or entrepreneurs who explore the economic aspects of the work.

A few examples below:

(a) the United States' aversion to the moral rights is one of the reasons for its late adhesion to the Berne Convention of 1886, which happened only in 1989;

(b) emphasis on author's economic rights by the World Trade Organization, in the Agreement on Trade-related Aspects of Intellectual Property Rights (TRIPs) Agreement of 1994. The TRIPs Agreement is silent on moral rights, which seems to intend to transform copyright into a merchandise like any other;

(c) emphasis on property rights in the *Livre Vert sur Le droit d'auteur et le défi technologique*, from 1988, by the Brussels Commission, named as "community bible of the matter", by Bernard Edelmana;[1]

(d) moral rights were omitted from the Directive No. 29, 2001, of the European Union (Directive No. 2001/29/EC), which deals with copyright and related rights, in the Information Society. Despite the direct omission, the Directive refers to various other legislations such as the legislation of the Member States, the Berne Convention and to both World Intellectual Property Organization (WIPO) Treaties: the WIPO Copyright Treaty (WTC) and the WIPO Performances and Phonograms Treaty (WPPT).

In a critical essay about this aversion stance Georges Koumantos rightly asks: *"Faut-il avoir peur du droit moral?"*[2]

---

[1] Bernard Edelman, *La personne en danger*, PUF, Paris, 1999.

[2] Georges Koumantos, "Faut-il avoir peur du droit moral?", *Revue Internationale du Droit D'Auteur*, 180, April (1999), 87–125.

In 2014, ALAI held its annual Congress in Brussels, to which this author contributed through the Brazilian Report – under the title "*Le droit moral au 21ème siècle. Le rôle changeant du droit moral à l'ère de l'information surabondante*".[3] The event content was very disappointing and, with the exception of Pierre Sirinelli, we have not seen a vehement defense of moral rights. On the contrary, it seems to us that the North American vision will dominate, with the exclusive emphasis on author's economic rights.[4]

We note our admiration for the resistant French authors who well ably defend the importance of moral rights, among whom we include Bernard Edelman,[5] André and Henri Jacques Lucas. Among the German jurists, we quote Adolph Dietz[6] and Eugen Ulmer.[7] On behalf of all Portuguese authors, we mention José de Oliveira Ascensão.

Actually, the classification of authors' rights as property is an impropriety. As analyzed in other works,[8] authors' rights do not have such nature. This classification was attributed to it a certain historical moment during the French Revolution and was justified by the circumstances. Authors' rights are not property since there are countless differences between both concepts. Given the relevance of moral rights, authors' rights are not a commodity and it should not be considered as a simple product or service. Being treated as simple merchandise would be incompatible with the dignity that lends it the differential of being the creation of the spirit.

Without such considerations in favor of authors' rights, Bernard Edelman's thought is disturbing, as he focuses his works on anthropocentrism and ethical personalism: "Market and technology will, perhaps mark the death of authors' rights and with it, the death of the culture he expressed."

---

3   Le droit moral au 21ème siècle. Le rôle changeant du droit moral à l'ère de l'information surabondante". www.aba-bva.be/IMG/pdf/alai_2014_brazil.pdf.

4   We inform that this Congress has counted without participation of South American legal experts. South America was represented only by Colombia, which host the previous annual meeting in Cartagena. We mention our perplexity in relation of the lack of interest in Latin-American Law, by not recognizing the richness of its legislation, legal theories and case law. We cite, in order to honor these legal experts, the substantial contribution of the Argentinians Delia Lipszig, president of the Interamerican Copyright Institute (IIDA – Instituto Interamericano de Derecho de Autor) and Carlos Alberto Villalb. Among the Brazilians, we honor those who have formed successive generations: Antonio Chaves, Walter Moraes, Carlos Alberto Bittar and Fábio Maria de Mattia.

5   Bernard Edelman, *Le crépuscule du droit d'auteur in* La personne en danger, PUF, Paris, 1999, p. 232. The importance of this authors' work was presented to me by the Portuguese legal expert Mário Emílio Bigotte Chorão, in connection with studies on bioethics, which is also our research subject. In this same work, the French author presents profound reflections on the importance of moral rights, pp. 227–42.

6   *Das Droit Moral des Urhebers im neuen französischen und deutschen Urheberrecht* [Moral rights of the author under French and German authors' rights] (Urheberrechtliche Abhandlungen des Max-Planck-Instituts für ausländisches und internationales Patent-, Urheber- und Wettbewerbsrecht, München, 7), C.H. Beck, München 1968. See also "Mutation du droit d'auteur, changement de paradigme em matière de droit d'auteur?" *RIDA*, October, 1988, 23 *et seq.*

7   *Urheber und Verlagsrecht* [Author and publishers' right] and *Enzyklopädie der Rechts- undStaatswissenschaft*, Springer Verlag, Berlin, 2013.

8   Among them, Silmara Juny de Abreu Chinellato, "Requisitos fundamentais para a proteção autoral de obras literárias, artísticas e científicas. Peculiaridades da obra de artes plásticas" ["Fundamental requirements to the protection of Authors' rights of Literary, Artistic and Scientific Works"], in: *Direito da arte* (eds Gladston Mamede/Marcílio Toscano Franca Filho/Otávio Luiz Rodrigues Jr.), Atlas, São Paulo, 2015, pp. 295–319.

Authors such as José de Oliveira Ascensão,[9] Delia Lipszyc,[10] Bernard Edelman, and this author,[11] have shown concerns with the opacity of the moral rights in the contemporary world, in the so-called "Information Society", or, as we prefer "Communication Society". The little importance given to the moral rights shows the need to increase the protection of the creator. Such protection becomes effective through moral rights.

Above all, the author is a skilled worker and the author's economic rights shall be considered as a form of work status. The Constitution of the Republic values work as one of its fundaments (Art. 1, IV), as well as the protection of the financial investment by producers and entrepreneurs who explore the work. Moral rights must not be neglected or left in the background or, sometimes simply forgotten. Only the moral rights fully honor the human person, who must always be revealed and kept at a different level, preventing the "technological uncivilization".

The choice of the theme of moral rights, object of our monographic study,[12] is an option for the defense of the author's personality, which is projected in the work and is revealed through the personality rights.

Its study was renewed by the promulgation of the Civil Code of 2002, and it honors the doctrine and jurisprudence to which the development of authors' rights owes so much. In this sense, the Faculty of Law of the University of São Paulo has the privilege of having created the first graduation authors' rights Law Course in 1971, thanks to Antonio Chaves. He started a true school of authors of the best lineage such as Walter Moraes, Carlos Alberto Bittar and Fábio Maria De Mattia.

The centrality in ethical values is an option of both the Civil Code and the Constitution of the Republic. This characteristic is shown through the principle of human dignity, enshrined in Art. 1, III, of the Constitution of the Republic, opportunely mentioned here.

The defense of the author honors the person and guarantees the survival, continuity and development of the cultural heritage of humanity. In the Information Society (or Communication Society) and in the technological age with the new challenges and fears, the ethical values inherent in moral rights deserve extra attention so they may be acclaimed in the "technological uncivilization".

---

[9] José De Oliveira Ascensão, "O futuro do 'direito moral'" ["The future of moral rights of the author"], *Direito e Justiça*, Vol. XVIII, Issue I, 2004, 41–63.

[10] Delia Lipszyc, "El derecho de autor y los derechos conexos ante los desafíos de un mundo cambiante" ["Copyright and Neighbouring Rights before the Challenges of a Changing World"], in: *Congreso Internacional – El derecho de autor ante los desafíos de un mundo cambiante. Homenaje a la profesora Delia Lipszyc* (ed. by Asociación Peruana de Autores y Compositores (ADPAYC)/Instituto Nacional de Defensa de la Competencia y de la Protección de la Propiedad Intelectual (INDECOPI)/Organización Mundial de la Propiedad Intelectual – OMPI), Palestra; APDAYC, Lima, 2006, pp. 55–87.

[11] "Direito de autor e direitos da personalidade: reflexões à luz do Código civil" ["Authors' right and personality rights: reflections on the Civil Code"], tese para concurso de Professor Titular de Direito Civil da Faculdade de Direito da Universidade de São Paulo, 2009, São Paulo. Unpublished. In the process of being published. Moreover, we mention our work to be consulted: O trabalhador autor [The Author Worker]. *Revista do Advogado. Homenagem a Walter Ceneviva.* (ed. Antonio Ruiz filho), São Paulo: AASP ed., Ano XL;. N. 145. April, 2020, pp. 203–9. It is also available at: https://www.migalhas .com.br/depeso/328786/o-trabalhador-autor.

[12] "Direito de autor e direitos da personalidade: reflexões à luz do Código civil", supra note 11.

2.   CHARACTERISTICS OF MORAL RIGHTS

One of the most important dichotomies of the authors' rights is its hybrid content, comprised of author's moral and economic rights, which would be enough to remove it from the nature of simple property. Moral rights are essentially personality rights of the author. Therefore, we believe that this is the appropriate qualification, and it seems unnecessary to create a separate category.

At this point, we disagree with Carine Doutrelepont[13] and Agnès Lucas-Schloetter.[14]

Based on its legal nature of personality rights, the moral rights are inalienable, imprescriptible, non-transferable and unseizable, not subject to renunciation or cession. They are also *erga omnes* rights, a quality that is not exclusive to the rights of the personality.

Brazilian law No. 9,610, of 19 February 1998[15] qualified them as inalienable and not subject to renunciation (Article 27), which repeats the content of the previous law.[16]

In addition to that, the Brazilian Civil Code qualifies them as non-transferable and not subject to renunciation, as provided in Article 11.[17]

The characteristic of being inalienable seems to be very expressive and relevant, taking into consideration the scope of its content.

According to Article 1911 of the Brazilian Civil Code, inserted in the Successions' rights book, "[t]he inalienable clause, imposed on assets by an act of liberality, implies no subjection to garnishment and incommunicability".

It is important to stress that personality rights, including author moral rights, cannot be claimed to be absolute rights, since there is no such right.

Although they are personal rights, exclusive to the holder, the rights of the personality shall be exercised considering "the self and the other". This concept is based on the thinking of Lévinas, who in this context influenced several authors, including this author.[18]

The restriction on the moral rights of the author affects the salaried author, who cannot claim unpublished rights; otherwise, the employment contract would become unattainable.

One more characteristic must be remembered: the list of moral rights is not exhaustive, as occurs with personality rights.

---

[13]   Carine Doutrelepont, *Le droit moral de l'auteur et le droit communautaire: analyse en droit comparé et em droit européen*, Bruylant LGDJ, Brussels/Paris, 1997.

[14]   Agnes Lucas-Schloetter, *Droit moral et droits de la personnalité: étude de droit comparé français et allemand*, Presses Universitaires d'Aix, Marseille, 2002.

[15]   We will name the Brazilian Law in question as authors' rights law. We are aware that WIPO (the World Intellectual Property Organization) has a document translated as "Law No. 9610 of 19 February 1998, on Copyright and Neighboring Rights". With all respect to this admirable work, we will not refer this Law to the denomination of the copyright system protection in virtue of the essence of our study, which is based on the system established on the protection of expression of the author's personality – the *droit d'auteur* or *Urheberrecht*.

[16]   Article 28 of the Law 5988, of 14 December 1973.

[17]   With the exception of cases which are provided by law, personality rights are non-transferable, cannot be renounced and their exercise shall not be voluntarily limited.

[18]   Incidentally, we also mention Diogo Leite De Campos, "O direito e os direitos da personalidade" [Law and personality rights], in: *Nós – Estudos sobre o direito das pessoas* [We – studies on the right of persons] (cord. Diogo Leite de Campos), Almedina, Coimbra, 2014, pp. 108–33.

In addition to that, Article 67 permits the necessary updating of the work, even when denied by the author.[19]

As for the protection of moral rights, the fundamental importance of the paternity right – right to attribution – is emphasized. Some authors, such as Greco and Vercellone,[20] consider it a priority, while others do not give due importance to non-patrimonial rights. Among those authors is the commercialist Tullio Ascarelli, whose work is dedicated to industrial property and considers the paternity right the main moral right,[21] while other moral rights could be reduced.

Paternity right or right to attribution would be best named "maternity right", since the author creates, gestates and gives birth to the work.

Although the terminology of paternity right is enshrined, Antonio Chaves' remark, that it should be a "maternity right", is opportune and praiseworthy. This proposal is justified by a fair analogy with pregnancy and childbirth.[22]

3. MORAL RIGHTS OF AUTHORS IN BRAZILIAN LAW NO. 9,610, OF 19 FEBRUARY 1998

Initially, it is important to highlight the absolute distinction between moral damages and moral rights. Damage is the consequence of the violation. It can be pure or have economic consequences. Both indemnities may be cumulative as correctly permitted by Precedent 37 of the Superior Court of Justice, dated August 2007: "Indemnities for material and moral damages arising from the same fact are cumulative."

Brazil is a signatory of the Berne Convention of 1886 and its revisions,[23] which already dealt with moral rights even though, and still today, in a non-systematic way.[24]

The main article is the 6*bis*, which enshrines the rights of paternity, non-modifiability and others:

---

[19] Art. 67: "Where, given the nature of the work, it is necessary to bring it up to date in new editions, the publisher may, if the author refuses to do so, entrust another person with doing so, on condition that the fact is mentioned in the edition". Available at: https://www.wipo.int/edocs/lexdocs/laws/en/br/br002en.pdf.

[20] Paolo Greco/Paolo Vercellone, "I diritti sulle opere dell'ingegno", in: *Trattato di diritto civile italiano* (ed. Filippo Vassai), I, Vol.11, T.3, UTET, Torino, 1974.

[21] Tullio Ascarelli, *Teoria de la concurrencia y de los bienes immateriales* [Theory of competition and of the intangible assets]. Translated by E. Verdera/L. Suárez-Llanos, Studia Albornotiana Publicaciones del Real Colegio de España en Bolonia, Bosch, Barcelona, 1970.

[22] Antonio Chaves, *Direito de autor. Princípios fundamentais* [Authors' rights. Fundamental principles], Forense, Rio de Janeiro, 1987, p. 52.

[23] Decree No. 75.699, 6 May 1975. It proclaims the Berne Convention for the Protection of Literary and Artistic Works, from 9 September 1886, revised at Paris on 24 July 1971. Available at: https://wipolex.wipo.int/en/text/283693.

[24] André Lucas and Henri-Jacques Lucas observe the timid and not very comprehensive treatment that the Convention devoted to moral rights, leaving the legislation of the member countries to expand, as occurs in France. They also remember that the rule of minimum duration of moral rights was enshrined in 1971, which does not exclude either the longest duration nor the perpetuity of moral right. They also reinforce the special rule regarding the autonomy of this right. Traité de la propriété littéraire et artistique, 3rd edition. Litec, Paris, 2006, pp. 966 *et seq.*

Independently of the author's economic rights, and even after the transfer of the said rights, the author shall have the right to claim authorship of the work and to object to any distortion, mutilation or other modification of, or other derogatory action in relation to the said work, which would be prejudicial to his honor or reputation.

Article 11*bis*, 2 also reserves the moral right in works authorized for broadcasting and any public communication.[25]

The Brazilian law of 1898 already treated moral rights, albeit in a non-systematic way. The Civil Code of 1916 also considered them, but in sparse rules in Chapter VI of Title II – Literary, artistic and scientific property. Moral rights were recognized, without the name that was enshrined in the subsequent law though: Law 5.988, of 14 December 1973, entirely dedicated to authors' rights.

Among the moral rights foreseen in the Civil Code of 1916, we mention: the prohibition to modify the work of art, literature or science (Article 659), protection of the author's name and indemnity for losses and damages in case of usurpation (Article 667 § 1), and sanctions for those who publish any unpublished works (Article 669).

Interestingly, Article 667 admitted the assignment of authorship, a norm that received much criticism and seems to not have been used. It should be noted that this rule resulted from the amendment of the National Congress and has been vehemently repudiated by the author of the Code, Clóvis Bevilaqua.

Law 5988 of 1973[26] treated this matter and, this time, in a systematic way. Its author was José Carlos Moreira Alves, tenured Professor at the Faculty of Law of the University of São Paulo and former Minister of the Supreme Federal Court.

The current Law No. 9610/98 regulates moral rights in Articles 24 *et seq.*[27]

---

[25]   (2) It shall be a matter for legislation in the countries of the Union to determine the conditions under which the rights mentioned in the preceding paragraph may be exercised, but these conditions shall apply only in the countries where they have been prescribed. They shall not in any circumstances be prejudicial to the moral rights of the author, nor to his right to obtain equitable remuneration which, in the absence of agreement, shall be fixed by competent authority. Available at: https://wipolex.wipo.int/en/text/283693.

[26]   Articles 25 to 28. Available at: https://www.wipo.int/edocs/lexdocs/laws/en/br/br002en.pdf.

[27]   Article 24. The moral rights of the author are understood to be the right: I. to claim authorship of the work at any time; II. to cause his name, pseudonym or conventional sign to appear or be announced as that of the author when the work is used; III. to keep the work unpublished; IV. to ensure the integrity of the work by objecting to any modification or any act liable in any way to have an adverse effect on the work or to be prejudicial to his reputation or honor as author; V. to amend the work either before or after it has been used; VI. to withdraw the work from circulation or to suspend any kind of use that has already been authorized where the circulation or the use of the work are liable to have an adverse effect on the reputation or image of the author; VII. to have access to the sole or a rare copy of the work that is lawfully in a third party's possession with a view to preserving the memory thereof by means of a photographic or similar or an audiovisual process, in such a way that the least possible inconvenience is caused to its possessor who shall in any event be indemnified for any damage or prejudice suffered. (1) On the author's death, the rights referred to under I to IV shall be transferred to his successors. (2) The State shall be under the obligation to defend the integrity and authorship of a work that has passed into the public domain. (3) In the cases referred to in subparagraphs V and VI, third parties shall be granted prior indemnification where appropriate.

Article 25: The director shall exercise the moral rights in an audiovisual work.

Article 26: The author may repudiate the authorship of an architectural work that has been altered without his consent in the course of its execution or after construction has been completed.

However, the norms are not limited to that chapter.

There are many other rules dealing with moral rights foreseen in several articles of the law, including Article 70, which provides for the right of the author to oppose the representation of the poorly rehearsed work and more: "Article 70. The author has the right to oppose a performance that has not been sufficiently rehearsed, and also to attend the show, for which purpose he shall have free access, during the performances, to the premises in which they take place."

This supervision includes monitoring the correlation between the execution of the work and the original text. The author has the right to oppose the introduction of improvised words and expressions by the actors.[28]

We should also state that Article 64, which deals with the sale of the work as a sales balance, which will be the object of further analysis in Section 4 below, when we take care of current issues.

Countries for instance such as France, Italy, Portugal and Germany (birthplace of personality rights) that are based on *droit d'auteur* value moral rights, in contradiction to those countries based on copyright, which mostly are the Anglo-Saxon countries, under the common law system.

It is important to emphasize that there is no compartmentalization between moral and economical rights, which may happen exceptionally only. The violation of moral rights has repercussions on economical rights and vice versa.

The lack of authorization of the author may be the cause of unannounced or undisclosed authorship, with impacts also on the economic rights.

The work modified without the author's authorization discredits it and distorts it with repercussions on economic rights.

Not asking for the author's authorization to transmit the work makes it impossible for him to refuse to do so. The purpose of the work, for example, may not interest the author. Thus, he has his work distorted and unpaid.

The author does not always want to authorize and license the publication of his work. The economic value of its work is not the sole purpose of an author. For this reason, is granted to the author the right to keep the work unpublished, for several reasons.

The contemporary monistic view honors both aspects and accepts the non-compartmentalization with results on the *quantum* of indemnity. Among German authors, we quote Eugen Ulmer who alludes to the "truncal aspect" of author's rights.[29]

With this hybrid but not compartmentalized view, it does not seem important to us that the Constitution of the Republic does not deal with moral rights. In addition to that, the TRIPs

---

Sole paragraph. The owner of the building shall be liable for any damage done to the author where, after the above repudiation, the said owner attributes the project in question to the author.

Article 27: Moral rights are inalienable and irrevocable.

[28] "Cacos" (improvization) is a theatrical term, which denominates sentences that are introduced by the actor or the actress in the original text, sometimes to complete it with a joke, other times to update the text with current news of the moment, notably with political-economic implications.

[29] We mention Eugen Ulmer's reflections, which are always opportune. According to Ulmer, the authors' rights involves a unity, by representing two aspects, one of moral rights, and the other of exploration (economic) rights, interests forming branch and stem that originates from the same tree's trunk. In this right, which is named "mother's right" (*Mutterrecht*), the unity of the authors' right will be guaranteed. Eugen Ulmer, *Urheber- und Verlagsrecht.* [Author and publishers' right]. *Enzyklopädie der Rechts- und Staatswissenschaft*, Springer Verlag, Berlin, 2013, p. 101.

Agreement does not mention it either, also because it is emphatically concerned with economic rights.

It should be noted that the importance of moral rights does not mean depreciation[30] of the economic rights, which are extremely important. Our criticism is that moral rights have been forgotten, overlooked and put in the background. Both rights are relevant.

Brazilian courts have made a great contribution. State and superior courts, notably the Superior Court of Justice, have considered the relevance of moral rights.

A very detailed judgment is the one involving the singer João Gilberto, who complains about the lack of authorization to reissue a musical album and about the violation of the right to ensure the integrity of the work by objecting to any modification, through an unauthorized agreement that he understood harmful to his interpretation.[31]

Another decision is the judgment issued in the case of the soap opera presented on TV, by Benedito Rui Barbosa, in which a biphasic standard is presented to determine the indemnification of moral rights: the relevance of the injured person and the circumstances of the specific case.[32]

It is worth remembering the judgment of the Superior Court of Justice addressing the artist Iara Tupinambá's interests, whose mural painted on the building of the Municipality of Belo Horizonte, Minas Gerais, was entirely destroyed when the headquarters were moved. The artist was not consulted about the possibility of transferring the mural or about any intervention of hers that could prevent the destruction of the work.[33]

Other judgments deal with the right of authorship, which may be just ignored in original works, or yet in derivative works without mention to the original work.

Among them, Appeal No. 1.422.699 – SP, which deals with the unauthorized reproduction of a Christmas crib, used in a photo to illustrate the seal of the Brazilian Post and Telegraph Company. There were convictions for moral damages – arising from violations of the moral rights of the author, and economic damages convictions as well. In the decision and content of the vote of the Judge Minister Humberto Martins, we were honored by having our article that analyzes the specificities of fine art works quoted.[34]

For us, the plagiarism concept implies the appropriation of the substance of someone else's work. In this circumstance, there is a double violation of moral rights: authorship and economic rights. This is a wide-ranging topic and was the subject of an article published by us in which we analyzed various aspects of this matter.[35]

---

[30]   The musician and performer is considered one of the creators of the musical movement called "bossa nova", to which belongs the song "The girl from Ipanema", well-known worldwide.

[31]   Recurso Especial No. 1.098.626-RJ. Judged on 13.12.2011, by the Third Chamber, Reporting Judge Minister Sidney Benneti, m.v. The expertise made by notable musicians, with great technical knowledge, was fundamental to support the winning opinion, in favor of João Gilberto.

[32]   Recurso Especial No. 1558638-SP. Judged by the 3rd Chamber in May, 2017, Reporting Judge Moura Ribeiro.

[33]   Revista dos Tribunais 711, p. 215. Reporting Minister Hélio Mosimann, judged on 28.9.1994, majority of votes.

[34]   Silmara Juny de Abreu Chinellato, "Requisitos fundamentais", supra note 8, pp. 295–319.

[35]   "Violações de direito autoral: plágio, 'autoplágio' e contrafação" ["Authors' rights violations: plagiarism, 'self-plagiarism' and infringment"], in: *Estudos avançados de direito autoral* (eds, Costa Netto, José Carlos et alii), Associação Brasileira de Direito Autoral, ABDA/ Elsevier, São Paulo, 2015, pp. 200–19.

Item IV of Article 24 deserves some criticism. Such article guarantees the author the right to the integrity of the work, opposing any modifications or the practice of acts that, in any way, may harm or affect the author in its reputation or honor.

Here is the wording:

> Article 24. The moral rights of the author are:
> IV. to ensure the integrity of the work by objecting to any modification or any act liable in any way to have an adverse effect on the work or to be prejudicial to his reputation or honor as an author;

The requirements for exercising the right are too many. In our view, the drafting of the standard could end in "objecting to any modification", as the requirements are inopportune and involve harmful interpretation to the author and the work.

One case to remember is the case of the Spanish Cecilia Gimenez, who, in August 2013, in the church of São Borja, Spain, modified the nineteenth century painting Ecce Homo, by Elias Garcia Martinez. Her goal was to embellish the original work. The requirements provided for by Brazilian law could give rise to the discussion that there was no damage to the work.

The painter's family intended to have the work wiped out for damaging the author's honor, but that did not happen, as the whole event resulted in generating euros for the city's tourism, by transforming it into a stamp for a winery and a film script.

Misinterpretation can give rise to great danger to the cultural heritage of humanity. The specific case causes many perplexities.

The wording of item VI of Article 24 also deserves criticism, according to which the author's moral rights are:

> VI. to withdraw the work from circulation or to suspend any kind of use that has already been authorized where the circulation or the use of the work are liable to have an adverse effect on the reputation or image of the author.

The cumulative requirements "where the circulation or the use of the work are liable to have an adverse effect on the reputation or image of the author" constitute an obstacle to the right of repentance.

The law could provide for the assignee or licensee's indemnity, without prior notice. Even if not expressly stated, the judicial mandate repudiates the unjust enrichment and the greater fundament of the civil rights being the damage indemnity according to the Civil Code's Articles 186 and 927, in the same sense as the previous codes.

Law 7,347, of 24 July 1985, regulates the public civil action,[36] expanding the list of those legally authorized to bring an action aimed at safeguarding works that have fallen into the public domain. In this sense, item III of Article 1 addresses the possible situations, regarding goods and rights of artistic, aesthetic, historical, touristic and landscape value.[37]

---

[36] "Art. 1 The provisions of this Law will govern, without prejudice to the citizen suit, the civil responsability claim for moral and property damages which were caused: 1 – to the environment; ll – to the consumer; III – to property and rights of artistic, aesthetic, historical, tourist and landscape value."

[37] "Art. 1 The provisions of this Law will govern, without prejudice to the citizen suit, the civil responsability claim for moral and property damages which were caused: 1 – to the environment; ll – to the consumer; III – to property and rights of artistic, aesthetic, historical, tourist and landscape value."

Consequently, there is a greater coverage than that resulting from Paragraph 2 of Law 9.610, of 1998.

Carlos Alberto Bittar was not only an outstanding academic, but also an experienced judge. He used his experience to deal with the indemnity criteria issues, which is a very difficult topic.

The proposal was to consider the severity of the infraction and the circumstances of each particular case. In addition to that, it was also considered the demotivation factor "in the defense of the transcendent values of the human person protected here".[38]

We present our proposal as a standard for establishing the indemnity amounts due resulting from breach of moral rights of the author.

1. One must consider the strict non-compartmentalization between economic and moral rights, with consequences in the *quantum* to be fixed. Important to note that the violation of personality rights, such as moral authors' rights, generates moral damage.
2. The disincentive function should be analyzed considering the perpetrator's assets. One should never consider the victim party's assets, as the poor would have a very small indemnity to receive, well below the impact of the damage. It would also be hateful discrimination.
3. You cannot assign the same contract value, even if authorized. It would serve to encourage the violation, as the perpetrator is not at risk of receiving refusal from the author. This guideline honors both the disincentive and the educational function.
4. The specific sanctions provided for in Articles 102 to 110 of Law 9.610/98 should also be considered, with emphasis on Article 108.[39]

We have not adopted the proposal of charging for moral damage, as an offense to any personality right. In any case, we must assess the circumstances of each specific case.

It also does not seem right for us to fix the value of the moral damage coming from the violation of personality rights (among which the moral rights of the author) in a *quantum* that represents twice the amount fixed for the patrimonial damage, based on the violation of author's economical rights.

If the value of the economic damage is negligible, it will also be fixed by the violation of moral rights of the author.

And if there is no violation of economic rights – although there are almost always both violations – there will be no compensation.

---

[38]   Carlos Alberto Bittar, *Direito de autor* [Authors' rights], 7th edition, revised, atualizada e ampliada por Eduardo Carlos Bianca Bittar, GEn-Forense, São Paulo, 2019, p. 161.

[39]   "Art. 108. Any person who, in the use of an intellectual work by any means fails to mention or announce as such the name, pseudonym or conventional mark of the author and performer, apart from having to answer for the moral prejudice, shall be bound to disclose their identity, I. in the case of a broadcasting organization, at the same times as those at which the infringement was committed, for three consecutive days; II. in the case of a graphic or phonographic publication, by the inclusion of an *erratum* in the copies not yet distributed, without prejudice to the conspicuous publication of a notice on three consecutive occasions in a major journal at the place of residence of the author, the performer and the publisher or producer; III. in the case of any other form of use, in the press according to the procedure referred to in the foregoing subparagraph." Available at: https://www.wipo.int/edocs/lexdocs/laws/en/br/br002en.pdf.

Thus, this does not seem to be the best guideline.[40]

There must be a systematic and teleological interpretation of the authors' rights. The law is in favor of the author, as expressed in Article 4, which reproduces the same thesis of Article 3 of the previous law: "Legal Acts relating to authors' rights shall be interpreted restrictively."

4.   CURRENT ISSUES

4.1   Inapplicability of Copyright Rules

Among the current issues, we mention the impropriety of applying the copyright law of the United States to the Brazilian cases. We have a rich and broad legislation, which is also different from copyright law. The author has more protection; hence, the scope of protection is different. In this way, authors will be at stake if the concrete case would be decided under authors' right fundaments of a different respectable legal system, and this interpretation is also not necessary, by considering *legem habemus*.

For these reasons, we understand that US copyright law is not appliable, being a different conclusion if compared to the appellate court decision of the Superior Court of Justice, which was published in 5.8.2015, in the "Recurso Especial" No. 1.512.647 – MG.

In that case, the film distribution company of educational material – legal courses – rebelled against the free disclosure of its courses by Orkut.[41] After a long discussion on contributory copyright infringement and on vicarious liability, the Superior Court of Justice established that Google had not contributed substantially and intentionally to the violation and that it had no purpose of profit-making, which is considered irrelevant to the Brazilian authors' rights law.

Moreover, we observe that the Brazilian system of civil responsibility is quite complete and does not need the transplant of forms of responsibility, as was carried out by the aforementioned decision. Furthermore, we observe the difference between systems that were founded in civil law and in common law, which has to be stressed in relation to the impropriety of this transplant.

We note that fundaments of US copyright law have not been applied in Brazilian case law. The conclusion of the aforementioned decision is an exception, but we understand that it deserves to be mentioned because it may represent a precedent to the detriment of Brazilian authors and law, which received a different basis.

4.2   Destruction of Works Due to New Legislation Repealing of Previous Law

Another issue that must be pointed out is related to the revision of legal codes, for instance, the Civil Code, which gives rise to the repeal of the prior law. The repeal of a legal code does not imply demerit of the legal theory, which was drawn up considering the prior law. On the contrary, we have a lot to learn from these legal experts. The work has value by itself and this

---

[40]   We invoke the Appellate court decision of the Supreme Federal Court (STF), pronounced in the Recurso Extraordinário No. 99.501-3, Reporting Judge Minister Francisco Rezek. This decision emphasizes that the moral prejudice cannot be placed depending on the proof of the actual material damage considering authors' rights. Furthermore, we also praise the lessons of Carlos Alberto Bittar.

[41]   Social network that preceded Facebook in terms of offering social interaction between its users.

understanding was not accepted by some Brazilian publishers. With the promulgation of the Brazilian Civil Code of 2002, we had the destruction of works, which were written according to our prior Civil Code (1916), without any prior notice to the author of the work.

Even though this deals with the destruction of the tangible medium and it may persist in any possible digital form, which would not always be appreciated by the users or consumers, the violation of the moral right of the author is inherent. We know that the literary work takes a long time to be edited in printed form, especially in times of financial crisis for publishers.

Moreover, the possibility of bringing the work up to date faced with new law also requires a lengthy study. Thus, the author, the interested public and the cultural heritage will be deprived of the work, without any prior notice regarding to the intention in order to deprive everyone of access to the tangible medium and, in consequence, to the intangible creation, the expressed work. We also emphasize that the digital version is relatively new and, therefore, would not reach a great number of works. Hence, not all interested parties appreciate this form of expression, preferring the printed version.

The correct interpretation is that the publisher must notify the author as well, when the intention is to destroy the physical medium (*corpus mechanicum*). The author must be given the opportunity to acquire copies of the work, which did not occur regarding some Brazilian publishers, in flagrant violation of moral rights and total disrespect to the author.

We remind that the Civil Procedure Code is recent (Law 13.105, of 16 March 2015), and it may represent new concerns related to the destruction of works, which were created when the previous Code was in force.

4.3   Third-Party Work Update

Another topic, which has caused us a great concern, is related to who brings a work up to date.

We understand that it must be done after the original text, and preferably, in a different letter, without incorporating the original text, otherwise it could impede the reader from knowing the original text. Thus, the original author faces the violation of his right to prevent modifications to his work, and at times, with a great prejudice to the new text, without the degree of technique and language requirements that would characterize the original text.

Furthermore, we must point out the violation of the reader's right – consumer, constituting a violation of the right to transparency (Article 4) and to information (Article 6, III), according to the Brazilian Consumer Defense Code – Law No. 8078, of 11 September 1990.

Lastly, we mention that who merely brings the legislation up to date, as well who reviews it, are not joint authors, according to the Brazilian authors' rights law (Law No. 9610 of 19 February 1998), in its Article 15, paragraph 1:

> Art. 15: Joint authorship of a work shall belong to the persons under whose names, pseudonyms or conventional signs it has been used.
> 1. A person shall not be considered a joint author if he has merely assisted the author in producing the literary, artistic or scientific work by reviewing it or bringing it up to date or by supervising or directing its publication or presentation in whatever form.

4.4 The Supposed Co-authorship Within the Academic Environment

In the academic community, we note that the supervisor of a master's dissertation, a doctoral thesis, or a thesis presented as a conclusion of a post-doctoral research, is not a co-author. Authors' rights protect the expression and not the idea, according to the Article 8, I, of the Brazilian authors' rights law (Law No. 9610 of 19 February 1998).

The idea is protected, if it will be expressed, characterizing a symbiosis. The supervisor could only be considered as a co-author if he or she would have participated in the expression of work of the supervisees, by writing the work partially, which would not be admissible. This is a matter related to the right of paternity.

4.5 Authors' Rights and Animals

When we reflect on the current issue of animal rights, we observe that the different legal nature of thing (*res*) has already been established by several Codes – among of them, we point out the recent French and Portuguese examples – which considers them as living beings, endowed with sensitivity. We ask ourselves whether it would be possible to consider the animal as owner of authors' rights or related rights, the same rights that are applied to artists and performers. In the current phase of development of authors' rights, it seems to us that the irrational animal cannot be considered either the author – of paintings, for example, of photography – as has already happened in a specific case starring the monkey Naruito – nor as a performer, as already verified in several audiovisual works, moreover, American and Brazilian ones.

The Brazilian authors' rights law is clear at the consideration of the author of a literary, artistic or scientific work as the natural person who has created it, in the caput of the Article 11, also extending the protection to the legal entity, in the cases foreseen by law (single paragraph) encompassing the collective work.

Article 7 defines intellectual works as creations of the mind.

With the evolution of the protection of animals, it may be possible that, in the future, authors' rights legislation will consider it, including them among those entitled to authors' rights.[42]

4.6 Technology and Moral Right of the Author: Artificial Intelligence

In the technological era, in the era of civilization or technological uncivilization, we must consider the various aspects of authors' rights and new technologies, including the contemporary concerns which were brought by artificial intelligence.

Who is the author of computer works? Is there an electronic personality?

In our view, the answer is negative. There would be devaluation (diminishing) and discrediting of the human person, who is also considered as a component of the legal or moral person.

---

[42] Regarding animal rights, under the Portuguese law, the pioneering work of Fernando Araújo, *A hora dos direitos dos animais* [The time of animal rights] was consulted (Almedina, Coimbra, 2003). In Brazil, the first book is a result of the PhD Thesis of Alfredo Domingues Barbosa Migliore, *Personalidade jurídica dos grandes primatas* [The great apes legal personhood], Del Rey, Belo Horizonte, 2012.

We are slowly making our way towards the personalization of the pre-implantation embryo, having already conquered, in much of the legal theory, after long and lengthy discussions, about the personality of the unborn child already conceived and implanted. The fastest path seems to be that of the hasty proposal, without grounds, of "electronic personality".

From our point of view, it represents a great exaggeration. Artificial intelligence is a reality but there will always be a natural or legal (moral) person to be held responsible.

Computer music has the intervention of a person who makes choices, according to our studies, in which we had spoken with authors who use computers to compose. He is the author and he can be held responsible for violating the authors' rights of others.

The removal of personalization is a very dangerous path, leading to a step backwards from recognizing the empowerment and greater importance of technology, to the detriment of the person. The change of the authority – once considered as a divine authority, and legitimized by mythologies, followed by the idea of human authority, may change again, according to Yuval Noah Harari's considerations.

According to him, "the future technological revolution could establish the authority of Big Data algorithms while undermining the simple idea of individual freedom".[43]

When we refer to the areas of industrial property and of authors' rights, it is inappropriate to refer to the electronic personality, or personification of the machine, in the opposite direction of what Hermogenian preached by emphasizing the primacy of the person.

We are doing ourselves a disservice, in this case, to the detriment of the author who creates with the assistance of machines, which has been happening for a long time, but always with human intervention.

We would be also moving backwards, leading to a possible civil irresponsibility.

This is a contemporary reality that law cannot ignore, but must reflect with moderation; artificial intelligence in the scope of intellectual rights cannot keep human creators at bay.

5.   CONCLUSION

Without prejudice to the economic rights of the author, we highlight the importance of moral rights of the author, personality rights, by means of which a person is emphasized and distinguished.

This consideration of importance is even more necessary in the technological era, the digital era in which the human person is relegated to a secondary level of respect and consideration as the main priority of law. Furthermore, the great "truncal aspect" between moral and exploration rights will be pronounced, with repercussions in the *quantum* of damages, in case of authors' rights infringement.

The moral rights of the author, by fully respecting the author in himself/herself, cause the prevention of a "technological uncivilization" prelude.

---

[43]   *21 lições para o século 21* [21 lessons for the 21st century]. São Paulo: Companhia das Letras. 2018. p. 72.

26. Moral rights in Commonwealth countries
Gillian Davies

1. INTRODUCTION

1.1 The Commonwealth

The Commonwealth of Nations, originally established in 1926, is a voluntary association of 56 sovereign states.[1] Nearly all the present member states are former British colonies or dependencies of those colonies. Today, no one government in the Commonwealth exercises power over the others; it is not a political union. Rather, the Commonwealth is an international organization in which countries with varying social, political, and economic backgrounds are regarded as equal in status, and cooperate within a framework of common values and goals, as outlined in the Singapore Declaration issued in 1971. Such common values and goals include the promotion of democracy, human rights, good governance, individual liberty, the rule of law, equality before the law, free trade, multilateralism, and world peace; these principles are promoted through multilateral projects and meetings on common interests and goals, including the Commonwealth Games, held once every four years.

Commonwealth countries are located all over the world, in Africa, Asia, the Americas, Europe, and the Pacific. They are diverse and include some of the world's both largest and smallest economies. Thirty-two of its members are classified as small states.[2]

The Commonwealth was formed in 1926, following the Balfour Declaration adopted at the Imperial Conference of that year, which recognized the full sovereignty of the British Empire's dominions at the time. It was known then as the "British Commonwealth". The original members were the United Kingdom, Canada, Irish Free State, Newfoundland, and South Africa. Australia and New Zealand did not adopt the status until 1942 and 1947, respectively. The present 56 Member States of the Commonwealth are listed below.[3] One common denominator between the countries within the Commonwealth to this day is that their legal systems and legislation were originally based on, and still have much in common with, the laws of the United Kingdom.

This is true also of both the theory and practice of copyright law. Prior to the independence of individual Commonwealth countries, as a general rule the British copyright laws of 1911

---

[1] As of 7 August 2022.

[2] For general information about the Commonwealth, see the Commonwealth Secretariat website: https://thecommonwealth.org.

[3] Antigua and Barbuda, Australia, The Bahamas, Bangladesh, Barbados, Belize, Botswana, Brunei, Cameroon, Canada, Cyprus, Dominica, Eswatini (former Swaziland), Fiji, Gabon, The Gambia, Ghana, Grenada, Guyana, India, Jamaica, Kenya, Kiribati, Lesotho, Malawi, Malaysia, Maldives, Malta, Mauritius, Mozambique, Namibia, Nauru, New Zealand, Nigeria, Pakistan, Papua New Guinea, Rwanda, Saint Kitts and Nevis, Saint Lucia, Saint Vincent and the Grenadines, Samoa, Seychelles, Sierra Leone, Singapore, Solomon Islands, South Africa, Sri Lanka, Tanzania, Togo, Tonga, Trinidad and Tobago, Tuvalu, Uganda, United Kingdom, Vanuatu, and Zambia.

and 1956 were extended to such countries and the copyright laws of these countries remain closely aligned and still have much in common with the present copyright law of the United Kingdom. For this reason, the history of the protection of moral rights (or more precisely, the lack of specific legislation on the subject) in Commonwealth countries is closely linked to that which prevailed in the United Kingdom.

The Commonwealth Secretariat, the intergovernmental agency which has served the member governments since its foundation in 1965, has its headquarters in London. Its role is to facilitate consultation and cooperation among member governments and countries to achieve its aims of development, democracy, and peace. The Head of the Commonwealth is King Charles III.

1.2   Common Law Legal Systems in Commonwealth Countries

As already mentioned, nearly all the present members of the Commonwealth are former British colonies or dependencies of those colonies and were at one time within the former British Empire. As a result, their legal systems were for many years until and indeed after they became independent closely aligned with that of the United Kingdom and may be described to this day as "Common Law Jurisdictions". In the days when members of the Commonwealth were still colonies of the British Empire, it was common practice for British legislation to be extended to and in force in Commonwealth countries and the common law, including judge-made case law, applied there too. The UK Copyright Acts of 1911 and 1956 were extended to the countries which are now members of the Commonwealth and so predominantly their copyright laws are based on the copyright tradition as opposed to the authors' right (*droit d'auteur*) approach of Continental Europe, where the concept of moral rights emerged in the late nineteenth and early twentieth centuries, predominantly in France. The courts of many Commonwealth countries "still, in practice, tend to accept and follow most English case-law authority".[4]

Moral rights were not protected under the 1911 and 1956 UK Copyright Acts. It was not until the adoption of the new Copyright Act of 1988 that such rights were finally legislated for and introduced, as such, into the UK law. Until then, with only limited exceptions, Commonwealth countries continued to follow the example of the UK legislator by not protecting moral rights by statutory means. Nevertheless, moral rights were already protected to some degree by the common law in the United Kingdom and elsewhere, as described below.

For the current situation regarding moral rights in the United Kingdom, see Section 3.

2.   MORAL RIGHTS, THE ROME ACT OF THE BERNE CONVENTION 1928 AND THE COMMONWEALTH

The Commonwealth was only established in 1926, so it was to be expected that its members as a group played no part in the discussions on the question whether moral rights should be protected under the Rome Act of the Berne Convention adopted in 1928. The only members

---

[4]   For a challenging overview of moral rights and the common law countries in the 1990s, see Gerald Dworkin, "The Moral Right of the Author", in the Proceedings of the ALAI Congress of Antwerp, September 1993, p. 81.

of the then British Empire present at the Rome Conference apart from Great Britain were Australia, Canada, India, the Irish Free State, and New Zealand.[5]

It was the Australian delegate, supported by his colleagues from other common law countries, who raised a point of procedure when the Italian delegation first put forward the new proposal that the protection of moral rights should be introduced into the Berne Convention (it had not been the subject of proposals in the preparatory documents).[6] In support of his proposal, in a special report distributed to delegates, the Italian delegate referred, inter alia, to changes in the doctrine and case law on the subject of authors' rights in, for example, France and Italy, and to resolutions of congresses of ALAI (Association littéraire et artistique interationale – International Literary and Artistic Association) on the subject of "moral rights". He drew attention also to the need to protect authors against compulsory licences and paying public domain. Finally, he also referred to existing legislation on moral rights in some countries.[7]

In response, the Australian delegate pointed out that in Australia the subject-matter of "moral rights" was based on the common law which the federal legislator in Australia had no competence over. Common law rights were a matter for the individual state legislatures; the federal legislator only had the power to legislate on copyright. Thus, should the Conference vote in favour of a text on moral rights, the federal legislator would not have the right to introduce it into Australian law.[8] According to the report, the Italian delegation subsequently held discussions with representatives of countries from the British Empire in order to avoid problems which might arise in connection with the British and other copyright laws of similar tradition based on the UK common law.[9]

The Australian and British delegations[10] subsequently confirmed that such discussions had taken place and thanked the Italian delegation for his spirit of conciliation. No further details about the discussions are given in the report of the Conference, but one can only assume that the copyright delegations considered moral rights to be protected by the common law and principles of equity in their countries. They took the view that the new moral right provisions introduced to the Convention in Article 6*bis* were compatible with such common law.

It was not surprising that the concept was new to the members of the British Empire delegations in 1928. It was only 20 years earlier, in 1908, that the theory of authors' moral rights as developed by the courts in France was described by the leading copyright (*droit d'auteur*) commentator in France of the time, Edouard Pouillet.[11] He wrote that: "The theory emerged in France from an accumulation of court decisions" and "the term 'droit moral' was in use after the turn of the century".[12] It is not to be wondered at that the UK Copyright Act 1911 did not refer to moral rights. At that time, the whole concept was in its infancy. Moreover, it is of

---

[5]   *Conférence de Rome, Rapports*, List of participants.
[6]   The proposal of the Italian delegation was supported by the delegations of Belgium, France, Poland, and Romania.
[7]   *Conférence de Rome, Rapports*, 236.
[8]   *Conférence de Rome, Rapports*, 238.
[9]   *Conférence de Rome, Rapports*, 238 and 239.
[10]   According to the Records of the Conference no other representatives of the British Empire were present.
[11]   E. Pouillet, *Traité théorique et pratique de la propriété littéraire et artistique,* 3rd edn (Paris, Marchal et Billard, 1908), para 204*bis*.
[12]   Pouillet, ibid., p. 103.

interest to note that specific legislation on the subject was not introduced in France until 1957,[13] even though there was a solid and growing body of case law on the subject.

In putting forward the proposal at Rome in 1928, the Italian delegation mentioned that moral rights were already protected by the Italian copyright law and recalled that the matter had been raised for consideration as early as 1908 at the Berlin Conference for the revision of the Berne Convention. However, the number of Member States of the Berne Convention with specific moral rights protection was still very limited in 1928.

2.1   Article 6*bis* Adopted at Rome

Article 6 *bis* of the Berne Convention, adopted at the Diplomatic Conference which took place in Rome in 1928, is still in force in paragraphs 1 and 3 of the present text of Article 6*bis* of the Paris Act 1971 of the Berne Convention. The original paragraphs 1 and 2 read as follows:

(1) Independently of the author's copyright, and even after transfer of the said copyright, the author shall have the right to claim authorship of the work, as well as the right to object to any distortion, mutilation or other modification of the said work which would be prejudicial to his honour or reputation.
(2) The determination of the conditions under which these rights shall be exercised is reserved for the national legislation of the countries of the Union. The means of redress for safeguarding these rights shall be regulated by the legislation of the country where protection is claimed.

It is important to emphasize that the text adopted at Rome was the result of a compromise which, by virtue of paragraph (2), left the Contracting States complete freedom to determine the legal means by which moral rights were to be protected.

2.2   Article 6*bis* Amended by the Stockholm Act 1967

A new paragraph 2, introduced to Article 6*bis* by the Stockholm Act 1967, deals with the duration of the rights, providing that moral rights shall be maintained *at least until the expiry of the economic rights* and, thereafter, where protection is claimed, shall be exercisable by the persons or institutions authorized by the legislation of the country where protection is claimed.

In the following sections we shall look at how in the first place the United Kingdom went about implementing the new Article 6*bis* in the years to come and also consider how moral rights were dealt with by other major common law countries. Finally, the extent to which the present 56 Members of the Commonwealth countries have recognized moral rights in their national legislations are discussed and the details presented in the Appendix to this *Handbook*, "Commonwealth Laws on Moral Rights".

---

[13]   Loi sur le droit d'auteur 1957.

3.   MORAL RIGHTS IN THE UNITED KINGDOM

3.1   Consideration of Moral Rights by the Gregory Committee 1952

As far as Great Britain was concerned, in 1928 and for many years thereafter, the term "droit moral" remained a "term unknown to the jurisprudence of the United Kingdom" as the Report of the Copyright Committee published in 1952 (the Gregory Committee) pointed out.[14] Amending the venerable UK Copyright Act 1911 to introduce the subject of moral rights had not been contemplated in the interval between the adoption of Article 6*bis* of the Berne Convention at the Rome Conference of 1928 and the setting up of the Gregory Committee in 1951 to advise on the reform of the UK Copyright Act. An enduring problem with the expression "moral right" in English-speaking countries was its literal translation from the French "*le droit moral*". As recently pointed out by a distinguished judge of England and Wales, the expression "failed to convey the special nature or particular content of a bunch of rights based on the legal recognition of respect for the special relationship of creator and creation".[15]

This did not mean that authors were without protection in respect of these rights under the common law. As the Gregory Committee pointed out with respect to Article 6*bis* of the Berne Convention:

> In the United Kingdom, protection [in respect of an author's honour and reputation] is given by the common law, in addition to various statutory provisions, and in the twenty years since this Convention was accepted [by the United Kingdom] no other Berne Union country has complained that the United Kingdom has failed to discharge its obligations under this Article.[16]

During its deliberations, the Gregory Committee also examined the amendments to Article 6*bis* introduced at the Brussels Conference for the revision of the Berne Convention which took place in 1948, but concluded that they did not add materially to the scope of the article. It noted further that the UK delegation at the Brussels Conference had made a statement that they were not prepared to accept any amendment which would enlarge the scope of the article.[17] On this basis, the Committee concluded that the additions made at Brussels did not impose any obligation on the United Kingdom involving legislation. Nevertheless, the Committee considered whether any amendment of the UK law was desirable for the purpose of meeting representations made to it for enlarging the extent of the protection of "droit moral" in the United Kingdom, irrespective of the obligations of Article 6*bis* of the Convention. It took account not only of the interests of authors, but also of those of artists and performers.

The Gregory Committee took the view that the issues raised did not lend themselves to cure by legislative action but were of a type that could be best regulated by contract between the parties concerned.[18] In the view of the Committee:

---

[14]   *Report of the Copyright Committee*, chaired by H.S. Gregory, 1952, para. 219. The report led to the Copyright Act 1956.

[15]   See Sir John Mummery, Preface to the first edition of G. Davies and K. Garnett, KC, *Moral Rights*, Sweet and Maxwell, 2010, p. ix.

[16]   Gregory Committee Report, supra note 14, para 220.

[17]   Ibid, para 221.

[18]   Ibid, para 224.

In a field so vague and ill-defined it seems to us to be impossible – even if it were desirable – to frame legislative proposals to meet all possible problems. In general, the common law of this country provides adequate remedies, and in addition there are certain statutory remedies to meet particular and defined cases.[19]

The Committee gave the example of Section 7 of the Fine Arts Copyright Act 1862 which gave artists a measure of protection against the unauthorized alteration of their drawings or the fraudulent affixing of signatures to them. It recommended that this protection should be continued, and that the protection available under the Act in respect of artistic works should be extended to apply also in the case of literary and musical works.[20]

The Committee therefore "reached the conclusion that no legislative action is necessary for the purpose of implementing the obligations imposed by Article 6*bis* of the Rome or Brussels Convention"; and did not recommend any legislation … for the purpose of conferring a wider measure of protection in respect of "droit moral".[21] Thus, the UK revised Copyright Act 1956 lacked specific provisions on moral rights. An indirect result of this decision was that these rights did not find their way into many of the copyright laws of Commonwealth countries by means of subsequent extension of the 1956 Copyright Act of the United Kingdom.

Surprisingly, it appears from the Report of the Committee that there was no direct consultation with member countries of the Commonwealth as such during its deliberations. It took written and oral evidence from a wide variety of UK organizations and interested parties but the only hint of direct consultation with the British Empire and Commonwealth was a representation in writing from the Imperial Arts League.[22] The same applies as regards moral rights. It is of interest to see that the French Embassy made representations in writing to the Committee. One can only wonder whether these concerned the subject of moral rights.[23]

3.2   The Whitford Committee Report 1977

The subject of moral rights was next addressed in the United Kingdom in the deliberations of the Whitford Committee, the report of which was published in the spring of 1977. The report described how the Berne Convention, following the Continental European tradition, divides authors' rights into economic and moral rights (the rights of "paternity" and "integrity"), "the former to enable him to earn money; the latter, in theory at least, only to protect his reputation". It drew attention also to the inalienability of such rights: Article 6*bis* of the Berne Convention making it clear "that an assignment of what we would call the copyright does not carry with it also an assignment of the author's moral rights".[24]

---

[19]   Ibid, para 225.
[20]   Ibid. The Committee recommended that the Act of 1862 be repealed, and provision for the protection recommended should be incorporated into the Copyright Act.
[21]   Ibid. para 226.
[22]   Gregory Committee Report, Appendix A, Part 1. However, oral evidence was received from the Industrial Property Department of the then Board of Trade, which at the time would have been responsible for intellectual property matters both national and international and represented the UK Government at e.g. the Rome 1928 and Brussels 1948 Diplomatic Conferences.
[23]   Gregory Committee Report, Appendix A, Part II.
[24]   Report of the Committee to consider the Law of Copyright and designs, March 1977 (Whitford Committee Report), para. 51.

The Committee noted, however, that such submissions as it had received on the subject were in favour of giving full protection to moral rights but also pointed out some disadvantages, in particular, the separation of rights in a single work could well give rise to difficulties. The Committee nevertheless approved the general philosophy of moral rights. Outlining the changes required in UK law to allow it to comply with Article 6*bis* of the Convention, the Committee expressed the view that:

> Although the Berne Convention limits our freedom of action this is the price we pay for joining in a multi-national agreement with some 60 other countries and thus giving our authors, composers, artists and film makers the enormous benefit of copyright protection in all those countries without formality, merely by virtue of their having created a work. In addition, our publishers know that when they first publish a work here, even if it is not by a Convention national, their investment is protected throughout the Berne Union.[25]

In its Summary of Recommendations,[26] and for the reasons outlined above, the Committee recommended that the United Kingdom should ratify the Paris Act 1971 of the Berne Convention which would, inter alia, involve amendments to the Copyright Act 1956 in order "to make proper provision for moral rights under copyright law" (referring to paragraphs 56 and 57 of the report).[27]

Thereafter, the subject of moral rights was dropped in the United Kingdom until the 1980s when work began on the next revision of the Copyright Act 1956 and the recommendations of the Whitford Committee on the subject came under consideration. The revision process was protracted and controversial and the issue of moral rights was not at the top of the agenda due to the impact on the copyright world resulting from technical and digital developments. It was not until 1988 that the United Kingdom finally adopted the new Copyright, Designs and Patents Act of that year bringing the UK law up to date. Among many changes, it introduced the protection of moral rights into the copyright law of the United Kingdom for the first time, thus accepting the basic recommendations of the Whitford Committee. The subject was highly contested and the resulting provisions were and remain the subject of controversy.

3.3   The Copyright, Designs and Patents Act 1988

It took many years of deliberation and uncertainty before the United Kingdom finally took the decision to introduce a chapter on moral rights in the new Copyright Act 1988. It had "taken a long time for moral rights to find their way onto the Statute Book"[28] (60 years from the inclusion of Article 6*bis* of the Berne Convention in 1928). The rights have been described:

> as a comparatively new transplant from the Civil law into English law. The rights only previously available in piecemeal legislation and in common law bits of contract and tort have been expanded and supplemented.[29]

---

[25]   Whitford Committee Report, para, 58.
[26]   Whitford Committee Report, Ch. 20 Summary of Recommendations
[27]   Whitford Committee Report, Summary, Ch. 2 – International Conventions, para 919 (vi).
[28]   Sir John Mummery, in G. Davies and K. Garnett, *Moral Rights*, 2nd edn, Sweet and Maxwell, 2016, Preface to the 1st edn, p. ix.
[29]   Ibid.

The 1988 Act introduced the following rights:

- The right to be identified as author of a work or director of a film to be identified as such in relation to his creations (the right of paternity or attribution);
- The right of a performer to be identified as such in relation to his performances;
- The right of any person not to have a work falsely attributed to him;
- The right to object to derogatory treatment of a work, a film or performance (right of integrity);
- The right not to be falsely attributed as author or director (false attribution of a work); and
- The right to privacy of certain photographs and films.[30]

Although included under the general heading "Moral Rights" in the new Copyright Act, only the paternity and the integrity rights of authors, film producers, and performers listed above correspond directly to the rights provided for in the Berne Convention and the more recent World Intellectual Property Organization (WIPO) Performances and Phonograms Treaty (WPPT) adopted in 1996. The right to privacy of certain photographs and films has nothing to do with moral rights, as such, and only a tenuous connection with copyright.

Unsatisfactory as the new statutory provisions are, the previously existing framework of statutory and common law remains in place and it should not be thought therefore that the new statutory "moral rights" represent the entire code of UK moral rights; the previous case law is still applicable.

Nevertheless, in the years since the 1988 Act was adopted, the law on moral rights has scarcely advanced in the United Kingdom. The legislation is of little substance itself and there have been very few moral rights disputes of any importance decided by the courts so the case law on the subject is sparse in the extreme.[31]

Two critical comments about the new moral rights provisions in the 1988 Act sum up the drawbacks of these new statutory rights:

> It is perhaps characteristic of the UK's lukewarm approach to moral rights in general that, as will be seen, the fundamental rights prescribed by the Berne Convention have been so hedged about by conditions and exceptions that the UK paternity and integrity rights are recognisable only as the sickly children of the Berne parent. The main criticisms of the statutory rights are the need to *assert* the paternity right in the first place, the numerous exceptions to the right in general, and the ease with which they can be given up by a waiver or made the subject of consent.[32]

Another sober assessment is that:

> Adopting a typically British legislative style, a detailed and complex moral rights code was favoured in preference to a simple restatement of the general principles set out in Article 6*bis* Berne which would have left the courts with too free a hand to work out how they should apply.[33]

---

[30]   The latter right is not a moral right as defined in the Berne Convention, but confers a personal right to privacy on the commissioner of such works.

[31]   See G. Davies and K. Garnett, KC, *Moral Rights*, 2nd edn, Sweet and Maxwell, 2016, Foreword, p. xi.

[32]   Ibid, para. 6-003 (emphasis added).

[33]   S. Ricketson, "The Moral Right of the Author, Moral Rights and the Common Law Countries" ALAI Congress Paper, September 1993.

By contrast, as my colleague, Kevin Garnett KC. and I have pointed out in our book on moral rights:

> Meanwhile, all around, and as if to bring the paucity of the UK rights into starker relief, there has continued to be an astonishing blossoming of moral rights in other countries. As this work will attempt to show, numerous countries around the world today take it as a matter of course that the bond between an author and his work is worthy of proper recognition and have enacted legislation accordingly. Moral rights protection is thus today no longer restricted to a few jurisprudentially exotic countries. The nature and extent of this development has left the UK standing on the platform with a few other stragglers, in particular, the USA, gazing after the moral rights train that has left the station with everyone else on board.[34]

4. MORAL RIGHTS PROTECTION IN INTERNATIONAL INSTRUMENTS OTHER THAN BERNE

4.1 Introduction

During the 1980s and early 1990s, it became clear to governments and interested circles that there was a need for new international regulations on intellectual property, generally, and on the application of the Berne Convention, in particular. As regards the Berne Convention, there was a need to update the level of protection afforded by the Convention to deal with the technical developments which had emerged since the adoption of the Paris Act of the Berne Convention in 1971. In the first place,

> the shortcomings of the Convention with respect to standards of protection and the lack of any mechanism therein for enforcing the obligations of Member States and for the settlement of disputes between them were brought into focus in the context of the international negotiations which took place at the time and resulted in the adoption of a new international treaty under the auspices of the World Trade Organization, the Agreement on Trade-related Aspects of Intellectual Property (the TRIPs Agreement) in 1994.[35]

Issues connected with the exploitation of works in the digital environment also needed to be addressed.

A new substantive revision of the Berne Convention was considered politically impossible at the time because it would require unanimity among the countries of the Union (100 Member States in 1994). Work therefore began under the auspices of WIPO on the elaboration of two new independent, multilateral treaties, which were adopted in 1996. The WIPO Copyright Treaty (WCT), providing extended protection in the digital environment for the rights of authors, and the WPPT, providing similarly extended protection for the rights of performers and producers of phonograms.

All three of these new treaties are concerned in one way or another with moral rights.

---

[34] Davies and Garnett, supra note 31, Foreword to the 2nd edn, 2016, p. xi.
[35] Ibid, para 4-009.

4.2   The TRIPs Agreement 1994

The TRIPs Agreement is an Annex to the Agreement establishing the World Trade Organization (WTO) adopted in 1994. It concerned intellectual property rights generally, including, inter alia, copyright and related rights. An important aspect of the Agreement is its provisions for the enforcement of intellectual property rights and for dispute prevention and settlement measures.

In relation to copyright, members of TRIPs are obliged to comply with the substantive provisions of the Berne Convention and not derogate from the existing obligations that members of the Berne Convention have to each other. However, this rule is subject to one important exception, namely that moral rights are expressly excluded from the scope of the TRIPs Agreement. Notwithstanding the TRIPs Agreement, however, the obligations of the countries of the Berne Union to each other under Article 6*bis* of the Berne Convention continue to apply in relation to moral rights.

4.3   WIPO Copyright Treaty 1996 (WCT)

The WCT is a special agreement within the meaning of Article 20 of the Berne Convention, and, as such, grants authors more extensive rights than those granted by the Convention itself. It entered into force on 6 March 2002.

So far as moral rights are concerned, the WCT merely safeguards the existing protection afforded to authors under the Berne Convention, preserving the status quo. This follows from Article 1 of the Treaty, which provides that all Contracting Parties to it shall comply with the substantive law provisions of the Paris Act of the Berne Convention, including Article 6*bis* on moral rights.[36]

4.4   WIPO Performances and Phonograms Treaty 1996 (WPPT)

The WPPT entered into force on 20 May 2002. It was adopted in response to the general:

> agreement that the level of protection provided for performers and producers of phonograms in the Rome Convention 1961 and the Phonograms Convention 1971 was inadequate in the light of contemporary technology and that there was a need for new international rules to provide adequate solutions to the questions raised by economic, social, cultural and technical developments.[37]

The Treaty aimed to update international copyright and related rights norms to better protect right owners (performers and producers of phonograms) in the digital age:

> The new information and communication technologies had created new means for creating, storing, performing and disseminating phonograms and performances, which were having a profound impact on their production and use.[38]

---

[36]   Ibid, para 4-010.
[37]   Ibid, para 4-011.
[38]   See the Preamble to the WPPT.

The WPPT mainly parallels the provisions of the WCT, but in respect of the protection of performers it is relevant to this chapter because it made history by providing a degree of protection for the moral rights of performers for the first time at international level. It protects their moral rights of paternity and integrity as regards live *aural* performances or performances fixed in phonograms. The use of the word "aural" is significant. The Treaty does not apply to *audiovisual* performances or performances fixed in audiovisual works.[39] However, the word *aural is not limited to musical works* but covers also speech and recitation of literary works, as well as the aural part of a dramatic performance and its fixation in a phonogram.

The WPPT requires a somewhat lower level of protection for performers' moral rights than that afforded to authors. In respect of the right to be identified as a performer, certain exceptions to the rule may be permitted for practical reasons, in identified circumstances. The right of integrity is also restricted; whereas authors may object to actions prejudicial to their honour or reputation, performers only have the right to object to actions which would be prejudicial to their reputation. The justification for this limitation is not clear but from the records of the Conference it appears that it may have been to exclude performers from objecting to parodies of their performances.[40]

4.5   The Beijing Treaty on Audiovisual Performances 2012

The WPPT failed to protect the rights of performers in the audiovisual fixations of their performances. A "Resolution Concerning Audiovisual Performances" was adopted at the conclusion of the Diplomatic Conference which adopted the WCT and WPPT, calling for the matter to be further considered. It took 16 years (1996–2012) before the matter was resolved and opposition to the protection of audiovisual performances on the part of the international and powerful film and broadcasting industries was overcome. The problem had first come to light more than 50 years previously in relation to the negotiations leading to the Rome Convention of 1961, when the protection of audiovisual performances was first and successfully opposed.

As regards moral rights, the rights of paternity and integrity are recognized in favour of performers with respect to live performances or performances fixed in audiovisual fixations as they enjoy rights in fixations of sound.[41]

Performers are defined in the same way as in the WPPT and the Treaty is based on the principle of national treatment.

5.   DEVELOPMENT OF MORAL RIGHTS LEGISLATION IN MAJOR COMMON LAW COUNTRIES 1928–2022

It took the United Kingdom no less than 60 years following the introduction of moral rights protection into the Berne Convention in 1928 to introduce specific moral rights legislation in its national copyright law. The concepts behind, and history of, moral rights legislation intro-

---

[39]   Agreement could not be reached at the Diplomatic Conference of 1996 on rights in audiovisual performances. Protection for such rights had to wait for the Beijing Conference Treaty on Audiovisual Performances, adopted in 2012.

[40]   See Davies and Garnett, supra note 31, para 4-011 for more details.

[41]   Beijing Treaty, Art. 2.

duced in the Copyright, Designs and Patents Act 1988 would have been new, not just to the British, but to many copyright practitioners, the legal professions generally, and governments responsible for copyright in Commonwealth countries. The 1911 and 1956 Copyright Acts of the United Kingdom, which were extended to many Commonwealth countries, contained no provisions on the subject. Since the concept of moral rights was not a feature of common law jurisdictions or of the law of the United Kingdom, in particular, common law countries, whether members of the Commonwealth or not, for the most part did not include moral rights in their copyright legislation.

Among Commonwealth countries, there were two striking exceptions to this rule: Canada and India. These are discussed briefly below.

5.1   Canada

Canada, with its law based on the common law system, was also influenced by the civil law system which prevailed in the province of Quebec and introduced the protection of moral rights into its copyright law as early as 1931. It was the first country with a jurisdiction mainly based on the English legal tradition to introduce moral rights as prescribed by the Berne Convention into its domestic law. It enacted specific moral rights legislation in anticipation of Canada's accession to the 1928 Rome revision Act of the Berne Convention in the same year.

The provision, which virtually reproduced Article 6*bis*(1) of the Rome Act of the Berne Convention verbatim, remained on the books until 1988, when the Copyright Act was amended to include a more detailed regime of moral rights.[42]

Nevertheless, in Canada prior to its accession to the Rome Act, moral rights had been recognized already by legislation and in the case law.

As David Vaver explained in 1998:

> The first vestige of moral rights in legislation appeared in 1915. An amendment to the Criminal Code made it an offence either to make any change in a copyright dramatic, operatic or musical work that was to be publicly performed for profit, or to suppress its title or authorship, without the consent of the author or his legal representative.[43]

The provision was carried over into the Copyright Act of 1921 and remained as Section 43 in the consolidation of the Copyright Act until the Act was revised again in 1988. David Vaver, in his report to ALAI in 1993, also drew attention to the extent to which Canadian judges had taken account of the common law in decisions concerning "moral rights" issues, starting with a case in the Canadian Supreme Court as long ago as 1911. In that case, the Court required a publisher to return a biographical manuscript which it had refused to publish, on condition that the author repaid any advances. In his judgment, the Chief Justice referred directly to the concept of moral rights stating that: "After the author has parted with his pecuniary interest in the manuscript, he retains a species of personal or moral right in the product of his brain".[44] Vaver also pointed out that: "Although the case was an appeal from a common law

---

[42]   David Vaver, "Report on Moral Rights, Canada", in The Moral Right of the Author, Proceedings of the Congress of Antwerp, ALAI 1993, p. 207 et seq.
[43]   Ibid.
[44]   *Morang & Co v. Le Sueur* (1911) 45 S.C.R. 95, 97–8, 99–100.

province, Ontario, the judge supported his comments by reference to French doctrine and jurisprudence."[45]

5.2   India

India was another pioneering Commonwealth country in respect of moral rights. Like Canada, it became a member of the Berne Convention in 1928 during the period of British rule and later ratified the Rome Act of 1928 – which introduced Article 6*bis* on moral rights into the Convention – depositing its instrument of ratification in 1931. "It has been said that s 57 of the 1957 Act lifts authors' status beyond the material gains of copyright and gives it a special status, its object being to put the moral rights of authors on a higher footing than the normal object of copyright."[46]

The concept of copyright protection for authors' works and the provision of exclusive intellectual property rights were unknown in India until the British colonial government imported the law of copyright. Previously, the creative works of authors were considered public property to which there was free access to impart knowledge, education, and entertainment. The history of copyright law in India began with the pre-independence British period.[47] The Indian Copyright Act of 1847 was a reproduction of the English Copyright Act 1842 and conferred copyright on books. Subsequently, the Indian Copyright Act 1914 was introduced, tailored to the local needs of India but modelled on the UK Copyright Act 1911. Moral rights were not mentioned in these colonial Acts.

After independence, however, the Government of India enacted the Copyright Act 1957, which introduced the concept of moral rights of authors. These rights were known as "Authors' 'special rights'" to promote the importance of quality of creative genius of artists and authors, which determine the maturity and vitality of any culture, and to protect the social interest.[48] Thus, the concept of rights similar to the "moral rights" protected by the Berne Convention was recognized.

Many years later, in 1994, the Copyright Amendment Act was adopted, amending the 1957 Act to partly introduce the model of protection of moral rights of the Paris Act of the Berne Convention. It modified the law on moral rights in several respects, introducing exceptions limiting the author's moral rights in respect of adaptations of computer programs and the display of works. The term of protection, which had been perpetual under the 1957 Act, was reduced to life plus 60 years. However, more recently in 2012, protection in perpetuity was re-introduced as regards the moral right of integrity.

A further important amendment introduced protection for the moral rights of performers in compliance with the WPPT 1996.[49]

The history of moral rights in India illustrates how elements of the Continental approach to moral rights can be combined with the common law approach without controversy.

---

[45] See Vaver, supra note 42, at p. 208.
[46] G.R. Raghavender, in Davies and Garnett, supra note 31, Ch. 28 – India – at 28-011.
[47] Ibid, para 28-001.
[48] Ibid, para 28-003; see *Mannu Bhandari v. Kula Vikas Pictures Pvt Ltd,* AIR 1987 Del 13.
[49] The author is indebted to G.R. Raghavender for the information on moral rights in India published in Davies and Garnett, supra note 31, Ch. 28.

5.3   Australia

Australia provides a final example of a major common law Commonwealth jurisdiction which now recognizes moral rights. In Section 2, I have described how Australia as a representative of the British Empire played a crucial role in defending the common law attitude to moral rights at the Rome Conference in 1928, when Article 6*bis* of the Berne Convention was adopted. The Australian delegate's contribution to the debates in Rome was vital to the recognition in the report on moral rights that Article 6*bis* was compatible with the common law, which provided sufficient protection to meet the requirements of the new article.

Many years were to pass before Australia adopted legislation on moral rights; meanwhile they continued to be protected under the common law. In 1988, the same year as the United Kingdom passed the new Copyright, Designs and Patents Act with its new provisions on moral rights, a report on the subject by the Copyright Review Board concluded by a bare majority of 5 to 4 that its existing laws (which were virtually identical to the UK case law) were sufficient to comply with Article 6*bis* of the Berne Convention and that there was no need to enact specific moral rights legislation. It stated that there was insufficient support from authors and artists, there would be practical problems if any such legislation were to be introduced, and there were probably too few instances of "moral rights abuse" to warrant new legislation. This decision was obviously controversial and was in direct conflict with the recommendations of the UK Whitford Report which had led the United Kingdom to legislate on moral rights only recently.[50] The conclusions of the Committee were much criticized; experts maintained that the Australian law as it stood was in breach of Article 6*bis* of the Berne Convention and called for specific legislation to repair the situation.[51]

Two years later, in an unusual governmental U-turn, Australia did introduce such legislation. It was a surprising development because in the 1980s and 1990s there had been an ongoing debate on the subject which most assumed had been ended by the publication of the report of the Copyright Review Board referred to above. Moreover, Australia had adhered to the Berne Convention in its own right in 1928 and signed the Rome Act in that year ratifying it in 1935 on the understanding that so far as moral rights were concerned, its domestic law provided sufficient protection by means of common law and statute to satisfy other states members of the Berne Convention.

The change of attitude arose from the minority recommendations of the 1988 Copyright Review Committee. The minority had argued that Australia stood in breach of Article 6*bis* of the Berne Convention in so far as (1) the right to claim authorship was only partly protected and (2) the protection accorded to both rights of attribution and integrity only survived the author in very limited circumstances. It was these recommendations which subsequently gathered support and, following the publication of further discussion papers, draft legislation was put to Parliament in 1997, the Copyright Amendment (Moral Rights) Act being finally enacted in 2000.

The resulting legislation created two basic rights for authors, a right of integrity and a right of paternity, expressed as three rights: the right of integrity enabling the author to object to certain treatments of the work; the right of attribution (paternity right); and the right not to have authorship of a work falsely attributed. Despite all the debate, the interest in moral rights

---

[50]   See supra notes 24 and 26, above.
[51]   See Gerald Dworkin, supra note 4, p. 90.

appears to have vanished following the adoption of the legislation as in the intervening 20 years there has been "almost no case law on the subject".[52]

6.   MORAL RIGHTS IN THE COMMONWEALTH TODAY

6.1   Introduction

Looking at the position of moral rights in mid-2022, for a common lawyer it is striking how these rights have come to be almost universally recognized in the Commonwealth. Embarking on research for this chapter, I was not aware of the extent to which moral rights are now recognized in the 56 Commonwealth countries. I compared the list of Commonwealth countries with the lists of Contracting States of the Berne Convention and the WPPT and discovered to my surprise that no less than 50 of the 56 Commonwealth countries are party to the Berne Convention (the vast majority being party to the Paris Act) and 24 are party to the WPPT. Moreover, I found that nearly all have either enacted national legislation for the protection of moral rights or are party to the Berne Convention.

   I then compared the protection afforded by the 50 Commonwealth countries with the Table of National Laws on Moral Rights published in Chapter 33 of the book *Moral Rights* published by my colleague Kevin Garnett and myself in 2016. Being six years out of date now, it does not cover the situation in all Commonwealth countries, but it does show an astonishing level of protection of moral rights in the legislations of a large majority of the 56 members of the Commonwealth, as the table of their national laws on the subject in the Appendix to this *Handbook* demonstrates.

   The Appendix provides the following information about the protection of moral rights in the 56 Member States of the Commonwealth:

1. Name of country;
2. Copyright legislation in force;
3. Beneficiaries;
4. Moral Rights recognized;
5. Term of protection;
6. Date of joining the Berne Convention; and
7. Date of joining the WPPT.

6.2   Copyright Legislation in Force

Under this heading, details of the legislation currently in force on moral rights in each country is given. However, no information about legislation on the subject is available from: Bangladesh, Eswatini (former Swaziland), Guyana, Kiribati, Nauru, the Solomon Islands, and Tuvalu. Nevertheless, Bangladesh, Guyana, Kiribati, Nauru, the Solomon Islands, and Tuvalu are party to the Berne Convention. Only Eswatini has no legislation and is not party to the Berne Convention.

---

[52]   Davies and Garnett, supra note 31, para 3-006.

6.3   Beneficiaries

Most laws protect authors and performers. Only South Africa does not protect performers. Some define authors in some detail, listing film directors and/or producers, or making exceptions, such as, for example, excluding authors of computer programs. These details are shown in the table in the Appendix.

6.4   Moral Rights Recognized

The various specific moral rights granted by each country are noted by abbreviations and symbols which are defined at the end of the table in the Appendix, for example "P" stands for the paternity right and "I" for the integrity right. Where a category of beneficiary, for example, performers, have no rights, "None" appears.

6.5   The Term of Protection

The term of protection varies considerably and details of the terms of duration are given under this heading. The majority, 30, provide for 50 years p.m.a. and seven for 70 years p.m.a; nine protect moral rights in perpetuity and other variants include 75 p.m.a, 95 p.m.a and "lifetime" of the author. Of those who provide for 70 years p.m.a. for authors, some provide only 50 years p.m.a. protection for performers.

6.6   Membership of the Berne Convention and WPPT

No less than 50 of the 56 countries of the Commonwealth are party to the Berne Convention (only six exceptions) and 24 are party to the WPPT.

Of the six exceptions, five, Maldives, Papua New Guinea, Seychelles, Sierra Leone, and Uganda, do, however, have legislation on moral rights.

There is also a small group of countries party to the Berne Convention who have no legislation on copyright: Guyana, Nauru, the Solomon Islands, and Tuvalu.

6.7   The Beijing Treaty

Most recently, a substantial group of Commonwealth countries have become parties to the Beijing Treaty on Audiovisual Performances with effect from its entry into force on 28 April 2020: Belize, Botswana, Gabon, Ghana, Grenada, Kenya, Kiribati, Mauritius, Namibia, Nigeria, Saint Vincent and the Grenadines, Samoa, Togo, Trinidad and Tobago, Uganda, and Vanuatu, to date.

7.   CONCLUSIONS

Historically, common law countries, with the honourable exceptions of Canada and India already referred to, were long suspicious of the concept of moral rights, fearing that they serve as a limitation on the copyright owner's economic rights and thus finding them "inimical to the proper functioning of the commercial interests to which the exercise of the economic rights of copyright give rise".[53]

Writing in 2016, my colleague Kevin Garnett KC and I suggested:

> Thus, it is only comparatively recently that some other major common law jurisdictions such as the UK, Australia and the USA, have given serious consideration to legislating to introduce at least the minimum moral rights provided for by Art 6*bis* of the Berne Convention, namely the paternity right and the right of integrity.[54]

Nevertheless, as we pointed out in our discussion of copyright in common law countries,[55] the moral rights of disclosure, paternity and integrity were not as alien to the common law as has often been asserted. With their roots in the Statute of Anne 1709, these rights were not without protection altogether in common law jurisdictions, even if there was little specific legislation relating to them. Thus, it was that the common law countries, not wishing "to be obstructive" and in view of the fact that their laws provided some limited, albeit incidental, protection for moral rights were able to sign up to the compromise text that subsequently became Article 6*bis* of the Berne Convention as revised at Rome: the compromise not only refrained from requiring national copyright laws to have express moral rights provisions, but also tacitly acknowledged that the protection then offered at common law and equity by the common law countries' was adequate.[56]

It is just as well for the widespread international acceptance of the need for twenty-first century copyright laws to include moral rights, that the influence of UK copyright legislation on the subject declined once the practice of extending the UK Copyright Act to former colonies and dependencies ceased with the 1956 Act. Even though the moral rights provisions of the UK Copyright Act 1988 Act have been much criticized, at the least they led to much debate and an increased interest in the subject in common law countries whose copyright laws had their roots in UK copyright law.

Now that over 30 years have passed since the 1988 Act was passed, it is much to be welcomed that moral rights have secured recognition in nearly all the common law countries which are members of the Commonwealth. It demonstrates a near universal recognition of the personal connection between the author and his work and a performer and his performance which transcends the economic rights derived from copyright protection.

---

[53]   Y. Gendreau, "Moral Rights", in G.F. Henderson (ed.), *Copyright and Confidential Information Law of Canada* (Scarborough, Carswell, 1994), pp. 161 and 162.

[54]   Davies and Garnett, supra note 31, para 3-004.

[55]   Ibid.

[56]   See S. Ricketson, *The Berne Convention for the Protection of Literary and Artistic Works 1886–1986* (Arnhem and London, Kluwer and Centre for Commercial Law Studies, Queen Mary College, 1986), paras 8.92–8.116

PART VI

AUTHORS AND MORAL RIGHTS

27. Maybe he thought I was dead: a tale of moral rights and image ethics in South Africa
John Peffer

Questions about who is an author and who is a subject vis-à-vis the moral rights and ethical responsibilities of artists took an interesting turn in 2018 when South African photographer Graeme Williams was touring the Johannesburg Art Fair and was surprised to see a work of his for sale in a booth set up by the Goodman Gallery – but under another name.[1] The work was a colour photograph Williams made during an African National Congress (ANC) rally at a sports stadium in Thokoza Township, Johannesburg on 25 November 1990.[2] Nelson Mandela had recently been released from prison and was addressing a crowd of supporters. On one side of a fence a group of policemen were sitting on top of an armoured personnel carrier. In the picture they are facing to the right as they watching Mandela, who is outside the frame of the picture, and they look bored. Below them and on the other side of the fence a group of children were marching along in the opposite direction, doing the high-stepping martial dance known in South Africa as the *toyi-toyi*, a dance associated with the struggle against apartheid. 'I could see that there was a possibility of a picture happening,' Williams later recalled, so he walked across the pitch and snapped off several images in quick succession as the marchers passed beneath the police, taunting them.[3]

This was a chance image, a decisive moment that appears from our present distance to be a picture symbolic of the revolutionary end of apartheid and of South Africa's transition to democracy. The picture is one of several that have become iconic in the sense that they are among the most well-known and emblematic pictures from the anti-apartheid struggle. The year 1990 was still the pre-digital era and one would only see what images they had after developing the film in the lab later. From the negatives Williams developed from 25 November 1990 the international news agency *Reuters* chose one that was subsequently 'widely syndicated'.[4] The picture of the children *toyi-toying* in front of the police was subsequently reprinted and seen around the world in multiple iterations, in various media and size formats and with some variation in the caption.

Initially the primary object was the immediate news value of the picture. Later the picture acquired more historic and symbolic value. In the early 1990s it was only one of 'thousands

---

[1]   The FNB Joburg Art Fair is an annual trade fair for art galleries in Africa. In 2018 it was held 7, 8, and 9 September at the Sandton Convention Centre.

[2]   Details on the original contexts of his image were shared in a series of emails to the author by Graeme Williams, on 22, 23, and 25 July 2020.

[3]   Email from Graeme Williams to the author (22 July 2020).

[4]   The original *Reuters* caption slightly misstated the location of the event by several kilometres: 'Tembisa, South Africa, 25 Nov 90 – South African Police watch from their troop carrier November 25 as African National Congress supporters dance below, at a rally held in Tembisa Township. The rally was addressed by ANC deputy president, Nelson Mandela. Graeme Williams REUTER'. My thanks to Williams for sharing the original print and caption as sent by wire to *Reuters*, from his archive.

of images coming out of South Africa', as the world's interest was transfixed by the fall of apartheid and the transition to democracy.[5] During the 2000s the image lived a second life after slightly differently framed negatives from the initial batch were digitally scanned and made available via international photo agencies. Williams claims this picture only 'started to be used more and more in the 2000s when publications and exhibitions started to focus/ look back on the transition era', and that was after he had begun to sift and re-release his own older images in this new context.[6] Wider connections, similarities and comparisons with other contemporary images and with other struggles elsewhere in the world began to be made by viewers. The work moved from newspapers into magazines and from there into commercial art galleries and public museums.

Over time views on the image became more retrospective, more reflective, and less about the initial and immediate context of events. In 2002, a version with more of the crowd in view was included in the exhibition 'Shooting Resistance: South African Photography 1976–1994' at Axis Gallery in New York, whose press release noted its '65 images by 24 leading South African photographers' may (among other things) illustrate how 'South Africa's historic struggle for civil rights resonates with American history'.[7] Similarly, in 2008 the Obama campaign chose Williams's picture to illustrate the then-candidate's world view in a special feature in the 6 October issue of *Newsweek* magazine dedicated to the McCain/Obama presidential contest in the United States. In *Newsweek* a quotation by Obama from when he had participated in a student rally in support of the anti-apartheid movement on campus at Occidental College in 1981 was overlaid on the Williams image: 'There is a struggle going on! A struggle that demands we choose sides. It's a choice between dignity and servitude. A choice between right and wrong.'[8]

In 2013 the image was reframed once again, this time as a diptych within a longer photographic essay titled, 'Over Time'. This essay was Williams's response 'to the increasing disregard for what Mandela and his friends achieved, and the general decay of values', two decades after Mandela's celebrated release from prison.[9] For the 'Over Time' project he returned to the sites of many of his earlier press photographs and made new images in a more reflective mode. The new pictures were shown in pairs with the older ones to contrast then and now. Next to the *toyi-toyi* image he juxtaposed a photograph of a mural made at the Thokoza stadium after 1990 that depicted the funeral of ANC activist Sam Ntuli. Ntuli was murdered in 1991 and the stadium was renamed in his honour. Today the mural itself is crumbling with age and neglect, and in the diptych the earlier image of the children taunting police ironically appears fresher, more immediate, as if better preserved for posterity than the commemorative mural that came later. 'Over Time' was featured on the Apartheid and After exhibition at Huis Marseille pho-

---

[5]   Email from Graeme Williams to the author (25 July 2020).
[6]   Email from Graeme Williams to the author (25 July 2020).
[7]   See the exhibition description from the Axis Gallery website: https:// axis .gallery/ exhibitions/ shooting-resistance/ accessed 15 August 2020.
[8]   N.a., 'Mr. Cool v.s. Mr. Hot, How They See the World' *Newsweek* (6 October 2008). The quotation was from a divestment rally at Occidental College in 1981. See Peter Dreier, 'Mandela Inspired a Generation of Activists, Including Obama' *Huffington Post* (10 December 2013) https://www.huffpost .com/entry/mandela-inspired-a- generation_b_4422712 accessed 15 August 2020.
[9]   Email from Graeme Williams to the author (25 July 2020).

tography museum in Amsterdam in 2014.[10] An earlier version of the juxtaposition project had been published in a feature on Williams in 2012, as part a special South Africa focus in the UK surf, skate and subcultures magazine *Huck*, where it was referred to by the title, 'Previously Significant Places'.[11]

Perhaps the most widely-seen presentation of the work, aside from the usage by the Obama campaign in 2008, was when it featured prominently on the blockbuster exhibit Rise and Fall of Apartheid organized at the International Center for Photography (ICP) in New York that travelled to Munich, Milan and Johannesburg between 2013 and 2015.[12] The ICP show presented an inventory of images documenting the apartheid state and its demise, in effect sealing their legacy status as a group, as an 'archive'. This also secured canonical status for them, facilitating their being seen even more as historic objects and as aesthetic objects beyond their information-bearing aspects. Williams's picture was illustrated in the catalogue and circulated widely as one of the lead images used in print and online press reviews of Rise and Fall.[13]

No longer only as documentary or as photojournalism, the *toyi-toyi* photograph was then shown as a work of fine art at the Goodman Gallery, this time as an even more generalized example of common gestures seen at popular protests. And for a moment its authorship changed hands. This brings us back to the upmarket Sandton Convention Centre and the JNB Joburg Art Fair in 2018, where the 'surprise' was that Williams was not an artist represented by the Goodman Gallery, permission to use his work had not been asked, and the work was not credited to him in the display. At the Joburg Art Fair the picture was being shown as part of a multi-photograph solo presentation by American artist Hank Willis Thomas. It was re-titled, 'Gravitas', credited solely to Thomas, and offered for sale for $36,000.[14]

Hank Willis Thomas's display at the Joburg Art Fair was a series of separately framed and hung pictures, and it included well-known and widely published images dating from the antiapartheid struggle made by veteran South African photojournalists Peter Magubane and Jan Hamman, as well as Williams. Magubane's photograph was of a Black resident in the racially

---

[10]   Press materials for the exhibition give the title of the work as 'Previously Important Places series 1990s–2013'. https://huismarseille.nl/tentoonstellingen/apartheid-after/ accessed 15 August 2020.

[11]   Andrea Kurland, 'Snapshots of the Rainbow Nation before and after Apartheid Fell' (August/ September 2012) 34 *Huck* https://www.huckmag.com/perspectives/reportage-2/south-africa/ accessed 15 August 2020.

[12]   The exhibition dates were 14 September 2012–6 January 2013 in New York; at Haus der Kunst, Munich, Germany, 15 February–26 May 2013; at Padiglione d'Arte Contemporanea Milano, Milan, Italy, 8 July–15 September 2013; and an extended run at Museum Africa in Johannesburg, South Africa, 13 February 2014–30 April 2015. According to the ICP website the exhibition examined, 'the legacy of the apartheid system and how it penetrated even the most mundane aspects of social existence in South Africa, from housing, public amenities, transportation, to education, tourism, religion, and businesses'. It included nearly 500 photographs, films, books, magazines, newspapers, and assorted archival documents and covers more than 60 years of powerful photographic and visual production that form part of the historical record of South Africa. https://www.icp.org/exhibitions/rise-and-fall-of-apartheid accessed 15 August 2020.

[13]   Anna Hiatt, 'The Rise and Fall of Apartheid in Pictures. An Exhibition in South Africa Is Attracting Record-Breaking Crowds' *The New Republic* (26 June 2014) https://newrepublic.com/article/118367/rise-and-fall-south-africas-apartheid-pictures accessed 15 August 2020.

[14]   Debora Patta, 'U.S. Artist Accused of Stealing Iconic Images from South African Photographers' *CBS News* (17 October 2018) https://www.cbsnews.com/news/artist-hank-willis-thomas-accused-of-stealing-from-south-african-photographers-peter-magubane-graeme-williams/ accessed 15 August 2020.

mixed neighbourhood Sophiatown in 1955, giving a thumbs-up sign as she was being forcibly removed from her home by police. The removals at Sophiatown are one of the most notorious incidents of apartheid segregation in South Africa. The Jan Hamman photograph was from the uprising in 1976 in Soweto when school kids were protesting the apartheid education system and police fired on the crowd, killing scores of children. In the centre of Hamman's image two young men kneel and raise their hands in peace signs over their heads. In the foreground a policeman is watching them (possibly pointing a gun) from behind the open door of a police truck, and in the background a large crowd of children looks on.

Hank Willis Thomas reprinted these images, outlined their central figures, and partly obscured their backgrounds using a white, thinly opaque reflective coating. This creative process was similar to other works of his that had been featured to much acclaim earlier that same year in the United States at the Jack Shainman Gallery in New York.[15] In New York Thomas had taken older news photographs from the history of civil rights protests in South Africa and the United States, isolated the main figures, and covered the rest with an industrial retro-reflective material that selectively revealed the background when brightly lit. At the Joburg Art Fair the descriptive flyer produced by the Goodman Gallery reproduced the 1976 picture by Jan Hamman of the young men in Soweto with hands raised, above the caption, 'HANK WILLIS THOMAS, *Winds of Change, 2018.*' Above this picture a text explained:

SOLO PRESENTATION HANK WILLIS THOMAS

For his solo presentation, Hank Wills Thomas presents a series of reflective vinyls featuring press photographs from Apartheid-era South Africa. The prints are made using a white-on-white retro-reflective process in which the images are barely visible until activated by viewers, who are invited to illuminate the works using cell phones or LED glasses. When light hits the images' surfaces, the background becomes highly reflective, while the image impressed on it remains comparably darker. The effect is a series of images that appear to change and invert depending on your angle of view, creating an instability that brings attention to the important role that a viewer plays in the life cycle of an image. Recalling the silk screen prints of Robert Rauschenberg and Andy Warhol, Thomas stresses the repetition of images in popular culture as a vehicle for creating value in society. For this series Thomas appropriates from numerous historic images of protest in order to shed light on stories, images and ideas that have been marginalized and/or excluded from our collective conscience.[16]

Thomas's use of creative appropriation follows from the long history of twentieth century avant-garde artists who have cut and pasted and remixed from mass culture for purposes of critical social commentary. In the early 1900s, Cubist artists collaged real world items into their paintings, and Dada and Surrealist artists incorporated everyday found objects into their compositions. In the 1950s and 1960s, Rauschenberg, in the Dada tradition, made seemingly random juxtapositions of found objects and images, some taken from newspapers and magazines, suggesting new visual associations. With some irony and a touch of camp, Warhol silk-screened and added garish colour to famous personalities, shocking news images

---

[15]   Julian A. Jimarez Howard, 'Hank Willis Thomas's New Show Literally Shines a Light on Whitewashed Histories' *Garage* (2 April 2018) https://garage.vice.com/en_us/article/59jdv5/hank-willis -thomas-jack-shainman-what-we-ask accessed 15 August 2020.

[16]   The wording of this text closely follows promotional materials for the artist placed online by the Shainman and Goodman galleries. See for instance the web page for Thomas's solo show at Shainman, *What we ask is simple*, 29 March–12 May 2018. https://jackshainman.com/exhibitions/what_we_ask_is _simple_20th accessed 15 August 2020.

of disasters, and common commercial products. American and European Artists of the 1970s and 1980s appropriated mass media images and advertisements to reveal and critique the construction of racialized and gendered identities by corporate culture, and to interrogate everyday notions of economic and social value in modern society.

Appropriation as part of revolutionary art practices of *détournement* of the meaning of oppressive symbols and monuments, and of parodying commodity images, has been an aspect of South African art history since at least the 1970s.[17] So has the translation of iconic photojournalistic images into other media, most notably in the case of Sam Nzima's photograph of 12 year old Hector Pieterson dying in the arms of Mbuyisa Makhubu after being shot by police in Soweto on June 16 1976, which has been reiterated on countless posters and silk-screened tee shirts during the struggle period and after.[18]

Thomas's overall conceptual project, as appropriation art, is heir to these antecedents of mining and re-authoring of others' works. It is also in line with the work of other contemporary American artists who have examined historic images of twentieth-century civil rights protests, removing them from their original contexts and considering them as aesthetic objects, in order to call attention to other aspects of the signage of protest beyond their original or literal meanings, making them less static, less iconic, and opening them for alternative and critical interpretations. For example in Glenn Ligon's 1988 'Untitled (I am a man)', the artist made a painting based on the silk-screened placard worn by striking Black sanitation workers in Memphis in 1968, turning the original multiple back into a personal object, and changing the colour from red to black on white.[19] In 2000, Ligon also added a museum 'condition report' pointing to all the scuffs and scratches on the surface, as if they were a forensic report indicating signs of injury to the human body, thus hinting at the ageing of civil rights discourse as well as shifting notions of Black masculinity. The same 'I am a man' placard from 1968 was also represented by Sharon Hayes as part of her series of performances on city streets circa 2009, where she anachronistically held up several signs dating from earlier eras of protest as a means to cite these earlier struggles and to bring attention to the rhetoric-in-common of diverse popular struggles particularly as they may intersect with present day rights demands by LGBTQIA+ persons.[20] And the same placard is the basis for a 20-painting series by Hank Willis Thomas titled, 'I Am a Man' (2009), that is now in the collection – and prominently on display in the lobby – of the Ford Foundation in New York. Thomas's piece uses the original text as a sort of anagram, which he remixed to create alternative inflections of meaning, some humorous and others more biting, such as Am I A Man, I Am Your Man, I Am a Woman, What a Man, I Am Many, I Am Amen ... and so on.

In his decontextualization of images from protest culture another characteristic of Thomas's work has been that he has removed his source images from their specific local contexts, thus making their meaning more ambiguous, more available for alternative interpretation and for juxtaposition with other kinds of images from other places. An example is his 2014 sculpture,

---

[17] John Peffer, 'Censorship and Iconoclasm: Unsettling Monuments' (Autumn 2005) 48 RES: Anthropology and Aesthetics 45.

[18] Ruth Kerkham Simbao, 'The Thirtieth Anniversary of the Soweto Uprisings: Reading the Shadow in Sam Nzima's Iconic Photograph of Hector Pieterson' (2007) 40(2) African Arts 52.

[19] https://www.nga.gov/collection/art-object-page.159784.html accessed 15 August 2020.

[20] Sharon Hayes, 'In the Near Future' (2009) http://shaze.info/work/in-the-near-future/ accessed 15 August 2020.

'Raise Up', based on a famous photograph from the 1960s by the South African Ernest Cole. In Cole's original picture a group of Black men stand naked with arms raised facing a wall. Each has a stack of papers on the floor behind him. These are recruits to South Africa's gold mines, undergoing an invasive and humiliating series of health inspections. Thomas transformed Cole's photograph into a bronze sculpture and removed the bodies below the shoulders, placing them on a long wall of cement. Now as a sculpture, the cement appears to be rising up about to engulf and suffocate the figures. The bureaucratic stack of papers is gone, information about apartheid, about the miners, and about Ernest Cole (who braved harassment by authorities in order to make this picture), is gone. This new ambiguity about the image prompted *New York Times* art critic Holland Cotter to wonder rhetorically if the new sculpture was 'a victory salute'. 'No', he concludes, because, 'in an American context the same figures suggest police suspects lined up at gunpoint'.[21]

Thomas has often taken images like this from one medium, usually photographs from popular media, and translated them using another medium or technology. He uses this inter-medial process to comment on the original or make it available for other kinds of discussion. For instance, when it facilitates a comparison of gestures commonly found at civil rights protests, or a pondering over the common experiences of subjection of Black bodies in the United States and elsewhere. This was the case with the 'retro-reflective' works that either obscured historic photographs in layers of coloured reflective coating, or, as with the South African pieces, used a pared-down palette of black and white. The over-painting was intended to bring selected elements of the original images into the foreground. The idea, according to Thomas, is that the historic protest images, 'are activated by flash photography playing with role reversal by having the viewer step into the position of image maker'.[22]

In addition to the common civil rights thematic, this novel viewing strategy is meant to call traditional notions of authorship into question. Authorship of the original pictures is shifted to the viewers-as-active-participants in acts of historical interpretation of canonical images. Thomas himself ultimately claims authorship since it is he who has captured our attention in this way and he who ultimately signed the work alone, had solo shows of the work, and keeps the artist's share of proceeds of sales.

In an interview on the occasion of the Frieze Art Fair in New York in 2018, Thomas elaborated how he believes the people depicted in historic images should also be seen as authors, of their own history, and this is something that is usually lost in the general glut of images available through the internet and mass media. These marginalized subjects are often absent from discussions of historic, iconic, and otherwise canonical photographs from the global history of human rights struggles:

> I think there is a metaphor for history and that sometimes we need to shine light on certain things to see them in a new way or to remember them. A lot of the images that are used and the people in them

---

[21]   Holland Cotter, 'A Memorial to the Lingering Horror of Lynching' *New York Times* (3 June 2018) https://www.nytimes.com/2018/06/01/arts/design/national-memorial-for-peace-and-justice -montgomery-alabama.html accessed 15 August 2020.
[22]   Hank Willis Thomas, artist bio posted by Jack Shainman Gallery https://jackshainman.com/artists/ hank_willis_thomas accessed 15 August 2020.

are not the people who normally get the light shined on them; and so it's really a reminder for myself, as well as for the viewers, to look deeper and not just for what's visible on the face reading.[23]

Furthermore, Thomas sees his privilege as a prominent fine artist as giving him a platform to call attention to these unsung people in the glut of historic images and likewise to take images otherwise lost to history and give them more permanence as art:

> One of the challenges I've always had with archival images is that if it's a news photograph or something that we've seen as a 'document,' there's an expiration date on the relevance ... When you take images that are seen as current events and easily dispersed and use the language of art history and lauded artists to frame them differently, I hope it gives these images new life.[24]

The reception of this body of work in the United States has been overwhelmingly enthusiastic, garnering a Guggenheim Fellowship and other prestigious awards, and with commentators generally emphasizing its relevance and its timeliness: 'Thomas's engagement with the politics of identity, history, the history of art, and popular culture is particularly apropos in today's political climate.'[25] In the United States the work has been understood as trenchant commentary on the ubiquity and lack of context for images of political struggle in the (digital) world today, prompting a reviewer for the art magazine *Garage* to write:

> This desire for sincere engagement with these histories explains Thomas's use of reflection – what could be seen as a gimmick instead breaks the fourth wall, implicating us in these historic scenes, forcing us to complete them. In some instances, he reveals the whitewashing of history by literally erasing context, selectively cropping the image, covering part of the scene in a white made transparent only when light is applied to reveal the image underneath.[26]

Interestingly, the same reviewer mentions some dissonance between the artist's intentions and the actual work on display, since 'despite their historical significance, viewers might struggle to identify each image's source', and noted further that, '[i]n an interview at the gallery, Thomas himself noted his own unfamiliarity with many of them prior to the inception of this project'. But this lack of context is resolved, they say, because it 'underscores the way these events are comprehended en masse by society', and because, 'Thomas provides a counterpoint, isolating and revealing the images, piece by piece'.[27]

That is not how things were perceived in South Africa. There, in addition to Williams's and Magubane's own unpleasant surprise at the Joburg Art Fair, press reviewers were uniformly critical of Thomas's process and pointed to what they saw as inconsistencies in his stated intentions.[28] According to the *Sunday Times* (Johannesburg), '[t]he only changes to the

---

[23] Uchenna Itam, 'Hank Willis Thomas Shines a Light' *The Standard* (2 May 2018) www .standardhotels.com/culture/Hank-Willis-Thomas-Interview-Shainman-Frieze accessed 15 August 2020.
[24] Ibid.
[25] Ibid.
[26] Julian A. Jimarez Howard, 'Hank Willis Thomas's New Show Literally Shines a Light on Whitewashed Histories' *Garage* (2 April 2018) https://garage.vice.com/en_us/article/59jdv5/hank-willis -thomas-jack-shainman-what-we-ask accessed 15 August 2020.
[27] Ibid. The article notes that 'Thumbnails have been compiled into a reference list accompanied by a brief didactic text, so that viewers can dig a little deeper into their context.' A similar list was claimed to have been produced by Goodman, but the gallery did not provide copies to the author upon request.
[28] Jan Hamman passed in 2004.

original photos are that they have been enlarged and drained of colour or had a colour wash added. Thomas did not ask permission to use the photos, which he sells for about R500,000.'[29] Where in the United States the conversation was mostly about the ambiguity of gestures of protest and about the restitution of protest history by the artist, instead the conversation in South Africa was about definitions of plagiarism, unauthorized alteration, and artists' rights to attribution. The *Sunday Times* noted how, in addition to works shown at the Art Fair, '[s]everal other Magubane images were used by Thomas in a collage ... unaltered except for a solid wash of colour over them'.[30] Fikile Magubane, the photographer's daughter, complained publicly about how the family was 'disappointed at how Magubane's work has been "defaced."'[31] Peter Magubane himself, then 86, 'said he regretted not being asked for permission to use his photographs'.[32] He remarked that '[s]everal people in the past have used my photos for their art, but they have always come to me first. I think it's respectful to do so. Maybe he thought I was dead.'[33]

Following complaints by Williams and by the Magubane family, Goodman Gallery removed the works in question from the Art Fair walls and from the gallery premises nearby. But a growing chorus of negative feedback continued to appear, in Graeme Williams's Facebook feed, in the South African press, in the international press, and in online fora including *Artforum*, *Quartz* business news, *artnet News*, *The Conversation*, *The Guardian*, *Al Jazeera*, and *CBS News*. Commentators on Facebook, doing their own social media sleuthing, pointed out that at a concurrent exhibit in China, Thomas had applied the same technique to historic images from Hong Kong and Tiananmen Square, also with minimal alteration beyond the addition of reflective screening material, and also lacking attribution.[34] Another, by scrolling through Thomas's Instagram feed, found that photojournalist Noel Watson's famous 'Security forces with dogs hold back a crowd protesting against Minister Piet Koornhof being given the "Freedom of Soweto"' (1980), had similarly been appropriated without credit or compensation. The same images by both Graeme Williams and Noel Watson's 'appeared alongside each other in the exhibition and book "The Rise and Fall of Apartheid."'[35] The implication was that the 'archive' referred to may have been the catalogue from that recent exhibition, whose

---

[29]   Alex Patrick, 'Shock at Whitewash of Iconic Photos by US Artist Hank Willis Thomas. US artist Alters Works by SA Greats with No Attribution or Say-so' *Sunday Times* (Johannesburg 23 September 2018) https:// www .timeslive .co .za/ sunday -times/ news/ 2018 -09 -22 -shock -at -whitewash -of -iconic -photos -by -us -artist -hank -willis -thomas/. The asking price, $36,000 is about 100 times the monthly subsistence wages of a family living near the poverty line in South Africa. It is a significant sum in South Africa and it is 30 times the rate Williams usually sold his picture for. The high asking price appears to have added to the annoyance of local photographers.

[30]   Ibid.

[31]   Ibid.

[32]   Ibid.

[33]   Ibid.

[34]   According to the descriptive text for the Hong Kong show: 'It is only when the works are illuminated by a beam of light that the full details and crushing impact of these historical photographs are revealed.' See Hank Willis Thomas, *My Life is Ours*, Ben Brown Fine Arts (Hong Kong) 20 September–27 October 2018. https://www.benbrownfinearts.com/ exhibitions/ 134/ works/ accessed 16 August 2020.

[35]   Facebook post from Dale Yudelman to Graeme Williams (11 September 2018).

images could just have been scanned to create the new works. The same images had also appeared side-by-side in press reviews of the Rise and Fall exhibition.[36]

In the United States the Visual Artists Rights Act (VARA) does not protect moral rights of attribution for news photographers, unless their work is produced in limited signed editions for exhibition.[37] Even so, it might be argued that Thomas's use of the source images was not sufficiently transformative under US Copyright law, pointing to the success of plaintiffs in a succession of cases against 1980s appropriation artist Jeff Koons.[38] In Johannesburg, *City Press* arts writer Charl Blignaut acknowledged Thomas's clearly stated intentions, 'to do something new with historical imagery', but nevertheless concluded that the 'argument that the work is a sufficiently changed version of the original and hence didn't need permission is arguably negated by the fact that the whitened out police are visible with a camera flash or if wearing special glasses, making the most significant change the fact that Thomas has presented the colour photo in black and white'.[39]

In South Africa the Copyright Act *does* contain a distinct moral rights clause stating:

> the author shall have the right to claim authorship of the work ... and to object to any distortion, muti-
> lation or other modification of the work where such action is or would be prejudicial to the honour or
> reputation of the author ... [and that] Any infringement of the provisions of this section shall be treated
> as an infringement of copyright ...[40]

Infringement of copyright occurs in South Africa when one reproduces 'the work in any manner or form' without permission, or makes an adaptation of the work and 'imports ... sells,

---

[36] See for instance Hiatt (n 13).

[37] Moral rights of attribution and integrity were granted by the United States Visual Artists Rights Act 1990 [17 U.S.C. Section 106A]. But in the definitions section of the United States Copyright Act [17 U.S.C. Section 101], for a photograph to qualify as a 'work of visual art' it must be 'a still photographic image produced for exhibition purposes only, existing in a single copy that is signed by the author, or in a limited edition of 200 copies or fewer that are signed and consecutively numbered by the author'. This precludes news photography, unless it is later repurposed in a limited edition or as gallery art.

[38] The Jeff Koons cases involved uncredited use of photographic images from magazines, translated with minimal or no alteration into sculptures and paintings by the artist. Henri Neuendorf, 'Jeff Koons Sued Yet Again over Copyright Infringement' *artnet News* (15 December 2015) https:// news .artnet .com/art-world/jeff-koons-sued-copyright-infringement-392667; Jessica Meiselman, 'How Jeff Koons, 8 Puppies, and a Lawsuit Changed Artists' Right to Copy' *artsy* (14 August 2017) https://www.artsy.net/ article/ artsy -editorial -jeff-koons -8 -puppies -lawsuit -changed -artists -copy; Rogers v. Koons, 960 F.2d 301 (2d Cir. 1992). Meiselman quotes from the decision in Rogers v. Koons: 'The copying was so deliberate as to suggest that defendants resolved so long as they were significant players in the art business, and the copies they produced bettered the price of the copied work by a thousand to one, their piracy of a less well-known artist's work would escape being sullied by an accusation of plagiarism.'

[39] Here the writer is conflating moral rights to attribution with related rights to copy and adapt from original works. Charl Blignaut, 'Two plagiarism Claims Stir up SA Art' *City Press* (Johannesburg 15 September 2018) https://www.news24.com/citypress/Trending/two-plagiarism-claims-stir-up-sa-art -20180915 ?fbclid=IwAR1CxwaMDQlu9EBA_Kv0Ow7s8z11bcbZ1VSkZaczPlsA1iSFy-kGp-Y8TFs accessed 16 August 2020.

[40] South Africa Copyright Act 98 of 1978 (as amended) Chapter 1, Section 20: 'Moral rights'. https:// www.wipo.int/edocs/lexdocs/laws/en/za/za002en.pdf and https://www.gov.za/documents/copyright-act -16-apr-2015-0942; see also Owen H. Dean, 'Protection of the Author's Moral Rights in South Africa' (April 1996) 59 Copyright World 38.

lets, or by way of trade offers or exposes for sale or hire in the Republic' any unauthorized copies.[41] In addition, according to intellectual property scholar Owen Dean, in South African common law (which is based on the *actio injuriarum* of Roman-Dutch law), 'personality rights of the author could overlap with or complement the author's moral rights in the event of his authorship of his work not being acknowledged or being disavowed and distortions, mutilations or other modifications being made to his work'.[42]

Facing increasing and embarrassing media reports, and potential legal jeopardy, the Goodman Gallery and Hank Willis Thomas settled amicably out of court with Peter Magubane and with Graeme Williams.[43]

Even though the legal case for right to attribution under South African law seems clear enough, more should be said about the cultural implications of this tempest at the Joburg Art Fair. The issue was perhaps as much about differences in recent historical experience as it was about differences between American and South African copyright law.

Earlier the same year as the Joburg Art Fair, an investigative report in the *Mail and Guardian* had already discovered several cases where iconic works of South African photojournalism were being sold without permission or compensation by digital image distribution outlets including Photononstop, Alamy, Diomedia, Mediabakery, Gallo, and Getty. The report focused on one 'Emilie Chaix', a French photographer whose stock in trade appears to be the scanning of iconic photographs (by others) from archives around the world – some of them made before she was even born! – and passing them off as her own.[44] This revelation had already set local photographers on edge even before Thomas's works had been placed on the wall by Goodman.

More crucially, though, according to *CBS News* correspondent Debora Patta, 'this debate must also include an understanding of South Africa's history, which includes black South Africans being dispossessed of their land, right to vote and artwork'.[45] Indeed, this is particularly sensitive terrain in the global South because historically local heritage has routinely been miscast as 'anonymous' or as folklore, and used as raw material by those who are structurally, economically, and geographically more privileged. As arts writer and academic Neelika Jayawardane wrote, 'in locations where our cultural, scientific, intellectual and artistic heritage has been erased, stolen and represented as the invention of our colonial masters, it

---

[41]   South Africa Copyright Act 98 of 1978 (as amended). See especially Chapter 1, Section 7, 'Nature of Copyright in Artistic Works' and Chapter 2, Section 23, 'Infringement'.

[42]   Owen H. Dean, 'Protection of the Author's Moral Rights in South Africa' (April 1996) 59 Copyright World 38, 43.

[43]   Despite requests to the Goodman Gallery and to Thomas by the author, it was not possible to determine whether settlements were also made with the other photojournalists (or their estates) whose work had been appropriated, including Ian Berry, Jan Hamman, Alf Kumalo, Noel Watson, and Ernest Cole. Liza Essers, Director of the Goodman Gallery, in an email reply to the author (19 August 2020): 'Settlement agreements, to the extent that they exist with any of the artists, are confidential in nature and the gallery is unable to comment.'

[44]   Kwanele Sosibo, 'Exposed: SA's Iconic Pics Plundered' *Mail and Guardian* (Johannesburg, 13 April 2018) https://mg.co.za/article/2018-04-13-00-exposed-sas-iconic-pics-plundered/ accessed 16 August 2020

[45]   Patta (n 14).

remains important to identify the lineage of our objects and ideas, precisely because we remain in danger of being seen as people who made nothing, innovated nothing and did nothing'.[46]

Indeed, many of the critical comments made at the time of the Art Fair referred to the harrowing lived experiences of the photographers, and to the history of South Africa and Africa broadly as places that have been the source of extraction without volition or proper compensation. Of particular relevance is the dialogue between Jayawardane and photojournalist Greg Marinovich published in the *Mail and Guardian*, to which I refer extensively below.

The media narrative cast the issue of attribution as an opposition between the American appropriator and South African photographers that are considered 'heroes' who braved the line of fire, and suffered imprisonment, harassment, and beatings by police and by white nationalists in order to expose the horrors of apartheid to the world.[47] '[I]t's important to remember both men [Williams and Magubane] risked their lives to document the history of South Africa', Patta said on *CBS News*.[48] Peter Magubane is particularly revered for having continued to cover protests during the 1960s and 1970s, despite bannings, beatings, and despite being jailed and placed in solitary confinement for many months. 'This man was there for every major struggle event. He was jailed for these images, his house was burned down. It's just courtesy [to ask to use the images]', said Magubane's agent David Meyer-Gollan.[49] Many of these photographers are still alive or are only recently deceased, the scars of living under apartheid are also still alive in the public memory at large, and the unattributed re-working of theses images was felt to be invasive, even beyond the legal concerns. For his part, Thomas, who is used to being lauded in the United States for his politically progressive works, understandably did not appreciate being typecast as 'the American colonialist'.[50] 'My mistake', he told the *Sunday Times*, 'is not knowing whose work I was referencing and, once I found out, my mistake was not going to the artist'.[51]

Nevertheless, as Greg Marinovich notes in an interview aired on South African television, Thomas claimed that '[a]n argument could be made that as an African-American, he is "taking back" the land appropriated by Williams, who is a white South African', when Williams took images of Blacks without permission. 'The optics, as they say, are that a young black man is striking a blow against the exploitation of township kids by reusing an image by an older white South African photographer without permission or redress.' 'That argument is utterly moot', Marinovich says, 'when the appropriated work is that of African photographers such as [Alf] Kumalo, [Peter] Magubane, etcetera.'[52] Thomas also did not make many allies in South Africa

---

[46]   M Neelika Jayawardane and Greg Marinovich, 'On Photographs and the Art of "remixing" Images' *Mail and Guardian* (Johannesburg, 5 October 2018) https://mg.co.za/article/2018-10-05-00-on -photographs-and-the-art-of-remixing-the-images/ accessed 16 August 2020

[47]   Patta (n 14). In an email to the author, Thomas likewise stressed how he admired the South African photographers (naming Williams specifically): 'We always had positive conversations and I admire him [Williams] very much. There was not disagreement with any artists the way it was depicted in the media ... any attempt to talk any of it in good faith was distorted [by the press] to put me in opposition to heroes, one who has been connected to my family for 40 years [Magubane], I decided to not try fix it in public.' Email from Hank Willis Thomas to author (9 August 2020).

[48]   Patta (n 14).

[49]   Patrick (n 29).

[50]   Ibid.

[51]   Ibid.

[52]   Jayawardane and Marinovich (n 46). The reference is to the 21 September 2018 episode of the *eNCA television* (South Africa) news show "Tonight with Jane Dutton". I was not able to access this episode, and therefore rely here on Marinovich's re-telling.

when in a defensive moment spliced for broadcast from his interview with *CBS News* he is heard conflating the right to comment with the right to use without permission or attribution, and raising the spectre of the draconian old regime: 'I think it is a dangerous moment when we try to tell people what they can and cannot talk about ... when they are making art ... censorship was one of the critical tools of the apartheid government and any oppressive regime.'[53] In his defence, he says his interest is in 'the history of photography and the landscape of photography, and how political movements across the world are connected'.[54] 'This is an image that was taken almost 30 years ago that has been distributed and printed hundreds of thousands of times all over the world. At what point can someone else begin to wrestle with these images and issues in a different way ... much the way that people would quote from a book?' he asked rhetorically, in *artnet News*.[55]

Perhaps we should, then, also consider these other 'moral' or ethical aspects, beyond what is found in the statutory moral rights given in copyright law. That would be to take the kinds of questions asked about popular images by Hank Willis Thomas, through his words and in his work, and apply those very same questions to his work itself. It would be to embrace what Goodman Gallery Director, Liza Essers, quoted in *The Guardian*, stated at the time of the Art Fair: 'Hank is questioning the ownership and authorship of documentary photography. The question of copyright or not is irrelevant to what Hank's asking. They're coming from completely different places of departure.'[56] What, then are these 'completely different places of departure', and how do they have a bearing on the questions of political representation, authorship, and ownership?

As Thomas points out: 'Questions of presentation, representation, ethics, appropriation, commodity, ownership, authorship, exploitation, and subjectivity have been raised within the field [of photography] since its beginnings and will be into the future.'[57] Art critic Jayawardane, writing for *Al Jazeera English*, agrees, stressing that these sorts of questions raised about photography have particular salience and urgency in the global South context, where people have historically not been represented well by the medium. Therefore, '[i]n places like South Africa, such issues are deeply felt, and it is necessary to maintain respectful boundaries and acknowledge people's intellectual and cultural contributions'.[58] Elsewhere Jayawardane notes how Thomas, in defending his work against South African critics 'may not have expressed himself well' and that 'some of the explanations and analogies he offered

---

[53]   Patta (n 14).

[54]   Ibid.

[55]   This was an awkward defence, considering quotations from books are generally expected to include citation of sources. Eileen Kinsella, 'Artist Hank Willis Thomas Pulls Work from a South African Art Fair after a Photographer Levels Plagiarism Charges. The artist says he hopes to have a debate with the photographer who cried foul' *artnet News* (13 September 2018) https://news.artnet.com/art-world/artist-hank-willis-thomas-pulls-work-from-art-fair-after-photographer-levels-plagiarism-charges accessed 16 August 2020.

[56]   Chris McGreal, 'Plagiarism or Remixing? South African Photographer Accuses Artist of Theft' *The Guardian* (13 September 2018) https://www.theguardian.com/artanddesign/2018/sep/13/graeme-williams-hank-willis-thomas-photograph accessed 16 August 2020.

[57]   M. Neelika Jayawardane, 'Theft or Artistic Prerogative? Do well-known artists have a right to appropriate other people's photographs to make "art"?' *Al Jazeera English* (13 September 2018) https://www.aljazeera.com/indepth/opinion/theft-artistic-prerogative-180912130325682.html accessed 16 August 2020.

[58]   Ibid.

about the works shown at the Goodman did not sit well with South African audiences'. This, she sees, 'is partly because of the realities of the socio-political landscape, which Thomas may not have read well'.[59] 'Knowing Thomas's ... artistic practice invites his audiences to be politically engaged, thoughtful consumers, subjects and citizens', she says. 'I do not believe that he intended to steal the photographers' works, nor do them dishonour. But I also know that intentions and the effects of actions are two different things.'[60]

One of the kinds of authority over images that Thomas has sought to question through his work are the ethical rights of the subjects of photographs that have been taken without permission in public places, that is, of almost all news photography. In interviews Thomas has challenged photojournalists' claims over ownership of images made of historic events made in public places, saying 'there are critical questions about who has the right to the image and whether it be subjects of the image, who I am most interested in. If the subjects of the image were compensated or remunerated. If they were asked. There's a lot of questions related to representation, objectification, exploitation.'[61] Greg Marinovich, the South African photojournalist, responds that, 'Thomas's original contention is that he should equally be allowed to use that image and any image, without reference or permission from the author or the subjects in the image. This seems like a contradiction.'[62] The people in the appropriated images were not asked or paid by Thomas either, and yet he, too, used their pictures, even highlighted them, and offered them for sale. Furthermore, there is nothing in the adaptation itself that indicates the children's rights to not be looked at in Thomas's version. These contradictions appeared to undermine his quite valid interrogation of subjects rights in the work, leading observers in South Africa to conclude, inaccurately, that this was a rationale that was more self-serving than sincere. It also distracted from the critical questions he sought to pose about subject's rights and authorship in historic photographs.

Nevertheless, the issues raised by Thomas are in fact important ethical concerns faced by news and documentary photographers generally. Lisa Henderson discusses this facet in an influential essay on access and consent in public photography, where she considers how subjects may implicitly give consent to have their picture taken but that this does not equate to 'consent to use', in any future context. 'What the practical contingencies of public photography therefore suggest', she writes, 'is the essentially exploitative relationship that prevails between photographers and subjects'.[63] Along these lines, reflecting on his own past work and issues of consent, Marinovich, a former member of the 'Bang Bang Club' of conflict photographers, recalls that '[s]ometimes people were aware of who that particular work was intended for, at other times they presumed or did not give a damn'.[64] Another consideration, one that is not common to all press images but is so in reference to the Williams image, is the fact that the children are marching on a raised platform at a political rally in a stadium. They are 'performing' publicly in full view of the phalanx of press photographers attending the

---

[59]   Jayawardane and Marinovich (n 46).

[60]   Ibid.

[61]   McGreal (n 56).

[62]   Jayawardane and Marinovich (n 46).

[63]   Lisa Henderson, 'Access and Consent in Public Photography' in Larry Gross, John Stuart Katz, and Ruby Jay (eds), *Image Ethics: The Moral Rights of Subjects in Photographs, Film, and Television* (Oxford University Press 1988), 104–5.

[64]   Jayawardane and Marinovich (n 46).

Mandela event and openly taunting the police. At least when used as a news picture the issues of consent in Williams's case are not very ambiguous.

Regarding the use of a person's image without their consent in a photograph taken in a public place as documentation of historic events, Dario Milo and Pamela Stein write in their guide to media law in South Africa that, 'if the image, name or likeness is being used for journalistic purposes as part of a story, such use is likely to enjoy protection'.[65] But, if used for purposes of trade or if depicting the subject in a manner that misrepresents them, rights of personality, identity, and dignity may apply in South African law.[66] Here again the legal definition does not address the popular 'moral' or ethical issues Thomas sought to raise.

Marinovich also recognizes (as does Thomas) that as older news images are taken out of the dailies and placed in new contexts, the values and expectations (and credit lines) surrounding them create new ethical dilemmas: 'Some of those images have been revived through digitization and find their way on to various virtual sites, and in academia or photo agencies' catalogues. Others are curated on gallery walls. Many images are spun around the world in a dizzying maze of online sites in unauthorized and unrecompensed versions.'[67] As these new contexts alter the valuation and meaning of the pictures, he says:

> there is now definitely a conversation to be had about initial intent and subsequent use/ misuse of these images, by both the original creators, the publications that may own copyright and others drawn to them as a source of artistic inspiration, or simply commercial exploitation ... [because] ... if the original intention of the photographer, and the understanding of the subjects (if they were given an explanation, or if there was a presumption based on the circumstances) was that these were news images, is it okay to repurpose some of those images for gallery walls, for sale as fine art works?[68]

In the new contexts of art galleries and museums, photographs become objects for contemplation, they are isolated from the larger mass stream of images and therefore another kind of consideration of privacy and different definitions of authorial agency may be called for. As subjects emerge from the crowd through this kind of isolation and highlighting of their presence, is there not also an expectation that they be understood as authors and agents of their own history, and worthy of protection? The tempest over Hank Willis Thomas's art in South Africa raised but did not resolve the conflict between the ethical rights of subjects and the legal moral rights of photographers when their pictures move from mass distribution as news to individual presentation on a gallery wall.

Another consideration is that today in the online realm there is a sense – one perhaps shared even more by a younger generation that has grown up with the internet – that images found openly in places online are just co-equal things 'out there' without much specific context. What one sees online appears to be freely available for use, and further what one 'finds' in this way is perceived as something one has actually produced oneself – that it is now 'mine' and it has in effect been authored and owned by me, the finder. This kind of conflation of seeing-is-owning is an effect of the spread of online culture. I think it was in part with a critical awareness of this contemporary trend that when asked about his image sources by the

---

[65]   Dario Milo and Pamela Stein, *A Practical Guide to Media Law* (LexisNexis South Africa 2013) 157.
[66]   Ibid 156–8.
[67]   Jayawardane and Marinovich (n 46).
[68]   Ibid.

the *Sunday Times*, Thomas could say frankly, 'I get it from archives and from the internet', and that 'he felt he had "inherited" the works'.[69] By which I think he meant it is now up to him (as an African-American man) and to his generation (of those seeking new ways forward in the progress of civil rights) to deal with these historic images for themselves. It is their 'inheritance' to find ways to navigate the historic images, to make new connections among them, and to make them speak differently, more equitably. 'If a photograph is 25 years old, 40, 100 years old, of public events where most people who are in the photograph are not given control over how they're depicted and what's happening', he asks 'when is it ours as a society to wrestle with?'[70]

Who exactly are these marginalized subjects of history to be found in archival photographs of historic events, that are 'not the people who normally get the light shined on them'? A possible answer may be found if we return to look more closely at the *toyi-toyi* picture, the Graeme Williams photograph that was recast as 'Gravitas' by Hank Willis Thomas. 'It is the simplicity of the message that has kind of given this image longevity and meaning to South Africans', says Williams of his original picture made at the rally in Thokoza Township in 1990.[71] Arguably the kind of high contrast seen in the picture, the aspect that makes it stand out from other pictures, is a result of the gestures that appear uplifting in isolation yet also appear vulnerable against a more violent threat in the background: heroic Black protesters versus looming white police; jubilant children versus bored (but looming) police. This is likely why the picture was chosen by the Obama campaign to represent its own world view, and why it was picked up as a lead image for the press reviews of the Rise and Fall exhibition.

Roland Barthes termed this quality often found in news photographs the *studium*.[72] This *studium* aspect is what allows many press pictures to be intelligible and to be of interest in the first place. It is what makes them 'good' pictures. And good news photographers are the ones who are not just in the right places at the right times. They are also those who have developed the skill and the sense, as Graeme Williams said about his own chance image, to know when 'there was a possibility of a picture happening'. This skill in knowing where a picture will happen, and having the good sense to point a camera at it, is one of the things that makes news photographers 'authors' of their pictures. Even if those things happening in the world might have happened on their own, they would not have been made into a picture for others elsewhere to see, nor would they have been framed in that particular way with that kind of interesting contrast.

For Barthes this *studium* is also that aspect of a picture that invites the viewer to 'to experience the intentions' of the photographer and in that way it also enables later viewers to feel (falsely, of course) *as if* they were a spectator on the spot, that they were there, too and part of the action. This 'feeling like they were there', we recall, is a stated goal of Thomas's retro-reflective technique. But *studium* elements are not obscure, hidden, or oblique. They are there and obvious for all to see, enabling a dispersed audience to gather together virtually in the viewing experience, to participate in the feeling of 'revealing'. This collective (Barthes

---

[69] Patrick (n 29).

[70] McGreal (n 56).

[71] Greg Marinovich, 'Graeme Williams vs Hank Willis Thomas: Acceptable artistic appropriation – or just plain old theft?' *Daily Maverick* (Johannesburg 17 September 2018).

[72] See Roland Barthes, *Camera Lucida* (Richard Howard tr, Noonday Press 1981) 23, 28, 40–1, et passim.

calls it 'cultural') intelligibility element can make certain news images quite powerful, but at the same time it relies on their conventionality, their lack of subtlety, and may even appeal to stereotyping and oversimplification. What is revealed is usually not all that far from what viewers already know or expect in advance. For instance, in Peter Magubane's image from Sophiatown one could say: 'See, that woman is giving the thumbs-up; but see, there is a man with a gun over there.' The revelation-through-contrast still holds its appeal whether one tends to be a supporter of the police or of protesters.

So it is justifiable to ask, when Thomas says his retro-reflective process 'puts you in the position of creating the picture', as if you made it yourself, if that is much different than if one 'discovers' a picture by being arrested by it in an art exhibit catalogue, or by scrolling through pictures on Google? Is this not also related to how Graeme Williams knew, as a veteran photojournalist, that 'a picture' was about to happen at stadium in Thokoza in 1990?[73] In the retro-reflective works, rather than the intended 'unveiling' of 'new social and cultural meanings',[74] Hank Willis Thomas it seems instead isolated these same elements, highlighting the same contrast of protagonist versus background that already made up the *studium* of the original pictures. He has given an ingenious visual demonstration of the common visual pattern of consumption of the pictures, or, if you will, of the stereotypes used by the media to package complex human experience, though he has not effectively isolated 'marginalized' subjects as claimed in his artist statements.

What is obscured by *studium*, but also obscured by the white or coloured washes in Thomas's retro-reflective series are often the onlookers and the police. And what is also not noted by most commentators is that some of the police are themselves Black. Most commentators only refer to the 'white police'. But the Black officers are there watching from above in the police vehicle in the Graeme Williams photograph, and they appear to be watching the marchers more intently than the white officers. They are there, too, in the background of the forced removals in Magubane's picture from Sophiatown. The policeman watching, menacing, and likely pointing a gun at the young men in Jan Hamman's picture from Soweto may in fact be a Black police-*woman*. If there are truly marginalized characters in these images surely these Black police, co-enforcers of apartheid, are among them. Or it may be the many faces looking on with fear or expectation but now erased into the backgrounds of Hamman's and Magubane's pictures, and equally erased in Thomas's modified versions. In my view, calling attention to those whose history is unsung, as opposed to those already highlighted as 'heroes' or 'victims', would make for a more nuanced approach to reviewing historic images, it would make them more messy, and it would make for a worthy artistic intervention.[75] Noting, for instance, that Black police participated in enforcing apartheid, and perhaps also relating this uncomfortable truth to images of post-apartheid protests against current economic inequity – where now it is

---

[73]   Iconic press photographs are often made in this way. They already exist as a potential image before the camera and before the event in front of the camera. John Peffer, 'Remarks on South African Photography and the Extraphotographic' (Spring 2012) 88 Africultures http://africultures.com/remarks -on-south-african-photography-and-the-extraphotographic-11101/ accessed 16 August 2020.

[74]   According to the text on the Goodman Gallery website describing Thomas's 2014 solo show History Doesn't Laugh, 'Thomas is known for his extensive use of archival visual records to work through ideas that address the social constructions of race, gender, and commodity ... [He] smartly decodes popular images with the intention of proposing and unveiling new social and cultural meanings.' https://www.goodman-gallery.com/exhibitions/413 accessed 16 August 2020.

[75]   John Peffer, *Art and the End of Apartheid* (University of Minnesota Press 2009) 258.

the Black police who are the State – would be to ask harder questions than merely isolating and reinforcing a simplistic white-police-versus-Black-protesters type of narrative. This would not be to diminish the abhorrence of apartheid. Indeed it would be to shine a light on how apartheid further humiliated non-white South Africans by pitting brother against brother, and to consider what the legacy of such things may be in the post-apartheid era. These stories are also there within the iconic pictures, waiting to be told, waiting for another author.

Neelika Jayawardane notes the unfortunate trend in the mainstream culture industry of looting African cultural patrimony without credit or compensation: 'Almost every other week, we hear how the director of a fashion photo shoot or a music video "borrowed" aesthetic concepts from artists and photographers from less culturally privileged locations', she writes, citing Beyoncé's use of the promotional image for 'Djibril Diop Mambéty's 1973 classic French New Wave-inspired Senegalese film, *Touki Bouki*'.[76] Other prominent recent examples include the serial theft of Solomon Linda's song 'Mbube/The Lion Sleeps Tonight', including ultimately for Disney's *The Lion King*, and Kendrick Lamar's alleged use without permission of works by British-Liberian artist Lina Iris Viktor in his 'All The Stars' video.[77] Contrasting the kinds of bottom-up remixing of mainstream culture elements that are performed by members of subcultures, against top-down corporate uses of images taken from those with less political and economic power, Jayawardane writes that '[t]he common thread ... is that the original photographer's or artist's intellectual and creative labour is erased by the powerful subjectivity of the star artists, performers, and the galleries and lawyers that represent their interests'.[78]

With the VARA in the United States, the implication is there is a hierarchy where 'lauded' fine artists who are supposedly making more subtle work merit preferential treatment as true 'authors', over works made by photojournalists. That is not the case in South African copyright law, where there is more equal protection for moral rights and copyrights of artists and photographers. On its face this seems to be a fortuitous layer of legal protection for local artists and photographers in the African context. And yet, interestingly, while the moral rights of attribution and integrity are clearly protected in South African copyright law, legal scholar Owen Dean has noted that '[a]uthors have, however, been slow to enforce these rights, or have not in the past had occasion to do so, because there are no South African cases in which the court has made any pronouncements or determinations in this regard',[79] and that situation does not appear to have changed much since he wrote on the subject in 1996. Perhaps it is because in order to avail oneself of this protection, those whose work has been appropriated would first need to have been made aware of the infringement. They would then also need to be financially capable of litigating against infringement. These may be too-difficult hurdles

---

76   Jayawardane and Marinovich (n 46).
77   Patta (n 14); Lynsey Chutel, 'Whose Wakanda is it Anyway? A Black Panther lawsuit is testing the cultural exchange between Africans and African-Americans' *Quartz Africa* (30 May 2018) https://qz.com/africa/1291390/kendrick-lamar-sza-sued-by-african-artist-over-copyright-for-black-panther-anthem-all-the-stars/ accessed 16 August 2020; Lynsey Chutel, 'Appropriate Appropriation? An African American artist's "remixing" of apartheid-era images is raising questions about appropriation' *Quartz Africa* (24 October 2018) https://qz.com/africa/1433855/apartheid-south-africa-photo-art-stirs-appropriation-controversy/ accessed 16 August 2020.
78   Jayawardane and Marinovich (n 46).
79   Owen H. Dean, 'Protection of the Author's Moral Rights in South Africa' (April 1996) 59 Copyright World 38, 43.

in a place like South Africa, with the effect of placing moral rights protection out of reach for many artists. For example, lost in the media hustle around Graeme Williams and Peter Magubane and Hank Willis Thomas – who each already had substantial name recognition – was the case of another Goodman Gallery artist Haroon Gunn-Salie, who openly appropriated news photographs showing police use of blue-water canons on protesters, without attribution, and about which nothing was done.[80] Arguably it was the influence of historical experience but also the media scandal between famous artists that turned the tables at the Art Fair, as much as any legal jeopardy.

South African scholar Kylie Thomas writes admiringly about how Hank Willis Thomas 'is profoundly critical of extractive economies that take black people's bodies and lives, using them for commercial gain without ever recognizing them as individuals'.[81] And she notes how the debate about appropriation art and South Africa's historic 'archive' of documentary images 'also casts light on just how difficult it is to critique globalized racial capitalism from within the market, itself a system that serves to replicate the inequalities [Willis] Thomas is seeking to contest through his work'. She concludes that, if he truly wishes to be considered a 'collaborative' artist and not just an 'appropriation' artist, then '[a]cknowledging the source of the images he uses in his work more fully would amplify rather than diminish the power of Thomas's political art'.[82] Jayawardane similarly writes: 'It would not have been difficult for the artists to contact the photographers, and ask them to do a truly collaborative project. It is my opinion that the artists' works, had they been collaborative and the original work attributed appropriately, and profits shared, would have been far richer and layered conversations on the nature of photography and audience interpretation of images.'[83] As we have seen, this would be to not just speak for (from a position of privilege), but to speak with and alongside as co-authors. It would be to bring questions of moral rights in the legal sense into closer alliance with moral responsibilities in the ethical sense.

---

[80]   Facebook post from Rodger Bosch to Graeme Williams (7 September 2018): 'That guy Haroon Gun Salie did the same with an image I shot, with his name underneath ... Last I saw it was in the National Gallery. It was an image I shot for AFP, and I thought they would take exception, but they didn't. I did make a bit of a fuss at the time, but probably not enough ... It was an image of people being sprayed by a water canon. So GS made everything in the frame monochrome, except the blue spray from the water cannon.'

[81]   Kylie Thomas, 'It's Time to Stop the Appropriation of South Africa's Visual Archive' *The Conversation* (US Edition, 1 October 2018) https:// theconversation .com/ its -time -to -stop -the -appropriation-of-south-africas-visual-archive-103694 accessed 16 August 2020.

[82]   Ibid.

[83]   Jayawardane (n 57).

28. Fictional stories by fictional people: Alan Smithee and moral rights

Darren Hudson Hick

About a year ago, I received an e-mail from this *Handbook*'s editor, Ysolde Gendreau, asking if I would be interested in contributing to the book a chapter on 'works, usually from the literary and cinematographic fields, that touch upon issues that reflect moral rights considerations' – in other words, how moral rights are treated in narrative fictions. The topic targeted the overlap in my research areas – philosophy of art and copyright law – so I accepted the invitation, suggesting that I would focus on the right of attribution, and more specifically the right to publish anonymously or pseudonymously. All I had to do was find a few cases, which one would think an easy enough task – after all, writers love to write about writers. 'Writer' is probably second only to 'grizzled detective' in the list of the most popular careers among fictional people. And, just as there is no shortage of authors who write anonymously or pseudonymously, there should be no shortage of *fictional* authors who do likewise. Among the (probably) many such works featuring anonymous and pseudonymous authors, I estimated, at least a handful of these stories *must* engage with the *right* to do so – again, one would think.

I was right about the wealth of pseudonymous and anonymous writers in fictions, but my confidence about the number who dealt with moral rights was quickly eroded. Because he was on my shelf, I turned first to Stephen King, whose 1989 novel *The Dark Half* is about a writer whose own fictional pseudonym, George Stark, is seeking to avenge his 'murder' by the protagonist. But there was nothing here about Stark's rights to the books, nor even his right to exist. Next, I turned to Miguel de Cervantes, whose opus *Don Quixote* is derailed by the titular character learning of the real-world publication of an unauthorized sequel to the first half (published in 1605) by the pseudonymous Alonso Fernández de Avellaneda. Quixote spends much of the second half of his eponymous novel (published in 1605) mocking the pseudonymous Avellaneda and his forgery, but Avellaneda never appears to defend himself.[1] *Don Quixote* flirts with what is now called 'metafiction' – a category of self-conscious experimental works of fiction *about* fiction, often featuring their own authors as characters. Now targeting this genre, I thought of Paul Auster, Jorge Luis Borges, and Philip K. Dick, and re-read a stack of their stories. In 1974, Dick published 'Orpheus with Clay Feet' under the pen name 'Jack Dowland'. The story is about a twenty-first century time-traveler, Jesse Slade, who travels back to 1956 to inspire his favorite science-fiction author, Jack Dowland, to write his favorite novel. But Slade so irritates Dowland that the author instead writes Slade's own story of time travel under the pen name 'Philip K. Dick', titling the story 'Orpheus with Clay Feet'. It's a fantastic and fantastical tongue-in-cheek metafictional story, but moral rights don't come up. The other metafictionalists likewise shrugged and offered nothing. My personal resources exhausted, I turned to the Internet, and quickly learned that any combination of my search

---

[1]   Both Cervantes and Avellaneda were writing long before the first modern copyrights or moral-rights laws were recognized in Europe.

terms promised to retrieve only lists of authors who published anonymously and pseudony-mously. In my darker moments, I considered simply inventing three cases that might suit my needs – a move the metafictionalists, at least, would applaud.

Eventually, however, after some months, I was able to identify three works that *did* fit the requirements: two films and a novel. None of these is, on its own, a particularly good work. The first film is awful – Roger Ebert gave it one very generous star. The second film is better, but unnecessarily convoluted and overacted. The novel is one long, incoherent rant. But, understood in context – particularly in the context of moral rights – each of these works turns out to be engrossingly fascinating.

1.   *AN ALAN SMITHEE FILM: BURN HOLLYWOOD BURN*

Our first case, *An Alan Smithee Film: Burn Hollywood Burn* (1997),[2] is the story of Alan Smithee, a director who is so dissatisfied with the changes that his producers make to his film that he steals the master negative and goes on the lam. Smithee, a veteran film editor, is hired by producers James Edmunds and Jerry Glover to direct their big-budget action movie, *Trio*, starring Sylvester Stallone, Whoopi Goldberg, and Jackie Chan (all played by themselves). As an inexperienced director, Smithee is given no control: the stars decide when to wrap the shot, the producers decide how to cut it. The result, in Smithee's eyes, is an abomination. So, when the opportunity presents itself, Smithee grabs the master negative and runs. The hijacking makes national news. Smithee spends his days driving around Los Angeles in his Range Rover, eating bologna sandwiches, and calling *Larry King Live*, threatening to burn the film, until he is taken in by the Brothers Brothers (Leon and Dion) and the 'African American guerilla film family', who see Smithee as one of their own.[3] At first, the Brothers Brothers try to convince Smithee that he has to return the film:

LEON: You don't understand, man: this is a *film*!
DION: Yeah, man. This is the shit we *live* for, man. There's a lot of people's sweat in those cans. Man, you can't burn that shit; you got to give that shit back! …
SMITHEE: They took the film *away* from me. They *stole* it. They *abused* me, they *raped* me, they threatened to *kill* me. …
SMITHEE: If we believe in film, and we do, then don't we have a responsibility to protect the world from *bad* ones?[4]

The Brothers Brothers ask why Smithee doesn't simply take his name off the film, and put the standard industry pseudonym in place of his own name. But, of course, that's exactly the problem: the standard industry pseudonym used by directors who are dissatisfied with their

---

[2]   *An Alan Smithee Film: Burn Hollywood Burn.* 1997. [film] Directed by A. Smithee. Burbank, CA: Hollywood Pictures.
[3]   One might reasonably expect some discussion of race or the disenfranchisement of African-American filmmakers to have come up in the film, or to be otherwise relevant to the plot. One would be disappointed.
[4]   *An Alan Smithee Film: Burn Hollywood Burn.* 1997. [film] Directed by A. Smithee. Burbank, CA: Hollywood Pictures.

films *is* 'Alan Smithee'. If he takes his name off the film, they'll just put it back on. Smithee *can't* disassociate himself from the film; all he can do is destroy it.

The Brothers Brothers act on Smithee's behalf to broker a deal with the studio. The meeting turns into a brawl when Leon demands Smithee get 'final cut' – control over the final form of the film – in exchange for the master. Glover has to stop Edmunds from pulling a gun on the Brothers Brothers:

GLOVER: I tried to explain to them that only Kubrick and Spielberg have final cut. That's it. The other directors *pretend* to have it. Sometimes certain studios *say* they have it when they don't, just to assuage directorial ego.[5]

Glover instead offers the Brothers Brothers a three-picture deal with final cut in exchange for the master to *Trio*.

EDMUNDS: You never offer them that. You never offer *any* director that. The offer *itself* goes right to their head. They're the fucking *enemy*. You *know* that, Jerry.
GLOVER: No, they're not. They're part of the workforce.[6]

Alan does, indeed, burn the negative.

Real-world attorney Robert Shapiro, who plays himself in the movie, says, 'Alan Smithee was a man who was willing to make the ultimate decision: he saved what he had not been allowed to create. He had to save himself by killing it. He was a hero.' Smithee, finally face-to-face with Larry King, defends his act:

SMITHEE: It was my child, but it wasn't my child.
KING: Do you have the right – the right to kill a child, even if it isn't your child?[7]

Rather than seeking to prosecute him, the producers put Smithee into the Keith Moon Psychiatric Facility. The media spectacle of Smithee's heist has absolved him in the eyes of the directors, who offer him final cut on his next film:

GLOVER: The possessory credit on the movie 'An Alan Smithee Film' would mean more now than Tom Cruise or Jim Carrey. Alan Smithee has *redeemed* 'Alan Smithee'![8]

Ironically, then, *Alan Smithee* actually killed 'Alan Smithee'. The film *An Alan Smithee Film: Burn Hollywood Burn* was directed by Arthur Hiller, but lists 'Alan Smithee' as director. Hiller applied to the Directors Guild of America for an 'Alan Smithee' credit after the film's writer, Joe Eszterhas (who also wrote *Basic Instinct* and *Showgirls*, which gets a jab in the movie), re-edited the film, and producers went with the Eszterhas cut – a radical move. Hiller

---

[5]   Ibid.
[6]   Ibid.
[7]   Ibid.
[8]   Ibid.

lamented, 'As [Eszterhas] knows, I feel he's turned it into an extended "Saturday Night Live" sketch. Maybe that will be the successful way, but it's not the one I poured my creativity into.'[9]

Hiller was not (like the fictional Smithee) an inexperienced director. Four years before the film was released, Hiller was in fact President of the Directors Guild of America. Best known for *Love Story* (1970), Hiller worked with some of the biggest names in Hollywood for the next two decades. Hiller was hardly a nobody. But, when it came to *Burn Hollywood Burn*, he wanted to be. The Directors Guild created the 'Alan Smithee' credit in 1968 for the movie *Death of a Gunfighter* (1969), and 'Smithee' has since been credited with dozens of films, television episodes, and music videos. But *Burn Hollywood Burn* was such an enormous media bomb, and made such a spectacle of the 'Alan Smithee' name, that the Directors Guild retired the name in 2000. Commenting on the move, director John Rich noted that the Alan Smithee credit had 'been damaged to the point that it's unworkable'.[10]

Had he been directing his film in, say, France, the character of Alan Smithee could simply have released his film anonymously or under a *nom de plume* of his choice. In France, Smithee would have been recognized as the *author* of the film, and so would have *droit moral*: moral rights, including the right of publication, the right of integrity, the right of withdrawal, and the right of attribution or 'paternity'.[11] This last right is a bundle that includes the right to have one's name associated with one's work, the right to prevent one's name from being falsely associated with a work that *isn't* one's own, and the right to publish one's work anonymously or pseudonymously.[12] But Smithee gets none of these rights in America. First, since Smithee was directing his film in America, it wasn't (*legally* speaking) *his* film. In America, the producer of a film, not the director, is usually recognized as its author.[13] To be an author just *is* to have and to exercise the power of determining the form of the work – to have (in film terminology) 'final cut', exactly what producers like Edmunds and Glover withhold from directors.[14] Second, America does not fully recognize moral rights in authors generally. Rather, the Visual Artist's Rights Act (VARA), folded into the US Copyright Act in 1990, only recognizes moral rights in the author of a 'work of visual art'. This includes a version of the right of integrity and the right of attribution, and includes the right to 'prevent the use of his or her name as the author of any work of visual art which he or she did not create',[15] but *excludes* any right to publish a work anonymously or pseudonymously. Releasing a work under a pseudonym effectively means forfeiting rights under VARA. And, regardless – ordinary language notwithstanding – a film does not qualify under VARA as a 'work of visual art', a term that is

---

[9]   Variety Staff, 'Hiller edits "Smithee" spin' *Variety* (7 May 1997) https://variety.com/1997/voices/columns/hiller-edits-smithee-spin-1117342044/ accessed 22 April 2020.

[10]   Amy Wallace, 'Name of Director Smithee Isn't What It Used to Be' *Los Angeles Times* (15 January 2000) https://www.latimes.com/archives/la-xpm-2000-jan-15-ca-54271-story.html accessed 22 April 2020.

[11]   Claude Colombet, *Grands principes du droit d'auteur et des droits voisins dans le monde: approche de droit comparé* (2nd edn, Litec 1992), 42–51.

[12]   Ibid [45].

[13]   Jane C Ginsburg and Pierre Sirinelli, 'Authors and Exploitations in International Private Law: The French Supreme Court and the Huston Film Colorization Controversy' (1991) 15 Colum-Vla J L & Arts 135, 136.

[14]   Darren H Hick, 'Authorship, Co-Authorship, and Multiple Authorship' (2014) 72 J Aesthetics & Art Criticism 147.

[15]   17 U.S.C. §106A(a)(B).

restricted to drawings, paintings, prints, sculptures, and photographs that exist only in single copies, or signed-and-numbered editions of 200 or fewer.[16]

The VARA was created in a gambit to allow the United States to join the Berne Convention, an international copyright treaty which it had avoided joining for more than a century. The Convention's requirement that member nations recognize moral rights was one of the central sticking points.[17] Although the creation of VARA and other provisions of The Berne Convention Implementation Act of 1988 (strictly speaking) fell short of the Convention's requirements, America's membership meant that other parties could expect their citizens' works to be protected in America, and the United States would further secure international protection for its citizens' copyrights, so a sort of devil's bargain was struck.

The severe limitation of moral rights under VARA is not entirely surprising. The visual arts are the only major domain in the arts, generally, without a powerful lobbying industry in America. Although independent advocacy groups with an interest in the visual arts exist, they simply do not compare to the juggernaut industries for film, music, and publishing, which have the financial wherewithal to influence legislation. Allan Adler, General Counsel and Vice President for Government Affairs at the Association of American Publishers, says:

> Contract law was also one of the reasons why publishers generally objected to the imposition of a layer of moral rights on top of the existing economic rights and property rights framework of US copyright law. They felt that contracts gave the parties both a great degree of flexibility in terms of how to develop and conduct their own relationship with respect to the publication of work … Many works in the United States are published either pseudonymously or anonymously, and that's generally dealt with between the author and the publisher as a matter of contract.[18]

Of course, this position will seem more palatable if you, like the publisher, are in the superior bargaining position.

Jeffrey M. Dine notes:

> The movie industry appears to be the most vocal opponent of moral rights in the United States. Movie producers are concerned about the divorce of copyright from moral right. In the United States, a movie's copyright lies in the producer. In the now famous *Huston* case, the French Cour de Cassation held that the heirs of John Huston, the director of the film *The Asphalt Jungle*, had standing to sue to prevent the French broadcast of the colorized version of the film. This decision epitomized the danger to producers of acceptance of moral rights doctrine as a limitation on the ability to derive economic benefits from the copyrights they hold.[19]

Acceding moral rights in film risks giving those rights to directors, since the recognition of copyright in a film's producer rests on contractual work-for-hire agreements and not on anything stated in the law. That is, Hollywood's film industry opposes moral rights because it risks taking control from the producers and giving it to the directors. As producer Jerry Glover

---

[16]   17 U.S.C. §101.

[17]   See Samuel Jacobs, 'The Effect of the 1886 Berne Convention on the U.S. Copyright System's Treatment of Moral Rights and Copyright Term, and Where That Leaves Us Today' (2016) 23 Mich Telecomm & Tech L Rev 169.

[18]   United States Copyright Office, Symposium Transcript: 'Authors, Attribution, and Integrity: Examining Moral Rights in the United States' (2016) 8 Geo Mason J Int'l Com L 1, 36.

[19]   Jeffrey M Dine, 'Authors' Moral Rights in Non-European Nations: International Agreements, Economics, *Mannu Bhandari*, and the Dead Sea Scrolls' (1995) 16 Mich J Int Law 545, 548–9.

notes in *Burn Hollywood Burn*, directors are just 'part of the workforce', and studios prefer it that way. The 'Alan Smithee' credit was protected by collective bargaining agreements between the Directors Guild of America and the studios.[20] The pseudonym was a director's best – or, at least, most public – way to snub his nose at his producers for overstepping their artistic bounds (though, notably, the same agreements prevent a director who *has* used a pseudonym from publicly criticizing the film). Having contracted away his rights to the work, the best that the character Alan Smithee *can* do to keep his name off the film is to steal it or burn it. *An Alan Smithee Film: Burn Hollywood Burn* is the story of what happens when moral rights are lacking.

2.   *ROMAN DE GARE*

Our second film is *Roman de Gare* (2007), directed by Claude Lelouch.[21] We meet the film's main character while he is driving – dangerously – through Paris streets, listening to news reports about 'dreaded serial killer' and 'pedophile rapist' Georges 'The Magician' Maury, escaped that very night in a prison break. Our character passes from city streets to the open highway. Maury, we learn, lured his victims with magic tricks. We already think there's a possibility that the driver is Maury. Our suspicions seem confirmed when he performs a seemingly innocent magic trick for a young girl at a highway travel plaza. It's in the same travel plaza lounge where he meets Huguette, abandoned there by her fiancé Paul. He uses a magic trick to meet her, too. The driver persuades Huguette to let him give her a ride.

Along the way, Huguette gets carsick, so the driver pulls into a rest stop and suggests they go for 'a walk in the woods'. Huguette declines, preferring a cigarette. The driver tells Huguette he is actually the ghostwriter for Judith Ralitzer – a famous novelist – having written her novels for seven years. He offers to make Huguette a character in Ralitzer's next novel, then abruptly confesses that this is all a fiction, and that he is actually Claude Ravier, a teacher who three days ago walked away from his students, his wife, and his children. We have learned about just such a teacher in what seemed to be a disconnected side story. So, is the driver 'Maury' or is he 'Ravier'? Given his apparent penchant for pretending to be other people, Huguette persuades 'Claude' to pose as her fiancé in a visit with her parents. Paul is a doctor – a general practitioner – and 'Claude' successfully poses as him during an overnight visit (with more ice-breaking magic tricks) until the real Paul shows up. And, back in Paris, the real teacher has turned up, too. 'The Magician' is caught as well, which leaves only the nameless ghostwriter. We discover that this is exactly who he is when he meets Ralitzer on her yacht.

Over wine, the ghostwriter outlines Ralitzer's next novel for her: 'The journey of a man across France. We won't ever know, until the end, of course, if he's a teacher who has abandoned his wife and kids, everything, a serial killer on the run, or a writer in search of a character' – the plot of the very film we are watching, in other words. Ralitzer asks which of these the main character is. He responds, 'He's a famous novelist's ghost. Who is ending

---

[20]   The Writers' Guild of America likewise protects screenwriters' rights to publish pseudonymously by collective bargaining agreements with film and television studios https://www.wga.org/contracts/know-your-rights/creative-rights-for-writers accessed 22 April 2020.

[21]   *Roman de Gare*. 2007. [film] Directed by Claude Lelouch. France: Samuel Goldwyn Films.

seven years of slavery.'[22] He tells Ralitzer that he will be putting his own name on the novel. We still don't know his name.

Ralitzer is angry, but apparently comes around. Eventually, we learn the ghostwriter is Pierre Laclos, and (after shoving him overboard) Ralitzer offers to let him stay and write the novel on her yacht. Laclos finishes the final chapter, Ralitzer reads it, and she immediately seduces him. Sometime during the night, Laclos disappears, apparently overboard, apparently drunk. With Laclos apparently dead, Ralitzer publishes the book, word for word, under her own name. Huguette, recognizing her story in the published novel, confronts Ralitzer on live television. Ralitzer replies, 'Who wrote *The Three Musketeers*? Dumas or his ghost? And who was Shakespeare, really? Did Michelangelo or his assistants paint the Sistine Chapel?' Ralitzer is taken into custody for Laclos's murder. Eventually, Laclos turns up alive and well. He explains that he knew that Ralitzer planned to put her own name on the novel: 'I knew that when I wrote "the end", you would get rid of me one way or another … I called your publisher from the yacht one night. That's when I understood that my days were numbered.' Ralitzer's name is cleared, and she is released. She immediately commits suicide. Her name is cleared of guilt, but now that it's clear who wrote her novels, her name is cleared of acclaim as well.

Like *Burn Hollywood Burn*, *Roman de Gare* asks: Who is the author? Who deserves to put her name on the work? Who deserves blame for the work, who deserves acclaim? Director Claude Lelouch says: 'This character in my film has been humiliated. Now the entire world will know the books were written by someone else. It's as if one fine day someone said, Claude Lelouch has never made any films. Shame is very painful to endure. For me it makes perfect sense that the character would kill herself.'[23] Curiously, then, *Roman de Gare* was originally publicized as the work of a new, young director, 'Hervé Picard', and early screenings ran without credits. Lelouch only revealed himself after the film was selected for inclusion in the Cannes Film Festival.

Lelouch says that 'Hervé Picard' was the name of his tennis coach.[24] But (curiously, again) in 2007, 'Hervé Picard' was *also* the name of a doctor in Paris – a general practitioner, like Laclos's assumed identity. Coincidence? Laclos himself is almost certainly a nod at Pierre Choderlos de Laclos, author of the epistolary French novel, *Les Liasons Dangereuses*, originally published anonymously (as 'M.C…… de L…') in 1782. Lelouch, whose work to date had received mixed reviews, confesses:

> I wanted to send a message to those who dismiss my work. I wanted one of my movies to be seen for what it really was and not as a Claude Lelouch film. Of course, film audiences are prejudiced when they see the latest offspring of a director who gives birth to a new film every year, such as Woody Allen, Pedro Almodóvar or the Coen Brothers. I wanted to feel young again and treat myself with this

---

[22]   It's a line that seems overblown in English. But in French, 'ghostwriter' is translated as 'nègre', as it has been since the eighteenth century, immediately calling to mind a condition of slavery. See: Jake Lamar, 'The N-Word Is Just as Bad in French' (*The Root*, 1 November 2010) https://www.npr.org/templates/story/story.php?storyId=130970738 accessed 22 April 2020.

[23]   Erica Abeel, 'indieWIRE INTERVIEW | "Roman de Gare" Director Claude Lelouch' (*IndieWire*, 21 April 2008) https://www.indiewire.com/2008/04/indiewire-interview-roman-de-gare-director-claude-lelouch-72574/ accessed 22 April 2020.

[24]   Alison James, 'Lelouch Toys with "Roman" Credits' *Variety* (4 May 2007) https://variety.com/2007/more/news/lelouch-toys-with-roman-credits-1117964302/ accessed 22 April 2020.

film, which could have turned out to be a punishment instead, if it hadn't seduced the public. Hence my choice of remaining anonymous.[25]

So, Lelouch submits, he wanted the work to receive its due praise or blame without attachment to his well-known name. *Droit moral* allows Lelouch this luxury, and it is also what allows Laclos the power to reclaim his identity and his pride at the expense of Ralitzer. In France, even if Laclos contracts away his copyrights, he cannot contract away his moral rights.[26] He is not *required* to attach his name to his work, but there is nothing that Ralitzer can do to stop him doing so, short of making him disappear.

So, if Lelouch wanted his film to stand on its own, why reveal himself on the eve of its debut at Cannes? He explains:

> The joke was very successful and I could have pushed it further even. I didn't stop because I didn't want to be a thief. If someone buys a ticket in a theater to see a film by Herv Picard, it's a scam to show them a film by Claude Lelouch. Besides, it became too complex when dealing with royalties and the protection of author rights, in particular for Pierre Uytterhoeven who wrote with me the adaptation and dialogue. You had to register with the CNC (National Film Office), the censorship Commission and other official organizations to whom I couldn't lie. I was defeated by the tax and legal institutions. As soon as the film was selected for Cannes we started to tell the truth.[27]

So, it's other things in the real world, Lelouch says, that got in the way, though his explanation seems contrived. He professes that he doesn't want to rip off audiences who want to see a Picard film, though no such filmmaker exists. More likely than Lelouch worrying about stealing from audiences, he's worried about the fictional Picard stealing from him. Having your film selected for the Cannes Film Festival is an enormous honor. Lelouch has had an uneven career, critically speaking. In 1966, he won the Palme d'Or – the highest award at Cannes – and for the next decade had several of his films selected for screening at the festival. But in the mid-1970s, Lelouch's fortunes began to ebb. By 2007, he'd had only one film selected for Cannes in 20 years.

Taken at his word, Lelouch appears to be saying that it doesn't matter who wrote the work, that it should be judged on its own merits. But in the end, he seems to take the lesson from his own film: it matters very much who wrote it. In a tongue-in-cheek interview, Lelouch was asked: 'Visually, how does Hervé Picard's work differ from your own?' He replied, laughing: 'Hervé Picard is a big plagiarist. He stole lots of things from me.'[28] Lelouch wasn't about to let him steal a Cannes selection.

One more curious thing. The title of *Roman de Gare* is translated for English-speaking markets as *Crossed Tracks*, which has the right Hitchcockean feel for the English-speaking market. 'Roman de gare' literally means 'train station novel' – something close to 'trashy paperback you buy to read on the train'. On its own, the original title doesn't make a lot of sense. Early in the film, Ralitzer is outlining the plot of a novel she is writing about terrorists

---

[25] Emanuel Levy, 'Roman de Gare: French Director Claude Lelouch' (*emanuellevy.com*, 21 April 2008) https://emanuellevy.com/interviews/roman-de-gare-with-french-director-claude-lelouch-2/ accessed 22 April 2020.

[26] Code de la Propriété Intellectuelle, Art. L121-1.

[27] Levy (n 25).

[28] Movieweb, 'Roman de Gare – Exclusive: Director Claude Lelouch Interview' (20 September 2010) https://www.youtube.com/watch?v=aIcVjF4Omho accessed 22 April 2020.

assassinating the American president by poisoning his wine supply. She is asked the title, and responds, 'For now, *Roman de Gare*'. (It's also the name of her yacht, but nobody mentions this.) As described, that novel *does* sound like a trashy paperback. But the movie isn't *about* that novel; that novel doesn't come up again. And who titles their novel – or, for that matter, their movie – with the derogatory term for its category? *Weepy Romance*. *Thinly Plotted Page-Turner*. *Mindless Horror Sequel*. Given Lelouch's penchant for playing with names, it's unlikely that it's mere coincidence that *Romain Gary* (a near homonym to *Roman de Gare*) is, in addition to being one of the most popular authors in France, a pen name for Roman Kacew, who also wrote under 'Émile Ajar' and a selection of other *noms de plume*. Gary's third novel as Ajar, *Pseudo*, is our third example.[29]

3.   *PSEUDO*

Although his name would be unfamiliar to most Americans, Romain Gary's biography sounds like a wild fiction, the sort of incredible story best suited for the Golden Age of Hollywood – a role for Douglas Fairbanks or Errol Flynn, perhaps. The details of Gary's childhood and ancestry are hazy – Gary himself invented several different versions – but we know that he was born 'Roman Kacew' in 1914 in Lithuania. Gary emigrated to France with his mother when he was a teenager, going on to study philosophy and law, and eventually training as a military pilot. But, when France signed an armistice with Nazi Germany in 1940, Gary joined the Free French Forces, the military branch of the French government-in-exile headquartered in London, and spent the war as a bombardier, collecting honor upon honor – his legend cemented when he successfully guided a blinded pilot through a bombing run over Germany. At the same time, Gary was writing his first novel, *Education européenne*, published in 1945 just as he began pursuing his new career as a diplomat in the reestablished French government, going on to serve as secretary for the French Delegation to the United Nations, and Consul General of France in Los Angeles – effectively 'French Ambassador to Hollywood'.[30] By the time he landed in California, Gary had published six novels, the latest of which – *Les racines du ciel* (1956) – won the Goncourt Prize, France's most prestigious literary award. The novel was translated into English as *The Roots of Heaven* (1957), and a Hollywood film adaptation followed the next year, scripted by Gary himself, directed by John Huston (the same director whose heirs would make Hollywood nervous about moral rights), and starring (appropriately enough) Errol Flynn. Up through 1974, Gary would publish another dozen novels, including the autobiographical *La pomesse de l'aube* (1960). Gary had amassed fluency in six languages, international fame, and an affair with – and eventually marriage to – French New Wave icon Jean Seberg (who would herself have an affair with Clint Eastwood, whom Gary would then dutifully but unsuccessfully challenge to a duel).[31]

---

[29]   Lelouch is not, somehow, unaware of Gary. Gary's name is mentioned in a character's eulogy after Ralitzer's suicide. Gary himself died by suicide in 1980.

[30]   David Bellos, 'Romain Gary: au revoir et merci' *Daily Telegraph* (London, 13 November 2010) 24, 25.

[31]   For more details, see Bellos (n 30). For even *more* details, see David Bellos, *Romain Gary: A Tall Story* (Harvill Secker 2010). For Gary's own version of his story, see Roman Gary, *La promesse de l'aube* (Gallimard 1960), translated to English by John Markham Beach as *Promise at Dawn* (Gallimard 1961), and twice adapted for film: by Jules Dassin in 1970 and by Eric Barbier in 2017.

In 1974, Gary reinvented himself once again with a new comic novel about a lonely Parisian statistician with a pet python, *Gros-Câlin*. Rather that publishing the book under his own name, Gary surreptitiously submitted the manuscript to his publisher under a pseudonym, 'Émile Ajar', complete with false biography. The novel was picked up and was an immediate runaway success, shortlisted for the Renaudot Prize, France's second-most-prestigious literary award. Afraid of the publicity that the Renaudot Prize would direct towards the thin guise of Ajar, Gary had Ajar gracefully remove himself from the running. Still, Gary successfully carried the façade of Ajar into a second novel a year later: *La vie devant soi* (1975), another enormous success. Renaudot or not, Ajar attracted the attention of both critics and the press, and people began to notice similarities between Ajar's writing and Gary's, both thematic and textual. When journalist Laure Boulay confronted Gary with evidence that he and Ajar were one and the same, Gary suggested that perhaps Ajar had plagiarized *him*: 'But, well, he's a young author. I'm not going to make a fuss about it.'[32] When Ajar's editor insisted on meeting him, Gary convinced his cousin's son, Paul Pavlowitch, to pose as Ajar. Pavlowitch went on to appear as Ajar in a series of interviews, following directions by Gary. The ruse, already precariously balanced, threatened to explode entirely when *La vie devant soi* was shortlisted for the Goncourt Prize. Ajar could *perhaps* demur from the Renaudot, but *nobody* turns down the Goncourt. However, a writer is only allowed to win the Goncourt Prize once; for Gary to accept it a second time, under the guise of Ajar, would be tantamount to fraud.[33] Gary directed Pavlowitch to turn down the Prize, but the message, apparently, was not delivered. So, *La vie devant soi* made history as the first time an author had won the Goncourt for a second time – though at this point the public was unaware of this fact. So, to completely upend public scrutiny, Ajar published his third book, *Pseudo* (1976), in which Ajar 'admits' his true identity of Paul Pavlowitch.[34]

Read seriously, *Pseudo* is the first-person confessional story of Pavlowitch, a delusional schizophrenic but talented author, struggling with his sense of identity and authenticity while trying to maintain the façade of his pseudonym, Émile Ajar. Pavlowitch wants to be left alone behind his anonymity, but Ajar's sudden and escalating celebrity makes it impossible. Ajar is an empty vessel, and the press abhors a vacuum. Read in retrospect (the English translation by David Bellos was published in 2010 as *Hocus Bogus*), it's clear that Gary (as Ajar [as Pavlowitch]) is trying to throw off any suspicion that he might be Gary in particular. And, since Pavlowitch *is* discoverably Gary's relative, Gary himself appears at several points in the book. The narrator sets up Gary as an enigmatic and self-obsessed figure, telling Pavlowitch that he needs to distance himself from Gary so the press doesn't think that Gary has helped him with his writing, and then expressing disappointment when the issue wasn't raised by Pavlowitch's interviewers. Late in the novel, Pavlowitch – by this point firmly established as delusional – accuses Gary of writing *La vie devant soi*, and (within a page) of trying to steal his prize:

---

[32]   Romain Gary, *The Life and Death of Émile Ajar* in *Hocus Bogus* (David Bellos tr, Yale University Press 2010) 175, 191.

[33]   For details on the ruse, see Bette H Lustig, 'Emile Ajar Demystified' (1983) 57 French Rev 203, and Gary's own *Vie et mort d'Émile Ajar* (1981), translated as Gary (n 32).

[34]   Émile Ajar, *Pseudo* (Mercure de France 1976).

> I rushed over to see my new lawyer. I told him [Gary] had stolen my manuscript, that he was trying to pass himself off as the author of my work, that he was spreading the rumor while appearing to deny it, by protesting too much, and that I wanted to sue.[35]

Pavlowitch has to explain away all of the textual similarities between Ajar's work and Gary's, and all of those places where Ajar has wandered or been pulled into the public eye, and in such a way as to redirect the scrutiny from Gary to Pavlowitch, all while working to cement Pavlowitch's mental instability. Most importantly, Gary has to find *some* reason that Ajar would withdraw *Gros-Câlin* from consideration for the Renaudot, and the odd circumstances immediately preceding *La vie devant soi* winning the Goncourt:

> I turned down the Goncourt prize in 1975 because of a panic attack. They had overcome my defensive gambit, got right inside it, and I was horrified by the publicity, which winkled me out of all my hidey-holes, and by my detectives asking questions at the hospital in Cahors.[36]

Ajar/Pavlowitch tries to explain his anxiety and confusion at his sudden media attention:

> Apparently I won the Goncourt prize as an authentic. For starters, I didn't even know the Goncourt prize existed. That's Point One. Then I withdrew from the Goncourt contest the day before the decision was made. Point Two.[37]

Later, in a mirror-version of the real world, Pavlowitch accuses Gary of deliberately failing to submit the letters of withdrawal on Pavlowitch's behalf: 'You kept the letters in your pocket, on purpose. You did it *on purpose*, to get me to win a literary prize, to put me on the right path … the only true path – your own!'[38]

Pseudo, at best, sits on the outer boundary of the category of fiction. Reading fiction involves an understanding that the thing you are reading is not the recounting of real events. *Pseudo* presents a wildly fictionalized account of real-world events. But importantly, the reader was never meant to know this. The reader was *meant* to read it as a non-fictional confession by the real-world Paul Pavlowitch. So *Pseudo* is a hoax, a lie. Read in retrospect, the text is *riddled* with enough nods and winks to suggest a sort of existential seizure. But *Pseudo* was an enormous success – both as a work of literature, and as a tool of misdirection. The press and the public bought it entirely. Gary went on to publish as both himself and as Ajar, successfully maintaining the charade for another four years, until his death by suicide in 1980. Gary had, at this point, already arranged for the posthumous publication of *Vie et mort d'Émile Ajar – The Life and Death of Émile Ajar* – in which he finally tells the true story.

4.   THREE LESSONS

There are, I think, three central lessons to be learned from this assemblage of works.

---

[35]   Romain Gary, *Hocus Bogus* (David Bellos tr, Yale University Press 2010) 155.
[36]   Ibid [7].
[37]   Ibid [31].
[38]   Ibid [148].

4.1   Lesson 1: Authenticity

First, notably, none of the works discussed here *overtly* deals with the moral right of attribution, nor even copyright or intellectual property in general – the terms never come up. (This, in part, explains the difficulty of identifying fictions that would suit the premise of the chapter you are reading.) To be fair, intellectual property law is hardly ideal fodder on which to turn a plot. It's a complex and often nitpicky domain of the law that varies substantially by jurisdiction, and which a writer can't assume her readers will already possess even a rudimentary understanding of. It's not murder, embezzlement, or blackmail, in other words. Indeed, despite their livelihood turning on it, most writers have at best only a basic grasp of intellectual property rights. Bestselling author Scott Turow tells the story of getting the contract for the film rights to his 1987 legal thriller *Presumed Innocent*:

> Draft contract arrives. And of course, it says that among the rights I am selling are my right to make a claim based on droit morale ... or moral rights. And so I called my lawyer, and I said, 'Well, what are moral rights?' And he said, 'Well, it has nothing to do with you. You're an American.' But I've always been conscious of the concept just because I'd been through law school. I never took a copyright class.[39]

Instead of dealing with intellectual property law directly, each of our works centrally grapples with issues of *authenticity* and *identity* – concepts that audiences will more easily appreciate, that writers (and artists in general) care *very* much about, and which the right of attribution is meant to embody.

Although initially arising from economic interests, moral rights in European law today are tied to the notion that traces of the author's personality are *imprinted* in her work, that the work carries the 'stamp of the author's personality' – that the work is an *extension of the author herself*.[40] Much of this understanding of moral rights comes from G.W.F. Hegel's *Philosophy of Right* (1820). Personality, Hegel argues, is the will's struggle to actualize itself – to make itself *real*, to impose itself on the world. And one discovers one's own personality – and so actualizes oneself – by marking the world with one's personality. The novel, the painting, the film, is *yours* because there's some of *you in it*. Indeed, it's only through imprinting oneself onto the world that one *learns* who one is. One's ownership of a thing, on Hegel's view, is contingent upon that thing representing the manifestation of one's personality, one's authentic self.[41]

To ask about authenticity and identity is, for an artist, to ask, 'Is this thing *my* work? Is it *me*?' Pierre Laclos, perhaps for the first time, recognizes his work *as his*, and is willing to fake his own death to protect his right to claim it as such. Alan Smithee, conversely, *rejects* the work *as his* – 'It was my child but it wasn't my child' – ultimately destroying the work to be freed from it. Émile Ajar's relationship with the work and his own identity is more complicated.

As Hegel's view suggests, authenticity is as much a matter of *learning* who you are as it is *showing* who you are, and – importantly – of having the freedom to do so. Romain Gary writes

---

[39]   US Copyright Office (n 18), 96.

[40]   See Calvin D Peeler, 'From the Providence of Kings to Copyrighted Things (and French Moral Rights)' (1999) 9 Indiana Int'l & Comp L R 423.

[41]   G W F Hegel, *Philosophy of Right* (first published as *Grundlinien der Philosophie des Rechts* 1820, T M Knox tr, Clarendon Press 1952) §§ 39–68.

in *The Life and Death of Émile Ajar*, 'I was tired of being nothing but myself. I was tired of the Romain Gary image I had been stuck with once and for all during the previous thirty years … To *renew* myself, to relive, to be someone else, was always the great temptation of my existence.'[42] Gary's enormous success restricts him from freely exploring his own identity, his own style, his own personality. Writing under a false name allows him to discover himself without the limits imposed by public and critical expectation. It also allows his work to be understood without being read through the lens of the author's recognized name. Gary writes: 'I knew, then, that [*Gros-câlin*], the first book of an unknown writer, would not sell well, but anonymity was more important to me than anything else. So the publisher couldn't be told.'[43]

Gary is neither the first nor the last writer to take on a pen name to allow him to explore his own personality, and to free the work from a constrained reading. Stephen King, who we briefly discussed early in this chapter, wrote several books under the pen name 'Richard Bachman'. When Bachman's first book, *Rage*, was released in late 1977, King was already attracting celebrity as the author of *Carrie* (1974), *Salem's Lot* (1975), and *The Shining* (1977). King published *horror*; Bachman published … whatever he wanted. King reflects: 'Bachman had become a kind of id for me; he said the things I couldn't.'[44] Bachman's early books – *Rage*, *The Long Walk* (1979), *Roadwork* (1981), and *The Running Man* (1982) – aren't horror, but (since his outing in 1985) that's the section of the bookstore you will find them in, usually filed under 'K'.

Having the freedom to publish your work under your own name – to claim responsibility, for good or for bad – or to publish under a pen name, or to retract your name from a work that you *don't* feel reflects who you are, is what is at the heart of the moral right of attribution. Authors (and artists generally) tend to report profoundly suffering under constraints to their sense of identity and authenticity of expression. Both Pavlowitch and Smithee end up in psychiatric care, and Laclos fakes his own death over the issue.

4.2   Lesson 2: The Real World

Certainly, there are workaday writers who labor from nine to five, plugging away at the keyboard, creating a product to be sold to the public. And, certainly, there are journeyman directors, hired to competently direct films or television episodes, but without working to put anything of *themselves* into the work. Writers have a word for creators like these: *hacks*. 'Hack' is a pejorative term. A hack writer produces undistinguished work, which is a weird thing to have a word for. There is no obvious equivalent for, say, construction workers or nurses or librarians, who are hired to competently apply their specialized knowledge and skills to perform a service or create a product that doesn't somehow embody their unique personalities. What a hack lacks is that apparent connection between her work and her identity – in short, a concern with *authenticity*. It would be strange for a hack writer to write a work about authenticity. Conversely, it should not be surprising that when a writer or director tells a story that *focuses* on issues of artistic identity and authenticity, that same writer or director will have a personal interest in those same issues. As such, as we have seen, the issues at the heart of our selected works have spilled out into the real world. Hiller takes on the 'Alan Smithee' name

---

[42]   Gary (n 32), 183.
[43]   Ibid [182].
[44]   Stephen King, 'The Importance of Being Bachman' in *The Regulators* (Penguin 1999) i, vi.

when his work is wrested from his control; Lelouch puts a pseudonym on his film when he
wants it to be judged on its own merits and puts his name back on it when he wants the credit;
Gary creates the story of a writer who hides behind a pseudonym to ensure that Gary himself
can hide behind the same pseudonym. As Pavlowitch says in *Pseudo*: '[L]iterature flows back
into life and renews it.'[45] Even Joe Eszterhas, the screenwriter who wrested control of *Burn
Hollywood Burn* from Arthur Hiller, reports:

> Afraid that Disney wouldn't release *An Alan Smithee Film: Burn Hollywood Burn*, I was ready to
> show it myself in church halls and school cafeterias.
> So I had a copy of the negative illicitly duped, and then I *stole it* (a federal offense)!
> I still have it in a closet in the baby's room, hidden underneath a big box of old toys.[46]

Eszterhas, after all, is a writer too, and so it should come as no surprise that he put some of
himself into that film – and absconded with the negative to ensure that his child couldn't be
killed by the producers.

4.3   Lesson 3: Moral Rights Are Not Absolute

Our final lesson arises from the fact that, in each of our cases, the creators' rights are challenged by industry convention, by competing legal rights, or by public interests. In short: moral
rights are not absolute; they exist in a complex dimension of overlapping rights and interests.

As a Hollywood director, Alan Smithee only has those rights that have been guaranteed him
by contract. In the world of film, these rights are secured by the 'Basic Agreement' between
the Directors Guild of America (DGA) and the producers' union, the Alliance of Motion
Picture and Television Producers (AMPTP). The Basic Agreement runs to nearly 600 pages,
and includes substantial detail about how directors and others may be credited in a film.[47]
Section 8-211 outlines provisions for directorial pseudonyms. Under these rules, a director
may apply to the DGA to use a pseudonym, and the DGA *may* grant permission. Then again, it
may not. If the DGA approves the use of a pseudonym, the producers *may* reject that request,
triggering a vote between representatives of the DGA and the AMPTP. Nothing would have
stopped Smithee from applying to use a *different* pseudonym, but nothing guarantees him the
use of one either. Smithee's rights are in the hands of others. Now, as we noted, because he is
making his work in America, and because his work is not a 'work of visual art', Smithee does
not have moral rights in the first place.

Pierre Laclos, the ghostwriter, is another story. Undoubtedly, Laclos has a business contract with Judith Ralitzer. He can sell the copyright to the novel he writes. But France makes
a distinction between the economic rights conferred by copyright ownership, which (like other
rights to property) can be transferred, sold, or otherwise contracted away, and moral rights,
which cannot. The authorial right of attribution is 'perpetual, inalienable and imprescriptible'.[48]
This would appear to place moral rights in a class with such other inalienable rights as the
right to life, the right to freedom of expression, and the right to be treated as a person. One

45   Gary (n 35), 129.
46   Joe Eszterhas, *The Devil's Guide to Hollywood* (St. Martin's Press 2006), 218.
47   Directors Guild of America, '2014-2017 Basic Agreement' https:// www .dga .org/ Contracts/
Agreements/Basic2014.aspx accessed 16 August 2021.
48   Code de la Propriété Intellectuelle, Art. L121-1.

might perhaps choose not to *exercise* one's rights, but this is a distinct matter from transferring such rights away. Simply put, it is not possible to be paid enough to voluntarily give up either one's right to personhood or one's right of attribution.[49] Indeed, the author's rights in France can only be transferred upon death and will never expire. But France is unique in this regard. In Germany, moral rights (*Urheberrechte*), including the right of attribution, may be temporarily contractually waived by an author. In France, Laclos would always be within his rights to demand his name be attached to what he has written, regardless of whether he had signed a contract to the contrary.[50] Conflicting findings in French courts suggest both that the ghostwriter can enter into a legally binding contract in which he voluntarily and permanently waives his right to attribution *and* that the ghostwriter has the legal right to withdraw consent to that contract and assert authorship at any time. The inability of an author to give up his right of attribution *should* by reason negate the contract, but courts have determined otherwise. So, Vanessa Nistor argues, in seeking to strike a balance between the inalienability of *droit moral* and maximal contractual freedom, the courts have failed to respect either, leaving authorial rights in a precarious position.[51]

The same inalienability of the right of attribution that allows Laclos to attach his name to his work *should* allow Claude Lelouch to maintain the ruse of 'Hervé Picard', though he laments a litany of practical barriers to his doing so, including tax issues arising from royalty payments, authorial rights for Lelouch's collaborator, Pierre Uytterhoeven, and registration with various official bodies, where use of a false name, he suggests, would amount to fraud. And, it seems, that same inalienability of the right of attribution *should* allow Paul Pavlowitch the pleasure of living anonymously behind the protective shield of 'Émile Ajar'. However, Pavlowitch's world, like ours, seems set against the notion of *anonymous celebrity*. The moral right of attribution operates as a 'negative right', meaning others cannot stop me from publishing under a *nom de plume* of my choice. In this way, the right to publish pseudonymously is like the right to free speech: you wrong me if you act to stop me. A 'positive right' differs from a negative right in that it places an obligation on others: not only to refrain from interfering, but to assist the rightsholder in securing the object of that right. Nothing compels you to help me speak freely. And so, it may be that the public must not interfere with Gary's (or Pavlowitch's or Lelouch's, or Laclos's) right to publish pseudonymously, but nothing compels the public to assist in the charade. The right to *publish* pseudonymously, after all, is not a right to *live* pseudonymously. If there is one overarching moral to this collection of stories, it is that having a right doesn't mean you don't have to keep fighting for it.

---

[49]   Drawing another parallel between the role of the ghostwriter and the condition of slavery.

[50]   Cour de cassation, Chambre civile 1, 13 February 2007, 05-12.016 https://www.legifrance.gouv .fr/affichJuriJudi.do?idTexte=JURITEXT000017635047 accessed 22 April 2020.

[51]   Vanessa Nistor (2015) 'L'affaiblissement du caractère inaliénable du droit moral: les conventions de nègre' (2015) 2 Le Nouvel Endroit 121.

29. Thou shalt not read: *ius abutendi* as a moral right of the author?

Rudolf Leška[1]

Divus Augustus carmina Vergili cremari contra testamenti eius verecundiam vetuit, maiusque ita vati testimonium contigit quam si ipse sua probavisset.[2]

1.   INTRODUCTION: WHEN AUTHORS DO NOT WISH TO SEE THEIR WORKS AVAILABLE

We tend to understand copyright as a vehicle for the monetization of a creative investment of labour, time or money. This approach, which is spreading universally and seems to be currently prevailing, is to some extent influenced by the Anglo-American concept of copyright as an economic instrument, rather than the continental approach which sees author's rights as natural, akin to the right to one's own brainchild. In the view of most of today's policy-makers, be it the European Union or the United States, copyright needs to be reformed to allow broad cross-border availability of protected works without questioning the author's intent to have his or her work globally available, and often without respecting the wish of the rightholder to legitimately increase profit through selected or consecutive distribution of the work in certain territories. But this is not the whole picture of copyright. The author also has the right not to use the work – for any conceivable reason – and to disallow its use by others.

Many authors have objected to unauthorized use of their works not because of money, but because they had no control over the accuracy and correctness of such copies. On the other hand, authors such as Wagner, Kafka, O'Neill, Beckett, Nabokov, Grass, Bernhard, Foucault, Kundera and many others produced works that, for one reason or another, they did not wish to be available to certain audiences at all. In the most extreme case, an author might wish to destroy all existing copies of the work to remove it from the heritage of humankind.

Copyright law contains tools that allow the author to prevent the circulation of a work. After all, textbooks define copyright as a 'right to exclude'. The author may simply refuse to grant a licence and withhold a divulgation of a work to keep it personal. As the US Supreme Court has taught us, this does not necessarily mean that the public would not be familiarized with

[1]   I would like to thank the University of Finance and Administration, VŠFS for the institutional support of long-term conceptual development in research. My thanks go to the patient editor of this book, Professor Gendreau, for inspiring this study, Natalia Kapyrina for a useful advice concerning the Soviet law, and to Milan Kundera for his continuous support of the cause of the arts and authors.
[2]   'His late Majesty Augustus overrode the modesty of Virgil's will and forbade the burning of his poems, and thus the bard achieved a stronger testimony than if he had commended his own works himself.' Pliny the Elder, *Natural History*, vol 5 (first published AD 77, Harris Rackham (tr), Harvard University Press 1961) 114.

the work.[3] Similarly in the European Union, some copyright exceptions allow the use of yet undisclosed works.[4]

Once a licence is granted, the author becomes essentially defenceless against any further exploitation of the work, with a few exceptions. Contract law might offer the right to terminate the agreement after a certain period of time[5] or the right to withdraw due to a change of mind (*droit de repentir*)[6] or for other reasons contractually agreed. Another solution can be provided by moral rights discussed elsewhere in this book (the right to oppose derogatory use, the right to oppose changes in the work, etc.).

2.   USING COPYRIGHT TO PREVENT THE AVAILABILITY OF A WORK

The right to exclude is a fundamental aspect of property rights, including copyright; many authors used this right in the past and continue to use it today to exclude large portions of their potential audiences from enjoying their works.

Literary history records many examples of various strategies that creators used to supress the circulation of their work for other than monetary reasons. In these strategies, I have identified four repeating patterns. The authors either (1) do not allow the work to be accessible to a certain audience;[7] (2) do not publish the work during their lifetime; (3) prohibit publication for a certain time after their death; or (4) destroy copies of the work.

What these examples share is the fact that whenever an author refuses to grant a licence or withholds a work from publication, the morality of such step is questioned. It seems counter-intuitive and unethical for some[8] that the author does not wish to share their work with the public or any part of it, regardless of any remuneration which might flow from such exploitation.

In the individualistic approach, one should not question the author's right not to publish a work, refuse to grant a licence, or even destroy all copies in his or her possession. But many

---

[3]   *Harper & Row v. Nation Enterprises* 471 U.S. 539 (1985), concerning Gerald Ford's memoirs.

[4]   Cf. Directive 2001/29/EC of the European Parliament and of the Council on the Harmonisation of Certain Aspects of Copyright and Related Rights in the Information Society [2001] OJ L167, Art. 5.

[5]   Cf. the US Copyright Act; 17 USC §§ 203, 304(c)(d).

[6]   Cf. Article L. 121-4 of the French Intellectual Property Code; § 42 of the German Copyright Act, etc.

[7]   Naturally, copyright owners often do not grant permission to certain uses in order to exploit the work more efficiently and to legitimately maximize their profit. This approach is typical for the theatre and film industry. For example, the publisher may restrict stage productions of a play if a blockbuster film based on the play is forthcoming. Another example includes distribution windows and geographical restrictions typical for film distribution which aim to gain higher revenue for the producer from different territories and distribution schemes. This type of economic behaviour exemplified by publishers and producers remains outside the scope of this study, which focuses on an analysis of the authors' own decisions not to use their work for other than pecuniary reasons.

[8]   In the privacy context, Goldman and Silbey call this 'copyright's memory hole'. Eric Goldman and Jessica Silbey, 'Copyright's Memory Hole' [2019] BYU L. Rev. 929. For the ethical analysis of territorial limitation of copyright (access to geoblocked audiovisual content) cf. Pavel Zahrádka, *Etická analýza zeměpisného blokování online přístupu k audiovizuálnímu obsahu* (Univerzita Palackého v Olomouci 2020).

arguments can be made that such behaviour contradicts the very essence of copyright and authorship. If a work is an author's brainchild, does this mean we can kill our own child? And furthermore, could we see the work as a peculiar kind of scarce property? Such as city apartments rented out through Airbnb, or a useful but unexploited patent? In these cases, legislators often allow for rent regulation or compulsory licensing. Indeed, the copyright law of every country contains at least some compulsory licensing scheme in the form of mandatory collective licensing, typically in the area of broadcasting and rebroadcasting or public performance of musical works. As a rule, these schemes, however, only apply to published or otherwise divulged works. This is related to the idea that once the author presents the work to the public, he or she is making it part of public heritage. Communist copyright law allowed much broader compulsory licensing. The communists saw works as belonging to the society rather than the author, although they allowed for 'appropriate' remuneration to the author.[9] The Czechoslovak Copyright Act of 1953 and the Czechoslovak Copyright Act of 1964 permitted also compulsory licensing in cases where the author could not grant a licence or refused to grant a licence to a published work 'without due cause'.[10] The Soviet law went even further and technically allowed (though extremely rarely utilized) compulsory licence even in cases of undisclosed works.[11] The Marxist theory, derived from classical German philosophy, considered an author's work to be a contribution to society, which means that society has a *right* to use the work. In fact, this can be understood as an elaboration of the German idea of the 'social obligation' of a property (*Sozialbindung des Eigentums*), including intellectual property.[12]

2.1   Works Made Available by the Author Only to Certain People

Some authors prevent the circulation of their work among certain audiences defined by territory (such as the communist countries), language (translation to a certain language), technology (film version of a novel) or other factor.

2.1.1   Thomas Bernhard

Thomas Bernhard, a polarizing Austrian novelist and playwright, directed his publisher Suhrkamp not to sell any books in Austria after the scandalous reception of his 1984 novel *Woodcutters* (*Holzfällen*) in his homeland. In the novel, Bernhard painted a rather unflattering image of the Viennese art scene; the composer Gerhard Lampersberg recognized himself in the character of Auersberger and commenced private criminal prosecution for libel ('*üble Nachrede*') and insult ('*Beleidigung*') under Sections 111 and 115 of the Austrian Criminal

---

[9]   'The purpose of the Copyright Act is to regulate legal relationships originating in connection with the creation of literary, scientific and artistic works in a way which ensures the protection of the interests of authors of such works and which provides an incentive to the creation of works of ideas serving the interests of the people and their cultural growth and at the same time ensures that the broadest masses of the working people will benefit from the creative work of the authors, so that their works become an effective instrument in the progress of socialist society.' §1 of the Czechoslovak Copyright Act of 1953 [Author's own translation].

[10]   There is, however, no known case where this mechanism was used. Rudolf Leška, 'From Marx to Google: Redefining the Role of Moral Rights in Czechia' [2019] Journal of Intellectual Property Law & Practice 331.

[11]   Section 106 of Part IV of Principles of Civil Legislation of 1961.

[12]   Cf. Eric Pahud, *Die Sozialbindung des Urheberrechts* (Stämpfli Verlag AG 2000).

Code.[13] Following the preliminary seizure of the printed books in Austria by the police, the angry author forbade Austrians from buying any of his books, as reported by the daily *Presse* on 9 November 1984. Although he changed his mind a year later and the criminal case ended with settlement of the parties after the revision court[14] lifted the seizure order,[15] the case remains one of the sourest battles fought between Bernhard and the Second Austrian Republic during his lifetime (and beyond). After another scandalous première of his play *Heroes Square* (*Heldenplatz*) in 1988, the author ordered his heirs in his will not to allow any stage productions in Austria – a ban circumvented by the establishment of the foundation Thomas-Bernhard-Stiftung.[16]

2.1.2   Milan Kundera

After emigrating from Czechoslovakia in 1975, Milan Kundera stopped writing his works in the Czech language and opted for French instead, starting with the novel *Slowness* (*La Lenteur*). More than that, he refused to translate his French novels into Czech or even to authorize a Czech or Slovak translation produced by anyone else, despite the fact that many illegal unauthorized fan translations circulated illegally on the internet.[17] His motives were not entirely clear; they might have been in part social (because he considered his Czech homeland to be 'ungrateful'), in part very pragmatic (he did not want anyone else to translate the works and on the other hand did not have the time to do it himself).[18] Nevertheless, in 2020 the author authorized Anna Kareninová and Elena Flašková to translate his most recent novel, *The Festival of Insignificance*, into Czech[19] and Slovak[20] respectively.

2.1.3   Richard Wagner

A special case is Wagner's last opera *Parsifal*, which he and his heirs did not allow to be staged outside of the festival theatre in Bayreuth, specially designed to accommodate his own works. The *Parsifal* case is well researched.[21] In principle, Wagner did not wish *Parsifal*,

---

[13]   Nina Birkner and York-Gothart Mix, 'Machtkämpfe in der "Gesellschaftshölle"?: Thomas Bernhards Holzfällen, Walter Gronds Der Soldat und das Schöne, die österreichische Kulturszene, die Kunstfreiheit und das Persönlichkeitsrecht' in Claude D. Conter (ed.), *Justitiabilität und Rechtmäßigkeit: Verrechtlichungsprozesse von Literatur und Film in der Moderne* (Brill, Rodopi 2010), 51.

[14]   Oberlandesgericht für Strafsachen Wien, Decision 27 Bs 566/84 of 21 December 1984.

[15]   Nina Birkner and York-Gothart Mix, 'Machtkämpfe in der "Gesellschaftshölle"?; Thomas Bernhards Holzfällen, Walter Gronds Der Soldat und das Schöne, die österreichische Kulturszene, die Kunstfreiheit und das Persönlichkeitsrecht' in Claude D. Conter (ed.), *Justitiabilität und Rechtmäßigkeit: Verrechtlichungsprozesse von Literatur und Film in der Moderne* (Brill, Rodopi 2010), 53, 56.

[16]   Georg Markus, 'Nestbeschmutzer, Blender oder Genie?' *Der Kurier* (Vienna, 9 February 2014) https://kurier.at/kultur/thomas-bernhard-nestbeschmutzer-blender-oder-genie/50.439.885 accessed 23 December 2020.

[17]   I wrote about illegal fan translations of J.K. Rowling and Milan Kundera in: Rudolf Leška, 'Pirátské překlady a paragrafy' (2006) 2(11) Plav 13.

[18]   Milan Kundera, 'O slavnosti a hostech. Dopis A. J. Liehmovi' *Lidové noviny* (Praha, 22 November 1990); Václav Bělohradský, 'Kunderův sen o absolutním autorství' *Právo* (Praha, 12 October 2006).

[19]   Alison Flood, 'Milan Kundera "joyfully" accepts Czech Republic's Franz Kafka Prize' *The Guardian* (London, 22 September 2020).

[20]   Alexander Balogh, 'Musela som poslať ukážku prekladu, ktorú potom Milan Kundera odobril' *Denník N* (Bratislava, 24 August 2020).

[21]   Cf. the studies of Manfred Rehbinder, 'Die Parsifal-Frage oder der Gedanke des Verbraucherschutzes im Urheberrecht' and Heinz Püschel, 'Rechte des Bühnenautors und Urheberrechtsschutzfrist aus his-

which he considered to be a 'stage-consecrating festival-play',[22] 'the last and the most sacred work'[23] to be staged elsewhere:

> I must find [for the work] a stage to consecrate and such a stage can only be my unique festival theatre in Bayreuth. Only and exclusively there may *Parsifal* be staged in the future. Never may be *Parsifal* presented at any other theatre for the amusement of the audience; ...[24]

Naturally, the best way to achieve this was through exclusive right to the work (ironically, the copyright to *Parsifal* was not originally owned by Wagner, but by the Bavarian king who generously waived his rights arising out of Wagner's previous copyright assignment and let the rights return to the author). The term of protection in the German Empire at the time was only 30 years p.m.a., which Wagner's heirs, his wife Cosima and son Siegfried, did not consider satisfactory. Their attempts to prolong the copyright protection whenever a new copyright law was discussed, specifically in 1901 and 1934, are beyond the scope of this chapter. More interestingly, Wagner's deeply religious, and indeed sacred, opera became the subject of a 'mystic' call for the eternal right of the author's family to control the very place of its staging. I find it important, however, that Richard Wagner never left a formal will[25] and his wishes were merely extrapolated by his widow (who declared herself to be the guardian of his will) from Wagner's letters and opinions published elsewhere.

Wagner always had many fervent followers; in 1913, they submitted a petition to the German Imperial Diet (with enthusiastic support of Wagner's widow) which proposed a special bill designed to protect mainly the moral interest of the (deceased) author. According to this proposal, a special eternal exclusive right would be introduced under which the author (the heirs) would be forever able to prevent the staging of a work which the author wished not to be staged and to prevent the staging of a work on a stage different from that conceived by the author. The proposed addition to the then valid Section 29 of the Law on Copyright in Works of Literature and Music[26] which stipulated a term of protection of 30 years p.m.a. consisted of the following four paragraphs:

---

torischer Sicht', both in Robert Dittrich (ed.), *Die Notwendigkeit des Urheberrechtsschutzes im Lichte seiner Geschichte* (Manz Verlag 1991). The *Parsifal* story is followed in detail by Anthony J. Steinhoff, 'Embracing the Grail: Parsifal, Richard Wagner and the German Nation' (2012) 30 German History 372. For extensive research of copyright issues related to Wagner cf. Sebastian Wündisch, *Richard Wagner und das Urheberrecht* (Berliner Wissenschafts-Verlag 2004) and the references therein.

[22]   *Bühnenweihfestspiel*. Translation according to The Concise Oxford Dictionary of Music.

[23]   '[D]ieses letzte und heiligste Werk'. Wagner in a letter to King Ludwig II of Bavaria dated 28 September 1880. The original is kept by the German Federal Archives (Bundesarchiv), File R 36 Deutscher Gemeindetag, Reichsjustizamt Nr. 6385, Bl. 35. Reprinted i.a. in Sebastian Wündisch, *Richard Wagner und das Urheberrecht* (Berliner Wissenschafts-Verlag 2004) 67.

[24]   'So muß ich ihm denn nun eine Bühne zu weihen suchen, und dies kann nur mein einsam dastehendes Bühnenfestspielhaus in Bayreuth sein. Dort darf der *Parsifal* in aller Zukunft einzig und allein aufgeführt werden; nie soll der *Parsifal* auf irgendeinem anderen Theater dem Publikum zum Amüsement dargeboten werden ...' Ibid [Author's own translation].

[25]   Anthony J. Steinhoff, 'Embracing the Grail: Parsifal, Richard Wagner and the German Nation' (2012) 30 German History 372, 374.

[26]   1901 Law on Copyright in Works of Literature and Music (*Gesetz betreffend das Urheberrecht an Werken der Literatur und der Tonkunst*) (RGBl. 1901, S. 227) (FRG).

(2)   If a published dramatic work has not been staged during the term of protection according to the author's express decision, the exclusive right of theatrical performance does not expire with the term of protection.

(3)   The same applies if, according to the author's express decision, the work has been staged before the expiration of the term of protection at only one location specified by the author.

(4)   In the case of paragraph 2, the performance right expires 10 years after the first performance permitted by the rightholder, in the case of paragraph 3, 10 years after the first performance at another stage permitted by the rightholder; in the case of paragraph 3, the right also expires if not exercised for 10 years.

(5)   In the cases of paragraphs 2–4, the Chancellor of the Empire is authorized to grant individual applicants the right to stage [the work] on a case-by-case basis.[27]

The Imperial Diet rejected the petition and thus *Parsifal*, together with the rest of Wagner's oeuvre, entered the public domain on 31 December 1913. This allowed opera houses around Europe to start the new year with a *Parsifal* production; in some instances, like in Barcelona, the opera opened on New Year's Eve just after midnight.[28] In some cities, like in Prague, two rivalling opera houses staged *Parsifal* at the same time – specifically, Prague's National Theatre and the New German Theatre both performed the opera on the very first day of 1914.[29]

There were, however, also several prior productions, either illegal, like in Amsterdam[30] or Monaco,[31] or legal in countries where the work had not been granted protection, like in the United States. The scholarship tends to repeat the claim that the American production was possible because the United States did not adhere to the Berne Convention.[32] This is, however, untrue; works of German nationals were at that time protected in the US under the bilateral

---

[27]   '(2) Ist ein erschienenes dramatisches Werk bis zum Ablauf der vorbezeichneten Fristen zufolge ausdrücklicher Verfügung des Urhebers der bühnenmäßigen Aufführung entzogen geblieben, so erlischt die ausschließliche Befugnis zur bühnenmäßigen Aufführung mit Ablauf der Schutzfrist nicht; (3) Das gleiche gilt, wenn bis zum Ablauf der Frist der ausdrücklichen Bestimmung des Urhebers zufolge Bühnenmäßige Aufführungen nur an einem vom Urheber bestimmten Ort veranstaltet worden sind; (4) Im Falle des Abs. 2 erlischt das Aufführungsrecht 10 Jahre nach der ersten vom Berechtigten gestatteten Aufführung, im Falle des Abs. 3 10 Jahre nach der ersten von dem Berechtigten außerhalb des Bestimmungsortes gestatteten Aufführung, im Falle des Abs. 3 erlischt es auch durch Nichtausübung innerhalb von 10 Jahren; (5) Der Reichskanzler ist ermächtigt, in den Fällen von Abs. 2-4 von Fall zu Fall Befugnis zur bühnenmäßigen Aufführung an Antragsteller zu verleihen.' Original in the German Federal Archives (Bundesarchiv), File R 36 Deutscher Gemeindetag, Reichsjustizamt Nr. 6385, Bl. 88. Reprinted i.a. in Sebastian Wündisch, *Richard Wagner und das Urheberrecht* (Berliner Wissenschafts-Verlag 2004), 98 [Author's own translation].

[28]   Heinz Püschel, 'Rechte des Bühnenautors und Urheberrechtsschutzfrist aus historischer Sicht' in Robert Dittrich (ed.), *Die Notwendigkeit des Urheberrechtsschutzes im Lichte seiner Geschichte* (Manz Verlag 1991) 222, 224.

[29]   Gary B. Cohen, 'Cultural Crossings in Prague, 1900: Scenes from Late Imperial Austria' (2014) 45 Austrian History Yearbook 1.

[30]   Anthony J. Steinhoff, 'Embracing the Grail: Parsifal, Richard Wagner and the German Nation' (2012) 30 German History 372, 375; Sebastian Wündisch, *Richard Wagner und das Urheberrecht* (Berliner Wissenschafts-Verlag 2004) 78–9.

[31]   Monaco was bound by the Berne Convention and the production was banned by the government, but one 'private' rehearsal took place in 1913 anyway. Cf. Heinz Püschel, 'Rechte des Bühnenautors und Urheberrechtsschutzfrist aus historischer Sicht' in Robert Dittrich (ed.), *Die Notwendigkeit des Urheberrechtsschutzes im Lichte seiner Geschichte* (Manz Verlag 1991) 222, 225.

[32]   Most recently, this erroneous claim was repeated by Anthony J. Steinhoff in 'Embracing the Grail: Parsifal, Richard Wagner and the German Nation' (2012) 30 German History 372, 375.

agreement of 1892.[33] Nevertheless, Wagner's publisher Schott did not properly register *Parsifal* with the Copyright Office, which was at that time a required condition for gaining protection. Interestingly, Wagner's estate tried to stop the production at the Metropolitan Opera by applying – to no avail – for an injunction at the US District Court for the Southern District of New York.[34] As a consequence, there was not only a stage production, but also a film production by the Edison Film Company, both entirely legal.[35]

This legislative attempt remains a curiosity in copyright history and it is now possible to stage *Parsifal* legally anywhere around the globe. All Wagnerians know, however, that to achieve full gratification, they have no other choice but to embark on a pilgrimage to see *Parsifal* in Bayreuth.

2.2   Works Made Available Only after the Author's Death

Various authors keep their work or works undisclosed during their lifetime, but do not leave any directions as to their publication once they pass away. This is, of course, a common fate of most unfinished works, which are left behind by almost every author who is active until the end of life. In some cases, the authors do not wish a finished work to be published in their lifetime due to various personal or political reasons, or they exercise their right of withdrawal due to a change of their opinion (*droit de repentir*). The work might, for example, lead to criminal prosecution or social ostracization of the author; it could also hurt the feelings of the close family, for example by portraying the author's lovers.

In some jurisdictions, notably in the civil law countries of continental Europe, this purpose is served by the moral right of divulgation or disclosure as a right distinct from economic rights. One can argue that this right is redundant as economic rights may well serve the very same purpose by themselves – by preventing the premature disclosure of a work to the public.[36] While this may be true in some instances, it is not always helpful and typically fails whenever a user invokes a copyright exception. Imagine a situation where a painter sells original painting to a collector. The collector, as the owner of the canvas, would be in most jurisdictions allowed to display the work publicly, but if the work had not been previously disclosed to the public, the moral right of divulgation would require the author's special consent.

One good example of this situation is the brilliant novel *Jottings for Beloved Lutécia* (*Písačky pre milovanú Lutéciu*) by the Slovak author Dominik Tatarka.[37] The partially autobiographical novel, written during the Soviet occupation of Czechoslovakia (1968–1990) when Tatarka was

---

[33]   Agreement of 15 January 1892 between the German Empire and the United States of America on the mutual protection of author's rights. 27 Stat. 1021 (US), RGBl. 1892, S. 473 (FRG).

[34]   Sebastian Wündisch, *Richard Wagner und das Urheberrecht* (Berliner Wissenschafts-Verlag 2004) 72–4. The application for preliminary injunction is preserved in the archives of the Richard Wagner Foundation. Cf. Nationalarchiv der Richard-Wagner-Stiftung, AFS 413-92.

[35]   Sebastian Wündisch, *Richard Wagner und das Urheberrecht* (Berliner Wissenschafts-Verlag 2004) 80 et seq.

[36]   Branka Marušić, 'Author's Right to Choose: Right of Divulgation in the Online Digital Single Market of the EU' in Tatiana-Eleni Synodinou, Philippe Jougleux, Christiana Markou, Thalia Prastitou (eds), *EU Internet Law in the Digital Era: Regulation and Enforcement* (Springer International Publishing 2020) 137–60.

[37]   An excerpt in English is available at https://www.litcentrum.sk/en/sample/jottings-beloved-lutecia accessed 10 December 2020.

not allowed to publish, follows his passionate extramarital relationship to a student of French literature, more than 40 years younger, who, as the reader later realizes, was a hired agent of State Security, the Czechoslovak intelligence agency. In exchange for her reports on Tatarka, she was allowed to study in Paris, Tatarka's beloved city, which he was not allowed to visit and which he identified with the persona of his lover (whom he called by the Latin name for Paris, Lutetia). The author did not wish to publish the text in his lifetime,[38] although an excerpt circulated against his will in the 1980s as a *samizdat*.[39] The full edition appeared long after his death once the publisher got the approval from the Tatarka family, which finally agreed with the publication of this very intimate text (1999 first edition, 2013 revised edition).

2.3   Works Prevented from Publication after the Author's Death

Other authors not only keep their work secret or known only to close acquaintances, but also prohibit any publication after their death, either for a certain period of time or forever. Even if copyright termination causes the work to enter the public domain, copies might still remain confidential based on the direction of the author or heirs – sometimes even without regard to the author's intentions.

2.3.1   Sigmund Freud
One prominent example is Sigmund Freud, the German-speaking Jew born in the Moravian town of Příbor. One part of his estate (mostly interviews with patients) stored in the Freud Collection at the Library of Congress will remain confidential until 2113.[40] In this case, the decision was made by Sigmund Freud Archives, Inc., which donated most of the material for the collection, and not the late author whose work had been in the public domain in Europe since 2010 because he died in 1939.

2.3.2   Adolf Hitler
In one very particular case, the Free State of Bavaria opposed the use of toxic writings authored by Adolf Hitler. Hitler's estate was confiscated by the decision of the specialized denazification tribunal in Munich[41] of 15 October 1948[42] and was later, in 1965, assigned to the Free State of Bavaria. This included the copyright to Hitler's works. Until this copyright expired in 2015, the Bavarian state repeatedly used its ownership to sue publishers of *My Struggle* (*Mein Kampf*) around the world for copyright infringement and never agreed to any publication, including in an annotated critical edition which appeared in Germany only in

---

[38] The author's statement was preserved in 1986 by a certain C. Guérin who recorded Tatarka's voice message for his lover, at that time already living in Paris. The tape is transcribed in: Dominik Tatarka, 'Entretien' in Dominik Tatarka, *Le Démon du consentement et autres textes* (Eur'Orbem Éditions Paris 2019) 181.

[39] Valér Mikula, 'Neznáma "navrávačka" Dominika Tatarku' (2020) 2(12) Rozum 36. The identity of Tatarka's lover was disclosed only recently because of her own response to this and following articles, in which she denies any intentional cooperation with State Security. Cf. Natalie Borodin, 'Heidelberg' (2021) 3(2) Rozum 4.

[40] Joseph L. Sax, *Playing Darts with a Rembrandt* (The University of Michigan Press 1999) 129.

[41] Spruchkammer München I.

[42] German Federal Archives Koblenz (Bundesarchiv Koblenz); File Bundesministerium der Justiz (BdJ), B 141/73827; Vol. 3602-2. Band 2.

2016.[43] Although the press often reported that the Bavarian state owned the rights because it inherited the original 1925 licence from the Eher publishing house (Franz Eher Nachfolger GmbH), which had been owned by the Nationalist Socialist German Workers' Party (NSDAP) and was seized by the post-war government, this is untrue. The Bavarian state based its standing in the judicial proceeding on having original ownership of Hitler's copyright rather than the ownership of a licence, as was shown during a trial in Czechia in response to an unlawful publication of the book.[44] This makes sense also legally, because even if the Bavarian state also owned the licence, the rights from the licence would cease to exist upon the merger with the rights of the author's successor. This opens the rather intriguing question of whether copyright can actually be expropriated in a continental jurisdiction like Germany, which understands copyright as a bundle of moral and economic interests.[45]

2.4   Destroyed Works

The most radical form of authors' rejection of their own work is a conviction that the work is, for one reason or another, not suitable to be presented to the public, and therefore all copies of the work must be destroyed – either by the author or by the heirs or executors of their will who are ordered to destroy all surviving copies.

3.   *IUS ABUTENDI*

3.1   Introduction

In most jurisdictions around the world, property is characterized through some, or all, of the following owner's rights: *ius utendi, ius fruendi, ius possidendi, ius disponendi, ius abutendi*. Although varieties occur, *ius abutendi* (*right to destroy*) is often expressly considered to be a part of the owner's absolute dominium over a substance.

Contrary to popular belief, *ius abutendi* was not recognized by Roman law.[46] As Földi explains:

> The word *abuti* can be found also in the works of the Roman jurists, and it meant mainly the misuse-like exploitation of a thing e.g. by the usufructuary. However, the *abuti* occurring in the fragment of Ulpian in D. 5, 3, 25, 11, which constitutes the source of the medieval *ius abutendi*, referred simply to the consumption of the *res consumptibiles* by the *bona fide* possessor.[47]

---

[43]   Adolf Hitler, *Mein Kampf – Eine kritische Edition* (Institut für Zeitgeschichte München–Berlin 2016).
[44]   Unpublished judgment of the Municipal Court in Prague (*Městský soud v Praze*) 31 C 104/2009 of 17 September 2010. For other cases concerning this work, cf. Marc Mimler, 'On How to Seal with Pandora's Box – Copyright in Works of Nazi Leaders' in Enrico Bonadio and Nicola Lucchi (eds), *Non-conventional Copyright* (Edward Elgar Publishing 2018) 432–54.
[45]   For the nationalization of copyright in India, cf. Mira T. Sundara Rajan, 'The Lessons of the Past: C Subramania Bharati and the Nationalisation of Copyright' [2009] Script-ed 201.
[46]   András Földi, 'Historic and Dogmatic Aspects of the Triad of Proprietary Rights' in Antonio Palma (ed.), *Scritti in onore di Generoso Melillo I* (Satura 2009) 353.
[47]   Ibid. References in the original text omitted.

The classical definition of property, *dominium est ius utendi fruendi et abutendi re sua, quatenus iuris ratio patitur*, first appears as late as the seventeenth century and was later enriched with *ius possidendi*.[48] Still, only some civil codes expressly recognize the owner's right to destroy their own property;[49] this particular aspect is typically lumped under a more general definition granting the owner an absolute right over the substance, or, more specifically, the right to dispose with the property.

Interestingly, in modern law-making, case law and scholarship, there is a certain hostility against the owner's broad right to destroy his or her possession. Lior Strahilevitz in his seminal article[50] engages in a lonely fight against this trend, which is in the US doctrine represented most prominently by property scholars such as Joseph Sax[51] and Edward McCaffery,[52] who argue for a radical limitation of the traditionally understood right to destroy, citing important public interest in the preservation of certain values and things. McCaffery even argues for a reform of the tax system which would punish waste and he answers the question *Must we have the right to waste?* 'decisively in the negative'.[53] I presume that this branch of property scholarship will gain even greater argumentative power with further development of our climatic crises and the shift of the social discourse towards environmentally oriented sustainable use of resources.

But what would be the implications of these theories if they were applied to immaterial works of art and their tangible copies?

3.2   *Ius Abutendi* in the Copyright Context: The Right to Destroy a Work?

3.2.1   By the owner of the copy

First and foremost, a work cannot be destroyed. A work of art, not only as a legal concept but as a phenomenon, cannot be destroyed, for art is immaterial and eternal. Only *copies* of a work can be destroyed – books may be burned, paintings cut to pieces and statues pulled down, but the work as such remains. This is the main reason why most jurisdictions around the world do not recognize an author's moral right to prevent the destruction of a copy of their work. One notable exception is the Visual Artists Rights Act (VARA) in the United States,[54] another one was the Indian Copyright Act.[55] A 'mere' destruction of a copy does not and cannot – at least in

---

[48]   Ibid.

[49]   The Czech Civil Code 89/2012 Sb. mentions the right of a bona fide possessor to destroy a property in Section 996, copying this text from Section 329 of the Austrian Civil Code ('ABGB') JGS 946/1811. The German Civil Code ('BGB') contains no such explicit provision.

[50]   Lior Strahilevitz, 'The Right to Destroy' [2005] Yale Law Journal 781.

[51]   Joseph L. Sax, *Playing Darts with a Rembrandt* (The University of Michigan Press 1999).

[52]   Edward J. McCaffery, 'Must We Have the Right to Waste?' in Stephen R. Munzer (ed.), *New Essays in the Legal and Political Theory of Property* (Cambridge University Press 2001).

[53]   Ibid.

[54]   The Visual Artists Rights Act of 1990 (VARA), (Pub.L. 101–650 title VI, 17 U.S.C. § 106A). Under §106A(a)(3)(b)B), 'author of a work of visual art shall have the right to prevent any destruction of a work of recognized stature, and any intentional or grossly negligent destruction of that work is a violation of that right'. Interestingly, the US legislator speaks about destruction 'of that work' although, as mentioned, only a copy of a work can actually be destroyed. US case law offers interesting examples of authors invoking damages for destruction of an original copy of their work.

[55]   As Rajan reported, the Indian Copyright Act of 1957 as interpreted by the Delhi High Court in the case *Amar Nath Sehgal v. Union of India*, 2005 (30) PTC 253 (Del), dated 21 February 2005, gave the

theory – destroy the work itself, which may survive in the memory of the author or humankind even if all copies are destroyed. After all, even the *Iliad* and the *Odyssey* were for a long time disseminated only through oral tradition.

Naturally, in the case of original copies of visual art or architecture, a destruction may cause irreparable harm. For this purpose, certain jurisdictions have enacted in their copyright laws at least the owners' duty to notify the author about their intent to change or destroy a building or a statue in order to allow the authors or their heirs to create documentation of the work before this change or destruction. As an incident from Czechia demonstrates, however, this provision may not be sufficient when a global corporation enters the picture. In this particular case, Tesco decided to destroy a building designed by the prominent architect and Perret Prize laureate Karel Hubáček and his colleague Miroslav Masák: the modernist Ještěd Shopping Centre in the city of Liberec, built in 1978–1979 and demolished in 2009 to make room for a thoroughly generic glass-steel-and-concrete Tesco store. In violation of Section 38d(b) of the Czech Copyright Act, the authors were not notified by the Tesco corporation about the destruction in advance.[56] Nevertheless, the authors decided not to pursue any formal legal complaint against the Tesco corporation.

3.2.2   By the author: infanticide

Shameful as it might be when the owner of the only copy or the original of a valuable work, mainly in the field of visual arts and architecture, decides to destroy it, as in the Sehgal and Hubáček cases discussed above, the situation becomes more interesting if said owner of the copy is, in fact, the author, engaging in an act that military terminology would describe as friendly fire.

Does the author possess the right to destroy copies of his or her works? This simple question may provoke a straight affirmative answer, but there are subtler ethical considerations to be taken into account. And to make the question even more complicated, does the situation change if the author, for whatever reason, does not destroy the copy or copies by themselves, but rather directs their heirs or testamentary executors to do this work for them? Should authors have the absolute right to demand the destruction of the copies? Is this a sort of a moral right?

L'ardente mio dramma ci scaldi ('my burning drama will warm us'), sings Rodolfo in Puccini's *La Bohème*, based on Murger's novel *Scenes of Bohemian Life*, before he puts his manuscript in the stove. Whether it is because they wanted to produce heat or because of their religious conversion, insanity, anger, critique from others, to perform an aesthetic act or mostly because of their own dissatisfaction with the result, we know of many examples of authors destroying their own manuscripts, 'demolishing them in an act akin to infanticide'.[57]

---

author the right to 'protect an artistic work from outright destruction'. The Indian court interpreted the moral right of integrity very broadly to also cover the destruction of the original embodiment of the work. Mira T. Sundara Rajan, 'Moral Rights in Developing Countries: The Example of India' [2003] Journal of Intellectual Property Rights 357, 449. According to Rajan, after the 1994 amendment of Section 57 of the Indian Copyright Act, a similar outcome would be unlikely as the code now expressly states that 'Failure to display a work or to display it to the satisfaction of the author shall not be deemed to be an infringement of the rights conferred by this section.'

[56]   Miloš Solař, 'Obchodní dům Ještěd v. Liberci: Památka! Nebourat!' (2005) 27(4) Dějiny a současnost 8.

[57]   Michael H. Miller, 'From Claude Monet to Banksy, Why Do Artists Destroy Their Own Work?' *The New York Times* (New York City, 11 March 2019) https://archive.nytimes.com/www.nytimes.com/books/98/02/08/reviews/980208.08rothstt.html accessed 23 December 2020.

Brahms reportedly destroyed large amounts of his unpublished oeuvre shortly before he died, including perhaps some 20 string quartets and his second violin concerto.[58] Leoš Janáček's 'Piano Sonata 1. X. 1905 From the Street' (*Z ulice*), one of the most beautiful piano pieces ever composed, which expresses the artist's sorrow felt over the body of a young carpenter shot to death by the imperial police during a demonstration in the city of Brno, was considered lost when the dissatisfied author destroyed its manuscript after the 1906 première – an act which he reportedly later regretted.[59] The pianist Ludmila Tučková, who performed the première, thankfully owned her own copy of the first two movements, which enabled a repeat performance in 1924 attended by the happy composer.[60]

In the literary world, there is the well-known case of the second volume of Gogol's *Dead Souls*, the manuscript of which he burned in 1852 after a priest convinced him that the book was sinful. Similarly to Janáček, he soon regretted the decision and died ten days later in agony.[61] While burning a manuscript is an irreversible act, there are other ways of destruction that may not last forever; the peculiar case of the English poet Dante Gabriel Rossetti shows that if you put notebooks in your wife's coffin, there is still a chance to dig them up seven years later.[62]

Destruction is much easier with original artwork; Tate, in fact, organized an entire online exhibition devoted to destroyed or lost pieces of art named 'The Gallery of Lost Art'[63] (which cannot be accessed today as it was, well, erased). Claude Monet destroyed 15 of his waterlily paintings before an exhibition because he was not satisfied with them,[64] van Gogh destroyed certain figure compositions in 1883 after being criticized by his brother Theo,[65] and Francis Bacon did the same constantly with his works 'as part of a sometimes pained and tortuous creative practice'.[66]

A tragic example where a living author is unable to carry out the task by himself represents the story of Josef Čapek, cubist painter and patriot who was arrested shortly after occupation of Czechoslovakia by German forces and spent more than five years in concentration camps, where he was murdered shortly before the end of war. He instructed his wife Jarmila to destroy dozens of paintings in one of his last letters – a task she faithfully executed.[67] Clearly, he did

---

[58] Edward Rothstein, 'Composing Himself: Brahms's Music Seems to Renounce, Again and Again, the Satisfaction of Desire' *The New York Times* (New York City, 8 February 1998) https:// archive .nytimes.com/www.nytimes.com/books/98/02/08/reviews/980208.08rothstt.html accessed 23 December 2020.

[59] Jiří Zahrádka, '1. X. 1905 – Myth and Fact of the Composition Destroyed by Janáček' in Ludvík Kundera and Jarmil Burghauser (eds), *1. X. 1905 Sonata for piano* (Editio Bärenreiter Praha 2005) 3.

[60] Ibid.

[61] Janko Lavin, 'Nikolay Gogol', *Encyclopædia Britannica* https://www.britannica.com/biography/ Nikolay-Gogol accessed 23 December 2020.

[62] Jan Marsh, 'Did Rossetti Really Need to Exhume his Wife?' *The Times Literary Supplement* (London, 15 February 2021).

[63] Cf. http://galleryoflostart.com/ accessed 23 December 2020.

[64] Michael H. Miller, 'From Claude Monet to Banksy, Why Do Artists Destroy Their Own Work?' *The New York Times* (New York City, 11 March 2019) https://archive.nytimes.com/www.nytimes.com/ books/98/02/08/reviews/980208.08rothstt.html accessed 23 December 2020.

[65] Roland Dorn, Albrecht Schröder and John Sillevis (eds), *Van Gogh und die Haager Schule* (Bank Austria Kunstforum, 1996).

[66] Jennifer Mundy, *Lost Art: Missing Artworks of the Twentieth Century* (Harry N. Abrams, 2014) 172, 173.

[67] Jan H. Vitvar, *Umění, kterému nikdo nerozumí* (Paseka, 2021) 33.

this only at the moment he was sure that he would not be able to sort the artworks in person and in this case the act is directly attributable to the author rather than his spouse.

Conceptual artists might use the destructive process by itself as an artistic manifesto. Perhaps the first such act might be Rauschenberg's well-known piece *Erased de Kooning Drawing* from 1953. Rauschenberg decided to approach the act of 'painting' from the opposite direction: by taking a finished drawing by de Kooning – which the author gave to Rauschenberg knowing his intent – and erasing it until it is hardly visible. He proved that 'erasure could create a new work of art',[68] and actually quite a valuable one, albeit hardly protected by copyright. Paradoxically, unlike the resulting blank piece of paper, the original drawing which was recently reconstructed by SFMOMA[69] is still copyright protected.

John Baldessari cremated all of his works painted between 1953 to 1966 that were still in his possession in the San Diego crematorium in 1970; he then baked them into wafers as part of his *Cremation Project with Corpus Wafers (Version 2)*.[70] Michael Landy went even further and destroyed everything (!) he owned, not only artworks, in a performative act named *Break Down*.[71] The anti-consumerist message of such performance is clear. A similar message, perhaps in a slightly wittier form, can be seen in Banksy's performative destruction of his work of art once it was purchased for $1.4 million by an anonymous buyer in a Sotheby's auction.[72] Another author, Cj Hendry, aptly titled her destruction act *Copyright Infringement*. Originally, she created a hyperrealist painting after Michael Halsband's photograph which took 'hundreds of hours to make'. After receiving a cease and desist letter from Halsband's lawyer she sold the recording of the destruction act at the Superrare website.[73]

All these examples clearly illustrate the inherent tension that we feel between violating the author's decision to destroy part (or all) of their own oeuvre, and the interests of society. As Landy puts it:

> it's not very difficult, for many people, to witness the destruction of household objects such as crockery. But to see the destruction of personal mementoes, letters, photographs, works of art – that is deeply disturbing.[74]

---

[68]   Jennifer Mundy, *Lost Art: Missing Artworks of the Twentieth Century* (Harry N. Abrams, 2014) 178. The process reportedly 'required several weeks of work and many different types of eraser to rub out the crayon, ink, charcoal and pencil of the original drawing'.

[69]   Digitally enhanced infrared scan of Robert Rauschenberg's *Erased de Kooning Drawing*: https://www.sfmoma.org/artwork/98.298/research-materials/document/EDeK_98.298_003/ accessed 23 December 2020.

[70]   Jennifer Mundy, *Lost Art: Missing Artworks of the Twentieth Century* (Harry N. Abrams, 2014) 179–83.

[71]   Alaistar Sooke, 'The man who destroyed all his belongings' *BBC Culture* (London, 14 July 2016) https://www.bbc.com/culture/article/20160713-michael-landy-the-man-who-destroyed-all-his-belongings accessed 23 December 2020.

[72]   Gina Martinez, 'It Appears We Just Got Banksy-ed. Art Piece Self Destructs after Being Sold for Over $1 Million' *Time* (New York City, 6 October 2018) https://time.com/5417659/banksy-art-self-destructs-1-million-sothebys/ accessed 23 December 2020.

[73]   Keith Estiler, 'Cj Hendry Destroys Basquiat and Warhol Artwork in NFT Stunt' *Hypebeast* (Hong Kong, 16 April 2021) https://hypebeast.com/2021/4/cj-hendry-copyright-infringement-nft-auction-superrare-release accessed 16 April 2021.

[74]   Alaistar Sooke, 'The Man Who Destroyed All His Belongings' *BBC Culture* (London, 14 July 2016) https://www.bbc.com/culture/article/20160713-michael-landy-the-man-who-destroyed-all-his-belongings accessed 23 December 2020.

In the most extreme approach, one could prohibit authors from destroying their own (copies of) works. Silly as it may sound if applied to every piece of paper with some scribblings on it, there are instances where a legal intervention might be debated. I doubt that copyright law should adopt such measures, even though the concept was proposed at times.[75]

Some scholars stressed the argument that an author's work belongs to the public. This is not a new idea at all; it has been attributed even to Goethe. What would be new, though, is the idea that the 'right' of the public might be used in certain exceptional instances even against the author. Kohler proposed that the prolongation of copyright term from 30 to 50 years p.m.a. should be bound with heirs' duty to exploit the work.[76] Buum argued that there should be a certain public moral right enforceable against the author in cases where he or she has approved, for monetary gain, the mutilation of their own work. As he explained, it is likely that Schubert would approve the pulp operetta *House of the Three Girls* (*Das Dreimäderlhaus*) by Heinrich Berté (in which Berté uses Schubert's music) 'if he had received 500 gulden for it'.[77] Although this case does not involve the destruction of a copy, it would be just a small step from his idea of enforcing some 'public rights' against the author who wishes to deal with their work in a manner that offends the public.

As painful as the destruction of art might be for the author's fans and art historians, an intuitive ethical judgment would suggest that it is entirely acceptable for authors to destroy what they have created. If authors have free rein to engage in 'lunatic' actions when creating a work, they should have the same right when destroying their expression embodied in their own property. Not even a Lockean argument based in natural law seems to oppose this notion, unless we claim that art is given to people by God rather than created by them ('Nothing was made by God for Man to spoil or destroy' writes Locke in his *Second Treatise of Government*).[78]

Even scholars like Sax agree that the artist should – generally speaking – 'be entitled to decide how the world will remember him or her'.[79] I believe that Sax uses here the term 'artist' deliberately to distinguish between artists and non-fiction authors in whose case, according to Sax, public interest might prevail, e.g., to preserve materials of historical interest possessed by public figures.

Strahilevitz believes that the right of disclosure 'necessarily protects the artist's ability to destroy a work prior to completion',[80] which might be right even if a work can be well

---

[75]   Buum reports about an anecdotical expression of Richard Strauss that there will be no good copyright law unless it will be punished by crime to make a kitsch like 'Dreimäderlhaus' (Solange ein Machwerk wie das 'Dreimäderlhaus' nicht mit Zuchthaus bestraft würde, hätten wir kein gutes Urheberrecht). Alfred Buum, 'Über das Droit moral, seine Ausübung und seine Dauer' (1965) 14 GRUR Auslands- und Internationaler Teil 418, 422. Unfortunately, it is not possible to verify this non-referenced quote of Strauss. For further discussion of Buum's study, see below.

[76]   Josef Kohler, '"Parsifal" und das Autorrecht', *Der Tag* (Berlin, 25 August 1912). Reprinted in: Sebastian Wündisch, *Richard Wagner und das Urheberrecht* (Berliner Wissenschafts-Verlag 2004) 115, 117.

[77]   Alfred Buum, 'Über das Droit moral, seine Ausübung und seine Dauer' (1965) 14 GRUR Auslands- und Internationaler Teil 418, 421. In his article, Buum also pleads for no damages for the infringement of moral rights, in order to avoid situations in which authors would sue for moral rights infringement to 'enrich' themselves.

[78]   John Locke, *Two Treatises of Government* (first published 1690, Cambridge University Press 1970) 308.

[79]   Joseph L. Sax, *Playing Darts with a Rembrandt* (The University of Michigan Press 1999).

[80]   Lior Strahilevitz, 'The Right to Destroy' [2005] Yale Law Journal 781, 834.

disclosed via a radio or live performance without providing any copy to the public. The question is whether the manuscript of such a work may be destroyed once it becomes, in a sense, part of the knowledge of humankind.[81] Even in this case, the answer should be affirmative though. Besides general ethical arguments in favour of the creator, it is possible to discuss also copyright-based arguments.

When VARA introduced the right to prevent destruction, did it implicitly provide the author's moral right to destroy the original copy of the work? Could we derive a moral right to destroy such a copy from the right of disclosure, as Strahilevitz suggests? And what if the author uses his or her right to access a copy in someone else's possession (the moral right of access) just to destroy it? Could he or she claim the moral right to do so, albeit with an obvious duty to compensate for the owner's material loss?

In addition, we have seen that the destruction itself might have enormous expressive value (Strahilevitz) – to suppress such 'speech' might likely amount to a violation of the artist's freedom of expression, specifically the freedom of artistic expression and 'creation'. As Milan Kundera wrote in his seminal essay, 'You're Not in Your Own House Here, My Dear Fellow' (*'Là, vous n'êtes pas chez vous, mon cher'*):

> For aesthetic wishes show not only by what an author has written but also by what he has deleted. Deleting a paragraph calls for even more talent, cultivation, and creative power than writing it does. Therefore, publishing what the author deleted is the same act of rape as censoring what he decided to retain.[82]

Kundera also supports this view with a very interesting argument on the right to privacy. He argues that 'shame is one of the key notions of the Modern Era'.[83] That is why, Kundera believes, Kafka did not want his letters read by anyone else than the addressees and actually burned many manuscripts before his death. We can well presume that the author has a reason why he or she does not want the work to be disclosed, and this reason must be respected – until disclosure, any work, personal or not, is exclusively the private matter of an individual. At the end, authors might wish to calculate with destruction or vanishing at the time the artwork is conceived in case of performance art or temporary works.[84]

The only available means for a legal intervention by society would be declaring a manuscript, painting, object or other tangible manifestation of a masterpiece to be part of cultural heritage or a historical monument, i.e., to employ public law rather than private law. Most countries have adopted cultural heritage laws which limit the owner's right to destroy, change or export such a monument. Such measures are nonetheless rarely used and the authorities might be reluctant to declare a contemporary piece of art to be a historic monument, particu-

---

[81]   This was the case of O'Neill's early play *Bread and Butter* written in 1914. After rejection by the producer, he tore his only copy to pieces. Prior to that, however, he had sent one copy for copyright registration; this copy was discovered and staged in 1998. Wilborn Hampton, 'In O'Neill's First Play, Sparks to Light His Future' *The New York Times* (New York City, 4 September 1998) https://www.nytimes.com/1998/09/04/movies/theater-review-in-o-neills-first-play-sparks-to-light-his-future.html accessed 23 December 2020.

[82]   Milan Kundera, *Testaments Betrayed: An Essay in Nine Parts* (Linda Asher tr, Faber and Faber 1996) 267. Part of this essay is introduced on p. xi of this book.

[83]   Milan Kundera, *Testaments Betrayed: An Essay in Nine Parts* (Linda Asher tr, Faber and Faber 1996) 257–8.

[84]   Noah Charney, *The Museum of Lost Art* (Phaidon Press 2018) 157 et seq.

larly if the author is still alive or even if he or she is the actual owner.[85] More than that, it is very likely that the authorities would not even be aware of the existence of a work which has never been disclosed.

Ultimately, there is only one person who has the legal capability to actually prohibit the destruction of a tangible materialization of a work – the author's spouse! Unless otherwise agreed between spouses, everything acquired during marriage is in most countries part of marital property; this usually includes artwork created by any of the spouses, but excludes the copyright in such works.[86] As we can imagine, a prudent spouse may dislike an author's destructive wishes and prevent the destruction on the basis of legal ownership of the object.

3.2.3   By the heirs

'[D]estruction of an expressive work by its creator is very different from destruction of a creative work by anyone else', admits Strahilevitz.[87] And indeed, most controversies are related to the post-mortem destruction of artwork by the heirs or executors. Whether it is Virgil's parchment, Nabokov's unfinished novel,[88] Kafka's oeuvre, Albee's manuscripts,[89] Pratchett's hard drive,[90] or a fictitious work,[91] the result is the same: the only existing copies of famous works were endangered by the wish of dying authors passed on to their heirs, executors or friends. Every such case places a serious burden on the person so directed. Under the strict individualistic and author-centric approach, defended in Kundera's essay or Strahilevitz's study, such last wishes of the authors should be sacrosanct.

---

[85]   This happens sometimes with works of architecture. For example, the famous *Ještěd Tower*, designed by Karel Hubáček (1924–2011), has been declared a cultural monument and submitted to the tentative list of UNESCO World Heritage sites during the architect's lifetime. Cf. https://whc.unesco.org/en/tentativelists/5152 accessed 23 December 2020.

[86]   I am not aware of any country in continental Europe where copyright would be considered to form part of matrimonial property, but US case law suggests the opposite; cf. *In re Marriage of Worth* (1987) 195 Cal. App. 3d 768, 241 Cal. Rptr. 135.

[87]   Lior Strahilevitz, 'The Right to Destroy' [2005] Yale Law Journal 781, 834.

[88]   The Original of Laura, Nabokov's last novel, remains as a 'rough draft'. Kept unpublished by his late wife Vera, it has been published recently with the consent of his only son by Vintage. Cf. Vladimir Nabokov, *The Original of Laura (Dying is Fun)* (Dmitri Nabokov ed., Vintage Books 2009). It should be noted, though, that unlike his mother, Dmitri Nabokov was not legally bound to testamentary wishes directed at his mother.

[89]   Michael Paulson, 'Edward Albee's Final Wish: Destroy My Unfinished Work' *The New York Times* (New York City, 4 July 2017) https://www.nytimes.com/2017/07/04/theater/edward-albees-final -wish-destroy-my-unfinished-work.html?mcubz=3 accessed 23 December 2020.

[90]   Sophie Haigney, 'Terry Pratchett's Unpublished Work Crushed by Steamroller' *The New York Times* (New York City, 30 August 2017) https://www.nytimes.com/2017/08/30/books/terry-pratchett -steamroller-unpublished-work.html accessed 23 December 2020. The crushed 'copy' of Pratchett's work remains available as an artifact of the late author's oeuvre.

[91]   The topic is exciting enough to also be adapted in literature, like in Morrison's *The Executor*, a 2018 novel with poems dealing with the moral dilemma of a literary executor whose friend, a poet, unexpectedly died: Blake Morrison, *The Executor* (Random House 2018). Cf. also author's essay: Blake Morrison, 'Up in Smoke: Should an Author's Dying Wishes Be Obeyed?' *The Guardian* (London, 10 March 2018) https://www.theguardian.com/books/2018/mar/10/up-in-smoke-should-an-authors-dying -wishes-be-obeyed accessed 23 December 2020. The dilemma of the main character is a bit different – he is directed to publish what the widow finds unpleasant – while he does not hesitate to destroy what he is directed to destroy.

Besides other interesting aspects, such wishes provoke controversial legal and ethical questions. Unlike with the destruction of the author's own property by him or herself, we feel extremely concerned by the fact that someone is destroying literary or other artistic property left by the author. Our ethical intuition seems to consider such literary works left by the author to be part of humankind's heritage in some way, perhaps even before the termination of copyright. From this perspective, it does not belong to the author, but neither is it rubbish destined for a bin; it is a *res omnium communes*[92] rather than a *res nullius*. Kohler likens the author to Prometheus who brings the light to the mankind:

> no great man lives outside of history. The hero is a Prometheus who brought the light to the people and who is at the same time a member of the mankind and his nation and he brings the light which he took from the gods to the mankind and what he achieved is the mankind's eternal present.[93]

Nordemann describes this difference in his essay pleading for eternal moral rights as follows:

> Free as a bird is a work after the lapse of the copyright term … only if it is absolutely with no master, if it does not belong to anyone anymore, similarly to an empty can on a landfill or a big boulder at the bottom of the Atlantic Ocean. However, even if it 'only' belongs to the public, certain very substantial restrictions on its use by anyone result from this.[94]

From his extremely property-oriented position, Strahilevitz offers four arguments in favour of the author's right:[95] (1) the incentive argument;[96] (2) economic rationale;[97] (3) the free speech argument;[98] and (4) the forced speech argument.[99] What I find compelling in Strahilevitz's paper, however, is something different – it is his elucidation of the fact that the testamentary destroyer incurs costs similar (even if lower) to the living destroyer,[100] a theory which can be

---

[92]   The Czechoslovak 1953 Copyright Act contained a provision which allowed the government to pronounce a public domain work to be an 'immaterial public monument' which could only be used under certain conditions (the Czechoslovak government never issued any such decision). Cf. §82 of the Act No. 115/1953 Sb. The Polish government decided to declare the Chopin's work for such a monument by a statutory instrument in 2001 as Sybilla Stanisławska-Kloc reports in Chapter 2 in this *Handbook*.

[93]   '… kein Großer lebt außerhalb der Geschichte. Der Heros ist ein Prometheus, der den Menschen das Licht gebracht, aber er ist zu gleicher Zeit ein Mitglied der Menschheit und seiner Volkes, und das Licht, das er bei den Göttern holt, bringt er der Menschheit, und was er schafft, ist ihr ewiges Angebinde.' Josef Kohler, '"Parsifal" und das Autorrecht' *Der Tag* (Berlin, 25 August 1912). Reprinted in: Sebastian Wündisch, *Richard Wagner und das Urheberrecht* (Berliner Wissenschafts-Verlag 2004) 115.

[94]   'Vogelfrei … ist ein Werk nach Ablauf der Schutzfrist nur, wenn es absolut herrenlos ist, wenn es schlechthin niemandem mehr gehört, wie eine leere Konservenbüchse auf dem Müllhaufen oder ein großer Felsbrocken auf dem Grunde des Atlantischen Ozeans. Schon wenn es aber "nur" der Allgemeinheit gehört, ergeben sich hieraus bestimmte, sehr erhebliche Einschränkungen für seine freie Benutzung durch jedermann.' Wilhelm Nordemann, 'Das Recht der Bearbeitung gemeinfreier Werke' (1964) 66 Gewerblicher Rechtsschutz und Urheberrecht 117, 119.

[95]   Lior Strahilevitz, 'The Right to Destroy' [2005] Yale Law Journal 781, 830 et seq.

[96]   In this hypothesis, there would be fewer literary products because authors would not venture to produce works which they would not be sure to finish during their lifetime.

[97]   By suppressing some works, the authors might create more post-mortem interest in the rest of their works, thus benefiting the heirs.

[98]   Directions to destroy property as 'speech' of the dead author, as explored above.

[99]   Forcing the author to speak 'when he would have preferred to remain silent'.

[100]   Lior Strahilevitz, 'The Right to Destroy' [2005] Yale Law Journal 781, 840.

perfectly applied to the arts: if authors during their lifetime forgo any interest in licensing or exploiting their works, they incur costs (monetary sacrifice) – similarly as living authors who destroy copies of their works.

Kundera supports this claim by focusing on the moral interests of the late author:

> As if such a decision [to destroy all work] were a priori absurd. As if an author could not have reasons enough to take his work along with him on his last voyage … I know, I know, you'll object he is mistaken, that he is giving in to an unhealthy depression, but your exhortations are meaningless. He's in his own house with that work, not you, my dear fellow![101]

This conflict is largely played out on the ethical level, as authors such as Kafka rarely leave behind any legally valid and binding directions to destroy their possessions. Sax argues that 'it is unfair for any creative genius to thrust the burden of decision on friends and family'[102] and that 'the responsibility is the artist's'.[103] I fully agree, believing that this is also in line with the general ethical intuition.

For a lawyer, true tension arises if one is confronted by a legally perfect and unambiguous will written by an unquestionably sane testator. A good example is Edward Albee's will drafted under the New York law,[104] which seems to leave little room for objection, except on public policy grounds, which would, on the other hand, conflict the principle *favor testamenti* (to interpret a last will as valid rather than invalid and to uphold the decision of the testator as much as possible). An unambiguous – even if controversial – law that would expressly consider the destruction of original copies of works to be against the public order might provide a helpful resolution to such a dilemma.[105]

As in other cases, here also the government could step in by proclaiming that certain manuscripts or other preserved works are public heritage, but *only if* the government has the necessary knowledge.

(a)   The death of Virgil

There is no doubt that not having Virgil's *Aeneid* would be an unimaginable loss for humankind. And yet, as the story goes, Virgil left directions to his friend Varius to burn all manuscripts of the *Aeneid*.[106] The problem is, however, that there is no surviving copy of the great poet's testament (or testaments, as he reportedly wrote several – as was common among Romans at the time), only reports of one.[107] Nevertheless, many scholars do not doubt the

---

[101]   Milan Kundera, *Testaments Betrayed: An Essay in Nine Parts* (Linda Asher tr, Faber and Faber 1996) 253.

[102]   Joseph L. Sax, *Playing Darts with a Rembrandt* (The University of Michigan Press 1999) 47.

[103]   Ibid.

[104]   The provisions of Albee's will related to the destruction the literary possessions has been published in: Michael Paulson, 'Edward Albee's Final Wish: Destroy My Unfinished Work' *The New York Times* (New York City, 4 July 2017) https://www.nytimes.com/2017/07/04/theater/edward-albees-final-wish-destroy-my-unfinished-work.html?mcubz=3 accessed 23 December 2020.

[105]   Italian legal romanist and politician Vittorio Scialoja also defends such solution in the modern law. Cf. V. Scialoia, 'Il testamento di Virgilio' (1930) 8 Athenaeum 168, 173.

[106]   The main source of information is *The Life of Virgil*, ascribed to Donatus, although his authorship is contested. Cf. Russel Mortimer Geer, 'Non-Suetonian Passages in the Life of Vergil' (1926) 57 Transactions and Proceedings of the American Philological Association 107.

[107]   Heinrich Naumann, 'Die Vergil-Legende' (1982) 35(1–2) Mnemosyne 148, 150–1.

veracity of the story,[108] although one theory suggests that this was Virgil's wish, but not part of his testament.[109]

According to Virgil's biographer Aelius Donatus, Virgil committed (*'legauit'*) his writings to certain Lucius Varius and Plotius Tucca[110] and directed Varius to burn what had not been finished. We also know that Virgil did not consider his *Aeneid* finished at the time of his death.[111]

According to Donatus, this was a testamentary direction, and as such was considered legally binding.[112] Augustus – according to Roman sources – opposed the idea of burning Virgil's manuscripts presented to him by Varius and ordered them to be published instead. And it was the divine Augustus himself[113] who lamented the ethical dilemma so posed:[114]

> *Ergone supremis potuit vox improba verbis*
> *Tam dirum mandare nefas? Ergo ibit in ignes*
> *Magnaque doctiloqui morietur Musa Maronis?*[115]

This story, as old as our ancient literary heritage, shows that the Romans must have felt similarly about an act of destroying a literary work as we do.[116] The poem attributed to Augustus terms such an act a 'nefas', i.e., something that is against divine laws (*'fas'* or *'ius divinum'*). Since the Romans believed that divine laws are supreme and superordinate to human laws (*'ius'*), Augustus solved the presented ethical and legal dilemma simply by giving preference to *'fas'* instead of *'ius'*.

The Austrian novelist Hermann Broch – who is by no coincidence one of Kundera's favourite writers – addressed the topic in his excellent account of the final hours of the Roman poet in his philosophical novel, interspersed with poems and poetic prose, *The Death of Virgil*.[117] This complicated novel discusses the relationship between an author's autonomy and politics as well as the essential questions of literary creation. It remains open to various interpretations, one of the most straightforward (and perhaps oversimplified) being a nihilist author's revolt

---

[108]   William T. Avery, 'Augustus and the "Aeneid"' (1957) 52(5) The Classical Journal 225.

[109]   This theory was presented in the press by Professor Edward Champlin. 'Virgil's Will: New Account' *New York Times* (New York City, 23 November 1981) https://www.nytimes.com/1981/11/23/nyregion/virgil-s-will-new-account.html accessed 23 December 2020.

[110]   Aelius Donatus, *Vita Vergilii* (David Wilson-Okamura tr, *Virgil.org* 2008) www.virgil.org/vitae/a-donatus.htm accessed 23 December 2020.

[111]   F.J. Miller, 'Evidences of Incompleteness in the Aeneid of Vergil' (1909) 4 The Classical Journal 341.

[112]   This notion of the binding nature of a testator's wishes was strengthened even further during the times of Augustus, who also enforced by his authority the legality of codicils. Inst. 2, 25.

[113]   According to Avery, the attribution of the poem to Augustus is false. Cf. William T. Avery, 'Augustus and the "Aeneid"' (1957) 52(5) The Classical Journal 225, 228.

[114]   Caesar Augustus, 'Ergone supremis potuit vox improba verbis' in Franciscus Buecheler, Alexander Riese (eds), *Anthologia latina sive Poesis latinae supplementum*, vol 1, part II, poem 672 (B. G. Teubner 1870) 132.

[115]   'So then, could that voice, with the loftiest of words, have / done something so wicked, / Commanded something so unspeakably cruel? Shall it go, / therefore, into the flames, / Shall learned Virgil's great poem fall silent?' Caesar Augustus, 'Ergone supremis potuit vox improba verbis' (David Wilson-Okamura tr, *Virgil.org* 2008) http://virgil.org/vitae/a-donatus-oldnumbering.htm accessed 23 December 2020.

[116]   Joseph A. Howley, 'Book-Burning and the Uses of Writing in Ancient Rome: Destructive Practice between Literature and Document' (2017) 107 The Journal of Roman Studies 213, 216–17.

[117]   Hermann Broch, *The Death of Virgil* (Jean Starr Untermeyer tr, Pantheon 1945).

against Augustus[118] and his tyranny – a metaphor supported by a critical reading of the *Aeneid*[119] and by Broch's own fate in US exile during the war. In the novel, Augustus disagrees with Virgil and declares the *Aeneid* to be public property similar to the Roman concept of dominion, stating that not even the gods may order it to be destroyed.[120]

Nita Krevans argues that the well-known Virgilian anecdote became an example and established a repeating pattern characterized by the presence of four key elements:

> First, the modesty of the poet designates the work as somehow imperfect – either incomplete, or generically imperfect. Second, the poet requests on his deathbed that the work be burned. Third, the biographer refutes the poet's judgement and provides evidence of the greatness of the work. Finally, a patron or friend intervenes to rescue the manuscript and publish it posthumously.[121]

(b)   *Debunking the Kafka myth – facts and law*

The Kafka story remains as powerful as Virgil's, but in this particular case we know much more and may submit the known facts to legal scrutiny under Czechoslovak law of succession applicable at the time. Although Kafka did not die in Czechoslovakia,[122] his inheritance was tried under Czechoslovak law. After unification of the Czechs and Slovaks in 1918, Czechoslovakia opted for legal dualism[123] in which two legal systems coexisted – one adopted from Austrian law (especially the Austrian Civil Code, ABGB[124]) that was valid in the Czech lands, and one adopted from the Hungarian law and valid in Slovakia and Carpathian Ruthenia. Because Kafka was a Czechoslovak citizen and a resident of Prague, his inheritance was thus subject to the ABGB.

Importantly, Kafka (just like Wagner) left no testament in any form. What some writers (including the lawyer Brod!) refer to as his 'testament' were in fact two simple unsent letters to Brod which he found in Kafka's drawer. Even without a testament, the testator might have written a codicil under which he would commit certain property as a bequest ('*legatum*') to a person other than his testamentary or statutory heirs.[125] Czechoslovak jurisprudence commonly accepted bequests in the form of a private letter, even if this letter was not delivered to

---

[118]   A fictional autobiography of the Roman poet by David Wishart also underlines the motive of animosity towards Augustus. Cf. David Wishart, *I, Virgil* (Sceptre 1995).

[119]   For a reading of the *Aeneid* as a song of liberty and revolt against Augustus, cf. Francesco Sforza, 'The Problem of Virgil' (1935) 49 The Classical Review 97. Scholars have long debated various readings of the *Aeneid* as either subversive or legitimizing, and Broch knew about both possible interpretations of the epos. For a summary of these opinions, cf. Sabine Grebe, 'Augustus' Divine Authority and Vergil's "Aeneid"' (2005) 50 Vergilius 35.

[120]   Hermann Broch, *The Death of Virgil* (Jean Starr Untermeyer tr, Pantheon 1945) 311.

[121]   Nita Krevans, 'Bookburning and the Poetic Deathbed: The Legacy of Virgil' in Philip Hardie and Helen Moore (eds), *Classical Literary Careers and their Reception* (Cambridge University Press 2010) 197, 201.

[122]   Even though some writers continue to erroneously state that Kafka died in Prague, he actually died in the Hoffmann Sanatorium in Kierling, which is today part of Klosterneuburg, Austria. The mistake also appears in numerous scholarly papers, e.g., Nili Cohen, 'The Betrayed(?) Wills of Kafka and Brod' (2015) 27(1) Law & Literature 1.

[123]   Act No. 11/1918 Sb.

[124]   Allgemeines bürgerliches Gesetzbuch (The General Civil Code), in Czech Všeobecný zákoník občanský. Act No. 946/1811 JGS.

[125]   Under Czechoslovak law valid in the Czech part of the country, a codicil could have been less formal and could have been executed besides a will or instead of a will.

the addressee. As part of such a bequest, the testator could have also given binding directions to the person receiving the bequest. Nevertheless, Kafka expressed in his letters only certain wishes (to destroy a part of his work, not all of it as is sometimes mentioned – specifically private papers and unfinished novels, including those that were in the possession of others[126]) without bequeathing anything to Brod and without naming him an executor. Brod was not legally bound by such wishes, and more than that, by carrying them out he would have committed offence against Kafka's parents as his statutory heirs,[127] as they were the legal owners of the manuscripts.[128]

Kundera understands that Kafka's letters were nothing more than a non-binding wish of a dying friend, and yet, he argues, such wishes should have been respected by Brod. In other words, he considers it immoral not to respect the dying wish of a literary friend. His main argument is that Kafka would have destroyed the manuscripts himself – which he could not, since he died in a sanatorium without access to them: 'As long as he is not dying, a writer has no reason to destroy something he has written.'[129] But even Kundera admits that he would not follow such directions diligently and would spare at least the unfinished novels.[130]

4.   SUMMARY

This chapter tried to explore whether the act of preventing access to a work by the author might be seen as a sort of moral right. Whether in their lifetime or by testamentary directions, authors utilize copyright and other legal instruments, such as inheritance laws, to deprive the public of the fruits of their creative labour either by limiting their audience or, in extreme cases, destroying all copies. This may be considered ethically debatable.

---

[126]   The letters, first published by Brod, are fully quoted i.a. in: Nili Cohen, 'The Betrayed(?) Wills of Kafka and Brod' (2015) 27(1) Law & Literature 1, 3. In his commentary, Brod argues that Kafka must have known that he would not destroy the manuscripts, since Brod had told him as much before. Ibid. For an in-depth analysis of Kafka's inheritance cf. Benjamin Balint, *Kafka's Last Trial: The Case of a Literary Legacy* (W.W. Norton & Company, 2018).

[127]   Professor Jiří Srstka, the director of the Czech literary agency DILIA, explains that their archived documents prove that the only heirs were Kafka's parents; after their death, it was Kafka's sisters, who were murdered in concentration camps, and their children. According to some sources, the family gave a 45% share of Kafka's copyright to Dora Diamant, his partner at the time of his death, which Srstka denies, arguing that there is no evidence supporting that in DILIA's archives. Cf. Interview with Jiří Srstka: Jana Machalická, 'Dílo není salám na krájení' *Lidové noviny* (Praha 22 January 2010). Jiří Srstka subsequently confirmed this in a personal interview with the author of the present chapter in spring 2021. DILIA statement seems credible since DILIA once was in charge of distributing Kafka estate's copyright royalties.

[128]   His parents also inherited the copyright to his writings, which expired in 1974.

[129]   Milan Kundera, *Testaments Betrayed: An Essay in Nine Parts* (Linda Asher tr, Faber and Faber 1996) 256.

[130]   'What would I myself have done in Brod's situation? For me a dead friend's wish is a law; on the other hand, how could I destroy three novels I infinitely admire, novels without which I find the art of our own century unimaginable? No, I would have been incapable of obeying Kafka's instructions dogmatically and to the letter. I would not have destroyed these novels ... But my disobedience ... I would have considered an *exception* I had made on my own responsibility, at my own moral risk, and made as a person *violating a law*, not denying or nullifying it.' Emphasis in the original. Milan Kundera, *Testaments Betrayed: An Essay in Nine Parts* (Linda Asher tr, Faber and Faber 1996) 275.

I believe that the investigated cases show that our ethical intuition as well as the general construction of the laws of property, copyright and inheritance strongly support the idea that while the works are fully in the hands of their authors while they are alive, their destruction by testamentary executors or heirs after the author's death is usually seen as immoral, if not illegal.[131] The reason why the general public is usually distressed by the idea of an heir destroying manuscripts of a renowned writer might well lie in the fact that once a work has been divulged or if a copy of the work survived its author, we tend to consider it as part of humankind's heritage. And in fact, even if a specific moral right protects first disclosure (which, in a sense, includes the *ius abutendi*), such right in most jurisdictions expires with the death of the author and copyright laws are generally designed to encourage publication by providing monetary incentive to the author and the heirs. And not only the heirs, but also to anyone who publishes work that has already become part of the public domain.[132]

The suggested resolution of the ethical conflict seems to be that an author should be free to withhold the work from the public before his or her death, and even to destroy its copies, but heirs should not obey a late author's wishes concerning the destruction of their manuscripts in order to save the *Aeneid* or Kafka's *Trial* for humankind. The inherent conflict posed by a dead author's wishes might be thus resolved by declaring such wishes *ex lege* void and unenforceable, forcing the authors to make such decisions during their lifetime and to execute them by themselves.

---

[131]   On the other hand, the author or his or her successors are entirely free to utilize copyright to limit the availability of a work, even by not using or licensing the work at all. This is in no way illegitimate and does not violate public policy; in other words, it is not a copyright loophole, but a part of the system which allows the copyright holder not to license a work.

[132]   Cf. the protection for previously unpublished works in the Copyright Term Directive. Directive 2006/116/EC of the European Parliament and of the Council of 12 December 2006 on the term of protection of copyright and certain related rights (codified version) [2006] OJ L372, Art. 4.

In conclusion: What's new with moral rights?

Ysolde Gendreau

I was working on the proof of one of my poems all the morning and took out a comma. In the afternoon
I put it back again. – Oscar Wilde

The figure of the overly fussy artist may well be at the root of the negative perceptions that moral rights persistently induce among their detractors.[1] What publisher, what producer wants to deal with the uncertainty that comes with an author who may step in at any time to ask for changes to his work or to prevent the slightest modification he can dream of? Against this possibility, the timeless motto of *pacta sunt servanda* stands as the warranty that agreements between authors and any person who puts in motion the exploitation of works – and beyond – will not be altered by considerations that fall outside the terms of the contracts. In a similar vein, members of the public who interact with works in various ways can find it difficult to be told after the fact that their actions infringe rights that they consider not to fall in their vague understanding of what constitutes copyright. It is easy to intuit that publishing a novel without authorization may break the law; it is less so when one uses music, and pays the royalties for it in the various venues where events take place, as a political campaign song.

Yet, depending on how they are perceived, moral rights have been around for more than a century. If one looks at their international presence, moral rights have been in the Berne Convention since the Rome Conference in 1928 and have thus not reached the century mark.[2] Some national legislations already contained moral rights provisions at that time, including most notably the Italian law that served as a catalyst for the Italian delegation at the Conference to press for their inclusion in the Convention.[3] Yet France, which is so often cited as *the* reference for moral rights legislation, only adopted provisions in 1957 when it went through the exercise of its first consolidation of the law since its founding Revolutionary decrees.[4] However, if one does not think in terms of explicit labels of moral rights but is willing to examine substance over form, it has been argued that the famous *Millar v. Taylor*[5] decision of the House of Lords embodies moral rights values.[6] Such an understanding would mean that copyright countries have not always been as inherently allergic to their objectives as they are said to be.

---

[1] See G. Koumantos, "Is There Any Cause to Be Afraid of Moral Rights?" (1999) 180 RIDA 86. For a typical negative assessment of moral rights, see J.A. Baumgarten, "On the Case Against Moral Rights" in P. Anderson and D. Saunders (eds), *Moral Rights Protection in a Copyright System* (Brisbane, Institute for Cultural Policy Studies, Griffith University 1992) 87.

[2] On the history of moral rights leading up to and including the Rome Revision Conference, see E. Adeney, *The Moral Rights of Authors and Performers – An International and Comparative Analysis* (Oxford, Oxford University Press 2006) 97–127.

[3] See G. Mazziotti, "Moral Rights in Italy: 'ieri, oggi e domani'" (2019) 14 JIPL&P 285, 286–7.

[4] See H. Desbois, "The Moral Right" (1958) 19 RIDA 121.

[5] (1769) 4 Burr. 2303, 98 ER 201.

[6] See G. Davies and K. Garnett, *Moral Rights* (2nd edn, London, Sweet & Maxwell 2016) 14–15. See also, Adeney, *supra*, note 2, 370, para 13.13.

The current technological environment provides a good opportunity to examine moral rights afresh to see if it sheds new light on their relevance. Moral rights have been extensively studied in an essentially analogue world, a simpler environment where the questionings – and the conclusions they beget – have more or less remained the same since the beginning. During that period, the ostensible signs of "progress" in their acceptability have been their inclusion in the Berne Convention, the succession of legislative interventions in copyright countries in the late twentieth century,[7] and their extension to performers in two international treaties around the turn of the twenty-first century.[8] This affirmative movement has been countervailed by their exclusion from the Agreement on Trade-related Aspects of Intellectual Property Rights (TRIPs Agreement) in 1994[9] – which is mirrored in the North American Free Trade Agreement (NAFTA)[10] – and the reluctance of the European Union to include them in its copyright harmonization endeavours.[11] The jury is thus still out on the full integration of moral rights in copyright law.

Naturally, moral rights are not the only component of copyright law that gives rise to debate. There is hardly unanimity on issues such as exceptions,[12] the updating of broadcasters' rights,[13] or the extent to which collective management can be involved in the exercise of copyright prerogatives.[14] The lack of unanimity over moral rights has resulted in a diversity of treatment that is often ignored by commentators (Section 1). Out of this diversity, however, important

---

[7]   Copyright, Designs and Patents Act 1988, ch. 48; Act to amend the Copyright Act and to amend other Acts in consequence thereof, RSC 1985, ch. 10 (4th Sup.) (Canada); Visual Artists Rights Act of 1990, Pub. L. No 101-650, Title VI. 104, Stat. 5089; Copyright (Amendment) Act 1994, Act No. 38 of 1994 (India); Copyright Act 1994 (NZ), Pub. Act 1994 No. 143 (NZ); Copyright Amendment (Moral Rights) Act 2000 (Cth), No. 159, 2000 (AU). On the philosophical impact of these adoptions, see C.P. Rigamonti, "The Conceptual Transformation of Moral Rights" (2007) 55 Am. J. Comp. L. 67; E. Adeney, "Of Moral Rights and Legal Transplants – Connecting Laws, Connecting Cultures" in G.W. Austin, A.F. Christie, A.T. Kenyon, and M. Richardson (eds), *Across Intellectual Property – Essays in Honour of Sam Ricketson* (Cambridge, Cambridge University Press 2020) 64.

[8]   WIPO Performances and Phonograms Treaty (WPPT) (1996), Art. 5; Beijing Treaty on Audiovisual Performances (2012), Art. 5.

[9]   "Members shall not have rights or obligations under this Agreement in respect of the rights conferred under Article 6bis of that Convention or of the rights derived therefrom": TRIPS Agreement, Art. 9(1).

[10]   North American Free Trade Agreement, Annex 1705.7.

[11]   Commission Staff Working Paper on the review of the EC legal framework in the field of copyright and related rights (19 July 2004), SEC 2004 (995) at p. 16. This position has not prevented a group of scholars, known as the Wittem Group, from including provisions on moral rights in Chapter 3 of the proposed European Copyright Code they designed in 2010: https://www.ivir.nl/copyrightcode/ See also G. Lea, "Moral Rights: Moving from Rhetoric to Reality in Pursuit of European Harmonisation" in E. Barendt and A. Firth (eds), *The Yearbook of Copyright and Media Law 2001/2* (Oxford, Oxford University Press 2002) 61.

[12]   The proliferation of literature on this issue is particularly abundant. As a start, see M. Senftleben, *Copyright, Limitations and the Three-step Test in International and EC Copyright Law* (Alphen aan den Rijn, Kluwer Law International 2004).

[13]   Since 2011, WIPO has been working on an update of the protection of broadcasters' rights since the 1961 Rome Convention. See Standing Committee on Copyright and Related Rights, Revised Draft Text for the WIPO Broadcasting Organizations Treaty, 42nd session, Geneva, 9–13 May 2022, SCCR/42/3, https://www.wipo.int/edocs/mdocs/copyright/en/sccr_42/sccr_42_3.pdf.

[14]   See M. Ficsor, "Collective Rights Management from the Viewpoint of International Treaties, with Special Attention to the EU '*Acquis*'" in D. Gervais (ed.), *Collective Management of Copyright and Related Rights* (3rd edn, Alphen aan den Rijn, Kluwer Law International 2016) 31.

lessons on the *raison d'être* of moral rights can be gleaned (Section 2), lessons that can help to infuse copyright law with a renewed relevance for our contemporary world.

1.   THE DIVERSITY OF MORAL RIGHTS

Anyone who starts to be interested in moral rights soon learns about the birth of this concept in the nineteenth century through French and German legal and philosophical discourses on the special nature of the author's creative process that makes the work an extension and embodiment of his personality.[15] Moral rights are thus firmly associated with the author's right conception of copyright, especially since the very word by which "copyright" is translated in European countries – all the local versions of "author's rights" – inherently favours such development. It does not take long thereafter before the differences between the two countries, the debate between French dualism and German monism, are acknowledged.[16] The world of moral rights can thus be divided in two groups: the countries that follow the French approach and those that are inspired by the German philosophy.

Probably for linguistic reasons, the French model is the better known of the two. This means that the characteristics that come with French moral rights are those that are most commonly associated with moral rights in general: "perpetual, inalienable, and imprescriptible".[17] Since the Berne Convention, which is regarded as a compromise between author's rights countries and copyright countries, mandates the protection of two prerogatives in its Article 6*bis*,[18] the combination of the two texts easily leads to the inference that the minimum regime of national moral rights legislations must correspond to these two prerogatives, the right of attribution and the right of integrity, that take on the characteristics of what is prescribed by French law. A broader examination of various national legislations that indeed protect moral rights reveals, however, that the global picture is quite different. On the contrary, there is no uniformity about moral rights around the world. The definition of moral rights (Section 1.1) is as diverse as the regimes (Section 1.2) that accompany them.

1.1   Diversity in the Definition of Moral Rights

It is trite law to say that the moral rights provision in the Berne Convention, Article 6*bis*, sets out the minimal standards that its Member States must provide in their national legislations. This principle has meant, however, that the international debate on moral rights has essentially focused on the implementation of these two rights to the point that, on a superficial level, it may almost seem that the right of attribution and the right of integrity indeed spell moral rights. When it provides for these two rights, a national legislature may then consider that it has fulfilled its obligations and can move on to other matters. Been there, done that.

---

[15]   See the very extensive description of this history in the first volume of S. Strömholm, *Le droit moral de l'auteur en droit allemand, français et scandinave – Étude de droit comparé* (Stockholm, P.A. Norstedt & Söners Förlag 1966).

[16]   See A. Lucas-Schloetter, *Droit moral et droits de la personnalité – Étude de droit comparé français et allemand* (Aix-en-Provence, Presses universitaires d'Aix-Marseille 2002).

[17]   Code of Intellectual Property, s. L. 121-1, para. 3.

[18]   One must not forget that moral rights considerations are also present in Articles 10(3) and 10*bis*(1) and that a specific reference is made to them in Article 11*bis*(2).

Of course, such an attitude is more often found in countries of the copyright tradition that have not been as enthusiastic about moral rights as their author's rights counterparts. Yet even when they are already considered in compliance with their international obligations, such copyright countries can be brought to revisit their moral rights system. Such a revision has taken place, for instance, in Canada, when its initial provision, a close paraphrase of the Berne text dating from 1931, was updated in 1988.[19] The adoption of the Visual Arts Rights Act of 1990,[20] in the United States, can be regarded as an exercise of legislative second thought, surprisingly soon after the earlier claims that US law needed no modification on account of moral rights to allow the country to adhere to the Berne Convention in 1989.[21] That important step in the recognition of moral rights in the United States nevertheless did remain, just as in Canada, within the confines of the right of attribution and the right of integrity.

Yet even an incomplete look at moral rights legislations around the world already reveals that moral rights exist in very different forms depending on the country where they are experienced.[22] Already, one can take note that in India they are not called "moral rights", but rather "special rights".[23] The very name of "moral rights", coined in 1872 by Morillot,[24] can indeed create a certain malaise among those who look at them suspiciously because of the high-ground posture they may associate with a word that belongs to the nomenclature of morality.[25] This invitation to look beyond the name that is given to them leads to the acknowledgement that moral rights interests can be protected through means other than legal systems that explicitly refer to them as such. That is why the different legal mechanisms that have been identified in the United States as measures that are partly equivalent to moral rights have been part of the discourse on moral rights in that country.[26] The same attitude was displayed in the United Kingdom:[27] until the Whitford Committee in 1972 recommended the adoption of the provisions that became part of the Copyright, Designs and Patents Act 1988,[28] the United Kingdom also considered that it met the requirements of the Berne Convention in this respect. Even more foreign to the moral rights doctrine is the Islamist legal tradition that can neverthe-

---

[19]   Copyright Act Amendment, 1931, 21–22 Geo. V, ch. 8; Act to amend the Copyright Act and to amend other Acts in consequence thereof, *supra* note 7.

[20]   *Supra* note 7.

[21]   "Final Report of the Ad Hoc Working Group on U.S. Adherence to the Berne Convention" (1986) 10 Colum. J.L. & Arts 513, 547.

[22]   See Axhamn, Chapter 16 in this *Handbook*.

[23]   This term has been in use since the first post-colonial Copyright Act in 1957. See G.R. Raghavender, "The Origin and Development of a Moral Rights Regime in India" (2019) 14 J.I.P.L.&P. 305, 306.

[24]   A. Morillot, "De la personnalité du droit de copie qui appartient à un auteur vivant" (1872) R. crit. lég'n et jur. 29.

[25]   See, for instance, E. Schéré, "Where is the Morality? Moral Rights in International Intellectual Property and Trade Law" (2018) 41 Fordham Int'l L.J. 773.

[26]   See Register of Copyrights, *Authors, Attribution, and Integrity: Examining Moral Rights in the United States* (Washington, US Copyright Office, April 2019) esp. 24–5.

[27]   See G. Dworkin, "The Moral Right of the Author – Moral Rights and the Common Law Countries" in ALAI (ed.), *The Moral Rights of the Author* (Paris, ALAI, 1994) 81, 89. Its quiver of measures even included, since 1862, a provision that condemns the unauthorized alterations of artistic works: Fine Arts Copyright Act, 25&26 Vict., ch. 68, s. 7. That provision was only repealed in 1956 to become s. 43 of Copyright Act, 4&5 Eliz. 2, ch. 74.

[28]   Copyright, Designs and Patents Act 1988, s. 77 ff.

less pretend that it also promotes authors' moral rights.[29] In all such circumstances, the essence of the process is to accept that reality matters more than labels.

When the situation is one where the law openly deals with moral rights, there is still the matter of how its constituents are enunciated. It must first be decided, just as in the world of exceptions to copyright law, whether the moral rights that are recognized will form a closed list of rights or will also serve as starting points for the recognition of other situations that will come within their ambit. Most countries seem to prefer the exhaustive approach, but some are willing to allow for an open system that goes beyond the interpretation of the identified rights.[30] Members of the Andean Pact are expressly allowed to add rights to the right of attribution, the right of integrity, and the right of divulgation or disclosure.[31] Closely related to this – rather rare – dilemma is the choice between a minimalist approach – to implement only what is required by the Berne Convention – and a more generous attitude, that is, to extend the scope of moral rights to other situations that have been identified over the years. Consequently, national laws may refer to other rights, such as the right of access,[32] or to specific situations within existing rights, such as the right in relation to works that may be destroyed.[33] The translation of the rights as they are currently known in the Western world into languages that do not have the same roots may also involve the use of terms that are slightly different, a process which may lead to interpretation issues. To wit, it can be argued that the Chinese right of alteration[34] can be viewed as equivalent to the right of retraction or withdrawal, as it is called in French law.[35]

Even if they are called the same, the contents of the moral rights may differ. Not only are they subject to the fluctuations of judicial interpretations both within and among countries, but legislators may decide to be more or less precise in their statements. Countries of the copyright tradition are well known for the various limitations that they bring to the rights themselves in their statutes.[36] Another technique is to target some categories of works. Particular rules can exist for architectural works and works made by civil servants, as it is allowed in the Andean Pact;[37] in Brazil, an author may prevent the performance of a work if he considers that it has not been sufficiently rehearsed.[38] To help navigate among the many possibilities of interpretation, pointers may come too from judicial guidelines that are more officially formalized by the courts than the usual system of court precedents.[39] All of these elements combine to produce definitions of moral rights that conjure up understandings which vary from country to country.

---

[29]   See Elmahjub, Chapter 3 in this *Handbook*.

[30]   Such seems to be the case, for example, in Brazil and in Japan. See Chinellato, Chapter 25 in this *Handbook*; Ueno, Chapter 22 in this *Handbook*.

[31]   Andean Community, Decision 351, Common Regime of Copyright and Neighboring Rights, 1993, Art. 12.

[32]   For example, Greece: Law 2121/1993, Copyright, Related Rights and Cultural Matters, s. 4(1)(d); Germany: Copyright and Related Rights Act of 9 September 1965, s. 25.

[33]   In the United States: Copyright Act of 1976, § 106A(3)(B).

[34]   See Yong Wan, Chapter 23 in this *Handbook*.

[35]   Code of Intellectual Property, s. L. 121-4.

[36]   In Canada, for instance, the right of attribution exists "where reasonable in the circumstances" and the right of integrity is infringed only if one can prove "prejudice [to the] author's or performer's honour or reputation". Copyright Act, ss. 14.1(1) and 28.2(1).

[37]   See Pabón Cadavid, Chapter 24 in this *Handbook*.

[38]   Law No. 9610/98 of 19 February 1998, s. 70.

[39]   Beijing High People's Court, *Guidelines for the Trial of Copyright Infringement Cases*, chapter IV, https://www.cpahkltd.com/en/info.aspx?n=20180423092240190497.

One must also be aware that names and status may change over the years. The easiest terminology example is that of the right of paternity, which, in our contemporary world, is evolving towards the more neutral right of attribution for want of outright calling it a right of maternity. The latter is used by commentators who study moral rights through the lens of feminist theories,[40] of course, but not exclusively.[41] The parenthood paradigm has always played an important role in the justification of moral rights and easily explains the willingness to refer to the destruction of works as infanticides.[42] The politico-legal status of moral rights is another prism through which they can be analysed and which can evolve over time. When they were born, the legal environment of moral rights did not include the equivalent of the 1948 Universal Declaration of Human Rights, whose Article 27(2) states that "Everyone has the right to the protection of the *moral* and material interests resulting from any scientific, literary or artistic production of which he is the author".[43] In a similar vein, the decision by the Constitutional Court of Colombia that declared moral rights as fundamental rights that allow their owners to avail themselves of a special procedure to vindicate them[44] confers on them a status that is reminiscent of the declaration by the French Court of Cassation that they are matters of *ordre public* and thus of immediate application for a foreign author.[45]

The statements that define moral rights are not the only intimations that moral rights can mean different things to different people: the mere evocation of moral rights also conveys various consequences that flow from their existence. Here again, the regimes that come with the rights offer a terrain of divergences.

1.2   Diversity in the Regimes of Moral Rights

Moral rights protect the special bond between an author and his work or between a performer and his performance. Once the circumstances in which this bond can be validated are identified, it becomes necessary to find out what this recognition means for the authors and performers. Some general characteristics apply to moral rights, irrespective of the definitions of the rights themselves, and here again their mere mention often provoke reactions that can be checked against the reality of various national experiences.

One of the main debates over moral rights pertains to their duration. Their perpetual nature is enshrined in some legislations, notably in France,[46] of course, but also in Poland[47] and in the Andean Pact,[48] for example. In the latter instance, this perpetuity is linked to the protection of cultural heritage and the existence of a *domaine public payant*.[49] Naturally, the idea that moral

---

[40]   See Craig and Dhonchak, Chapter 4 in this *Handbook*.
[41]   See Chinellato, Chapter 25 in this *Handbook*.
[42]   See Leška, Chapter 29 in this *Handbook*.
[43]   Emphasis added.
[44]   See Pabón Cadavid, Chapter 24 in this *Handbook*.
[45]   Cass. Civ. 1st, 28 May 1991, (1991) 149 RIDA 197 (Huston case). See Y. Gendreau, "The Continuing Saga of Colourization" (1993) 7 IPJ 340.
[46]   Code of Intellectual Property, s. L. 121-1 (3).
[47]   Act of 4 February 1994 on Copyright and Neighbouring Rights, Journal of Laws 1994, No. 24, text 83, s. 16.
[48]   Andean Community, Decision 351, Common Regime of Copyright and Neighboring Rights, 1993, s. 11.
[49]   Supreme Decree No. 23907, Regulation of the Copyright Act, 7 December 1994, s. 7.

rights might still be asserted today over the works of authors who have long been dead can be considered an example of their unrealistic nature.[50] The Berne Convention refers to two possibilities as minimum duration rules: a preference for a duration that is coterminous with the economic rights and the recognition that the rights may, in some circumstances, end with the author's death.[51] It is quite easy to identify countries where the moral rights end at the same time as the economic rights,[52] but some countries may even distinguish, among the rights, which ones end at that time and which ones last longer.[53] The longer the term of copyright protection, the more difficult it becomes, then, to determine clearly who exercises the moral rights and in whose interest this exercise is done.[54] As the debate on orphan works shows, this preoccupation can also plague economic rights even when they are not eternal.

The stereotypical image of the ownership of moral rights is that only authors – physical persons – can enjoy and exercise moral rights. The very personal relationship between an author and his works that moral rights embody warrants it. However, various rules that may apply during the life of these rights create twists that show that it is not always observed as strictly as one may imagine.

The first example of a situation where the right is exercised by someone other than the author – and even during his lifetime – is when the work is published anonymously or under a pseudonym.[55] The rights remain the author's, of course, but there is already here an opportunity for a legal entity to play a role in its management. A similar nod to corporate involvement exists when the moral rights in works can be exercised by artists' associations and collective management associations[56] or, when the work is in the public domain but the moral rights remain protected, by the state.[57]

Of course, the best-known situation where the existence of moral rights as the quintessential symbol of human authorship can come in conflict with the copyright ownership rules is that of the work made for hire of US law, where an employer, usually a legal entity, is declared to be the author of the work made by its employees.[58] That rule has been the primary source of antagonism between moral rights and US copyright law. Its recognition as an obstacle to the full presence of moral rights in the US Copyright Act is reinforced by the exclusion of works made for hire in the application of the moral rights that have been introduced in the *Act* by the Visual Artists Rights Act of 1990.[59] Yet, some "authors' rights" countries that have adopted

---

[50]   On the difficulty of exercising moral rights beyond the term of protection of economic rights in France, see A. Lucas, H-J Lucas, A. Lucas-Schloetter, and C. Bernault, *Traité de la propriété littéraire et artistique* (5th edn, Paris, LexixNexis 2017) 597–9.

[51]   Berne Convention, Art. 6*bis* (2).

[52]   Copyright Act, ss. 14.2 (authors) and 17.2 (performers).

[53]   Copyright Law of the People's Republic of China, ss. 20–1.

[54]   In an unusual move, the Canadian Parliament provided for the devolution of moral rights whereas it is silent as to the devolution of the economic rights. It even specified that the rule was to apply to the second generation of successors in titles: Copyright Act, s. 14.2(2) and (3).

[55]   In Greece: Law 2121/1993, Copyright, Related Rights and Cultural Matters, s. 11.

[56]   On this issue, see M.M. Walter, "Dualistic Aspects in Monistic Systems of Moral Rights" (2019) 14 J.I.P.L.&P. 318. See also Stanisława-Kloc, Chapter 2 in this *Handbook*, footnote 145.

[57]   In Brazil: Law No. 9610/98 of 19 February 1998, s. 24(VII)(2); in Greece: Law 2121/1993, Copyright, Related Rights and Cultural Matters, s. 29(2).

[58]   Copyright Act of 1976, § 201(b).

[59]   Copyright Act of 1976, § 106A(3)(B).

the work for hire concept nevertheless allow such deemed authors to enjoy moral rights,[60] while others display mixed feelings about such an outcome.[61]

Mixed feelings also seem to be at play with respect to collective works in France. Because the law declares that the person under whose name the (collective) work is "edited, published, and divulged" enjoys all the rights that an author – here a physical person – would have, this right owner, who is deliberately not called an "author", necessarily enjoys the moral rights associated with the work as a whole.[62] It is no surprise that doctrine considers that courts would assess infringements to moral rights over such works with less concern for their rights owners than if the rights of flesh-and-blood authors were at stake.[63] The uneasiness about collective works in French law can be regarded as a forerunner of the more contemporary forms of collaborative creation that have emerged. The presence of computer programs, which are so often developed by teams whose makeup can vary over the years, within the copyright sphere since the 1980s is perhaps the next major – and this time global – development towards a world where corporate entities can be identified as persons that can exercise moral rights. It has become increasingly easier – indeed more necessary in some circumstances – to work in teams to create works and this reality cannot be avoided.[64] Just as trademark law has evolved to provide protection to individuals, legal persons, and broader communities, the same recognition factor that moral rights guarantee can eventually be extended beyond the initial category of beneficiaries, i.e., individual authors, so long as the focus remains on the creation link between the works and those who have a legitimate interest in its validation.

The inalienability that is traditionally associated with moral rights is another feature that can be debunked upon closer inspection. Because it interferes with the full enjoyment of the economic rights over the work and with the freedom to dispose of a copy of the work as one wishes, it is a further fundamental characteristic that provokes negative reactions towards moral rights. Yet, however beneficial to authors it can be, it is far from being a universal truth. Even the Berne Convention does not mandate such rule. It does not take much investigation to observe that it is a principle that is more honoured in the breach than the observance.[65]

Observance of the inalienability of moral rights is probably at the root of the development of waivers to moral rights in copyright countries. It allows statements that declare moral rights cannot be assigned, but can nevertheless be waived.[66] If one broadens the examination to the identification of some form of contractual dealings over moral rights, however, then instances of transactions bearing upon the exercise of moral rights can even be found in some authors'

---

[60]   Ueno, Chapter 22 in this *Handbook*. A similar situation exists in China: Copyright Law of the People's Republic of China, s. 11(3).

[61]   Mireille van Eechoud, "Netherlands § 4 [1][b][ii]", in L. Bently and B. Ong (eds), *International Copyright Law and Practice* (New York, Lexis Nexis 2021): "Whether this provision vests moral rights is controversial."

[62]   Code of Intellectual Property, s. L. 113-2, para. 2.

[63]   P. Kamina, "France § 4 [1][b][i][B]", in L. Bently and B. Ong (eds), *International Copyright Law and Practice* (New York, Lexis Nexis 2021).

[64]   See Synodinou, Chapter 13 in this *Handbook*; Kamina, Chapter 12 in this *Handbook*.

[65]   See A. Kelli, T. Hoffmann, H. Pisuke, I. Kull, L. Jents, and C. Ginter, "The Exercise of Moral Rights by Non-Authors" (2014) 6 Juridiska zinatne 108; Leška, Chapter 29 in this *Handbook*; Hick, Chapter 28 in this *Handbook*.

[66]   Such is the case in Canada, for example: Copyright Act, s. 14.1(2).

rights countries.[67] Works by more than one author offer prime opportunities for such negotiations.[68] The availability of contractual modifications in the context of moral rights need not mean that the author is doomed to accept anything that the other party may want to foist upon him since it is possible for the legislator to impose some conditions on these arrangements.[69] The agreements that are negotiated in the US film industry provide worthy examples of what may be obtained when bargaining is allowed.[70] They represent, however, a very iconic form of moral rights substitutes that may not be altogether transferred in the world of statutory moral rights. One must acknowledge that an official sanction of the "contractualization" of moral rights creates greater pressure on authors than its tolerance in a world where it is not supposed to happen. At the same time, it would be naïve to believe that a legislative ban on this "contractualization" of moral rights necessarily entails that it is fully observed; but one can hope that at least it helps to minimize the occurrence of the most egregious cases.

The reality of moral rights today is thus different from what their initial proponents had in mind, though the initial philosophy of protection of personal interests endures strongly and continues to infuse them with meaning. Moral rights still represent the human dimension of copyright protection. That emphasis on the author's personality can coexist with the economic purpose of the right, as in dualist and – even more so – copyright countries or can colour more strongly the entire protection scheme, as in monist countries.[71] Moral rights today are no longer limited to authors: they are now part of performers' protection schemes. Both the World Intellectual Property Organization (WIPO) Performances and Phonograms Treaty (WPPT) of 1996 and the Beijing Treaty on Audiovisual Performances of 2012 boast provisions on the protection of moral rights.[72] If the texts that ensure the recognition of creators and inventors in industrial property legislations cannot be categorized as moral rights in the same manner as those that protect authors and performers,[73] one can nevertheless acknowledge that intellectual property as a whole does not shy away from the opportunities to call attention to the human elements in its structure. Could it be because their significance matters for the justification of intellectual property law?

2.   THE RELEVANCE OF MORAL RIGHTS

Even if they are not the main components of authors' rights/copyright legislations, moral rights remain an important element of their structure. The variety of national regimes indicates, however, that their status as a Berne Convention right has not led to a common understanding of the notion to the same extent as the right of reproduction and the right of public performance whose evolutions feed the debates on the development of the law. Their relationship with economic issues is at the heart of this differential treatment (Section 2.1), and the explosion of

---

[67]   For examples in Greece, Stamatoudi, Chapter 18 in this *Handbook*; in Poland: Stanisławska-Kloc, Chapter 2 in this *Handbook*.
[68]   See Synodinou, Chapter 13 in this *Handbook*.
[69]   See Yong Wan, Chapter 23 in this *Handbook*, text accompanying footnotes 64–5.
[70]   See Dougherty, Chapter 10 in this *Handbook*.
[71]   See de la Durantaye, Chapter 9 in this *Handbook*.
[72]   WPPT, Art. 5; Beijing Treaty on Audiovisual performances, Art. 5.
[73]   See Lee, Chapter 6 in this *Handbook*; Wilkinson, Chapter 8 in this *Handbook*; Spedicato, Chapter 7 in this *Handbook*.

digital creation and diffusion has paradoxically intensified the discourse on the role of human creativity in copyright law (Section 2.2).

2.1   The Economic Dimension of Moral Rights

That moral rights can wreak havoc with economic rights is a truth universally acknowledged. This disturbance is at the heart of the negative perceptions that one can have of moral rights. Exceptions and limitations to copyright also chip at the scope of economic rights; yet, while they can encounter resistance, they are not dismissed or fought in the same manner because they are seen as necessary components of copyright law. New exceptions are identified over the years and, while their individual necessity may be challenged, the general justification of exceptions and the need to adapt them to technological and social developments are taken for granted.

The difference between the two situations is easy to identify: exceptions are avowedly meant to impact on the economic value of the rights that they encroach, whereas the purpose of moral rights is not per se to attack the exploitation potential of protected works. Would moral rights thus be more devious?! That would be an unwarranted attribution of dishonesty to a body of rights that is merely meant to provide additional support to authors' interests. Instead of bemoaning an interference with economic rights in the name of the protection of non-economic considerations, perhaps it would be time to see that these so-called non-economic considerations indeed have an economic dimension.[74]

The remedies that are associated with moral rights are not limited to injunctions: authors can obtain monetary relief for their infringement. As a starting point for the recognition of their pecuniary character, this may not be the strongest argument. However, contrary to some other traditionally non-economic rights such as the right against defamation, their inextricable twinning with the economic rights in works helps to secure them a stronger foothold in the world of personality rights. Just like the US publicity rights that have emerged from privacy concerns to gain a notional autonomy thanks in part to their essentially commercial dimension, it may become more acceptable over the coming years to acknowledge the economic nature of moral rights. This process may be slower in the case of moral rights because of their terminology: the word "moral" can make it more difficult to acknowledge this aspect of their nature outside the usual discussions on moral damages.[75]

Outside of the traditional debate on the monist/dualist orientations within moral rights[76] where the monist approach is based on a greater integration of the economic and moral rights, some authors have identified indicia that support the recognition of the economic dimension of

---

[74]   Even Morillot, the father of the term "moral rights", recognized an economic dimension within them: "*Et cependant ces droits, tout en restant moraux, personnels, et non susceptibles d'une estimation pécuniaire directe, peuvent avoir des conséquences pécuniaires fort importantes.*" [And yet these rights, while remaining moral, personal, and incapable of direct monetary evaluation, can have very important monetary consequences.] Morillot, *supra* note 24, 31.

[75]   For an excellent discussion on moral damages in intellectual property law, see T.F. Cotter, "Damages for Noneconomic Harm in Intellectual Property Law" (2021) 72 Hastings L.J. 1055, where the author posits a special treatment for, among others, moral rights.

[76]   See de la Durantaye, Chapter 9 in this *Handbook*.

moral rights.[77] Textual elements in the international conventions form one group of evidence, while more general considerations provide contextual underpinning.

It has been pointed out that the making available right of the WIPO Copyright Treaties of 1996 uses the same expression, i.e., "making available", as in the description of the right of disclosure, the moral right component that allows an author to determine when and how a work is disclosed.[78] The similarity between moral rights and economic rights on that basis can be heightened when one considers two other elements of the international copyright texts: the right of publication (which can be said to have inspired the right of making available, but which can claim an older existence) and the texts on the term of protection. Article 3(3) of the Berne Convention refers to the "availability" of the copies as a sign of publication; the French version speaks of "*la mise à la disposition*" of the copies. As for Article 7, it identifies the starting point of most terms of protection that are not based on the author's life by referring to the time when "the work has been made available to the public".[79] Such similarities could be dismissed as anecdotal were it not for some more fundamental theoretical analysis.

Another indication of a convergence of moral rights and economic rights lies in the types of rights that are discussed when moral rights are at stake. An example is the issue of the *droit de suite* or resale royalty right that was included in the Berne Convention by the Brussels Act of 1948.[80] The status of this right within copyright law is not as solid as other rights, given that it is only subject to reciprocity rather than to national treatment. The Standing Committee on Copyright and Related Rights of WIPO has been discussing its future since 2015.[81] The resale royalty right is designed to bring income to authors when their artistic works are resold beyond their initial sale by the artist. As the value of the work increases over time, the artist can thus obtain a share of this increase. It is clearly a mechanism that is designed to be a source of income for artists, thus a pecuniary right. Yet, discussions of this right in the United States, for example, have often been held together with debates on moral rights. The Visual Artists Rights Act of 1990, which introduced moral rights for authors of some artistic works, mandated a study on the resale royalty right[82] and a 2014 government hearing also dealt with the two issues at the same time.[83]

---

[77]   The question is bluntly put in M. Rushton, "The Moral Rights of Artists: Droit Moral ou Droit Pécuniaire?" (1998) 22 J. of Cultural Economics 15.

[78]   See M.T. Sundara Rajan, "Moral Rights of Economic Rights?" in N. Wilkof and S. Basheer (eds), *Overlapping Intellectual Property Rights* (Oxford, Oxford University Press 2012) 209.

[79]   Berne Convention, Art. 7(2) and (3).

[80]   Berne Convention, Art. 14*ter*.

[81]   "Proposal from Senegal and Congo to include the resale right (droit de suite) in the agenda of future work by the Standing Committee on Copyright and Related Rights of the World Intellectual Property Organization", Standing Committee on Copyright and Related Rights, 31st session, Geneva, 7–11 December 2015, SCCR/31/5, 4 December 2015, https://www.wipo.int/edocs/mdocs/copyright/en/sccr_31/sccr_31_5.pdf.

[82]   Visual Artists Rights Act of 1990, Pub. L. 101-650, 608n. The focus on artistic works certainly enabled this amalgam.

[83]   *Moral Rights, Termination Rights, Resale Royalty, and Copyright Term: Hearing Before the Subcomm. on Courts, Intellectual Prop., & the Internet of the H. Comm. on the Judiciary,* 113th Cong. 4 (2014). Of course, reports bearing only on the resale royalty right have also been produced. See, for instance, *U.S. Copyright Office, Resale Royalties: An Updated Analysis (2013)*, http://www.copyright.gov/docs/resaleroyalty/usco-resaleroyalty.pdf.

The argument that the exercise of moral rights sends a strong signal that the work has a value for both the author and society, over and above the more mundane exercise of economic rights,[84] deserves attention. An author who remains complacent when his work is damaged or when it is marketed without proper attribution harms his bargaining position when the time comes to negotiate sales, assignments and licences over his works. Reputation remains important in the determination of the price of works. Who wants to pay a high price for a work that is not valued by its author? From a broader perspective, such carelessness would not help the author develop a reputation within his artistic milieu nor in the one in which he aspires to be. Moreover, "from the public's point of view, an artist's body of work is an important component of his 'personality'. That is, for an artist, reputation and personality become one and the same."[85] Such assertion brings one back to the theoretical justifications not only for moral rights, but also for copyright itself.

2.2   Moral Rights as Enhancers of Copyright Protection

There will always be debates about "the purpose" of copyright law. Between the promotion of "the progress of science and useful arts" and the protection of the authors' personality as it is expressed through their works, the identification of the goal of copyright law will continue to inspire its interpretation as it faces new challenges. Digital technology, as expected, provides fertile ground for this constant soul searching.[86] As pressing technological issues are debated, moral rights seem to attract less attention in this environment, almost as if they were irrelevant. Yet, the concerns that moral rights address have accompanied debates when new technologies have appeared in copyright law. The purpose of this section is not to revisit justifications for copyright law, but rather to highlight events where a special attention was paid to moral rights preoccupations either deliberately or unknowingly.

The first example comes from the British Fine Arts Copyright Act of 1862[87] which introduced photographs among the works that can be protected by copyright. Two provisions in its Section 7 were designed to prevent the sale of artistic works under another artist's name and the sale of altered copies of the works under the artist's name. While, as it was duly noted, the term "moral rights" had not yet been coined by Morillot, moral rights scholars today are willing to consider this event as a forerunner of the moral rights doctrine[88] even if it took place in a copyright country.

At the opposite end of the spectrum of moral rights awareness is the tailoring of moral rights rules for cinematographic works in France. The US "business" of film making is well known for its mistrust of moral rights. It has made the industry a force in the rejection by the United States of the Havana Convention, one of several Inter-American conventions that were

---

[84]   See Watt, Chapter 11 in this *Handbook.*

[85]   H. Hansmann and M. Santilli, "Authors' and Artists' Moral Rights: A Comparative Legal and Economic Analysis" (1997) 26 J. of Legal Studies 95 109–10.

[86]   On the important social function of moral rights in the global information society, see M.A. Wilkinson, "The Public Interest in Moral Rights Protection" [2006] Mich. St. L. Rev. 193.

[87]   25 & 26 Vict., c. 68.

[88]   Adeney, *supra* note 2, 371–4, paras 13.17–13.26; R. Deazley, "Breaking the Mould? The Radical Nature of the Fine Arts Copyright Bill 1862" in R. Deazley, M. Kretschmer, and L. Bently (eds), *Privilege and Property – Essays on the History of Copyright* (Cambridge, Open Book Publishers 2010) 289, 303.

developed for the Americas between 1889 and 1946,[89] which recognized moral rights.[90] The film industry in that country did develop its own protection standards outside an avowed moral rights framework,[91] but that did not prevent an open clash of values with the French statutory regime in the *Huston* case.[92] The latter is known for applying moral rights to cinematographic works in the same manner as they form part of the protection of other categories of works. However, it does contain a slight variation that often escapes attention: moral rights in cinematographic works are "suspended" during the making of the work and can only be exercised once the work is finished.[93] Because of the presumptions of authorship that apply to such works,[94] this means that the authors of scenarios and of the pre-existing works that may be at the origin of the film – in cases, say, of adaptations from novels – cannot assert their rights during the production of the film. It is one of the rare cases of bending of the moral rights rules in France because of the nature of the work to which they are meant to apply.

Closer to our technological times, a similar need to adjust moral rights to a new type of work was felt with respect to computer programs. Many characteristics of computer programs raise difficulties with such rights: their "unartistic" nature, their utilitarian objectives, the importance of teamwork in the creation process, etc. The absence of moral rights standards in the TRIPs Agreement, where one of the major objectives was to enshrine the copyright protection of computer programs, made it easy for countries that are not strong advocates of moral rights to skirt the issue. No exception in the moral rights regime was created for computer programs in the Canadian Copyright Act,[95] for example. However, some countries could not avoid revisiting their rules for moral rights in that context. Such was the case in France, where the law narrows the scope of the right of integrity and denies the right of withdrawal to authors of computer programs.[96] The EU position that moral rights need not form part of the harmonization process[97] also created a fertile ground for a motley collection of moral rights rules for computer programs.

There is an interesting jump in the awareness of moral rights issues when one compares computer programs with the developments of artificial intelligence. Even before artificial intelligence became the buzzword it is today, one copyright provision was noteworthy for its prescience. Section 9(2) of the UK's Copyright, Designs and Patents Act 1988 has been famous for its ground-breaking statement: "In the case of a ... work which is computer-generated, the author shall be taken to be the person by whom the arrangements necessary for the creation of the work are undertaken." The need to identify an author in order to protect the work and thus

---

[89]   On these Inter-American texts, see D. Lipszyc, *Copyright and Neighbouring Rights* (Paris, UNESCO Publishing 1999) 605–14.

[90]   Adeney, *supra* note 2, 101, paras 5.12 and 5.13.

[91]   See Dougherty, Chapter 10 in this *Handbook*.

[92]   See Torremans, Chapter 20 in this *Handbook*. See also Y. Gendreau, "Colourizing Movies: Some International Ramifications" (1989–1990) 5 Intellectual Property Journal 297.

[93]   Code of Intellectual Property, s. L. 121-5, para. 5. See A.-E. Kahn, "La notion de droit moral dans le cadre de l'œuvre audiovisuelle" in I. Marinone and I. Moine-Dupuis (eds), *Cinéma et droit d'auteur – Réflexions historiques et juridiques sur la paternité du réalisateur* (Villeneuve d'Ascq, Presses universitaires du Septentrion 2022) 31.

[94]   Code of Intellectual Property, s. L. 113-7.

[95]   R.S.C. 1985, c. C-42, ss. 14.1, 14.2, 28.1, 28.2.

[96]   Code of Intellectual Property, s. L.121-7.

[97]   See I. Sirvinskaite, "Towards Copyright 'Europeanification': European Union Moral Rights" (2010–2011) 3 J. Int'l Media & Ent. L. 263, 279–84.

give it all the rights the law provides, including the moral rights, was obviously felt to be of paramount importance to ensure that copyright law is properly working. Many copyright discussions today on artificial intelligence revolve around the notion of authorship as the essential prerequisite for copyright protection, and the existence of moral rights in a given situation directly flows from that finding. Indeed, there is a constant dialogue between the status of author and the protection of moral rights in these interrogations since the answer to the question "who would exercise the moral rights over the work produced by artificial intelligence?" also informs the authorship issue.[98]

When a new technology begets a different type of work, screening it through the prism of moral rights is part of the overall assessment of its legitimacy within the copyright protection scheme. The haste to protect computer programs in the 1980s has meant that moral rights were given short shrift to facilitate their acceptance as a new category of work, but the subsequent developments of the Internet and of artificial intelligence have brought moral rights back into the discussion.[99] Other international developments may have created a more propitious environment for that exercise. One of the highlights of the WPPT was the recognition of moral rights to performers.[100] A similar achievement was accomplished with the Beijing Treaty on Audiovisual Performances of 2012.[101] The extension of moral rights to performers on the international level fills a void that existed since the Rome Convention of 1961 and thus sends the signal that copyright and related rights protection is incomplete without moral rights.

3.   CONCLUSION

Whether they are consciously named as such or not, moral rights seem to be part of the fabric of many authors. They have led authors to fight duels in the nineteenth century[102] and to engage in mass shootings in the twentieth century.[103] Contemporary structures of creation, such as the Creative Commons system, integrate some of its objectives.[104] Authors of fiction works, whether books or films, incorporate them to different degrees in their story lines.[105] Even in industrial property rights, one can find preoccupations with the values that moral rights bring

---

[98]   See Branco and Nunes, Chapter 15 in this *Handbook*. Even in "traditional" discussions on moral rights, commentators make the point of discussing authorship issues in their moral rights analysis: see G. Davies and K. Garnett, *Moral Rights* (2nd edn, London, Sweet & Maxwell 2016) 85–102, paras 6-009–6-050.

[99]   Even before the 1996 WIPO treaties, the existence of rights management information has given rise to speculations as to the moral rights function of such information. See Y. Gendreau, "Digital Technology and Copyright: Can Moral Rights Survive the Disappearance of the Hard Copy?" [1995] Entertainment Law Review 214, 219. See also, Mazziotti, *supra* note 3, 292; Raghavender, *supra* note 23, 310.

[100]   WPPT, Art. 5.

[101]   Beijing Treaty on Audiovisual Performances, Art. 5.

[102]   See Pabón Cadavid, Chapter 24 in this *Handbook*, Section 3.

[103]   On this extraordinary copyright event (a university professor considered his colleagues had not been fair to him in their publications), see N. Tamaro, "Réflexions d'un civiliste autour de *Fabrikant* c. *Swamy*: l'initiative d'une procédure et le droit moral" (2008) 20 Cahiers de propriété intellectuelle 597.

[104]   See Giannopoulou, Chapter 14 in this *Handbook*.

[105]   *Supra* note 65.

to the protection of creative activities.[106] Moral rights provide a public recognition of the social value of creativity,[107] a value that is certainly not declining in society.

Why is it then so difficult to embrace moral rights? Clues can be identified. As simplistic as it may seem, their name is perhaps their first obstacle. While so many countries call them by their name, recall that one copyright country, India, has seen fit to call them "special rights".[108] The word "moral" creates uneasiness and may convey a holier-than-thou repute that is difficult to find engaging. What is usually identified as a reason for rejecting them, however, is their potential to thwart economic transactions. International resistance to their integration as a binding legal norm is well documented. Even the adhesion of the United States to the Berne Convention in 1989 cannot be truly perceived as an endorsement of its Article 6*bis* since it was followed by the TRIPs Agreement, driven by the United States, that specifically excluded it from its ambit.[109] Admittedly, it is not necessary to point solely at the US copyright tradition to identify an unwillingness to integrate moral rights in the copyright regime: the EU, an authors' right coalition but for one, is not interested in the harmonization of moral rights for its internal market.[110] Two international related rights instruments since the TRIPs Agreement have incorporated moral rights, the WPPT and the Beijing Treaty on Audiovisual Performances; but apart from the fact that they represent an extension of moral rights in the sphere of international law, that progression may seem marginal because it can be regarded as an overdue adjustment.

Without a strong persuasive force in international law that would put it on the same footing as, for instance, the three-step test in the world of exceptions, moral rights have been able to develop freely in order to fit within national idiosyncrasies. US law can have a patchwork of state legislations, common law remedies, and federal moral rights within its Copyright Act only for a limited number of artistic works. UK law can include what would elsewhere be considered personality rights over one's image in its notion of moral rights.[111] If they have been able to become an essential part of the laws in authors' rights in countries, it may well be because, unlike what has taken place in the copyright countries, scholars in that field have been expounding them ever since their beginnings. In France, for example, at least one doctoral dissertation on moral rights was written even before the Berne Convention[112] and Eugène Pouillet, an important figure of early twentieth-century authors' rights doctrine, could cite another one in addition to other writings in the 1908 edition of his treatise.[113] On the other side of the Channel, court cases and legislation that embody moral rights values existed too at that time,[114] but there was no similar doctrinal construction to support and flesh them out. Today,

[106]   *Supra* note 73.
[107]   Carnegy-Arbuthnott, Chapter 1 in this *Handbook*.
[108]   See Raghavender, *supra* note 23.
[109]   TRIPs Agreement, Art. 9(1).
[110]   See, *supra* note 11 and the text that accompanies it.
[111]   Copyright, Designs and Patents Act 1988, s. 85.
[112]   G.A. Lebret, *Du droit des auteurs et des artistes sur leurs œuvres* (Paris, Edition A. Lahure 1878).
[113]   E. Pouillet, *Traité théorique et pratique de la propriété littéraire et artistique et du droit de représentation* (3rd edn, Paris, Marchal & Billard 1908) 256–8, para. 204*bis*.
[114]   *Prince Albert v. Strange*, (1849) 47 E.R. 1302; Fine Arts Copyright Act of 1862, 25 & 26 Vict., c. 68. Similarly, case law and doctrine existed in Canada well before the Copyright Act was amended to implement the Rome Act of the Berne Convention. See E. Adeney, "Moral Rights: A Brief Excursion into Canadian History" (2001) 15 Intellectual Property Journal 205.

moral rights exist around the world according to rules that stretch their clichéd image well beyond their description by their original developers.

Is it possible to make moral right as unavoidable as exceptions in copyright law without taking umbrage at the tailoring they may require? If their philosophical underpinnings remain stuck in strict nineteenth-century perceptions, it cannot happen. It is time to update these beginnings and be willing to open up to contemporary considerations that can fully justify the multifaceted variations that already exist.[115] Doctrinal research has already started: the formidable copyright laboratory that EU law provides to test concepts before they can migrate to an even broader international environment has enabled scholars who wanted to lay the foundations for a supranational EU copyright law to envisage moral rights within their Wittem Code.[116]

To make such a project work, one must come to terms with the nature of moral rights within copyright law and this may be where the problem lies. The traditional perspective on moral rights relies on the protection of the author's personality within copyright law, but does not really go beyond that objective. Without losing it from sight, it is possible to bring this objective further to a dual function.[117] Moral rights create a balancing act within copyright law just as exceptions do. They act as a check on the exercise of the economic rights over works, hence the need to keep them "reasonable". What allows them to play that role is their other purpose: they contribute to the legitimacy of the entire copyright scheme, including, yes, the economic rights. That dimension of moral rights is just as important, if not even more so, than its balancing function and should thus guide the application of the rights themselves. It may seem contradictory to suggest that the same concept can act both as a political driving force and as a technical break on the overall copyright protection. It would not be the first time that a duality characterizes moral right: the existence of the monist/dualist approaches, the tug between purely personalist and economic dimensions have always been part of their history, albeit at different times and with different intensities. However, the recognition of this paradox may help to unlock the development of moral rights – and of copyright law – in an age where it is challenged by technology as never before. Legal norms for moral rights are already in place, so it could mean that it is up to the courts (and doctrine?) to develop moral rights in light of our current technological environment.[118] As concluded an eminent specialist of moral rights:

---

[115] Calls for such an evolution have already been made. See P. Goldstein, "Moral Rights on the Internet" in F. Brison, S. Dusollier, M.-C. Janssens, and H. Vanhees (eds), *Moral Rights in the 21st Century – The Changing Role of the Moral Rights in an Era of Information Overload* (Brussels, Larcier 2015) 296; M.T. Sundara Rajan, *Moral Rights – Principles, Practice and New Technology* (Oxford, Oxford University Press 2011). They are in contrast with earlier doctrine that was less optimistic. See A. Françon, "Protection of Artists' Moral Rights and the Internet" in F. Pollaud-Dulian (ed.), *Perspectives on Intellectual Property*, vol. 5: The Internet and Authors' Rights (London, Sweet & Maxwell 1999) 73; G. Lea, "Moral Rights and the Internet: Some Thoughts from a Common Law Perspective" in F. Pollaud-Dulian (ed.), *Perspectives on Intellectual Property*, vol. 5: The Internet and Authors' Rights (London, Sweet & Maxwell 1999) 87.

[116] *Supra* note 11. See also A. Strowel, *Le droit d'auteur européen en transition numérique – De ses origines à l'unification européenne et aux défis de l'intelligence artificielle et des Big Data* (Brussels, Larcier 2022) 172–5, paras 127–9.

[117] The phenomenon has also been studied according to the concept of overlapping rights and considered particularly relevant for the digital environment. See Sundara Rajan, *supra* note 78.

[118] See the prescient article by G. Pessach, "The Author's Moral Rights of Integrity in Cyberspace – A Preliminary Normative Framework" (2003) 34 I.I.C. 250 and the detailed analysis in the doctoral dissertation by P. Scoffoni, *Le droit moral de l'auteur à l'ère numérique – Etude comparée des sys-*

If modern copyright law has a certain tendency to cover all and everything, in the very interest of authors of literature and art, music and film, we must adapt our positions to the new situation, in order to save the principle as such.[119]

---

tèmes américain et européens, Aix-Marseille Université, 2013, available at https://www.academia.edu/21563384/Author_s_Moral_Rights_in_the_Digital_Age_a_Comparative_Study_of_the_American_and_European_Systems.
[119] A. Dietz, "Legal Principles of Moral Rights (Civil Law) – General Report" in ALAI (ed.), *The Moral Rights of the Author* (Paris, ALAI 1994) 19, 80.

Table A1.1   Appendix: Commonwealth laws on moral rights – August 2022

COUNTRIES	LEGISLATION	BENEFICIARIES	MORAL RIGHTS	TERM OF PROTECTION	BERNE CONVENTION	WPPT
Antigua and Barbuda	Copyright Act 2003	Authors Films: Director, Performers	P. I* P. I* None	50 years pma	17 March 2000 Paris Act	Not member
Australia	Copyright Act 1968 (consolidated as of June 2015)	Authors Films: director, producer (if an individual) & screenwriters Performers	P. I* As above P. I*	70 years pma P: 70 years from qualifying event; I* death of last surviving author P: 70 years from qualifying event I*: Death of the performer	14 April 1928 Paris Act	26 July 2007
The Bahamas	Copyright Act 1998, as amended in 2004	Authors Authors of visual art only Performers	P. I* None	70 years pma As above	10 July 1973 Brussels Act	Not member
Bangladesh	No information				4 May 1999	Not member
Barbados	Copyright Act 1999 (as revised to 2006)	Authors (other than of computer programs) Films: Directors Performers	P. I* As above None	50 years from qualifying event As above	30 July 1983	13 December 2019
Belize	Copyright Act 2000	Authors Performers	P. I* None	50 years pma	17 June 2000 Paris Act	9 February 2019
Botswana	Copyright and Neighbouring Rights Act (No. 6 of 2006)	Authors Performers	P. I* P. I*	50 years pma 50 years from qualifying event	15 April 1998 Paris Act	27 January 2005
Brunei	Copyright Order 1999	Authors Performers	P. I* P. I*	50 years pma 50 years from qualifying event	30 August 2006 Paris Act	2 May 2017
Cameroon	Law on Copyright and Neighbouring Rights 19 December 2000	Authors Performers	D, P, I, R P. I	Perpetual Perpetual	21 September 1964 Paris Act	Not member

COUNTRIES	LEGISLATION	BENEFICIARIES	MORAL RIGHTS	TERM OF PROTECTION	BERNE CONVENTION	WPPT
Canada	Copyright Act (consolidated, 31 March 2015)	Authors Performers	P. 1* P. 1*	Same duration as economic rights As above	10 April 1928 Paris Act	13 August 2014
Cyprus	Copyright Law No. 59 of 3 December 1976 as amended to 1993	Authors Performers	P. 1* None	50 years from qualifying event	24 February 1964 Paris Act	2 December 2005
Dominica	Copyright Act 2003	Authors Performers	P. 1* P. 1*	70 years from qualifying event 50 years from qualifying event	7 August 1999	Not member
Eswatini (former Swaziland)	Unknown				Not member	Not member
Fiji	Copyright Act 1999	Authors (except of computer programs and c-generated works) Directors of Audio-Visual works Performers	P. 1* P. 1* None	50 years from qualifying event	1 December 1971 Brussels and Stockholm Acts	Not member
Gabon	Decree No. 000452/PR/MCAEP 2066, on the Establishment of the Regulation on the Management of Copyright and Neighbouring Rights	No details	No details	No details	26 March 1962	20 May 2002
The Gambia	Copyright Act 2004	Authors Performers	P. 1* P6. 1*	50 years from qualifying event (25 for works of applied art) Unclear	7 March 1993	Not member
Ghana	Copyright Act of 17 May 2005	Authors Performers	P. 1* P. 1*	Perpetual Perpetual (independent of economic rights)	11 October 1991 Paris Act	16 February 2013

COUNTRIES	LEGISLATION	BENEFICIARIES	MORAL RIGHTS	TERM OF PROTECTION	BERNE CONVENTION	WPPT
Grenada	Copyright Act No. 21 of 2011	Authors Performers	P. I* P6. I*	50 years from qualifying event (25 for works of applied art) Unclear	22 September 1998 Paris Act	Not member
Guyana	No information				25 July 1994	Not member
India	Copyright Act 1957, as amended in 2012	Authors Computer programs Performers	P. I* PP6. I*	Perpetual Unclear	1 April 1928 Paris Act	25 December 2018
Jamaica	Copyright Act 1993, as amended in 2015	Authors Performers	P. I* P6. I*	95 pma 95 years after performance	1 January 1994 Paris Act	12 June 2002
Kenya	Copyright Act of 31 December 2001	Authors Performers	P. I* P. I*	50 years pma Life of performer	11 June 1993 Paris Act	Signed 20 December 1996 (not ratified)
Kiribati	No information				2 January 2018	22 June 2021
Lesotho	Copyright Order 1989 (Act No. 13 of 1989)	Authors	P. I*	50 years from end of year of qualifying event	28 September Paris Act	Not member
Malawi	Copyright Act 1989 (No. 9, 26 April 1989)	Authors Employed authors Performers	P. IP. I None	50 years from date of qualifying event As above	12 October 1991 Paris Act	Not member
Malaysia	Copyright Act 1987, (Act 332, as at I January 2006)	Authors Performers	P. I* P6. I* None	50 years from authors' death 50 years from date of qualifying event	1 October 1990 Paris Act	27 December 2012
Maldives	Copyright and Related Rights Act 2010	Authors Performers	P. I P. I*	50 years from qualifying event (25 for works of applied art) 50 years from qualifying event	Not member	Not member
Malta	Copyright Act 2000 as amended in 2011	Authors Performers	P. I* P6. I*	70 years from qualifying event 50 years from qualifying event	21 September 1964 Rome Act & Paris Act (Arts 22–36)	14 March 2010

COUNTRIES	LEGISLATION	BENEFICIARIES	MORAL RIGHTS	TERM OF PROTECTION	BERNE CONVENTION	WPPT
Mauritius	Copyright Act 2014 (Act No. 2 of 2014)	Authors Performers	P. 1* P6. 1*	50 years from date of qualifying event (25 years for works of applied art) 50 years from fixation	10 May 1989 Paris Act	Not member
Mozambique	Law No. 4/2001 of 27 February 2001 (Copyright Law)	Authors Performers	D, P, I None	Perpetual	22 November 2013 Paris Act	Not member
Namibia	Copyright and Neighbouring Rights Protection Act 1994	Authors Performers	P. 1* None	50 years pma	21 March 1990 Paris Act	Not member
Nauru	No information				11 May 2020 Paris Act	Not member
New Zealand	Copyright Act 1994 (reprinted 2014)	Authors Directors of Audiovisual works NB Authors in employment, of computer programs and performers	P9. 1* P. 1* No rights	50 years from qualifying event As above	24 April 1928 Rome Act	17 March 2019
Nigeria	Copyright Act Ch. C 28 as codified 2004	Authors Performers	P. 1* None	Perpetual	14 September 1993 Paris Act	4 January 2018
Pakistan	Copyright Ordinance No. XXXIV 1962, amended 29 September 2000	Authors Performers	P. 1* None	50 years from qualifying event	5 July 1948 Rome Act + Stockholm Act (Arts 22–38)	Not member
Papua New Guinea	Copyright and Neighbouring Rights Act (No. 21) of 2000	Authors Performers	P. 1* P. 1*	50 years pma 50 years from qualifying event	Not member	Not member
Rwanda	Law No. 31/2009 of 26 October 2009 on the Protection of Intellectual Property	Authors *Collective Works* Natural or legal person who has taken the initiative and direction of works Performers	P. 1* As above P6. 1*	Perpetual As above As above	1 March 1984 Paris Act	Not member

COUNTRIES	LEGISLATION	BENEFICIARIES	MORAL RIGHTS	TERM OF PROTECTION	BERNE CONVENTION	WPPT
Saint Kitts and Nevis	Copyright Act 2000	Authors (other than of computer programs and reports on current events) Film Directors Performers	P. I* P. I* None	50 years from qualifying event (same as economic rights) (false attribution 20 years from end of year from death of person) As above	9 April 1995 Paris Act	Not member
Saint Lucia	Copyright Act 1995, as amended by Act No. 7, 2000	Authors Film Directors Performers	P. I* P. I* P6. I*	50 years from qualifying event False attribution 20 years pma As above 50 years from end of year of performance	24 August 1993 Paris Act	20 May 2002
Saint Vincent and the Grenadines	Copyright Act (No. 21) of 2003	Authors (other than of computer programs and reports on current events) Directors of audiovisual works Performers	P. I* P6. I*	50 years from qualifying event False attribution life of author and 20 years pma As above	29 August 1995 Paris Act	12 February 2011
Samoa	Copyright Act 1988 (as consolidated in 2011)	Authors Performers	P. I* None	75 years from qualifying event (25 for works of applied art)	21 July 2006 Paris Act	Not member
Seychelles	Copyright Act 2014	Authors Performers	P. I* P6. I*	50 years from qualifying event (25 for works of applied art) 50 years from date of performance	Not member	Not member
Sierra Leone	Copyright Act (No. 8) of 2011	Authors Performers	P. I. P6. I*	Perpetual Unspecified	Not member	Not member
Singapore	Copyright Act 1987 (amended to 31 March 2015)	Authors Performers	P (false attribution) P (false attribution)	70 years from qualifying event As above	21 December 1998 Paris Act	17 April 2005

COUNTRIES	LEGISLATION	BENEFICIARIES	MORAL RIGHTS	TERM OF PROTECTION	BERNE CONVENTION	WPPT
Solomon Islands	No information				4 July 2019	Not member
South Africa	Copyright Act 1978 (Act No. 98, as amended in 2002)	Authors	P. 1* (limited integrity right for authors of films and computer programs)	50 years from end of qualifying event	3 October 1928 Brussels Act + Paris Act (Arts 22–38)	Not member (Signed 12 December 1997)
Sri Lanka	Intellectual Property Act (No. 36) 2003	Authors Performers	P. 1* None	70 years from qualifying event (25 years for works of applied art)	20 July 1959 Paris Act	Not member
Tanzania	Copyright and Neighbouring Rights Act 1999	Authors Performers	P. 1*	50 or 70 years from end of year of the qualifying event	25 July 1994 Paris Act	Not member
Togo	Law on the Establishment of the Code of Artisanic Handicraft in the Togolese Republic 2012 (Arts 67 & 68)				30 April 1975	21 February 2003
Tonga	Copyright Act 2002	Authors Performers	P. 1* P6. 1*	50 years pma 50 years from end of year of qualifying event	14 June 2001 Paris Act	Not member
Trinidad and Tobago	Copyright Act 1997 (as amended in 2000 and 2008)	Authors Performers	P. 1* P. 1*	50 years pma 50 years from end of year when performance fixed or took place	16 August 1988 Paris Act	28 November 2008
Tuvalu	No information				2 June 2017	Not member
Uganda	The Copyright and Neighbouring Rights Act 2006	Authors Performers	P. 1 P. 1	Perpetual 50 years from performance	Not member	28 April 2022
United Kingdom	Copyright, Designs and Patents Act 1988, as amended	Authors Film directors Employed authors Computer programs Performers	P9. 1* P9. 1* Limited I None P. 1*	70 years from the qualifying event As above As above 50 or 70 years from end of year of the qualifying event	5 December 1987 Paris Act	14 March 2010

COUNTRIES	LEGISLATION	BENEFICIARIES	MORAL RIGHTS	TERM OF PROTECTION	BERNE CONVENTION	WPPT
Vanuatu	Copyright Act No. 42 of 2000	Authors Performers	P. I* P6. I*	50 years from qualifying event (25 for works of applied art) 50 years from qualifying event	6 May 2020	6 August 2020
Zambia	Copyright and Performance Rights Act 1994 (No. 44), as amended in 2010	Authors (except of computer programs) Film directors	P. I* P. I*	Lifetime As above	2 January 1992	Not member

Notes: Definitions of the abbreviations and symbols used in the table

D: *Right of disclosure:* Right to decide whether, in what form and on what terms, a work will be made available to the public for the first time.

I: *Right of Integrity:* Right to object to any distortion, mutilation or other unauthorised modification of, or other derogatory action in relation to the work/performance.

I*: Right of Integrity limited to the right to object to any distortion, mutilation, or other modification of the work/performance which would be prejudicial to the honour or reputation of the author/performer.

P: *Right of Paternity:* Right to claim authorship of the work and to object to false attribution of authorship as well as the right not to be mentioned as the author.

P6: The right of the author/performer to have his name mentioned is recognised to the extent and in the manner required by proper usage and practice.

P9: The paternity right must be asserted by the author. The right does not apply to publication in newspapers, magazines, encyclopaedias or collective works of reference.

R: *Right of Retraction:* Right to withdraw the work from publication or from circulation. In such case, the author is obliged to pay compensation for any loss or prejudice caused to any person who has previously been authorised to use the work.

Source: In preparing this Table, the author has drawn on the information about national laws worldwide published in G. Davies and K. Garnett, KC, *Moral Rights*, Sweet and Maxwell, 2010, Ch. 33, and the WIPO website.

Index

abuse of moral rights, Greece *see* Greece, moral
    rights protection, moral rights abuse
access rights
    Greece, moral rights protection 329–30, 334
    Latin America, reinforced protection 420–21
    multiple ownership 220
    see also disclosure rights
adaptations *see* modifications
Adeney, E. *xiii* 22, 23, 25, 135, 145, 233, 270,
    271, 275, 402, 409, 516, 517, 527, 528,
    530
Adler, A. 8, 67, 191
advertising
    US motion picture industry, credits and
        rights of attribution 182
    value for value of future works 188–9, 193–4
AI *see* artificial intelligence
Akester, P. 161, 292
alienable rights
    China 401–2
    relational autonomy 2–3, 4–5, 7, 8, 10
    trademarks, intellectual creations underlying
        136–7
    see also inalienability issues
alteration rights
    alternative dispute resolution 340–41
    China 401, 407–8, 411, 520
    corporate entities, digital rights-management
        information 206
    exceptions and limitations to moral rights,
        Germany 279–80
    Greece, consent and contractual limitations
        333–4
    relational autonomy 4–5
    see also modification
alternative dispute resolution 339–54
    adjudicative forms 354
    alterations, objections to 340–41
    arbitration 345, 347–8, 349, 350–54
    benefits over court litigation 344
    and changing technological environment
        342–3
    consensus-based forms 353
    Court of Arbitration for Art (CAFA) 346
    criticism of 344–5
    divulgation rights 341
    fair trial right 344–5
    ghostwriting 341

Independent Film and Television Alliance
    346
institutionalised assistance 354
integrity rights 341–2
Internet and de-contextualisation 342
jurisdictional issues 347–8
legal obstacles, potential 346–52
legal tools 343–6
mediation and conciliation 345, 347, 349,
    353
neutral evaluation and expert determination
    345, 353
parody or quotation disputes 341
paternity rights 341
personal relationship of authors 339–40
providers 345–6
and public order 349–50
reproduction of sound recordings in bad
    quality 341–2
rights and obligations on which the parties
    are not free to decide themselves 349
selection of suitable processes 352–4
Singapore Convention 344, 349
substantive issues 349–52
third party violations 341
tort-based disputes 341
traditional moral rights 340–42
user-generated content on social media
    342–3
Waiting for Godot productions 341
waiver of moral rights 340, 350, 351, 352,
    354
WIPO Arbitration and Mediation Center
    345–6
An Alan Smithee Film: Burn Hollywood Burn and
    author's rights 480–84, 491–2
    see also fictional stories by fictional people
Angelopoulos, C. 212, 292
animal rights
    Brazil 441
    Naruto monkey case 258–61, 262, 264
anonymous works *see* pseudonyms
anti-discrimination law, and EU, copyright
    and dualist vs. monist approaches,
    harmonization issues 163, 164
AOIC standard (author's own intellectual
    creation), industrial design 121
arbitration 345, 347–8, 349, 350–54
    see also alternative dispute resolution